Jewish Worship

JEWISH WORSHIP

by

ABRAHAM E. MILLGRAM

The Jewish Publication Society of America
Philadelphia
5732:1971

Library of Congress Catalog Card Number 77-151316
Manufactured in the United States of America
Designed by
Sol Calvin Cohen

*The author wishes to express
his sincere appreciation to the following,
who have kindly granted permission
to use their copyrighted material:*

The Soncino Press Limited, London, England,
for selections from THE BABYLONIAN TALMUD,
*translated under the editorship of Isidore Epstein, 1935–1950;
and selections from* MIDRASH RABBAH,
*translated under the editorship
of H. Freedman and Maurice Simon, 1939–1951.*

Yale University Press, New Haven,
for selections from
THE MIDRASH ON PSALMS,
translated by William G. Braude, 1959.

To my beloved children:

HILLEL & DEVORAH

ELIJAH
MICHAEL
JEREMIAH

PREFACE

It is doubtful whether any product of the Jewish heritage has succeeded in reflecting as succinctly and as accurately the basic commitments of rabbinic Judaism as does the worship of the synagogue. No wonder the *Siddur* has intrigued both laymen and scholars. Rabbis have sensed this interest and have introduced expositions on selected liturgic items into the synagogue worship. Publishers, too, have seen fit to include enlightening information about the more important prayers in their recently published prayer books. They have also published a number of books on the Jewish liturgy. Unfortunately, these publications have not always dealt with the liturgy as a living, growing organism. It is the writer's hope that this book will meet the obvious need for a comprehensive yet nontechnical work on the history and content of Jewish worship.

The Jewish liturgy was not born in a vacuum, nor did it thrive in a spiritual wilderness. Like all liturgies it has developed in response to religious needs and has grown in the framework of religious living. It has impinged on community institutions and national aspirations; it was molded by theological commitments and artistic expressions. Hence a book on Jewish liturgy must reckon with the whole gamut of Jewish life. The writer therefore did not resist the temptation to venture into some of the bypaths of Jewish life and history. But he always made sure to return to the main highway.

This book was written primarily for the intelligent Jewish layman who has some acquaintance with the synagogue worship but has had no formal training in the specialized field of the liturgy. He is often puzzled and even confused by the seemingly unordered and often incomprehensible prayers of the tradition. The writer hopes that the book will prove enlightening to the layman and will help to make the synagogue worship more meaningful and perhaps even more relevant.

It is also hoped that the book will be of interest to non-Jews, many of whom are intrigued by the mystery of the Jewish people's survival in the face of unimaginable odds. This survival, they rightly feel, has been powered by commitments to ideas and ideals about God, the good life, and the hope for an ideal society which the Jews called the kingship or the sovereignty of God. An insight into these areas of Jewish historic commitment can best be gleaned from a study of the history and content of the prayers of the synagogues. Many a Christian is also in search of information that will shed light on his own faith, the primary sources of which are to be found in pharisaic Judaism. For a concise yet authentic summary of rabbinic Judaism almost no other Jewish classic equals the *Siddur*, the core of which was composed by the rabbis of the Talmud.

It is also hoped that the book will prove useful in the classroom, both in the house of worship and on the college campus.

There are several things that this book is not. It is not sufficiently encyclopedic to embrace everything related to Jewish worship. Nor does it deal with the history or content of every prayer. To include everything that competent scholars have said about the various elements of synagogue worship and to discuss every prayer would have made this book into a bulky reference work, instead of a readable book for both Jewish and non-Jewish laymen.

Nor is this book a guide to Jewish worship. Laws regulating the synagogue services are hardly dealt with. The writer's aim was only to provide the intelligent layman with an introduction to Jewish worship in the framework of its history.

The writer did not adhere rigidly to the formal definitions of a number of technical terms. Thus the words *liturgy* and *worship* were used interchangeably despite their specific definitions.* Likewise the terms *dogma*, *doctrine*, *tenet*, and *belief* were used freely without sharp distinctions. Chronology, too, was not permitted to violate the logical treatment of a subject; the writer preferred to trespass into a period that was later than

* Worship *usually refers to "the inner movement" of the worshiper's soul, while* liturgy *usually refers to the outward manifestation of worship. Yet they are inseparable, because liturgy creates worship as truly as worship expresses itself in liturgy.*

the one under discussion rather than to leave a theme dangling in an unfinished state.

The writer also took the liberty of repeating some material which he thought would prove helpful to the reader. Just as the *Siddur* often repeats a prayer in order to save the worshiper the effort of turning back to where the prayer appeared for the first time, so the writer too chose occasionally to repeat what was already said in a previous chapter rather than refer the reader to the earlier account. Reliance on cross-references would make the reading of the book both boring and burdensome.

Another seemingly strange decision was to prefer direct quotations from the sources to the smooth paraphrases one usually meets in modern books on the liturgy. The archaic idiom of the biblical and rabbinic classics are more authentic than the paraphrases, which often gloss over those classic expressions which the writers think will be unpalatable to their readers. Excerpts from the *Siddur* were taken from *The Standard Prayer Book*, translated by S. Singer, and excerpts from the *Mahzor* were taken from *Service of the Synagogue*, translated by Herbert M. Adler and Arthur Davis. These translations are occasionally too literal to be elegant. However, they are faithful to the text, and they refrain from adorning the text with vague and sugary phrases. The writer took the liberty of substituting the word *Torah* for *the Law* and *Praised art Thou* for *Blessed art Thou* in all benedictions. These corrections are in line with the consensus of modern scholarly opinion.

Quotations from other classic sources were taken from the following standard texts:

1. The Torah: The Five Books of Moses (Philadelphia: The Jewish Publication Society of America, 1962).
2. "The Prophets" and "The Writings," in The Holy Scriptures (Philadelphia: The Jewish Publication Society of America, 1917).
3. The Babylonian Talmud, 35 vols. (London: The Soncino Press, 1948).
4. *Midrash Rabbah*, 10 vols. (London: The Soncino Press, 1939).

5. *The Midrash on Psalms*, 2 vols. (New Haven: Yale University Press, 1959).

Where the word *Blessed* appears in theses sources, it is followed by the word *Praised* in brackets; where the word *law* appears, it is followed by *Torah* in brackets.

Except for several pioneering works that should be known by the general reader, even if only by name, the Bibliography is limited to books and monographs in the English language.

Cross-references were provided at the bottom of the pages to direct the attention of those who read only selected chapters to additional information on the subject of their special interest.

The Notes at the end of the book contain, in addition to references and sources, additional information on some subjects which will prove helpful to teachers in the enrichment of their teaching.

The Index was designed to serve the additional function of a glossary of foreign and technical terms. Numbers in bold type refer to pages on which one will find definitions of the indexed items.

A Word of Thanks

I am indebted to a number of people who read all or part of the manuscript and made helpful suggestions. Among these are my dear friend, colleague, and for many years my co-worker in the field of Jewish education, Rabbi Samuel Schafler; my good neighbors in Jerusalem Rabbi and Mrs. David A. Goldstein; and a young colleague Rabbi Aryae Wineman. The most valuable help, however, came from my wife and my children, Hillel and Devorah, whose criticism and encouragement sustained me during many a moment of doubt and discouragement.

One of the members of the Jewish Publication Society's Publication Committee, my lifelong friend Dr. Azriel Eisenberg, not only read the whole manuscript but made many insightful suggestions. My gratitude to Dr. Eisenberg is deep and profound.

Another lifelong friend to whom I am deeply indebted is the Society's editor emeritus, Dr. Solomon Grayzel. When I was leaving for Israel in the summer of 1963 I went to bid him farewell. He reminded me of his suggestion, which he had made on several occasions, that I write a book on the *Siddur*. I had not acted on that suggestion because I had been too preoccupied to do justice to so important a work. Now he repeated his suggestion and urged me to give it serious thought. I promised him that I would. I hardly need add that had it not been for Dr. Grayzel's repeated urging this book would not have been written.

Finally, I am grateful to the Society's gifted staff: its distinguished editor, Dr. Chaim Potok, its competent copy editor, Kay Powell, and its capable executive director, Lesser Zussman, for their meticulous work of editing and producing this book.

One more word of thanks, this time to an institution—the National and University Library, located on the campus of Hebrew University in Jerusalem. It was there that I did my research and my writing. The library's splendid collection of books and the courteous help of the staff made my work an enjoyable adventure.

נשלם תודה לאל שהיה לי לעוזר,
ירושלים עה"ק, תובב"א,
י"א לחודש תמוז, תש"ל

אברהם עוזר בר' ישראל מנחם הלוי מילגרם

A. E. M.

Jerusalem
July 15, 1970

CONTENTS

ILLUSTRATIONS

INTRODUCTION

THE *SIDDUR*: A PRECIOUS SPIRITUAL POSSESSION

Judaism has given birth to several religious institutions which have revolutionized man's world outlook and man's way of life. Among these are the Sabbath and the synagogue. Equally important are the religious literary classics that Judaism has begotten—for example, the Bible and the Talmud. But the religious classic that has been closest to the heart of the Jew is the Jewish book of common prayer, known as the *Siddur*.

The Jewish Book of Common Prayer

In modern times many Jews have lost touch with their spiritual patrimony. The Bible and the Talmud, the cornerstones of Judaism, have unfortunately shared the proverbial fate of the classic which people talk about but hardly ever read. The contents of these monumental religious works are, for all practical purposes, unknown among the mass of the Jewish people. As might be expected, the *Siddur* has fallen into a similar obscurity. It is a terra incognita even to the Jew who comes periodically into the synagogue. That is why rabbis find it necessary to announce the pages at public services. To be sure, many a Jew leafs through the prayer book, especially during the long High Holy Days services. But this hardly arouses any sustained interest. Such a casual examination only reveals that the *Siddur* contains many prayers and benedictions, all in a strange language, totally incomprehensible to the uninitiated. On closer examination one also discovers in the *Siddur* many psalms and other biblical selections, as well as excerpts from the Talmud, all seemingly thrown together without any order or plan. Yet one feels intuitively that there must be a reason for the particular prayers included in the *Siddur* and for their sequence; there must be meaning to a literary work that has grown out of a people's cumulative religious experience, extending over so many centuries; there must be some relevance to these prayers, since they have satisfied the religious yearnings of saints and scholars during so long a period and in so many varied countries and cultures. Added to this intuitive feeling is the tangible contiguity that the Jew still maintains with the *Siddur*. Each time he enters a synagogue he is handed a *Siddur;* each time he opens it his curiosity about its contents is newly aroused. To be sure, this curiosity is usually of a fleeting nature. Nonetheless it keeps recurring, and the Jew's curiosity about the *Siddur*'s contents is never totally extinguished.

In recent years the Jew's interest in the *Siddur* has been stimulated by developments within and without the Jewish community. Forces, mainly sociological, have catapulted the synagogue into a position of centrality in the American Jewish community. The *Siddur*, which is the instrument of synagogue worship, has thus become an object of interest to the many Jews who have become affiliated with the synagogue. Equally important has been the impact of religious movements outside of Judaism. Some Christian theologians have given profound thought to the subject of liturgy and have delved deeply into the meaning and role of worship in the life of modern man. These theological explorations have resulted in a number of striking changes in the traditional liturgy of some churches. Among the most widely known are the changes in the Roman Catholic liturgy introduced at the Vatican Council II.[1] Among the provisions of the Schema on Liturgy is the radical departure from the ancient custom of using only Latin in the sacraments. The use of the vernacular in these rituals promises to have a profound effect on the prayer habits of the Catholic worshiper. Some liturgic changes have impinged directly on the Jewish people. Thus Pope John XXIII eliminated from the Catholic liturgy the offensive reference to the Jews as "perfidious." Reading about these and other developments among his neighbors, many a Jew asks himself: What about the liturgy of the synagogue? Are the prayers of the synagogue still relevant, or do they require adjustments or perhaps even radical changes?

The SIDDUR: *A Precious Spiritual Possession*

A Unique Product of the Jewish Genius

The *Siddur* has been the subject of exaggerated praise as well as abundant abuse. To some the *Siddur* represents the summit of spiritual nobility and intellectual profundity; to others it represents only a kind of curiosity shop, with varied bric-a-brac thrown together haphazardly. The disparaging views do not represent the traditional attitude of the Jewish people, who have chosen to call their book of devotions *Seder Tefillot* (The Order of Prayers), or simply *Siddur*. And this name is altogether reasonable, because the Jew of former days was able to find in the *Siddur* all the prayers designated for public and private worship, the prayers prescribed for weekdays and Sabbaths, for holy days and fast days. And the prayers were arranged in such a way that he could locate them as he needed them with relative ease. What greater order could anyone reasonably expect from a prayer book?

Though the prayer book is orderly enough to merit the name *Siddur*, the nature of its development and maturation is hardly orderly, for it did not emerge as a finished product, logically arranged and authoritatively fixed by a council of scholars. It is the end product of a slow historic process extending over a period of many centuries. The collective experience of the Jewish people was slowly and painstakingly distilled and deposited in the *Siddur*. It contains a succession of liturgic accretions, each reflecting the theological thinking, the cultural tastes, and the historical conditions of its period. The *Siddur* is therefore a most intriguing work. It is not only a handbook for Jewish prayer, but also a faithful record of Jewish thoughts, ideals, hopes, and anxieties during the many centuries of its growth. The *Siddur* may be regarded as both the Jewish book of common prayer and the spiritual history of the Jewish people.

Another characteristic of the *Siddur* has been its relative relevancy because of its traditional hospitality to new prayers. While other religious classics, like the Bible and the Talmud, were permanently closed to new material once they were completed, the prayer book always remained open-ended. All other classics could be enriched only through commentaries, glosses, and other marginal notes; the *Siddur* remained open to new prayers and could thus meet the needs arising from new situations. It was, in a sense, the loose-leaf classic of the Jewish people. This flexibility gave the *Siddur* the added dimension of timeliness, a quality which enabled it to serve the needs of the Jewish people up to the modern era. And it suited the spiritual needs of the Jewish people most admirably. The learned and the unlettered, the saint and the sinner, the sensitive and the brutish all found in it the spiritual nourishment they needed. From his childhood to his dying day the Jew availed himself of this spiritual companion and always found in it the appropriate fare for his soul.

A Mirror of the Jewish Soul

The *Siddur* is one of the crowning achievements of the religious teachings of the Pharisees, who translated the abstract teachings of the prophets into the living experience of their day and transformed the ritual symbolism of the sacrificial cult of the Temple into the worship of the synagogue which was characterized by inwardness and simplicity. The prophets repudiated mere outward ceremony as a means of approaching God, and the rabbis of the Talmud implemented the prophetic teachings by composing the essential prayers of the synagogue.

The *Siddur* has also been called a treasure-house of the Jewish spirit. Actually it is more than that. It is also the blueprint of the Jewish religious life at its noblest level. The daily routines of the Jew, his yearly cycles, and the milestones of his life from infancy to death are all accounted for in the *Siddur*. It enters into the Jew's living experiences on every level. By means of suitable benedictions and prayers, the *Siddur* infuses the Jew's daily activities with an element of sanctity. Such routine acts as eating and drinking, rising in the morning and retiring at night, dressing and washing one's hands are all within the purview of the *Siddur*.

The prayers and benedictions, the psalms and hymns, the joyous thanksgivings and mournful dirges which constitute the component parts of the *Siddur* evoke not only emotions, but also national memories and hopes. The prayers of the *Siddur* are the precipitates of the profoundest Jewish historic experiences. Through its contents one can glimpse the panorama of Jewish history from the earliest time to our own day. The redemption from Egyptian slavery, the victory of the Hasmoneans over their Syrian oppressors, the destruction of the Temple by the Romans, the massacres of whole Jewish communities by the Crusaders, the modern struggle for a national home in the land of Israel are but a few of the historic events that are celebrated or lamented in the prayers of the synagogue. But the *Siddur* can bring one into contact with the broad sweep of Jewish history only if he knows the story of the Jewish people, at least the peak events that gave rise to the national outbursts of joyful thanksgiving or sorrowful mourning. For example, if one is to grasp the meaning of the twelfth benediction of the *Tefillah*,* which begins with the malediction "For slanderers let there be no hope," he must know the events that followed the rise of Christianity and the anti-Jewish activities of some of the early Christians.† If one is to appreciate the bitterness of the Sabbath morning prayer "O Father of mercy . . . remember those loving, upright, and blameless ones who laid down their lives for the sanctification of the divine name," one must be informed about the massacres perpetrated by the Crusaders.‡

Among the authors of the many beseechments, thanksgivings, and dirges that fill the pages of the *Siddur* are many of the shining lights of the Jewish spirit. To be sure, most of the prayers were composed by men who preferred anonymity. But among those who can be identified, one finds priests and prophets, psalmists and sages, philosophers and poets, mystics and martyrs. What a glorious assortment of personalities the Jewish worshiper meets in the *Siddur!*

But most rewarding is the glimpse into the soul of the Jewish people that one gains through an acquaintance with the *Siddur*. In the prayers one can sense the pulse of the Jewish

* *See pp. 101 ff.*
† *See pp. 437–40.*
‡ *See pp. 446 ff.*

heart, the innermost feelings of the Jewish people in their moments of exaltation and dejection. One can also discern the Jewish people's aspirations and disillusionments, its ideals, and its profoundest beliefs. As a devotional compendium the *Siddur* is characterized by its numerous supplications and beseechments directed to the God of Abraham, Isaac, and Jacob, its many utterances of gratitude to the Almighty for His blessings and His love, its repeated outpourings of grief over sins committed, and its unending expressions of confidence that the Father in heaven will in His compassion forgive Israel's transgressions and will restore His people to its former glory. Through the *Siddur* one can also fathom the essence of Judaism and grasp "its strong doctrines of duty and righteousness, its moral earnestness, its cheery confidence in the world's possibilities of a sufficing and ennobling happiness, its faith in the purity and perfectibility of human nature, in brief, its ethical optimism."[2] It is a treasure-house of prayers, hymns, psalms, affirmations of faith, and eternal hope. These vital characteristics have raised the *Siddur* from the status of a useful handbook of worship to one of the most sacred books of Judaism, second only to the Bible.

A Beloved Treasure

The Jew of old knew his *Siddur* and he loved it. He enshrined it in his heart as the most beloved of all his religious possessions, exceeding even the Holy Scriptures. This sentimental relationship between the Jew and his *Siddur* is due in large measure to its personal orientation. The Bible, Solomon Schechter has pointed out, is the record of God's revelation to Israel. The *Siddur*, however, is the record of Israel's self-revelation to God. In it the Jew opens his heart to his Maker and reveals to Him his deepest yearnings and his highest aspirations. And the Jew was amply rewarded for his love of the *Siddur*. It gave him the healing balm of solace and hope. While the scholars searched for knowledge and guidance in the heavy tomes of the Talmud, the mass of the people incessantly read and reread the *Siddur* and found in it treasures of spiritual and intellectual riches. The *Siddur* has therefore been far more than a handy tool of worship to the Jew. Tools deteriorate with time and usage. But the *Siddur's* span of life has been almost coextensive with that of Israel. If we accept the thesis that God has planted eternal life in Israel's midst, then the *Siddur* promises to live eternally.

What Is Prayer?

The word *prayer* has become an esoteric term which at best conveys to modern man only vague, if not distorted, concepts. When modern man tries to define prayer he more often than not comes up with faded and even biased definitions that only compound the existing confusion. Before launching on a discussion of the *Siddur*, one must of necessity clarify the essential meaning of prayer and more specifically the Jewish concept of worship in its various manifestations.

Prayer is not, as some think, the invention of religious leaders. It preceded prophets and priests, temples and houses of prayer. Prayer is essentially the product of man's yearning for the most intimate of all human communication, for the opportunity to open his heart and his mind in adoration and supplication to the divine presence. This longing to pour out one's heart before God is natural and even necessary, provided one believes that there is a God who created the universe and is concerned with man, the crown of His creation. The roots of this yearning are to be found in man's sense of insufficiency, especially in time of stress, and in his desire to liberate himself from the burden of sin and the enslavement to evil. On a higher level there is man's eternal search for the ideal, a search which leads him to the Source of all good and of ultimate perfection.

Prayer is also born of man's sense of wonder, from his awareness of God's marvelous creation and the miracles that daily bear witness to God's goodness and love. One of the introductory benedictions of the daily morning service describes the marvel of the human body and its normal functions, and it concludes with the benediction "*Praised art Thou, O Lord, who healest all flesh and doest wonderfully*." There are also the eternal mysteries of life and death, birth and growth, the cycles of the seasons and the recurring regeneration of man's spirit and hope. When man begins to marvel at these mysteries, he naturally exclaims, as does the Jew in his daily prayers: "We give thanks unto Thee and declare Thy praise . . . for Thy miracles, which are daily with us, and for Thy wonders and Thy benefits, which are wrought at all times, evening, morn, and noon."

Prayer is also rooted in man's response of gratitude for God's blessings of life and sustenance, health and happiness, for the power to triumph over adversity and to recover from illness. Man is grateful for the sunshine and the rain in their season, for children and grandchildren, for hope in the future and anticipation of redemption. For these normal blessings man often wants to express his gratitude to God "whose loving-kindnesses never cease." Prayer is thus the bridge between earth and heaven, between man's despair and his eternal hope, between his depression of the soul and his spiritual elation.

The rabbis defined prayer as "the service of the heart." This does not imply that the rabbis identified prayer with emotionalism, for prayer is equally rooted in man's convictions concerning God's reality. The prayers of the synagogue contain not only outpourings of the heart but also many affirmations of the nature of God, His relationship with Israel, His concern for every human being, and man's duty to live in accordance with God's revealed will. Prayer thus presupposes convictions of the mind even as it engages the emotions of the heart.

The literary aspect of prayer is also a most engaging subject. Some prayers of the *Siddur* give evidence of having been born of rapture and delight and written in the excitement of the moment. These are often the most exalted religious lyrics of the liturgy. Others are evidently the result of concentrated creative efforts—these, too, are frequently examples of exquisite religious art. But some prayers are contrived and neatly confined within formal and complicated literary patterns of composition. Whatever their formulations, they have the potentiality of eliciting a response in the heart or mind of the worshiper.

The rabbis assigned to prayer a place of primacy in the life of the Jew. The Jew is required not only to participate in the prescribed daily services in synagogue and at home, but also to pronounce blessings on all events and experiences. As the famous scholar M. Steinschneider aptly put it: "the [Jew's] whole life became a divine service with interruptions." And these rabbinic prayers have withstood the vicissitudes of time and fashion and have survived the onslaughts of both persecution and prosperity. It is only in our times that these prayers have been challenged. If the challenge is to be met successfully an understanding of these prayers is urgently needed.

The Heart Has Many Chambers

The heart has many compartments, more than its morphology would suggest. Hence one finds different types of prayers emanating from the various human motivations. The most obvious type of prayer is that of supplication whereby the worshiper beseeches God to grant him certain boons.[3] These prayers are usually called petitions.

Prayers of Petition

Ideally, man should pray only for God's help in the achievement of noble goals. This high level of worship, however, can be reached only by saintly souls; ordinary men, as a rule, pray for the practical needs of life. They pray for health, sustenance, security, and long life. When their hearts are heavy with worry and fear, they pray for assurance and protection. When their bodies are afflicted with pain and disease, they pray for healing and recovery.

Among the primary supplications of religious persons are also prayers that seek forgiveness of sin. Nothing burdens a sensitive soul more than a feeling of sin. It gnaws at the very roots of his conscience, and does not permit him to forget that he has betrayed his God and repaid Him evil for His blessings. But forgiveness presupposes the acknowledgment of one's transgressions accompanied by repentance. Out of this presupposition was born the confessional prayer, examples of which are to be found in the Bible, especially in the postexilic books Ezra and Nehemiah and Daniel. Thus Nehemiah confesses his sins in the first of his recorded prayers:

> I beseech Thee, O Lord, the God of heaven . . . let Thine ear now be attentive, and Thine eyes open . . . while I confess the sins . . . which we have sinned against Thee. . . . We have dealt very corruptly against Thee, and have not kept the commandments . . . which Thou didst command Thy servant Moses [Neh. 1:5–7].

Prayers of petition have been relegated by some to the lowest rung of the ladder of worship. Actually, supplication is the heart of all prayer, and those who would remove supplications from the prayer book would only succeed in stripping it of its religious vitality and in emptying it of all personal relevance. For the truly religious person presents all his concerns to God as a child appeals to his father. To cut this direct line of communication between the worshiper and the divine is to cut the heart out of worship.

It is not to be denied, however, that petitionary prayer can be vulgarized, as, for example, when people beg God for favors and indicate why they deserve special consideration. Then there are what the rabbis called vain prayers, which anticipate God's suspension of the natural laws in order to meet the wants of the worshipers. The rabbis illustrate this type of prayer:

> If a man's wife is pregnant and he says, [God] grant that my wife bear a male child, this is a vain prayer. [The child's sex can be altered only by a miracle.] If he is coming home from a journey and he hears cries of distress in the town and says, [God] grant that this is not in my house, this is a vain prayer. [If the distress is already there it can be reversed only by a miracle.] [Ber. 54a].

Some prayers are not only vain but utterly unworthy and degrading. When students pray for athletic victory or for easy examinations, they are reducing prayer to the level of the ludicrous. But most disturbing are the prayers that are outright immoral. Among these are prayers that tend to intensify hatreds and foster passions of vengeance against enemies. Such degrading prayers should be contrasted with the teaching of the saintly Rabbi Judah He-Hasid: "In time of war, the prayer should not be for victory of one side over the other, but it should be for peace—that the Holy One, blessed be He, influence their hearts that they make peace." [4]

The prayer of the devout is neither vulgar nor selfish. It is not vain and surely not immoral. The devout person stands before God in utter humility and prays for God's help to rise above his afflictions both physical and spiritual and to achieve his highest potentials.

THANKSGIVING AND PRAISE

Supplication for personal or communal needs, common belief notwithstanding, is not the be-all and end-all of prayer. In fact most of the synagogue prayers are expressions of gratitude for God's manifold blessings. The psalmist's exclamation "O give thanks unto the Lord, for He is good/For His mercy endureth for ever" (Ps. 118:1), might be regarded as the keynote of the synagogue prayers. The Jew's first prayer of the day, recited on waking in the morning, is a prayer of thanksgiving: "I thank Thee, O everliving King, for having restored my soul to me in mercy. Thy faithfulness is very great." Similarly is the prayer recited on the Sabbath and festivals a hymn of thanksgiving:

> Though our mouths were full of song as the sea, and our tongues with exultation as the multitude of its waves, . . . we should still be unable to thank Thee and to praise Thy name, O Lord our God and God of our fathers, for one thousandth or one ten-thousandth part of the bounties which Thou hast bestowed upon our fathers and upon us.

Most significant is the fact that on the Sabbath and festivals prayers of petition have been all but eliminated so that the Jew might the better enjoy his Sabbath rest and his festival celebration.

The grace after meals * is obviously a prayer of thanksgiving; in it one finds a listing of some of the gifts that God has granted His people. The opening prayer is appropriately a

* *See pp. 292 ff.*

thanksgiving for the food. What follows may be regarded as a listing of the major divine gifts to Israel—the land of Israel, the Torah, the covenant (of Abraham), the Temple service, and the messianic promise.

Actually, the Jewish liturgy provides a blessing of gratitude for every experience,* and the rabbis teach that one should bless God for evil as well as for good (Ber. 54a). Thus an eighteenth century rabbi speaks about his practice of thanking God for everything:

> It was ever my wont to thank God for whatever happened to me. If some misfortune, small or great, befell [me] . . . I would acclaim with joy the justice of the decree. And I would put my happy thanks into words. . . . Similarly, on occasion of any good, small or great, I would offer thanks for the Lord's bountiful kindness. And He who knows my inmost secrets can testify of me that . . . I have ever rendered this service of praise unto God out of the great love of Him which is fixed in my heart, which has made it thankful for evil as for good, seeing that both are His handiwork.[5]

According to the rabbis, the prayers of thanksgiving are so central in the liturgy that they are destined to outlast all the other prayers. When the Messiah comes, said the rabbis, "all prayers will cease except the prayer of thanksgiving."[6]

Closely connected with gratitude is the desire to offer praises, not as a means of pleasing God, but as another means of expressing one's gratefulness for the daily wonders and miracles. To be sure, God is "exalted above all blessing and praise" (Neh. 9:5), yet the pious man feels a powerful urge to praise God and to extol His majestic glory. Many of the psalms are dedicated to the praise of God and "His marvellous works among all the peoples" (Ps. 96:3). The refrain "Hallelujah. (Praise ye the Lord)" opens and closes many of the psalms. Indeed, the Hebrew name of the Book of Psalms is *Tehillim*, or Hymns of Praise.

Sensitive people of every generation find themselves in a

* *See pp. 91–92.*

spiritual dilemma. They urgently desire to "recount the glories of God," but they are keenly aware of their inadequacy, which the psalmist expresses so eloquently: "Who can express the mighty acts of the Lord/Or make all His praise to be heard?" (Ps. 106:2). The rabbis, too, faced this dilemma. On the one hand, they interpreted the verse "He is your glory and He is your God" (Deut. 10:21) to mean that God is to be worshiped in words of praise.[7] On the other hand, they feel that any praise of God is essentially a falsification of God's true greatness and is therefore an affront. They objected to excessive praise of God, which is ultimately a dwarfing of God's greatness. One of the sages rebuked a synagogue reader who heaped a lot of praise on God. He asked the reader: "Have you concluded all the praise of your Master? Why do we want all this? Even with these three that we say [great, mighty and awesome], had not Moses our Master mentioned them in the Torah [Deut. 10:17] and had not the Men of the Great Synagogue come and inserted them in the *Tefillah*, we should not have been able to mention them." [8]

Actually this dilemma has never been resolved. The pious have continued to utter God's praises while at the same time they have continued to acknowledge the inadequacy of their utterances. As Solomon Ibn Gabirol put it so aptly in the concluding verses of his poem "Morning I Shall Seek Thee":

Little to Thy glory
Heart or tongue can do;
Small remains the story,
Add we spirit too.
Yet since man's praise ringing,
May seem good to Thee,
I will praise Thee singing,
While Thy breath's in me.[9]

Study as a Form of Worship

Jewish worship embraces the study of Torah. To people who are not steeped in Judaism this concept seems strange if not contradictory. The rabbinic definition of prayer as "the service of the heart" seems to exclude study which is strictly a matter of the mind. But this dichotomy does not exist in Judaism.

Solomon Schechter, in his essay on "Rabbi Elijah Wilna, Gaon," writes:

> To learn Torah meant for the Gaon . . . a kind of service to God. Contemporaries who watched him when he was studying the Torah observed that the effect wrought on the personality of the Gaon was the same as when he was praying. With every word his countenance flushed with joy; with every line he was gaining strength for proceeding further.[10]

The Gaon of Wilna was not an exception; he was a normal product of Judaism. Every Jewish scholar studied Torah with devotion, and many of them were wont to wear their tallitot and tefillin during their study. The ordinary Jew tried to emulate the scholars by studying the popular texts in the spirit of divine worship. The study of Torah was a central element of the synagogue worship, and the Torah was regularly read and expounded. The homily was a normal element of the service. The humblest Jew was afforded an opportunity not only to listen and to learn but to study the Torah on his own as part of his daily worship. Thus the rabbis taught:

> In what way can the words, *In His law* [*Torah*] *doth he meditate day and night* [Ps. 1:2] be obeyed? Rabbi Joshua answered: By the reading of the *Shema*, for when a man reads the [three paragraphs of] the *Shema* morning and evening, the Holy One, blessed be He, reckons it for him as if he had labored day and night in the study of Torah.[11]

This concept of the study of Torah has fostered among the Jewish people a zeal for learning which in time became a religious enthusiasm. To quote George Foot Moore:

> This conception of individual and collective study as a form of divine service has persisted in Judaism through all ages, and has made not only the learned by profession but men of humble callings in life assiduous students of the Talmud as the pursuit of the highest branch of religious learning and the most meritorious of good works.[12]

THE IDEAL PRAYER

Religious emotion flows not only through verbal expression, but also through song and dance. The psalmists therefore call on those who would worship God wholeheartedly to "Praise Him with the timbrel and dance" (Ps. 150:4).

> *Give thanks unto the Lord with harp,*
> *Sing praises unto Him with the psaltery of ten strings,*
> *Sing unto Him a new song;*
> *Play skilfully amid shouts of joy* [*Ps. 33:2–3*].

In the Pentateuch we are given a graphic picture of how "Moses and the Israelites sang" (Exod. 15:1) when they were rescued "out of the hand of the Egyptians" at the Sea of Reeds. And Moses' sister, Miriam, "took a timbrel in her hand, and all the women went out after her in dance with timbrels" (Exod. 15:20).

Song and dance have been a form of worship from days immemorial. In the synagogue, too, many of the prayers have been rendered in traditional tunes. On some occasions dance was utilized as a form of worship, especially during the annual celebration of the Rejoicing with the Torah, when the congregation abandons all rules of formal propriety and goes out in song and dance in honor of the Torah. The Hasidim * are particularly emphatic on the importance of "dancing before the Lord." In their synagogues singing and dancing occupy an important place in the service.

According to some, however, the highest form of worship, surpassing personal supplications, thanksgiving and praise, and the ecstasy of song and dance, is simple silence. When one directs his heart to God and utters no words of petition, his prayer is pure and humble. He does not suggest to God what He is to do. Nor does he indulge in excessive praises or thanksgiving which inevitably fall short of God's greatness and loving-kindness. Silence, according to this view, is man's ideal approach to God. The Midrash records a homily in support of this view:

* *See pp. 510–11.*

> Rabbi Abin said: When Jacob of the village of Neboria was in Tyre, he interpreted [the verse], *Praise is silence*[13] *for Thee, O God* (Ps. 65:2) as meaning that silence is the height of all praises of God. For God is like a jewel without price: however high you appraise it, still you undervalue it.[14]

The Spiritual Crisis of the Modern Jew

Notwithstanding the rapid secularization of modern life, there is an increasing interest in prayer. This interest, however, is largely intellectual. Its source is not religious faith, but rather widespread bewilderment because of the loss of faith. The modern Jew has abandoned the static traditions of the ghetto and has replaced them with the shifting values of modernity. But instead of feeling a sense of liberation, he often suffers from a spiritual void in his heart and a tormenting silence in his soul. Glaring contradictions bespeak this inner turbulence. Thus Felix Frankfurter, the eminent jurist and Supreme Court justice, left the synagogue as a youth and never returned to it. Yet he instructed that the Kaddish * prayer be recited at his funeral. Although he had declared himself an absolute agnostic, he asked that this intensely religious glorification of God be recited at his grave. He saw in it, said he, a way of "leaving the world as a Jew."

The modern Jew lives far more comfortably than his forebears. He is a beneficiary of the advances in science and technology. Yet he is not to be envied. Ease and comfort have not led to a nobler life. Some claim that there has been an inverse ratio between the quantity of the modern Jew's gadgets and the quality of his life. The more sensitive Jews have diagnosed their inner torments as a spiritual hunger which prayer might satisfy. But they cannot pray. Not only have they lost the habit of prayer, but they have lost the belief in the efficacy of prayer. Nonetheless, their interest in prayer has been aroused. They really want to know what there is to be known about prayer in general and about Jewish prayer in particular.

Despite his poverty the premodern Jew was in some ways a

* *See pp. 153–56.*

happier person. Under trying circumstances he knew what to do. "The righteous," said the prophet, "live[s] by his faith" (Hab. 2:4). The Jew of old had a deep and abiding faith in the God of his fathers. He found solace and strength in the certainty that God heard his prayer. In time of distress he poured out his heart to God in the confident belief that if he was deserving, God in His infinite wisdom and compassionate love would answer his prayer. Abraham Lincoln, though far from being a faithful churchman, often followed the same path. "I have been driven many times to my knees," said he, "by the overwhelming conviction that I had nowhere else to go. My own wisdom and that of all about me seemed insufficient for the day." [15] Most modern Jews, however, have lost this certainty, and with it they have also lost the art of prayer. When crisis comes, bewilderment and emptiness of soul are their lot.

Is Prayer Answered?

The premodern Jew fully believed that God hears and answers prayer. Thus Moses prayed in behalf of his sister, Miriam, and her leprosy was cured (Num. 12:13–14). The prophet Elijah prayed in behalf of a lifeless child and the child was restored to life (1 Kings 17:20–22). The people of Nineveh repented and "cried mightily unto God" and were saved from the impending doom (Jonah 3:5–10). The psalmists lived by this assumption:

> *The Lord is nigh unto all them that call upon Him,*
> *To all that call upon Him in truth.*
> *He will fulfil the desire of them that fear Him;*
> *He also will hear their cry, and will save them*
> [*Ps. 145:18–19*].

The rabbis of the Talmud reiterated this article of faith on numerous occasions. Thus we have the statement by Rabbi Hiyya bar Abba:

> When you pray and pray again, know that your prayer is heard, and that there will come a time when God will do what you ask. And the proof? *Wait for the Lord; be strong, and let thy heart take courage; yea, wait thou for the Lord.*
> [Ps. 27: 14].[16]

Among the medieval mystics, especially those of the Lurianic school,* there was a belief that prayer, if recited by the right person, at the right time, and with the proper concentration, has a powerful effect even in realms far beyond the mundane affairs of man. Such prayer, the mystics believed, could determine events of transcendent importance, such as bringing to an end Israel's exile. Many a mystic attempted to force God's hand by means of such prayer, but these attempts usually ended in disaster, because, said the kabbalists, some indispensable conditions of the perfect mystical prayer must have been missed.

Some Theological Questions and Answers

In modern times the traditional views on prayer have come under serious attack, and many a modern Jew has questioned the efficacy of prayer. Among these are even some who pray regularly but are nonetheless troubled by grave spiritual problems. If God answers prayer, they ask, how is it that the unending prayers for the coming of the Messiah and the redemption of Israel have remained unanswered these two thousand years? To be sure, the pious have an answer for this paradox. The deliverance of Israel, they say, affects the whole people and is therefore conditioned upon the repentance of the whole people. This is a foolproof argument, since it can never be established that every Jew has repented of his sins and has returned wholeheartedly to God.

But modern man is skeptical and he asks the old question: If God is omniscient, how can He answer prayer? If He responds to prayer, then He cannot know in advance the fate of anyone, for the fate of any person may change as a result of his prayer. Here, too, the theologians meet the challenge with a strong theological argument. They say that when God endowed man with free will, He ipso facto suspended His all-embracing knowledge in order to await man's actions, among which prayer is included.

But all theological speculations fade in the light of the Nazi holocaust. There are many who ask: Did God hear the agonizing cry of the millions of innocent victims in Buchenwald,

* *See pp. 488 ff.*

Auschwitz, and the other Nazi death factories? Where was God's answer to the prayers of the million innocent children who were doomed to death by the Nazis? If God can "hide His face" during such a mass slaughter, how can anyone be sure that prayer is ever efficacious?

In Defense of Prayer

The truly devout person is not staggered by the challenge of the moderns or the grim testimony of the holocaust. To begin with, he denies man's ability ever to understand God's ways. The devout person faces the fact of the Nazi holocaust as did the prophet Isaiah, who was similarly challenged by the holocaust of his day. He lived among the survivors of the mass slaughter perpetrated by the Babylonians during the destruction of the First Jewish Commonwealth in 586 B.C.E. The prophet, too, was challenged by the disturbing question: Where was God's answer to the prayers of the innocent victims during the mass slaughter at the time of the destruction of the holy Temple? The prophet's response was that man cannot possibly comprehend the ways of God:

> *For My thoughts are not your thoughts,*
> *Neither are your ways My ways, saith the Lord.*
> *For as the heavens are higher than the earth,*
> *So are My ways higher than your ways,*
> *And My thoughts than your thoughts* [*Isa.* 55:8–9].

The theological answers unfortunately do not satisfy the modern Jew. Not that they are illogical, but they are spoken in a language which is not modern in its idiom. Living in a world of rapid technological advances, he expects his question to be answered with experimental, demonstrable proof. But the laboratory of prayer is in the heart, and the process of searching for an answer is largely subjective. To sense the compelling reality of prayer, one must first develop the habit of prayer; to comprehend the power of prayer, one must experience the nearness of God. Most modern men, however, have become alienated from God and therefore cannot sense in their own hearts the essential efficacy of prayer. It should be noted, however, that some thoughtful men have discovered that the technological gods have clay feet. They provide life with neither purpose nor meaning. Some modern Jews have therefore responded to the prophet's call: "Return, O Israel, unto the Lord thy God" (Hos. 14:2), and many more may follow. How to hasten this response to the prophet's call is the central challenge for rabbis and Jewish religious educators.

"The Righteous Lives by His Faith"

For the devout person the proverbial "leap of faith" is decisive. He is convinced that the world has dimensions of reality unknowable to man. In the fact of creation and in the mystery of life he clearly sees the "hand of God." He discerns positive, moral forces at work in many spheres of human relationships. He sees God's moral purpose in the world of nature, in the history of the nations, and in the life of man. He therefore rejects any suggestion that the Creator is unconcerned with His creation. In short, the pivot of the pious Jew's faith is that the universe is not an accidental development. It is a purposeful divine creation. Man's sojourn on earth must therefore be purposeful. What nobler purpose can a Jew adopt than to do God's will? If it is God's will that man should engage in worship, as is indicated in the Torah, that is reason enough for the devout Jew to develop the habit of prayer and to engage in regular worship.

The Mystic Experience

The pious man is also a mystic at heart. He is uplifted by the experience of prayer. He does not expect the cosmic order to be altered for his sake. For him the privilege of having a "dialogue with God" is its own reward. Prayer is thus fully efficacious for the devout person. As a seventeenth century scribe enjoined his sons: "The real end of the prayers is not the petitions they contain, but the act of petition, the act of praying with genuine emotion. This is the true service, this is the true recognition of the sovereignty of Him to whom prayer is addressed." [17]

A Spiritual Force

But the pious Jew also knows from experience that the rewards of prayer exceed his anticipations. Not that God grants his every request, for God's answer is often negative. What is more, many prayers are not worthy of an answer. But the act of prayer tends to spiritualize the life of him who prays, and it tends to commit him to acts of moral significance.[18] It helps him to discover his life's orientation and sensitizes him to the ideals and aspirations of his faith. It enables the worshiper to listen more attentively to his inner voice of conscience and paves the way for following more closely the guidelines of moral action. The devout person knows from experience that prayer is the catalytic agent that often awakens in him ethical and moral forces.

To be sure, prayer does not by itself make a man godly, but it does tend to bring man a little nearer to God; prayer does not automatically make one a saintly person, but it does expose him to saintly ideals. Passions and temptations overwhelm even the most constant of worshipers, but it takes greater temptations for the devout to stumble into Satan's baited trap. As Abraham Joshua Heschel has put it: "Prayer may not save us, but it makes us worthy of being saved." [19]

Earnest prayer can help relieve anxieties of the soul and can awaken new resources of strength. It can calm the perplexities of the mind and thus endow the worshiper with new strength to overcome paralyzing fears. Prayer enables the devout to face crucial challenges and helps him to emerge from these confrontations unbroken. By sharing his frustrations and conflicts with God, the worshiper not only finds a measure of relief, but also discovers new sources of strength. When a Jew of old faced the new week on Saturday night, and his courage failed him because the anticipated trials seemed unendurable, he recited the Havdalah prayer:

> *Behold, God is my salvation;*
> *I will trust, and will not be afraid;*
> *For God the Lord is my strength and song;*
> *And He is become my salvation* [*Isa. 12:2*].

From this prayer he often drew much of the strength which enabled him to face the sad uncertainties of the new week. When a paratrooper in wartime is about to jump into the vast unknown, he often feels a powerful urge to pray. And his prayer usually releases in him new sources of courage to face the dangers ahead. In time of bereavement, prayers have often enabled mourners to overcome their deep sense of loss and to rise up from the depths of their gloom to face life with revived strength and hope.

One might speculate on the psychological and even the physiological factors that accompany these phenomena. For the devout person, however, it is enough to note that on numerous occasions in his own life prayer has been eminently effective. He is therefore prepared to follow the rabbinic injunction and offer prayers even when a sword is on his neck.

How to Pray

The rabbis often discussed the question of sincere prayer. How is one to worship God? How can one utter sincere prayer worthy of engaging divine attention and response? Their answer was simple and definitive: "A man must begin to pray only in a mood of humility—not in a mood of frivolity, nor in a mood of lightness, nor in a mood of banter—so that the Holy One, blessed be He, will listen to his prayer." [20] The rabbis also forbid the anticipation of a favorable divine response, however long and earnest one's prayer is. "If one prays long," says the Talmud, "and looks for the fulfilment of his prayer, in the end he will have vexation of heart" (Ber. 32b).

The lesson on how to pray is dramatically taught by the rabbis through an incident in the life of one of the great teachers of the Mishnah:

> When R. Eliezer fell ill, his disciples went in to visit him. They said to him: Master, teach us the paths of life so that we may through them win the life of the future world. He said to them . . . when you pray know before whom you are standing [Ber. 28b].[21]

Rabbi Eliezer's teaching on how to pray has been accepted by the Jewish people as a guiding rule. His advice, "know before whom you are standing," is prominently inscribed on the ark or the reading desk of most synagogues. Its purpose is to remind the worshipers that the element of intimacy, which often characterized the relationship between the Jew and God, must not be allowed to degenerate into vulgar familiarity. While sanctimonious pretentions are not encouraged in the synagogue, neither is a spirit of levity acceptable. Reverence and humility are the proper moods for prayer.

One must also strive for a mood of holiness. The term *holiness*, though elusive, is nonetheless indispensable to ideal worship. To be in a state of holiness implies an awareness of the mysterious and the godly; it infers a sense of awe which often kindles a feeling of ecstasy. Rabbi Eleazar, who lived in Worms in the eleventh century, admonishes his son: "My son! Exert all thy bodily powers to attain to holiness, to subdue thy will unto God!" [22] In a similar vein does Nachmanides, the great thirteenth century scholar and mystic, admonish his son:

> And when thou prayest, remove all worldly considerations from thy heart, . . . cleanse thine inmost thoughts and meditate before uttering thy devotions. . . . By this course thy deeds will all be upright, and thy prayer pure and clean, innocent and devout, and acceptable before the Lord.[23]

KAVVANAH, THE KEY TO PRAYER

The rabbis struggled against the all too human tendency to emphasize form rather than substance, the tendency to recite prayers rather than to pray with heart and mind. They strove to spiritualize the forms of worship by stressing the element of kavvanah. Unfortunately, the term *kavvanah* has no exact equivalent in the English language. It has been translated as *concentration*, *devotion*, *intention*, or *inwardness*. It means all these things and more. It arose from the Jewish religious experience and represents a uniquely Jewish attitude to religious devotion. Its nuances can be caught only from its historic and literary contexts. The closest we can come to a definition of the term is to say that it implies a total concentration on the act of prayer, so that one reaches a state of worship that encompasses all one's heart and all one's soul and all one's might. To achieve a state of kavvanah is obviously not easy. It is natural for the mind to be distracted and to wander. The prophets loudly denounced perfunctory worship, and their successors, the rabbis of the Talmud, continued this struggle. They pronounced the general principle that the performance of all religious duties requires kavvanah, especially that of prayer. The medieval Jewish philosopher Bahya Ibn Pakuda, in his classic work, *The Duties of the Heart*, gives this theme great emphasis:

> If one prays with his tongue and his heart is otherwise engaged, his prayer is like a body without a spirit, or a shell without a kernel. . . . Therefore, my brother, arrange the contents of your prayer in proper form in your heart. Let it correspond with the words which you utter. Let both the words and the thought be directed to God.[24]

Spontaneity and Regularity in Prayer

There are several dimensions to sincere prayer, and a devout person ardently strives to measure up to all of them. Among these, spontaneity is of crucial importance. The pious man often feels that fixed prayers tend to imprison his piety. They tend to fetter his devotions within established formulas, often reducing his supplications to a mere outward performance of a religious duty.

The rabbis of the Talmud were keenly aware of these dangers. The Mishnah quotes a definitive statement by one of the sages: "If a man makes his prayer a fixed task, it is not a [genuine] supplication" (Ber. 4:4). And the Talmud defines "a fixed task" as prayers which consists of an established liturgy with nothing new added (Ber. 29b). When Rabbi Gamaliel II canonized the early synagogue prayers,* some of his contemporaries strongly dissented (Ber. 4:3). They saw the dangers

* *See pp. 86–88.*

inherent in the regulation of devotions. Nonetheless, the rabbis felt that regularity of worship and fixed forms of prayer were indispensable elements of man's religious life. They therefore prescribed prayers and benedictions for all occasions, so that the whole of a Jew's life was to be hallowed by a continuous act of sanctification.

The rabbinic logic is to be found in the essential nature of man. The rabbis felt that one cannot wait for the rare moments of inspiration when one can engage in prayers of self-expression. There is a real danger that in the process of waiting one may become totally weaned from the art of prayer and incapable of praying even when that rare moment of inspiration arrives. Waiting for inspiration will thus result in not praying at all. This has been substantiated by the experience of many people. Not only have they ceased to pray, but the moments of inspiration also ceased to stir their hearts. To quote Israel Abrahams: "What can be done at any time and in any manner is apt to be done at no time and in no manner." [25] One must see prayer in the framework of an art:

> A musician must practice by prearranged schedule, regardless of his inclination at the moment. So with the devout soul. It may not rely on caprice or put its hope in chance. It must work. The man . . . who postpones worship for the right mood and the perfect setting—a forest or mountain peak, for example—will do little of meditating or praying. After all, how often does one find himself in a "cathedral of nature," and when he does who shall say that he will be in a worshipful temper? [26]

On the other hand, regular prayer, or prayer of empathy, as Abraham J. Heschel has termed it, though routinized into a habit, does on many occasions yield to meaningful worship. Besides it is not true that regulated prayer always degenerates into barren ritualism and therefore precludes inwardness and spirituality.

> Empathy is evocative; it calls up what is hidden. Every one of us bears a vast accumulation of unuttered sorrows, scruples, hopes, and yearnings,

> frozen in the muteness of our natures. In prayer, the ice breaks, our feelings begin to move our mind, striving for an outlet. Empathy generates expression.[27]

The man who prays regularly, utilizing the fixed prayers prescribed in the *Siddur* is obviously apt to be performing a routine ritual. But when that sought-after moment of devout prayer does arrive, when the heart truly yearns for God and for His help, the routine exercise becomes a soulful communion with God.

When the rabbis finally resolved to fix the prayers, they left room for a measure of spontaneity. They provided for privately composed prayers within the framework of the prescribed services. When the worshiper completed the silent *Tefillah*,* he was to add a personal prayer. The Talmud records a number of prayers that some of the sages composed for their private use. But the ordinary worshiper seldom emulated the rabbis. He was content to recite the prescribed prayer and to pour into them the yearnings of his heart.

Preparation for Prayer

When the rabbis established the "Order of the Prayers," they foresaw the danger of the prayers becoming mere mouthings of fixed formulas. To meet this danger they not only provided for personal prayers, but they also insisted on due preparation. "The pious men of old," says the Mishnah, "used to wait an hour before praying in order that they might concentrate their thoughts upon their Father in Heaven" (Ber. 5:1). The rabbis realized that a man cannot possibly make the transition from business transactions or idle talk to reverent prayer quickly. Nor can one spontaneously cross over from grief to exultation. The Talmud therefore teaches that a person whose mind is not at ease must not pray. One of the sages, relates the Talmud, would not pray when he was agitated (Eru. 65a). A bridge of preparation is indispensable.

In later centuries special prayers were composed to aid in "directing the heart to God," such as the introductory sup-

* *See pp. 101 ff.*

plications known as *Reshuyot*, which ask permission to recite the prayers that follow. The medieval Hebrew poets Solomon Ibn Gabirol and Judah Halevi excelled in their elaborate introductions. The recitation of the Ashre (Ps. 145) during the afternoon service was meant to induce the worshipers to meditate awhile before beginning the essential service itself. It is related that the Tzanzer Rebbe was asked by one of the Hasidim: "What does the Rebbe do before praying?" "I pray," said he, "that I may be able to pray properly." [28]

Music, an Aid to Devotion

The ancients discovered another antidote to the routinization of prayer. Appropriate music, they found, stirs the heart and infuses devotion into one's prayer. Thus the psalmist exhorts those who come to the Jerusalem Temple: "Sing unto the Lord with thanksgiving/Sing praises upon the harp unto our God" (Ps. 147:7). And the saintly Judah He-Hasid, who lived in the latter half of the twelfth century, elaborated on this theme:

> Say your prayer in the melody that is most pleasant and sweet in your eyes. Then you shall pray with proper concentration [kavvanah]; because the melody will draw your heart after the words that come from your mouth. Supplication in a melody makes the heart weep, and praise in a melody makes the heart happy. Thus you will be filled with love and joy for Him that sees your heart, and you will bless Him with great love and with joy.[29]

Praying with the Congregation

The institution of congregational worship is one of the great Jewish contributions to mankind.* To be sure, a man can worship privately and can order his devotional life within the framework of his God-given personality. But the rabbis felt that the Jew who worships privately treads a spiritually lonely road. He lacks the spiritual uplift that one gains from corporate worship. The rabbis therefore taught that prayer is most efficacious when offered with a congregation. They interpreted the verse "But as for me, let my prayer be unto Thee, O Lord,

* *See pp. 63 ff.*

in an acceptable time" (Ps. 69:14) to mean "when the congregation prays" (Ber. 7b–8a). One of the sages said that God's presence is in the synagogue, "for it is said: 'God standeth in the congregation of God' [Ps. 82:1]" (Ber. 6a).

It often happens that congregational services distract the worshiper from devotional concentration, or kavvanah. Occasionally, one is tempted to converse with his neighbor, especially when the service is not sufficiently decorous. Nonetheless, the rabbis preferred congregational to private prayer. One obvious reason is that it permits one to participate in a number of essential prayers which can be recited only at a group service.[30] Another is that it enables one to participate in the instructional part of the service which is a central feature of Jewish worship. One can follow the reading of the scriptural portions and can listen to the religious discourse.

But more noteworthy is the psychological factor. A person who worships with a congregation derives much spiritual strength from sharing his experiences with the group. Corporate worship sustains the weak and supports the wavering. It enables one to pray with heightened devotion and greater kavvanah.

For the Jew, group worship has the added value of fusing more firmly his tie with the community of Israel. At a public service the Jew experiences a tangible association with his people, an experience which tends to rivet the links that bind him with Israel. Only in the synagogue does the Jew experience fully that feeling of commonality, that warmth of association, and that sentiment of belonging which strengthen his identification with the Jewish people.

The creation of a strong feeling of identity with the Jewish people is especially important to the Jew because his people is scattered abroad and constantly exposed to the pressures of the dominant non-Jewish cultures. These pressures usually cause a spiritual and cultural erosion which threatens the Jewish people with total disintegration. Congregational worship thus assumes a significance which transcends the devotional needs of the individual Jew; it is also an effective weapon in the Jew's eternal battle for survival.

Praying for the Congregation

One of the remarkable characteristics of Jewish prayer is its formulation in the plural. The worshiper prays for the community of Israel. Not that the private needs of the individual are unimportant; but the individual's well-being is so intertwined with that of the community of Israel that the well-being of both is regarded as identical. Another underlying principle is that a man should "associate others" in his petitions. This principle is presented in an incisive talmudic pronouncement:

> A man should always associate himself with the congregation [even when reciting a private prayer on a journey]. How should he say [his prayer]? 'May it be Thy will, O Lord *our* God, to lead *us* forth in peace etc.' [Ber. 29b–30a].

This rabbinic statement is remarkable. Even a man who is far removed from a congregation, praying on a lonely road for his personal safety, must not pray for himself alone, but for the group. In this vein the Talmud teaches:

> One who passes through a place infested with beasts or bands of robbers says a short *Tefillah* [in place of the prescribed Eighteen Benedictions *]. What is a short *Tefillah*? . . . "The needs of Thy people Israel are many and their wit is small [i.e., they do not know how to ask for their needs]. May it be Thy will, O Lord our God, to give to each one his sustenance and to each body what it lacks. Blessed [Praised] art Thou, O Lord, who hearkenest unto prayer" [Ber. 29b].

The prayers of the synagogue are almost entirely in the plural. Even when a person cannot join a congregation and worships in the privacy of his home, the prayers are in the plural: "Cause us to return, O our Father, unto Thy Torah; draw us near, O our King, unto Thy service, and bring us back in perfect repentance unto Thy presence." "Forgive us, O our Father, for we have sinned; pardon us, O our King, for we

* *See pp. 101 ff.*

have transgressed; for Thou dost pardon and forgive." "Heal us, O Lord, and we shall be healed; save us and we shall be saved; for Thou art our praise."

The community of Israel is often called the "house of Israel." As a man prays for his family's well-being and thus finds his personal fulfillment through his family, so does the Jew find his salvation through the community of Israel.

The Language of Prayer

Liturgies are usually the offspring of the heart, and their purpose is primarily to inspire and uplift. The language of prayer is, therefore, as a rule literary, not scientific. Whether it expresses adoring gratitude or humble petition, it draws on poetic imagery rather than pedantic exactitude. The language of Jewish prayer is endowed with an additional characteristic derived from its slow evolution. The rabbis opposed the writing down of the prayers. This kept the liturgy in a fluid state for almost a thousand years * and permitted them to develop an incisive idiom. Original wording gave way to happier phrasing, wordy formulations were contracted, and excessively brief prayers were elaborated. The prosaic yielded to the poetic, the didactic to the imaginative, the artificial to the genuine language of the heart. Inevitably, much of worth was lost in this selective process which spanned so many generations. The residue, however, is much the finer because of the slow but thorough sifting and refining. To be sure, some excessive oriental praise of God remained in the *Siddur*. But that was unavoidable since the *Siddur*'s development took place largely in Palestine and Babylonia, which were then and still are part of the oriental world.

The Holy Tongue

Hebrew was the preferred language of prayer, and to this day Hebrew has remained for the most part the language of the *Siddur*. The rabbis of the Talmud repeatedly stressed the principle that Hebrew should be employed as the language of worship. Not only is Hebrew the holy tongue, the language of

* *See pp. 368–70.*

the Torah, but according to one of the sages, it is also the language most suitable for prayer: "R. Jonathan taught that there are four languages: the Roman is best for battle; the Greek best for song; the Persian best for lamentation; and the Hebrew best for prayer." [31]

Another teacher of the Talmud is quoted as having laid down the principle that secular matters may be uttered in the holy language, whereas sacred matters must not be uttered in secular language (Shab. 40b). The rabbis even opposed the use of Aramaic in prayer, notwithstanding the fact that Aramaic was considered a semiholy language because a substantial part of the Holy Scriptures are in the Aramaic tongue.[32] Thus Rabbi Yohanan is of the opinion that "if anyone prays for his needs in Aramaic, the Ministering Angels do not pay attention to him, because they do not understand that language [and therefore cannot transmit these prayers to the throne of glory]!" (Sotah 33a). But this extreme view did not prevail. Prayer in other languages was not ruled out. Not only were a number of Aramaic prayers admitted into the liturgy, but the Mishnah actually ruled that the *Shema* and the *Tefillah* * which constitute the essence of the Jewish liturgy "may be recited in any language" (Sotah 7:1).

The use of the vernacular in the liturgy did not really become a problem until modern times, when the mastery of Hebrew reading ceased to be universal among the Jews. Formerly all male children were thoroughly prepared for the synagogue ritual. The children were taught not only to read the Hebrew prayers but also to comprehend their contents. Conversely, the Bible was studied not only for meaning but also for usage in the synagogue services. The traditional chants of the Torah and the prophetic portions were intensively drilled in the Jewish schools. In modern times, however, when Jewish education is neither universal nor intensive, the majority of Jews cannot even read the Hebrew prayers, let alone understand their contents. The advisability of using the vernacular in the synagogue ritual has therefore become a live issue. If kavvanah is the road to efficacious prayer, it is argued, then let

* *See pp. 96 ff., 101 ff.*

the prayers be read in the vernacular. Otherwise, the words uttered are nothing more than mysterious incantations.

These powerful arguments have been met by equally logical and convincing reasoning. The holy tongue, say the defenders of the tradition, has been used as the language of Jewish prayer for thousands of years; it contains sentiments and nuances that no other tongue can possibly reproduce. To tamper with the Hebrew or even the several ancient Aramaic prayers is to destroy the authenticity of the prayers themselves. Thus the Kaddish prayer, which is recited by mourners,* and the Kol Nidre prayer chanted on the Day of Atonement † happen to be in Aramaic. If translated even into Hebrew, let alone into any other vernacular, they would be stripped of their historic garb and of their powerful appeal to the heart of the people. A Hebrew hymn, when recited by the congregation, evokes in the hearts of worshipers a feeling of oneness with the entire people of Israel throughout the world and throughout the ages.

Moses Maimonides gives a rational reason for the rabbinic institution of praying in the Hebrew tongue. There is a real danger arising from the scattering of the Jews over wide areas and many kingdoms. They might split up into many splinter groups in accordance with the different languages spoken by them. Therefore, says Maimonides, Ezra and his synod formulated the prayers in pure Hebrew so that all Israelites might pray in union.[33] And a modern Reform rabbi, writing in his congregational bulletin, speaks eloquently on the same theme:

> Hebrew is the language of prayer. . . . While God does understand every language, as the Sages said centuries ago, the Jew has discovered Hebrew to be the most appropriate vehicle for communion with the deity, the most perfect instrument for placing before Him the yearnings of the heart and the needs of the soul. Many of the traditional prayers and petitions defy translation. Who can render into English

* *See pp. 153 ff.*
† *See pp. 244 ff.*

> "*Ribono Shel Olam*"? "Master of the Universe" does not convey the overwhelmingly religious content of these untranslatable Hebrew words, which are unique to the Jew. And this is true of the entire liturgy, which loses much of its power and inspired character when rendered in another tongue.[34]

An Intelligent Piety

All liturgies are rooted in the nature of man and his relationship to the universe in which he lives. One can trace a number of these common roots to ancient man's fears of the inhospitable world that he inhabited. In periods of danger or distress he instinctively turned to the gods for protection and succor. And in time of deliverance and exaltation he naturally praised and thanked the gods for their benevolence. In time liturgies were developed and rituals took shape. To be sure, the concepts of the deities differed from people to people. But they were adequate within their specific cultures.

There were, from time to time, some sensitive souls who were not fully satisfied with the existing liturgies and rituals. They searched for the significance of life and the role of the gods in the affairs of man. This spiritual search often led them, as it still does, to an intellectual impasse. These exceptional men were often troubled by the mysteries of life and death, and not infrequently they experienced the anguish of loneliness. Out of these spiritual struggles came many of the noblest prayers both in Judaism and in other faiths. But less gifted men, who constitute the overwhelming majority of mankind, when faced with similar perplexities of the spirit cannot find the appropriate words to express the yearnings of their hearts. They naturally turn to priests and prophets for the formulation of their prayers.

The liturgy of the synagogue, though sharing many of its characteristics with the liturgies of other faiths, is nonetheless unique. This uniqueness can be grasped partly through a knowledge of its incomparable history. Although the Jewish liturgy had its beginnings in the sacrificial cult of the Jerusalem Temple, it developed into a revolutionary form: public prayer, now shared by many other faiths. It was Judaism that eliminated the sacrificial cult and the priest as an intermediary between the worshiper and the Deity. The Jews were the pioneers in the daring concept that the people can collectively pray directly to God. Since people cannot compose original prayers, the Jews utilized the prayers composed by the gifted —the psalmists and the sages. These prayers remained oral for over a millennium, during which they slowly took shape. In order that these prayers might emanate from their heart, the rabbis insisted on devotion and concentration during worship. This combination of an established liturgy and an earnestness of heart saved the Jewish prayers from becoming mere incantations and resulted, as George Foot Moore put it, in "an intelligent piety."[35] For an understanding of this religious odyssey involving the growth and development of the *Siddur* and for an appreciation of its spiritual dimensions, this book was written.

PART I

THE FOUNDATIONS OF JEWISH WORSHIP

1 HEBREW WORSHIP IN ANCIENT DAYS: THE TEMPLE CULT

The *Siddur* differs radically from any other book of prayer past or present. It differs in content not only because of differences in belief and tradition, but also because of its unique history. It was not composed by an official body charged with the task of producing a prayer book for the synagogue. The *Siddur* grew slowly over a period of many centuries. To grasp its unique development and its singular character we must cast our eyes far back in history, for its roots are sunk deep in the soil of the Jewish past, reaching back more than three thousand years. The story of the *Siddur* must begin with a brief account of the ancient mode of worship which prevailed during the days of the First and Second Temples.

A Glance at Thirteen Hundred Years of History

The period under review extends from the time when the Hebrew tribes gained their freedom from Egyptian bondage, about 1200 B.C.E., to the time when the Second Jewish Commonwealth ended catastrophically in the year 70 C.E. The Temple of Jerusalem was then destroyed, and the sacrificial cult came to an abrupt end. More accurately, the Temple ritual was suspended, and it has remained so for almost two thousand years.

This long period of almost thirteen hundred years saw the children of Israel molded into a nation. The inspired genius Moses led them from Egyptian bondage to Mount Sinai, where they received the Torah, and then to the borders of the Promised Land. Moses' successor, Joshua, led the erstwhile slaves into the land of Canaan. They conquered the land and settled in it. In the process of settling down the Hebrews were transformed from a group of nomadic tribes subsisting on domesticated animals to a settled nation sustaining itself on agricultural crops of field and orchard. This was a social revolution of vast dimensions. They also came into close contact with the cultic practices of the native population. The Hebrews imitated some of these practices, thus introducing crude, idolatrous rituals—including fertility rites and witchcraft. These practices shocked the Hebrew prophets, who protested vigorously and repeatedly. The end result of the prophetic activities was the banishment of the immoral practices of Baal worship from the Hebrew ritual. Only a few elements of the foreign worship were absorbed and assimilated. But the essential character of the Hebrew faith and worship was not corrupted.

The thirteen centuries extending from the Exodus from Egypt to the fall of Jerusalem in the year 70 C.E. also witnessed the founding of the Hebrew monarchy and its firm establishment under King David and his son Solomon. After Solomon's death the kingdom split, but the Davidic dynasty continued to reign in the southern kingdom of Judea, where Jerusalem was both the seat of government and the center of worship. It was there that Solomon built the Temple and installed a hereditary priesthood. The Jerusalem Temple eventually established itself firmly as the supreme holy place. It became the sole sanctuary where offerings could be brought and the great festivals celebrated.

The two Hebrew kingdoms—Israel in the north and Judea in the south—came to tragic ends. The northern kingdom lasted only two centuries. It was destroyed in 721 B.C.E. by Assyria, the contemporary world power, and it was never again restored. Its population, usually referred to as the Ten Tribes of Israel, was exiled and, in all probability, assimilated into the peoples of the empire. This gave rise to the myth of the "Lost Ten Tribes" who have been repeatedly "discovered" and identified with the most unlikely peoples, such as the Japanese, the American Indians, the British, and others.

The southern kingdom of Judea, however, managed to maintain itself for an additional century and a half. These were crucial years, during which several of the prophets uttered their exalted prophecies. When the catastrophe finally came in the year 586 B.C.E., the prophetic teachings had already immunized the Judeans against the shock of their spiritual and national calamity. The Babylonian conquerors destroyed Jerusalem, burned the Temple, and took a part of the population into captivity. But these exiles, unlike the Israelites of the northern kingdom, succeeded in accomplishing what no ancient people had ever achieved. They maintained their national identity and their ancestral faith despite the loss of their national homeland and the destruction of their central sanctuary. The prophets had foretold the impending misfortune and had repeatedly proclaimed the coming disaster as a just retribution for the people's sins. The Jews accepted this interpretation of their calamity; they repented of their past backsliding and relied on the prophets' comforting promise of restoration. They adjusted to their new life in exile and awaited their return to the Holy Land, where they would rebuild the Temple and resume their traditional worship.

Half a century passed and the hoped-for opportunity arrived. King Cyrus, the Persian, conquered Babylonia and permitted the exiled Jews to return to Jerusalem and to rebuild their Temple. To be sure, not many returned. Most of the exiles had established themselves in relative comfort. Besides, the road to Jerusalem was hazardous. Still, about forty thousand Jews did return. This nucleus of pioneers rebuilt the Temple altar and resumed the traditional worship. The leadership of Ezra and Nehemiah succeeded in bringing them a measure of normality, both political and spiritual. Ezra's leadership was especially momentous. His impact on the character of Judaism has been considered second only to that of Moses.

When Alexander the Great conquered the Near East and arrived in Jerusalem in 332 B.C.E., he found a peaceful Jewish community. Its religious life revolved around the Temple, and its political life was administered largely by the Temple hierarchy. This peaceful situation was disrupted by one of Alexander's successors, Antiochus IV of Syria, who initiated a policy of religious coercion. He hoped to bring unity into his realm by unifying all his subjects in a single state religion. When Antiochus forcefully introduced his pagan worship into the Jerusalem Temple, the Jews, under the leadership of the Hasmonean family, rebelled. They defeated the government forces, and in 165 B.C.E. they won their independence.

The Hasmonean dynasty reigned till it was replaced by the Roman procurators in 63 B.C.E. It is reported that when Pompey entered Jerusalem and penetrated the Holy of Holies he was amazed by its "emptiness." He found no images of gods. This was incomprehensible to him, as it had been to many a pagan before him. The Roman procurators were not only oppressive but callous to the religious sensibilities of the Jews. Jewish restiveness finally erupted in a violent rebellion. The heroic but unequal struggle lasted three years, ending catastrophically in the year 70 C.E. The Roman legions conquered Jerusalem, burned the Temple, and wreaked cruel vengeance on the population.

The Sacrificial Cult in Primitive Society

During that vast period of Jewish history the essential religious act of Jewish worship was the offering of sacrifices at local shrines as well as at the central sanctuary. The offering was usually an animal which was ritually slaughtered; its parts were either eaten at the sanctuary or burned on the altar. An elaborate ritual guided the performance of the sacrificial rites from the moment the victim was selected to the time of its final consumption. The number and variety of sacrifices was quite impressive: there were public and private sacrifices, voluntary and obligatory offerings. Among the sacrifices listed and described in the Bible are trespass offerings, sin offerings, purification offerings, peace offerings, thanksgiving offerings, and others. Then there were public morning and evening sacrifices, "additional" offerings on Sabbaths and festivals, and many others that filled the elaborate catalog of the priestly functions. And each sacrifice had its specified ritual, known to the Kohanim (priests) in all its particulars and performed by them with undeviating exactitude.

The sacrificial form of worship is incomprehensible to most modern men. It seems crude and devoid of spirituality. The popular view that it is nothing more than a kind of witchcraft practiced by primitive man because of his intellectual and spiritual immaturity is far from correct. All available evidence supports the view that ancient man was not less intelligent than modern man. But his education—using the term in its broadest sense—was different. Not only did he know less about the world he lived in and about the universe beyond, but his way of thinking was radically different. What modern man labels as superstition was for ancient man the "facts" of life. His concept of the gods was generally an extension of his daily experience. The gods were like men and women, but usually immortal. They possessed human frailties such as hunger, envy, and ambition. They loved and hated, fought and took vengeance, very much like human beings. But the gods were all-powerful and could reward and punish as they saw fit without regard to any law. Man, by contrast, was mortal, weak, and helpless. He naturally tried to win the favor of the gods by offering sacrifices at the holy places in accordance with the hallowed procedures best known to the priests.

It is significant that this form of worship, which modern man finds so difficult to comprehend, is as old as history. This is confirmed by the study of primitive man and is also indicated in the biblical story of the first generations of man. Cain and Abel, the Bible relates, brought sacrifices to God. So did their descendants throughout that primitive period. The sacrificial cults were not only ancient but natural; they were not imposed on primitive society by the priests. It was altogether natural for primitive man to express his thankfulness to the gods for the bounty of the harvest. When his fields yielded their harvest and his flocks delivered their "fruit of the womb," primitive man naturally felt grateful to the gods who bestowed upon him these blessings. He expressed his gratitude by bringing, as Cain did, "an offering to the Lord from the fruit of the soil" and as Abel "brought the choicest of the firstlings of his flock" (Gen. 4:3–4).

In bringing an offering to the shrine of worship primitive man was also expressing his submission to the gods who control the forces of nature which make for plenty or scarcity, for life or death. When primitive man suffered from a sense of guilt, a feeling of having offended a deity, he longed for reconciliation. How was he to propitiate the gods and once more become worthy of divine favor? It was natural for primitive man to bring an offering—usually something precious from the fruits of the earth or the increase of his flocks or even, in some cults, the most precious of gifts, one of his children—a practice the Bible protested most vigorously against. But abhorrent as human sacrifice is, it is not unnatural.

The sacrificial cult was also a most gratifying and even fascinating form of worship. The devotee not only felt that he had performed his duty and made his peace with the deity, but he experienced a personal contact and even union with the deity. It was customary for the officiating priest to bless the offering and to consecrate it. This brought the supplicant into actual contact with the deity. When he finally partook of the sacrificial meal, he felt rejuvenated and reinvigorated. He had absorbed, in a literal sense, some of the divine essence. It is no wonder that the cult was so attractive and even exciting to primitive man, that it elicited his scrupulous and dedicated attachment for millennia on end, until the Jews founded the synagogue and instituted public prayer as the chief form of worship.

The Sacrificial Cult in Israel

When the Hebrews entered the Promised Land and subdued it, they brought with them a nomadic culture based on a sheep-raising economy. But when they settled in the land of Canaan, their social organization underwent a revolutionary change. It became predominantly agricultural. This change affected every phase of their life, including their way of worship. They did not abandon their relatively simple desert rituals and observances. They only adapted them to the new circumstances. They also added some new features borrowed from their neighbors. For example, the sacrifice of the paschal lamb had its origin in the nomadic days when the Passover feast marked the yeaning of their flocks. As it happened, the first ripe grain was harvested in the land of Canaan at the same season of the year. The Hebrews continued to practice the ritual of the paschal lamb, but they added to it the agricultural offering of the first fruits in the form of the unleavened bread. Later, it should be noted, these rituals became associated with the Exodus from Egypt and assumed a significance that transcended both the nomadic and the agricultural roots of these observances.

At first the Hebrews brought their offerings at various local shrines. Almost every locality had its place of worship in the form of a bamah, or high place. Some of these shrines were especially sacred since their fame was based on ancient traditions. Bethel, for example, was reputed to have been founded by no less a historic figure than the patriarch Jacob (Gen. 28: 10–22). Similar sanctity adhered to shrines in Beersheba, Hebron, and other places. The Hebrews went to these shrines on Sabbaths and New Moons, and especially during the annual festivals. They offered their sacrifices and rejoiced before their God. At times admixtures of heathen practices contaminated the purity of the simple religion which the Hebrews had brought with them from the desert. The imitation of Canaanite fertility rites, witchcraft, and even human sacrifice threatened the ethical and moral character of the Hebrew faith. The religious leaders were shocked by these immoralities. They raised their voices repeatedly against these heathen practices. Throughout the period of the First Jewish Commonwealth the prophets battled unceasingly against idolatry and its abominations. This remarkable development in Jewish worship will again be touched upon later in this chapter.

The Centralization of Worship in Jerusalem

When the Hebrews conquered the land of Canaan, the city of Jerusalem successfully resisted the invaders. For almost two centuries Jerusalem remained outside the reach of the Hebrews. Its location in the mountains of Judea and its powerful fortifications had rendered it almost impregnable. It was finally conquered by King David, who made it the capital of his kingdom and designated it as the religious center of the Hebrews. This designation, however, did not assume reality till his son Solomon built a magnificent Temple and brought into it the ark of the covenant, which contained the tablets with the Ten Commandments inscribed upon them. The presence of the holy ark greatly heightened the sanctity and prestige of the Jerusalem Temple and helped make it the most important sanctuary of the nation. But even the Temple of Solomon did not succeed in displacing the local shrines where idolatrous practices often flourished. It was only in the days of King Josiah (637–608 B.C.E) that the Jerusalem Temple became the sole place of worship for the whole nation. It took a violent religious revolution to bring this about. What happened is dramatically related in the Bible. Hilkiah the high priest, we are told, "found the book of Law" in the Temple and sent it to the king. This book is identified by most scholars as the Book of Deuteronomy. When the king read the book, he was deeply moved. He assembled the people and read to them the book that had been discovered in the Temple:

> And the king . . . made a covenant before the Lord, to walk after the Lord and to keep His commandments, and His testimonies, and His statutes . . . that were written in this book; and all the people stood to the covenant [2 Kings 23:3].

King Josiah carried out the terms of the covenant. He destroyed every vestige of idolatry in the whole land of Judea and even in the northern cities of Israel. He destroyed the altars on the high places, the shrines, and all the witchcraft in the land. Only the Jerusalem Temple and its purified ritual remained. For this thoroughgoing religious revolution the Bible singles out King Josiah for highest praise:

> And like unto him was there no king before him, that turned to the Lord with all his heart, and with all his soul, and with all his might, according to all the law of Moses; neither after him arose there any like him [2 Kings 23:25].

The results of this drastic revolution were truly momentous. With the suppression of the local shrines, the allurements of idolatry and witchcraft could be controlled and eradicated.

The priesthood was now confined to the family of Aaron, and the code of the Book of Deuteronomy was solemnly adopted as the law of the land. The festivals now assumed historic significance in accordance with the teachings of the Book of Deuteronomy. The festivals now celebrated primarily the occasions when God revealed Himself as the Redeemer of Israel from the Egyptian bondage, as the Giver of the Torah at Mount Sinai, and as the Guardian of Israel during their precarious wanderings in the desert for forty years. These festivals were now observed exclusively in the Jerusalem Temple. To be sure, thc festivals also retained their agricultural associations, but their main emphasis was on the historical events that gave birth to the Hebrew nation. Needless to say, such a drastic revolution was bound to meet with lapses and reverses. After Josiah's death there was considerable backsliding. But ultimately these reforms endured.

Spiritualization of the Temple Service

The prophetic struggle was not limited to the elimination of the local shrines and the eradication of the heathen idolatries from the religious services. Concomitant with these vigorous teachings was the powerful protest against the tendency to observe the rituals of the Temple service scrupulously without their having any impact on ethical and moral conduct. The prophets did not denounce the Temple ritual as such. They accepted the cult as the normal way of worship. But they insisted that religious ceremonies and sacred symbols are useless unless they are accompanied by reverent sentiments and ethical conduct. To many people, however, the ritual possessed magical powers that released them from the burden of guilt and insured them success in their enterprises. They piously brought their sacrifices to the Temple—and then pursued their own ways as before. These perverted concepts of worship, it should be noted, are as prevalent today as they were in ancient days. There are many today whose uttered words of prayer are nothing more than incantations to insure well-being and success. To the prophets such worship was a desecration of the holy Temple and a profanation of its divine ritual. They insisted that offerings in the Temple that are not accompanied by moral conduct are an effrontery and an abomination. Indeed, the test of true worship was not the multitude of offerings in the Temple, but the multitude of good deeds performed outside the Temple. These teachings were proclaimed by the prophets in words that still echo loud and clear and still stir the conscience of man.[1]

The Effect of the Babylonian Captivity on the Temple Service

When the Babylonians conquered Judea in 586 B.C.E., they took the cream of the population into captivity. It was this exiled remnant of the people that finally caught the full meaning of the prophetic teachings. The prophets had predicted the catastrophe as a punishment for the prevailing idolatry and impiety. Now that the prophecies were realized, their meaning became obvious, and the people not only grasped but also accepted the theological interpretation of their calamity. This was historically decisive. For despite their desperate need for some religious anchorage the exiles refrained from building a local shrine in Babylonia even on a temporary basis. The prophetic war against local shrines had been decisively won, and the centralized worship in Jerusalem had been firmly established. The exiles focused their hopes upon the return to the land of Israel and to the city of Jerusalem, where the holy Temple might be rebuilt.

To fill the spiritual vacuum in their lives they devised a makeshift adjustment which ultimately proved to be a most astounding product of the Jewish religious genius. They developed a way to worship God without a sacrificial cult, without a Temple, and without a hereditary priesthood. This unexpected development will be discussed in a later chapter.*

Equally victorious was the prophetic war on the idolatrous practices, which were characteristic of the scattered shrines and high places. Idolatry was never again encountered in Jew-

* *See pp. 63 ff.*

ish worship. When the Babylonian exiles returned to the land of Israel in 538 B.C.E., the Jewish spiritual leaders were able to direct their efforts to the goal of creating a holy people who conducted themselves in accordance with the holy teachings of the Torah. The new emphasis was on the study of Torah, the worship of God, and righteous behavior. As to idolatry, the very thought of it had become abhorrent to the Jews.

The new Temple that the Jews constructed after their return from Babylonia was only a poor replica of the glorious Temple of Solomon. But its preeminent position was firmly established, and its ritual was exalted by music, psalms, and other concomitant rites. The Temple service was spiritually uplifting and deeply meaningful to the people. When it was destroyed by the Romans in the year 70 C.E., the cornerstone of Jewish religious life crumbled. That Judaism survived and even thrived is one of the historic miracles that demonstrate the remarkable religious genius of the Jewish people and their incredible vitality in the face of seemingly insuperable odds.

The Temple Service during the Second Commonwealth

The period of the Second Commonwealth was decisive in the development of the Jewish religious personality. The initial part of this period is poorly documented and suffers from large lacunae. But the latter part of this period is amply documented, and detailed descriptions of the Temple service have survived. A brief account of the Temple ritual is not only in order but is necessary for an understanding of the synagogue worship, because after the Temple fell the synagogue became heir to some of the Temple's rites and ceremonies.

By the beginning of the Common Era the Temple service had developed into an elaborate ritual accompanied by choral singing and instrumental music. The core of the service was the sacrificial offering. A person burdened with a feeling of guilt could find release by bringing an offering and confessing his sin. The Kohen (priest) was more than a functionary. He made the atonement for the sinner, and thereby the sin was forgiven. There were also other private sacrifices such as the thanksgiving, peace, and restitution offerings. Some of the sacrifices were expiatory, others were propitiatory; some were animal sacrifices, others were produce offerings.

More important were the public offerings. These were the heart of the Temple ritual. Preeminent among these were the daily sacrifices, which were brought every morning and afternoon, and the "additional" (Musaf) sacrifices brought on Sabbaths, New Moons, and festivals. There were also the special sacrifices prescribed for the Day of Atonement to expiate the sins of the whole community. This ritual was accompanied with a confession of "all the iniquities and transgressions of the Israelites, whatever their sins" (Lev. 16:21).[2] The Bible does not prescribe any prayers as part of a sacrificial ritual, except the prayer for those who brought the first fruits to the Temple. After that ceremony the farmer was to say: "Look down from Your holy abode, from heaven, and bless Your people Israel and the soil You have given us, a land flowing with milk and honey, as You swore to our fathers" (Deut. 26:15).

The ritual of the daily sacrifice, the *Tamid*, is described in detail in the rabbinic sources. At sunrise the sacrificial victim was slaughtered. The Kohanim then assembled and drew lots to determine who should offer the incense and who should deposit the parts of the victim on the altar. Those Kohanim on whom no lots had fallen divested themselves of their priestly garments and were free to leave. The chief officiating Kohen, alone in the sanctuary, offered the incense. When the people who stood in the court saw the cloud of smoke from the burning incense, they prostrated themselves, spreading out their hands in silent prayer. After the Kohanim placed the parts of the victim on the altar, the officiating Kohanim, standing on the steps in front of the Temple, lifted their hands and pronounced the threefold blessing (Num. 6:22–27).[3] The burning of the offering now took place, followed by the Levitical choir's singing of the psalm of the day to the accompaniment of musical instruments.[4] This concluded the morning service, and the Kohanim proceeded to perform the private sacrifices.

While each public sacrifice had its own characteristic ritual, the procedure described above was more or less basic to all. Thus the daily afternoon sacrifice was practically a repetition of the morning ritual. The Sabbath and festival rituals were more elaborate and the sacrifices were more numerous, but in essence the rituals were substantially like the daily offerings.

The Temple service was performed with impressive pomp and evoked deep feelings of reverence. The ritual gave the suppliant a feeling of closeness to the divine. Indeed the Hebrew word for sacrifice is *korban*, the root meaning of which is "coming near" (to the divine presence). Neither the Kohanim nor the people at large saw any contradiction between the offering of animal sacrifices and the recitation of the accompanying psalms, despite the constant emphasis in the psalms on God's desire of the pure heart and the good deed. Evidently the symbolic meaning of the cult was clear to the people. Moreover, the cultic regulations were validated in the Holy Scriptures and were therefore God's revealed will. It is no wonder that when the Temple was threatened with defilement, as in the days of the Hasmoneans, many Jews were ready for martyrdom. Nor is it surprising that many prayers of the synagogue still deal with the loss of the Temple and that a substantial portion of the Jewish liturgy still centers on the hoped-for restoration of the Jerusalem Temple and its sacrificial ritual. To this day Jews turn their faces toward the site of the Temple during prayer, and they still fast annually in mourning memory of its destruction.

The Uniqueness of the Temple Service

The Temple ritual was outwardly similar to those of the neighboring peoples. Nonetheless, it was radically different. The most conspicuous difference was the total absence of the idolatrous practices, which are repeatedly condemned in the Bible as abominations in the sight of God. The idolatrous practice of "passing children through the fire" did not exist in the Jerusalem Temple.[5] In like manner all magical incantations and demonology were totally absent.[6] The eminent biblical scholar Yehezkel Kaufmann, in his monumental work *The Religion of Israel,* emphasizes the point that

> in the pagan world in general, word and incantation were integral parts of the cult; act was accompanied by speech. . . . [In the Jerusalem Temple] all the various acts of the priest are performed in silence. . . . This silence is an intuitive expression of the priestly desire to fashion a non-pagan cult.[7]

Equally significant is the absence of fertility rites from the rituals of the Jerusalem Temple. The relentless battle of the prophets against all licentious practices in connection with worship had been completely successful. The sex orgies which characterized many of the pagan rituals were shocking abominations to the Jews.[8]

But the most important distinction of the Temple rites in Jerusalem was the uncompromising ethical monotheism which was the basis of the service. The ritual was dedicated to the one and only God who had no intermediary beings in the heavens above or on the earth below. Prophets, priests, and even heavenly beings were only the agents of the one God. And God was spiritual in essence. Hence no divine images were to be found in the Jerusalem Temple. Physical representations of divine beings were not tolerated even in the city of Jerusalem outside the Temple. The Jews were willing to suffer the presence of the hateful Roman legions in Jerusalem but reacted violently against the eagles on the Roman standards, because they saw in them physical representations of the pagan gods. The cardinal principle of God's unity and spirituality infused the sacrificial rites with associations of God's holiness and His desire of righteous living. The place of honor was occupied in the Temple by the ark which contained the Tablets of the Covenant on which were inscribed the Ten Commandments. That the Temple cult was permeated with ethical implications is evident from the biblical demand that one make restitution before sacrificing a guilt-offering. And in case it was a transgression committed unwittingly and no one suffered from it, repentance had to precede the sacrifice (Lev. 5:20–26). The efficacy of the sacrifice was dependent on ethical and religious acts and was not merely an outward ceremony.

The devotional spirit of the Temple service can also be judged from the adjunctive elements around the sacrificial rites. Among these were the singing of psalms by the Levites and the participation of the people who responded with such refrains as "For His mercy endureth for ever" or "Praise ye the Lord."

Frequently overlooked is the fact that the Temple service was in essence national and democratic. The ritual, though performed by a hereditary priesthood, did not belong exclusively to the priestly hierarchy; nor did the privilege of supporting the service belong exclusively to a single class of rich patrons. The Temple service was financed largely by an annual poll tax of half a shekel paid by all Jews both in Palestine and the dispersion.[9] The privilege of paying this poll tax was wrested from the hands of the rich and was cherished by the people as a precious prerogative.

In the actual service, too, the whole nation participated along with the Kohanim. There was a system known as the *Ma'amad*, which consisted of delegations from the outlying sections of the country who "stood by" during the service. The *Ma'amad* participated as representatives of the whole nation. Symbolically, every Jew was present in the Temple during the performance of the ritual and every Jew personally took part in the rites. The humble farmer, no less than the man of wealth or of princely birth, had a share in the support of the service and symbolically participated in the performance of the holy ritual.

The national character of the Jerusalem Temple was also recognized by the Jews of the Diaspora. A considerable portion of the Jewish people were already dispersed in many countries. These Jews could not visit the Temple during the pilgrimage festivals. They paid their annual poll tax, which served as a proxy for the required personal participation in the Temple service.

The Rationalization of the Sacrificial Cult

As long as the Temple existed, the sacrificial rites were regularly performed and the cult retained its unchallenged position. No one questioned that it was God's will that He be worshiped by means of this ceremonial. However, when the Temple was destroyed and the sacrificial cult became only a historic memory, the rabbis sensed the incongruity of divine worship by means of slaughtering animals, sprinkling blood on the altar, and similar priestly rituals. Yet they accepted the Temple cult as a divine service. How could they do otherwise—is it not commanded in the Torah? The rabbis therefore reexamined the Temple ritual from their own vantage point. They "searched" in the text and found an answer to their perplexing problem. They discovered in the sacrificial rites unsuspected religious and ethical teachings. Why, ask the rabbis, is it commanded in the Torah that the meal-offering should be of fine flour mingled with oil? To teach us that our daily life (which is compared to flour) should be mingled with the ethical teachings of the Torah (which is compared to oil).[10] And why are the crop and feathers removed from a bird offering (Lev. 1:16), while an animal is offered up whole (Lev. 1:13)? Because the bird flies and eats food which is not its master's, while the domesticated animal is reared on the master's crib. This is to teach us that the worshiper must be clean from the stains of violence and robbery.[11]

Philo, the Alexandrian Jewish philosopher who lived at the turn of the first century of the Common Era, similarly interpreted the sacrificial rites. The animals chosen for sacrifices, said Philo, are the meek of the animal kingdom. This is to teach us that God loves the humble and rejects the proud and the aggressive. The provision that the victim must be without blemish is to teach us that he who worships God must strive for perfection and his conduct must be irreproachable.

Obviously not every detail of the ritual could be infused with symbolic meaning of a spiritual nature. But this did not disturb the rabbis. The absence of significant meaning was in itself a spiritual lesson; it taught the duty to obey God's commandments even when one could not grasp their significance. Obedience of God's Torah is in itself a principle of transcendent value.

Centuries later, Moses Maimonides (1135–1204) took the bold step of rejecting the sacrificial cult outright, saying that the whole ritual was meaningless and inappropriate for the worship of God. According to Maimonides, Moses approved the sacrificial cult because he realized that the Hebrews were not ready for any higher form of worship. His acceptance of the sacrifices was a pedagogic means of weaning the erstwhile slaves from their primitive practices. The Temple ritual was only an intermediate stage in the process of educating the Jewish people in the proper method of divine worship.

But Maimonides' rational approach did not satisfy everyone, even in his own generation. The orthodox approach demanded adherence to every word of the Torah; the sacrificial rites are commanded in the Bible, and it is the sacred duty of God's people to obey His commandments. The Temple cult, according to this view, was only suspended. When the Temple is rebuilt during the messianic days, the sacrificial rites will be restored. Until then, it is the duty of the Jewish people to keep alive the memory of the Temple service and to perform these rites symbolically by reciting the biblical and rabbinic descriptions of the sacrifices at the daily, Sabbath, and festival services. These selections have been included in the prayer book and to this day are part of the synagogue service. To be sure, some moderns find these selections incongruous. They find the prayers for the restoration of the sacrificial cult unpalatable. But the traditional prayer book, used in most synagogues, is strongly associated with the ancient cult.

The synagogue service has also inherited a number of colorful rituals that go back to the Temple service. These will be discussed in later chapters. Students of the Jewish liturgy have rightly concluded that some of the foliage of the synagogue worship has grown up in the rich soil of the Jerusalem Temple. After the fall of the Temple some of its rituals were deliberately transplanted to the synagogue service and have remained an organic part of the Jewish liturgy.

2
PRAYER IN BIBLE AND TEMPLE DAYS

Bible and Temple days embrace a staggering stretch of history, an era which extends from the formative days of Jewish history when the Hebrew tribes left Egypt (about 1200 B.C.E.) to the time when Judaism achieved its maturity in the first century of the Common Era. As stated in chapter 1, the central form of worship during that time was an elaborate sacrificial ritual. The priestly rites at the Jerusalem Temple are treated in the Bible in great detail and in utter seriousness, as they are in the rabbinic literature of later times.

Prayer in Bible Times

In addition to the sacrificial rites there was a collateral form of worship, unofficial but fully recognized—private prayer. The Bible records private prayers by almost every important personality with whose life and activity it deals. The religious men and women turned to God in prayer, and their prayers, as recorded in the Bible, touch the heart and stir deep religious sentiments.

In general, the personal prayers in the Bible—exclusive of the psalms, which will be treated separately *—are very much like the prayers that we would utter today. Solomon's prayer at the dedication of the Jerusalem Temple may serve as an example. It contains all the elements of prayer—praise and thanksgiving, confession and intercession:

> O Lord, the God of Israel, there is no God like Thee, in heaven above, or on earth beneath; who keepest covenant and mercy with Thy servants,

* *See pp. 59 ff.*

> that walk before Thee with all their heart; . . . Behold, heaven and the heaven of heavens cannot contain Thee; how much less this house that I have builded! Yet have Thou respect unto the prayer of Thy servant, and to his supplication, O Lord my God, to hearken unto the cry and to the prayer which Thy servant prayeth before Thee this day; that Thine eyes may be open toward this house night and day. . . . And hearken Thou to the supplication of Thy servant, and of Thy people Israel, when they shall pray toward this place; yea, hear Thou in heaven Thy dwelling-place; and when Thou hearest, forgive. [1 Kings 8:23, 27–30].

Like all the prayers uttered by biblical personalities or ascribed to them, Solomon's prayer is addressed directly to God. There are no priests or other intermediaries, nor does Solomon offer any sacrifices to win God's favor. Solomon supplicates God with words that come from the heart, and his prayer is uttered in the utmost faith that if he is deserving his prayer will be heard and answered.

To be sure, some biblical prayers contain primitive elements, such as prayers that are conditional in content. The suppliant formulates his prayer in the framework of a vow to do something which he assumes is pleasing to God if his prayer is answered. The classic example of this type of prayer is Jephthah's vow before going to war against the Ammonites:

> If thou wilt indeed deliver the children of Ammon into my hand, then it shall be, that whatsoever cometh forth of the doors of my house to meet me, when I return in peace . . . shall be the Lord's, and I will offer it up for a burnt-offering [Judges 11:30–31.][1]

The Bible also contains a number of prayers in which the suppliants argue with God and persuade Him by their logical arguments to alter His intent. God graciously yields to the logic of the prayer and changes His original decree. Abraham's plea for Sodom and Gomorrah is the classic example. Abraham argues with the Almighty:

> Will You sweep away the innocent along with the guilty? What if there should be fifty innocent within the city; will You then wipe out the place and not forgive it for the sake of the innocent fifty who are in it? Far be it from You to do such a thing, to bring death upon the innocent as well as the guilty, so that innocent and guilty fare alike. Far be it from You! Shall not the Judge of all the earth deal justly? [Gen. 18:23–25].

Unfortunately, Abraham's logic was not backed by the facts of the situation, and his plea did not save the doomed cities.[2]

These primitive elements in some of the biblical prayers, however, are the exceptions. Most biblical prayers are so sophisticated in their formulation that they have been adopted as patterns of prayer for all time. These prayers usually consist of two basic elements—introductory words praising God for His might and mercy, and a concluding petition, often universal in scope. King Solomon's prayer, only part of which was quoted above, follows this pattern.

Not all biblical prayers are petitionary. Many of them concentrate solely on praising God or thanking Him for His mercies and blessings. One such prayer is the Song of Moses which he and the Israelites sang after safely crossing the Sea of Reeds and escaping from the pursuing Egyptians:

I will sing to the Lord, for He has triumphed gloriously;
Horse and driver He has hurled into the sea.
The Lord is my strength and might;
  He is become my salvation.
This is my God and I will enshrine Him;
The God of my father, and I will exalt Him
  [*Exod. 15:1–2*].

The ancient Hebrews found no contradiction between the two forms of worship: the sacrificial rites of the Temple and the informal words of prayer uttered by individuals. They coexisted without infringing upon each other. In those early times prayer was essentially a spontaneous "cry" to God for help. It was based on the intuitive feeling or the deep conviction that God gives ear to the supplications of the devout and answers the prayer that comes from the heart.

In connection with the Temple functions only one brief prayer is prescribed in the Bible. When the farmer brought his first fruits to the Temple, he was to recite a formula in which he briefly summarized the story of the bondage in Egypt, the redemption, and the "land flowing with milk and honey" which God had given to the children of Israel.* To these formulated prayers one may add a number of blessings which achieved official usage and later found their way into the *Siddur*. One of these is part of the blessing which Jacob bestowed on Joseph's sons: "God make you like Ephraim and Manasseh" (Gen. 48:20), which is to this day the paternal blessing that the Jew bestows on his sons on Friday evenings. Another biblical blessing that has been repeated innumerable times is the blessing which the Kohanim pronounced in the Temple. It, too, has been incorporated into the synagogue worship:

> The Lord bless you, and keep you!
> The Lord deal kindly and graciously with you!;
> The Lord bestow His favor upon you and grant you peace! [Num. 6:24–26].[3]

During the period of the First Jewish Commonwealth prayer was generally spontaneous, free, and independent. Except for the brief formula recited by the farmers, the priestly blessing, and some of the psalms, prayers occupied no place in the official worship of the Temple. The introduction of public prayer as a form of worship was, as we shall see, one of the great contributions of the Jewish people to world culture. But this took place during the Second Commonwealth.

The Book of Psalms

Of all biblical prayers, none have stirred the hearts of Jews and non-Jews as profoundly as the psalms. These moving

* *See p. 50.*

prayers have therefore become an important element in the worship of synagogue and church, in the family circle, and in the privacy of personal supplication.

The Book of Psalms is a collection of 150 prayers which constitute one of the books of the Bible.[4] In Hebrew the book is called *Tehillim,* or Hymns of Praise. In English it is generally called the Psalter, deriving its name from the Greek *psalterion,* a certain type of harp. As mentioned above,* some of the psalms were recited or sung at the Jerusalem Temple as an adjunct to the sacrificial rites.

The psalms differ from the other biblical prayers. While the latter are ascribed to certain historic personalities and are incidental to the narratives of their lives and deeds, the psalms focus on the prayers themselves. The authors who composed the psalms are incidental or altogether forgotten. And while the personal prayers in the Bible generally fit the occasions with which they are associated, the psalms do so only in part. Their contents are universal and their applicability is eternal. They do not belong to any individual author or to any specific occasion; they echo the deepest feelings and yearnings of the human heart and therefore belong to all people everywhere.

The psalms bespeak an intense and absolute conviction that God is near and is concerned with the fate of men and nations. This conviction is not in any way like the theologian's dogmas, which are rationally fortified to resist every logical challenge. The psalmists' convictions, like those of every pious man, are primarily of the heart. They are rooted in a deep and unquestioning love of God, the King, the Creator, and above all the merciful Father. The psalms speak to the heart of man in words of sublime tenderness and utter simplicity; they therefore reach into the heart of the suppliant and arouse his noblest sentiments. They express vividly and powerfully the psalmists' firm faith, hope, and trust in the God of Israel, the God of redemption and salvation. At times despondency bordering on despair overcomes the psalmist, but only to throw into greater relief his overflowing faith in the living God, whose salvation never fails.

* *See p. 50.*

The psalmists weep over man's suffering, especially that of the righteous, and exult in God's salvation. The psalmists were Israel's princes of the spirit, unsurpassed and unequaled. The psalms vary in form, content, and quality, as is inevitable in a collection, and several of the psalms would hardly be missed. This has in no way affected their universal acclaim, however, because the psalmists have succeeded in giving expression to man's yearning for God as no one else has ever done. As literature they exhibit a high degree of perfection of form, wealth of metaphor, and rhythm of thought. No wonder people everywhere have adopted the psalms, incorporated them into the core of their liturgies, and pronounced them the noblest of religious poetry. "After reading the hymns and prayers of other religions, no unprejudiced critic would deny that the Hebrew Psalms stand out unique among the prayers of the whole world by their simplicity, their power, and the majesty of their language." [5]

Most of these exalted prayers were composed during the days of the First Jewish Commonwealth.[6] Tradition ascribes the authorship of the psalms to King David, who has on this account been called "the sweet singer of Israel." Actually, it is difficult and in most cases impossible to know for sure when each psalm was written and exactly who was its author. But we do know that psalms were composed in the earliest days of Hebrew history, and the tradition that ascribes most of the psalms to King David cannot be dismissed out of hand. Religious lyrical poetry is to be found among the Israelites and their neighbors as early as the second millennium B.C.E. Hence it is not improbable that some or even many of the psalms actually originated with King David. It is equally probable that some of the psalms are even older. Nor is it improbable that some of the psalms are of a later date. One psalm is definitely dated. Psalm 137 opens with the touching and telling words: "By the rivers of Babylon, / There we sat down, yea, we wept, / When we remembered Zion." This psalm was obviously written during the deportation of the Jews to Babylonia in 586 B.C.E. But the other psalms are not dated at all. Judging by the superscriptions, or the introductory verses, no less than seventy-three psalms are ascribed to King David, while fifty are anonymous. The remaining twenty-seven psalms are ascribed to various authors, mostly obscure Temple singers.[7]

A number of psalms were used at the Jerusalem Temple for the enrichment of the sacrificial ritual. Some of them were sung, often to the accompaniment of instrumental music. Processions to the Temple and within the Temple courts were also accompanied with the chanting of certain psalms. One psalm clearly describes a Temple procession:

They see Thy goings, O God,
Even the goings of my God, my King, in holiness.
The singers go before, the minstrels follow after,
In the midst of damsels playing upon timbrels [*Ps. 68:25–26*].

The worshipers in the Temple court participated only in a peripheral manner. The Levites recited or chanted and provided the instrumental accompaniment. The worshipers listened and occasionally responded with "Amen!" or the refrain, "Blessed be the name of His glorious kingdom forever and ever!" When Psalm 136, called the Great Hallel, was recited by the Levites, the people responded after each verse with the refrain, "For His mercy endureth forever!"

During the great festivals of Passover, Pentecost, and Tabernacles, the Levites sang the six psalms of the Hallel.[8] These psalms are still recited in the synagogue on these festivals, as well as on New Moon days and on Hanukah.* When the Hallel was chanted in the Temple, the people responded after each verse with a loud Hallelujah! (Praise ye the Lord!), and when Psalm 118 was recited, the people repeated after the Levites the twenty-fifth verse: "We beseech Thee, O Lord, save now! / We beseech Thee, O Lord, make us now to prosper!"

The Jewish people increasingly took the psalms to their heart, loved them, and never tired of them. When the synagogue became the spiritual home of the Jewish people, many of the psalms were incorporated into every service. Fully half the psalms became part of the *Siddur*, and in the daily morning

* *See pp. 270–72.*

service alone more than twenty psalms are included. The psalms thus became the spiritual girders of the synagogue worship.

The Origin of the Synagogue

When the Babylonians captured Jerusalem in 586 B.C.E. and destroyed the Temple, the Jews were suddenly faced with a situation of deep tragedy. The Temple, which had been dedicated by King Solomon more than five hundred years before, had risen in importance and had become the sole shrine where public worship was permissible. With its destruction and the deportation of the elite to Babylonia, the sacrificial cult with its impressive ceremonial suddenly vanished, leaving a religious void of wide dimensions.

Offerings could be brought only in the Jerusalem Temple; no substitute shrine, temporary replica of the Jerusalem Temple, or even makeshift altar could be erected outside the sacred spot where the Temple had stood. The Jews in Babylonia found themselves completely cut off from communion with God. The accepted methods of imploring God's help, of finding absolution from sin, of thanking God for His merciful salvation, of celebrating the holy days all vanished with the suddenness of a dream. The Jews were trapped in a spiritual dead end. The situation called for a radical solution. Otherwise, the remnant of the Jewish people was doomed to extinction.

As we look back to that perilous era we are impressed with the remarkable coincidence that the sixth century B.C.E. was an extraordinary period of revolutionary religious developments in many diverse areas. That century saw the emergence of religious movements and institutions that have affected the lives of men and nations to this day. Confucius in China, Gautama Buddha in India, and Zoroaster in Persia laid the foundations of religious movements that still guide the lives of hundreds of millions of people. During the same century the prophets Jeremiah and Ezekiel were delivering their prophecies concerning the fate of the Jewish people, and the Jewish exiles in Babylonia were successfully meeting their deadly challenge and laying the foundations of a new religious institution that was destined to endow divine worship with undreamed-of spiritual potency.

As noted above, the psalms were either private occasional prayers or were mere embellishments of the sacrificial rites. They were not part of a public prayer service. The concept of people assembling for joint prayer was then beyond man's experience and imagination. How did this new and most remarkable institution develop? This question cannot be answered with any sense of certainty or exactitude. The origin of the house of prayer, later known as the synagogue, is recorded neither in the Bible nor in the postbiblical records. Only scattered hints can be discovered in the vast rabbinic literature. But these vague hints enable us to make some plausable conjectures. The most logical of these is that the synagogue had its origin in spontaneous informal gatherings among the Jewish exiles in Babylonia. With a little imagination we can reconstruct the situation and clearly see how this remarkable new religious institution was born.

The religious void which was created by the destruction of the Jerusalem Temple called for a new type of religious experience. But no new form of worship could be deliberately devised; this would have implied the abolition of the divinely ordained sacrificial ritual of the Temple. What did develop was merely the custom of gathering informally on Sabbaths and festivals, a custom that is common wherever there are immigrants from a common homeland. The Jews would gather periodically for mutual support in their foreign surroundings. At these gatherings they would encourage each other in their faith and in their hope of a speedy restoration. These makeshift, informal gatherings in small domestic settings—never planned as worship meetings—ultimately developed into a permanent religious institution. At the time, however, no one could possibly have foreseen that from such humble seeds would grow so majestic a tree, under whose shade hundreds of millions of people would find rest, stimulation, and nourishment.

Let us for a moment visualize the process that gave birth to the synagogue. It is not difficult to imagine the confusion among the Jewish captives in Babylonia. What was a Jew in Babylonia to do on a Sabbath or a festival? It was quite natural for some of them to visit the home of a local leader, a prophet, or a priest. In the land of Israel it had been customary to visit the prophet on Sabbaths and New Moon days.[9] And there were both prophets and Kohanim among the exiles. Thus Ezekiel was both a prophet and a Kohen. Now, what would a religious leader do on a Sabbath or festival when he was visited by his fellow Jews? It is not illogical to surmise that he would read to the people from the prophecies that had forewarned them of the approaching disaster. It would have been fitting also to utter some words of comfort and hope or to read some comforting words uttered by other prophets. A prophet might also read from the Torah about the Egyptian bondage of their forefathers and about their delivery. This was especially appropriate on the festival of Passover. This reading would have been particularly comforting to the exiles: the God who redeemed their forefathers would also redeem them if they prove themselves worthy.

The prophet or local leader might also expound the holy text that he had read and apply its message to the situation at hand. It is also reasonable to assume that the psalms which the Levites used to sing at the Temple on the day corresponding to the day of the gathering would be recited by the leader and that the people would respond with the traditional responses. And since it was not unusual for people when stirred by special occasions to recite personal prayers, it is not beyond probability that a special prayer might be composed for the occasion by the leader or by someone in the group. But such a prayer recited in the presence of a group would no longer be purely personal; it would probably be a prayer in behalf of the group. The first person singular would then be replaced by the first person plural. The prayer would say "Help *us*, O Lord" instead of "Help *me*, O Lord." Thus came into being the characteristic Jewish prayer which is in the plural.

Another remarkable development at these informal gatherings was a form of prayer which later became an integral part of both Jewish and non-Jewish worship. It is reasonable to assume that a prophet like Ezekiel not only read the prophecies that foretold the destruction of the Temple, but also indicated the causes of the national catastrophe. The prophets had often reproached the Jews for repeatedly breaking their covenant with God. If they were to obtain mercy and redemption, it was necessary to confess their sins and repent. God would then have mercy on His people, redeem them from their exile, and cause them to rebuild the holy Temple in Jerusalem. It is thus that the basic prayer formula of confession and repentance was born—a formula which is common in Jewish liturgy, especially in the service of the Day of Atonement. To be sure, this prayer form is not unknown in preexilic days. We find King David praying: "I have sinned greatly in what I have done; but now, O Lord, put away, I beseech Thee, the iniquity of Thy servant" (2 Sam. 24:10). But in postexilic times we find the confession of sins followed by repentance to be a regular liturgic form. In the postexilic Book of Daniel we are told that Daniel "prayed unto the Lord . . . and made confession" saying:

> O Lord, . . . we have sinned, and have dealt iniquitously, and have done wickedly, and have rebelled, and have turned aside from Thy commandments and from Thine ordinances. . . . Now therefore, O our God, hearken unto the prayer of Thy servant, and to his supplications, and cause Thy face to shine upon Thy sanctuary that is desolate, for the Lord's sake. O my God, incline Thine ear, and hear; open Thine eyes, and behold our desolations, and the city upon which Thy name is called; for we do not present our supplications before Thee because of our righteousness, but because of Thy great compassions [Dan. 9:4–5; 17–18].

This prayer, it will be noted, is communal in tone and content. Daniel prays for the people of Israel and consistently uses the first person plural: "*We* do not present *our* supplications before Thee because of *our* righteousness, but because of Thy great compassions." The same characteristics are to be found in the prayers of Ezra and Nehemiah, who lived after the return from the exile.

The Jews in Babylonia continued to attend these makeshift religious gatherings with increasing regularity because they filled the religious void created by the destruction of the Temple. In time these informal meetings became normal religious functions of the community. The people who participated in these religious gatherings, and especially their children, who were raised as participants at these meeting houses, gradually came to regard public prayer as official religious ritual and the gatherings at the prayer houses as religious requirements. Thus a basic institution of Judaism was born, and with the passage of time this institution became a normal part of the religious life of the Jews. In later years, when the Jews returned to Jerusalem and rebuilt the Temple, many of them continued to attend the prayer meetings. As time went on the prayers began to assume definite forms, and a synagogue liturgy began to develop.

Thus was born the institution of the synagogue, an institution so remarkable and so original that it has aroused the wonder and admiration of scholars and historians, both Jewish and non-Jewish. C. Travers Herford speaks of the synagogue in glowing terms: "In all their long history, the Jewish people have done scarcely anything more wonderful than to create the synagogue. No human institution has a longer continuous history, and none has done more for the uplifting of the human race." [10]

Study of Torah as Worship

Seeds scattered but not tended often wither and produce no harvest. This might have been the fate of the practice of periodically reading and explaining scriptural selections at the informal worship periods during the Babylonian exile had it not been for the work of Ezra the Scribe. It was he who provided the powerful impetus that transformed the informal readings from the Torah into a central institution of Judaism.

Ezra was a Babylonian Jew who arrived in the Holy Land

at the head of a second wave of emigrants. This took place in the year 458 B.C.E., seventy-five years after the first wave of emigrants in the days of King Cyrus. When Ezra arrived in Jerusalem he was shocked to find the Jewish community in a state of disintegration. The Bible tells us that he rent his garments, fasted, and prayed. Then he initiated a number of far-reaching reforms, the climax of which was launched at an assembly of the whole people to whom he read the Torah. This event is dramatically told in the Bible:

> And Ezra opened the book in the sight of all the people . . . and when he opened it, all the people stood up. And Ezra blessed the Lord, the great God. And all the people answered, 'Amen, Amen.' . . . And [Ezra and his associates] read in the book, in the Law of God, distinctly; and they gave the sense, and caused them to understand the reading [Neh. 8:5–8].

The act of teaching the Torah to the whole people was a characteristic of Judaism from its very beginning. The Ten Commandments were given at Mount Sinai to the whole assembly of Israel. In ancient times this was a revolutionary concept. In those days it was common practice for the priestly clans to be the custodians of the traditional knowledge and to keep this knowledge strictly to themselves. Judaism broke away from this practice and made the Torah available to all the people.[11] To quote George Foot Moore, when Ezra introduced the public reading and teaching of the Torah as an element of worship, he introduced a process that

> has no parallel in the ancient Mediterranean world. The religion of the household in Egypt or Greece or Rome was a matter of domestic tradition, perpetuated by example rather than by instruction . . . ; the religion of the city or the state was a tradition of the priesthoods in whose charge the public cultus was. . . . If the usage of the sanctuary was reduced to writing it was done privately or for the convenience of the priests themselves. The possession of a body of sacred

Scrolls of the Law, The Israel Museum, Jerusalem. PHOTO: ALFRED BERNHEIM

> Scriptures, including the principles of their religion as well as its ritual and the observances of the household and the individual, of itself put the Jews in a different case.[12]

The reading of the Torah in the synagogue service has developed a procedure which follows the precedent set by Ezra and his associates. To this day the scroll is unrolled and held up in the sight of the congregation, and the congregation rises as was done by the assemblage in Ezra's day: "And Ezra opened the book in the sight of all the people . . . and when he opened it, all the people stood up." As in the days of Ezra a benediction is recited before the reading ("And Ezra blessed the Lord, the great God. And all the people answered, 'Amen, Amen.' ") The Torah is read as it was read by Ezra and his associates—"distinctly," in a distinctive traditional chant. The "sense" used to be transmitted with the help of a meturgeman, a translator, who stood near the reader and translated each verse into the vernacular.[13] The teachers of the synagogue followed Ezra's example and "caused [the people] to understand" the Torah through explanations and homilies.

Ezra not only set the pattern for reading the Torah at public services on Sabbaths and festivals, but he also brought the Torah to the people at other convenient occasions. He introduced the custom of reading the Torah on Mondays and Thursdays, when the farmers used to come to town to sell their produce and to purchase their household goods.[14] Mondays and Thursdays are no longer market days, but the custom instituted by Ezra has persisted to this day: the Torah is still read regularly at Monday and Thursday morning services.

The Teachers of the Synagogue

The period from the return of the exiles from Babylonia in 533 B.C.E. to the arrival of Alexander the Great before the gates of Jerusalem in 332 B.C.E. is one of relative obscurity in Jewish history. These two centuries of Persian rule were relatively peaceful, and the tranquility resulted in a paucity of historic documents. This has led some to believe that these centuries were uneventful. But this is not so. Important changes in the religious life of the Jewish people took place, though we cannot describe them with any degree of certainty. We can only conjecture about them from the changed conditions that we find at the end of this era. One of the significant developments was in the area of the liturgy which began to take shape during this period. To be sure, there were no official written prayers for public worship. But prayer outlines and general formulations did develop during this period.

Tradition credits Ezra with the founding of an organized body of religious leaders known as the Men of the Great Assembly. Although their activities are relatively obscure, the rabbis of the Talmud credit this body with the composition of some of the principal prayers of Jewish worship. Thus we read in the Talmud: "The Men of the Great Synagogue . . . instituted for Israel blessing and prayers, sanctifications and *habdalahs*" (Ber. 33a). Another passage of the Talmud credits that body with fixing the order of the weekday *Tefillah* or the Eighteen Benedictions. "Rabbi Yohanan said: A hundred and twenty elders, among whom were many prophets, drew up eighteen blessings in a fixed order" (Meg. 17b). Moses Maimonides explained the phrase "in a fixed order" to mean that the Men of the Great Assembly decided that

> the first three benedictions should deal with praise of God, the last three benedictions should deal with thanksgiving, and the middle benedictions should consist of petitions for the principal needs of both individuals and the community as a whole [*Mishneh Torah: Tefillah* 1:3–4].

But the specific wording of the prayers was not composed for a long time to come.

If the contribution of the Men of the Great Assembly is undefined and relatively obscure, that of their spiritual successors, the Pharisees, is well documented and most impressive. The Pharisees were the authors of the Jerusalem and Babylonian Talmuds; they gave rabbinic Judaism its definitive shape. Most important for our discussion, they were the teachers of the synagogue. The Pharisees saw the dangers of Hellenism, which had swept the Near East, and they resolved to fight it with all their might. Their chief weapon was the spread of Torah among the people, and the arena of their spiritual combat was the synagogue. The Pharisees were the teachers of the people, and their method was to supply interpretive translations of the Torah readings in the Aramaic vernacular and edifying expository discourses based on the scriptural readings at the services. And the people, both the simple and the learned, followed the teachings of the Pharisees and gave them loyal support against their opponents.

There are some who trace the art of preaching to the prophets. But it should be noted that the prophets were not officials of an institution, and their addresses were not delivered on stated occasions or in fixed places devoted to religious functions. The prophets spoke as the spirit moved them, anywhere and any time. Some of the prophetic orations were undoubtedly delivered on Sabbaths and festivals, but not as part of public services. Yet in a sense the prophets were the forerunners of the synagogue preachers, for their utterances were religious addresses and may be regarded as the remote progenitors of the rabbinic homilies of later times.

As the teachers of the synagogue, the Pharisees developed the homily and firmly established it as a characteristic element of Jewish worship. In this way they helped endow Judaism with its essentials of piety—"conformity to the will of God and communion with God [which] are the two outstanding features of a spiritual religion."[15] Exposition of the Torah provided the necessary guidance for "the conformity to the will of God," and prayer provided the means of the Jew's continuing dialogue with God.

The Liturgy of the Temple Service

The sacrificial ritual continued to be the essence of official worship. But there grew up a concomitant liturgy in the Temple itself. To be sure, this Temple liturgy was only incidental to the sacrificial rites. However, it assumed importance in the synagogue worship, into which it was later incorporated.

The liturgy of the Temple as it developed during the Second Commonwealth is described in the Talmud by an eyewitness.[16] At dawn, after the Kohanim had performed the initial act of the morning sacrifice, they went down to the Chamber of Hewn Stones and conducted a service. This chamber was not a synagogue, as some have surmised. It was the seat of the Great Sanhedrin, the supreme legislative and judicial body. But the Kohanim found it convenient to assemble there for their daily service. The service consisted essentially of an affirmation of the faith, made up of the Ten Commandments and the three biblical paragraphs of the *Shema*. The first of these paragraphs was based on the well-known verses: "Hear, O Israel! The Lord is our God, the Lord alone. You shall love the Lord your God with all your heart and with all your soul and with all your might . . ." (Deut. 6:4–9). The next paragraph dealt with the reward for following the teachings of the Torah and the punishment for disobedience: "If, then, you obey the commandments that I enjoin upon you this day, loving the Lord your God and serving Him with all your heart and soul, I will grant the rain for your land in season, the early rain and the late . . ." (Deut. 11:13–21). The third selection contains the commandment enjoining Israel to become a holy people through the observance of God's commandments: "The Lord spoke to Moses, saying: Speak to the Israelite people and instruct them to make for themselves fringes on the corners of their garments... [to] look at it and recall all the commandments of the Lord and observe them . . . and to be holy to your God . . ." (Num. 15:37–41).

Before the recital of these three paragraphs, the Kohanim recited the benediction known as *Ahavah Rabbah*—"With great love hast Thou loved us, O Lord our God. . . ." Essentially this prayer thanks God, who loved Israel and gave them the Torah. After this prayer and the three biblical paragraphs of the *Shema*, the Kohanim recited three additional benedictions. The Mishnah specifies what these benedictions were. The first corresponded to the benediction *Emet Ve-Yatziv* (True and firm), which is still recited after the *Shema*. This prayer affirms the worshiper's belief in the tenets expressed in the *Shema*. The other two benedictions probably corresponded to two prayers which have been preserved in the *Tefillah*. One begins with the word *Retzeh* (Accept, O Lord) and petitions God to accept the sacrificial offering of the day. The other begins with the words *Sim Shalom* (Grant peace) and follows immediately after the priestly benediction in the reader's repetition of the *Tefillah*.[17] The Kohanim then returned to the altar and completed the sacrificial ritual. The final act of the morning worship was the bestowal of the priestly blessing on the people who were assembled in the Temple court.[18] The Levites then recited the special psalms of the day.[19]

On Sabbaths the liturgy of the Temple was essentially the same, except that there was an additional blessing for the outgoing division of Kohanim who had completed their tour of duty.

A most elaborate liturgy in the Temple took place on the Day of Atonement. It was solemn and impressive. The high point of the service was the public confession by the *Kohen Gadol* (the high priest) of his personal sins, the sins of his family and his tribe, and finally the sins of the whole house of Israel. In each of these confessions the *Kohen Gadol* pronounced the ineffable name of God. On hearing the Tetragrammaton, the people would "kneel, bow their heads, and fall on their faces," and respond loudly, "Praised be the name of His glorious kingdom for ever and ever." The *Kohen Gadol*'s confession was followed by prayers for God's forgiveness. The *Kohen Gadol* then read three relevant sections from the Bible wherein the children of Israel are commanded to observe the Day of Atonement,[20] and he recited eight benedictions, which correspond in essence to some of the blessings in the daily *Tefillah*.[21]

A detailed description of the Temple ritual on the Day of Atonement is included in the synagogue liturgy of today. It is called *Seder Avodah*, the Order of the Service (at the Temple). In many synagogues it is still customary for the congregation to "kneel and fall on their faces" when the reader recites the words describing this ancient rite. In some congregations only the reader performs the ritual, while the congregation stands in silence and reverently watches the Temple rite enacted by proxy. Obviously the Tetragrammaton is not pronounced in the synagogue service.

Another elaborate Temple ritual with a liturgic element took place on the festival of Sukkot. It was probably the most spectacular of all services. The people, with palm branches and citrons in hand, marched around the altar every day of the festival and chanted the verse from the Hallel: "We beseech Thee, O Lord, save now! / We beseech Thee, O Lord, make us now to prosper!" (Ps. 118:25). The climax of the Sukkot ritual was the ceremony of the Drawing of the Water. During this service the Levites chanted the fifteen pilgrimage psalms (120–134), each of which begins with the superscription "A Song of Ascents" *(Shir Ha-Ma'alot).*

It is significant that with the notable exception of the Ten Commandments almost every part of the priestly liturgic services is now part of the synagogue liturgy.[22] The question has often been raised whether these psalms, prayers, confessions, and benedictions that were used in the Temple during the last years of its existence grew out of the Temple ritual and later found their way into the synagogue service, or whether these liturgic elements of the Temple service originated in the synagogue and were taken over by the priesthood in the Temple. One cannot give a definitive answer, but the general consensus among scholars favors the latter assumption. The essence of the Temple service was the sacrificial ritual, which was performed in silence, without any prayers whatever. To be sure, the priestly blessing is of Temple origin. Also, the daily Levitical psalms in all probability originated in the Temple. The same may be said of the Hallel (Psalms 113–118), which was chanted by the Levitical choirs on the festivals. But the daily morning service conducted by the Kohanim in the Temple precincts had its origin in the synagogue. When the Pharisees had succeeded in their teaching that prayer and Torah reading constitute essential elements of a Jew's religious life, the Kohanim too adopted them as part of their life. They therefore interrupted the morning sacrificial rites to partake in a prayer service. And on Yom Kippur, when a large number of Jews assembled in the Jerusalem Temple, it was found necessary to incorporate some elements of the synagogue service into the Temple ritual. Otherwise a Jew would have been torn between his desires to attend the Temple ritual and to participate in a prayer service. The *Kohen Gadol*, therefore, incorporated into the Yom Kippur ritual his prayers for forgiveness.

The Coexistence of the Temple and the Synagogue

By the first century of the Common Era the synagogue was a well-established institution, despite the central position occupied by the Jerusalem Temple. The synagogue usually had an edifice of its own erected by the community or by individual patrons. Palestine was dotted with synagogues. The Talmud states that there were no less than 394 synagogues in Jerusalem before the Temple was destroyed.[23] In the Diaspora, too, every Jewish community had its synagogue, and the larger communities had several places of worship. In the Roman Empire Jews had the privilege of abstaining from participation in the state cult. But in order to enjoy this privilege a Jew had to be part of the Jewish community, and the Jewish community was, in the eyes of both Jew and Gentile, the local congregation, the physical representation of which was the synagogue.[24]

Radically different though the services of the Temple and the synagogue were, they nonetheless coexisted harmoniously. The teachers of the synagogue never denied the authenticity and the centrality of the Temple service, and the Kohanim never denied the religious importance of the synagogue service. There was no competition between the two institutions. Each performed its own functions with the full approval and support of the other. While the Temple occupied the center of sanctity and its ritual was the divinely sanctioned means of obtaining forgiveness for sins, it was the synagogue that occupied a position of immediacy in the lives of the people, because it permitted every worshiper personally to supplicate God and provided everyone with the opportunity to hear God's Torah read and explained by revered and dedicated teachers.

The ascendancy of the synagogue as a spiritual force in the life of the Jews was especially pronounced in the Diaspora. In Judea, and especially in Jerusalem, the Jew had a choice; he could offer sacrifices or prayers in accordance with his personal preference. In most cases he did both. Outside the Holy Land the Jew had no such choice. The synagogue therefore assumed a central position. The Jews in the Diaspora never denied the official status of the Temple service. It was for them, too, the divinely ordained means of worship. They collected among themselves the annual poll tax of half a shekel and forwarded the money to Jerusalem. But the payment of the tax was hardly a substitute for personal worship. Even an occasional pilgrimage to Jerusalem was a special occasion in the life of a Jew; only the well-to-do could indulge in such a luxury, probably only once in a lifetime. The house of prayer and study therefore became the de facto institution of religious worship among the Jews of the dispersion. It took little effort for these Jews to convince themselves that offering praise and thanksgiving to God was, under their circumstances, acceptable to God. To be sure, prayer and study were not as efficacious as the ritual in the Jerusalem Temple, but it was a suitable substitute, as the psalmist so clearly indicated: "Let my prayer be set forth as incense before Thee, / The lifting up of my hands [in prayer] as the evening sacrifice" (Ps. 141:2).

The Temple and the synagogue exerted on each other a reciprocal influence of considerable dimensions. As mentioned above, the Kohanim actually interrupted their daily sacrificial rites in order to partake in a prayer service within the precincts of the Temple. This speaks eloquently for the overwhelming popular acceptance of daily prayer as a normal aspect of the religious life. The influence of the Temple rites on the synagogue can be gauged from the institution known as *Ma'amadot* * (delegations of lay representatives who attended the daily sacrifices) [25] which developed during the latter days of the

* *See pp. 77–78.*

Second Commonwealth. Since the daily sacrifices were in behalf of the nation, it was felt that all the people should be present at the offerings. This was obviously impossible. So they devised a system of representation. The land was divided into twenty-four districts called *Ma'amadot.* The representatives of these districts took turns in attending the sacrificial services in Jerusalem. As the turn of each district came—twice annually for a week's duration each—its deputation traveled to Jerusalem and represented, not its district alone, but the whole nation. This representative system would have inevitably degenerated into a mere symbolic participation by proxies. But those who remained at home also gathered in their local synagogues at the very time when their deputation attended the Temple ritual and recited the psalms that were chanted at the Temple service. The link between the daily morning and afternoon synagogue services with the corresponding morning and afternoon sacrifices in the Temple was thus firmly forged. On Sabbaths and festivals there was an additional offering in the Temple, known as the Musaf. The connection between this Temple rite and the Sabbath and festival Musaf (additional) services in the synagogue was similarly established. The influence of the Temple ritual on the liturgy of the synagogue is thus greater than commonly acknowledged. This will become more evident in the next chapter.

The harmonious relationship between the Temple and the synagogue services is dramatically presented in a report by an eyewitness who lived in Jerusalem during the existence of the Temple and survived its fall. Rabbi Joshua ben Hananya, himself a Levite and a chorister at the Temple, is quoted in the Talmud as follows:

> When we used to rejoice at the place of the Water-Drawing, our eyes saw no sleep. How was this? The first hour [was occupied with] the daily morning sacrifice; from there [we proceeded] to prayers; from there [we proceeded] to the additional sacrifice, then the prayers to the additional sacrifice, then to the House of Study, then the eating and drinking, then the afternoon prayer, then the daily

evening sacrifice, and after that the Rejoicing at the place of the Water-Drawing [all night] [Suk. 53a].

Thus Kohanim and rabbis, Levites and ordinary Israelites were committed to both the Temple and the synagogue. During the great festivals, multitudes came to Jerusalem from the countryside as well as the scattered communities of the Diaspora to participate in the Temple ritual.[26] But they also flocked to the synagogues for prayer and instruction, not only on the great festivals, but also on Sabbaths and even on weekdays. When the Temple was destroyed, the people and their synagogue leaders, the Pharisees, mourned the great loss no less than the Kohanim. It was a national tragedy of transcendent magnitude for all.

3
NATIONAL TRAGEDY AND SPIRITUAL CONSOLIDATION

The story of the Jewish people during the early centuries of the Common Era hinges largely on the national catastrophe of the year 70 C.E. In that year the Romans succeeded in suppressing the Jewish rebellion. They burned the Temple and inflicted cruel vengeance on the hapless survivors. Jewish captives, we are told, choked the slave markets of the world.

The destruction of the Temple and the sudden cessation of its time-honored worship was a stunning blow. All at once the Jewish people found themselves without their hallowed sanctuary and its divine service. A spiritual hollowness encompassed them and threatened their survival as a religious community. It would have proved fatal had it not been for the collateral religious institution, the synagague, which already existed in every Jewish settlement. The synagogue stood ready to meet the religious needs of the people, and it was ideally suited to the new situation of Jewish national and spiritual homelessness.

The Reorganized Sanhedrin at Yavneh

The Jewish people was fortunate in having had the Pharisees as their spiritual leaders. The Pharisees provided them with guidance during those chaotic days, and they instilled in the people a spirit of hope and confidence in the future. Chief of these religious leaders was Rabbi Yohanan ben Zakkai. His prestige stemmed from his superior scholarship and his revered saintliness. It is told that Rabbi Yohanan ben Zakkai had realized the hopelessness of the war. Unable to stem the war fever, he decided to anticipate the inevitable defeat. With the help of a group of intimate disciples, he plotted a dangerous stratagem. He pretended to have died, and his disciples arranged a "funeral." They carried the "corpse" outside the walls of the besieged city for burial. The guards allowed the "mourners" to pass through the gates. No sooner were the "mourners" outside the city walls than the "corpse" arose and proceeded to the headquarters of the Roman general, Vespasian. Rabbi Yohanan ben Zakkai pleaded for a seemingly insignificant boon. He asked for the right to establish a school in the small town of Yavneh. Little did Vespasian suspect that by yielding to this harmless plea he was issuing an insurance policy, guaranteeing the life of the Jewish people for thousands of years, far beyond the life-span of the Roman Empire (Git. 56 a–b).

When Jerusalem fell and the Temple went up in flames, Rabbi Yohanan ben Zakkai and his disciples mourned bitterly, but the great teacher did not permit the mourning to dampen the spirit of bold action. He gathered the scholars and reconstituted the Sanhedrin, which had been the supreme legal and judicial body of the Jewish people. The reconstituted Sanhedrin lacked the authority and prestige that the Sanhedrin possessed when it held its sessions in the Temple. But the personality of Rabbi Yohanan ben Zakkai and the urgent need of leadership gave it wide acceptance and enabled it to bring order out of the existing chaos. One of the decisive acts of Rabbi Yohanan ben Zakkai and his Sanhedrin was to pronounce the principle that the utterance of prayer, the study of Torah, and the performance of good deeds were as acceptable to God as the sacrifices of the Temple. The Midrash records an incident that reflects the spirit of Rabbi Yohanan ben Zakkai's teaching:

> Once as Rabbi Yohanan ben Zakkai was coming forth from Jerusalem, Rabbi Joshua followed after him and beheld the Temple in ruins. "Woe unto us!" Rabbi Joshua cried, "that this, the place where the iniquities of Israel were atoned for, is laid waste!" "My son," Rabbi Yohanan said to him, "be not grieved; we have another atonement as effective as this. And what is it? It is acts of lovingkindness, as it is said, *For I desire mercy and not sacrifice*" [Hos. 6:6].[1]

The study of Torah is even more frequently emphasized as the equivalent of the Temple offerings. The rabbis teach this with poetic power:

> R. Joshua ben Levi [a scholar of the second century] taught that David said to the Holy One, blessed be He: Master of the universe, I have heard men say, "When will this old man die, so that Solomon his son will come and build the appointed shrine to which we shall ascend in pilgrimage?" Nevertheless, I rejoiced despite what they said, because the Holy One, blessed be He, assured me: "*A day in thy courts is better than a thousand elsewhere* (Ps. 84:11)—that is, I prefer a single day in which thou occupiest thyself with Torah to the thousand burnt-offerings which thy son Solomon will offer up before Me on the altar."[2]

The superiority of the study of Torah to Temple offerings is given special emphasis by the rabbinic saying "Even proselytes, if they occupy themselves with Torah, are equal in worth to the high priest."[3]

But the major emphasis of the sages was that prayer is the equivalent of Temple offerings. The three foundation pillars of the world are, in the words of Rabbi Simon the Just, the study of Torah, divine worship, and acts of loving-kindness (Avot 1:2). Rabbi Simon lived in the fourth century B.C.E. and by divine worship he meant the Temple ritual. After the fall of the Temple the word *Avodah* (Temple service) was given a new meaning. What is meant, ask the rabbis, by the biblical command to serve God "*with all your heart*" (Deut. 6:5)? Just as the worship at the Temple altar is called *Avodah* so is prayer called *Avodah*, that is, "the service of the heart" (Ta'an. 2a). The ultimate and clinching proof that prayer is an alternate means of efficacious worship is the oft-quoted words of Hosea (14:3): "So will we render for bullocks the offspring of our lips." The rabbis even claimed that prayer transcends sacrificial offerings. "R. Eleazar said: Prayer is more efficacious even than good deeds" (Ber. 32b), and "Prayer is dearer to God than . . . all sacrifices" (*Tanhuma Ki Tavo*).

It is thus that Rabbi Yohanan ben Zakkai, his disciples, and their successors, the sages of the Talmud, succeeded in transferring much of the authority, prestige, and function of the Temple ritual to the synagogue service. And like the prophets of old the rabbis demanded that prayer be more than a ritual. Prayer is to be preceded by repentance and followed by righteous conduct. Divine forgiveness was vouchsafed only to those who combine worship—consisting of prayer and study of Torah—with mitzvot, good deeds. And worship is efficacious only if it is truly the "service of the heart." This principle is prominently proclaimed in the High Holy Days service: "Repentance, prayer, and acts of righteousness avert the severe decree"; that is, worship which is preceded by repentance and followed by righteous deeds is efficacious.

Having made the substitution, the Jewish people found itself restored to spiritual health. It was now prepared for the interminable exile. Geography was no longer a barrier to a Jew's communion with God. No longer were they religiously tied to the Temple in Jerusalem. Nor were they dependent on a hereditary priesthood. In place of the Temple there was the ubiquitous synagogue. And religious leadership was open to anyone who possessed knowledge and piety. The synagogue fitted ideally the rabbinic concept of God as King of the universe. The rabbis ask, "Why is 'place' [*makom*] the name of God? Because in whatever place righteous men stand, there God is with them, as is said, *In every place where I cause My name to be mentioned, I will come unto thee and bless thee* (Exod. 20:21)."[4] The synagogue, like the tabernacle in the desert days, accompanied the Jewish people in all their wanderings. It crossed national boundaries and followed the Jew to the utmost corners of the earth. Physically the synagogue was often no more than a single room with a few simple appurtenances, frequently even shabby in appearance. But spiritually and intellectually it was resplendent. It provided the Jew with purposeful living and spiritual fulfillment. Neither poverty nor persecution could degrade the Jew so long as he could go to his synagogue. There he poured out his heart in prayer and lifted up his head in dignity as he studied God's Torah.

Preservation of the Memory of the Temple

The Temple ritual was commanded in the Bible. It was part of the divine legislation and therefore eternally binding. Hence the sacrificial cult could not be abrogated. Indeed how could the rabbis abolish the Temple ritual without denying the divine character of the Torah? Rabbi Yohanan ben Zakkai and his successors were thoroughly convinced that the Temple service was suspended for only a brief period. The Temple would soon be rebuilt and the ritual reinstated. It was therefore logical for them to take deliberate steps to preserve the memory of the sacrificial cult. They accomplished this in several ways. First of all they transferred to the synagogue as many of the Temple rites as they could. Obviously they could not transfer the sacrificial rites to the synagogue, because sacrifices could be offered only in the Temple located on the holy site of Mount Moriah. This is biblically legislated and cannot be altered even in time of emergency. But there were a number of rites which were not essential elements of the Temple service. These the rabbis detached and transferred to the synagogue service for the duration of the emergency. Even the names of some synagogue services and the times for holding them were associated with the Temple ritual. The times when the sacrifices were offered at the Temple were regarded as especially propitious for prayer. The rabbis therefore established the schedule of some of the synagogue services to correspond with the Temple sacrifices. While the morning service in the synagogue was merely called Shaharit (morning service), the afternoon service was called Minhah, which is the name of the afternoon offering in the Temple. Also the "additional" services on Sabbaths and festivals were called Musaf, which corresponds to the Musaf (additional) sacrifices offered at the Temple on these days. More significant is the transfer of the psalm of the day to the synagogue liturgy. The Levites used to recite a special psalm each day of the week after the daily morning sacrifice.* These seven psalms were incorporated into the daily synagogue service with a suitable introductory superscription for each of the psalms.[5]

The rabbis also transferred to the synagogue a number of impressive Temple rites. Among these are the blowing of the shofar at the Rosh Hashanah services, and the processions with lulav (palm branch) and etrog (citron) on Sukkot (Tabernacles).

By far the most important of these rabbinic enactments was the preservation of the Kohanim as a separate class within the community of Israel. This was so successful that even today, almost two millennia after the fall of the Temple, most Jews know whether they are of priestly, Levitic, or ordinary Israelitish descent.[6] And those who are Kohanim (of priestly descent) or *Levi'im* (of Levitical descent) have a number of special duties and privileges. They have a priority status at the reading of the Torah. The first one to be called to the Torah must be a Kohen, if one is present, and the second one must be a Levite, if one is present. In the absence of a Kohen, a Levite is called as a substitute. Similarly it is the prerogative of a Kohen, if one is present, to lead in the recitation of the grace after meals. But the most impressive duty of the Kohanim is that of

* *See p. 50.*

blessing the congregation during some of the services. This duty, it will be recalled, was biblically assigned to the Kohanim.[7] After the fall of the Temple, the priestly blessing was incorporated into the daily service and has been regularly pronounced by the reader during the repetition of the *Tefillah*. During the festivals[8] the Kohanim go up to *dukhan*, as their ancestors used to ascend the step (*dukhan*) leading to the Temple portico, and pronounce the priestly blessing. As to the Levites, their only sacerdotal function in the synagogue has been to pour water on the hands of the Kohanim before they bless the congregation.[9]

Of all the rabbinic enactments aimed at preserving the memory of the Temple rituals, the one that most affected the synagogue liturgy was the inclusion in the daily service of descriptions of the sacrificial rites. Reciting these, the rabbis taught, was equivalent to the actual performance of the rituals. The Talmud relates in a poetic vein that Abraham was worried about the fate of his descendants. How will they be forgiven for their sins when the Temple is no longer in existence? God answered him: "I have already fixed for them [in the Torah] the order of sacrifices. Whenever they will read the section dealing with them, I will reckon it as if they were bringing Me an offering, and forgive all their iniquities" (Meg. 31b).

The most dramatic example of this rabbinic principle is the elaborate description of the Temple ritual for the Day of Atonement, which has been incorporated into the synagogue service of that day. The *Avodah*, as this prayer unit is called, is a detailed account of the Temple rites as they were performed by the *Kohen Gadol*.* It includes the kneeling and falling on the face by the congregation, or by the reader as proxy for the worshipers. The wording of this ritual in the prayer books is of medieval composition. But the practice of verbally "performing" the Temple rites on Yom Kippur goes back to the rabbinic period.

The recital of the laws of the sacrificial cult is also part of the daily morning service and of the Musaf services on Sab-

* *See pp. 252–54.*

baths and festivals. These texts are taken from the Bible and the Talmud, and they occupy a substantial part of the prayer book.[10]

In addition the rabbis saturated the synagogue liturgy with prayers for the restoration of Zion, the rebuilding of the Temple, and the resumption of the sacrificial rites. Most of the Eighteen Benedictions of the weekday *Tefillah* are devoted to this theme.[11]

The synagogue proved itself a most effective preserver of the ancient sanctities in the national memory of the Jewish people. During the millennia of exile the Jews gathered daily in their synagogues and prayed for the restoration of the Temple. They symbolically performed the Temple rites and scrupulously safeguarded the identity of the Temple functionaries. They thus kept themselves in constant readiness for the resumption of the sacerdotal rituals in the rebuilt Temple.

Rabbi Gamaliel II and the Canonization of the Liturgy

By the turn of the first century of the Common Era the essence of the synagogue service was already in a coherent and recognizable state. The general order and contents of the synagogue prayers had already become a tradition, albeit an oral one. But there was no authoritative formulation, and even the order of the prayers was still in a fluid state. Great variety was the rule. The time had come for a measure of consolidation. The calamity of the war and the cessation of the Temple ritual called for a deliberate effort to bring order into the confusing rituals of the synagogue.

The man who was, more than anyone else, responsible for bringing order into the liturgy was Rabbi Gamaliel II, who succeeded Rabbi Yohanan ben Zakkai as the head of the Sanhedrin at Yavneh. Rabbi Gamaliel's prestige derived from the fact that he was a descendant of the saintly scholar Hillel, who had been head of the Sanhedrin that used to meet in the Temple. Because of Hillel's fame the post became hereditary, and for four generations the heads of the Sanhedrin had been Hillel's descendants. The post now reverted to the dynasty in the person of Rabbi Gamaliel. The new nasi (prince), as the Jews called the head of the Sanhedrin, correctly evaluated the sad state of his people. He feared for their total disintegration. He therefore concluded that the urgent need of the hour was national unity and that consolidation of the liturgy was of immediate urgency.

At first the new nasi was thwarted in his efforts. He did not command the unswerving loyalty of his colleagues, as had his predecessor. Nor did he possess the necessary tact for the bold action that he was to initiate. The Talmud records an incident in which Rabbi Gamaliel humiliated one of his colleagues in the Sanhedrin. Rabbi Joshua had dissented from a decision of the nasi, claiming that the calculations of the calendar as pronounced by Rabbi Gamaliel were erroneous. This meant that the Day of Atonement, according to Rabbi Joshua, would fall on a different day from the one officially set. Rabbi Gamaliel not only insisted on the observance of the Day of Atonement on the date set by his office, but ordered Rabbi Joshua to appear before him on the day which, according to Rabbi Joshua's calculations, was the Day of Atonement, dressed in his workday clothes, with his staff and purse. Rabbi Joshua, a humble and beloved scholar, obeyed. But this and similar humiliations brought the Sanhedrin to Rabbi Joshua's defense, and they deposed Rabbi Gamaliel. Rabbi Gamaliel accepted his humiliation with dignity. He proved to his colleagues that his actions were not motivated by pride but by concern for the unity and survival of his people, and after he went to Rabbi Joshua and begged for his forgiveness, the Sanhedrin reinstated him as nasi.

Under Rabbi Gamaliel's firm leadership the synagogue service took on its definitive shape. The nasi and his colleagues examined the many parallel versions of the prayers and decided on the preferred phraseology. The weekday *Tefillah* (the Eighteen Benedictions) was given its official order, and the individual benedictions were given their general formulations. Except for some verbal changes and amplifications, the regulations as adopted by Rabbi Gamaliel and his colleagues have remained essentially the same to this day. But the growth of the liturgy was not halted. A balance between order and rigidity was achieved through the rabbinic tradition which called for the oral transmission of the prayers.* The liturgy was thus kept sufficiently fluid to permit a measure of change.

As intimated above, there were dissenters who challenged the decisions of Rabbi Gamaliel. For example, Rabbi Gamaliel had prescribed that the three daily services were incumbent on every Jew. Rabbi Joshua, who had dissented earlier in the calendar matter, disagreed and claimed that only the Shaharit (morning) and Minhah (afternoon) services were obligatory. The Maariv (evening) service, Rabbi Joshua insisted, was optional. His reasoning was sound: in the Temple there were only the morning and the afternoon offerings, and only the synagogue services which correspond to the Temple rituals, said Rabbi Joshua, are binding on every Jew. The Maariv service is therefore optional. But the Bible speaks of three daily services. The psalmist prayed "evening, and morning, and at noonday" (Ps. 55:18), and Daniel prayed "three times a day" (Dan. 6:11). Rabbi Gamaliel's view prevailed. It received additional support from the rabbinic tradition that the obligation to pray three times daily originated with the patriarchs.[12]

The work of Rabbi Gamaliel and his associates achieved its goal. Order was brought into the spiritual life of the Jewish people. The disaster resulting from the fall of Jerusalem and the destruction of the Temple no longer threatened the survival of the Jewish people. To be sure, Judaism had received a deadly blow under whose crippling impact it staggered and tottered. But Judaism rallied from its misfortunes and was ready for the long exile that awaited it.

* *See pp. 368 ff.*

4
THE FRAMEWORK OF JEWISH WORSHIP

The Jewish book of prayer came to be known as the *Siddur*, which means order (of the services). The uninitiated, however, finds in the *Siddur* nothing but confusion. G. E. Biddle describes the *Siddur* from the point of view of a stranger as "an inextricable confusion":

> There appears to be no design in the composition, little sense of order, no central culminating point, scant feeling for proportion, no just estimation of values, no salient features—nothing, in short, by which [the stranger] may get a grip of the thing! an inextricable confusion; a prodigious tangle!
>
> But the confusion is not so badly confounded after all, presupposing that sympathy and respectful attention are exercised. The student will then gradually discern more and more of order *within* the chaos, and will find that, in common with all human productions, this noble volume is explainable and explicable without great difficulty in accordance with the genius of the people to whom it owes its origin. For the Jewish Prayer Book is what it is because its compilers and contributors were *what they were*. Its pages completely exhibit well marked features of Jewish character.[1]

The Simple Structure of the Jewish Liturgy

It is our purpose to examine the structure and content of the Jewish liturgy as it had developed by the end of the first century, when Gamaliel's work was completed. Our approach will be, as G. E. Biddle suggested, sympathetic and respectful. But we must stress at the outset that the rabbis were not systematic theologians. Their work, be it in the field of law or ethics or liturgy, is not a masterpiece of orderliness. Unlike most non-Jewish liturgies, which are orderly and symmetrical, the liturgy of the synagogue is organic in its formulation rather than logical. This is due to its slow, gradual development, which depended on historic situations and on prolonged usage rather than logical rules of organization. In the Jewish tradition the door was always open to new prayers, and the judge of their admissibility was not an official body of theologians guided by a system of logical rules, but the community of Israel. Prayers that reflected the yearnings of the people and did not negate the doctrines of Judaism found acceptance. And when that acceptance was sustained over a long period, a prayer became part of the prayer book. There was no official blueprint with which new prayers had to conform. A mass of liturgic material, varied in content and value, accumulated around the principal prayers which were canonized in the first century. This accumulation gave the *Siddur* its eclectic character. It is thus that one finds in the *Siddur* not only supplications, thanksgivings, and praises, but also credal recitations, ethical disquisitions, legal enactments, and poetical works both of high lyrical quality and of artificial linguistic manipulations hardly of prayerful value. But the basic structure of the Jewish liturgy is simplicity itself, provided one starts with the salient facts that the contents of the *Siddur* revolve not around one central pivot but around three such pivots, and that the resulting three central prayer units are radically different from each other in content and organization. Each of these prayer units is in its own way a noble product of the religious genius of the Jewish people.

The central cores of the *Siddur* consist of (1) the *Shema* and its benedictions, (2) the *Tefillah*, which is basically a series of personal and national supplications, and (3) readings from the Scriptures, often accompanied by homilies. Around these three central units there is a literary accumulation of vast proportions. Before discussing the three essential prayer units, it is necessary to digress and examine a basic ingredient out of which the Jewish prayers are built. This structural element of Jewish worship is known as the benediction, or Berakhah.

It recurs incessantly in all parts of the liturgy, both private and public. Any attempt to comprehend the pattern and content of Jewish worship must therefore begin with an analysis of the ubiquitous benediction.

The Hebrew Benediction

A pious Jew sees God's providence in every experience. He therefore praises and thanks God continually. Before partaking of bread he recites a benediction: "Praised art Thou, O Lord our God, King of the universe, who bringest forth bread from the earth." And before sipping from the wine cup, he pronounces a benediction: "Praised art Thou, O Lord our God, King of the universe, who createst the fruit of the vine."

The benediction is essentially an utterance of gratitude for God's beneficence, for the privilege of experiencing His manifold manifestations in nature, and for the privilege of performing the commandments of the Torah. Since God's manifestations are to be found everywhere at all times, the pious Jew recites numerous benedictions. Indeed, it is the goal of the pious Jew to recite daily not less than one hundred benedictions.

The rabbis formulated benedictions for practically every contingency—for the usual experiences of daily life, such as rising from sleep, dressing, eating, and drinking, and for the unusual happenings, such as escaping from danger, recovery from illness, or seeing something marvelous in nature. Thus the sight of a comet or lightning calls for the benediction "Praised art Thou, O Lord our God, King of the universe, whose strength and might fill the world." On seeing mountains, rivers, or deserts, the pious Jew recites a benediction praising God "the Author of Creation." When one sees crowds of men, God is praised for He is "wise in secrets," referring to the fact that no two human beings are alike in their features or personalities. And on emerging safely from a dangerous situation, the Jew praises God, "who bestows benefits upon the undeserving."[2] When S. Y. Agnon was informed that he had been awarded the Nobel Prize, he recited the blessing enjoined upon one who hears good tidings: "Praised art Thou . . . who is good and doeth good," and when he arrived in Stockholm to receive the Nobel Prize and saw the king of Sweden, he recited the blessing "Praised art Thou . . . who hast given of Thy glory to mortals." When a pious Jew receives bad news, he praises God, "the faithful Judge," for even in time of severe trial, one is to recite a blessing as did Job when he declared: "The Lord gave, and the Lord hath taken away, / Blessed be the name of the Lord" (Job 1:21). Even when a Jew was led to the stake—a not infrequent occurrence in the Middle Ages—he was to recite a benediction:

> Praised art Thou, O Lord our God, King of the universe, who sanctified us with His commandments, and commanded us to love the revered and awful Name—that was, is, and will be—to hallow Thy name among the many. *Praised art Thou, O Lord, who hallowest Thy name among the many.*

It is not an unwarranted assumption that these repeated benedictions tended not only to deepen the Jew's awareness of God's beneficence, but also to bestow an aura of holiness on the ordinary experiences of life. Thus eating bread became not only an occasion for worship but an act of consecration. Life as a whole tended to become a religious adventure, or, as the rabbis called it, a partnership with God in the achievement of the divine goal of turning the world of men into the kingdom of God.

The Benediction: A Foundation Stone of Jewish Prayer

As mentioned above, the benediction is the basic structural element out of which the Jewish liturgy is constructed. Every aspect of public and private prayer is saturated with benedictions. Moses Maimonides classified the benedictions into three categories—blessings for experiences of enjoyment, blessings for the privilege of performing religious commandments, and blessings that express petition, thanksgiving, or praise. Each of these benedictions has its own formula and structure.

1. Blessings for experiences of enjoyment are the simplest of the benedictions. They open with the formula *Praised art Thou, O Lord our God, King of the universe* and conclude with a

reference to the experience which called for the blessing, as in the benediction before eating bread (*who bringest forth bread from the earth*).

2. Blessings for the privilege of performing religious commandments open with an expanded formula—*Praised art Thou, O Lord our God, King of the universe, who sanctified us with His commandments and commanded us*—and conclude with the specific commandment which is being executed, as in the benediction recited during the kindling of the Sabbath lights (*to kindle the Sabbath lights*).

3. Blessings that express petition, thanksgiving, or praise are the essential prayers of public and private worship. These benedictions differ from the preceding ones in form and content. They begin and conclude with the formula *Praised art Thou, O Lord*. The body of the prayer is framed between these opening and closing formulas. Thus the first benediction of the Maariv service reads:

> *Praised art Thou, O Lord our God, King of the universe,* who at Thy word bringest on the evening twilight, with wisdom openest the gates of the heavens, and with understanding changest times and variest the seasons, and arrangest the stars in their watches in the sky, according to Thy will. Thou createst day and night; Thou rollest away the light from before the darkness, and the darkness from before the light; Thou makest the day to pass and the night to approach, and dividest the day from the night, the Lord of hosts is Thy name; a God living and enduring continually, mayest Thou reign over us for ever and ever. *Praised art Thou, O Lord, who bringest on the evening twilight.*

When the service contains a series of benedictions, only the first benediction starts with the introductory formula. The assumption is that the introduction of the first benediction applies to every one in the series. Thus the second benediction in the Maariv service starts directly with the prayer:

> With everlasting love Thou hast loved the house of Israel, Thy people; a Torah and commandments, statutes and judgments hast Thou taught us. Therefore,

> O Lord our God, when we lie down and when we rise up we will meditate on Thy statutes: yea, we will rejoice in the words of Thy Torah and in Thy commandments for ever; for they are our life and the length of our days, and we will meditate on them day and night. And mayest Thou never take away Thy love from us. *Praised art Thou, O Lord, who lovest Thy people Israel.*

The Origin and Development of the Benediction

The Talmud ascribes the origin of the benediction to the Men of the Great Assembly (Meg. 17a). In fact the formula "*Blessed [Praised] be Thou, O Lord*" is found in the Bible. Thus "David blessed the Lord before all the congregation; and David said: '*Blessed [Praised] be Thou, O Lord*, the God of Israel our father, for ever and ever' " (1 Chron. 29:10).[3] However, by the second century of the Common Era, the blessing had already assumed its traditional formulation. The rabbis of the Talmud summarized the rules governing the component parts of the blessing as follows:

> Rab taught: In making a blessing a man is required to say, "Blessed [Praised] art Thou, O Lord," for a blessing wherein the Lord's name is not mentioned is no blessing; as Scripture says, *I have set the Lord always before me* (Ps. 16:8).
>
> Both R. Ze'era and R. Judah taught: A blessing wherein God's kingship is not mentioned is no blessing, for it is said *I will extol Thee, my God, O King* (Ps. 145:1). R. Berechiah commented: What you say applies only to blessings such as the blessing over fruit, or the blessing at the performance of commandments. In general worship, however, as long as a man mentions the name of God he has done his duty.[4]

The introductory words of the benediction as finally formulated by the rabbis thus consist of two basic elements: (1) the mention of the divine name—*Praised art Thou, O Lord*—and (2) God's kingship—*our God, King of the universe*. This applies, as Rabbi Berechiah said, only to benedictions recited privately when enjoying God's beneficence or performing God's commandments. At regular services, both public and private, only the first part—*Praised art Thou, O Lord*—is obligatory.

The mention of God's name in a blessing called for a congregational response. This is in accordance with rabbinic interpretation of the biblical verse, "For the name of the Lord I proclaim; / Give glory to our God" (Deut. 32:3). When the Tetragrammaton was pronounced by the Kohanim in the Temple, the response was "Blessed be the Lord, the God of Israel, / From everlasting to everlasting. / Amen, and Amen" (Ps. 41:14). In the synagogue the word *Adonai* (Lord) is substituted for the name of God, and the congregational response to a blessing is only "Amen!" [5]

The benediction as it has come down to us is somewhat clumsy—in the first part of the benediction God is spoken to directly: "Praised art *Thou*, O Lord." But in the last part God is spoken of in the third person: "who sanctified us with *His* commandments." The strange and ungrammatical form of this benediction is due to a later insertion of the word *Thou* into the original benediction which used to read: "Praised is the Lord, our God, King of the universe who sanctified us with His commandments," etc. But the rabbis were intent on emphasizing the nearness of God to each worshiper. So they inserted the word *Thou* in order to give the worshiper the feeling of being in direct communion with God. Thus the awkward structure of the benediction came into being. In the rabbinic view the violation of a grammatical rule is a small price for so great a spiritual advantage as that of experiencing direct communion with the divine.

The Importance of the Benediction in Jewish Worship

The rabbis laid great stress on the exact wording of the benediction. Although the prayers continued to be oral and the reader formulated the prayers in accordance with his own diction,[6] the opening and closing formulas of the benediction were precise and not subject to any extemporizing. The reader had to use the exact wording.

The meaning of the benediction formula is quite clear except for the opening clause, which is often translated as *Blessed art Thou.* This seems to imply that God is in need of human blessings. This misleading inference is due to the literalness of the translation. The opening word—*Barukh*—is an expression of praise rather than blessing, and a more accurate translation of the opening clause is *Praised art Thou, O Lord.*

The phrase that follows—*our God*— is the Jew's proclamation of his acceptance of God's sovereignty, which is in accord with the first of the Ten Commandments. The last phrase—*King of the universe*—is an affirmation of God's sovereignty in the affairs of mankind. Implicit in these words is the Jewish doctrine that ultimately the kingship of God will be established on earth. Justice and mercy, righteousness and truth, peace and love will in time replace the forces of evil that often hold sway in the affairs of man.

In benedictions recited during the performance of religious duties, the formula includes the added words—*who sanctified us with His commandments.* These words set forth the principle that the goal of Judaism is to transform the Jewish people into a "holy nation" (Exod. 19:6) and that the achievement of this objective is possible through the performance of the divine commandments of the Torah.

The benediction thus affirms some of the fundamental doctrines of Jewish theology. The pious Jew reaffirms these doctrines innumerable times, until they become part of his consciousness and, in some cases, part of his way of life. That the Jews did not succeed in becoming truly a "holy nation" is surely not because of the rabbis' failure to emphasize this objective of Judaism. Unfortunately, the evil inclination in man is often stronger than the constant affirmations of these doctrines in the liturgy of the synagogue.

The *Shema*— First Core Unit of the Jewish Liturgy

The synagogue service consists of three essential cores, each of which has developed independently and is singular in content and structure. Any effort to reconstruct their respective developments must rely on a considerable amount of conjecture, because their origins go back to remote antiquity and their basic formulations took place largely during a period in Jewish history which is short on records and long on hearsay.* Yet much of the reconstructed history of these prayer units is based on sound scholarly foundations.

The first of these core elements of the synagogue liturgy is the Jewish affirmation of faith, known as the *Shema*. It consists of three biblical selections, and it derives its name from the initial word of the opening verse. The selections are preceded by two introductory benedictions and are concluded by one benediction. How these three biblical selections came to be chosen we do not know. When the rabbinic sources began to discuss the synagogue service, during the first century of the Common Era, these three selections were already firmly fixed in the liturgy and were already regarded as being of ancient origin. One tradition even ascribes their selection to Moses.

The Biblical Selections of the *Shema*

The first of the three selections of the *Shema* (Deut. 6:4–9) proclaims the unity of God as a central principle of Judaism, and it asserts the Jew's primary duty to "love the Lord your God with all your heart and with all your soul and with all your might." The Jew must forever keep these central doctrines before his eyes and diligently teach them to his children. The far-reaching import of this biblical selection is self-evident. It is not surprising that the early architects of the synagogue liturgy chose this paragraph as a cornerstone of the liturgic structure.

The second paragraph (Deut. 11:13–21) is related to the first in that the two selections have in common this injunction: "Bind them as a sign on your hand and let them serve as a symbol on your forehead; inscribe them on the doorposts of your house and on your gates" (Deut. 6:8–9; Deut. 11:18, 20). But more important is the thought relationship between the two selections. If the first emphasizes the doctrine of God's unity

* *See pp. 70–71.*

and stresses the duty to love God with one's whole heart and soul, the second selection affirms the theological doctrine of reward and punishment.

> If, then, you obey the commandments that I enjoin upon you this day, loving the Lord your God and serving Him with all your heart and soul, I will grant the rain for your land in season, the early rain and the late. . . . Take care not to be lured away to serve other gods and bow to them. For the Lord's anger will flare up against you, and He will shut up the skies so that there will be no rain and the ground will not yield its produce; and you will soon perish from the good land that the Lord is giving you [Deut. 11:13–21].

If the Jews love God and serve Him with all their hearts and with all their souls, as indicated in the first paragraph of the *Shema*, they will be rewarded. However, if they deny the one God and worship other gods, they will be punished. This paragraph is thus a logical extension of the first.

The third selection (Num. 15:37–41) places in the center of the Jewish creed the duty to strive for holiness through the performance of God's commandments. A special commandment is decreed here, that of the fringed garment (tzitzis): "Thus you shall be reminded to observe all My commandments and to be holy to your God" (Num. 15:40). This last paragraph of the *Shema* reaches the very heart of Judaism. The one God, the Redeemer and the Holy One of Israel, is to be loved, His commandments observed, and His essential nature emulated. Thereby the Jews will become a "holy nation."

The Benedictions of the *Shema* in the Morning Service

The three paragraphs of the *Shema* became the cornerstone of Jewish worship. They were recited daily, morning and evening. The opening paragraph was also the prayer of Jewish martyrs in their last agonizing moments, as it has been the last prayer of Jews who died of natural causes. And like a work of art, the *Shema* was enclosed in a frame known as "the benedictions before and after the *Shema*."

The daily morning service began with the reader's call to

worship: "Praise ye the Lord who is to be praised," to which the congregation responded: "Praised be the Lord who is to be praised for ever and ever." Since the morning service was usually held at sunrise, it was natural to start with a benediction which thanks God for the miracle of the daily sunrise. This benediction—*Yotzer Or* (He who creates light)—deals with the general theme of creation and expresses the Jew's gratitude for God's creative acts that are always with us. It should be reiterated that only the general contents of the benedictions were determined at Yavneh; however, the opening and closing formulas were fixed for all time. Thus the opening benediction as formulated by Saadia Gaon,* who lived in the tenth century, reads:

> *Praised art Thou, O Lord our God, King of the universe, who formest light and createst darkness, who makest peace and createst all things.*[7]
>
> In great mercy Thou givest light to the earth and to those who dwell thereon, and in Thy goodness renewest the creation every day continually. *Praised art Thou, O Lord, Creator of the luminaries.*[8]

The second benediction—*Ahavah Rabbah* (With great love)—is the introductory prayer to the *Shema*. It thanks God for His love of Israel, which was made evident through the giving of the Torah at Mount Sinai. It is a fitting introduction to the affirmation of faith. It reads in part:

> With abounding love hast Thou loved us, O Lord our God, with great and exceeding pity hast Thou pitied us. . . . Thou hast chosen us from all peoples and tongues, and hast brought us near unto Thy great name for ever in faithfulness, that we might in love give thanks unto Thee and proclaim Thy unity. *Praised art Thou, O Lord, who hast chosen Thy people Israel in love.*

The concluding benediction, which follows the three paragraphs of the *Shema*, is a sort of epilogue in which the worshiper affirms his belief in the teachings of the Torah. This benediction—*Emet Ve-Yatziv* (True and firm)—ends with

* *See pp. 385–88.*

words of thanksgiving for the redemption of Israel from the Egyptian bondage. The benediction reads in part:

> True and firm, established and enduring . . . is this Thy word unto us for ever and ever. It is true, the God of the universe is our King, the Rock of Jacob, the Shield of our salvation: throughout all generations He endureth and His name endureth; His throne is established, and His kingdom and His faithfulness endure for ever. His words also live and endure. . . . O Rock of Israel, arise to the help of Israel, and deliver, according to Thy promise, Judah and Israel. Our Redeemer, the Lord of hosts is His name, the Holy One of Israel. *Praised art Thou, O Lord, who hast redeemed Israel.*[9]

The Benedictions of the *Shema* in the Evening Service

In the first paragraph of the *Shema,* the Jew is instructed to speak of the teachings of the Torah "when thou liest down and when thou risest up." Accordingly, it was regarded as the duty of every Jew to recite the *Shema* both morning and evening. In the latter service the benedictions of the *Shema* are basically the same as their counterparts in the morning service.[10] The evening service starts with the reader's call to worship. Then follows the opening benediction, which is similar to its counterpart in the morning service except that it praises God the Creator of the night. This benediction was quoted in full earlier in the chapter.*

The next benediction, *Ahavat Olam* (With everlasting love), is the introduction to the *Shema.* It is a shorter version of the corresponding benediction in the morning service. It, too, thanks God for His love of Israel as it manifested itself by His giving them the Torah at Mount Sinai. This benediction, too, was quoted in full earlier in the chapter.†

The concluding benediction—*Emet Ve-Emunah* (True and faithful)—is again a variant of its counterpart in the morning service. It, too, confirms the truth of the doctrines proclaimed

* *See p. 93.*
† *See pp. 93–94.*

in the *Shema* and ends on the same theme—God is the Redeemer of Israel.

In the evening service there is an additional benediction—*Hashkivenu* (Cause us to lie down). It used to be the conclusion of the service:

> Cause us, O Lord our God, to lie down in peace, and raise us up, O our King, unto life. . . . Guard our going out and our coming in unto life and unto peace from this time forth and for evermore. *Praised art Thou, O Lord, who guardest Thy people Israel for ever.*

The *Shema* is thus concluded, both morning and evening, on the optimistic note that God is the ever-faithful Redeemer and Guardian of Israel. He redeemed Israel from the bonds of Pharaoh, and He will surely redeem the children of Israel from all oppressors. In their exile, where persecution and humiliation were so common, the Jews derived from the *Shema* and its benedictions the courage to resist temptations of the dominant faiths and the strength to endure incessant persecutions. The Jews read the *Shema* and its benedictions twice daily and were continually reassured that ultimately the God who redeemed their fathers from Egyptian bondage would also redeem them and vindicate their faith and steadfastness.

The *Tefillah*— Second Core Unit of the Jewish Liturgy

The *Tefillah* is the second of the three major focuses of the Jewish liturgy. It consists of a series of benedictions or short prayers, nineteen for weekday services and only seven for Sabbaths and festivals. The name *Tefillah* (Prayer) is appropriate for this core unit of the service, because it was regarded by the rabbis as the Jewish prayer par excellence. As we shall see, the *Tefillah* unites all the major elements of prayer—praise and thanksgiving, confession and petition.

Another name often applied to this prayer unit is Amidah, the prayer that is recited in a *standing* posture. During the recital of these benedictions the congregation always stands silently and reverently.

THE ORGANIZATION OF THE *Tefillah*

The *Tefillah* is divided into three sections: (1) the three introductory benedictions, (2) the three concluding benedictions, and (3) the thirteen intermediate benedictions.[11] The three initial benedictions concentrate on the praise of God. They pay homage to the God of Abraham, Isaac, and Jacob, the great, mighty, and revered God, who nourishes the living, quickens the dead, and is the Holy One of Israel.[12] These initial benedictions also emphasize a number of theological doctrines which the rabbis regarded as basic in Judaism. Especially crucial was the concept of God as the Quickener of the dead. This doctrine assumed central importance because it was challenged by the opponents of the Pharisees. By including this benediction in the *Tefillah* ("*Praised art Thou, O Lord, who quickenest the dead*") the rabbis effectively excluded from the synagogue all those who opposed the pharisaic doctrine concerning the revival of the dead during the messianic era.

The three concluding benedictions concentrate on thanksgiving. Actually only one of these benedictions deals with the theme of thanksgiving, but this one stands out as the most prominent. The first of these final benedictions expresses the hope that God will accept the congregation's prayers; the second thanks God for His beneficence; and the last benediction is a prayer for peace.

These three benedictions have a historic unity in that they had a common origin in the Temple service. The first benediction was originally a prayer for God's acceptance of the sacrificial offerings. After the destruction of the Temple the benediction was adapted to the new situation, and it expresses the hope that God will accept the congregation's prayers and that He will restore the Temple service. The second benediction thanks God for His many blessings. It reads in part:

> We give thanks unto Thee, for Thou art the Lord our God and the God of our fathers for ever and ever; Thou art the Rock of our lives, the Shield of our salvation through every generation. We will give thanks unto Thee and declare Thy praise for our lives which are committed unto Thy hand, and for our souls

> which are in Thy charge, and for Thy miracles, which are daily with us, and for Thy wonders and Thy benefits, which are wrought at all times, evening, morn, and noon. . . . *Praised art Thou, O Lord, whose name is all-good, and unto whom it is becoming to give thanks.*

The third benediction is an extension of the priestly blessing which the reader bestows at this point on the congregation, as did the Kohanim at the end of the sacrificial ritual in the Temple. The priestly blessing concludes with the words "The Lord bestow His favor upon you and grant you peace" (Num. 6:26). The congregation picks up the last word and responds with a prayer for peace:

> Grant peace, welfare, blessing, grace, loving-kindness, and mercy unto us and unto all Israel, Thy people. Bless us, O our Father, even all of us together, with the light of Thy countenance; for by the light of Thy countenance Thou hast given us, O Lord our God, the Torah of life, loving-kindness and righteousness, blessing, mercy, life, and peace; and may it be good in Thy sight to bless Thy people Israel at all times and in every hour with Thy peace. *Praised art Thou, O Lord, who blessest Thy people Israel with peace.*

The thirteen intermediate benedictions are congregational petitions for such boons as wisdom and understanding, forgiveness of sins, restoration of Israel, good health, and sustenance.[13] The thirteen petitions have an integral logic. The first three are prayers for religious blessings—ability to study the Torah, repentance, and forgiveness of sins. The next three deal with private and communal misfortunes—delivery from persecution, sickness, and famine. Thus the first six benedictions deal with current needs, religious and mundane. The following six benedictions deal with matters of the future, mainly messianic hopes, and the last benediction is a prayer for God's acceptance of Israel's prayers.

The overall structure of the *Tefillah* is also in accord with the traditional pattern: one is to approach the divine presence first with words that praise God, who is merciful and beneficent; then one is to present his petitions; then he is to conclude with a prayer thanks for God's mercies.

Though the origin of the *Tefillah* was independent of the *Shema*, the rabbis welded the two prayer units into one service. To emphasize the unity of these two essential parts of the service, the rabbis prohibited any break between the last benediction of the *Shema* and the first benediction of the *Tefillah*.[14] The two units are complementary parts of one service.

The Origin of the *Tefillah*

The development of the *Tefillah* is shrouded in mystery. Its formative period goes back to the days of the Persian rule in Palestine,* a period which is particularly lacking in Jewish historic documents. According to a previously quoted rabbinic tradition, "a hundred and twenty elders, among whom were many prophets, drew up eighteen blessings" (Meg. 17b). Elsewhere in the Talmud we read: "It was the Men of the Great Synagogue who instituted for Israel blessings and prayers, sanctifications [Kedushot] and *habdalahs*" (Ber. 33a).[15] With such skimpy source material it is almost impossible to reconstruct the early formulation of these benedictions and to trace their development accurately. Although some scholars have applied great ingenuity to this task, it is generally agreed that little that can be called definitive has come out of these praiseworthy efforts. One thing is certain: it was only after the destruction of the Temple that the order of the benedictions and the exact wording of their concluding blessings were established. Also, the general content (though not the exact wording) of each benediction was decided upon.† The *Tefillah* was thus left largely in a fluid state. It was decreed at that time that the prayers should be in the plural, so that even if a petition did not apply to a particular worshiper it applied to others in the congregation. When one prayed in private he was to pronounce the prayers in the plural too, for a Jew is always part of the community of Israel. Thus the benediction "Heal us, O Lord, and we shall be healed" was to be uttered not only by the sick,

* *See pp. 70–71.*
† *See p. 87.*

but by every Jew. A person in good health prayed for the sick of the community of Israel.

The redaction of the *Tefillah* at Yavneh is recorded in the Talmud, but again rather vaguely:

> Our Rabbis taught: Simeon ha-Pakuli arranged the eighteen benedictions in order before Rabban Gamaliel in Jabneh. Said Rabban Gamaliel to the Sages [on a subsequent occasion]: Can any one among you frame a benediction relating to the *Minim* [Judeo-Christians]? Samuel the Lesser arose and composed it [Ber. 28b].

This cryptic statement indicates that not only was the *Tefillah* arranged and edited at Yavneh, but also that a new benediction * was composed by Samuel the Lesser. This benediction became necessary at that time because of the critical situation created by some Jews who had joined the new sect of Nazarenes, or early Christians. These erstwhile Jews became a threat to the precarious existence of the Jewish people. The Judeo-Christians not only dissociated themselves from the Jews in order to escape the harsh Roman persecutions that followed the war, but in the heat of the controversy some of them turned against the Jews and acted as informers for the Romans. The bitterness they aroused is quite understandable. But the Judeo-Christians were indistinguishable from the rest of the Jews, because they lived in accordance with rabbinic laws and participated in the synagogue services. This rendered them especially dangerous during that critical period.

Rabbi Gamaliel resorted to a unique and effective stratagem. By adding to the *Tefillah* a benediction which contains a malediction against the Judeo-Christians, the sectarians were effectively eliminated from the synagogue. Any reader who failed to recite this benediction or any worshiper who failed to respond to it with the customary "Amen" was immediately recognized as a Judeo-Christian. This benediction, the twelfth in the order of the *Tefillah*, used to read somewhat as follows: "For apostates may there be no hope, and may the *Minim* [Judeo-Christians] and heretics speedily perish. . . . *Praised art*

** See pp. 439–40.*

Thou, O Lord, who breakest the enemies and humblest the arrogant." [16]

With the addition of this benediction against the Judeo-Christians, the weekday *Tefillah* achieved its official number of eighteen benedictions and thus derived its alternate name, *Shemoneh Esreh*, or the Eighteen Benedictions. The number was obviously fortuitous. It just happened that the number of benedictions of the *Tefillah*, as edited and arranged by Rabbi Gamaliel and his associates, was eighteen. But in later times some tried to find special significance in that number. Thus we read in the Midrash:

> Moses upon being asked, "Whence do we know how many prayers we are to offer?" answered: "Mark how many times the Ineffable Name occurs in this Psalm [29]." Told, "Eighteen times," Moses answered: "You must offer Eighteen Benedictions." [17]

Saadia Gaon, who lived about eight centuries after Rabbi Gamaliel II, gives twelve reasons why eighteen is a distinguished number in the Jewish prayer ritual. Some of these are that the patriarchs, Abraham, Isaac, and Jacob, are mentioned together eighteen times in the Torah; that eighteen prayers are mentioned in the Torah; and that there are eighteen festival days in the Jewish calendar. Hence the *Tefillah* is composed of eighteen benedictions.

The *Tefillah* for Sabbaths, Festivals, and Holy Days

On Sabbaths and festivals, petitions were generally avoided. This was also the practice in the Temple, where personal offerings were not accepted on holy days. The Sabbath and festival *Tefillah* therefore consisted only of the first three benedictions of praise, the last three benedictions of thanksgiving, and a single benediction in the middle. This benediction declares the sanctity of the day and concludes with the formula "*Praised art Thou, O Lord, who sanctifiest the Sabbath*" or "*who sanctifiest Israel and the festivals.*"

On Sabbaths and festivals there is also an additional (Musaf) service, corresponding to the additional sacrifice in the Temple. The Musaf service is essentially an additional *Tefillah* in which there is a description of the special Temple offering of the day and a prayer for the restoration of the Temple and its ritual.

The High Holy Days of Rosh Hashanah (New Year) and Yom Kippur (Day of Atonement) also had only seven benedictions in their *Tefillah*.[18] But the Musaf *Tefillah* of Rosh Hashanah has three intermediate benedictions instead of only one. These three benedictions deal with God's kingship over the whole universe, His remembrance of Israel, and His hearing of the sound of the shofar on Rosh Hashanah.*

As we have said, except for its concluding formula the specific wording of each benediction remained fluid for a long time to come. Since variety of expression was not frowned upon and the readers had the right to word the benedictions freely as long as they expressed the prescribed essence of the prayers, only scholars were permitted to act as readers, for only they could be relied upon to formulate the prayers without violating the rabbinic regulations regarding their proper contents.

The Service of the Heart

The *Tefillah* fulfills the commandment "You shall serve the Lord your God" (Exod. 23:25), which, according to the rabbis, refers to the Temple service. By reciting the *Tefillah* mornings and afternoons at the time when the sacrificial ritual was performed in the Temple, the Jew fulfills his duty to "serve the Lord." [19] He replaced the "service of the altar" with the "service of the heart." At a later time the *Tefillah* was also added to the Maariv service.† The *Tefillah* thus became part of every service, morning, afternoon, and night.

The *Tefillah* occupied a special place in the heart of the Jew. He recited the Eighteen Benedictions with genuine reverence. During this prayer he stood in silence and experienced the awe of the divine presence. The *Tefillah* therefore became the heart of the Jewish service—and deservedly so, because the Eighteen Benedictions express simply and succinctly the highest and noblest of the Jew's yearnings. "In their religious spirit," says

* *See pp. 240–42.*
† *See pp. 159–61.*

George Foot Moore, the Eighteen Benedictions "resemble the Psalms, from which their diction is chiefly drawn." And like the psalms, these benedictions were truly the Jewish prayers par excellence.

Teaching the Torah— Third Core Unit of the Jewish Liturgy

In ancient times the priestly clans were the professional keepers of the tradition. The religious lore, as it applied to the official ritual or to the conduct of man in his private and public relationships, was restricted to the priesthood. This knowledge was kept a professional secret and was passed on in strict secrecy to their priestly offspring or to others selected to serve as priests. To teach the whole religious lore to all the people not only was unknown, but this revolutionary idea would have shocked all within hearing if it had ever been mentioned. To make the teaching of the tradition a cardinal principle of the faith, which today is accepted quite casually as normal and natural, was in ancient times one of the most revolutionary innovations imaginable. And it is to this daring cultural leap of the synagogue that some scholars trace the beginnings of modern democracy.

The Torah imposes on every Jew the duty to study God's Torah. In the *Shema* we read: "Recite them [the words of the Torah] when you stay at home and when you are away, when you lie down and when you get up" (Deut. 6:7). But since not every person is equipped with the ability to study, the rabbis ordained that it was the duty of the scholars to teach the people at every opportunity. The Pharisees, who were the popular teachers of those days, performed their duty assiduously and developed the public teaching of the Torah into a permanent institution. Thus teaching and learning developed from a purely professional occupation into a universal Jewish preoccupation. Since the object of this preoccupation was a sacred literature, the Jew's attitude toward the study of Torah was one of deep reverence. The study of Torah became a form of divine worship and an integral part of the synagogue liturgy. Actually, the prayer elements of Jewish worship developed around the teaching of Torah, and to this day the ceremonial accompanying the reading of the Torah at public services is the climax and the most impressive part of the synagogue ritual.*

The process that gave rise to this most marvelous of Jewish religious institutions was discussed in an earlier chapter.† Its formal development was ascribed to the forceful and fruitful leadership of Ezra and his colleagues and to their successors, the Pharisees. As was pointed out, the general pattern consisted of the reading of scriptural selections, their translation verse by verse, and their elucidation with a homily.

The Benedictions of the Torah

By the end of the first century, the reading of the Torah in the synagogue had become a firm institution. It was preceded and followed by a benediction. The first benediction read: "*Praised art Thou, O Lord our God, King of the universe*, who hast chosen us from all peoples and hast given us Thy Torah. *Praised art Thou, O Lord, who givest the Torah.*"

The benediction after the Torah reading was: "*Praised art Thou, O Lord our God, King of the universe*, who hast given us the Torah of truth, and hast planted in our midst everlasting life. *Praised art Thou, O Lord, who givest the Torah.*"

In these benedictions the Jew not only thanks God for the privilege of receiving the Torah, the greatest of divine gifts, but also confirms several basic doctrines of rabbinic Judaism. These doctrines will be discussed in a later chapter.‡ At this point it will suffice to mention them briefly.

In the first benediction the Jew confirms that God gave them the Torah; the Torah is thus declared to be the word of God." But the Torah is not a frozen and lifeless instrument. The concluding phrase, "who givest the Torah," underscores the pharisaic teaching that the divine revelation is a continuing process. The rabbinic interpretations of the Torah, known as the Oral Torah, are also divine and binding.

* *See pp. 178–81.*
† *See pp. 67–70.*
‡ *See pp. 391 ff.*

In the second benediction the Jew affirms that the Torah has endowed Israel with everlasting life. By studying the Torah and by living in accordance with its teachings the Jewish people becomes an eternal people. Conversely, when the Jews cease to study the Torah and stray from its teachings they are doomed to extinction.

The benediction before the reading of the Torah is introduced by the traditional call to worship. This is seemingly strange, because the Torah reading takes place after the *Tefillah*. Why call the congregation to worship when they are in the midst of it? This call to worship, however, is intelligible in terms of the basic organization of the liturgy. The congregation is officially called to worship before the *Shema* because that was originally the start of the service. As mentioned above, the *Tefillah* was attached to the *Shema*, and no break between them was permitted; hence no call to prayer was possible before the *Tefillah*. However, the Torah reading maintained its independent character, and a call to worship at the start of the reading was logical.

It should also be noted that in ancient times there was only one call to worship before the reading of the Torah. The Torah benedictions were recited only once, as we read in the Mishnah: "The one who reads first in the Torah and the one who reads last make [respectively] a blessing before reading and after" (Meg. 21a). Those who were called between the first and the last read without any benedictions. The current practice, in which everyone called to the reading of the Torah recites both benedictions, is a later innovation. It satisfied the craving of the pious to recite a minimum of a hundred benedictions daily,* but one may not pronounce God's name in vain. So a valid reason for repeating the benedictions by each person called to the Torah was discovered in the fact that some people come late and miss the opportunity of hearing the opening benediction and responding to it with the traditional "Amen." Then there are surely some who have to leave before the end of the reading. For the sake of these probable latecomers and early-

* *See p. 144.*

leavers the recitation of the Torah benedictions by each person called to the Torah was instituted.

When the rabbis, under the leadership of Rabbi Gamaliel, were arranging and editing the synagogue liturgy, the practice of reading the Torah during the services and elucidating the text by translation into the vernacular and by popular homilies was already an ancient institution, traced back to Ezra. Already the reason for calling a specific number of people on Sabbaths and festivals was a mystery to the rabbis. Why do we call seven people to the Torah on the Sabbaths and only six on Yom Kippur? Why five on the festivals, four on the intermediate days of the festivals, and three on weekdays and at the Sabbath afternoon services? Since the rabbis did not know how and why these customs developed, they gave some farfetched reasons. They said, for example, that the number of people called to the Torah corresponds to the number of words in the three verses of the priestly blessing, that is, three, five, and seven (Meg. 23a)—which, of course, does not account for the six that are called on Yom Kippur and the four called on the intermediate days of the festivals. This type of explanation is evidence of the ancient origin of the customs associated with the reading of the Torah. However, there is much that is known about the Torah reading traditions, and these will be presented herewith.

The Torah Portions Read in the Synagogue

The choice of the Torah selections read at the various services is the result of a long historic process. The first prescribed portions were those read on holidays and fast days. It was natural to read and explain selections that dealt with these special occasions. In time these selections became the traditional readings for those occasions. We therefore find in the Mishnah a list of the Torah readings for the festivals (Meg. 3:4–6). This list also includes assigned readings for the minor festivals of Purim, Hanukah, New Moons, and the four special Sabbaths before Passover. These prescribed portions are brief. Some consist of only a few verses, indicating that they probably served merely as a basis for a homily in which the preacher explained the festival and the manner of its observance.

The portions read on ordinary Sabbaths were neither specific nor consecutive. The *rosh ha-kenesset* (the head of the congregation) would choose from the Torah a selection which he thought suitable for the occasion; or if the Torah reader was also the preacher that day, he would choose a selection that was suitable for his homily. But the Torah reader was not permitted to "skip from place to place in the Torah" (Meg. 4:4). (This regulation applied only to the reading on a single Sabbath; the readings on different Sabbaths were not consecutive.)

Reading the Torah consecutively, so as to complete the whole Pentateuch within a given time, is first described as a ruling of Rabbi Meir, who lived in the second century:

> The place [in the Torah] where they leave off in the morning service on Sabbath is the place where they begin at [the Sabbath] *Minhah;* the place where they leave off at *Minhah* [on Sabbath] is the place where they begin on Monday; the place where they leave off on Monday is the place where they begin on Thursday; the place where they leave off on Thursday is the place where they begin on the next Sabbath [Meg. 31b].

The accepted practice, however, follows the opinion of Rabbi Judah Ben Ilai, who held that they ought to begin each Sabbath morning where they left off the preceding Sabbath morning (ibid.). From this we deduce that there was no fixed cycle of readings. Later, after the compilation of the Mishnah at the end of the second century, definite cycles were established. In Palestine the cycle was three years. The Pentateuch was divided into 154 portions which were read consecutively; thus the Five Books of Moses were completed once in three years (Meg. 29b). The section read on the Sabbath was called a sidra. In Babylonia an annual cycle was developed. The Pentateuch was divided into fifty-four sections; each of these sections (called a parashah) was about three times as long as that of the Palestinian triennial cycle.

Translation of the Torah Reading into the Vernacular

In the first century it was customary in the Palestinian synagogues to accompany the reading of the Torah with a translation into the vernacular. This was appropriate because Hebrew was no longer the spoken language of the Jewish people. The Jews in Palestine and Babylonia spoke Aramaic, and in Egypt they spoke Greek. As mentioned above,* the rabbis interpreted the biblical account of Ezra's reading of the Torah as follows: " '*And they read in the book*,' " say the rabbis, "this indicates the [Hebrew] text; '*with an interpretation*': this indicates [that the text was accompanied with a translation]" (Meg. 3a).

The custom in Palestine was to call to the Torah a reader and a translator (meturgeman).[20] The reading of the Torah and its translation were done verse by verse. A tenth century source describes this procedure, which was hardly different from the custom that prevailed centuries earlier:

> The one called to the Torah reads and another translates, verse by verse . . . and a third person stands between the reader and the translator . . . to help the reader and the translator, and to prompt them before they read or translate. . . . If there is one who does not know how to read well, or is shy, then the third one helps him. But if he doesn't know at all how to read, he may not be called to read or to translate. . . . And if the reader erred, the translator may not correct him. Similarly if the translator erred, the reader may not correct him. Only the third one may correct the reading or the translating.[21]

The task of the translator was not an easy one. To begin with, he was not permitted to have anything written before him—the translation was regarded as part of the Oral Torah. He was not permitted to translate word by word, lest he distort the sense of the text, nor was he permitted to elaborate on the text. His was to be a free though exact translation. If he took any liberties with the translation he was to be "silenced and admonished." Rabbi Judah Ben Ilai is quoted: "He who

* *See p. 70.*

translates a verse with strict literalness is a falsifier, and he who makes additions to it is a blasphemer" (Tos. Meg. 4.9). Nonetheless, the meturgeman was more than a translator, for his translation invariably incorporated many rabbinic interpretations of the text.

The Privileged Status of the Kohen and the Levite

As mentioned in an earlier chapter,* precedence is given to one who is of priestly descent and after him to one who is of Levitical descent, if they are present (Horayot 3:8). But, the Mishnah concludes: "If the bastard, however, was a scholar and the *Kohen Gadol* an ignoramus, the learned bastard takes precedence over the ignorant *Kohen Gadol*." This principle, however, is effectively nullified by a rabbinic teaching that damns anyone who shames a person in public. The practice has therefore been to follow the set hierarchy and to call to the reading of the Torah first a Kohen and then a Levite, if they are in attendance, without regard to their scholarship ratings. Public judgments about people's relative scholarship are forbidden at all times, especially during divine worship.

The tradition of reading the Torah on Monday and Thursday mornings, discussed in an earlier chapter,† was explained on the basis of both practical and theological considerations. The practical explanation has already been mentioned: Mondays and Thursdays were formerly market days, on which many Jews from the outlying districts came to town for trading purposes. The designation of these days for Torah reading offered the logical opportunity to teach Torah to the masses. With the passage of time conditions changed, and market days were no longer necessarily held on Mondays and Thursdays. A new motivation was found in the fact that this practice spaces the reading in such a way that the words of Torah never go unheard in the congregation for three consecutive days.

The Reading of the Haftarah

Along with the prescribed reading from the Pentateuch it was customary to read on Sabbaths and festivals a supplementary

* *See p. 84.*
† *See p. 70.*

selection from the Prophets. In the days of the Mishnah this was already a familiar practice (Meg. 4:10). The Christian Bible (Luke 4:16–21) relates that while attending a synagogue service Jesus was called to read in the Torah. He was handed the Book of Isaiah, which he opened to the sixty-first chapter. He read the verses, rolled up the scroll, and handed it to the attendant. Then he sat down and expounded the reading.

This incident indicates that the prophetic readings had not been fixed. As stated before, they were chosen by either the head of the synagogue or by the reader, and their choice was determined mainly by its appropriateness as a follow-up to the reading from the Pentateuch. A common or similar theme was sought. Thus the Torah reading that contains the Song of Moses has as its Haftarah a prophetic selection that contains the Song of Deborah. Obviously the readings from the Prophets could not possibly be continuous, as were those from the Pentateuch.

As was the case with the readings from the Torah, the Talmud lists specific prophetic readings only for the festivals and the special Sabbaths (Meg. 31a–b). The prophetic readings for the ordinary Sabbaths were not yet fixed by the second century. Indeed, the rabbis could not possibly have fixed the prophetic readings till the Pentateuch readings were set. Their interdependence, as mentioned above, was due to the accepted principle that the contents of the Haftarah had to be related to the theme of the Torah section. However, when the Pentateuch readings ceased to be readings "in course" and became readings "in cycle," it became possible to assign definite prophetic selections to each Torah reading.

The incorporation of teaching the Torah into the liturgy had a singular effect on the Jewish people. The Jews, said the Moslems, were the "people of the book," because every Jew was acquainted with the Scriptures and was a devotee of learning. And in the Middle Ages, when illiteracy was not unknown even in the ranks of the nobility, practically every Jew could read his Hebrew prayers and could follow the reading of the Torah with a fair amount of comprehension. Today, too, though the heritage is no longer a determining factor in the life of the Diaspora Jew, the hunger for learning has remained a powerful motivation in the Jew's life, so that the university campus has become the universal goal among the Jews.

The Homily in the Ancient Synagogue

In the early centuries of the Common Era the homily had already assumed the main features of its classic form. Generally delivered after the reading from the Torah, it interpreted and applied the scriptural reading to the daily life of the people. The homily was known as *derashah*, an act of "searching" in the Torah for its innumerable teachings. The preacher was called *darshan*, one who "searched" in the Torah for new insights and new light on the problems of the day. The actual preaching procedure is illustrated by an incident reported in early rabbinic sources going back to the first century:

> [Once] in Rabbi Joshua's old age, his disciples came to visit him. "My sons," he said to them, "what new interpretation have you had in the study house?"
>
> "We are thy disciples," they replied, "and it is thy waters we drink."
>
> "Heaven forbid!" he exclaimed. "There is no generation bereft of Sages. Whose Sabbath was it?"
>
> "It was the Sabbath of Rabbi Eleazar ben Azariah," they answered.
>
> "And on what [text] was the agadic discourse today?" he asked.
>
> "It was," they replied, "on the section, *Assemble the people, the men and the women and the little ones*" (Deut. 31:12).
>
> "And how did he interpret it?" he asked them.
>
> They said to him: "This is how he interpreted it: As to *the men*, they came to study; as to *the women*, they came to listen. Why do *the little ones* come? So that a goodly reward might be given to those who bring them." [22]

The rabbinic preaching technique was not quite as simple as the above incident would suggest. Rabbi Joshua's disciples only reported the gist of the homily. Actually the construction of the homily was governed by strict rules. The preacher did not, as some believe, roam freely all over the Bible picking up

Bible, 13th Century, Schocken Library, Jerusalem. PHOTO: ALFRED BERNHEIM

his texts as they suited him. Nor did he correlate the texts on the pure coincidence of their having in common a word or a phrase. The rules of the homily limited the preacher in the choice of the initial biblical text, because it had to tally linguistically with a text in the Haftarah. There had to be some words or phrases that were common to both the opening text and the Haftarah text. This served as a bridge on which the preacher crossed over from the opening text to the Haftarah and thence to the Torah section of the day. The opening text was usually from the Writings, which were, as a rule, part of the service. To be sure, the preacher also drew on additional texts from the Scriptures, mostly on the basis of linguistic similarities. But the major consideration was the necessity of bridging the opener with the Haftarah and then with the Torah portion of the week.

The general construction of the homily thus consisted of the following elements:

(1) An opening biblical verse, usually from the Writings, which was explained, connected with the Haftarah and with the Torah reading.

(2) The body of the homily, in which the central ideas were supported by additional quotations from the Bible and by parables, allegories, or fables.

(3) The conclusion, which contained a summary of the ideas drawn from the text and a final prayer in the Aramaic vernacular, ending with the familiar words of the Kaddish: * "May His great name be blessed for ever and ever." [23]

The body of the homily dealt with either halakic (legal) matters, or haggadic (ethical, moral, or theological) issues. But when the homily was finished, the Pentateuch, the Prophets, and the Writings, which comprise the Written Torah, had been skillfully interwoven with each other and with rabbinic teachings, which constitute the Oral Torah. A homily, thus constructed, demonstrated clearly and convincingly the unity

* *See pp. 153–54.*

of the Written Torah and the Oral Torah and their common divine authority.

The preachers obviously had no formal training in homiletics,[24] but judging by their signal success it is evident that many of the Pharisees were masters of the art of preaching. We read in the Talmud about two rabbis whose respective types of preaching had unequal success:

> R. Abbahu and R. Hiyya b. Abba once came to a place; R. Abbahu expounded *Aggada* [popular, nonlegal matters] and R. Hiyya b. Abba expounded legal lore. All the people left R. Hiyya b. Abba and went to hear R. Abbahu, so that the former was was upset. [R. Abbahu] said to him: "I will give you a parable. To what is the matter like? To two men, one of whom was selling precious stones and the other various kinds of small ware. To whom will the people hurry? Is it not to the seller of various kinds of small ware?" [Sotah 40a].

The delicacy of Rabbi Abbahu, the successful preacher, is admirable. But the text clearly demonstrates the drawing power of the popular, nontechnical sermon. Eloquence and relevance rather than erudition and scholarship attract the masses and hold their attention. The fact that the Pharisees, who were both the scholars and the teachers of their day, succeeded in gaining the loyal following of the people is due largely to their wisdom in delivering their learned (halakic) lectures in their academies and their edifying (haggadic) sermons in the synagogues.

The Rabbis as Teachers

The objective of the Pharisees was moral and theological instruction. And they were remarkably successful. Their sermons gave the people comfort and encouragement, fortitude and faith. They taught the people the doctrines of Judaism and the laws of the Torah. In the grievous days that followed each of the Roman wars, the Pharisees comforted the people and gave them hope of redemption and salvation. They preserved the unity of the Jewish remnants and nurtured the soul of the people with the study of the Torah and a sustaining faith in God. It was the successful teaching of the Pharisees that enabled the Jews to declare in the words of the psalmist:

The law of the Lord is perfect, restoring the soul;
The testimony of the Lord is sure, making wise the simple.
The precepts of the Lord are right, rejoicing the heart;
The commandment of the Lord is pure, enlightening the eyes
[*Ps. 19:8–9*].

PART II

THE *SIDDUR*: ITS ORGANIZATION AND CONTENTS

5

A GLANCE AT EIGHT CENTURIES OF JEWISH HISTORY

When the Roman legions finally succeeded in penetrating the defenses of Jerusalem and putting the Temple to the torch, they celebrated their victory by the usual triumphal parade in Rome. They built the Arch of Titus, a monument still admired by tourists, and they struck coins with the inscriptions "*Judaea Capta*" and "*Judaea Devicta*," which occupy an honorable place in numismatic collections. But Judea was not as defeated as the Romans had concluded. On the spiritual side, Yohanan ben Zakkai and his disciples and then his successor, Rabbi Gamaliel II, and his colleagues carried on unceasing educational activities which united and consolidated the remnants of the Palestinian Jewish community. Their fruitful work was continued by their successors. So well did they perform their educational task that the Jews have lived on the spiritual treasures laid up by these singular men of scholarship and piety for almost two thousand years.

On the military plane, too, the Roman victory was not as decisive as the Romans had imagined. The patriots who survived the war harbored bitter feelings and sought vengeance from the enemy. The Jews were also sustained by an ardent faith in the approaching victory over the "kingdom of wickedness." The Messiah, they were sure, would soon come and lead them to victory over wicked Rome. The Temple would then be rebuilt and the holy ritual restored. They were ready to acclaim the Messiah and to follow him in physical combat against the oppressor.

The Second Revolt against Rome

In the year 132 C.E. an "anointed" leader did arise, and the second war with Rome was launched. It was bloodier than the first and its outcome more decisive. Bar Koziba, the heroic leader of the war, was a man of remarkable ability. His devoted followers called him Bar Kokhba—Son of a Star. With the support of Rabbi Akiba, the leading scholar of that generation, Bar Kokhba succeeded in rousing the people to furious revolt. The immediate cause seems to have been, from the Roman point of view, rather petty: the Romans "merely" tried to stop the Jews from circumcising their male children. But this was not so petty from the Jewish point of view. Circumcision was the sign of Abraham's covenant with God. Interference with this ancient and sacred rite was a declaration of war against Judaism.

The revolt began with a fury that took the Romans by surprise. The rebels captured Jerusalem, struck coins with the hopeful inscription "Jerusalem liberated," and hurriedly erected an altar on the site of the Temple. There is even some evidence suggesting that sacrificial rites were resumed. The battles were stubbornly fought with tremendous losses on both sides. Once more Rome suffered some telling defeats, and once more Rome found it necessary to bring its ablest general, Severus, all the way from Britain. After three years of desperate and heroic battles the overwhelming power of Rome prevailed, and Rome wreaked stern vengeance on the Jewish survivors. A plow was drawn over the site of Jerusalem and a new pagan city, Aelia Capitolina, was built in its place. On the site of the Temple a pagan shrine was erected. There stood two statues face to face: one was the image of Hadrian the Conqueror, and the other was of Jupiter Capitolinus, the god who gave him the victory. No Jew was allowed to set foot in the new city except once a year, on the anniversary of the fall of the Temple, to mourn the national calamity.

But the suppression of the revolt was an inconclusive triumph for Hadrian. To complete the victory he took stern measures to make sure that there would be no new Jewish rebellion. Persecutions aimed at the total destruction of this troublesome people were launched. The method of achieving this goal was to suppress the sources of Jewish vitality: the teaching of Torah, the ordination of rabbis, and the practice of religious rites, especially the circumcision of children, were strictly forbidden. Death was the penalty for anyone who dared defy these crushing edicts. So the blood of martyrs began to flow freely. Among those who died "for the sanctification of God's name" was the famous Rabbi Akiba, who rejoiced at his fate of martyrdom because, as he put it, he had finally succeeded in serving God "with all his soul," as prescribed in the *Shema*. The embellished story of the torture and death of ten outstanding religious leaders, Rabbi Akiba among them, is related in a touching martyrology recited on the Day of Atonement. Pious Jews have shed many tears during the centuries over this martyrology.

The tragedy of the disastrous war affected every phase of Jewish life. The land lay wasted, depopulated, and impoverished. The prospect of a speedy restoration of the nation and its holy Temple was now bleaker than ever. So the remnants of the nation's spiritual leaders settled down to wage the peaceful battles of the Torah in the academies, which were now moved from devastated Judea northward to Galilee.

The persecutions were not sustained beyond Hadrian's lifetime. But their surcease did not restore vitality to Jewish life in Palestine. The land was still rich in scholars, and the post of nasi (the head of the Sanhedrin) was still held in reverence. But the land was too devastated, poverty-stricken, and depopulated to sustain a vital center of Jewish life and a distinguished scholarly leadership. This sad state resulted in two developments of historic importance—a consolidation of the spiritual and intellectual assets of Palestinian Jewry and the rise of the Babylonian Jewish community to spiritual leadership and scholarly ascendancy.

The Compilation of the Mishnah

It was not long after the disastrous Bar Kokhba rebellion that a leader of wisdom and prestige took the bold step of gathering, sifting, and editing the accumulated Oral Torah, which had been growing and expanding for more than five centuries. Rabbi Judah Ha-Nasi (the Prince) saw the hopeless decline which he could not stem, and he feared that the pressures of disintegration, set loose by the agonies of the war and the persecutions that followed it, would lead to the loss of the precious heritage. What Gamaliel II, his grandfather, had done a century before—after the first war with Rome—Rabbi Judah Ha-Nasi now did on a larger scale for the Oral Torah. It should be mentioned that his work was made considerably easier by the pioneering work of his predecessors Rabbi Akiba and Rabbi Meir. Rabbi Akiba began the work of systematizing the Oral Torah and arranging it into logical categories. A generation later (in the mid-second century) Rabbi Meir revised his teacher's work and elaborated on it. But it was Rabbi Judah Ha-Nasi who really succeeded in collecting and editing the vast accumulation of learning and tradition. The result of his monumental efforts was the compilation of the Mishnah, which later became the core of the Talmud. The Mishnah is organized into six "orders" which deal with six broad areas of law. Each order is divided into tractates, chapters, and paragraphs. The first order is called *Zera'im* (Seeds) and deals with agricultural law; the first tractate of this order is Berakhot (Blessings), which deals with the general theme of prayer. The reasoning behind this arrangement is probably that it is a Jew's duty to bless God before he enjoys the produce of the field. This tractate on blessings is the main source of our knowledge about the development of the Jewish liturgy. It is both a fertile and rocky field of vast proportions. It has been plowed by scholars for many centuries and will surely be worked intensively by many scholars in the future.

The Ascendancy of the Babylonian Jewish Community

The second outcome of the impoverishment and decline of Palestinian Jewry was the rise of the Babylonian Jewish community to leadership in the Diaspora. The origin of this community goes back almost eight hundred years to the time when the First Jewish Commonwealth was destroyed in the year 586 B.C.E. The cream of the nation was then deported to Babylonia, and thus the long-lived and creative Babylonian Jewish community came into being. Some of those Jews returned to Palestine after Cyrus, king of Persia, issued his declaration in 538 B.C.E., encouraging the Jews to return to their homeland and rebuild their Temple. Most Jews, however, remained in the land of exile. After eight centuries of historic silence, they wakened from their seeming dormant state. They rose up with surprising vitality and assumed a position of leadership in Jewish life that lasted about eight centuries.

This rise to leadership was due in large measure to the favorable circumstances that prevailed in Babylonia. The Jews were relatively numerous and prosperous, and they enjoyed considerable autonomy in their internal affairs. The recognized head of the Jewish community was the exilarch or *resh galuta* (head of the exile), who claimed descent from the House of David. His office was sanctioned by the government, which allowed him to exercise civil rule in the Jewish communities and gave him the power of taxation. Jewish law was applied in the courts, and Jewish tradition held sway in the communities. The exilarch maintained a palace of almost royal splendor and was treated by the government as a prince and dignitary of high standing. His position among the Jews was one befitting a prince of the House of David.

Early in the third century Babylonian Jewry began to dominate Jewish scholarship. The intellectual leaders of that generation, Rav and Samuel, were the recognized authorities of their day, and the academies of Sura and Nehardea (later moved to Pumbedita) were the most famous seats of learning. For eight centuries men of scholarship and piety headed these academies. Their discussions during the three centuries from approximately 200 to approximately 500 C.E. centered mainly on the Mishnah. These discussions and legal conclusions were accepted as authoritative and binding not only on the local Jewish communities but on Jews everywhere. By the beginning of the fifth century, however, it again became clear that the accumulated mass of tradition needed consolidation if it was to be preserved. And again men of scholarly stature and courageous temperament provided the leadership. Rav Ashi, head of the Sura Academy in the mid-fourth century, began the huge task of collecting and editing the Oral Torah. The result of his efforts was further reviewed and amplified during the following generations. It is not known exactly when the Babylonian Talmud was reduced to writing, but by the end of the sixth century manuscripts of the Talmud were available. The Babylonian Talmud became the leading authority in all areas of Jewish life. In Jewish schools everywhere the Talmud became the chief focus of intellectual concentration, superseding the study of the Bible. Indeed, the Bible and the Mishnah were comprehended mainly through the interpretations that emerged from the involved discussions in the Babylonian academies.

The Age of the Geonim

The study of the Talmud has occupied the best minds of the Jewish people up until modern times. But only a keen mind after many years of concentrated study could find its way through the labyrinthian paths of the large tomes of the Talmud. The renowned scholar Solomon Schechter aptly described the Talmud as a "bottomless sea with innumerable undercurrents."[1] To master the Talmud required a lifetime of scholarship and the assistance of the many commentaries that grew up around the text. With the writing down of the Babylonian Talmud in the sixth century, the prestige of the Babylonian academies reached its height. Jewish communities in North Africa and Europe dispatched their inquiries to the geonim, who headed the academies, and as a rule the responses by their excellencies were accepted as authoritative. A statement in a rabbinic response to the effect that such-and-such was "the custom of the two academies" was usually accepted as final and binding. The ascendancy of the Babylonian community was thus achieved through the superiority of its scholars and its academies. It is not surprising, therefore, that despite the powerful hold that local traditions maintained upon the scattered Jewish communities,* the Jewish liturgy reflects many Babylonian customs and traditions.

The Babylonian academies continued to function for more than five centuries after the compilation of the Talmud. And

* *See p. 373.*

since the religious influence of the heads of the two Babylonian academies was generally decisive among the Jewish people everywhere, this period, extending to about 1000 C.E., is usually called the geonic period. The geonim were proud of the Talmud. It was produced in their academies and was recognized as the classic exposition of Jewish law and the peak of Jewish scholarly achievement. The geonim naturally regarded themselves as the guardians of the Talmud, and they exerted a steadying influence on Jewish life.

In the field of liturgy the efforts of the geonim were directed mainly toward preserving the tradition as developed and handed down by the sages of the Talmud. They resisted innovations, additions, or improvements of the services. They strongly opposed expansion of the benedictions that precede and follow the *Shema* and fought against the introduction of newly composed religious poems into the *Tefillah*. To be sure, they ultimately failed in these efforts because—as we shall see—the insertion of new material into the benedictions of the *Shema* and of new poetic compositions into the *Tefillah* proved overwhelmingly popular. But the geonim did succeed in stemming the tide and preventing what might have become a flood. They saved the synagogue liturgy from an inundation that might have destroyed the tradition altogether. The great scholar Louis Ginzberg therefore concludes that the influence of the geonim on the development of the liturgy was decisive.[2]

The Rise of Mohammedanism and the Karaite Schism

This historical overview, sketchy though it is, cannot be concluded without mentioning two movements of abiding significance to Judaism, both of which had their start during the geonic period. The first is the birth of Mohammedanism, which began its meteoric rise on the seemingly unpromising Arabian Peninsula in the early seventh century. Within a hundred years it was the ruling power over vast territories extending from the Atlantic Ocean to the Persian Gulf and beyond. Though its origin and basic tenets are sufficiently close to Judaism that it may be called a daughter religion, Mohammedanism soon turned against Judaism as well as against Christianity and treated them both as tolerated strangers. As we shall see later, in addition to winning many adherents, the new faith also stimulated the development of an enviable Arab culture. This in turn exerted a powerful influence on the Jews, resulting in spiritual developments of historic magnitude. But this is beyond our present concern.

The second relevant development was a schism within the Jewish people which threatened their very survival. In the early eighth century a challenge to rabbinic Judaism was hurled by Anan ben David. He denied the authority of the Talmud and demanded a return to the Bible, which alone, according to Anan and his followers, is the word of God—all else is extraneous material which the rabbis imposed on the Jews. The Karaites, as these sectarians were called, eventually broke away from the mainstream of Judaism and have lived apart, following, they say, the genuine Judaism of the Bible. They purged their liturgy of the prayers developed since the days of Ezra and substituted biblical selections. The schism split the Jewish people into two camps that were so effectively separated that they ceased to exert any manifest influence on each other, including their respective liturgies.

By the end of the tenth century the gaonate had already begun to disintegrate; the heads of the schools were no longer men of stature. With the passing of Hai Gaon in 1034, Babylonia lost the last of its distinguished scholars. The glory of the Torah had moved westward to European centers, where it shone brightly for many centuries; the impact of the new centers of learning on Jewish liturgy will be the theme of later chapters in the book.

One of the great achievements of the talmudic and geonic eras was in the field of the liturgy. The skeleton of the prayers, which had been fashioned in Yavneh during the first century of the Common Era, took on sinews and was covered with flesh and skin. It was during this period that the first prayer book of the synagogue was published.

6
EXPANSION OF THE WEEKDAY SERVICES

More than seven centuries elapsed between the redaction of the prayers at Yavneh under the direction of Rabbi Gamaliel II and the official writing down of the first *Siddur*. During that vast stretch of time, usually called the talmudic and geonic periods of Jewish history, the synagogue liturgy did not remain frozen. To be sure, the decisions of Yavneh were not challenged. Nonetheless, great changes did take place. These changes consisted mainly of enlargements of existing prayers, insertions of new prayers, and the additions of a number of prayer units of considerable dimensions. The heads of the Babylonian academies often resisted expansions of the traditional services. Occasionally they even resorted to praising the virtues of brevity, invoking the example of Moses' prayer in behalf of his sister Miriam, which consisted of only five monosyllabic Hebrew words—"O God, pray heal her!" (Num. 12:13). But these efforts were ineffective. The pious zeal of the people demanded more prayers. So the liturgy continued to expand, and the prayers continued to multiply until the accretions exceeded by far the basic core that was defined at Yavneh.

The Enlargement of the *Shema* Benedictions

The benedictions of the *Shema*, notwithstanding their general formulation at Yavneh, were expanded considerably during the centuries under discussion. Originally these benedictions were rather brief. The first benediction was limited to praising God, who "in mercy gives light to the world and those who dwell upon it, and in goodness renews each day continually the work of creation." The second benediction, too, was brief. It only spoke of God's love of Israel, as demonstrated by His revelation at Sinai, and it praised Him for choosing "His people Israel in love." The benediction after the *Shema* only dealt with the affirmation of the tenets contained in the three paragraphs of the *Shema* and concluded with Israel's gratitude for the deliverance from Egypt. These benedictions contained no prayers for the future redemption of Israel; this theme was amply provided for in the *Tefillah*. During the geonic period, however, the *Shema* benedictions were expanded and enriched with petitions for the deliverance of Israel. Thus we find in the first benediction before the *Shema* an insertion: "O cause a new light to shine upon Zion, and may we all be worthy of its light." And in the second benediction we find the prayer "O bring us in peace from the four corners of the earth, and make us go upright to our land." But the most conspicuous insertion was that of a Kedushah, a prayer about God's holiness which the angels on high and the community of Israel jointly pronounce. This significant addition will be discussed below in conjunction with a similar prayer that was added to the *Tefillah*.*

These enlargements of the benedictions before and after the *Shema* were not the result of any planned action. They were part of a historic process which prevailed, as mentioned above, in the face of geonic opposition—not because they were inappropriate or repetitious, but because the geonim watched over the talmudic tradition and resisted all change, including accretions. But their opposition was to no avail. The *Shema* benedictions grew; the insertions were thoroughly integrated; and today no distinctions are made between the original text and the later additions.

The Nineteenth Benediction of the *Tefillah*

The forces making for the expansion of the liturgy also affected the *Tefillah*. To be sure the number of benedictions, their order, their general content, and the exact wording of the concluding formula of each benediction had all been deter-

* *See pp. 134–37.*

mined at Yavneh. And these decisions were respected. Nonetheless, many insertions found their way into the *Tefillah.*

To begin with, a fitting framework was provided in the form of introductory and concluding verses from Psalms. The Talmud tells us that Rabbi Yohanan, a Palestinian teacher of the third century, said: "In the beginning [of the *Tefillah*] one has to say: *O Lord, open Thou my lips* [*And my mouth shall declare Thy praise* (Ps. 51:17)], and at the end one has to say: *Let the words of my mouth* [*and the meditation of my heart be acceptable before Thee, O Lord, my Rock, and my Redeemer* (Ps. 19:15)]" (Ber. 4b). These verses have been incorporated into the official prayers, and to this day they are the opening and closing words of the *Tefillah.*

But a far more important change was instituted during this period. A nineteenth benediction was added to the *Tefillah.*[1] At first it was accepted in only one locality; later it became an integral part of the *Tefillah* everywhere. The origin of this benediction goes back to the geonic period, when the exilarchate was at the height of its prestige. The exilarch was the temporal head of the Babylonian Jewish community. He was held in high esteem among the people, especially since he was a descendant of the royal House of David. It is not surprising that some Jews felt it appropriate to include in the *Tefillah* a special prayer for the offspring of the House of David. The benediction that was composed reads: "Speedily cause the offspring of David, Thy servant, to flourish, and let his horn be exalted by Thy salvation, because we wait for Thy salvation all the day. *Praised art Thou, O Lord, who causest the horn of salvation to flourish.*" This new benediction was inserted after the fourteenth benediction, which implores God: "Do Thou in Thy mercy return to Thy city, Jerusalem."

At first the inclusion of this nineteenth benediction was a local Babylonian custom. But in those days the prestige of the Babylonian Jewish community was at its height and its hegemony among the Jews throughout the world was practically unchallenged. Any practice adopted in the Babylonian academies was followed in all Jewish communities. The nineteenth benediction was therefore incorporated in the *Tefillah* everywhere and became a permanent part of the synagogue liturgy. The name *Shemoneh Esreh* (Eighteen Benedictions) thus became a misnomer. But it has persisted throughout the centuries, and the *Tefillah* is still known by its original name designated in Yavneh: the Eighteen Benedictions.

The Kedushah

But the most significant addition to the liturgy after its redaction at Yavneh was that of the Kedushah, a prayer in which the community of Israel together with the heavenly hosts proclaim God's holiness. This prayer is obviously mystic in nature. Still, it had its origin in Babylonia, the home of the great rabbinic academies, where the study of Jewish law reached the peak of its classic development. That Jewish mysticism should have developed in Babylonia is seemingly contradictory. However, it is an undisputed fact that both the intense concentration on legal study and the deep speculations on esoteric theories flourished side by side without contradiction or conflict. The coexistence of the rational and the mystical even in one and the same person is not as unusual as some believe. Thus Joseph Karo, the author of the classic Jewish code of law, the *Shulhan Arukh*, was also an extraordinary mystic who communed with a heavenly mentor and recorded his conversations with this angel.

During the rabbinic period the Babylonian mystics were engrossed in speculations regarding the nature, appearance, and functions of the heavenly chariot and the angelic sanctification of God, as described in the sixth chapter of Isaiah and in the first and third chapters of Ezekiel. Thus the prophet Isaiah speaks of the celestial choir, and how the angels declare God's holiness:

> *And one* [*angel*] *called unto another, and said:*
> *Holy, holy, holy, is the Lord of hosts;*
> *The whole earth is full of His glory* [*Isa. 6:3*].

The triple sanctification of God's name by the celestial hosts suggested to the early mystics that Israel, too, should proclaim God's holiness using these and similar mystic expressions derived from Holy Writ. In Ezekiel, too, the heavenly hosts are described as praising God. They exclaim: "Blessed be the glory of the Lord from His place" (Ezek. 3:12). This angelic exclamation, too, the mystics thought worthy of use by the community of Israel in emulation of the heavenly hosts. A third verse, this time from Psalms, was regarded by the mystics as a fitting climax for the proclamation of God's holiness. The psalmist declares God's eternal sovereignty:

The Lord will reign for ever,
Thy God, O Zion, unto all generations.
Hallelujah [*Ps. 146:10*].

These three verses became the essential elements of the Kedushah. And in order that the Kedushah might recapture the mystic spirit and ecstasy that are reflected in their biblical contexts, the mystics provided appropriate introductions and connecting sentences. Quite logically, the Kedushah is placed immediately before the third benediction, which deals with God's holiness, and concludes with the blessing "*Praised art Thou, O Lord, the holy God.*"

The mystics were highly successful in their efforts, for the Kedushah communicates a feeling of tangible yet ineffable holiness of God. When the Kedushah is recited during the reader's repetition of the *Tefillah*, the devout worshiper senses the awesome nearness of God. He experiences the mysterious, or, as Rudolf Otto called it, the numinous element that permeates the Kedushah. This feeling of awe and ecstasy is given added reality in the worshipers' posture and bodily movements during the recitation of the Kedushah. They stand erect with their feet together as is implied in Ezekiel's vision: "and their feet were straight" (Ezek. 1:7). And when the words, *Kadosh, Kadosh, Kadosh* (Holy, Holy, Holy) are recited, they lift their heels, giving expression to their aspirations for the higher, spiritual forces in life. Unfortunately, the Kedushah is difficult to translate.* The available renditions in modern prayer books, though generally faithful to the Hebrew text, have lost much of the distinctive flavor of the original Hebrew formulation. Somehow the refinements and subtleties of the Hebrew are missing, and

* *See p. 574.*

without these untranslatable nuances the mystic power of the Kedushah is lost. As a consequence, those who rely on the translation of the Kedushah for their comprehension of the prayer seldom grasp the reason why Jews who know the Kedushah in the Hebrew strive ardently to worship with a congregation in order to be able to recite the Kedushah.

But not all Jews can attend synagogue services daily. Most Jews find it necessary to recite their prayers in solitude. These Jews are not altogether deprived of the privilege of reciting the Kedushah, because this doxology has found its way into two additional prayers of the morning service—in the first benediction before the *Shema* and in a prayer which is recited near the end of the morning service, known by its initial words as *Uva Le-Zion Go'el* (A redeemer will come to Zion).[2] By the inclusion of the Kedushah in these prayers, especially in the first benediction before the *Shema*, every Jew was enabled to declare God's holiness in the mystic words of the prophet Isaiah. But this recitation was not a substitute for the recital of the Kedushah by the community of Israel during a public service.

As indicated above, the inclusion of the Kedushah in the daily prayers first gained currency only in Babylonia. In Palestine there was considerable resistance to this innovation at the outset. For centuries the Kedushah was not part of the Palestinian liturgy. But as the Church intensified its persecutions of the Palestinian Jews and as the degradation and poverty of the Palestinian Jews increased, their prestige among the scattered Jewish communities correspondingly dwindled.* At the same time the hegemony of the Babylonian Jews grew, and for many centuries it remained unchallenged. Eventually the Palestinian Jews yielded and accepted this innovation. At first their acceptance was limited to the Sabbath and festival services,[3] but in time they yielded completely and began to recite the Kedushah at every service.[4] Once the Kedushah was accepted by the Palestinian Jews it became for them too the spiritual summit of the service, and it was recited by them with devotion as great as that of the Babylonian Jews. From these two centers of

* *See pp. 126–28.*

religious influence the practice of reciting the Kedushah in the daily service spread to all Jewish communities.

Prayers for Rain

During the talmudic and geonic times a number of other additions were made to the *Tefillah*. These accretions do not rank in importance with that of the nineteenth benediction, or the Kedushah, but they are of sufficient significance to have become integral parts of the liturgy.[5]

The first of these accretions to the *Tefillah* consists of two short sentences related to the agricultural conditions in Palestine. The first praises God who causes "the wind to blow and the rain to fall." The second supplicated God to "grant dew and rain for a blessing." In the Mishnah (Ber. 5:2) we are informed that "the miracle of the rainfall" is to be said in the second benediction in which God is praised: "Thou sustainest the living with loving-kindness." The petition for rain is to be said in the ninth benediction, in which God is beseeched to "bless the seasons of this year with all manner of produce."

These additions to the *Tefillah* may seem rather piddling. But in ancient Palestine these two sentences were of crucial concern. They touched on a recurring life-and-death issue. The rainy season in Palestine is limited to a few months of the year, and the rains are notoriously fickle and unpredictable. They are preceded by winds that are at times so violent as to turn the hoped-for rain into a calamity. To this day people in Israel live through the winter months in fear of either drought or destructive storms. In ancient days drought was dreaded because it meant famine, plagues, and even death. The Mishnah (Ta'an. 2:1) vividly describes the terror that overwhelmed the people when the rains were late in coming. A general fast was proclaimed; the ark was taken into the public square, ashes were placed on it and on the heads of the community leaders, and then everyone put ashes on his own head. The elders addressed the people, calling on them to repent. Then prayers were recited with great devotion. No wonder it was felt that when God is praised in the first three benedictions of the *Tefil-*

lah for sustaining the living with loving-kindness, the "miracle" of rain should also be mentioned and that later in the *Tefillah*, when the congregation implores God to "bless the seasons . . . with all manner of produce," a prayer for rain should be added. Not just rain, but "rain for a blessing." The wind was accepted as a necessary precursor to the rain, but they prayed that the wind be "for a blessing." * These two insertions were to be recited only during the winter months, which are the rainy season in the Holy Land.

The *Modim* of the Rabbis

Another addition to the *Tefillah* is the *Modim De-Rabbanan*, or the Thanksgiving Prayer of the Rabbis, which the congregation says silently when the reader recites the regular thanksgiving *(Modim)* benediction. The origin of the *Modim De-Rabbanan* is intriguing. The Talmud asks: "While the Precentor recites the paragraph 'We give thanks' [*Modim Anahnu Lakh*] what does the congregation say?" The Talmud then quotes the prayers of four talmudic sages, and Rabbi Papa concludes: "Consequently let us recite them all" (Sotah 40a). And so it has been ever since. The individual prayers of the rabbis, as quoted in the Talmud, were combined, and what emerged was the "*Modim* of the Rabbis" as we have it in the *Tefillah*.

This prayer of thanksgiving is included in all prayer books. It is usually printed in a column parallel to the *Modim* benediction and in smaller type, to indicate that it is said silently while the reader recites the *Modim* benediction of the *Tefillah*.

The Variant Version of the Last Benediction

The last benediction of the *Tefillah* appears in two versions. The initial words of the main version, which appears in the morning service, are *Sim Shalom* (Grant peace). The alternate version used in the afternoon and evening services [6] begins with the words *Shalom Rav* (Abundant peace). There is no logical reason why one should be recited in the morning and the other

* *See pp. 221–22.*

in the afternoon and evening. The only reason that scholars have been able to offer is one of rabbinic tact. The two versions had coexisted in different localities for a long time and both were valid. Instead of choosing one version and rejecting the other, the rabbis wisely made a compromise. They retained both versions and assigned one to the morning service and the other to the afternoon and evening services.

The Concluding Prayer of the *Tefillah*

Reciting only the prescribed congregational prayers did not satisfy the religious cravings of the pious. Some wanted to address their personal beseechments to God. The sages of the Talmud were aware of this religious need, as we read in the Talmud: "R. Eliezer says: He who makes his prayer a fixed task [has no true devotion (Ber. 4:4)]. . . . Rabbah and R. Joseph both say: Whoever is not able to insert something fresh in it" (Ber. 29b). Everyone was therefore urged to compose one or more personal prayers. The preferred time for these private supplications was immediately after the *Tefillah*. The Talmud records a number of devotional prayers composed by some of the sages for their personal use after the *Tefillah*.[7] But only few people are articulate enough to formulate their own prayers—most people cannot find the fitting words for the outpouring of their hearts. Such people are usually content to recite the prayers composed by others, provided these prayers express their own sentiments. Thus a number of the personal prayers quoted in the Talmud have found their way into the prayer book. One of these private prayers became the "personal" prayer of every Jew. It was composed by a teacher of the Talmud, Mar the son of Rabina, for his own use. It reads as follows:

> My God, keep my tongue from evil and my lips from speaking guile. May my soul be silent to them that curse me and may my soul be as the dust to all. Open Thou my heart in Thy law [Torah], and may my soul pursue Thy commandments. . . . As for all that design evil against me, speedily annul their counsel and frustrate their designs [Ber. 17a].

This prayer, with some later accretions, became the concluding prayer of the *Tefillah* and serves as a substitute for the personal prayer one is supposed to add to the set prayers of the *Tefillah.*

The Abbreviated *Tefillah*

One often gets the impression that the Jewish liturgy kept on expanding without any consideration for the convenience of the average Jew, who was usually subject to the pressures of earning a livelihood and had no time for lengthy services. This impression, however, is contradicted by the rabbinic provision for an abridgment of the *Tefillah* when time does not permit one to recite the prescribed prayers. It is for such people that the rabbis suggested "an abbreviated eighteen [benedictions]" (Ber. 4:3). This suggestion is defined in the Talmud:

> What is meant by "an abbreviated eighteen"?
> Rav said: An abbreviated form of each blessing;
> Samuel said: Give us discernment, O Lord, to know
> Thy ways, and circumcise our heart to fear Thee,
> and forgive us so that we may be redeemed, and keep
> us far from our sufferings, . . . before we call mayest
> Thou answer: blessed [praised] art Thou, O Lord,
> who hearkenest to prayer [Ber. 29a].

While Rav interprets Rabbi Joshua's suggestion to mean that each of the benedictions is to be recited but in a shorter form, Samuel combines the twelve middle benedictions into one, retaining only central phrase from each and concluding with the blessing of the sixteenth benediction. This abbreviation by Samuel preceded by the first three and followed by the final three benedictions constitute the short *Tefillah.* It is called by its initial word *Havinenu* (Give us discernment) and is to be found in most prayer books. But Jews have generally preferred to recite the whole *Tefillah.* The Eighteen Benedictions have become the heart of all Jewish services, and Jews have held back from any tampering with the *Tefillah*, even if sanctioned by the rabbis. What prevails in religious worship is not always the recommendation of the authorities; the collective sentiment of the people usually fashions a tradition.

The Introductory Prayer Sections

While the enlargement of the *Shema* benedictions and the accretions to the *Tefillah* met with considerable opposition from those who sought to maintain the status quo, the addition of several large prayer units to the morning service was achieved without any resistance whatsoever. These large additions were readily accepted because they did not tamper with the prayer units established at Yavneh. Furthermore, these prayers were initially optional. Why object to anyone's adding a number of private prayers to the prescribed congregational service? But as usual the optional prayers in time became obligatory. Thus the morning service was greatly expanded. It was augmented by two lengthy introductory sections known as the *Pesukey De-Zimra* (Verses of Praise) and the *Birkhot Ha-Shahar* (Early Morning Benedictions), each of which was almost equal in length to the combined prayers of the *Shema* and the *Tefillah*.

The Verses of Praise

How did these two lengthy introductory sections come into being, and how did they find their way into the official liturgy? The origin of the *Pesukey De-Zimra* can be traced to the practice of "the pious" who used to spend an hour in preparation for prayer.* It is assumed that they spent that hour in reading psalms and other biblical selections in order to put themselves into a prayerful mood. The Talmud quotes one of the sages as saying: "May my portion be of those who recite [the Verses of Praise] every day" (Shab. 118b). These Verses of Praise were in time formalized into a definite, well-rounded liturgic unit, the heart of which consists of the last six psalms of the Psalter (Psalms 145–150). The hundredth psalm is also included in this unit. It used to be recited in the Jerusalem Temple whenever a thanksgiving offering was brought to the altar. These seven psalms are preceded and followed by a number of collected biblical prayers or passages.[8]

* *See p. 28.*

This prayer unit is introduced and concluded by appropriate benedictions. The opening benediction, known by its initial words as *Barukh She-Amar* (Praised be He who spoke), reads in part:

> Praised be He who spoke, and the world existed: praised be He: praised be He who was the Creator of the world: . . . praised be He who liveth for ever, and endureth to eternity. . . . *Praised art Thou, O Lord our God, King of the universe.* O God and merciful Father, praised by the mouth of Thy people . . . with the songs of David Thy servant: . . . praised and glorified be Thy great name for ever and ever. *Praised are Thou, O Lord, a King extolled with praises.*

The closing benediction, known by its initial word as *Yishtabah* (Praised be [Thy name]), reads in part:

> Praised be Thy name for ever, O our King, . . . for unto Thee, O Lord our God and God of our fathers, song and praise are becoming, hymn and psalm, . . . praises and thanksgivings from henceforth even for ever. *Praised art Thou, O Lord, God and King, great in praises, . . . who makest choice of song and psalm, O King and God, the life of all worlds.*

When Saadia Gaon published his *Siddur* in the early tenth century, he included this unit of prayers in an appendix. He stated apologetically that these benedictions were not found in the Talmud but that he included them because "our nation has voluntarily taken upon itself . . . to read psalms . . . with an introductory and concluding benediction." In subsequent prayer books, however, the *Pesukey De-Zimra* were placed directly before the official call to prayer (the *Barkhu*). No apologies were necessary anymore. This prayer unit had already become firmly established as an official part of the morning service. For the past thousand years these psalms, their accrued lectionaries, and their opening and closing benedictions have been part of the morning prayers, and no one questions their legitimacy as an obligatory part of the service.

The Early Morning Benedictions

The second prayer unit that was added to the morning service is known as the *Birkhot Ha-Shahar*, the Early Morning Benedictions. The section is heterogeneous in its contents owing to its rather complicated course of development.

The Morning Blessings

The first part of this extensive prayer unit is a group of blessings which were originally prescribed for private use at the time of one's rising from sleep. As one performed the normal acts of dressing and washing, he was to recite the appropriate blessings, as we read in the Talmud:

> When he wakes he says: "My God, the soul which Thou hast placed in me is pure. Thou hast fashioned it in me, Thou didst breathe it into me, and Thou preservest it within me and Thou wilt one day take it from me and restore it to me in the time to come. So long as the soul is within me I give thanks unto Thee, O Lord, my God, and the God of my fathers, Sovereign of all worlds, Lord of all souls. Blessed [Praised] art Thou, O Lord who restoreth souls to dead corpses." When he hears the cock crowing he should say: "Blessed [Praised] is He who has given to the cock understanding to distinguish between day and night." When he opens his eyes he should say: "Blessed [Praised] is He who opens the eyes of the blind." When he stretches himself and sits up, he should say: "Blessed [Praised] is He who looseneth the bound." When he dresses he should say: "Blessed [Praised] is He who clothes the naked" [Ber. 60b].

Fifteen blessings are recorded in the Talmud. The last of these is accompanied by a fitting prayer for starting the day:

> When he washes his face he should say: "Blessed [Praised] is He who has removed the bands of sleep from mine eyes and slumber from mine eyes. And may it be Thy will, O Lord, my God to habituate me to Thy law [Torah] and make me cleave to Thy

> commandments, and do not bring me into sin, or into iniquity, or into temptation, or into contempt, . . . and let me obtain this day and every day grace, favour, and mercy in Thine eyes, and in the eyes of all that see me. . . . Blessed [Praised] art Thou, O Lord, who bestowest lovingkindness upon Thy people Israel" [Ber. 60b].[9]

This substantial group of blessings offered a splendid opportunity to start the day with a goodly number of blessings toward the goal of one hundred, which Rabbi Meir in the second century had established as a daily minimum (Men. 43b).[10] Unfortunately, the recommendation by the rabbis that these blessings be recited with each act of rising and getting ready for the day's work was widely neglected, because many Jews did not know these blessings by heart. Nor—since prayers could not be written down—did they have a handy manual. They were strictly part of the Oral Torah. It therefore occurred to some anonymous rabbi to transfer these morning blessings to the public service, where the reader recited them at the beginning of the service and afforded the less knowledgeable an opportunity to hear them and to respond with the traditional "Amen!"

In a responsum of Rabbi Amram Gaon, who lived in the ninth century, it is stated that in Spain it is customary for the reader to recite these blessings on behalf of those who do not know them. The reader recites all the blessings "with a loud voice," and the worshipers answer "Amen!" to each blessing. Moses Maimonides, who lived in the twelfth century, objected to this practice on logical grounds. He writes:

> The people in most of our cities have the custom of reciting these blessings in the synagogue, consecutively. . . . This, however, is an erroneous practice which should not be followed. No blessing should be recited unless there is an obligation to do so [that is, when the act is performed].[11]

That Maimonides' opinion is logical cannot be gainsaid. Why should a blessing for hearing the cock crow be recited in the synagogue long after the cock has crowed? Why should a blessing for opening one's eyes be recited in the synagogue long after one has awakened from his sleep? But custom is stronger than logic. The private blessings not only remained in the synagogue ritual, but they were expanded to include a number of related blessings. They snowballed into what is now a lengthy introductory section to the morning service.

This growth of the morning blessings was not altogether haphazard. There were logical and historical reasons behind each phase of this process of expansion. The talmudic prayer mentioned above that is prescribed for everyone to recite immediately after waking from his morning sleep is known by its initial words: *Elohai Neshamah* (My God, the soul). Although the Talmud prescribes that "when he wakes he says: 'My God, the soul which Thou hast placed in me is pure,' " etc., there were people who objected to reciting this prayer upon awakening. How can one, they asked, utter a prayer with God's name in it before washing one's hands? The prayer was therefore transferred along with the morning blessings to the synagogue services. It was placed before the morning blessings and has served as a fitting introduction to them.

But the transfer of the *Elohai Neshamah* prayer to the synagogue services left a void in the religious life of the people. They missed a prayer to recite upon waking from sleep. Another prayer was therefore composed, known by its initial words as *Modeh Ani* (I thank [Thee]). This prayer is based on a statement in the Midrash which reads:

> It is written, *They are new every morning; great is Thy faithfulness* (Lam. 3:23). Rabbi Simeon ben Abba interpreted this: Because Thou renewest us every morning, we know that great is Thy faithfulness to redeem us (Gen. Rab. 78:1).[12]

The *Modeh Ani* prayer, based on this rabbinic saying, reads: "I thank Thee, everliving King, who hast mercifully restored my soul within me; great is Thy faithfulness." This brief formula was enlarged by the addition of a biblical verse which the Talmud directs every Jew to teach his child as soon as the child begins to talk (Suk. 42a): "*Moses commanded us a Law, an inheritance of the congregation of Jacob* [Deut. 33:4]."

Every Jew who was brought up in an observant home remembers this brief morning prayer which his mother taught him in his early childhood, and many a Jew has continued to recite it every morning for the rest of his life.

Another addition to the morning blessings is of mishnaic origin, as we read:

> R. Judah used to say, A man is bound to say the following three blessings daily: ["Blessed (Praised) art Thou . . .] who hast not made me a heathen, . . .[13] who hast not made me a woman, and . . . who hast not made me a brutish man." R. Aha b. Jacob once overheard his son saying, "[Blessed (Praised) art Thou . . .] who hast not made me a brutish man," whereupon he said to him, "And this too!" [14] Said the other, "Then what blessing should I say instead?" [He replied,] " . . . who hast not made me a slave" [Men. 43b].[15]

Since it was customary for most people to attend to their normal calls of nature in the early morning, before the service, it is not surprising that a talmudic benediction prescribed for such occasions found its way into the morning ritual, immediately before the morning blessings. Thus we read in the Talmud:

> Abaye said: . . . When he comes out [of a privy] he says: "Blessed [Praised] is He who has formed man in wisdom and created in him many orifices and many cavities. It is fully known before the throne of Thy glory that if one of them should be [improperly] opened or one of them closed it would be impossible for a man to stand before Thee." How does the blessing conclude? . . . R. Papa said: . . . "Who healest all flesh and doest wonderfully" [Ber. 60b].

This benediction was obviously a private prayer, associated with one of the normal acts of rising in the morning. It, too, was neglected by the unlettered. Hence it was transferred to the synagogue service and was logically placed next to the other private blessings.[16]

The Obligation to Study Torah

A third accretion to the morning benedictions consists of three blessings on the study of Torah. Every Jew is obliged to study Torah every day. According to the rabbis, a Jew should divide his study into three parts, one for the study of the Bible, one for the Mishnah, and one for the Babylonian Talmud (Kid. 30a). But what is the unlettered or the very busy man to do? Is he to be deprived of observing this divine commandment? The obvious solution of this problem was to follow the precedent set by the morning blessings and to incorporate study selections into the service ritual. Three small selections, chosen from the Scriptures, the Mishnah, and the Babylonian Talmud were incorporated into the introductory section immediately before the morning blessings. These selections consisted of the priestly benediction (Nun. 6:24–26) and two rabbinic selections from the Mishnah and the Babylonian Talmud (Pe'ah 1:1 and Shab. 127a) that deal with a number of ethical duties. Among these are the duty to honor one's parents, to visit the sick, and, above all, to study the Torah. Since the study of Torah is a religious obligation, it is to be preceded by a fitting blessing. Actually three blessings, corresponding to the three areas of study, were prescribed:

1. *Praised art Thou, O Lord our God, King of the universe,* who sanctified us by His commandments, and commanded us to occupy ourselves with the words of the Torah.

2. Make pleasant, therefore, we beseech Thee, O Lord our God, the words of Thy Torah in our mouth and in the mouth of Thy people, the house of Israel, so that we with our offspring and the offspring of Thy people the house of Israel, may all know Thy name and learn Thy Torah. *Praised art Thou, O Lord, who teachest the Torah to Thy people Israel.*

3. *Praised art Thou, O Lord our God, King of the universe,* who hast chosen us from all nations and given us Thy Torah. *Praised art Thou, O Lord, who givest the Torah.*

The Torah was thus studied symbolically by everyone. To be sure, one can hardly call this study; one only reads the same specified selections every morning. Nonetheless it satisfied the conscience of those who could not do any actual studying.

THE ABBREVIATED *Shema*

After the expanded group of morning blessings there is another group of prayers, at the center of which is an abbreviated *Shema.* This prayer unit originated in Persia during one of the periodic agonies of persecution which befell the Jewish community. These persecutions lasted about two centuries, from the middle of the fifth century to the middle of the seventh century. The fanatic Magians were offended by the Jewish emphasis on the unity of God. It negated the dualistic doctrines of the Zoroastrians. The recitation of the *Shema* at the synagogue services was, therefore, proscribed.* The rabbis met this emergency by instructing the people to recite the *Shema* privately before coming to the public services. To facilitate this strategy, the rabbis composed a short prayer unit with the first verse of the *Shema* at its center.

This prayer unit begins with a proclamation of Israel's faith in the God of their fathers. It clearly reflects the persecutions that gave rise to the prayer unit: "At all times let a man fear God as well in private as in public,[17] acknowledge the truth, and speak the truth in his heart; and let him rise early and say: . . ." This opening declaration is followed by a rabbinic prayer originally composed for use on the Day of Atonement (Yoma 87b):

> Sovereign of all worlds! Not because of our righteous acts do we lay our supplications before Thee, but because of Thine abundant mercies. . . . Happy are we! How goodly is our portion, how pleasant is our lot, and how beautiful our heritage!

* *See p. 398.*

> Happy are we who, early and late, morning and evening, twice daily, declare:
> *Hear, O Israel, the Lord our God, the Lord is One.*

The proclamation of God's unity is followed by a prayer which expands on the central theme of the persecutions, and concludes with a benediction on the duty of the Jew to sanctify God's name publicly, that is, to accept martyrdom if necessary. The prayer ends, as does the last benediction of the *Shema*, with a supplication for the restoration of Israel.

The persecutions in Persia lasted till the Moslems overran the country in 637 C.E. The regular synagogue services were then restored, and the *Shema* with its benedictions were reinstated in their traditional place in the service. But the prayers instituted during the emergency were not dropped. They were added to the *Birkhot Ha-Shahar*, where they have remained to this day. Two centuries of usage are sufficient to convert a temporary enactment into an honored tradition. Besides, these prayers are among the most exalted in the Jewish liturgy.

Symbolic Participation in the Temple Ritual

Still another prayer unit was added to the Early Morning Benedictions. It consists of selections from the Scriptures and rabbinic sources which describe the daily sacrificial ritual at the Jerusalem Temple. The last of these selections deals with the thirteen rules governing the interpretation of the Torah as taught by Rabbi Ishmael, a leading scholar of the second century. It will be recalled * that reading about the Temple ritual was regarded as equivalent to actual participation in the sacrificial worship. The pious Jew was thus enabled to fulfill his duties of the Temple worship before embarking on the main prayer service of the *Shema* and the *Tefillah*.

Although the Early Morning Benedictions, embracing the several prayer units mentioned above, developed either by chance or by historic circumstances, they have a measure of coherence and in a way are characteristic of Jewish worship. They contain, in abbreviated form, (1) the *Shema*, (2) a series of blessings which equal in number the benedictions of

* *See p. 85.*

the weekday *Tefillah*, and (3) symbolic study of the Torah. The *Birkhot Ha-Shahar* also contain a reminder of the Temple rites which is a traditional part of every service.[18]

To conclude this rather involved discussion, the Early Morning Benedictions were placed at the very beginning of the morning service. This was not only logical but necessary. The Verses of Praise were already part of the regular morning service. When the Early Morning Benedictions were transferred to the synagogue, they were naturally attached to the existing service, that is, before the Verses of Praise. The *Birkhot Ha-Shahar* thus became the opening prayers of every morning service.

Preparation for the Morning Prayers

By the end of the geonic period the Verses of Praise and the Early Morning Benedictions had become part of the statutory prayers of the morning service. Pious people therefore felt a need for some scriptural readings or hymns to attune their hearts and minds to the morning prayers. But it took several centuries before the new introductory elements were officially introduced. The first of these, known by its initial words as *Mah Tovu* (How fair), consists of several scriptural verses which express the worshiper's joy at coming into the house of prayer and his feelings of reverence for the divine presence that one senses in the synagogue. These biblical verses are recited as one enters for worship. The opening verse was originally uttered by the gentile prophet, Balaam, who came to curse Israel but blessed them instead: "How fair are your tents, O Jacob, / Your dwellings, O Israel" (Num. 24:5). Jacob's tents, say the rabbis, are the houses of prayer, and Israel's dwellings are the houses of study. The other scriptural verses are taken from Psalms:

But as for me, in the abundance of Thy
lovingkindness will I come into Thy house;
I will bow down toward Thy holy temple in the
fear of Thee [*Ps. 5:8*].

Lord, I love the habitation of Thy house,
And the place where Thy glory dwelleth [*Ps. 26:8*].

O come, let us bow down and bend the knee;
Let us kneel before the Lord our Maker [*Ps. 95:6*].

But as for me, let my prayer be unto Thee,
O Lord, in an acceptable time;
O God, in the abundance of Thy mercy,
Answer me with the truth of Thy salvation
[*Ps. 69:14*].

These introductory verses are followed by two hymns that are known by their initial words as *Yigdal* (Magnified [be the living God]) and *Adon Olam* (Lord of the universe). The former was composed by Daniel ben Judah, who lived in the fourteenth century, and is based on Maimonides' Thirteen Articles of Faith.* The latter was introduced into the morning service as late as the fifteenth century. Its authorship is unknown, though some have attributed it to the gifted poet Solomon Ibn Gabirol. The *Adon Olam* has become one of the most popular hymns in the synagogue. Its popularity is due, in large measure, to its pious sentiments and its simplicity of language. It speaks of God as the Sovereign and Creator of the universe, the omnipotent, ever-living, and only God. From these lofty theological concepts, the hymn goes over to intimate sentiments of piety:

He is my God, my living Redeemer
My Rock in time of travail and sorrow.
He is my banner and my refuge,
My cup of life whenever I call.
Into His hand I commend my spirit, when I sleep
and when I wake,
And after death, too, the Lord is with me; I will
not fear.

The introductory verses and hymns did not become part of the statutory prayers. Nevertheless they have been included in the *Siddur* as part of the morning prayers. In the course of time many melodies were composed for the hymns. This has made them popular and has facilitated their utilization in other services as concluding hymns.

* *See pp. 420–23.*

With the introduction into the morning service of the scriptural verses of the *Mah Tovu* and the hymns of *Yigdal* and *Adon Olam*, the extensive prayer sections which precede the *Shema* were completed.

"A Redeemer Will Come to Zion"

As we have seen, two large liturgic units were added as introductory prayers to the daily morning service. A similar development took place in regard to the closing prayers which follow the *Tefillah*. On Mondays and Thursdays the opening section of the Torah portion of the coming Sabbath was read. This practice, discussed in a previous chapter,* had been instituted long before the talmudic period. During the period under discussion, however, an important prayer—known by its initial words as *Uva Le-Zion Go'el* (A redeemer will come to Zion [Isa. 59:20])—was introduced into the liturgy.† It had its beginning in the talmudic period, when it was customary for the congregation to stay after the conclusion of the *Tefillah* to hear selections from the Prophets read, translated into the Aramaic vernacular, and expounded by the rabbis. After this study period it was customary to read "words of praise of the Holy One, blessed be He" and words of comfort regarding God's promise of redemption.

An allusion to the custom of reading and expounding the Prophets after the morning service is to be found in the talmudic comment on the statement in the Mishnah: "From the day the Temple was destroyed there is no day without a curse" (Sotah 9:12). In the Babylonian Talmud there is a comment on the above: "And the curse of each day is severer than that of the preceding. . . . How, in that case, can the world endure?—Through the doxology [Kedushah] recited after the Scriptural reading" (Sotah 49a). This cryptic reference to "the scriptural reading" speaks of the practice described above. It needed no explanation in the Talmud since it was then well known to everybody. The verses of comfort that followed

* *See p. 70.*
† *See pp. 193–94.*

the reading were in time formalized and came to be known by the initial words of the opening verse: *Uva Le-Zion Go'el.*

The reading and expounding of prophetic selections extended the service considerably. In normal times this was a most desirable practice; the people gladly accepted the additional period of study. However, when hard times came and the struggle for a livelihood became intense, they could no longer indulge in a lengthy service. The daily reading from the Prophets was abandoned, but the reading of the prayer *Uva Le-Zion Go'el* remained in the service. By that time, however, this prayer had already absorbed a significant addition. This took place during a period of severe persecution,* when it was forbidden to recite the Kedushah during the reader's repetition of the *Tefillah.* The rabbis therefore inserted the Kedushah into the prayer *Uva Le-Zion Go'el* so that the congregation could continue to recite this mystic prayer at a time when the government censors were no longer present in the synagogue.[19]

The Kaddish

The story of the daily morning service as it developed during the talmudic and geonic periods cannot be concluded without a brief discussion of the recurring prayer known as the Kaddish. This doxology is popularly regarded as an intercession in behalf of the deceased, but there is nothing in the Kaddish to suggest any association with the dead.

Originally the Kaddish was associated with the study of Torah. At the conclusion of a discourse in the synagogue or the schoolhouse, the preacher or teacher would utter a few words of consolation. This hopeful peroration was followed by the formal dismissal now known as the Kaddish. It was addressed to the assembly in the Aramaic vernacular. In his dismissal the teacher proclaimed God's greatness and holiness and alluded to the messianic hope, which God would surely fulfill in accordance with the prophetic words: "Thus will I *magnify* Myself and *sanctify* Myself, and I will make Myself known in

* *See pp. 444–45.*

the eyes of many nations; and they shall know that I am the Lord" (Ezek. 38:23). And when God's greatness and holiness become known among the nations, Israel's exile will be terminated and Israel's martyrdom will be vindicated. The Kaddish reads as follows: "Magnified and sanctified be His great name in the world which He hath created according to His will. May He establish His kingdom during your life and during your days, and during the life of all the house of Israel, even speedily and at a near time, and say ye, Amen." [20]

The congregation responded to this dismissal formula with an enthusiastic exclamation: "Amen! Let His great name be blessed forever and unto all eternity!" This response had been used in the Temple ritual, especially during the Day of Atonement, in a slightly variant Hebrew version.[21]

The congregational response to the Kaddish came to be regarded, especially among the mystics, as the essential element of the doxology. To quote but one talmudic comment: "Whenever the Israelites go into the synagogues . . . and respond: 'May His great name be blessed!' the Holy One, blessed be He . . . says: Happy is the king who is thus praised in this house" (Ber. 3a).

During the geonic period two paragraphs were added. These additions are also in the Aramaic vernacular, but they contain several Hebrew words and phrases. They are still in the spirit of the dismissal formula. These paragraphs read:

> Blessed, praised, and glorified . . . be the name of the Holy One, blessed be He; though He be high above all blessings . . . which are uttered in the world; and say ye, Amen!
>
> May there be abundant peace from heaven, and life for us and for all Israel; and say ye, Amen! [22]

The ancient custom of dismissing the assembly with the words of the Kaddish has been preserved to this day in what is known as the scholars' Kaddish or the *Kaddish De-Rabbanan.* This special Kaddish is recited after a study period or a religious discourse. It contains the following interpolation: "Unto Israel, and unto the rabbis, and unto their disciples . . . and unto all who engage in the study of the Torah . . . unto them and unto you be abundant peace . . . and salvation from the Father who is in heaven, and say ye, Amen!" But the person who recites the *Kaddish De-Rabbanan* is no longer the teacher or preacher but mourners who happen to be in attendance. This transfer of role came about when it became customary to honor a deceased scholar at the close of the seven days of mourning with a learned discourse delivered at the house of mourning. And the discourse was followed by the usual dismissal, the Kaddish. But this custom ruffled the sensibilities of some in the community, because the absence of such a discourse at the end of the mourning period implied that the deceased was wanting in scholarship. In order to obviate this public embarrassment it was ordained that a discourse be delivered or a religious text be studied during the mourning period of every deceased Jew.* This democratically inspired practice spread to all Jewish communities.

The next step in the change of the Kaddish from being a dismissal formula to that of a mourners' ritual derives from the fact that there was a widespread belief based on a legend that Rabbi Akiba had helped to redeem the soul of a deceased man from the tortures of Gehenna by teaching his son to recite the Kaddish at a congregational service. So it came about that people ceased to regard the Kaddish as a dismissal formula after a religious discourse and began to regard it as a doxology of great merit for the redemption of the soul of the deceased. This doxology, if recited by the children of the deceased during the year after burial, can save the dead from the punishment visited upon sinners during the year after burial. It was logical therefore for a person who delivered a religious discourse at a house of mourning to let the mourners recite the Kaddish for the benefit of their deceased relative.[23]

Still another logical step in the transformation of the Kaddish into a mourners' prayer is the reasoning that if the Kaddish is recited by mourners after a study period, which is regarded as divine worship in Judaism, why not also recite the Kaddish after every public prayer period, which is likewise divine wor-

* *See pp. 183–84.*

ship? It thus came about that during the year after burial the mourners were allowed to recite the Kaddish at the conclusion of every service and at several other designated places in the service.[24] And the congregation responded each time with the efficacious formula: "Amen! Let His great name be blessed forever and until all eternity!" [25] The mourners' Kaddish thus became a permanent part of the synagogue liturgy.

It should be added that the claim of the mystics that the recitation of the Kaddish helps to redeem the deceased at the judgment on high has evoked many condemnations throughout the generations. Especially in modern times, when rationalism has had a strong impact on theological thinking, this view has been strongly condemned. The modern emphasis has been on the value of the mourners' bearing public witness of their faith in God. Even in time of anguish the mourners stand up and publicly declare God's glory and holiness, as did Job during his severe trial: "The Lord gave, and the Lord hath taken away; Blessed be the name of the Lord" (Job 1:21).

The Reader's Kaddish

There is also a Kaddish that is recited by the reader at several points in the service. He recites what is called the Full Kaddish at the end of each service and an abbreviated or Half Kaddish at the end of each prayer unit within the service. How this reader's Kaddish came into being we do not know, but its psychological and theological rationalizations are fairly clear. As indicated above, the congregational response to the Kaddish was regarded by the mystics as very pleasing to God. In addition, the Talmud records the opinion of the third century sage, Rabbi Joshua ben Levi, who said: "He who responds, 'Amen! May His great Name be blessed,' with all his might, his decreed sentence is torn up" (Shab. 119b). Accordingly, it is quite logical for the pious to seek opportunities to make this efficacious response. This requires additional recitations of the Kaddish. It takes little ingenuity to draw the simple parallel that just as the Kaddish was recited by the teacher or preacher after a religious discourse, so should the reader of the prayers recite the Kaddish at the conclusion of every congregational service. So this was added to each service thus enabling the people to respond with the formula *Yehe Shemei Rabba*, etc. An appropriate paragraph, in which God was beseeched to accept Israel's prayers, was substituted for the one that invoked God's blessings on the scholars. It read: "May the prayers and supplications of all Israel be accepted by their Father who is in heaven; and say ye: Amen!" This reader's Kaddish is known as the *Kaddish Titkabel*, that is, the Kaddish that contains the additional paragraph which begins with the word *Titkabel* (May the prayers . . . be accepted).

But this concluding Kaddish did not fully satisfy the craving of the pious to recite that marvelous response that so pleases the Almighty and, in addition, has the power to nullify one's "decreed sentence." Why not conclude every prayer unit with the Kaddish? To distinguish the conclusion of a prayer unit from that of the whole service, only part of the Kaddish is used, that is, only the first three paragraphs. Thus the abbreviated or Half Kaddish found its way into many places of the service.

With the addition of the Kaddish in its various forms, the morning service had practically achieved its classic formulation. It had expanded far beyond its original framework, assumed at the time of its redaction at Yavneh. The daily morning service had more than doubled its original size. It had reached a point where writing down the prayers and making them available to the ordinary worshiper became a real necessity.

The Afternoon Service

The daily afternoon service derives its name, Minhah, from the afternoon offering at the Jerusalem Temple.* This service, too, expanded during the centuries under discussion, but not as abundantly as the morning service. The chief accretion was a psalm which was recited as an introductory prayer. This psalm (145) † in turn was introduced by two verses, each of which

* *See pp. 50, 84.*
† *See pp. 193–94.*

begins with the word *Ashre* (Happy are they that . . .). The psalm is therefore called Ashre, that is, the psalm that is introduced by verses which begin with the word *Ashre* (Happy). These introductory verses read:

> *Happy are they that dwell in Thy house,*
> *They are ever praising Thee* [*Ps. 84:5*].
>
> *Happy is the people that is in such a case.*
> *Yea, happy is the people whose God is the Lord*
> [*Ps. 144:15*].

The Ashre prayer also contains an extra verse at its conclusion:

> *But we will bless the Lord*
> *From this time forth and for ever.*
> *Hallelujah* [*Ps. 115:18*].

The reason for adding the Ashre to the Minhah service is similar to that for adding the Verses of Praise to the morning service. Before starting the official prayers, which in the Minhah are the Eighteen Benedictions, one should engage in acts of preparation for prayer. One cannot enter the synagogue and immediately start to worship. The recitation of a psalm helps to put one into a prayerful mood. The choice of Psalm 145 is due to the high regard that the sages had for it, as we read in the Talmud: "Whoever recites [this psalm] three times daily, is sure to inherit the world to come" (Ber. 4b).[26] And what pious Jew does not aspire to a share in immortality? Added to the promised reward is the psalm's alphabetical acrostic. Each verse starts with one of the letters of the alphabet, beginning with the aleph and ending with the taw, that is, from A to Z. Because the psalm is thus easily memorized, many worshipers can recite it by heart. But the acrostic suffers from one fault: the letter nun (N) is missing, an omission that commentators have explained—but not without strain. The mystery of this omission has recently been cleared up with the help of one of the Dead Sea Scrolls wherein the psalm is quoted. The missing verse is in its rightful place, and it reads:

> *Faithful* [Ne'eman] *is God in His works*
> *And loyal in all His doings.*[27]

The recitation of the Ashre at the Minhah service completes the quota of three daily recitations of the psalm, for the Ashre is also recited twice in the morning service—once as part of the Verses of Praise and a second time near the end of the service before the prayer *Uva Le-Zion Go'el.*

By the end of the geonic period the Minhah service consisted of the opening psalm and the *Tefillah,* which was recited silently by the congregation and then audibly repeated by the reader with the Kedushah in the third benediction. Like all services, the Minhah had its fair share of Kaddish recitations—the Half Kaddish before the *Tefillah,* the *Kaddish Titkabel* after it, and the mourners' Kaddish at the conclusion of the service.

But the Minhah service, despite its brevity, ran into occasional difficulties because of its inconvenient timing. It was usually recited at dusk, and there was always the danger that the sun would set before the service was concluded. In order to finish the Minhah before sunset it was at times necessary to abbreviate the service. On such occasions a quicker service, known as a Loud Kedushah, was in order. Instead of the *Tefillah*'s being recited twice (silently by the congregation and then audibly by the reader), the emergency procedure calls for the reader to recite the first three benedictions with the Kedushah, while the congregation stands silently and follows the reading. Then everyone completes the *Tefillah* quietly. The *Tefillah* is thus recited only once, and the service is correspondingly shortened to meet the emergency.

The Evening Service

If the expansion of the Minhah service during the talmudic and geonic periods was rather limited, the Maariv service not only expanded considerably, but also underwent a change in its essential character. As already mentioned,* the evening service consisted of the *Shema* and its benedictions. When the worshiper concluded the last of the benedictions, "*Praised art*

* *See pp. 100–101.*

Thou O Lord, who guards His people Israel," the Maariv was finished. Even as late as the ninth century, the evening service did not extend beyond this point. This was altogether logical because the recitation of the *Tefillah* was meant to correspond to the Temple offerings.* Since there were no evening sacrifices at the Temple, there was no *Tefillah* in the evening service. But the people missed the *Tefillah*, because it contained so many of their personal supplications. Without these prayers the heart of the service seemed to be missing. An attempt was made to fill this void by adding a prayer which consisted of eighteen biblical verses, each of which contains God's name.[28] But this was a pale substitute for the vital, pulsating Eighteen Benedictions which are the climax of the morning and afternoon services. It is not surprising, therefore, that some people added the *Tefillah* to the Maariv. This practice became so nearly universal that by the end of the geonic period the Eighteen Benedictions were officially adopted as part of the evening service. Since the recitation of the *Tefillah* was not obligatory at this service, the reader was not required to repeat it for the benefit of the unlettered.† As to the substitute for the *Tefillah*, that is, the eighteen biblical verses (*Barukh Adonai Le-Olam*), they have remained in the service to this day. Having established themselves as an integral part of the ritual, they did not yield their place to the *Tefillah* but have coexisted with it.[29]

By the end of the geonic period it also became customary to start the Maariv service with two introductory verses, known by their initial words as *Ve-Hu Rahum* (But He, being full of compassion):

But He, being full of compassion, forgiveth iniquity,
and destroyeth not;
Yea, many a time doth He turn His anger away
And doth not stir up all His wrath [*Ps. 78:38*].

Save, Lord;
Let the King answer us in the day that we call
[*Ps. 20:10*].

* *See p. 107.*
† *See pp. 144, 427.*

These introductory verses served the same purpose as the Verses of Praise in the morning service and the Ashre in the afternoon service. They were added to help put the worshiper into a prayerful mood before the official call to worship.[30]

The main elements of the Maariv service as they developed during the period under discussion were (1) two introductory verses *(Ve-Hu Rahum)*, (2) the call to prayer *(Barkhu)*, (3) the *Shema* and its benedictions, (4) the eighteen biblical verses *(Barukh Adonai Le-Olam)* with their concluding blessing, and (5) the silent *Tefillah*. The evening service also had its share of Kaddish recitations. As usual, the Half Kaddish was said at the start of the service and again before the *Tefillah* to indicate that a full prayer unit—the *Shema* and its benedictions—had been concluded. After the *Tefillah*, the *Kaddish Titkabel* was recited to indicate that the service had been concluded except for the mourners' Kaddish, which followed.

7
THE CRYSTALLIZATION OF THE SABBATH SERVICES

The focal point in the Jew's religious life was the Sabbath. Its observance was decreed in the Ten Commandments, and it embraced not only abstention from labor—both economic and domestic—but also active participation in certain spiritual and intellectual activities. The prohibitions were not burdensome because they were part of a habitual life pattern learned in childhood, and the intellectual and spiritual activities of the day provided stimulation and inspiration. Hence the Sabbath day was to the Jew more than a divine commandment; it was a "holy day" and an "everlasting sign" of the covenant between God and Israel.[1]

The Sabbath was a unique development in the spiritual history of mankind. As George Foot Moore put it categorically: "Nothing corresponding to it existed in the Greek and Roman world, nor, so far as is known, elsewhere in antiquity." [2] Since the Sabbath was not attached to the Temple, as were the festivals, it assumed special importance in the scattered Jewish communities outside Palestine. Keeping the Sabbath in the face of social and economic disadvantage and in the face of many restrictions on pleasurable activities has become, to this day, the touchstone of the Jew's steadfastness as a member of the community of Israel.

As might be expected, the spiritual activity that loomed highest on the Sabbath day was that of public worship. This brought the Jew to the synagogue for substantial stretches of time. The synagogue was thus afforded the opportunity to perform its central function of providing the Jew with inspiration and edification through prayer and instruction. During the talmudic and geonic periods, the Sabbath liturgy grew and expanded, and the Torah instruction centering on the scriptural readings was formalized and intensified. By the end of the geonic period the essential structure of the Sabbath liturgy had already been shaped, and, like the liturgy of the weekday services, was ready for the inevitable step—its publication for use by every Jew.

The Friday Evening Service

During the centuries under discussion the Friday evening service grew, but not excessively. Like the weekday Maariv service,* it acquired a *Tefillah*, but unlike it, it also acquired an abbreviated repetition of the *Tefillah*.[3]

The Seven Benedictions

The *Tefillah* which was added to the Friday evening service was that of the regular Sabbath liturgy. This *Tefillah* consisted of only seven benedictions. The first three and the last three benedictions were identical with those of the weekday *Tefillah*. The middle benediction affirmed the sanctity of the Sabbath day. The reason generally given for omitting the thirteen

* *See p. 160.*

intermediate benedictions on the Sabbath is that they contain supplications for personal and communal needs. Such prayers are not suitable for the Sabbath, because the Jew is expected to banish all distressing thoughts on the holy day. Furthermore, the *Tefillah* was considered a substitute for the sacrificial offerings, and on the Sabbath there were no personal offerings in the Temple. Hence the thirteen intermediate benedictions, which contained prayers for health and sustenance, for national well-being and redemption, were replaced on the Sabbath by just one benediction devoted primarily to the affirmation of the day's sanctity.[4] The intermediate benediction of the Sabbath *Tefillah* reads:

> Our God and God of our fathers, accept our rest; sanctify us by Thy commandments, and grant our portion in Thy Torah; satisfy us with Thy goodness, and gladden us with Thy salvation; purify our hearts to serve Thee in truth; and in Thy love and favor, O Lord our God, let us inherit Thy holy Sabbath; and may Israel, who hallow Thy name, rest thereon. *Praised art Thou, O Lord, who hallowest the Sabbath.*

The contraction of the nineteen benedictions of the weekday service to only seven on the Sabbath makes sense in terms of theological reasoning. But the reason for adding a repetition of the *Tefillah* on Friday evening is to be found in the social conditions of that period. The repetition, which is in the form of a digest of the seven benedictions, is known by its initial words: *Magen Avot* (Shield of the fathers). Its origin goes back to the geonic period, when Jews who lived on the outskirts of the towns, especially farmers, would often arrive late in the synagogue on Friday evenings. These latecomers would stay on after the completion of the congregational service in order to finish their prayers. Since it was not safe to go home alone after dark, the congregation deliberately prolonged the service to enable the stragglers to catch up with the congregation and thus have company on their way home.[5]

Another addition to the Friday evening service that arose during that period for the identical purpose consisted of the reading of a mishnaic chapter (Shab. 2) dealing with the laws of kindling the Sabbath lights. This mishnaic chapter, known by its initial words as *Bameh Madlikin* (With what [materials may the Sabbath lamp] be kindled?), is hardly inspirational. However, it was considered appropriate because of its timeliness. Some modern congregations have abandoned the reading of this text because it disrupts the prayer mood and introduces legal material that has little bearing on modern life. However, there are many congregations that cling to the tradition and read this chapter of the Mishnah. Tradition is stronger than logic and survives even when conditions render it irrelevant.

The Congregational Kiddush

A more dramatic addition to the Friday evening service was the recitation of the Kiddush at the synagogue service. The Kiddush consists of the blessing over wine followed by a benediction declaring the sanctity of the Sabbath. The Kiddush is fundamentally a home ceremony and as such will be discussed in a later chapter.* However, it was introduced into the synagogue service to meet a current need. During the geonic period the synagogue also served as a hostel for Jewish travelers. These homeless strangers would eat and sleep on the synagogue premises. Most of these transients were poor and did not recite the Kiddush because wine was expensive in Babylonia. The custom therefore arose of reciting the Kiddush at the end of the Friday evening service so that those who could not recite it at their meals would hear it and respond with the traditional Amen.

The Jewish community of Babylonia, as already indicated, enjoyed preeminent prestige among the Jews of the Diaspora. Its customs were usually adopted and followed everywhere. The recitation of the Kiddush at the Friday evening service was therefore adopted in the scattered Jewish communities, as were the digest of the Friday evening *Tefillah (Magen Avot)* and the mishnaic chapter *(Bameh Madlikin)*. They have remained in the Friday evening service to this day. This despite

* *See pp. 297–99.*

the relative safety provided by modern street lighting and the absence of hostel facilities in the modern synagogue.[6]

By the end of the geonic period, the Friday evening service consisted of (1) the call to service, followed by (2) the *Shema* and its benedictions,[7] (3) the silent Sabbath *Tefillah*, (4) the abbreviated repetition of the *Tefillah (Magen Avot)*, and (5) the Kiddush. The Kaddish recitations were the same as those of the weekday Maariv service.*

The Sabbath Morning Service

The Sabbath morning service did not escape the prevailing pressures for the expansion of the liturgy. From time to time new prayers were added to the "inheritance of the synagogue." These additions were not made in the spirit of reform, for the basic elements of the service approved at Yavneh were never challenged. New prayers became part of the liturgy only after they had proved themselves worthy. The test of a new prayer was usually its staying power in the face of the conservative forces which resisted change. When a new prayer passed this difficult test, it became part of the tradition and remained in the liturgy even after the conditions that brought it into being had ceased to exist.

The original elements of the Sabbath morning service have already been referred to. These consisted of the *Shema* and its benedictions, the *Tefillah* (reduced on the Sabbath to seven benedictions), and the study elements consisting of scriptural readings and homilies.† There were also the Early Morning Benedictions and the Verses of Praise which were discussed in an earlier chapter.‡ Since there had been in the Temple an additional or Musaf offering, an additional or Musaf *Tefillah* was added to the Sabbath morning service. The Verses of Praise, too, were enlarged by the addition of several psalms, and the concluding benediction of the *Pesukey De-Zimra* was expanded by the addition of an unusually beautiful prayer, the *Nishmat*.

* *See p. 161.*
† *See pp. 89 ff.*
‡ *See pp. 141 ff.*

Additional Verses of Praise

The enlargement of the *Pesukey De-Zimra* on the Sabbath was altogether natural. The Jew had plenty of time, and he indulged himself with a number of additional psalms, among them Psalm 136, which was known as the Great Hallel.* However, one of the weekday psalms (100) was deliberately eliminated. This psalm used to be recited in the Temple at the time of thanksgiving offerings. Since these offerings were never brought on the Sabbath, their accompanying psalm was not read at the Sabbath services. But this deletion was amply compensated for. Nine psalms were added to the Verses of Praise,[8] and the closing benediction was enriched with an exalted prayer known by its initial word as *Nishmat*. The introductory words of the prayer read: "The breath of every living being shall bless Thy name, O Lord our God, and the spirit of all flesh shall continually glorify and exalt Thy memorial, O our King; from everlasting to everlasting Thou art God." The introductory part of the *Nishmat* is followed by an ancient prayer, which the Talmud associates with the prayers for rain. Thus we read in the Talmud:

> What blessing do they say [for the rain]? . . . R. Johanan concluded thus: "If our mouths were full of song like the sea . . . we could not sufficiently give thanks unto Thee, O Lord our God, etc." up to "shall prostrate itself before Thee. *Blessed [Praised] art Thou, O Lord, to whom abundant thanksgivings are due*" [Ber. 59b].

The fact that the Talmud only quotes the beginning and the end of the prayer indicates that the prayer was already well known and that many people knew it by heart.

How did the *Nishmat* prayer become part of the Sabbath morning liturgy? Originally this prayer was the concluding benediction of the Great Hallel (Psalm 136). When this psalm was included in the Sabbath Verses of Praise, its accompanying benediction was also included. It was not placed im-

* *See p. 210.*

Nuremberg Prayer Book, 1331, Schocken Library, Jerusalem. PHOTO: ALFRED BERNHEIM

mediately after the psalm, however, but added to the concluding benediction of the Verses of Praise *(Yishtabah)*.*

In the traditional prayer book the *Nishmat* prayer was usually printed in bold type. Many people have therefore assumed that the *Nishmat* prayer was the official opening of the main Sabbath morning service. Actually, it was only an adjunct to the *Yishtabah* benediction which concluded the Verses of Praise.

The *Nishmat* prayer, as intimated above, is an eclectic prayer. It consists of three distinct parts. The opening sentences, till "to Thee alone we give thanks," are introductory. Then comes the ancient prayer for rain which begins with the words "Though our mouths were full of song as the sea" and ends with the words "the bounties which Thou hast bestowed upon our fathers and us." The last part is from "Thou didst redeem us from Egypt" to the end.[9]

The New Synagogue Poetry (Piyut)

Early in the geonic period a new form of synagogue poetry became popular in the synagogue worship. This poetry was destined to absorb the poetic talents of the Jewish people for many centuries. The talent that once produced the psalms and later the rabbinic prayers was channeled into the composition of the new sophisticated prayer-poems known as piyutim. Like the psalmists and the sages of the Talmud, the synagogue poets, or payetanim, expressed their religious feelings by uttering praises and thanksgiving to God for His many acts of loving-kindness, and implored His mercy and blessing upon the community of Israel. They wrote about God's justice and mercy, the sinfulness of man and the open door of repentance, the evanescence of man's worldly existence and the life everlasting to come, Israel's martyrdom and the hope of messianic redemption, and, above all, the glory of God and His merciful forgiveness of sin. But the way they expressed these religious sentiments was so different from the classic prayers of the synagogue that one finds it difficult to detect a relationship be-

* *See p. 142.*

tween these piyutim and the simple yet noble prayers of the psalmists and the sages of the Talmud.

The composition of religious poetry for use during worship was not altogether new.[10] The Temple processions during the festival of Sukkot were accompanied by litanies known as Hoshanot.* These litanies usually consisted of a series of divine appellations, each introduced and followed by the refrain "Hoshana" (Save, we beseech Thee!). The divine appellations were, as a rule, arranged in an alphabetical acrostic, and they usually contained a primitive rhyme which was achieved through the use of a common grammatical suffix at the end of each phrase or line. Similar litanies were in use during the Temple days on fast days in drought periods. Instead of the refrain Hoshana, they used the word *Anenu* (Answer us).

After the destruction of the Temple, it was not uncommon for local poets to express their religious sentiments in the form of prayer-poems, some of which were read in the local synagogues. But it was not till the early geonic period, when a powerful impetus was provided in the form of bitter persecutions that threatened the survival of Judaism, that the new poetry really assumed its sophisticated form and entered the synagogue worship on a massive scale. It was then that the Jewish religious genius was harnessed and ingenious schemes were improvised to circumvent the harsh antisynagogue legislation.

Early in the fourth century, Christianity triumphed. Constantine the Great raised the new faith to the rank of a state religion, and the state was no less than the world power of Rome. The formerly persecuted Church now attained tremendous power and became the persecutor of the mother faith. For three centuries the Church was dominant in the Holy Land; its power came to an abrupt end in 636 C.E., when the Moslems overran the Near East. In 553 C.E. Emperor Justinian issued an edict forbidding the reading, study, and teaching of rabbinic lore. The rabbis were forbidden to interpret the Scriptures in the synagogue or to explain the observances of the festivals. The edict also forbade the recital of the es-

* *See pp. 219–20.*

sential prayers of the *Shema* and the *Tefillah*. By crippling the liturgy of the synagogue and silencing the teaching of the Torah, the edict seemed to sound the death knell of Judaism.

But the rabbis were not to be silenced, at least not completely. They resorted to a stratagem which enabled them partially to circumvent the law. They smuggled their teaching into the synagogue by means of poetic compositions, the reading of which was not forbidden. In order not to be detected by the government overseers, the poems utilized veiled allusions to biblical, talmudic, and midrashic passages which were fairly clear to most of the Jewish worshipers but were utterly mystifying to those who were not initiated into rabbinic lore. This clandestine method of teaching is accurately described by a twelfth century rabbi, Rabbi Judah ben Barzillai Albargeloni, who wrote:

> There was a time when the Jews were forbidden by their oppressors to engage in the study of the Torah. The learned men among them, therefore, introduced the custom of mentioning in the course of the prayers the laws of the festivals and the laws of the Sabbath and religious observance, and exhorting the common people in regard to them by means of hymns, thanksgivings, rimes and piyutim.[11]

The piyutim were obviously didactic, and the utilization of innumerable veiled allusions was a technique not likely to inspire poetic expression. External form thus became a salient feature of the new poetry. One of the favorite techniques of achieving poetic fame was the acrostic. To be sure, this form of poetic composition antedated the payetanim. There are several psalms in which successive verses start with successive letters of the alphabet—among them the Ashre (Psalm 145).[12] But the composers of the piyutim improved on the psalmists. They composed piyutim with acrostics in which the alphabet ran backwards, from Z to A, and spelled out words which in turn were independent prayers. Thus we have an ingenious acrostic in a lament by Judah Halevi which consists of seventy-three verses, the initial letters of which make up an independent poem.[13] And the poets also "signed" their poems with acrostics in which the initial letters of successive verses spelled out the author's name. These acrostics became a favorite with the people. To this day some piyutim with clever acrostics are specially honored in the synagogue. The ark is opened and the congregation rises during their recitation. This despite the fact that some of these piyutim are at best only mediocre.[14]

In addition to veiled allusions and transparent acrostics, the piyutim were subjected to other artificial conventions, such as rhyme and rhythm. At the beginning these were rather simple, but in time they became structurally involved, highly artificial, and increasingly restrictive. They placed a special premium on cleverness rather than poetic sentiment. A further complication was the tendency of many poets to take liberties with the Hebrew language. They made up new words the meaning of which only few could guess. There is a paradox in the excessive indulgence in these poetic conventions. On the one hand, they circumscribed the spirit and sentiment of the piyutim. On the other hand, they intrigued the synagogue worshipers. The more involved the acrostic and the more disguised the allusions and the more ingenious the rhyme, the greater the author's fame. Authors were therefore encouraged to indulge in these clever contrivances, and the piyutim tended to become increasingly formal and correspondingly less inspirational. The enigma is doubly compounded when we consider the fact that the piyutim were specially written for use as devotional literature. No wonder we occasionally read some harsh criticism of the piyutim. Among these critics are not only rationalists like Maimonides and Abraham Ibn Ezra, but also pietists like Rabbi Solomon de Medina (Rashdam), who lived in Salonika in the sixteenth century, and the famous eighteenth century talmudist Rabbi Jacob Emden.

Rabbi Solomon de Medina, in answer to a question about a dispute which had arisen in a synagogue of mixed (Ashkenazic and Sephardic) membership in regard to the choice of piyutim for the services, states emphatically that the Ashkenazic piyutim are beyond the comprehension of the worshipers. That is why Ashkenazim talk during the service. These piyutim should be omitted because they are "an abomination." Still better, he suggests, is to adopt the Sephardic rite, because their piyutim were composed by such poets as Judah Halevi, Solomon Ibn Gabirol, and Abraham Ibn Ezra. These piyutim are understandable, like the classic prayers of the rabbis. To use the Rashdam's own words: "It seems to me that it is far better to omit these piyutim . . . since in our time hardly anyone understands their translation or meaning . . . unlike our fixed prayers which are written in clear and simple Hebrew." [15]

But the harshest attack on the piyutim is to be found in Rabbi Jacob Emden's commentary on the *Siddur* in the section on the benedictions after the Haftarah. Rabbi Jacob Emden speaks of the the piyutim as "mere gibberish" and ridicules the people who read them with devotion. He says that "the long piyutim which the innocents babble . . . even the angels cannot possibly comprehend. . . . The strange and outlandish expressions that have been incorporated into the piyutim are ludicrous in style, without sense." [16]

As already mentioned, the geonim who headed the Babylonian academies regarded themselves as the guardians of the talmudic tradition. Understandably, they opposed the introduction of extraneous material into the liturgy. They objected especially to the insertion of piyutim into the essential prayers of the synagogue. But the popularity of the piyutim swept aside their opposition, and by the tenth century we find Saadia Gaon (882–942) not only writing piyutim, but including some of them in the compilation of his prayer book. To be sure, he is rather apologetic about his breach of geonic policy. "I found," says Saadia, "that people are accustomed to recite [piyutim], hence I included [some piyutim]." Indeed, the writing of clever piyutim became so fashionable that even outstanding scholars tried their hand at it. The end result was that the piyutim multiplied and became increasingly intriguing—but hardly inspiring.

Yet we dare not overstate the negative aspects of the new synagogue poetry. Despite all its shortcomings the piyut had such famous defenders as Rabbenu Gershom (960–1040), "the Light of the Exile," and the distinguished Rabbi Jacob ben

Moses Mölln (Maharil) (1365–1427).* More important, the piyutim had some redeeming features which assured at least some of them a permanent place in the synagogue liturgy. Thus Solomon Schechter speaks warmly of the piyutim composed in Central Europe:

> From the literary point of view the merit of these liturgic productions by the saints of Ashkenaz [Central Europe] is certainly not very great. They are wanting in literary grace, faulty in grammar, and awkward in their diction. . . . But, on the other hand, they have a depth of feeling and a certain inwardness, *Gemüt*, which is hardly to be found with poets of the synagogue of any other school. It is especially the hymns for the various Sabbaths between the Passover and the Feast of Weeks which reveal a religious fervor and a love for God knowing no bounds.[17]

Similarly does Leopold Zunz, the pioneer in the study of the development of Jewish liturgy, speak of the piyut in words of high admiration. He states that a "treasure of religion and history, of poetry and philosophy, and prophecy and psalms is revived in the piyut . . . of the Middle Ages." [18]

It should not be overlooked that among those who composed piyutim were some truly great poets. If many of the piyutim were (to use Leopold Zunz's remark about Saadia Gaon's poetry) "not by the grace of God," there were also those (written by such poets as Solomon Ibn Gabirol and Judah Halevi) whose poetry possessed beauty and grandeur. The "poetic tenderness" of the former's poetry and the "inspiring majesty" of the latter's are the crowning glory of medieval Hebrew poetry.

But the great majority of the synagogue poets excelled primarily in the technical conventions of the time. However, as was pointed out by Solomon Schechter, they compensated for their shortcomings by their saintly piety. This saintliness quali-

* *See p. 373.*

fied many of them to be regarded the spiritual descendants of the psalmists and the talmudic sages. From this viewpoint, some of the piyutim rightly belong in the synagogue liturgy, alongside the essential prayers of Israel.

When the Moslems conquered Palestine in 636 and the persecutions initiated by Justinian came to an end, there was no longer any need for any clandestine teaching. Homilies could freely be delivered in the synagogue, and the Torah reading could be translated and explained. But the writing of piyutim with veiled allusions to the teachings of Judaism continued with ever-increasing vigor, and the synagogue worshipers received them with sincere acclamation. The sheer quantity of these poems became staggering. Israel Davidson's monumental *Thesaurus of Mediaeval Hebrew Poetry* lists over thirty-five thousand piyutim by almost three thousand authors.[19] And this includes only the piyutim gathered from printed sources.

From its birthplace in Palestinc the new poetry spread westward to southern Italy, to Rome, and to Central Europe. It spread eastward to Babylonia and ultimately reached the scattered Jewish communities everywhere. And the piyut, says Zunz,

> embellished . . . the whole of the Jew's religious life, and found access into every prayer and service—and not only in the synagogue but also in the household. It would visit families, partake in their meals on the day of Sabbath and on the termination of Sabbath, on days of joy and sorrow, on birthdays and anniversaries of death.[20]

But the piyutim never displaced the rabbinic prayers and the psalms. These remained the essential prayers of the synagogue. Not an iota of the synagogue tradition was altered by the intrusion of the piyutim. The liturgic tradition as developed by the sages of the Talmud remained the sacred core of the service. To be sure, the liturgy was interrupted by the new piyutim, but the congregation always returned to the rabbinic prayers which have remained to this day the foundation of the synagogue tradition.

Early Piyutim in the Sabbath Service

During the talmudic and geonic periods the Sabbath morning service was embellished with a number of piyutim that have won for themselves a permanent place in the liturgy. Among these are the piyutim that were interpolated into the first benediction before the *Shema*, the benediction that praises God "who forms [*Yotzer*] light and creates darkness." It will be recalled that a Kedushah had already been woven into the text of this benediction.* The new material elaborated on the general theme of creation and the Sabbath which followed it.

The piyutim inserted in this benediction are called *Yotzrot*, deriving their name from the key word of the benediction—*Yotzer*, (Who forms [light]). The authors of these piyutim are unknown, as is the exact time of their composition. But scholars are agreed that they are of Palestinian origin and go back to rabbinic times.

Three piyutim, generally known by their initial words, were incorporated into the first benediction before the *Shema*. The first of these—*Hakol Yodukha* (All do thank Thee)—is a relatively simple song of praise based on the concluding words of the opening blessing: "[Thou] makest peace and createst all [things]." The piyut picks up the last word, *hakol* (all) and elaborates on the theme of God the Creator of *all* things. It is a kind of Midrash on the opening blessing.

The second piyut—*El Adon* (God, thc Lord of all)—is an alphabetic acrostic based on a section of the benediction which begins with the words *El Barukh Gedol De'ah* (The blessed God, great in knowledge). This section of the benediction is itself an acrostic in which each word begins with a succeeding letter of the alphabet. In the piyut each word is expanded into a full verse. In this way the piyut enlarges both the benediction and its thought content.

The third piyut—*La-El Asher Shavat* (To the God who rested [from all His works])—also elaborates on the benediction and glorifies the name of God the Creator. It also in-

* *See p. 136.*

cludes an extended formula for the observance of the Sabbath.

These three piyutim, or *Yotzrot*, were not immediately accepted into the liturgy. It was only in postgeonic years that they appear as official prayers of the synagogue. The delay was probably due to the objections of the Babylonian geonim, who opposed the insertion of piyutim into the main body of the liturgy. Eventually, however, the Sabbath *Yotzrot* became integral parts of the service. They have shown tenacity even in the face of the modern tendency to omit piyutim because they prolong the service unduly. In all probability these three piyutim will continue to occupy an honored place in the Sabbath morning service.

The first benediction before the *Shema* has thus undergone an inordinate expansion. At first it was only the opening benediction of the morning service that was recited at sunrise. It praised God the Creator: "*Praised art Thou, O Lord our God, King of the universe who formest light and createst darkness, who makest peace and createst all things.*" It concluded with the blessing "*Praised are Thou, O Lord, Creator of the luminaries.*" The benediction was then expanded to include some additional passages, such as the supplication "O cause a new light to shine upon Zion, and may we all be worthy soon to enjoy its brightness." Then the Babylonian mystics interpolated a Kedushah, and the Palestinean poets added the *Yotzrot* for the Sabbath service. As a result the original benediction grew from a few lines to several pages. By the time one reaches the end of the benediction one hardly associates it with its opening blessing.

The writing of piyutim continued throughout the Middle Ages and up to modern times. While the ancient Romans sang of "arms and the man" and the medieval minnesingers sang of romantic love, the synagogue poets continued to emulate the psalmists and sang of "mercy and justice" (Ps. 101:1). While the medieval troubadours sang of the nobility and of their heroic deeds, the Jewish poets sang incessantly of God and His loving-kindness, of Israel and its expected redemption. While the songs of both the minnesingers and the troubadours were light and joyous, the piyutim were serious and often sad. But they were always confident of God's redeeming power and of Israel's eventual vindication in the sight of all mankind.

The Sabbath Morning *Tefillah*

The Sabbath morning *Tefillah* did not grow noticeably during the talmudic and geonic periods. As mentioned,* it consisted of only seven benedictions, the first three and the last three identical with those of the weekday *Tefillah*. The intermediate benediction, which affirmed the sanctity of the Sabbath, was introduced by a short postgeonic piyut known by its initial words: *Yismah Moshe* (Moses rejoiced [with the Sabbath]). Then came a biblical quotation regarding the importance of keeping the Sabbath, which is "a covenant for all time" and "a sign for all time between Me and the people of Israel" (Exod. 31:16–17).

The most significant expansion in the Sabbath morning *Tefillah* is to be found in the Kedushah. Basically this doxology was not changed; its essential elements remained the same as in the weekday service.† But the brief phrases that connect the biblical verses were expanded. Thus we find after the second verse of the Kedushah an eloquent supplication for Israel's redemption. The Kedushah picks up the last word of the verse and continues with a touching prayer:

> From *Thy place* shine forth, O our King, and reign over us, for we wait for Thee. When wilt Thou reign in Zion? Speedily, even in our days, do Thou dwell there, and for ever. Mayest Thou be magnified and sanctified in the midst of Jerusalem Thy city throughout all generations and to all eternity. O let our eyes behold Thy kingdom, according to the word that was spoken in the songs of Thy might by David, Thy righteous anointed:
>
> *The Lord shall reign for ever,*
> *Thy God, O Zion, unto all generations. Hallelujah!*

* *See p. 162.*
† *See pp. 134–36.*

With the completion of the *Tefillah* the congregation is ready for the most uniquely Jewish part of the ritual—the reading from the Scriptures.

Reading from the Scriptures

The central feature of the Sabbath morning service was the reading from the Torah and the Prophets. These were usually followed by a homily. This worship unit was given definitive form during the centuries under discussion. The ritual of taking the Torah out of the ark and then returning it to the ark was standardized, the portions of the Torah and the Prophets were fixed, and several miscellaneous prayers were assigned a permanent place after the reading of the scriptural selections.

The Ritual of Taking Out and Returning the Scroll to the Ark

The most striking ritual of the Sabbath morning service is the taking out of the Torah from the ark, and, after the reading, the returning of the scroll to the ark. The obvious purpose of the ritual is to demonstrate the centrality of the Torah in Judaism. Despite the weekly repetition of the ritual, the ceremony has retained its freshness. It is dramatic, yet it is not ostentatious. And its liturgy is a fitting framework for the central element of the worship, that of studying Torah.

The ceremony contains several liturgic selections dating back to geonic times. The first is known by its initial words: *En Kamokha* (There is none like unto Thee). It is usually chanted by the reader and the congregation prior to the opening of the ark. The *En Kamokha* consists of four biblical verses which extol God and His everlasting kingship:

> *There is none like unto Thee among the gods, O Lord,*
> *And there are no works like Thine* [*Ps. 86:8*].
>
> *Thy kingdom is a kingdom for all ages,*
> *And Thy dominion endureth throughout all generations* [*Ps. 145:13*].
>
> *The Lord reigneth; the Lord hath reigned; the Lord shall reign for ever and ever.*[21]

The Lord will give strength unto His people;
The Lord will bless His people with peace [*Ps. 29:11*].[22]

The ark is now opened, and the congregation rises. As the Torah is taken out of the ark, two biblical verses, known by their initial words—*Vayehi Binso'a* (And it came to pass, when [the ark] set forward), and *Ki Mi-Tzion* (For out of Zion)—are chanted. The first of these verses refers to the Hebrews in the desert going forth to battle. They take the ark with them, and Moses prays for victory. The second verse is Isaiah's prophecy regarding the messianic age when Torah will go forth from Zion. "When the Ark was to set out, Moses would say: Advance, O Lord! May Your enemies be scattered/And may Your foes flee before You!" (Num. 10:35). "For out of Zion shall go forth the law,/And the word of the Lord from Jerusalem" (Isa. 2:3).

The climax of this moving ritual has now been reached. The reader, holding the scroll of the Torah, faces the congregation and chants: "Hear, O Israel! The Lord is our God, the Lord alone [Deut. 6:4]. One is our God; great is our Lord; holy is His name. O magnify the Lord with me,/And let us exalt His name together [Ps. 34:4]." The ritual is concluded with a procession from the ark to the reader's desk. During the procession the congregation chants:

> Thine, O Lord, is the greatness, and the power, and the glory, and the victory, and the majesty; for all that is in the heaven and in the earth is Thine; Thine is the kingdom, O Lord, and Thou art exalted as head above all [1 Chron. 29:11].
>
> *Exalt ye the Lord our God,*
> *And prostrate yourselves at His footstool;*
> *Holy is He.* [*Ps. 99:5*].
>
> *Exalt ye the Lord our God,*
> *And worship at His holy hill;*
> *For the Lord our God is holy* [*Ps. 99:9*].

Since the last two verses call upon the congregation to exalt God "for the Lord our God is holy," it is logical for the congregation to respond with a prayer which exalts God and His attribute of holiness. Such a prayer is obviously the Kaddish.* What follows is exactly that—a Hebrew version of the Kaddish: "Magnified and hallowed . . . exalted and extolled above all be the name of the supreme King of kings, the Holy One, blessed be He, in the worlds which He hath created . . . in accordance with His desire. . . ." A short concluding supplication was added to this Hebrew version of the Kaddish. The merciful Father (*Av Ha-Rahamim*) is beseeched to have mercy on Israel, to remember the covenant with the patriarchs, and to grant His people "salvation and mercy."

When the reading of the Torah portion is completed,[23] two men are honored with the "lifting" and the "rolling up" of the scroll. This ritual follows precisely the precedent set by Ezra.† The person who lifts up the scroll unrolls it sufficiently to expose at least three columns of the script. This corresponds to what was done by Ezra who "opened the book in the sight of all the people" (Neh. 8:5). When the worshipers see the Torah uplifted, they recite a text which is replete with theological affirmations: "This is the Teaching that Moses set before the Israelites [Deut. 4:44] at the Lord's bidding through Moses" (Num. 9:23).[24] The person who lifts the scroll is seated, and the second person rolls it up, ties it with a special band, and places the various appurtenances upon it. The appurtenances consist of the mantle, the breastplate, and the crown, or finials.‡ The Torah scroll is now ready for its return to the ark. But it is held for a while. First the Haftarah is read, and a number of special prayers are recited.

The ritual of returning the scroll to the ark is introduced with the Ashre (Ps. 145).§ The reader then takes the scroll and proclaims: "Let them praise the name of the Lord,/For His name alone is exalted" (Ps. 148:13). And the congregation responds:

His glory is above the earth and heaven.
And He hath lifted up a horn for His people,

* *See pp. 153 ff.*
† *See pp. 67–70.*
‡ *See pp. 338–39.*
§ *See pp. 157–59.*

A praise for all His saints,
Even for the children of Israel, a people near unto Him.
Hallelujah! [*Ps. 148:13–14*].

As the reader carries the scroll to the ark, the congregation chants Psalm 29, which is the congregation's response to the reader's original call to praise God:

Ascribe unto the Lord, O ye sons of might,
Ascribe unto the Lord glory and strength.
Ascribe unto the Lord the glory due unto His name.
Worship the Lord in the beauty of holiness [*Ps. 29:1–2*].

When the scroll is placed in the ark, the reader and congregation recite several fitting verses, known by the initial words as *Uvnuhoh Yomar* (And when [the ark] halted, [Moses] would say). The initial verse of this prayer follows in the Bible immediately after that which was recited when the Torah was taken out of the ark. This prayer reads:

And when [*the ark*] *halted, he would say:*
Return O Lord,
You who are Israel's myriads of thousands!
[*Num. 10:36*].

Arise, O Lord, unto Thy resting-place;
Thou, and the ark of Thy strength.
Let Thy priests be clothed with righteousness;
And let Thy saints shout for joy.
For Thy servant David's sake
Turn not away the face of Thine anointed
[*Ps. 132:8–10*].

For I give you good doctrine;
Forsake ye not my teaching [*Prov. 4:2*].

She is a tree of life to them that lay hold upon her,
And happy is every one that holdeth her fast
[*Prov. 3:18*].

Her ways are ways of pleasantness,
And her paths are peace [*Prov. 3:17*].

Turn Thou us unto Thee, O Lord, and we shall be turned;
Renew our days as of old [*Lam. 5:21*].

Reading from the Torah

The reading of the Torah was not only expanded during the centuries under discussion, but it was also standardized. As mentioned in an earlier chapter,* the practice in Palestine had been to complete the reading of the Pentateuch triennially. Each verse was translated into the vernacular "for the benefit of the unlearned men, for the women, and the children." In Babylonia, however, the custom was to complete the reading of the Pentateuch annually, and the portions read were correspondingly longer. Since the hegemony of Babylonian Jewry was recognized among the Jewish communities throughout the world, the annual cycle of Torah reading gained increasing acceptance: in time it displaced the triennial cycle even in Palestine. To be sure, the triennial cycle like all rooted traditions died hard. In some isolated communities whose members stemmed from Palestine, it persisted for many centuries. In Fustat (Old Cairo), for example, the triennial cycle was still in use in the Palestinian congregation as late as the seventeenth century.[25]

With the universal acceptance of the annual cycle of Torah reading the congregations began to feel the pressure of time. It was thus that the ancient tradition of translating the Torah reading into the vernacular was abandoned. In place of translating the Torah during the synagogue reading, Jews were directed to prepare for the Sabbath service at home by reading the prescribed Torah portion and its Aramaic translation, verse by verse. The second century Aramaic translation, known as Targum Onkelos (The Onkelos Translation), was adopted in Babylonia as the official text for this purpose. And like so many other Babylonian practices, this custom, too, spread everywhere. Thus the meturgeman disappeared from the synagogue, except for a few Yemenite synagogues in Israel where the translator still stands near the reader and performs his duty as of old. The Yemenite Jews are a patient people; they read the long portion of the annual cycle, and the meturgeman translates each verse into Arabic. They start their Sabbath

* *See p. 112.*

service at sunrise and do not mind if the service is prolonged.

The Official Torah Reader

Another ancient tradition fell by the wayside during these centuries. Formerly everyone called to the Torah read his portion. As late as the twelfth century the Jewish traveler Petahia of Ratisbon reports with admiration:

> There is no one so ignorant in the whole of Babylon, Assyria, Media, and Persia, but knows the twenty-four books [of the Bible], punctuation, grammar, the superfluous and omitted letters, for the preceptor does not recite the scripture lesson, but he that is called up to the scroll of the law recites it himself.[26]

Unfortunately, there were many communities where not all Jews knew how to read from the scroll of the Torah. As a result some were never called to the Torah. This was easily corrected by having a reader on hand to read for those who could not read for themselves. The person called to the Torah recited the appropriate benedictions, while the reader read the Torah selection. But this practice, too, was objectionable—a public distinction was made between the learned, who read their portion, and the unlearned, for whom the reader substituted. This was contrary to the democratic tradition of the synagogue.

A similar situation once existed during the Temple days. The Mishnah reports that some farmers who brought their first fruits to the Temple in Jerusalem were embarrassed by their ignorance:

> Originally all who knew how to recite would recite, whilst those unable to do so would repeat it [after the priest]; but when they refrained from bringing [because they were ashamed at this public avowal of their ignorance], it was decided that both those who could and those who could not [recite] should repeat the words [after the priest] [Bik. 3:7].

Following the example of this ancient precedent, the rabbis decreed that an official reader would read for everyone, for the scholar and for the ignorant alike. The person called to the reading of the Torah recited the prescribed benedictions, and the reader read on his behalf. As a result, the privilege of being called to the reading of the Torah became available to everyone.*

Reading from the Prophets

The democratic principle which provided equality of opportunity in regard to being called to the Torah did not extend to the reading of the prophetic lesson or the Haftarah. No professional reader was provided, nor is one provided in the modern synagogue. The person called to the reading of the Haftarah was expected to read the selection himself.

As mentioned in an earlier chapter,† the choice of the prophetic lesson was originally left to the reader, especially when he was the one who was designated to deliver the homily. He chose a selection that lent itself to the lesson he intended to teach. By the time of the geonic period this fluid state no longer prevailed. When the Torah reading for each Sabbath had been established, it followed naturally that the prophetic readings would cease to be optional. Specific selections were assigned to each Torah portion. These selections from the Prophets usually contained something related to the Torah portion of the week.[27] The selections for the special Sabbaths and the festivals had been established for a long time, because the Torah readings for those occasions were defined long before the portions for the ordinary Sabbaths. Now the Haftarah for every Sabbath was designated, and they have been chanted at the Sabbath services ever since.

The most interesting liturgic development in connection with the reading of the Haftarah is that of the benedictions that are recited before and after it. While the Torah benedictions are germane to the general themes of Torah and revelation, the Haftarah benedictions are, to a large extent, unrelated

* *See pp. 558–60.*
† *See pp. 114–16.*

to the theme of prophecy. The Torah benedictions appropriately deal with God's choice of Israel to receive the Torah, and they underscore that the Torah is true and is the source of Israel's eternal life. Both Torah benedictions conclude with the identical words: "*Praised art Thou, O Lord, who givest the Torah.*" Not so with the Haftarah benedictions. To begin with, there are five benedictions. The first, which precedes the reading of the Haftarah, is relevant to the prophetic reading: "*Praised art Thou, O Lord our God, King of the universe*, who hast chosen good prophets, and hast found pleasure in their words which were spoken in truth. *Praised art Thou, O Lord*, who hast chosen the Torah, and Moses Thy servant, and Israel Thy people, and prophets of truth and righteousness."

The four benedictions which follow the reading deal with a variety of praises, supplications, and thanksgivings, and they conclude with a blessing on the sanctification of the Sabbath. To grasp the wide sweep of their content one must read the benedictions, even if only hastily:

> *Praised art Thou, O Lord our God, King of the universe*, Rock of all worlds, righteous through all generations, O faithful God, who sayest and doest, who speakest and fulfillest, all whose words are truth and righteousness.[28] Faithful art Thou, O Lord our God, and faithful are Thy words, and not one of Thy words shall return void, for Thou art a faithful and merciful God and King. *Praised art Thou, O Lord, God, who art faithful in all Thy words.*
>
> Have mercy upon Zion, for it is the home of our life, and save her that is grieved in spirit speedily, even in our days. *Praised art Thou, O Lord, who makest Zion joyful through her children.*
>
> Gladden us, O Lord our God, with Elijah the Prophet, Thy servant, and with the kingdom of the House of David, Thine anointed. Soon may he come and rejoice our hearts. Suffer not a stranger to sit upon his throne, nor let others any longer inherit his glory; for by Thy holy name Thou didst swear unto him, that his light should not be

> quenched for ever. *Praised art Thou, O Lord, the Shield of David.*
>
> For the Torah, for the divine service, for the prophets, and for the Sabbath day, which Thou, O Lord our God, hast given us for holiness and for rest, for honor and for glory. For all these we thank and bless Thee, O Lord our God, blessed be Thy name by the mouth of every living being continually and for ever. *Praised art Thou, O Lord, who sanctifiest the Sabbath.*

The Haftarah benedictions are evidently more than the usual blessing one would expect at the conclusion of the prophetic lesson; they are in all probability a complete prayer unit similar to the Sabbath *Tefillah*. The concluding benediction on the sanctification of the Sabbath is obviously the same as the essential benediction of the Sabbath *Tefillah*. The other benedictions, too, contain elements that are parallel to those of the Sabbath *Tefillah*. Scholars have therefore concluded that these benedictions go back to ancient days before the canonization of the prayers at Yavneh. At that time there were several versions of the *Tefillah* for the Sabbath, including, in some synagogues, the benedictions now used with the Haftarah.[29] Although these were not selected at Yavneh as the official *Tefillah* for the Sabbath service, they were not discarded: they were assigned for use at the end of the Scripture readings. This is not an unusual procedure for the rabbis. The prayer book contains several cases where two traditions, both of them regarded as meritorious, were preserved in the ritual—for example, the benedictions immediately before the *Shema* in the morning and the evening services are parallel versions.[30] The Haftarah benedictions, too, are an ancient pre-Yavneh formulation of the Sabbath *Tefillah* which was preserved and read after the Haftarah.

Special Prayers

During the geonic period it became customary to offer a number of special prayers before returning the scroll of the Torah to the ark. The homily used to be delivered at this point. When the Babylonian practice of reading the Pentateuch in a one-year cycle was accepted, however, and the services had been expanded by the addition of the Early Morning Benedictions, the Verses of Praise, and piyutim and other prayers, the delivery of the homily was rescheduled for the afternoon, after the customary Sabbath siesta. But the custom of utilizing the break in the service, after the reading from the Scriptures, for the recital of a number of special prayers was continued.

The *Yekum Purkan* Prayers

By the tenth century the Babylonian academies had already passed their peak of glory. Spiritual leadership was gradually passing into the hands of European scholars. To be sure, the hegemony of the Babylonian Jewish community was still unchallenged. Some outstanding scholars still presided over the academies even during those declining years—Saadia Gaon, Sherira Gaon, and Hai Gaon were personalities of profound scholarship and great influence. Nonetheless, it was becoming increasingly evident that leadership in Jewry was shared by scholars of other communities. As the prestige of the Babylonian academies declined, the flow of income became increasingly sluggish. The Babylonian academies, feeling the stress of declining income, sent emissaries to the scattered Jewish communities to press for greater generosity. But the income was still not commensurate with the academics' needs.

During the eleventh century, when the very existence of the gaonate was threatened, a prayer was composed in behalf of the academies, the geonim, and the exilarch. The purpose was not only to awaken God's mercy, but also to stir up the people's generosity. The recital of the prayer at every Sabbath service, it was hoped, would arouse the people's awareness of the academies' importance and their needs. Since the prayer was directed to the worshipers as much as to the Almighty, it was composed in the Aramaic vernacular. In time it became a permanent part of the liturgy.

The *Yekum Purkan* prayer mainly deals with the institutions that prevailed in Babylonia during the geonic period. It invokes God's blessing on the geonim who were "the heads of the academies," on the exilarchs who were the "chiefs of the captivity," and the judges who held court "in the gates" of the cities. The fact that today Jews no longer speak Aramaic and that the geonim, the exilarchs, and their academies no longer exist has had no effect on the *Yekum Purkan*'s secure place in the Sabbath liturgy. The worshipers reinterpret the prayer in terms of modern conditions and invoke God's blessings on the spiritual and lay leaders of modern Jewry.

There is a second *Yekum Purkan* prayer which came into being in postgeonic times, after the Babylonian academies had ceased to hold sway over Jewish life in the Diaspora. Some claim that it is of geonic origin, that it was part of the original *Yekum Purkan* prayer but was detached for added emphasis on the local situation with which this prayer deals. The second *Yekum Purkan* prayer, too, was composed in the Aramaic language and is identical in style. It became a twin rather than a mere supplement. It speaks directly to the congregation, addressing it in the second person, and bestows abundant blessings on the worshipers:

> May salvation from heaven, grace and loving-kindness, mercy and long life . . . be vouchsafed unto all this holy congregation, great and small, children and women. May the King of the universe bless you, prolong your lives, increase your days and add to your years, and may you be saved and delivered from every trouble and mishap. May the Lord of heaven be your help at all times and seasons; and let us say, Amen.

The two *Yekum Purkan* prayers are concluded with a third prayer, this one in Hebrew. It begins with the traditional opening words used in special blessings bestowed on people—*Mi She-Berakh* (May He who blessed [our fathers Abraham, Isaac, and Jacob]). It invokes God's blessings on the patrons of the synagogue and the philanthropic institutions associated with it. The *Mi She-Berakh* is the most popular of the three prayers. In the modern synagogue it is often read in the vernacular because of its direct appeal to the worshipers and the ethical responsibilities it spells out for the people:

> May He who blessed our fathers, Abraham, Isaac, and Jacob, bless this holy congregation, together with all other holy congregations; them, their wives, their sons and daughters, and all that belong to them; those who unite to form synagogues for prayer, and those who enter therein to pray, those who give . . . bread to the wayfarers and charity to the poor, and all such as occupy themselves in faithfulness with the wants of the congregation. May the Holy One, blessed be He, give them their recompense; may He remove from them all sickness, heal all their body, forgive all their iniquity, and send blessing and prosperity upon all the work of their hands, as well as upon all Israel, their brethren; and let us say, Amen.

Prayer for the Government

Another special prayer recited before returning the scroll to the ark is the traditional prayer for the government. Contrary to common belief, this prayer is not a modern innovation. Nor was it, as some believe, imposed on the synagogue by the Russian czar or any other monarch. This prayer is ancient in origin and is sanctioned by biblical authority. The prophet Jeremiah, in his famous letter to the Jewish captives in Babylonia, exhorted them: "Seek the peace of the city whither I have caused you to be carried away captive, and pray unto the Lord for it; for in the peace thereof shall ye have peace" (Jer. 29:7). It is related that when Alexander came to Palestine at the head of his conquering army, he was met at the gates of Jerusalem by Simon the Just. The latter, we are told, greeted the conqueror and asked if he would "destroy the House wherein prayers are said for you and your kingdom that it be never destroyed?" (Yoma 69a). A similar appeal was made by the Jews of a latter day to Petronius, Emperor Caligula's agent, who had come to Jerusalem to place the emperor's statue in the Temple. The Jews pleaded against this desecration of the Temple and pointed to their loyalty, as evidenced by the fact "that they offered sacrifices twice daily for Caesar and the Roman people." [31]

But it was not pure patriotism or political necessity that motivated the Temple offerings in behalf of Caesar. It was rather due to ordinary prudence reinforced by a talmudic teaching: "Rabbi Hanina . . . said: Pray for the welfare of the government, for were it not for the fear thereof, one man would swallow up alive his fellow-man." (Avot 3:2).

But the traditional prayer for the government as we now have it appears for the first time in a fourteenth century commentary on the prayer book.[32] The prayer for the government is here assigned a fixed place in the Sabbath morning service. "After the reading of the Torah is completed," says the compiler of that prayer book, "it is customary to ask for a blessing on the king, and to pray to God to help him and strengthen him against his enemies." The author then cites Jeremiah's letter to the Jewish captives in Babylonia, and he adds that to "pray for the peace of the city" is "to pray that God enable the king to vanquish his enemies." It should be noted that the compiler of the prayer book does not present this prayer as an innovation. He speaks of it as an established custom. The prayer was probably in use during the geonic period, though not in exactly the same words. The traditional prayer for the government opens with the words of the psalmist (Ps. 144:10):

> *He who gives salvation unto kings* and dominion unto princes, whose kingdom is an everlasting kingdom, *who delivered His servant David from the hurtful sword* . . . may He bless, guard, . . . and aggrandize [name of king or prince]. May the supreme King of kings in His mercy exalt him . . . and inspire him . . . with benevolence toward us and all Israel our brethren. . . . May the redeemer come to Zion. May this be His will, and let us say, Amen.

The prayer thus names the kings and princes, and in one of the early English translations of the prayer book,[33] published just before the American Revolution, the prayer for the government specified "our most Sovereign Lord King George the

Third, our most Gracious Queen Charlotte, the Royal Highness George, Prince of Wales, and all the Royal Family." Prayer books published in Russia included the names of the czar, the czarina, and the czarevitch. Rabbi Max Lilienthal objected to the prayer's references to monarchs and their families, and in 1846 he introduced a new prayer of his own authorship in its place. The Reform and Conservative branches of Judaism have followed in his footsteps. In most Orthodox synagogues the traditional prayer, *Ha-Noten Teshu'ah* (He who gives salvation), has been retained but without the specification of royal names.

The Additional (Musaf) *Tefillah*

The *Tefillah* in the morning and afternoon services, it will be recalled, correspond to the two daily Temple offerings. On Sabbaths there was an additional (Musaf) sacrifice. Hence there is an additional (Musaf) *Tefillah* in the Sabbath service.

The Musaf *Tefillah* consists of the same seven benedictions as in the Shaharit service, with several insertions before the central benediction. The most prominent of these is a piyut known by its initial words as *Tikanta Shabbat* (Thou didst institute the Sabbath). The piyut starts out with a reverse alphabetical acrostic in which each word begins with a successive letter of the alphabet from Z to *A*. This part of the prayer deals only with the Sabbath. However, the next section of the prayer, which was added at a later time, not only refers to the Musaf offering in the Temple, but also includes a pledge to reinstitute the sacrificial cult after the restoration of Israel to the Holy Land:

> Lead us up in joy unto our land . . . where we will prepare unto Thee the offerings that are obligatory for us; . . . and the additional offering of this Sabbath day we will prepare and offer up unto Thee in love, according to the precept of Thy will, as Thou hast prescribed for us in Thy Torah. . . .

In modern times the pledge to reestablish the Temple cult has become a subject of controversy. Some Jews cannot conceive of themselves worshiping God by means of animal offerings. But the cult is clearly commanded in the Torah, and according to rabbinic doctrine a scriptural commandment cannot be abrogated. Orthodox Jews have therefore retained the traditional version. Non-Orthodox congregations, however, have revised this prayer. Reform synagogues eliminated from their prayer book all references to the sacrificial cult. Conservative synagogues retained references and descriptions of the sacrificial cult but eliminated the pledge to reinstitute the sacrificial form of worship. In the *Tikanta Shabbat* prayer the pledge was changed to a historical reminder of past practice. The prayer beseeches God "to lead us up in joy unto our land . . . where our fathers prepared unto Thee the offerings that were obligatory for them; . . . and the additional offering of the Sabbath day they prepared and offered up unto Thee in love, as Thou didst prescribe in Thy Torah. . . ." The problem, however, is purely academic and in all probability will remain so for the foreseeable future.

The Kedushah of the Musaf *Tefillah*

The Kedushah of the Musaf *Tefillah* was somewhat enlarged. In addition to the three biblical verses which are basic there is a fourth verse, that of the *Shema*. According to one theory this enlargement took place during a period of severe persecutions when the recitation of the *Shema* was proscribed.* To circumvent the watchful eyes and ears of the government overseers who attend the services to enforce the edict, a recitation of the *Shema* was interpolated in the Musaf Kedushah.[35] The censors watched the Shaharit service, during which the *Shema* was normally recited, but they did not stay to the end of the Sabbath morning service. The Musaf Kedushah was therefore emended to include the *Shema*. The prayer picks up the last phrase of the angelic chant, "Blessed be the glory of the Lord from His place," and continues: "*From His place* may He turn in mercy and be gracious unto a people who, evening and morning, twice every day, proclaim with constancy the unity of His name, saying in love: *Hear, O Israel, the Lord our God,*

* *See p. 444.*

the Lord is One." Once more the Kedushah picks up the last word of the verse and proceeds with a forceful declaration of Israel's everlasting faith in God:

> *One is our God; He is our Father;*
> *He is our King; He is our Savior.*
> *In His mercy He will let us hear a second time,*
> *In the presence of all living (His promise),*
> *"To be unto you for a God."*

And the congregation responds: "I, the Lord am your God" (Exod. 6:7). This brings thc special interpolation to an end, and the Kedushah resumes with the consoling words of the psalmist: "The Lord will reign for ever, Thy God, O Zion, unto all generations. Hallelujah!" (Ps. 146:10). The worshiper has thus traveled emotionally from the celestial realms where the hosts on high, in awe and trembling, declare God's holiness, to the earthly realities of Israel's yearning for redemption, and Israel's eternal faith in God the Redeemer.

The Sabbath Afternoon Service

During the period under discussion the Sabbath afternoon service took on its definitive form, which has survived to this day. The service consisted of five parts: (1) the introductory Psalm 145 (Ashre) followed by the prayer *Uva Le-Zion Go'el* (A redeemer will come to Zion), (2) the reading from the Torah of the first section of the coming Sabbath's portion, (3) the *Tefillah* (essentially the same as that of the other Sabbath services), (4) three verses from Psalms, each of which begins with the word *Tzidkatkha* (Thy righteousness), and (5) the study of a chapter of Avot (Fathers) or the recital of certain psalms, depending on the season of the year.

The recital of the Ashre needs no additional comment; this psalm is recited at the beginning of every Minhah service.* Nor does the addition of the *Uva Le-Zion Go'el* need an exhaustive explanation—it is read for the same reason as in the weekday morning service.† Prophetic selections used to be

* *See pp. 157–59.*
† *See pp. 152–53.*

read in the synagogue on Sabbath afternoons, and the reading was concluded with the comforting promise that "a redeemer will come to Zion" and will fulfill the prophecies uttered by the prophets of old. In time the reading of the prophetic selections fell into disuse, but the recital of the prayer *Uva Le-Zion Go'el* has remained in the liturgy.

The *Tefillah* of the Sabbath afternoon service differed little from that of the other Sabbath services. However, the central benediction, which proclaims the holiness of the Sabbath, is preceded by an introductory piyut, known by its initial words as *Attah Ehad* (Thou art One):

> Thou art One and Thy name is One, and who is like Thy people Israel, a unique nation on earth? . . . The day of rest and holiness [which] Thou hast given unto Thy people . . . [is] a perfect rest wherein Thou delightest. Let Thy children perceive and know that this their rest is from Thee, and by their rest may they hallow Thy name.

The three verses[36] recited after the *Tefillah* are distinguished by the initial word which is, in each of them, *Tzidkatkha* (Thy righteousness). These verses have the same implication as the *Tzidduk Ha-Din* (The righteousness of God's judgment), which is recited during a burial service. They suggest the acceptance of God's judgment, however painful it may be. The reason for reciting these verses is the tradition that Moses, Joseph, and King David died on Sabbath afternoons. By reciting these verses Israel both reaffirms God's righteousness and memorializes three of its great heroes. Since these verses are not in harmony with happy occasions, they are omitted on Sabbaths of special community rejoicing, such as the presence of a bridegroom in the congregation.

Study of Avot (Fathers)

Raba, one of the leading sages of the Talmud, is reported to have said: "He who wishes to be pious must [in the first instance particularly] fulfil the . . . matters [dealt with in the tractate] Aboth" (B.K. 30a). The tractate Avot (Fathers) is a small treatise which contains the favorite sayings of the sages of the Mishnah. These ethical maxims were frequently repeated by their disciples and were finally collected and appended to the Mishnah. The maxims of this treatise cover a period of almost six centuries, from the days of Simon the Just, who lived in the fourth century B.C.E., to the days of the completion of the Mishnah at the end of the second century of the Common Era. The ethical teachings are concise and deal with the moral goals of rabbinic Judaism. The treatise has always appealed to the heart and mind of the Jew, and it became a favorite of the Jewish people. In time the study of this tractate was routinized, so that a chapter was studied every Sabbath afternoon during the summer months. Since study is a form of worship, it was quite appropriate to include this treatise in the prayer book as a supplement to the Sabbath Minhah service.

Originally this treatise was studied only on the Sabbaths between Passover and Shavuot. But there are six Sabbaths between the two festivals and the treatise contained only five chapters, so a sixth chapter was added. This chapter, known as *Kinyan Torah* (The Acquisition of Torah), is a collection of rabbinic sayings dealing with the study of Torah, a theme that is especially appropriate for the Sabbath before Shavuot. But the Jews loved the treatise Avot and were not satisfied with studying it only once a year. So the study of Avot was extended to all the Sabbaths of the summer season, from the first Sabbath after Passover to the Sabbath before Rosh Hashanah. The treatise was thus studied annually over and over again. Every Sabbath the Jew would rise from his Sabbath afternoon siesta, go to the synagogue for the Minhah service, and then study the prescribed chapter of the week.

Each chapter was introduced with the reassuring words: "All Israel have a portion in the world to come, as it is said: Thy people also shall be all righteous. . . ." (Isa. 60:21). And each chapter was concluded with the equally reassuring words:

> Rabbi Hananya . . . said: The Holy One, blessed
> be He, was pleased to make Israel worthy; wherefore
> He gave them a copious Torah and many

commandments, as it is said; The Lord was pleased, for His righteousness' sake, to make the teaching great and glorious [Isa. 42:21].

The study of the tractate Avot was already an established institution during the geonic period. Rabbi Amram Gaon states that "it is a tradition at the Babylonian academies to study the tractate Avot and the chapter *Kinyan Torah* after the Sabbath Minhah service."

When the summer months end and the afternoons become too short for study, it is customary to replace the tractate Avot with the reading of a number of psalms. Obviously reading takes less time than studying. The reading of the psalms starts on the first Sabbath after the fall holidays, when the portion of the Torah deals with the creation of the world. And what psalm is more fitting than the 104th—*Barkhi Nafshi* (Bless the Lord, O my soul)—which is a magnificent paean on God the Creator?

This psalm is followed by a group of fifteen short psalms (120–134) known as the pilgrim psalms, each of which begins with the introductory phrase *Shir Ha-Ma'alot* (A song of ascents). These psalms used to be sung by the pilgrims when they ascended to Jerusalem for the festival celebrations at the Temple. They were also sung by the Levites in the Temple on the festival of Sukkot, during the ceremony of the Drawing of the Water.*

The reading of the psalms after the Sabbath Minhah service goes back to ancient times, as we read in the Talmud: "In [the academy of] Nehardea they closed the prescribed lesson [of the Pentateuch] with [a reading from] the Hagiographa at *minhah* on the Sabbath" (Shab. 116b). These readings after the Sabbath Minhah service consisted of a number of psalms. But why did the rabbis choose the pilgrim psalms? The obvious reason is that these psalms, which are among the most inspiring, had lost their place in Jewish worship. When the Temple was destroyed they were no longer sung by pilgrims or Levites. It was especially appropriate to institute the

* *See p. 204.*

reading of these psalms on the first Sabbath after Sukkot, the festival when these psalms used to be sung by multitudes of pilgrims and by the Levites at the ceremony of the Drawing of the Water. The reading of Psalms 120–134 is thus both a memorial of the Temple rituals and an expression of hope that the land of Israel will be restored to the people of Israel and that these psalms will again be sung by pilgrims and Levites.

Just as Psalm 104 *(Barkhi Nafshi)*, having been recited on the Sabbath after Sukkot, continues to be read on every Sabbath afternoon throughout the winter months, so the pilgrim psalms too are read every Sabbath afternoon till the spring festival of Passover, after which the days begin to lengthen and time becomes available for the resumption of the study of the tractate Avot.

The Saturday Evening Service

Saturday night is technically only a week-night, but because of the depressed mood which replaced the joy of the Sabbath, its liturgy took on a number of distinctive characteristics. Fundamentally the service is a weekday Maariv service with several additions that give it an identity of its own. The first addition is the Havdalah prayer, which emphasizes the distinction that God has made "between the holy and the profane . . . between the seventh day and the six days of creation." It was appropriately interpolated in the fourth benedictions of the *Tefillah* as an introduction to the thirteen intermediate benedictions suspended during the Sabbath. The Havdalah is again recited near the end of the service for the benefit of the homeless wayfarers for whom the synagogue used to serve as a hostel.* This time the blessings over wine, spices, and light were added, as in the Havdalah which is recited at home.†

Another enrichment of the Saturday evening service consisted of a number of prayers which aimed at cheering the crestfallen Jew with words of comfort and hope. The Jew had to gird his loins for the struggles of the week ahead. Particu-

* *See p. 164.*
† *See pp. 299–301.*

larly bitter was the unceasing battle for a livelihood in the face of discrimination. In order to bolster the Jew's courage and to give him the fortitude necessary to face the uncertainties ahead, the Saturday evening service was begun with a fitting introductory psalm:

> *Blessed be the Lord my Rock,*
> *Who traineth my hands for war,*
> *And my fingers for battle;*
> *My . . . fortress,*
> *My high tower, and my deliverer* [*Ps. 144:1–2*].

At the end of the service, too, a number of comforting selections from the Prophets and the Writings used to be read, and they were followed by the prayer *Uva Le-Zion Go'el*.[37] These readings are no longer part of the liturgy. Only a remnant has survived—Psalm 91 and the concluding prayer, *Uva Le-Zion Go'el*.* The latter, however, does not contain the first two verses (Isa. 59:20–21). This omission is ascribed to the rabbinic tradition that the messianic era will not be ushered in during the nighttime. Hence this prayer starts directly with the Kedushah—*Ve-Atah Kadosh* (Thou art holy, O Thou that art enthroned upon the praises of Israel [Ps. 22:4]).

But words of comfort and the promise of God's blessings during the week ahead have not been totally eliminated from the Saturday evening service. On the contrary, a long series of biblical blessings which promise worldly goods as well as national redemption are read after the *Tefillah*. The first of these is the blessing that Isaac bestowed on his son Jacob: "May God give you / Of the dew of heaven and the fat of the earth, / Abundance of new grain and wine" (Gen. 27:28). The blessings conclude with the words: "Cursed be they who curse you, / Blessed they who bless you" (Gen. 27:29).[38] With these blessings fresh in his mind, the Jew left the synagogue for his home, where he again recited the Havdalah and chanted a number of appropriate hymns.† These, too, served to bolster his spirit and enabled him to go forth and face the trials of the weekdays ahead.

* *See pp. 152–53, 193–94.*
† *See pp. 499–501.*

8
THE LITURGY OF THE MAJOR FESTIVALS

The liturgy of the major festivals—Passover, Pentecost, and Tabernacles—differs sufficiently from that of the weekly Sabbath service to justify an independent treatment. The Sabbath, it will be recalled, is associated with two events, both of which are independent of the Temple and the land of Israel. The biblical reasons for the observance of the Sabbath are the creation of the world and the Exodus from Egypt. The observance of the Sabbath is thus based on the duty to emulate God and rest on the Sabbath, and the duty to be a free person not only by resting but also by engaging in spiritual activities.*

Not so with the three festivals. They are closely connected with the land of Israel and with the Temple service. Each of the festivals is linked with an agricultural harvest in the land of Israel. Passover, or the Feast of Unleavened Bread, coincided with the barley harvest; Pentecost, or the Feast of Weeks, coincided with the wheat harvest; and Tabernacles, or the Feast of the Ingathering, fell at the time of the vintage. While the Sabbath was observed primarily at home and, during the Second Commonwealth, at the local synagogues, the three festivals were observed primarily in Jerusalem, the national center of worship. The Bible commands: "Three times a year—on the Feast of Unleavened Bread, on the Feast of Weeks, and on the Feast of Booths—all your males shall appear before the Lord your God in the place that He will choose" (Deut. 16:16). Every Jew was expected to make a pilgrimage to the central shrine on each of the festivals and to attend the prescribed sacrificial worship and its concomitant

* *See pp. 161–62.*

rituals. When the Temple was destroyed, rituals that lent themselves to detachment were transferred to the synagogue services.

Historic Background

In ancient days the three festivals had already become associated with important historic events. The festivals thus assumed additional religious significance and were endowed with transcendent importance, especially in the Diaspora.

The Passover

The first of the major festivals, the Passover, has been associated historically with the redemption of the children of Israel from Egypt, "the house of bondage." The festival celebrates this decisive event as "the season of our freedom." Passover thus became the annual occasion for dramatizing the ideal of freedom as a religious objective in the life of the Jew and in the collective life of the Jewish people. The abhorrence of slavery and the love of freedom were thus woven into the fabric of the Jew's personality and became a powerful drive in the collective aspirations of the Jewish people. Although the Jew was often oppressed and persecuted, he maintained within his congested ghetto the spirit of freedom and dignity. In the eyes of the Gentiles he was a degraded and inferior person; in his own estimation he was an aristocrat, a descendant of Abraham, Isaac, and Jacob, and one of the people whom God had redeemed from slavery. In time, he was sure, God would again redeem the Jewish people from exile and degradation. This ultimate redemption would vindicate the Jewish people in the eyes of the whole world. The Exodus from Egypt is therefore an ever-recurring theme in the Jewish liturgy, and it reaches its climax during the festival of Passover, especially during the elaborate home service know as the Seder.*

In the ancient Temple the essential act of the Passover observance was the family offering of the paschal lamb and its festive consumption by the family group at the Temple site. Also basic to the observance of the Passover was the absten-

* *See pp. 301 ff.*

tion from eating leavened bread during the seven days of the festival—which is frequently called the Feast of Unleavened Bread. This dietary aspect of the Passover observance has been traced to the agricultural origin of the festival. But as early as the biblical account unleavened bread was associated with the Exodus from Egypt, for it was a reminder of the haste in which the Hebrews left Egypt, as we are told in the Bible: "For seven days thereafter you shall eat unleavened bread . . . for you departed from the land of Egypt hurriedly—so that you may remember the day of your departure from the land of Egypt as long as you live" (Deut. 16:3).

The Feast of Weeks

The second major festival is Shavuot, or the Feast of Weeks. The Bible directs: "[You shall keep] the Feast of the Harvest, of the first fruits of your work, of what you sow in the field" (Exod. 23:16). As in all the festivals, a religiohistorical meaning was woven into its texture, and the festival thus assumed preeminent significance in the life of the Jews. The Feast of Weeks became the anniversary of God's revelation to Israel at Mount Sinai, when Moses received the Ten Commandments in the midst of overwhelming supernatural events. This theophany took place in the presence of all the children of Israel, and it constituted a holy and everlasting covenant between God and Israel. It is significant that there is no intimation in the Bible that the feast of Shavuot commemorates the revelation at Sinai. Nor is there any mention of a connection between the festival and the giving of the Torah in any other of the early sources. In the Talmud, however, the association of Shavuot with the revelation at Mount Sinai is already referred to as an established tradition, fully accepted and unchallenged.[1] When the date of the giving of the Torah was calculated on the basis of the biblical account, it was found to coincide with the agricultural festival of the first fruits.

In comparison with the other two festivals, the celebration of the Feast of Weeks has been rather pale. Shavuot has been celebrated for only one day, while Passover and Tabernacles have been observed for a whole week. Ritually, too, Shavuot has not been as rich: Passover has had its colorful Seder and the strict prohibition of leavened bread; Sukkot, the "feast of rejoicing," was celebrated with an abundance of ceremonials, such as the booths and the processions with palm branches and citrons. The Feast of Weeks, however, had no distinctive ceremonials except the bringing of bikkurim, the first fruits, to the Temple in Jerusalem. To be sure, this ceremony was most impressive. Yet it attracted relatively few pilgrims. And in later times when a new celebration was born, Simhat Torah (Rejoicing with the Torah), it was not attached to Shavuot, which commemorates the giving of the Torah. Instead, the new festival was attached to Sukkot. The reason for this seemingly strange development is the coincidence that in accordance with the annual cycle, the reading of the Pentateuch was completed at the end of the religious year, which is in the fall.

As indicated above, Shavuot had but one striking ritual—the bringing of the first fruits to the Temple.[2] The procession to the Temple Mount is described in the Mishnah:

> How were the *Bikkurim* taken up [to Jerusalem]? All [the inhabitants of] the cities that constituted the *Ma'amad* [district] [3] assembled in the city of the *Ma'amad*, and spent the night in the open place thereof without entering any of the houses. Early in the morning the officer said: *Come ye, and let us go up to Zion unto the Lord our God* (Isa. 2:3). Those who lived near Jerusalem brought fresh figs and grapes, but those from a distance brought dried figs and raisins. An ox with horns bedecked with gold and with an olive crown on its head led the way. The flute was played before them until they were nigh to Jerusalem. . . . The governors and chiefs and treasurers of the Temple went out to meet them. . . . The flute was playing before them till they reached the Temple Mount. . . . Even King Agrippa would take the basket and place it on his shoulder and walk as far as the Temple Court. At the approach to the Court the levites would sing the song: *I will extol Thee, O Lord, for Thou hast raised me up and hast not suffered mine enemies to rejoice over me* (Ps. 30:2) [Bik. 3:2–4].

This ritual was impressive. But it disappeared when the Temple was destroyed. In addition, the Jewish people ceased to be farmers, and harvests ceased to be of special significance. Hence the religiohistoric basis of the festival, the giving of the Torah, became the primary reason for the celebration of the Feast of Weeks. The Torah assumed surpassing significance in the life of the Jews; study of Torah became the passion of the people and transfigured the Jew and his sense of values. Scholarship became his chosen preoccupation, and the scholar became the aristocrat of the community. The Torah and its mastery therefore became the central themes of the festival services.

The Feast of Tabernacles

The third of the major festivals was the Feast of Tabernacles. In ancient times it was the climax of the year's celebrations. This joyous celebration took place at the time of the general harvest, the vintage, and the oil pressing. The ritual was elaborate: seventy sacrifices were offered in the Temple. Added to the week's celebration was an Eighth Day of Solemn Assembly, on which only one offering was brought. A number of midrashic homilies deal with the theme of Judaism's concern for the welfare of the seventy heathen nations in whose behalf Israel offered sacrifices on the Feast of Tabernacles [4] before offering a sacrifice in its own behalf.

More impressive was the ceremony in which each worshiper carried a citron (etrog) and a palm branch (lulav), to which were tied myrtle and willow twigs in fulfillment of the biblical injunction: "You shall take the product of *hadar* [goodly] trees, branches of palm trees, boughs of leafy trees, and willows of the brook" (Lev. 23:40). And when the first and the twenty-fifth verses of Psalm 118 were pronounced during the Temple service, the people waved the palm branches in unison. It has been suggested that this Temple ceremony was originally connected with a ritual aimed at bringing rain to the parched earth, for in Palestine the waving of the palm branches suggested the wind that precedes the rain. At the time of the Temple, however, this ritual had long since lost its association with rain, and its symbolic meaning was one of thanksgiving to God for His bounty. After the completion of the sacrificial offerings, the etrog and lulav were carried in a joyous procession around the altar, while the people sang with loud, firm voices: "We beseech Thee, O Lord, save now! / We beseech Thee, O Lord, make us now to prosper!" (Ps. 118:25).

Another distinctive ceremony of the Sukkot service at the Jerusalem Temple was the Libation of Water at the morning services. The water was brought in a golden flask from the fountain of Siloam and poured by the officiating Kohen into the basin near the altar. This was the most joyous of the Temple ceremonies. The Mishnah says that "he who has not seen the rejoicing at the place of the Water-Drawing has never seen rejoicing in his life" (Sukkah 5:1). The ceremony was accompanied by a torchlight procession, dances, singing, and the chanting by the Levitical choir of the fifteen pilgrim psalms, the songs of ascents (Pss. 120–134), to the accompaniment of musical instruments. This ceremony, too, was of ancient origin and was probably connected with rain-bringing rites. But in Temple days this ceremony already had a new meaning. It was a symbolic act performed in compliance with the prophetic verse "With joy shall ye draw water / Out of the wells of salvation" (Isa. 12:3). But the Libation of Water ceremony, like the sacrificial rites, ceased when the Temple was destroyed.

The most obvious of the symbols connected with the Feast of Tabernacles was the erection of booths (sukkot) to dwell in during the festival. This, however, was not associated with the Temple service. It was incumbent on every Jew, wherever he dwelt, even outside the Holy Land, to build a sukkah and to dwell therein during the festival. In all probability the sukkah had its origin in the temporary shelters that used to be erected for vintners during the vintage season. When these booths were no longer in common use, they survived as a religious symbol which dramatized the children of Israel's forty years of wandering in the desert, where life was impossible but for God's special protection. The memory of this national experience and of God's providence has had a telling effect on the morale of the Jewish people during their wanderings in exile.

It filled their hearts with trust in God's providence. As God had seen their forefathers through the desert in the days of Moses, so would he see the Jewish people through their wanderings in their exile. He would surely sustain them and bring them back to the Promised Land. "You shall live in booths seven days," says the Bible, "in order that future generations may know that I made the Israelite people live in booths when I brought them out of the land of Egypt, I the Lord your God" (Lev. 23:42–43).

When the Temple was destroyed and its elaborate rituals could no longer be observed, those elements of the service which lent themselves to detachment from the sacrificial cult were transferred to the synagogue and the home. The Passover Seder was transferred from the Temple precincts to the home; the Sukkot procession around the Temple altar with etrog and lulav became the synagogue procession around the reader's table; and the chanting of the Hallel psalms (113–118) by the Levitical choir in the Temple became an integral part of the festival liturgy of the synagogue.

The Second-Day Festival of the Diaspora

The three major festivals are observed for an additional day in the Diaspora. Thus Passover is celebrated in Israel for seven days, of which only the first and the seventh are observed as full festivals. In the Diaspora, however, Passover lasts eight days and the first two days and the last two days are observed as full festivals. In Israel there is only one Seder, while in the Diaspora the Seder is celebrated twice, on the first and the second evenings of the festival. Similarly, the festival of Shavuot is observed in Israel for only one day, while in the Diaspora it is observed for two. And in Israel the festival of Sukkot lasts eight days, of which the first and the eighth are observed as full festivals, in the Diaspora it lasts nine days, of which the first two days and the last two days are observed as full festivals. The eighth day of the Sukkot festival is known as Shemini Atzeret, the Eighth Day of Solemn Assembly, and the ninth day is Simhat Torah, the Rejoicing with the Torah. The additional days of the festival observed in the Diaspora are called *Yom Tov Sheni Shel Galuyot*, the Second-Day Festival of the Diaspora.[5]

How did this Second-Day Festival of the Diaspora arise? And how did it affect the synagogue liturgy? To understand the development of the discrepancy between the practice in Israel and that of the Diaspora, it is necessary to digress somewhat and examine certain aspects of the Jewish calendar.

The Jewish calendar is rather complicated. The months are based on the moon's cycle, while the year is based on the sun's cycle. Since the lunar month consists of approximately twenty-nine and a half days, twelve such months do not add up to a full solar year of 365 days. It is therefore necessary to add a thirteenth month approximately every third year.

The determination of the start of a new month is complicated by the fact that the lunar month includes a fraction of a day. The months are therefore of unequal length. Some are twenty-nine days and some are thirty days. In ancient times the beginning of a month was determined by the evidence of witnesses who saw the "birth," or appearance, of the new moon. The power to declare that a new month had begun was lodged in the hands of the Palestinian patriarch and his court, the Sanhedrin. When a new month was officially declared, the news was immediately relayed to all Jewish communities so that they might know exactly when to observe the religious festivals. The method of spreading the information was by fire signals from mountaintop to mountaintop. This method was effective for the communities in Palestine, but for the Jews of Babylonia, Egypt, and more distant lands, emissaries were employed. These emissaries could not always reach their destinations in time, however, so the Jews in the Diaspora found it necessary to institute the observance of an additional day on each festival in order to make sure that they were observing the festivals in their proper time.

The power to fix the calendar gave the patriarch and his court in Palestine a position of centrality. Even when the Jews learned how to calculate the moon's cycle with exactitude, the patriarch and his court continued the traditional procedure of taking testimony and announcing each month in accordance with the evidence of the witnesses. But the Palestinian authorities could not forever maintain their monopoly on fixing the calendar. When Christianity became the state religion of Rome and began to oppress the Jews in Palestine, the emissaries could no longer be sent out each month to inform the scattered Jewish communities of the dates set by the patriarch and his court. In the fourth century the patriarch Hillel II took the decisive step of officially publishing a calendar based on astronomical calculations. He thus abolished the old system of determining the start of each month and made it possible for Jews everywhere to calculate accurately the beginning of each month and to intercalate the additional month of a leap year. This ended the limited hegemony of the Palestinian Jewish community, but it did not terminate the practice of observing additional festival days in the Diaspora. The Talmud enlightens us as to why the Second-Day Festival of the Diaspora was not abrogated:

> R. Zera said: . . . we are now well acquainted with the fixing of the new moon and, nevertheless, we do observe two days. Abaye said: . . . In early times they used to light bonfires [as signals], but on account of the mischief of the Samaritans,[6] the Rabbis ordained that messengers should go forth. . . . Now that we are well acquainted with the fixing of the new moon, why do we observe two days?—Because they sent [word] from there [Palestine]: Give heed to the customs of your ancestors which have come down to you [Bezah 4b].

The Jews of the Diaspora did not need much persuading. The observance of the extra festival days had been firmly established by usage during many generations, and traditions tend to perpetuate themselves even when their raison d'etre no longer exists.* As for the liturgy of the Second-Day Festival of the Diaspora, there is little to say—it is an almost exact rep-

* *See pp. 371–72.*

lica of the liturgy of the first day. The main differences are in the Torah and Haftarah readings, which are specific for each day of the festival. There are also some special piyutim for each day.

In modern times the Reform synagogues have abolished the Second-Day Festival of the Diaspora. They even limited the observance of Rosh Hashanah to one day, despite its two-day observance in Israel. Among the American Conservative congregations there is considerable agitation for the abolition of these extra days of festival observance. Those who want to abolish these duplicate festival days argue that it is incongruous to observe the eighth day of Passover when in Israel even the pious go to work and do not abstain from eating non-Passover foods. They also point to the burden that the extra festival days place on the Jews of the Diaspora. These extra days, they say, are in the legal category of edicts which the majority cannot observe, and therefore should be abandoned. The Orthodox branch of the American Jewish community fully accepts the observance of the Second-Day Festival of the Diaspora, and in all probability will continue to adhere to the talmudic dictum "Give head to the customs of your ancestors."

The Liturgy of the Major Festivals

Except for minor accretions in postgeonic times, the liturgy of the major festivals was fully formulated during the talmudic and geonic times. The festival services are generally like those on the Sabbath. They contain the Early Morning Benedictions, the Verses of Praise, the *Shema* and its benedictions, the *Tefillah* with its Kedushah, the scriptural readings, and the Musaf *Tefillah* with its Kedushah. However, the festival services also contain a number of distinguishing characteristics that have endowed them with a quality all their own. To begin with, the liturgy of the festivals has been embellished with many piyutim that have been interpolated in the benedictions that precede and follow the *Shema*, and in the first three benedictions of the *Tefillah*. The traditional prayer books of former generations were full to overflowing with such piyutim. The piyutim inserted into the *Tefillah* were usually introduced by a special formula known by its initial words: *Misod Hakhamim* (With words from the learned). This formula goes back to the eighth century or earlier. Its purpose was to ask permission for breaking into the normal sequence of the *Tefillah* benedictions with new liturgic compositions. This introductory formula reads: "With words from the learned and the discerning, will I open my lips in song and chanting to thank and praise the One who dwells on high." It should be noted, however, that the modern prayer books, including some that are used in Orthodox synagogues, have eliminated the festival piyutim, so that hardly a trace of them is left.

The Essential Benediction of the Festival *Tefillah*

A second characteristic of the festival liturgy is the central benediction of the *Tefillah*. It is introduced by two preliminary prayers which are already mentioned in the Talmud. The first begins with a confirmation of the doctrine that God chose Israel from among all the peoples of the earth and in His love gave them the festivals.[7] At this point a reference to the observance is interpolated. For Passover it reads: "this day of the Feast of Unleavened Bread, the season of our Freedom"; for Shavuot: "this day of the Feast of Weeks, the season of the giving of our Torah"; and for Sukkot the special passage reads: "this day of the Feast of Tabernacles, the season of our gladness."

This introductory statement is followed with a familiar prayer known as *Ya'aleh Ve-Yavo,* derived from the first essential words of the opening sentence: "Our God and God of our fathers! May our remembrance *rise up and come* [*Ya'aleh Ve-Yavo*] . . . before Thee." Here again the specific festival is mentioned: "on this day of the Feast of Unleavened Bread" or "the Feast of Weeks," etc. After praying for such boons as "remembrance of Messiah the son of David Thy servant, of Jerusalem Thy holy city, and of all Thy people the house of Israel," the prayer continues: "Remember us, O Lord our God, thereon for wellbeing; be mindful of us for blessing, and save us unto life . . . for our eyes are bent upon Thee, because

Thou art a gracious and merciful God and King." [8] The logic of the *Ya'aleh Ve-Yavo* prayer is to be found in the reasoning that just as the Jewish people *remembers* the historic events associated with each of the festivals and observes them in accordance with God's injunction, so may God *remember* the people of Israel and grant them redemption and personal blessings.[9]

The introductory prayer and the *Ya'aleh Ve-Yavo* are followed by the essential benediction of the festivals. It concludes with the blessing "*Praise art Thou, O Lord, who hallowest Israel and the festivals.*" If the festival falls on a Sabbath, the blessing is expanded to include the sanctification of the Sabbath. It reads: "*Praised art Thou, O Lord, who hallowest the Sabbath and Israel and the festivals.*"

The Hallel

Equally distinctive of the festival liturgy is the recital of the Hallel (Pss. 113–118) immediately after the morning *Tefillah*. These six psalms are sometimes called the "Egyptian Hallel," a name derived from Psalm 114, which deals with the Exodus from Egypt: "When Israel came forth out of Egypt . . . / The sea saw it, and fled; / The Jordan turned backward." By calling these psalms the Egyptian Hallel, the rabbis distinguished them from the Great Hallel, which consists of Psalm 136 (Pes. 118a).[10]

Originally these six psalms were part of the Temple ritual. When the Temple was destroyed the Hallel was transferred to the synagogue. In the Temple the Hallel was recited only on the first day of Passover at the Seder, on the eight days of Sukkot, and on the eight days of Hanukah (the latter in remembrance of the Temple's rededication after the Hasmonean victory). At a later time the Hallel was added to the Shavuot service as a substitute for the pilgrim psalms (Pss. 120–134) that used to be chanted when the first fruits were brought to the Temple. At about the beginning of the third century, or perhaps even earlier, the Babylonian Jews initiated the practice of reciting the Hallel on the last six days of Passover and on the New Moon days. To distinguish these new occasions from those on which the Hallel had been traditionally recited, the Babylonian Jews abridged the Hallel by omitting verses 1–11 from Psalms 115 and 116. Thus arose the distinction between the Full Hallel and the Half Hallel.[11] This development is succinctly related in the Talmud:

> Rab once came to Babylonia and he noticed that they recited the *Hallel* on New Moon; at first he thought of stopping them but when he saw that they omitted parts of [the Hallel], he remarked: It is clearly evident that [this practice] is an old ancestral custom with them [Ta'anit 28b].

Rav did not interfere with the Babylonian Jews because he saw that they did not act out of ignorance. As has happened with so many other local Babylonian customs, the practice of reciting the Half Hallel on the last six days of Passover and on New Moon days spread to other Jewish communities and in time became part of the synagogue liturgy everywhere.[12]

In accordance with established rabbinic traditions the recitation of a group of psalms is preceded and concluded by a benediction, as is the case with the Verses of Praise, which are preceded by the benediction of *Barukh She-Amar* (Praised be He who spoke) and are concluded by the benediction of *Yishtabah* (Praised be [Thy name]). The Hallel psalms, too, are introduced by the simple benediction "*Praised art Thou, O Lord our God, King of the universe, who sanctified us by His commandments, and commanded us to read the Hallel.*" The concluding benediction is more elaborate:

> All Thy works shall praise Thee, O Lord our God, and Thy pious ones, the just who do Thy will, together with all Thy people, the house of Israel shall . . . thank, bless, praise . . . and ascribe sovereignty unto Thy name, O our King. . . . *Praised art Thou, O Lord, a King extolled with praises.*[13]

The Readings from the Scriptures

The Torah readings at the Sabbath services are in sequence; the aim is to complete the reading of the Pentateuch annually or triennially. But the Torah readings at the festival services are selective. They deal with the historic events that are commemorated by the festivals and with the nature of their respective observances. Only five persons are called to the Torah,* indicating that the festivals rank in their sanctity below that of the Sabbath, when seven are called to the Torah reading. The person called for the prophetic portion reads a special Torah selection, which necessitates the use of two scrolls. This selection deals with the offerings that were sacrificed at the Temple service during the festival. Reading about the special offerings of the day keeps alive the memory of those services. It also serves as a substitute for the actual performance of the biblical commandments regarding the sacrificial rituals. And the prophetic lessons, too, deal with themes related to the festivals.

All the scriptural readings, both from the Pentateuch and from the Prophets, were designated during the centuries under discussion and have been scrupulously followed up to the present day.

The ceremony of taking the scrolls of the Torah out of the ark and returning them after the reading is similar to that of the Sabbath service.† But the special prayers recited on the Sabbath before returning the scroll to the ark, that is, the *Yekum Purkan* prayers and the prayer for the government, are omitted.[14]

On each of the festivals it is also customary to read one of the five small scrolls *(megillot)* of the Bible. They are read on the Sabbath of the intermediate days of Passover and Sukkot and on the second day of Shavuot. The Song of Songs is read on Passover, the Book of Ruth on Shavuot, and the Book of Ecclesiastes on Sukkot. There is a sort of logic to the reading of these scrolls on the festivals. The Song of Songs deals with youth and love, and Passover falls in the spring, which is associated with youthfulness. In addition, the Song of Songs contains a reference to the Exodus, or at least to Pharaoh: "I have compared thee, O my love, to a steed in

* *See pp. 111–12.*
† *See pp. 178–81.*

Prayer Book, Italy, 1441, Schocken Library, Jerusalem. PHOTO: ALFRED BERNHEIM

Pharaoh's chariots" (Song of Songs 1:9). Similarly, Shavuot is associated with the wheat harvest, and the Book of Ruth mentions that harvest: "So she kept fast by the maidens of Boaz to glean unto the end of barley harvest and of wheat harvest" (Ruth 2:23). Another good reason for reading the Book of Ruth on Shavuot is that Ruth accepted the Torah when she became a Jewess, just as the Hebrews did at Mount Sinai. Still another reason offered is that King David, a descendant of Ruth, was, according to an ancient tradition, born on Shavuot, and died on Shavuot at the age of seventy. Similarly, there are good reasons for the reading of the somber Book of Ecclesiastes on the festival of Sukkot. According to the rabbis this book was written by King Solomon in his old age, which is often associated with autumn. Another reason given is that the depressing tone of the book is calculated to dampen the excessive exuberance of the "season of our rejoicing" which might lead to some laxity.

The tradition of reading the Song of Songs on Passover and Ruth on Shavuot goes back to the geonic period, while the reading of Ecclesiastes on Sukkot is a relative latecomer, since it originated in postgeonic times. With its inclusion in the liturgy, all the five *megillot* were given a place in the synagogue worship.[15]

The Festival Musaf *Tefillah*

The festival Musaf, like its counterpart on the Sabbath, concentrates on the Temple ritual. It serves to keep alive the historic memory of the ancient observance of the festivals, and it supplicates God to restore Israel to the Holy Land, where Jews will be able to observe the festivals in accordance with biblical directives. The special elements of the Musaf *Tefillah* are concentrated in the essential benedictions. The other benedictions, the three that precede and the three that follow the central benediction, are exactly the same as in all services. The Kedushah, too, contains nothing to distinguish it from that of the Sabbath Musaf.

The essential benediction starts exactly as in the *Tefillah* of the morning service: it thanks God for choosing Israel and for giving them the festivals "for gladness . . . and for joy." What follows, however, is distinctive and significant. It starts with a declaration absolving God from the onus of having exiled the Jewish people from the Holy Land and preventing them from observing the Temple rites: "On account of our sins we were exiled from our land . . . and we are unable to go up . . . and fulfill our obligations in Thy [Temple]." After accepting the justice of God's dispensations, the prayer logically proceeds to supplicate God's mercy:

> May it be Thy will, O Lord our God and God of our fathers, merciful King, that Thou mayest again . . . have mercy upon us and upon Thy sanctuary, and mayest speedily rebuild it and magnify its glory. Our Father and King . . . gather our dispersed from the ends of the earth. Lead us with exultation unto Zion Thy city, and unto Jerusalem the place of Thy sanctuary with everlasting joy.

Then comes a firm pledge similar to the one of the Sabbath Musaf service,* that the restoration to Zion will be followed by the observance of the authentic ritual as prescribed in the Bible:

> And there we will prepare before Thee the offerings that are obligatory for us, the continual offerings . . . and the additional [Musaf] offering of the [Feast of Unleavened Bread] we will prepare and offer unto Thee in love according to the precept of Thy will, as Thou hast prescribed for us in Thy Torah.

The next section of the prayer deals with the obligation to go up to Jerusalem during each of the festivals and personally participate in the Temple ritual.

> Our God and God of our fathers, merciful King, have mercy upon us, . . . rebuild Thy house as at the beginning and establish Thy sanctuary upon its site; grant that we may see it in its rebuilding, and make us rejoice in its reestablishment; . . . and there we

* *See pp. 191–92.*

> will go up to appear and prostrate ourselves before Thee at the three periods of our festivals according as it is written in Thy Torah: *Three times a year—on the Feast of Unleavened Bread, on the Feast of Weeks, and on the Feast of Booths—all your males shall appear before the Lord your God in the place that He will choose* [Deut. 16:16].

The third paragraph is the regular festival benediction, which concludes, like the benediction in the earlier *Tefillah*, "*Praised art Thou, O Lord, who hallowest Israel and the seasons.*"

The Priestly Blessing

Among the Temple rituals that were transferred to the synagogue was the priestly blessing. Those who are of priestly descent, the Kohanim, go to an adjoining chamber where the descendants of the tribe of Levi pour water on the Kohanim's hands. This is a symbol of the purification rites of the priests in the Temple. The Kohanim then ascend the *dukhan*, or platform, in front of the ark. Before turning around to face the congregation, they pull their prayer shawls over their heads and over their outstretched hands in the symbolic posture of bestowing a blessing.[16] They chant each word of the priestly blessing after the reader: "The Lord bless you and keep you! / The Lord deal kindly and graciously with you! / The Lord bestow His favor upon you and grant you peace!" (Num. 6:24–26). This impressive ritual is performed before the last benediction of the reader's repetition of the Musaf *Tefillah*. It is to be regretted that this ceremony has been discarded in many American synagogues. The reason given for its deletion from the liturgy of many traditional synagogues is that there are few Kohanim who are sufficiently observant to qualify for this sacred rite. In such synagogues the reader recites the priestly blessing, as he does at the repetition of every *Tefillah* on weekdays, Sabbaths, and festivals.

The Intermediate Days of the Festivals

The Bible requires full observance for only the first and last days of the Passover and Sukkot festivals. The intermediate days, known as Hol Hamoed, are only semifestivals. The liturgy on these days reflects their in-between status. The morning services resemble the weekday worship. In the Ashkenazic synagogues the tefillin are worn during the morning prayers. But the festival prayer *Ya'aleh Ve-Yavo* * is inserted into the seventeenth benediction of the *Tefillah*. More significant is the reading of the Hallel psalms immediately after the *Tefillah*, and the reading of a selection from the Torah dealing with the Temple offering of the day. As might be expected, the Musaf *Tefillah* is read silently by the congregation and is duly repeated by the reader. It is exactly the same as the Musaf of the full festival service. The Hol Hamoed service thus consists of the weekday Shaharit with the addition of the *Ya'aleh Ve-Yavo* prayer, the Hallel psalms, an appropriate reading from the Torah, and finally the Musaf *Tefillah*.

On the Sabbath that falls during the intermediate days, the same procedure is followed. To the regular Sabbath *Tefillah* is added the *Ya'aleh Ve-Yavo* prayer and the Hallel psalms. The Torah reading is not in sequence, it is a special selection.[17] Then comes the festival Musaf *Tefillah*, in which a number of phrases are inserted to include the additional Sabbath offering.

Special Prayer Units in the Festival Liturgy

The festival services have been enriched with a number of special prayer units. Some of these were transferred from the Temple ritual and some were developed independently during the talmudic and geonic periods. Those transferred from the Temple service, like the Hallel psalms mentioned above, are among the most dramatic and most colorful of the synagogue service. The others are logical derivations from the religious message of each festival. Among the former was the family Seder which was celebrated on the first night (in the Diaspora on the first two nights) of the festival. This most impressive ritual will be discussed in a later chapter devoted to the domestic liturgy.†

* *See pp. 209–10.*
† *See pp. 301 ff.*

Counting the Omer

One of the prayer units that has its roots in the ancient Temple service is the counting of the omer. In the Temple days the grain harvest was initiated with an elaborate ritual, the climax of which was the waving of a measure (omer) of barley at the altar by the officiating Kohen. This measure of barley was reaped on the second day of Passover and brought to the Temple for the ceremony. The grain harvest thus initiated lasted seven weeks, starting with the barley harvest on Passover and ending with the wheat harvest on the Feast of Weeks. The Bible is quite specific about the start and the end of the grain harvest:

> And from the day on which you bring the sheaf of wave offering—the day after the sabbath—you shall count off seven weeks. They must be complete: you must count until the day after the seventh week—fifty days; then you shall bring an offering of new grain to the Lord [Lev. 23:15–16].

After forty-nine days had been counted, the fiftieth was the Feast of Weeks—or, as the Greek Jews called it, Pentecost (that is, the fiftieth day).

When the Temple was destroyed, the ceremony of the waving of the measure of barley on the second day of Passover disappeared from the ritual. However, the counting of the forty-nine days of the grain harvest remained a part of the liturgy. The counting begins on the second day of Passover, and on the fiftieth day the Feast of Weeks is celebrated. The counting of the omer is a regular part of the service. Beginning with the second evening of Passover, at the conclusion of the Maariv service [18] the congregation rises and counts the omer. Since this rite is a specific commandment of the Torah, it is introduced with a formal benediction: "*Praised art Thou, O Lord our God, King of the universe, who sanctified us by His commandments, and commanded us concerning the counting of the omer.*" The benediction is followed by the actual counting, by day and week; for example: "This is the twenty-third day, making three weeks and two days of the omer."

The counting is followed by a prayer that God restore the Temple service, where "we will serve Thee . . . as in the days of old." [19]

Hoshanot

The most impressive Temple ritual that was transferred to the synagogue was the prayer unit known as Hoshanot. The word *Hoshanot* is derived from the Hebrew words *Hosha Na*, "Save Now!"—a refrain which is repeatedly recited on Sukkot, after the Musaf *Tefillah*. On the seventh day of Sukkot the Hoshanot service is greatly expanded, and its ceremonial is considerably elaborated. The seventh day is therefore called Hoshana Rabba, the Great *Hosha Na*, or the day when the refrain *Hosha Na* is frequently repeated by the congregation. The special emphasis on the seventh day goes back to the Temple days. The Mishnah informs us:

> Every day [of the first six days of the Festival] they went round the altar once, saying, "We beseech Thee, O Lord, save now; we beseech Thee, O Lord, make us now prosper (Ps. 118:25). . . . But on that [seventh] day they went round the altar seven times [Suk. 4:5].

The synagogue ritual, too, consists of a procession around the reader's desk. A scroll of the Torah is taken from the ark and is held at the reader's desk by someone specially chosen for this honored function. The reader leads the procession and chants the appropriate piyutim or Hoshanot for the day, as was done during the Temple days, when the people circled the altar and chanted Hoshanot. Everyone who has a lulav and an etrog joins the procession led by the reader. Others stand at their seats and follow the service.

The ritual is essentially of the talmudic and geonic period, though some of the piyutim are of postgeonic origin. The Hoshanot piyutim are characterized by their alphabetical acrostics, with each phrase or verse followed by the refrain "*Hosha Na!*"

During the first six days of the festival only a few piyutim are recited each day, and there is only one procession around the reader's desk. On the seventh day the Hoshanot ritual is quite elaborate. All the scrolls of the Torah are taken from the ark, and when the reader leads the procession, chanting the designated Hoshanot prayers, the men holding the scrolls follow him. After them come the men carrying their palm branches and citrons. Seven such processions take place.

In remembrance of the Temple ritual, which involved the decoration of the altar with willow branches, worshipers provide themselves before the service with bundles of willow twigs. These twigs are popularly called Hoshanot because of their use during the recitation of the Hoshanot prayers. When the congregation reaches the piyut with the refrain *Kol Mevaser*, *Mevaser Ve-Omer* (A voice brings news and says), which proclaims the hope of the Messiah's arrival during the coming year, every worshiper beats the willow twigs on the floor. This ceremony, like the waving of the palm branches, may once have been connected with rain-bringing rituals. But that was in prehistoric times; its meaning in the synagogue ritual is the remembrance of the Temple service, the awareness of the Temple's destruction, and the hope of its restoration.

Hoshana Rabba is also regarded as the last day of the season of divine judgment initiated on Rosh Hashanah. On that day final decisions regarding the fate of each person are reached in the heavenly court. Consequently, the synagogue service of Hoshana Rabba is an occasion for final pleas for divine mercy. In its solemnity the morning service has come to resemble those of the High Holy Days.* The reader wears a white robe as on Yom Kippur, and some of the chants are derived from the Day of Atonement service. Scores of piyutim have been composed for Hoshana Rabba, and the reading of the Hoshanot on that day is almost interminable. They are a last desperate effort to obtain absolution from the sins of the past year and to receive a merciful judgment from the court on high. When the Hoshana Rabba service comes to an end, there is a feeling of relief in the heart of everyone. God has surely forgiven the transgressions of His people.

* *See pp. 224 ff.*

Prayers for Rain and Dew

The eighth day of Sukkot is treated in the liturgy as an independent festival. Its name is Shemini Atzeret, the Eighth Day of Solemn Assembly, and wherever the name of the festivals are specified in a prayer, the name of Shemini Atzeret is included. This one-day festival is devoid of historic associations. Its raison d'etre is the need for a solemn day to moderate and subdue the high spirits of the people which prevailed during the preceding seven days of joyous celebration.

The liturgy of this day is exactly like that of the other festival services except for the inclusion of a special prayer unit known as *Geshem*, prayers for rain. These special prayers are mentioned in the Mishnah and are further discussed in the Talmud (Ta'anit 2b). In those days the ritual was merely the introduction of the formula "Thou causest the wind to blow and the rain to fall," which was to be recited before the second benediction of the *Tefillah* * throughout the winter season. This first mention of the wind and rain was regarded as an important occasion, because rain in Palestine was a matter of life or death. And the rains in Palestine are fickle. They are preceded by winds which can become destructive storms; the rains can become disastrous floods. Rain has therefore preoccupied the hearts of the people, and it still receives many headlines in the Israeli press each winter. Rain is regarded in the Talmud as one of God's greatest miracles, equal to that of the resurrection of the dead (Ber. 33a). That is why the second paragraph of the *Shema* features rain and drought as God's means of dispensing justice.†

Since the *Geshem* prayers are so important, the reader puts on a white robe and cap as on the Day of Atonement, and he intones the introductory Kaddish in the Yom Kippur mode. The synagogue poets produced many piyutim for the occasion, among them some that list the months and their signs of the zodiac. Prayer books of earlier generations used to have the symbols of the zodiac as adornments for these piyutim, but modern prayer books no longer contain most of these piyutim

* *See pp. 137–38.*
† *See pp. 97–98.*

and have thus been deprived of the few decorations that used to brighten the old festival prayer books. The only piyut retained in most modern prayer books is the one which actually introduces the rain formula. It contains six short stanzas imploring God to remember the merits of Abraham, Isaac, Jacob, Moses, Aaron, and the Twelve Tribes, and for their sakes to bless the land with rain. This sixfold invocation is followed by the reader's pronouncement of the essential formula:

> For Thou art the Lord our God, who *causest the wind to blow and the rain to fall*—
> For a blessing and not for a curse—[Cong.] Amen!
> For life and not for death—[Cong.] Amen!
> For plenty and not for scarcity—[Cong.] Amen!

The corresponding prayer for *Tal* (dew) is recited at the Musaf *Tefillah* of the first day of Passover. By that time the rainy season is past. The service is similar to that of *Geshem*, but the piyutim are obviously different from those of the *Geshem* service. The last piyut, which introduces the new formula, consists of six similar stanzas and is geared to the new formula: "*Thou causest the wind to blow and the dew to fall.*" In the *Tal* prayers, too, most modern synagogues recite only the sixfold invocation which concludes the prayer unit.

The prayers for rain in the winter and for dew in the summer are recited in synagogues everywhere, even in lands where the abundance of rain would suggest prayers for their curtailment and where rains are needed in summer rather than winter. But spiritually the Jew has never ceased to dwell in the Holy Land, and he still continues to pray as if his home is in the subtropical land of his forefathers, where the winter rain is the key to abundance and blessing.

Simhat Torah

The final day of the fall holiday season is Simhat Torah, the Rejoicing with the Torah. This ninth day of Sukkot is actually the Second-Day Festival of the Diaspora for Shemini Atzeret. In Israel the Rejoicing with the Torah takes place on Shemini Atzeret.

The origin of Simhat Torah goes back to the talmudic time when the Babylonian custom of reading the Pentateuch in one year was established. The completion of this annual cycle of Torah reading at the end of the religious year called for a joyous celebration. During the geonic period the name Simhat Torah came to be generally applied to the second day of Shemini Atzeret, and some of the main features of its observance were then established.[20]

During the morning service every worshiper thirteen years of age and over is called to the reading of the Torah. The portion of the Torah is therefore read over and over again. Several special honors are reserved for the notables of the congregation, especially the scholars. One of these honors is to be called up "with all the boys," a privilege that is usually reserved for the rabbi. A prayer shawl is spread like a canopy over the reader's table, and all the children gather under it. The person called up "with all the boys" pronounces the Torah benedictions, and the children repeat them after him. In this significant act the Torah is symbolically handed down from generation to generation. Jacob's blessing is then bestowed on the children:

> *The Angel who has redeemed me from all harm—*
> *Bless the lads.*
> *In them may my name be recalled,*
> *And the names of my fathers Abraham and Isaac,*
> *And may they be teeming multitudes upon the earth*
> [*Gen. 48:16*].

Another great honor is to be called up as *Hatan Torah* (the Bridegroom of the Torah). This signal honor of completing the Torah is usually reserved for a scholar. He is summoned with a special piyut in which blessings are showered upon him. The *Hatan Torah* represents the community of Israel, which is forever "wedded" to its beloved "bride," the Torah. At this point the cycle of Torah reading is officially completed.

No sooner is the reading completed than the new cycle is begun. To be called for the reading of the first section of the Pentateuch is also regarded as a great honor. The person called is known as *Hatan Bereshit* (the Bridegroom of Genesis). A special piyut is also recited in his honor. Finally the last person is called to read the prophetic portion. This selection is logically the first chapter of the Book of Joshua, corresponding to the first chapter of the Book of Genesis, which was just read.

The spirit of the service is one of abundant joy. Decorum is thrown to the winds. An outsider visiting a synagogue on Simhat Torah is usually appalled by the prevailing pandemonium and is shocked by the seeming spirit of levity.* For the Jews, however, this abandon is additional evidence of their abundant love of the Torah and their joyous appreciation of the privilege of studying it.

9
THE LITURGY OF THE HIGH HOLY DAYS

The High Holy Days encompass more than Rosh Hashanah (the religious New Year) and Yom Kippur (the Day of Atonement). They comprise a whole season devoted to penitence and contrition. They are inaugurated by a month of orientation and are concluded on Hoshana Rabba,† the seventh day of Sukkot. The liturgy of this lengthy period of almost two months is marked by many special prayers and distinctive penitential services aimed at the reconciliation of man with God. Most of these prayers had their origin during the crucial post-Yavneh period, when the liturgy of the High Holy Days took on its definitive form.

The chief emphasis of this season is on the concept of "returning to God," who in His mercy receives the penitent sinner, forgives his sins, and allows him to start the New Year spiritually clean and morally reborn. God's justice and mercy

* *See pp. 571–73.*
† *See pp. 219–20.*

come into focus. God is pictured in vivid, poetic symbolism as the King of the universe who passes judgment on every creature and decides the fate of every human being. But the divine decrees are not passed in haste. They are not sealed immediately on Rosh Hashanah, which is the Day of Judgment. The gates of prayer and repentance remain open till the Day of Atonement. Immediate judgment is passed only on the extremely righteous and the extremely wicked. But the overwhelming majority belong somewhere between. Judgment of them is mercifully deferred to Yom Kippur. God is long-suffering and waits for the sinner to return from his evil ways. In the words of the prophet, God pleads:

> Cast away . . . your transgressions, wherein ye have transgressed; and make you a new heart and a new spirit. . . . For I have no pleasure in the death of him that dieth, saith the Lord God; wherefore turn yourselves, and live [Ezek. 18:31–32].

The High Holy Days fill the pious Jew with awe. He prays for his very life, that it not be terminated prematurely during the coming year. He trembles in anticipation of the divine verdict. These days are therefore called the *Yamim Nora'im*, the Days of Awe. However, there is hope for him who heeds the words of the prophet and casts away his transgressions. God sets aside His attribute of justice in favor of His attribute of mercy and receives the penitent sinner in love and compassion. The door of repentance is open to everyone. The Jew is therefore told to meditate on his deeds of the past year. If there are good deeds among them, he is to resolve to add to them; if there are evil deeds among them, he is to repent and "return to God." He has ten days in which to pray for God's forgiveness. These ten days, from Rosh Hashanah to Yom Kippur, are called the *Asseret Yemei Teshuvah*, the Ten Days of Penitence.

The call to repentance is emphasized even in the synagogue appurtenances. To symbolize the spiritual purity which results from teshuvah, the color white predominates during the Ten Days of Penitence: the rabbi and the cantor wear white robes; the Torah scrolls are dressed in white mantles; the ark is draped with a white curtain; and the reader's table is covered with a white cloth. "Though your sins be as scarlet," says the prophet, "they shall be as white as snow" (Isa. 1:18).

Rosh Hashanah and Yom Kippur are officially regarded as festivals, and their liturgy has much in common with that of the major festivals. Yet it is in many ways quite unique, because Rosh Hashanah and Yom Kippur are primarily "holy convocations" with hardly any historical associations. Their emphasis is on spirituality and holiness rather than historic and national memories. To be sure, the historic events observed on the festivals are not nationalistic; they are observed as divine manifestations in the history of Israel and are fully religious in concept and ritual. But Rosh Hashanah and Yom Kippur emphasize not God's role in Israel's history, but God's role as King of the universe and as Judge of every human being. The liturgy of the High Holy Days is therefore the most fervent and solemn of all Jewish worship convocations.

The Month of Elul

The penitential period, as indicated above, begins a full month before Rosh Hashanah. The whole month of Elul is a period of spiritual orientation and preparation for the Days of Awe. From the beginning of the month until the initiation of the New Year on the first of Tishri, the shofar, the ram's horn, is sounded daily at the conclusion of the morning congregational service. This is calculated to rouse the worshipers to an awareness of the approaching High Holy Days. A special psalm (27) is recited daily at the end of the morning and evening services to assure the people of God's forgiveness: "The Lord is my light and my salvation; whom shall I fear? / The Lord is the stronghold of my life; of whom shall I be afraid?" (Ps. 27:1). This psalm is interpreted by the rabbis as referring to the New Year's Day and to the Day of Atonement.[1]

The *Selihot* Services

The most important and most characteristic act of preparation for the Days of Awe is the special midnight service known as *Selihot*,[2] which takes place about a week before Rosh Hashanah.

The *selihah* is a penitential prayer in which the worshiper supplicates God to forgive his sins. It differs from the piyut described in a previous chapter * in that the piyut aims in part at instruction, while the *selihah* aims mainly at directing man's heart to his Maker. The piyut is replete with allusions to rabbinic texts; the *selihah* quotes biblical verses that speak of God's mercy. The *selihah* is preoccupied not only with the sins of the worshiper, but also with the suffering of Israel. These prayers repeatedly point up the afflictions, persecutions, and humiliations that have been Israel's lot in exile. Overshadowing all is the theme of Israel's undying faith in God's mercy, and Israel's absolute conviction that the ordeal of the exile will ultimately come to an end and that redemption will replace the anguish of the dispersion. These characteristics of the *selihah* relate it closely to the psalm.

Some of the penitential prayers are among the oldest in the liturgy. Some are quoted in the Talmud as already well known, thus indicating that they are of ancient origin. The Mishnah (Ta'anit 2:4) quotes one such litany, in which all the important biblical characters, from Abraham up to Ezra, are listed as examples of God's mercy. The litany is part of the *Selihot* service. Its opening lines read:

> He who answered Abraham on Mount Moriah, He will answer us.
> He who answered his son Isaac when he was bound on the altar, He will answer us.
>
> He who answered Jacob at Bethel, He will answer us.
> He who answered Joseph in the dungeon, He will answer us. . . .
> He who answered our fathers at the Red Sea, He will answer us.

Equally ancient is the Aramaic litany still recited in the *Selihot* service:

> O merciful One, who answerest the poor, answer us.
> O merciful One, who answerest the lowly in spirit, answer us.
> O merciful One, who answerest the brokenhearted, answer us. . . .

* *See pp. 168 ff.*

The Development of the *Selihot* Services

During the geonic period special predawn *Selihot* services were instituted for each of the intermediate days between Rosh Hashanah and Yom Kippur. In the late geonic period these penitential services were extended to the days immediately before Rosh Hashanah. As might be expected, these *Selihot* services were at first brief. However, as the centuries rolled by and the persecutions became increasingly intolerable, the production of penitential prayers increased. These prayers also developed in complexity and assumed a formal structure. But they never lost sight of their primary purpose—to supplicate God for His forgiveness. Like the whole of the synagogue liturgy, these prayers remained strictly part of the oral tradition and were not collected and published till late in the Middle Ages.

The mystics found good reason of an esoteric nature in support of the predawn penitential services: * God's attribute of mercy is preeminent during the still hours before sunrise. The pious would therefore rise before dawn and betake themselves to the synagogue for the *Selihot* service. Ordinary Jews, however, could not subject themselves to such a rigorous regimen. They were satisfied with one *Selihot* service, the one that usually takes place on the Saturday night preceding Rosh Hashanah.[3] For the convenience of the multitude, this *Selihot* service is held at midnight instead of the predawn hours.

Midnight, too, is authoritatively sanctioned as a suitable time for penitential prayers. The psalmist affirmed its merit when he said: "At midnight I will rise to give thanks unto Thee / Because of Thy righteous ordinances" (Ps. 119:62).

The Thirteen Divine Attributes

Every *Selihot* service, be it midnight, predawn, or a prayer unit in any of the High Holy Days services, follows a set pattern. It is introduced by prayers composed of clusters of biblical verses and is concluded by several litanies, such as were quoted above. Between these are two well-developed units—the Thirteen Divine Attributes and the confession of sins.

* *See pp. 504–505.*

The Thirteen Divine Attributes originated in the biblical account of the golden calf. The Bible relates that Moses prayed in behalf of the children of Israel and that God forgave them. Moses prayed again: "Show me, I pray Thee, Thy glory." God answered his prayer and made known to him "all His goodness":

> The Lord came down in a cloud, . . . and proclaimed: "The Lord! the Lord! a God compassionate and gracious, slow to anger, abounding in kindness and faithfulness, extending kindness to the thousandth generation, forgiving iniquity, transgression, and sin [acquitting the penitent] . . ." [Exod. 34:5–7].

These divine attributes are again mentioned in the Bible in connection with the twelve spies whom Moses had sent to the land of Canaan. The spies returned with a discouraging report. Thereupon the people cried: "If only we had died in the land of Egypt. . . . Let us head back for Egypt" (Num. 14:2,4). This threat to go back to Egypt was open rebellion not only against Moses, but also against God:

> And the Lord said to Moses: "How long will this people spurn Me, and how long will they have no faith in Me despite all the signs that I have performed in their midst? I will strike them with pestilence and disown them, and I will make of you a nation far more numerous than they!" [Num. 14:11–12].

Upon hearing God's intent, Moses prayed for his people. He recited the Thirteen Attributes of God's mercy, and concluded with the plea: "Pardon, I pray, the iniquity of this people according to Your great kindness, as You have forgiven this people ever since Egypt" (Num. 14:19). The Bible concludes: "And the Lord said: 'I pardon, as you have asked' " (Num. 14:20).

In the *Selihot* service the congregation repeats the supplications of Moses in the hope that their prayers will prove as efficacious as those of Moses. Several times the Thirteen Divine Attributes are repeated and are concluded with Moses' prayer as quoted above.

That the recitation of the Thirteen Divine Attributes is highly efficacious is supported by a talmudic statement: "Rabbi Johanan said: . . . the Holy One, blessed be He, . . . said to him [Moses]: Whenever Israel sin, let them [read the passage containing the Thirteen Attributes] and I will forgive them" (R.H. 17b).

The Confession of Sins

But the recitation of the Thirteen Divine Attributes is not meant to be a magic formula which automatically results in absolution. Penitential prayers must be accompanied with contrite remorse. Penitence presumes a confession of one's sins and a resolve not to repeat them. The recitation of the Thirteen Attributes of God's mercy is therefore followed by the *Vidui*, the confession of sins. In the liturgy of the High Holy Days there are two confessions of sins. The first is known by its initial word as *Ashamnu* (We have trespassed) and is frequently called the short confession. The second, known by its initial words as *Al Het* (For the sin [that we have committed before Thee]), is also known as the long confession.* In the *Selihot* service only the short confession is included. It is an alphabetical listing of sins expressed in generic terms and, as is customary in the Jewish liturgy, in the plural. Any one of these sins may have been committed by someone in the congregation, and the assembly shares the responsibility and prays for its forgiveness. Moral corruption is not the concern of the sinner alone; it is also the concern of the whole social organism. Hence the congregation recites the confession in unison, and each worshiper beats his breast at the mention of each sin, symbolically expressing his remorse: "We have trespassed; we have been faithless; we have robbed; We have spoken slander. . . ."

The *Ashamnu* is repeated several times, each time introduced by: "We are not arrogant and stiff-necked, that we should say before Thee, O Lord our God and God of our fathers, we are righteous and have not sinned; verily, we have sinned." The confession is followed by the restatement of the rabbinic theodicy: "We have turned away from Thy commandments and

* *See pp. 247–50.*

good judgments, and it hath not profited us. But Thou art righteous in all that is come upon us; for Thou hast acted truthfully, but we have wrought unrighteousness."

The *Selihot* service, as it has come down to us from the geonic period, is a well-knit, logically structured service. It is opened, like the Minhah service, with the Ashre (Ps. 145) and the Half Kaddish, and is concluded with the Full Kaddish (*Titkabel*).*

More important than its structure is its profound effect on the worshiper. At the *Selihot* service before Rosh Hashanah he senses both the nearness of God and His transcendent glory. He feels the purifying and revitalizing force of prayer at its deepest level and usually emerges from the *Selihot* service spiritually reinvigorated, in a state of readiness for the approaching Days of Awe.

The Rosh Hashanah Services

Rosh Hashanah has both personal and universal implications. The fate of each individual as well as the fate of each nation is determined on this day of divine judgment. The spirit of the day is therefore solemn, and the time devoted to prayer far exceeds that of the festivals. According to some, Rosh Hashanah is observed for two days because one day is not enough for all the supplications and all the searching of the heart that are called for on so holy an occasion. The two days are regarded as one long "day" of forty-eight hours. This is a sound psychological rationalization of the two days of Rosh Hashanah, but it is not altogether sound historically. The second day of Rosh Hashanah owes its origin to the uncertainty about the calendar which gave rise to the Second-Day Festival of the Diaspora.† Originally Rosh Hashanah was observed in Palestine for only one day. However, European Jews who immigrated to the Holy Land in the eleventh century clung to their Diaspora custom of observing Rosh Hashanah for two days. They succeeded not only in maintaining their imported

* *See pp. 156–57.*
† *See pp. 205–208.*

tradition, but also in imposing it on the rest of the Jews in the Holy Land. The two-day Rosh Hashanah thus became universal, and the legal fiction of its being a long "day" of forty-eight hours rationalized its two-day observance in Palestine.

The liturgy of the two days varies but little. Obviously the Torah and Haftarah readings are different on each day. So are some of the piyutim. In all other respects the service on the second day is a repetition of that of the first day.

The general framework of the Rosh Hashanah service is like that of the festivals. It consists of a Shaharit (morning) service, scriptural readings from the Pentateuch and the Prophets, and a Musaf (additional) service. Within this framework, however, there are significant differences. The most distinctive of these are the shofar service and the unique construction and contents of the Musaf *Tefillah*. The Hallel psalms, which are a characteristic element of the festival liturgy, are not part of the Rosh Hashanah service, because the ancient Temple ritual of the New Year's observance did not include the recital of these psalms.

The Shaharit Service

The Shaharit service of Rosh Hashanah, as mentioned above, is similar to that of the festivals. The Early Morning Benedictions, the Verses of Praise, and the *Shema* with its benedictions are identical to their corresponding parts in the festival services. The *Tefillah*, too, is similar to that of the festivals in that it consists of seven benedictions, of which the first three and the last three are identical with those of every *Tefillah*. But here we meet with several differences. In the opening and closing benedictions there are several brief interpolations which had their origin in the geonic period or earlier. Their theme is the elemental desire to live. The first two of these additions just pray for life; the last two qualify the petition with the pivotal adjective "happy."

The prayers inserted in the first two benedictions read: "Remember us unto life, O King, who delightest in life, and inscribe us in the book of life, for Thine own sake, O living God"; and "Who is like unto Thee, Father of mercy, who in mercy rememberest Thy creatures unto life?" The prayers inserted in the last two benedictions of the *Tefillah* read: "O inscribe all the children of Thy covenant for a happy life"; and "In the book of life, blessing, peace and good sustenance may we be remembered and inscribed before Thee, we and all Thy people the house of Israel, for a happy life and for peace." These petitionary insertions do not disturb the essential nature of the benedictions. They enrich the content of the benedictions and relate them to one of the central themes of the season.

There is also a slight but deliberate change in the blessing of the third benediction. Instead of reading "*Praised art Thou, O Lord, the holy God*," the blessing concludes: "the holy King." The change involves only one word, but this word underscores one of the key themes of the service, God's sovereignty in the world. It is He who rules the destinies of men and nations in justice and mercy. The four inserted short prayers and the change in the blessing of the third benediction are maintained in the *Tefillah* of every service throughout the Ten Days of Penitence.[4]

The first substantial prayer that gives the liturgy of Rosh Hashanah its distinctive character is a supplication ascribed to Rav, the famous third century talmudic sage. The prayer consists of three short paragraphs, each of which begins with the word *Uvkhen* (Now, therefore). The threefold prayer implores God to hasten the day when all mankind will be united into "a single band" to do His will, to restore Israel to its homeland, and to banish iniquity and wickedness from the earth. This ancient prayer is part of every *Tefillah* on Rosh Hashanah and Yom Kippur.

As was indicated in earlier discussions of the *Tefillah*,* it is the intermediate benediction that distinguishes the *Tefillah* of each special occasion. This benediction singles out the essential nature of the occasion and in its closing blessing pronounces the sanctity of the day. This benediction of the Rosh Hashanah *Tefillah* stresses the theme of God's sovereignty:

> Our God and God of our fathers, reign Thou in Thy glory over the whole universe, and be exalted above all

* *See pp. 162–64.*

> the earth . . . that whatsoever hath been made may know that Thou hast made it, and whatsoever hath been created may understand that Thou hast created it, and whatsoever hath breath in its nostrils may say: The Lord God of Israel is King, and His dominion ruleth over all.
>
> Our God and God of our fathers, sanctify us by Thy commandments, and grant our portion in Thy Torah; . . . O purify our hearts to serve Thee in truth, for Thou art God in truth, and Thy word is truth, and endureth for ever. *Praised art Thou, O Lord, King over all the earth, who sanctifiest Israel and the Day of Remembrance.*

The reader's repetition of the Shaharit *Tefillah* is considerably longer. In addition to the Kedushah there are also a large number of piyutim, many of them from the geonic period.[5] These piyutim emphasize God's sovereignty, as is indicated in one of the frequent refrains: "*The Lord is King; the Lord was King; the Lord will be King for ever and ever.*" Man's insignificance is contrasted with God's eternal and infinite glory, and man's urgent need to return to God with his whole heart is repeatedly stressed.

The Shaharit service is concluded with the well-known litany *Avinu Malkenu* (Our Father, our King). It is recited by the reader and the congregation, line by line, immediately after the *Tefillah*. The litany consists of forty-four invocations, each initiated with the call "Our Father, our King." About half these invocations are of ancient origin, ascribed to Rabbi Akiba, a leading second century scholar. Others are as late as the fourteenth century. The *Avinu Malkenu* is recited throughout the Ten Days of Penitence except on the Sabbath. The reason for its omission on the Sabbath is that the litany was originally part of the liturgy for fast days. Its association with fast days made it unsuitable for the Sabbath, which is dedicated to pleasant and joyful experiences. The litany begins with a brief confession of sins and concludes with a stirring cry for God's acceptance of the congregation's supplications:

> Our Father, our King! we have sinned before Thee.
> Our Father, our King! we have no King but Thee.

> Our Father, our King! deal with us for the sake of Thy name. Our Father, our King! let a happy year begin for us. . . .
>
> Our Father, our King! be gracious unto us and answer us, for we have no good works of our own; deal with us in charity and kindness, and save us.

The Scriptural Readings

The selections from the Pentateuch and the Prophets that are read on Rosh Hashanah deal primarily with God's remembrance of each person and each nation. That is why Rosh Hashanah is also called *Yom Ha-Zikkaron,* the Day of Remembrance, and why the essential benediction in each *Tefillah* concludes with the formula "*who sanctifiest Israel and the Day of Remembrance.*" It will also be recalled that the first two prayers inserted in the *Tefillah* are built around the theme of God's remembrance of each person. "Remember us unto life" are the opening words of the first of these prayers. "Who in mercy rememberest Thy creatures unto life" are the concluding words of the second prayer. It is a basic principle of Judaism that before God no man is forgotten.

On the first day of Rosh Hashanah the Torah portion consists of the twenty-first chapter of Genesis:

> The Lord took note of [*remembered*] Sarah as He had promised. . . . Sarah conceived and bore a son to Abraham in his old age. . . . Abraham gave his newborn son . . . the name of Isaac. And when his son Isaac was eight days old, Abraham circumcised him, as God had commanded him [Gen. 21:1–4].

And the Haftarah, too, deals with the theme of divine remembrance. God remembers Hannah after many years of childlessness: "And the Lord *remembered* her. And . . . [Hannah] bore a son; and she called his name Samuel" (1 Sam. 1:19–20). Hannah takes the boy to the priest Eli to be brought up to serve in the Temple during his whole life.

On the second day of Rosh Hashanah the Scripture readings continue with the same theme. The readings for the day are specified in the Talmud: "Nowadays that we keep two days [of Rosh Hashanah] . . . on the next [second] day . . .

we say, *And God tried Abraham* [Gen. 22:1], with '*Is Ephraim a darling son to me*' [Jer. 31:20] for *Haftarah*" (Meg. 31a).

In the Torah portion, the word *remember* is not in the text. But the account of Isaac's binding implies a plea for God's remembrance of the children of Israel, whose forebears Abraham and Isaac made such superhuman sacrifices as tokens of their total faith in God. Abraham suppressed his fatherly love and Isaac offered himself for martyrdom. This is explicitly stated in the Musaf service:

> *Remember* unto us, O Lord our God, the covenant and the loving-kindness and the oath which Thou hast sworn unto Abraham our father on Mount Moriah; and may the binding with which Abraham our father bound his son Isaac on the altar appear before Thee, how he suppressed his compassion in order to perform Thy will with a whole heart.

During the Middle Ages, when martyrdom became a recurrent experience among the Jews, this biblical selection assumed foremost importance in the liturgy. Isaac became the prototype of Jewish martyrdom, the model to be emulated by every Jew. When confronted with the choice of apostasy or martyrdom, the Jew is to offer his life willingly for the sanctification of God's name.

The Haftarah on the second day of Rosh Hashanah centers on God's remembrance of Israel. In the Haftarah God speaks tenderly of Ephraim, or the ten exiled tribes of which the tribe of Ephraim was the leader:

> *Is Ephraim a darling son unto Me?*
> *Is he a child that is dandled?*
> *For as often as I speak of him,*
> *I do earnestly* remember *him still;*
> *Therefore My heart yearneth for him,*
> *I will surely have compassion upon him, saith the Lord*
> [*Jer. 31:20*].

These comforting words were understood as a divine promise to remember Israel and to restore the Jews to the Holy Land.

The restoration of Israel is thus the culminating theme of the Rosh Hashanah scriptural readings, just as it is the final prayer of the *Shema* benedictions.

The Shofar Service

The shofar, or ram's horn, was in use among the Hebrews long before it became a liturgic instrument in the synagogue. In ancient times the sound of the shofar summoned the people to rally against an enemy. In time of drought and pestilence, the shofar roused the people to repentance and prayer. When a king was anointed, the shofar announced the initiation of his reign. And on Yom Kippur of the jubilee year the shofar proclaimed "release throughout the land" (Lev. 25:10).

Most important for the development of the shofar's role in the liturgy of Rosh Hashanah was the ancient practice of announcing the new moon with the sounding of the shofar. When the first day of Tishri assumed special spiritual significance, the sounding of the shofar on that day also assumed deeper meaning, and it became intimately associated with the central theme of the religious New Year. So much so that in the Bible the day is called "a day when the horn is sounded" (Num. 29:1). The shofar thus became a sacred religious symbol, and its unmusical sounds have become the means of stirring the worshiper's soul during the Rosh Hashanah services.[6]

The shofar ritual was originally located in the early part of the Rosh Hashanah service. It was shifted to the Musaf service after the Bar Kokhba rebellion because the Romans had become very sensitive to the danger of another Jewish uprising. Once when they mistook the shofar's sound for a call to arms, they responded with military force. The sounding of the shofar was therefore transferred to the Musaf service, which comes at a time of day which the Romans did not regard as suitable for starting an insurrection.[7] When the restrictions were finally removed, the ritual of blowing the shofar was not moved back to its original place in the Shaharit service.

As we shall note later in this chapter,* the Musaf contains three prayer units which constitute the core of that *Tefillah*.

* *See pp. 240–42.*

At the completion of each, the shofar was blown. A preliminary sounding of the shofar was also introduced after the reading of the Torah. Since the benediction is pronounced before the first sounding of the shofar, it was natural that the preliminary blowing of the shofar, when the benediction was pronounced, should in time assume the major emphasis of the ritual.

The blowing of the shofar on Rosh Hashanah was carefully regulated by the rabbis of the Talmud. Every detail was fully discussed and meticulously defined. Three musical phrases were prescribed for the shofar service—the tekiah, the teruah, and the shevarim. Only the first two are mentioned in the Bible (Num. 10:5–7), and these were recognized by the rabbis as the essential sounds. But there was a difficulty in regard to the definition of these terms. There was unanimous agreement that the tekiah was a single long blast, but there were differences of opinion as to the nature of the musical phrase represented by the teruah. A third musical phrase, the shevarim, was therefore introduced. It is literally "a broken sound," that is, a tekiah broken into three shorter blasts (R.H. 34a). The shofar sounds, as finally established, consist of three groupings each of which has a long blast (tekiah) at its beginning and at its end. The first grouping has in the middle a broken (shevarim) blast and a stuttering (teruah) blast. The second grouping has in the middle only a broken (shevarim) blast. And the third has in its middle only a stuttering (teruah) blast.

The rabbis not only regulated the ritual of the shofar service but filled it with much spiritual significance. To be sure, the blowing of the shofar was biblically enjoined and was therefore obligatory irrespective of any theological or ethical meaning. But the rabbis always sought instruction in the prescribed rituals.* The shofar therefore became the symbol and assurance of God's mercy and forgiveness. Psalm 47, read before the sounding of the shofar, conveys this message. "God is gone up . . . amidst the sound of the horn" (Ps. 47:6). This, the rabbis say, means that at the sound of the shofar God transfers His mode of judgment from justice to mercy. The concept

* *See pp. 54–55.*

is concretized to mean that when God hears the shofar sounded in the synagogues, He leaves His throne of justice, as it were, and occupies the throne of mercy.*

How does the sound of the shofar cause God to leave His seat of justice? The sound of the shofar brings to God's remembrance the ram that was offered as a sacrifice in place of Isaac on Mount Moriah. This awakens God's mercy on behalf of Isaac's children.

The sound of the shofar also brings to God's remembrance that exalted moment in the annals of Israel when "a very loud blast of the horn" (Exod. 19:16) was heard at Mount Sinai, and the children of Israel entered into an everlasting covenant with God. On that eventful occasion they responded with the memorable words: "All that the Lord has spoken we will faithfully do!" (Exod. 24:7). This remembrance, too, awakens God's attribute of mercy on behalf of the children of Israel.

And the shofar brings to God's remembrance His promise to redeem Israel from the evils and suffering that plague them. A shofar will then be sounded to announce the establishment of God's kingship on earth.[8]

But the most rational interpretation of the shofar ritual was given by Moses Maimonides, according to whom the shofar's sound speaks to the congregation and says:

> *Awake, awake, O sleepers, from your sleep!*
> *O slumberers, arouse ye from your slumbers!*
> *Examine your deeds; return in repentance; and remember your Creator.*
> *Those of you who forget the truth in the follies of the times, and go astray the whole year in vanity and emptiness, which neither profit nor save, look to your souls.*
> *Improve your ways and works.*
> *Abandon, everyone of you, his evil course and the thought that is not good.*[9]

The sounding of the shofar is preceded by the usual benediction: "*Praised art Thou, . . . who sanctified us with His*

* *See p. 397.*

commandments and commanded us to hear the sound of the shofar," and by the Sheheheyanu benediction, which thanks God who "*has kept us in life, and has preserved us, and enabled us to reach this occasion.*" Just one concluding verse is recited after the blowing of the shofar. It is a shout of joy, a release of tension, deriving from a feeling of confidence that God has heard the sound of the shofar and will surely judge the congregation in mercy: "Happy is the people that know the joyful shout; / They walk, O Lord, in the light of Thy countenance" (Ps. 89:16).

As mentioned above, the shofar is also sounded during the reader's repetition of the Musaf *Tefillah* after each of its three special prayer units. But these shofar blasts are only listened to respectfully. The initial ritual has all but exhausted the emotional potential of the worshipers.

The Musaf Service

The Musaf *Tefillah* of Rosh Hashanah is unusual. Instead of seven benedictions, it contains nine. Its three introductory and three concluding benedictions are similar to those of all services. Between these, however, there are three impressive prayer units, each of which concludes with an independent blessing. The three prayer units are based on the following talmudic guidelines attributed to Rabbi Akiba:

> R. Judah said in the name of R. Akiba: . . . the Holy One, blessed be He, said . . . recite before Me on New Year [texts making mention of] kingship, remembrance, and the *shofar*—kingship, so that you may proclaim Me king over you; remembrance, so that your remembrance may rise favourably before Me; and through what? Through the *shofar* [R.H. 16a].

These prayer units conform to a simple organizational pattern. Each unit consists of one or more introductory prayers followed by ten brief biblical selections, mostly of one verse each, and a final supplication that ends with a blessing. The prayer units deal with God's sovereignty (*Malkhuyot*), God's remembrance (*Zikhronot*), and the shofar sounds associated with historic events (*Shofrot*). These three themes correspond to the three names by which Rosh Hashanah is traditionally known: *Yom Ha-Din* (the Day of Judgment),[10] *Yom Ha-Zikkaron* (the Day of Remembrance), and *Yom Teruah* (the Day of Sounding the Shofar). Each of these themes is also related to God's role in the messianic days, when God will be Sovereign over the whole world, when He will remember Israel and redeem the people from their exile, and the shofar will be sounded to announce the coming of the Messiah.

The biblical verses which compose the center of these prayer units follow a specific design.[11] Each group consists of three selections from the Pentateuch, three from the Writings, three from the Prophets, and a concluding one from the Pentateuch.

The first of the three prayer units (*Malkhuyot*) deals with God's universal sovereignty and stresses the optimistic view that God will ultimately establish His kingship over the whole universe. The introductory prayer of this liturgic unit is the well-known *Alenu* prayer, which has won the hearts of the Jewish people and has become the concluding prayer of every service. The *Alenu* prayer is a fitting introduction to the *Malkhuyot* because it proclaims God's sovereignty. Logically enough the second paragraph of the *Alenu* declares Israel's faith that all nations will ultimately accept God's sovereignty and that God's kingship will be established forever. This exalted hope reads, in part:

> We therefore hope in Thee, O Lord our God, that we may speedily behold the glory of Thy might, when Thou wilt remove the abominations from the earth, and the idols will be utterly cut off, when the world will be perfected under the kingship of the Almighty, and all the children of flesh will call upon Thy name, when Thou wilt turn unto Thyself all the wicked of the earth. . . . For the kingship is Thine, and to all eternity Thou wilt reign in glory; as it is written in Thy Torah, "The Lord will reign for ever and ever" [Exod. 15:18]. And it is said, "And the Lord shall be King over all the earth; in that day shall the Lord be One, and His name one" [Zech. 14:9].

The ten biblical selections of this prayer unit stress God's kingship. The concluding prayer is identical with the intermediate benediction of the Shaharit *Tefillah*. Its blessing is the "sanctification of the day": *"Praised art Thou, O Lord, King over all the earth, who hallowest Israel and the Day of Remembrance."*

The second prayer unit (*Zikhronot*) deals with God's role in remembering the deeds of nations and individuals, and in determining their destinies in justice and mercy. God remembers all and judges all in accordance with their deeds. In due time He will remember His covenant with Israel and redeem His people from exile and suffering. Accordingly the concluding blessing reads: *"Praised art Thou, O Lord, who rememberest the covenant."*

The third prayer unit (*Shofrot*) deals with the symbolic role of the shofar. The ram's horn was sounded at Mount Sinai when God revealed Himself to Israel, and it will be sounded at the time of the coming of the Messiah, who will initiate God's kingship on earth. The ten biblical selections of this prayer unit contain references to various occasions when the shofar was sounded and to the grand occasion when the sound of the shofar will usher in the messianic days. The concluding prayer ends with the blessing *"Praised art Thou, O Lord, who in mercy hearkenest to the shofar sounds of Thy people Israel."*

The Musaf *Tefillah*, with its three prayer units, is the longest *Tefillah* in the synagogue liturgy. And the reader's repetition is still longer because of the many piyutim that have been added during the centuries. Many of these piyutim originated during the talmudic and geonic periods. It is impractical to list, let alone discuss, each of these piyutim. Suffice it to say that so many piyutim have accumulated in the Rosh Hashanah liturgy that the morning service usually lasts five to six hours.

The Ten Days of Penitence

The Ten Days of Penitence, as stated above, embrace the period from Rosh Hashanah to Yom Kippur. More specifically, the term refers to the seven intermediate days when acts of penitence are engaged in, though not as intensively as on the High Holy Days proper. By the end of the geonic period the liturgic elements of these penitential days had already been developed. The pious would rise daily before dawn and betake themselves to the synagogue for the penitential prayers of the *Selihot* services. Those who did not participate in the predawn *Selihot* services would take note of the season's penitential nature during the regular services. As noted earlier,* four brief paragraphs were inserted into the *Tefillah* and slight changes were made in the third and eleventh blessings. After the morning *Tefillah* the litany *Avinu Malkenu* was recited, and after the morning and evening services the twenty-seventh psalm was recited, as it had been during the month of Elul.† After the morning service the shofar was sounded to remind the congregation that it is incumbent on every Jew to repent of his misdeeds and to prepare for the great and decisive Day of Atonement.

The theme of repentance, or teshuvah, was reinforced on the Sabbath before Yom Kippur by the prophetic reading which calls on the children of Israel to return to their God. This Sabbath is called *Shabbat Shuvah*, the Sabbath on which the prophetic selection starts with the word *Shuvah* (Return, [O Israel, unto the Lord thy God]). This Haftarah consists of the last nine verses in the Book of Hosea and the last three verses of the Book of Micah. In the opening verse the prophet's message is succinctly stated: "Return, O Israel, unto the Lord thy God; / For thou hast stumbled in thine iniquity" (Hos. 14:2). In the concluding verses the prophet Micah utters words of reassurance: "Who is a God like unto Thee, that pardoneth the iniquity, / And passeth by the transgression of the remnant of His heritage? (Micah 7:18).

The climax of the intermediate days was reached on the day before Yom Kippur. The Minhah service was usually held early in the afternoon, and the confession of sins which is so characteristic of the Yom Kippur liturgy was recited in the *Tefillah*.

* *See pp. 232–33.*
† *See p. 226.*

The nature of this confession will be discussed below * in connection with the Yom Kippur *Tefillah*. After a festive meal in preparation for the fast, everyone went to the synagogue to spend many hours in penitent prayer.

The Day of Atonement

Yom Kippur, the Day of Atonement, is of ancient origin. Its solemn nature is already indicated in the Bible, where a fast is prescribed for the day. This is the only fast enjoined in the Pentateuch:

> The tenth day of this seventh month is the Day of Atonement. It shall be a sacred occasion for you: you shall practice self-denial; . . . you shall do no work throughout that day. For it is a Day of Atonement, on which expiation is made on your behalf before the Lord your God [Lev. 23:27–28].

These biblical injunctions helped make the Yom Kippur services the ones which are the most widely observed. And the spiritual appetite of the Jews on that day has truly been voracious. Not only was an extra service added, that of Neilah (the closing service), but also the regular services have been so expanded that they usually last from early morning to sunset.[12]

The basic liturgy of the day was almost fully developed during the geonic period—so much so that a discussion of the liturgy during the geonic period will seem to describe the Yom Kippur service of our own day.

The Kol Nidre "Prayer"

The Yom Kippur services begin before sunset with a legal declaration known as Kol Nidre (All Vows). This convocation is technically a session of a religious tribunal. The congregation, as it were, appears before a bet din—an ecclesiastical court—for absolution from rashly assumed vows and obligations. How can one appear before God on the holiest day of

* *See pp. 247–50.*

the year when he is spiritually sullied by unfulfilled vows? How can one utter prayers when his utterances have proved themselves to be meaningless? In order to start the Day of Atonement with a clear conscience the congregation gathers in the synagogue before sunset, when a court session can still be convened. In the spirit of the solemn occasion the men put on their prayer shawls.[13] Everyone rises, and the ritual begins.

The language of the Kol Nidre prayer is Aramaic. In former days the scholars used a Hebrew version, while the ordinary people preferred the Aramaic version because it was their vernacular. As might be expected, the popular Aramaic version triumphed and became the established form of the ritual.

The purpose of the Kol Nidre is, as mentioned above, to annul vows that people make recklessly and then, through forgetfulness or negligence, fail to fulfill. These vows, it should be stressed, are limited to obligations "between man and God." In general the rabbis viewed with disfavor all self-imposed vows of abstinence. One of the sages is quoted as having said: "Are not the things prohibited in the Torah enough for you that you add prohibitions of your own?" Yet people frequently make vows to perform certain rites or to abstain from certain pleasures, either as penance for sins or for reasons of special piety. It is for such vows that the Kol Nidre prayer was instituted. Vows and obligations that involve duties "between man and man" are not encompassed in the Kol Nidre ritual. This principle is clearly stated in the Mishnah:

> *Of all your sins you shall be clean before the Lord* (Lev. 16:30)—for transgressions as between man and the Omnipresent the Day of Atonement procures atonement; but for transgressions as between man and his fellow the Day of Atonement does not procure atonement until he has pacified his fellow [Yoma 8:9].

Notwithstanding this pronouncement, some people, through ignorance or malice, have perverted the intent of the Kol Nidre prayer and its high moral motivation, and have attacked the Jewish people and Judaism as perfidious and corrupt.* The Kol Nidre has also encountered opposition from within the

* *See p. 454.*

Jewish community. The Babylonian geonim opposed the Kol Nidre ritual,[14] and in modern times the Reform movement tried to expurgate it from the prayer book. But the Kol Nidre has prevailed against all its opponents.

The bet din, or religious tribunal, consists of the reader and two other men chosen for their piety and learning. Two Torah scrolls are taken from the ark and are held by the two chosen men at the reader's desk. The Kol Nidre is then chanted by the reader in an ancient melody that is solemn and stirring. The tune affects the congregation profoundly and creates the emotional setting for the Yom Kippur services. Three times the Kol Nidre is chanted by the reader, while the congregation stands in reverent attention:

> All vows, obligations, oaths, and anathemas . . . which we may vow, or swear, or pledge, or whereby we may be bound from this Day of Atonement until the next, we do repent. May they be deemed abolished, forgiven, annulled, and void. . . . The vows shall not be reckoned vows; the obligations shall not be obligatory; nor the oaths be oaths.

The reader and the congregation then repeat three times the biblical verse "The whole Israelite community and the stranger residing among them shall be forgiven, for it happened to the entire people through error" (Num. 15:26). Finally the reader pronounces the Sheheheyanu benediction, thanking God "*who has kept us in life, and has preserved us, and enabled us to reach this season.*"

The mood of reverence and awe that pervade the congregation during the Kol Nidre rite is difficult to describe. One may perhaps capture part of that mood by reading the story of the distinguished philosopher Franz Rosenzweig.[15] As a young man, he relates, he had decided to apostatize. But before taking the decisive step of baptism, he participated in the synagogue services of the Day of Atonement. Young Franz Rosenzweig joined the worshipers in a small Orthodox synagogue in Berlin and this religious experience charged his soul with such deep and lasting spiritual insights that he not only changed his mind about baptism, he became the foremost spokesman for Judaism in his generation. What impressed him especially was the Kol Nidre ritual. He found himself in direct communion with God, without any intermediaries, divine or human. During the devotions of the day he experienced God's nearness and the reality of his own membership in the house of Israel. On that fateful Yom Kippur in 1913, Rosenzweig rediscovered his Jewishness and resolved to devote his life to the study and the teaching of Judaism.

It is this type of experience that the congregation shares during the Kol Nidre ritual. It is an experience of deep mystery and holiness, of awe and reverence, of total readiness for the ensuing services.

The Yom Kippur Evening Service

The Maariv service on the evening of Yom Kippur is substantially the same as that of Rosh Hashanah, except that the blessing of the essential benediction in the *Tefillah* is unusually long. It reads:

> *Praised art Thou, O Lord, Thou King, who pardonest and forgivest our iniquities and the iniquities of Thy people, the house of Israel, who makest our trespasses to pass away year by year, King over all the earth, who sanctifiest Israel and the Day of Atonement.*

In the *Tefillah* there are also two prayer units, which are essential parts of every service of the Day of Atonement. One is a confession of sins and the other a group of penitential supplications known as *Selihot*.

The Confession of Sins

Many Westerners view confession of moral failure as an act of humiliation. Not so in the Jewish tradition. Confession of sins is the first step on the road to atonement. Divine forgiveness, which reconciles the worshiper with God, must be preceded by a cleansing of the soul. Confession of sins also awakens one's heart to earnest prayer. It enables one to stand before

God and plead for His mercy. The rabbis therefore prescribed the inclusion of the confession in each of the five Yom Kippur services (Yoma 87b). To be sure, the frequent repetition of the confession results in a dwindling of effectiveness. By the third or fourth repetition the confession tends to become meaningless. In modern times satiety sets in even sooner. Yet the rabbis could not conceive of any Yom Kippur service without a confession of sins.

Confession of sins as a means of atonement did not originate with the rabbis. It goes back to very ancient times. The classic biblical example is King David's humble admission of his guilt. He confessed to the prophet Nathan and said: "I have sinned against the Lord." And Nathan's response is equally memorable: "The Lord also hath put away thy sin; thou shalt not die" (2 Sam. 12:13).

But a confession of sins does not automatically beget absolution. Confession is not a magic ritual. It must be followed by teshuvah, a *return* from one's errant ways. A firm resolution to amend one's way of life is essential if one's confession is to lead to forgiveness.

The oldest formula of the confession seems to have been the simple statement "I have done wrong, I have transgressed, and have sinned." These words were used by the *Kohen Gadol* in his confession on the Day of Atonement (Yoma 3:8). The Yom Kippur confession of sins remained in a fluid state for a long time. The Talmud quotes the confessions that some of the sages used to recite on the Day of Atonement. Thus Rabbi Hamnuna formulated his confession in these humble words:

> My God, before I was formed, I was of no worth, and now that I have been formed, it is as if I had not been formed. I am dust in my life, how much more in my death. Behold I am before Thee like a vessel full of shame and reproach. May it be Thy will that I sin no more, and what I have sinned wipe away in Thy mercy, but not through suffering [Yoma 87b].

Rav's confession is quoted as follows:

> Thou knowest the secrets of eternity [and the most hidden mysteries of all living. Thou searchest the

> innermost recesses, and triest the reins and the heart. Naught is concealed from Thee, or hidden from Thine eyes. May it then be Thy will, O Lord our God and God of our fathers, to forgive us all our iniquities and to grant us remission for all our transgressions]. [Yoma 87b].

In the geonic period, when the confession of sins, or *Vidui*, was formalized, the private confessions of Rabbi Hamnuna and Rav were incorporated into it, and they are still part of the liturgy.

The heart of the confession of sins consists of a litany with a long list of sins, generally known as the *Al Het* (For the sin), or the long confession. As he recites each of the sins the worshiper beats his breast as a symbol of contrition. As we have said, the confession is in the plural, or corporate in nature. The underlying principle is that although no one in the congregation is guilty of all those sins, every Jew is responsible, at least in part, for the sins of every other Jew. No one sins in a social vacuum; all of society is partly responsible for the transgressions of the individual.

The sins in the long confession are not arranged in a logical sequence. Their order is determined by a double alphabetical acrostic which yields forty-four transgressions, a number which happens to coincide with the number of lines in the *Avinu Malkenu* litany.* More significant is the fact that the sins listed in the long confession are all ethical in character, with the sins of the tongue especially prominent.[16] The nature of this confession can be judged from the initial two couplets:

> For the sin *which we have committed before Thee*
> *under compulsion, or of our own will;*
> And for the sin *which we have committed before Thee*
> *in hardening of the heart;*
> For the sin *which we have committed before Thee*
> *out of ignorance;*
> And for the sin *which we have committed before Thee*
> *with utterance of the lips; . . .*
>
> *For all these, O God of forgiveness, forgive us, pardon*
> *us, grant us remission.*

* *See pp. 234–35.*

The *Al Het* is preceded by a "short confession," also an alphabetical acrostic, known by its initial word *Ashamnu* (We have trespassed). This confession was discussed above in connection with the midnight *Selihot* service.* Both the *Al Het* and the *Ashamnu* were composed during the geonic period and are to this day an important part of the Yom Kippur liturgy.

THE *Selihot* OF THE YOM KIPPUR SERVICES

The second prayer unit that distinguishes the evening service of Yom Kippur is that of the *Selihot*, or penitential prayers. The basic organizational pattern of this prayer unit is like that of the midnight *Selihot* service. It begins with a group of interlocked biblical verses dealing with God's infinite glory and His merciful loving-kindness. These verses lead up to the climax of the *Selihot* prayers, the Thirteen Divine Attributes of mercy. Then comes the confession of sins, including both the *Ashamnu* and the *Al Het*. Finally there are several litanies similar to those quoted above.† In ancient days, when prayer was recited from memory, these litanies were popular because they are arranged in alphabetical sequences which make them easy to memorize. Everybody could easily follow the reader and respond with the simple refrains. These responses were, in all probability, the loudest and most enthusiastic elements of the service.

The *Selihot* prayer unit was later expanded by the interpolation of additional penitential piyutim, some of which date back to the geonic period. One of these is the introductory piyut, known by its initial word as *Ya'aleh* (Let [our prayers] ascend). Despite its intricate structure, which includes an alphabetical acrostic as well as rhymes and refrains, this piyut is a touching plea for divine acceptance of the congregation's beseechments during the Day of Atonement. Among the other piyutim interwoven in the *Selihot* of the evening service is the favorite piyut *Ki Hineh Ka-Homer* (Lo! as the clay):

Lo! as the potter mouldeth plastic clay
To forms his varying fancy doth display;
So in Thy hand, O God of love, are we:
Thy bond regard, let sin be veil'd from Thee.[17]

* *See pp. 230–31.*
† *See p. 227.*

In the succeeding stanzas the metaphor of the potter is replaced by that of the mason, the smith, the seaman, the embroiderer, and the smelter. Each stanza concludes with the refrain imploring God to regard His covenant with Israel rather than Israel's transgressions.

Since the Day of Atonement is the last of the penitential days, as well as the climax, the liturgy includes all the special prayers of the Ten Days of Penitence. The litany *Avinu Malkenu* is recited after the *Selihot*, and the service concludes, quite appropriately, with the twenty-seventh psalm:

> *Though a host should encamp against me,*
> *My heart shall not fear;*
> *Though war should rise up against me,*
> *Even then will I be confident* [*Ps.* 27:3].

The Shaharit and Musaf Services

The Yom Kippur liturgy consists of five services. The first is the evening Maariv service already described. Of the other four services, the morning (Shaharit), the additional service (Musaf), and the afternoon service (Minhah) correspond to the Sabbath and festival services which are similarly named. In addition to these, there is a closing service (Neilah), a service not found in the liturgy of any other festival.

The basic pattern of all these services corresponds to the general structure of the festival services.* Thus the morning service consists of the Early Morning Benedictions, the Verses of Praise, the *Shema* with its benedictions, the *Tefillah*, the readings from the Scriptures, and the Musaf *Tefillah*. Within this general pattern, however, there are so many special prayers that the Yom Kippur services stand out as the most unusual services of the synagogue.

A distinctive characteristic of the Yom Kippur liturgy is to be found in the many piyutim woven into the benedictions of the *Shema* and into the benedictions of the reader's *Tefillah*. So full of interpolations is the reader's *Tefillah*, in both the Shaharit and the Musaf services, that the basic seven benedictions are almost lost in the superabundance of piyutim.† In ad-

* *See pp. 208 ff.*
† *See pp. 168 ff.*

dition to the many piyutim there are a number of large prayer units. In the Shaharit *Tefillah* we have the *Selihot*[18] and the confession of sins. These have already been discussed in connection with the Yom Kippur evening service. In the Musaf *Tefillah* we have the *Avodah*, or Temple service, which is one of the central components of the Yom Kippur liturgy.

The *Avodah*

The Yom Kippur service in the Jerusalem Temple was the most impressive ritual of the sanctuary. For those present in the Temple court it must have been the most awesome of all their religious experiences. The Mishnah Yoma has preserved a detailed description of the intricate rites of the day. The Mishnah begins with an account of the *Kohen Gadol*'s preparation for the ritual:

> Seven days before the Day of Atonement the *Kohen Gadol* was removed from his house to the Cell of Counsellors [in the Temple] and another *Kohen* was prepared to take his place in case anything happened to him [the *Kohen Gadol*] that would unfit him [for the service]. . . . [The elders] read before him [throughout the seven days] out of the order of the day. They said to him: Sir *Kohen Gadol*, read you yourself with your own mouth, perchance you have forgotten or perchance you have never learned [Yoma 1:1,3].

The Mishnah continues in this spirit and relates in detail how the ritual was conducted from its beginning to its joyful conclusion.

In the synagogue liturgy there is a long piyut known as the *Avodah*. In the liturgy of the German and East European Jewish communities this piyut is known by its initial words: *Amitz Ko'ah* (Thou art mighty). This piyut was composed by Rabbi Meshullam ben Kalonymus, who lived in Italy in the tenth century. The piyut is quite complicated in structure, containing a fourfold alphabetical acrostic, as well as the poet's name in an acrostic signature.[19] The *Avodah* follows the pattern established by earlier poets. Rabbi Meshullam ben Kalonymus starts with a brief account of the creation and quickly leads up to Aaron, the first *Kohen Gadol.* Then follows the priestly service in the Jerusalem Temple, in which the poet describes the *Kohen Gadol*'s preparation for the great day, his ablutions before and during the service, and his special garments during the ritual. The *Avodah* poem then tells how the *Kohen Gadol* made confession for himself, for his tribe, and for the house of Israel. In each confession the *Kohen Gadol* pronounced the Tetragrammaton, which no other Jew ever utters—even the *Kohen Gadol* uttered it only on this awesome occasion:

> And when the Kohanim and the people that stood in the court heard the glorious and awful name pronounced out of the mouth of the *Kohen Gadol*, in holiness and in purity, they knelt and prostrated themselves and made acknowledgment, falling on their faces and saying: Praised be His name whose glorious kingdom is for ever and ever.

Three times the people in the Temple court heard the Tetragrammaton pronounced by the *Kohen Gadol*, and three times they kneeled and prostrated themselves.

In the synagogue the Tetragrammaton is not pronounced. But when the reader utters the words "they knelt and prostrated themselves" everyone kneels and prostrates himself as if he has heard the Tetragrammaton pronounced by the *Kohen Gadol.* Three times the congregation kneels and prostrates itself, and each time it repeats the formula, "Praised be His name whose glorious kingdom is for ever and ever."

Kneeling and prostration are no longer generally practiced in synogague worship. Hence the congregation's "falling on their faces" during the *Avodah* is especially impressive, one of the high points of the day's worship. Unfortunately, in many American synagogues the reader alone kneels and prostrates himself. In these synagogues the congregations have become mere spectators.

On the Day of Atonement the *Kohen Gadol* also entered the Holy of Holies, a chamber which no one ever entered except the *Kohen Gadol* during this service. One can imagine the

Kohen Gadol's frame of mind when he entered the Holy of Holies: his heart was filled with awe and trepidation. And when he emerged in peace, his profound sense of relief expressed itself in prayer and festivity. The *Avodah* describes his sense of elation.

> The *Kohen Gadol* also made a festive day for all his friends, after he had entered the holy place in peace, and had come forth in perfect peace. And thus was the prayer of the *Kohen Gadol* upon the Day of Atonement when he came out of the Holy of Holies in perfect peace: May it be Thy will, O Lord our God and God of our fathers, that this year that hath now arrived be unto us and unto all Thy people, the house of Israel, a year of plenteous store; a year of blessings; . . . a year in which Thou wilt bless our going out and our coming in; . . . a year of peace and tranquility; . . . a year in which Thy people, the house of Israel, may not be in need of support, one from the other, nor from another people, in that Thou wilt set a blessing upon the work of their hands.

The *Avodah* concludes with a medieval piyut: "Happy the eye that saw all this; our soul grieves at the mere mention of it."

Why, it will be asked, did the rabbis see fit to include this detailed description of the Temple service in the synagogue liturgy? The most obvious answer is the rabbinic principle that the sacrificial rites have not been rescinded, only suspended because of the destruction of the Temple. During this emergency situation one can perform his Temple duties by reading about them, since the utterance of one's lips is equivalent to actual performance of the rites.* In addition, the rabbis wanted to keep alive the memory of the land of Israel and the longing for its restoration. They were also determined to maintain the Jewish sense of historic continuity. Reciting the *Avodah* and sharing with their ancestors the experience of kneeling and prostrating themselves in the court of the Temple have been effective means of deepening the sense of interdependence between the Jewish present and the Jewish past.

* *See pp. 81–83.*

The Scriptural Readings

The scriptural readings on Yom Kippur are distinctive and unusual because of their contents and their historic backgrounds.

The Mishnah Yoma, which deals with the observance of the Day of Atonement during the Second Commonwealth, describes one of the rituals performed after the completion of the offerings of the day:

> The *Kohen Gadol* [then] came to read. . . . The synagogue attendant would take a scroll of the Torah and give it to the head of the synagogue, and the head of the synagogue gave it to the [*Kohen Gadol*'s] assistant, and the assistant gave it to the *Kohen Gadol*, and the *Kohen Gadol* stands . . . and reads [the section beginning] "After the death" . . . [Yoma 7:1].

The biblical selection that the *Kohen Gadol* read (Lev. 16) is the Torah portion that is read in the synagogue on Yom Kippur.

The Mishnah's account does not imply that the Torah reading on Yom Kippur was determined by the Temple Kohanim. Reading from the Torah was not a part of the Temple ritual. What the Mishnah tells us is that two thousand years ago this Torah portion was already part of the Yom Kippur synagogue liturgy. At the prayer service held in the Temple precincts,* the custom had developed of honoring the *Kohen Gadol* by having him read the scriptural selection. In other places of worship—and there were many of them in Jerusalem—any competent person could read the Torah portion.

The choice of this selection from Leviticus is altogether fitting: it deals with the Temple ritual on Yom Kippur and the *Kohen Gadol*'s central role in it. The description of the ritual in the Mishnah Yoma and in the *Avodah* piyut of the Musaf service are only elaborations of this biblical chapter. In addition to describing the sacrificial offerings, the *Kohen Gadol*'s confessions, and his special garments, this chapter also contains general instructions for the observance of the day.

* *See pp.* 72–76.

In the afternoon, at the start of the Minhah service, there is a second reading from the Torah, followed by a reading from the Prophets. The third person called to the Torah reads the Haftarah. The Torah selection is unusual—it deals with neither the Day of Atonement nor any of its rituals. Its theme is, of all things, sexual perversion and incestuous marriages, both of which the Bible calls "abominations." It is because of such moral decay that the land spewed out the peoples who formerly inhabited it, and the Bible warns that a similar fate awaits the Jews if they sink morally to these low levels.

Why is this biblical selection read on Yom Kippur? The reason usually given is that the purity of a people's family life is the foundation of its moral and spiritual well-being. The rabbis felt that this important teaching of Judaism should be impressed on the people's consciousness during the most important synagogue service of the year.

There is also a social factor that has given this Torah reading special relevance. The Mishnah tells us that during the days of the Second Temple, the *Kohen Gadol* was not the only one who "made a festive day for all his friends." After the completion of the Yom Kippur services, the youths and maidens of Jerusalem assembled in the vineyards outside the city for a joyous celebration, so the mishnaic account goes:

> Rabbi Simeon ben Gamaliel said: There never were in Israel greater days of joy than the fifteenth of Ab and the Day of Atonement. On these days the daughters of Jerusalem used to walk out in white garments which they borrowed in order not to put to shame any one who had none. . . . The daughters of Jerusalem came out and danced in the vineyards, exclaiming at the same time: "Young man, lift up thine eyes and see what thou choosest for thyself. Do not set thine eyes on beauty, but set thine eyes on [good] family." Grace is deceitful, and beauty is vain; but a woman that feareth the Lord, she shall be praised. (Prov. 31:30) [Ta'an. 4:8].[20]

From this it is clear that the afternoon of the Day of Atonement was an official courting season in Jerusalem; hence the reading of the biblical selection that deals with the "abominations" of incestuous marriages and sexual perversions was timely.

Although the courting festivities on the afternoon of Yom Kippur were discontinued after the Roman conquest of Judea, the crucial importance of the family as the cornerstone of a wholesome society renders this reading still relevant.

The Readings from the Prophets

The selections from the Prophets read on Yom Kippur stand out for their lofty moral teachings. The morning Haftarah is from Isaiah (57:14–58:14). The prophet proclaims the principle that ritual is only a means to the achievement of the good life. The following verses from the Haftarah speak more eloquently than all the commentaries:

> *Is such the fast that I have chosen?*
> *The day for a man to afflict his soul?*
> *Is it to bow down his head as a bulrush,*
> *And to spread sackcloth and ashes under him? . . .*
> *Is not this the fast that I have chosen?*
> *To loose the fetters of wickedness,*
> *To undo the bands of the yoke,*
> *And to let the oppressed go free,*
> *And that ye break every yoke?*
> *Is it not to deal thy bread to the hungry,*
> *And that thou bring the poor that are cast out to thy house?*
> *When thou seest the naked, that thou cover him,*
> *And that thou hide not thyself from thine own flesh?*
> [*Isa. 58:5–7*].

The Haftarah for the afternoon is the most unusual of prophetic readings in the synagogue. It consists of the Book of Jonah, a book frequently associated by the uninformed with a fish story and glibly dismissed as an ancient fable. Yet many scholars consider the Book of Jonah as the peak of prophetic moral instruction. Its multiple message contains some of the most important teachings of Judaism. Among these are the doctrines that:

1. The God of Israel is the God of all nations
2. Every human being, irrespective of race or nationality, is precious in the sight of God
3. God is merciful and forgiving, waiting for the sinner to turn from his ways
4. Every human being has the potentiality of abandoning his evil ways and returning to God
5. It is the duty of everyone to assume moral responsibility

An adequate discussion of the Book of Jonah would involve not only the retelling of the story, but also an analysis of the text in order to bring out the teachings listed above, as well as other moral lessons. Although this is impossible within the confines of this book, it is hoped that readers will take the time to peruse the few pages in the Bible constituting the Book of Jonah and draw their own conclusions. The book's relevance to the message of the Day of Atonement is obvious. The repentance of the people of Nineveh and God's forgiveness of their sins are the essential message of Yom Kippur.[21]

The Afternoon and the Closing Services

The essence of each of the last two services of the Day of Atonement is its *Tefillah*. The Minhah service consists only of the above-mentioned scriptural readings and the *Tefillah*. The Ashre (Psalm 145) and the *Uva Le-Zion Go'el* prayers * which introduce the Sabbath and festival Minhah service are omitted. So is the *Avinu Malkenu* which is recited after the Minhah *Tefillah* during the Ten Days of Penitence. These, however, are not real omissions; as we shall see, they have simply been transferred to the Neilah service. The Minhah *Tefillah* is the same as that of the morning service, except for the piyutim in the reader's repetition.

The liturgy of the Neilah service is quite exceptional. Its uniqueness derives from the concept that the gates of prayer close at the end of the Day of Atonement. This poetic image has endowed the Neilah service with a sense of urgency. The

* *See pp. 193–94.*

Prayer Book, Italy, 1441, Schocken Library, Jerusalem. PHOTO: ALFRED BERNHEIM

congregation feels that now is the last chance to pour out one's heart before the divine throne of mercy. To be sure, Judaism teaches that the gates of prayer are always open to the contrite heart and that God's mercy is forever available to the penitent. Nonetheless, the Yom Kippur service reaches a tense climax during the closing service. Even those who have retired from the synagogue because of weakness induced by the fast usually return to participate in the Neilah service. A tangible feeling of mysticism and holiness envelops the congregation. The sun is setting, the shadows are lengthening, and the worshipers make their supreme effort to reach the divine throne and to move the merciful One to grant atonement to His penitent children.

The Neilah service is opened with the Ashre psalm (145) and the *Uva Le-Zion Go'el* prayer. In the *Tefillah* there is a slight but significant emendation in the repeated prayers to be "inscribed in the book of life." * These prayers now read: "*Seal* us in the book of life" and "*Seal* all the children of Thy covenant for a happy life." At Neilah time, the Ten Days of Penitence come to an end and the final seal is placed on the divine decree. The ark is kept open throughout the reader's repetition of the *Tefillah*, symbolizing the open gates of prayer, and the piyutim reiterate the theme of "the closing gates":

Open the gate for us,
Yea, even at the closing of the gate,
For the day is nearly past;
The day is passing thus;
The sun is low, the day is growing late:
O let us come into Thy gates at last.

After the reader's repetition of the *Tefillah*, the congregation's devotions become most ardent and reach their climax. The litany *Avinu Malkenu* is recited for the last time; then the reader and congregation join in the recitation of three biblical sentences whereby they rededicate themselves to the essential theological doctrines of Judaism. The first is a loud, clear affirmation of faith: "Hear, O Israel, the Lord our God, the Lord is One." Although these words are repeatedly recited morning and evening throughout the year, they ring out pow-

* *See pp. 232–33.*

erfully on this occasion and are charged with stirring associations. These words have been the last words of countless martyrs who died for the sanctification of God's name and are the last words that a Jew utters on his deathbed when he is preparing to meet his Creator. This vigorous statement of faith is followed by its traditional sequel: "Praised be His name whose glorious kingdom is for ever and ever." Three times it is repeated by reader and congregation. Finally, the climactic declaration is made: "The Lord, He is God." This affirmation of the one and only God and the implied denial of all idolatry is repeated seven times. This affirmation was made by the Israelites at the time of Elijah's challenge to the priests of Baal. After Elijah's triumph, the people exclaimed: "The Lord, He is God; the Lord, He is God" (1 Kings 18:39). This declaration is followed by a long blast of the shofar, and the worship of the most sacred day of the year is at an end. The long blast of the shofar symbolizes the forgiveness that God has surely granted. This certainty fills the hearts of the worshipers with renewed hope and faith.

The congregation lingers in the synagogue for a few additional minutes to participate in the brief weekday Maariv service and to exchange hearty greetings. But this lasts only a few moments, and the synagogue is soon emptied of its worshipers. Everyone is on his way home to break the fast. Immediately after satisfying their hunger, the pious start to build their sukkot for the Feast of Tabernacles, which is only a few days off.

10
THE LITURGY OF THE MINOR FESTIVALS AND FAST DAYS

The rhythm of the Jewish year accentuates a number of minor festivals and fast days. These have been observed throughout the centuries but not as rigorously as the Sabbath, the major festivals, and the holy days. Among these minor festivals are the monthly observance of Rosh Hodesh, or the New Moon, and the joyous celebrations of Hanukah and Purim. Among the fast days other than the Day of Atonement are the Ninth of Av and its three subsidiary fast days, the Tenth of Tevet, the Seventeenth of Tammuz, and the Fast of Gedaliah. Other fast days still observed in limited circles are the Fast of Esther and the Fast of the Firstborn.

The synagogue liturgy gives due recognition to these lesser stars in the galaxy of religious and national observances. Scholars, saints, and poets created appropriate prayers for each occasion. Foremost among the liturgic authors were, as always, the rabbis of the Talmud. Their prayers have been sifted, expanded, and enriched during the subsequent centuries. By the end of the geonic period most of the prayers for the minor festivals and fast days had already attained their classic form and were fully established as the tradition of the synagogue.

The Semifestival of the New Moon

In terms of frequency of observance and deep historic roots the monthly celebration of Rosh Hodesh (the New Moon) takes precedence over all the semifestivals. The Jewish month, as noted earlier,* is based on the lunar cycle. The new month begins when the crescent of the new moon is sighted. In ancient times Rosh Hodesh was regarded as an important holiday and observed with great seriousness. Work was suspended, special sacrifices were offered in the Temple, the shofar was blown, and feasting was the order of the day. The prophet Isaiah, in his vigorous protest against the lack of congruity between sacrificial offerings and ethical living, coupled the New Moon with the Sabbath: "New moon and Sabbath, the holding of convocations— / I cannot endure iniquity along with solemn assembly" (Isa. 1:13).

When the Temple was destroyed and the sacrificial ritual of the New Moon day was no longer possible, the importance of the Rosh Hodesh observance deteriorated. But it continued to

* *See pp. 205–206.*

play a key role in the religious life of the Jews, because the New Moon established the dates on which the festivals were to be observed. This was of crucial importance, because a dispute based on the calendar could easily split a religious community into bitterly contending sects. The person who could fix the day of the New Moon was ipso facto a central pillar of authority throughout the Jewish Diaspora. When the Temple was in existence this power was lodged with the head of the Sanhedrin.

The procedure of fixing the date of the New Moon is graphically recorded in the Mishnah (R.H. 2:5–7). On the thirtieth of each month the head of the court would examine the witnesses who claimed to have seen the crescent of the new moon. When he was satisfied with the evidence, he would call out: "The New Moon is consecrated," and the people assembled in the Temple court would respond: "It is consecrated; it is consecrated." The shofar was blown, and the festivities, including the Temple rites, would begin. If no witnesses appeared, the New Moon day was celebrated on the following day.

After the destruction of the Temple the power to declare the New Moon day was transferred to the head of the court at Yavneh. When leadership in Jewry passed from the patriarch in Palestine to the geonim in Babylonia, the power to determine the day of the New Moon and the intercalation of an extra month in a leap year remained in the hands of the patriarch; this maintained the prestige of the patriarch and his court. However, when the dissemination of information regarding the New Moon and the leap year was prohibited by the Christian authorities in Palestine, the patriarch, Hillel II, was faced with the sad choice of either holding on to the sole prerogative of authority left to his court or saving Judaism from the threat of chaos arising from uncertainty about the calendar. He decided to sacrifice his personal interest. In the year 359, Hillel II published a calendar based on astronomical calculations, thus freeing Jewish communities from reliance on the head of the Palestinian high court. No longer was the fixing of the New Moon dependent on eyewitnesses who saw the crescent of the new moon. Hillel II undermined his own authority and that of the Palestinian court, but he achieved his aim of maintaining the unity of the scattered Jewish people.

Although the importance of Rosh Hodesh as a religious festival declined and it retained only the shadow of its former prominence, its liturgy has remained impressive and testifies to its former glory.

The Liturgy of Rosh Hodesh

The Rosh Hodesh service contains three liturgic elements, which raise it to the level of the intermediate days of the major festivals. In the *Tefillah* of each service there is the *Ya'aleh Ve-Yavo* prayer.* More significant is the recitation of the Half Hallel † after the *Tefillah* of the morning service. The third special liturgic element is a Musaf *Tefillah*. The Musaf consists of the usual seven benedictions, the central one dealing with the Temple offerings of the New Moon day. When Rosh Hodesh falls on a Sabbath, its Musaf replaces that of the Sabbath, and the prayer *Tikanta Shabbat* ‡ is replaced by the Rosh Hodesh prayer *Attah Yatzarta* (Thou didst form [Thy world from of old]). The Sabbath on which Rosh Hodesh falls is also distinguished by a special Haftarah, the last chapter of Isaiah, in which the prophet pictures the bright future of Israel's redemption:

> *And it shall come to pass,*
> *That from one new moon to another,*
> *And from one sabbath to another,*
> *Shall all flesh come to worship before Me,*
> *Saith the Lord [Isa. 66:23]* [1]

Blessing the New Month

Actually, the liturgy of the New Moon involves three distinct observances. In addition to marking the New Moon day, as described above, there is also a preliminary service known as Blessing the New Month and a supplementary service known as *Kiddush Levanah*, the Consecration of the Moon. The origin of the ritual of Blessing the New Month goes back to the fourth century, when the calendar was made public by Hillel II.

* *See pp. 209–10.*
† *See pp. 210–11.*
‡ *See pp. 191–92.*

Actually, Blessing the New Month is only an announcement, for there is no special benediction in this service. Once astronomical calculations became the basis for fixing the date of the New Moon, it became possible to alert the people to the approaching New Moon day. The appropriate place and time for such a public reminder was obviously during the Sabbath service before the New Moon day. During the eighth century, however, the Jewish sectarians known as the Karaites * denied the validity of all rabbinic enactments and insisted on the strict and literal adherence to the biblical legislation. They decried the new rabbinic procedure of determining the New Moon day by calculation and loudly proclaimed their compliance with the old system. The act of announcing the New Moon on the Sabbath therefore became a demonstrative refutation of the Karaites. It publicly proclaimed in advance the exact moment of the appearance of the new moon. To emphasize the validity of the new system, the rabbis added to the announcement of the New Moon special prayers for the coming month. This made the advance announcement and the calculations upon which it was based a religious act, a part of the synagogue service. The resulting prayer unit had for its central theme the hope of Israel's redemption. The monthly reappearance of the moon became the symbol of Israel's restoration. As the moon emerges from its total eclipse into brightness, so will Israel be redeemed from its exile and brought back to the land of its fathers. The "blessing" of the new month became increasingly popular with the worshipers and in time came to be regarded as especially efficacious.

Blessing the New Month was originally concise. It began with a brief introductory prayer and finished with an equally brief prayer, neither of which contained a blessing in the technical sense.† The following was the entire Blessing the New Month:

The Introductory Prayer

He who wrought miracles for our fathers, and redeemed them from slavery to freedom, may He speedily redeem us, and gather our exiles from the four

* *See p. 130.*
† *See pp. 91 ff.*

corners of the earth, even all Israel, united in fellowship; and say ye, Amen.

The Announcement of the New Moon

The New Moon of —— will be on ——. May it come to us and to all Israel for good.

The Concluding Prayer

May the Holy One, blessed be He, renew it unto us and unto all His people, the house of Israel, for life and peace, for gladness and joy, for salvation and consolation; and let us say, Amen.

At a much later time, probably as late as the eighteenth century, a private prayer, composed by Rav in the third century for recitation after the *Tefillah*,[2] was added. The words "to renew unto us this coming month for good and for blessing" were interpolated so as to relate it to the occasion.

THE CONSECRATION OF THE MOON

Blessing the New Month is basically an announcement; the Consecration of the Moon, or *Kiddush Levanah*, is a real service with a regular benediction. This service is in accord with rabbinic tradition: whenever one witnesses an important or stirring natural phenomenon, he is obliged to pronounce a benediction.* It is the duty of a religious Jew to offer praise and thanksgiving to the Creator each time he becomes aware of the miracle of creation. The appearance of the new moon with its blessings of light and hope obviously calls for a benediction.

The name of this service, it will be noted, does not speak of the new moon, because the service is held several days after the appearance of the new crescent. The official ruling is that the *Kiddush Levanah* should be held at least three days after the new moon and not later than the fifteenth day of the month. Prior to the third day the moon does not provide enough light to enable the people to read their prayers by its light. After the fifteenth day the moon is already waning. One cannot greet it as a new phenomenon.

* *See pp. 91–92.*

The service of *Kiddush Levanah* has a mystic, haunting air about it. On a clear moonlit weekday evening, immediately after the Maariv service, the congregation assembles in front of the synagogue and proceeds with the service. There is no reader. Yet it is a public service, because a quorum of ten men is required. The service opens with a benediction of talmudic origin, based in part on a verse from Psalms: "By the word of the Lord were the heavens made; / And all the host of them by the breath of His mouth" (Ps. 33:6). The benediction as quoted in the Talmud reads:

> Praised [art Thou, O Lord our God, King of the universe] who created the Heavens with His word, and all their host with the breath of His mouth. He appointed unto them fixed laws and times, that they should not change their ordinance. . . . The moon He ordered that she should renew herself as a crown of beauty for those whom He sustains from the womb [i.e., the children of Israel], and who will, like it, be renewed in the future. . . . Blessed [Praised] art Thou, O Lord, who renewest the moons [San. 42a].

The benediction is followed by two short formulas addressed to the moon. The first declares: "Blessed be thy Creator." This greeting is repeated in four different forms. The second formula is a survival from ancient days, when dancing was part of the New Moon celebration. The formula reads: "Even as I dance before you and I cannot touch you, so shall all my foes be unable to touch me for evil." The people then greet each other with the traditional shalom aleichem (peace be with you). In the geonic period this was the end of the service.

Of the three services connected with the new moon, Blessing the New Month is best known because it is part of a Sabbath service, when many people are in attendance. The observance of the actual New Moon day is known only to a few, because it usually falls on a weekday, when relatively few people attend the synagogue services. The *Kiddush Levanah* is now hardly known at all. Only few congregations still gather outside their synagogues to consecrate the moon. Most modern prayer books do not even include the prayers for this service.

In the geonic period, however, all the services connected with the new moon were rendered with equal seriousness. They were all regarded as part of the rabbinic legislation which was accepted as part of God's revelation at Sinai.

The Feasts of Hanukah and Purim

If the services for the new moon, despite the preliminary blessing and the supplementary consecration, have waned considerably, the minor festivals of Hanukah (the Feast of Lights) and Purim (the Feast of Lots) have waxed greatly in their significance. To be sure, they have remained in the category of minor festivals; people are not required to suspend their normal activities, nor does the liturgy provide for a Musaf (additional) service. But their striking relevance to Jewish experience throughout the centuries has raised these minor festivals to positions of importance in the religious calendar of the Jewish year.

Hanukah marks the deliverance of the Jewish people from the Syrian Greeks, who sought to impose on them the paganism of the Hellenistic world. The historic events which are the basis of the Hanukah festival go back to the second century B.C.E., when Antiochus IV, king of Syria, proscribed the observance of Jewish religious practices: the Temple ritual, the teaching of the Torah, the observance of the Sabbath, and the circumcision of children. The Temple was converted into a pagan shrine. This mortal blow at the very survival of Judaism was met by an uprising, led by the Hasmonean family under the daring leadership of Judah Maccabeus. When the Syrians were defeated in the year 165 B.C.E. and the Jerusalem Temple was cleansed and rededicated to the Jewish traditional worship, a grand celebration was held. These festivities then became an annual event known as the Feast of Hanukah, in commemoration of the rededication of the Temple to the service of God. Since the festival is observed by the kindling of lights, it has also been known as the Feast of Lights. The festival lasts eight days, starting on the twenty-fifth day of the month of Kislev, which corresponds approximately to the month of December. Vivid accounts of the persecutions, the battles, and the miraculous salvation have been preserved for us in the first, second, and third Books of the Maccabees, which are part of the Apocrypha, and in the Scroll of the Hasmoneans, a seventh century composition that was used in some Italian synagogues as part of the festival liturgy. Some of these accounts are historic, others are apocryphal; but all of them are dramatic and exciting.[3]

Purim, the older of the two festivals, commemorates the deliverance of the Persian Jews from the slaughter which Haman had plotted against them. The story is eloquently told in the biblical Book of Esther, which is read at the evening and morning services of the festival. The name Purim, we are told in the Book of Esther, is derived from the word for lots (*purim*), which Haman had cast for determining the day of the slaughter. But Haman's plans were foiled by Mordecai and Queen Esther. Thus the days of doom were "turned . . . from sorrow to gladness, and from mourning into a good day," and they became "days of feasting and gladness, and of sending portions one to another, and gifts to the poor" (Esther 9:22). The designated day of celebration was set for the fourteenth of Adar, which corresponds approximately to March. However, the Jews of Shushan, the capital, were preoccupied for an additional day with their struggle against those who sought to destroy them and could not celebrate till the fifteenth of Adar. Since Shushan was a fortified city, all cities that were fortified in those ancient days celebrate the Feast of Lots a day later. Obviously there is no record of any American city's having been walled twenty-five centuries ago, so Purim is observed everywhere in America on the fourteenth of Adar. But there are some cities in the Old World where Purim is celebrated on the fifteenth of Adar—Jerusalem is one.

The similarities between Hanukah and Purim have often been noted. Hanukah stresses the danger of extinction of the Jewish people through the persecution of Judaism, while Purim underscores the danger of physical annihilation. In modern times Hanukah reminds the Jew of the danger that faces Russian Jewry because of the religious persecutions by the Communists, while Purim reminds the Jew of the Nazi holocaust, which aimed at the annihilation of the Jewish people by physical destruction. In their liturgy, however, the two festivals are quite dissimilar. Purim is observed for only one day, while Hanukah is observed for eight days. Purim is marked by merriment and levity both in the synagogue and in home observances, Hanukah by relative sobriety and earnestness. To be sure, Hanukah is a joyous festival, but its observance is not boisterous, as is that of Purim. Its prayers and rituals are joyous but not hilarious.

The Liturgy of the Feast of Lights

The liturgy of Hanukah is not the outcome of a long historic development. It derived its momentum from the stirring religio-national experiences of the successful war against the pagan oppressors and was inaugurated after the victory over the Syrian Greeks. Some scholars have tried to relate the liturgy of Hanukah to historic and social considerations not directly connected with the revolt and the reconsecration of the Temple. They base their speculations on the fact that a number of the characteristics of the festival are seemingly unrelated to any other Jewish observances. The very number of eight days of observance is exceptional—all other Jewish festivals and holy days are either of one day's or seven days' duration.[4] The number of lights—eight—is also a break with the traditional seven-branched menorah which was rekindled in the Temple on the occasion of the victory over the pagans. Some have therefore sought antecedents for the Hanukah festival outside the events of the successful war against the Syrian Greeks. Some have tried to associate the ritual of Hanukah with ancient Semitic rites performed at the winter solstice. Others have tried to trace the antecedents of Hanukah to the festival of Sukkot. They claim that the rededication of the Temple took place only two months after the time of the Sukkot festival and that the observance of Hanukah was only a delayed Sukkot observance. Hence the celebration of eight days, which correspond to the seven days of Sukkot and the one day of Shemini Atzeret. This theory also accounts for the recitation of the Full Hallel at each morning service of Hanukah.[5]

Whatever the antecedents of Hanukah may have been, the fact remains that its message and ceremonies are all associated with the victory over the enemies of Judaism and the resumption of the Jewish worship in the Temple.[6] Since the rededication of the Temple was the center of the festivity, it was natural to copy the Temple ritual of similar happy celebrations. The Hallel which was part of the ritual for the other festivals was especially suitable for the occasion. It was therefore adopted and is still part of the synagogue liturgy for Hanukah. The Full Hallel is used, because the Half Hallel did not come into existence till almost four centuries later.* The kindling of lights is associated with the central act of the rededication of the Temple, which consisted of the rekindling of the fire on the altar and the rekindling of the menorah in the Temple. Since the kindling of the Hanukah lights is primarily a home service, it will be discussed in the next chapter, which deals with the liturgy of the home.†

In addition to the Hallel, a special prayer, known from its initial words as *Al Ha-Nissim* (For the miracles), was added to the thanksgiving benediction of the *Tefillah* of every service. This prayer is of geonic origin. It is already mentioned in an eighth century work.[7] The *Al Ha-Nissim* thanks God for the deliverance from the hands of the Syrian Greeks:

> Thou didst deliver the strong into the hands of the weak, the many into the hands of the few, the impure into the hands of the pure, the wicked into the hands of the righteous, and the arrogant into the hands of them that occupied themselves with Thy Torah.

The liturgy also provided for special scriptural readings at every morning service of the festival. These Torah readings consist of the biblical accounts of the dedication of the altar in the days of Moses and the gifts brought by the twelve princes of Israel (Num. 7). On the Sabbath of Hanukah, the Haftarah (Zech. 2:14–4:7) speaks of the prophet's vision about the Temple menorah, which in the minds of the people is associated with the menorah which was lighted and dedicated to

* *See pp. 210–11.*
† *See pp. 316–19.*

God's service by the Hasmoneans. The Haftarah concludes with the oft-quoted prophetic words "Not by might, nor by power, but by My spirit, saith the Lord of hosts" (Zech. 4:6).

Occasionally there are two Sabbaths on Hanukah. The Haftarah read on the second Sabbath deals with the building of Solomon's Temple (1 Kings 7:40–50).

When the Temple was destroyed in the year 70 C.E., the observance of Hanukah was almost unaffected, because its liturgy was centered on the synagogue and the home. It was thus able to continue as before. The lights were kindled at home every evening of the festival, the *Al Ha-Nissim* prayer continued to be recited in the *Tefillah* of every service, the Hallel continued to be read during the morning service, and the Torah selections continued to be read at each morning service. These rites have remained the characteristic elements of the Hanukah liturgy to this day.

The Liturgy of the Feast of Lots

The religious basis for the festival of Purim is that God saved the Jews from the plot of Haman, just as He had saved the children of Israel from the evil designs of Pharaoh and other tyrants. It is for this reason that the Book of Esther was canonized and included in the Bible—despite the fact that God's role in the saving of the Jews is hardly mentioned in the Book of Esther. Indeed, God's name does not appear in the story. But the healthy religious instinct of the Jewish people dictated an interpretation of those historic events that placed God in the center of that national drama. In rabbinic times, the event was given further emphasis. A whole tractate of the Talmud known as Megillah (literally, the Scroll) is devoted to the theme of Purim. As in the case of Hanukah a special prayer, *Al Ha-Nissim* (For the miracles), was added to the thanksgiving benediction of the *Tefillah*, thanking God for the deliverance of the Jews from the hands of Haman. This prayer reads:

> We thank Thee also *for the miracles*, for the redemption, for the mighty deeds and saving acts, wrought by Thee . . . for our fathers in days of old, at this season.

> In the days of Mordecai and Esther, in Shushan, the capital, when the wicked Haman rose up against them, and sought to destroy, to slay, and make to perish all the Jews, both young and old, little children and women, on one day, . . . then didst Thou in Thine abundant mercy bring his counsel to nought . . . and didst return his recompense upon his own head. . . .

The climax of the Purim service is the reading of the *Megillah* (Scroll). Actually, there are five scrolls in the Bible.[8] But *the* Scroll, without specification, always refers to the Book of Esther, because in the days of the Mishnah the Book of Esther was the only scroll read in the synagogue. Hence the Talmud speaks of the Book of Esther as the Scroll, and so it has been called ever since.

The regulations governing the reading of the *Megillah* are of great antiquity. The Talmud ascribes them to the Men of the Great Assembly (Meg. 2a), who lived in the fifth century B.C.E. Everyone is duty bound to read or hear the reading of the *Megillah*, because everyone was saved by the great deliverance. Hence everyone congregates in the synagogue on Purim eve to celebrate the joyous occasion. The prevailing spirit is one of cheer and gaiety. The reader recites three benedictions: one for the divine command "concerning the reading of the *Megillah*," another for "the miracles" performed "for our fathers in days of old, at this season," and the Sheheheyanu, for God's having "preserved us and enabled us to reach this season." The *Megillah* is read in a special chant. It proceeds rather laboriously, because children are permitted to drown out the name of Haman with the help of noisemakers of all sorts. Not infrequently they drown out more than the name of Haman. Whole passages are not heard distinctly. The pious, who really want to hear every word of the *Megillah* in accordance with the explicit directions of rabbinic law, protest loudly. But the noisemakers are as a rule louder, and they usually prevail, to the delight of the children and many grown-ups. A spirit of levity thus predominates. Non-Jews who happen to be present are baffled by this strange coexistence of noise and worship, thanksgiving and levity. For the Jew, however, this boisterous festivity is a form of worship. The gaiety is inspired by gratitude for God's ever-present salvation. It has also served as a welcome release from the sober and serious quality of Jewish life in the ghetto. Besides, the Jew has always felt that God is not lacking in a sense of humor, Ernest Renan's opinion notwithstanding. In addition, the Jew's relationship with God has always been more intimate than the visiting non-Jew suspects.

The reading of the Torah, it will be remembered, is concluded with a benediction praising God "who gave us the Torah and planted everlasting life in our midst." * The reading of the *Megillah*, too, is concluded with a suitable benediction that is prescribed in the Talmud:

> Blessed [Praised] art Thou, O Lord our God, king of the universe, [the God] who espoused our quarrel and vindicated our cause and executed our vengeance and punished our adversaries for us and visited retribution on all the enemies of our soul. Blessed [Praised] art Thou, O Lord, who avenges Israel on all their enemies [Meg. 21b].

At the evening reading there is also a hymn of ancient origin which is sung after the recital of the above benediction: "Who broughtest the counsel of the heathen to nought, and madest the devices of the crafty of none effect, when a wicked man, an arrogant offshoot of the seed of Amalek, rose up against us." And the hymn concludes, to the satisfaction of all:

> *Accursed be Haman who sought to destroy me;*
> *Blessed be Mordecai the Jew;*
> *Accursed be Zeresh, the wife of him that terrified me;*
> *Blessed be Esther my protectress; and may Harbonah*
> *also be remembered for good.*

There are several other manifestations of the Purim observance. On the Sabbath preceding the festival, a special selection from the Torah is read for the maftir: "Remember what Amalek did to you on your journey, after you left Egypt—how, undeterred by fear of God, he surprised you on the march, when you were famished and weary, and cut down all the stragglers

* *See pp. 109–11.*

in your rear" (Deut. 25:17–18). In the Jewish tradition Haman and all archenemies of Israel are regarded as the spiritual descendants of Amalek. It is the duty of Jews to remember Amalek and to be on guard. The Sabbath before Purim is known as *Shabbat Zakhor*, the Sabbath when the selection beginning with the word *Zakhor* (Remember) is read. And the Haftarah on that Sabbath, too, deals with Amalek (1 Sam. 15:2–34): "Thus saith the Lord of hosts: I remember that which Amalek did to Israel . . . when he came up out of Egypt" (1 Sam. 15:2). King Saul, the Haftarah relates, gathered an army and went up against the Amalekites. He utterly defeated them and took their king captive, along with much booty. The prophet Samuel rebuked the king for taking booty and foretold the fall of his dynasty.

Another characteric of the Purim liturgy was the enrichment of the morning service with many piyutim. In modern times these piyutim have fallen into disuse, but during the geonic period and especially during the Middle Ages they were read avidly. The people enjoyed blessing Mordecai, damning Haman, and praising God for the happy event. For them, the Purim drama and its actors were alive and relevant to the pressing problems of their own lives.

Other characteristics of the festival were feasting, the exchange of delicacies, gifts for the poor, masquerading, and dramatic enactments of the great deliverance or of other plots of biblical inspiration. But these are hardly liturgic in content. They should be left to the folklorists.

The Major and Minor Fast Days

Many calamities have befallen the Jewish people during their long history. Some of them are commemorated by annual fast days.[9] Four fast days are listed by the prophet Zechariah, all of which had their origin in the destruction of the First Temple in 586 B.C.E.[10] These fast days assumed added significance when the Second Jewish Commonwealth fell in 70 C.E. As might be expected, the liturgy of these fast days not only bewailed the misfortunes of the past, but also pleaded for Israel's redemption from exile. Another fast day mentioned in the Bible is the Fast of Esther (Esther 9:31), which commemorates the threatened slaughter of the Persian Jews in the fifth century B.C.E. These five fasts have been considered obligatory. Still another biblical fast day, though not mentioned directly in the Bible, is the Fast of the Firstborn. This fast is still observed by many but, as we shall see, not by fasting but by feasting.

The Fast of Tishah Be-Av

The most widely observed of all these fast days is Tishah Be-Av, the Ninth of Av. It commemorates a series of major disasters which, by coincidence, occurred on this day. This fast day has therefore been called the Black Fast, in contradistinction to that of the Day of Atonement, often called the White Fast. The Mishnah (Ta'an. 4:6) lists five calamities that befell the Jewish people on the Ninth of Av: on that day it was decreed that none of the Hebrews who left Egypt, except Caleb and Joshua, should enter the Promised Land (Num. 14:21–24); the First and the Second Temples were destroyed; Bethar, the last Jewish stronghold during the Bar Kokhba rebellion, fell on that day; and on that same day a year later Jerusalem was ploughed over by the Romans.[11] To these should be added another calamity—in 1492 the Jews of Spain were despoiled and expelled, thus ending a glorious era in the annals of Jewish history.

The fast of Tishah Be-Av is therefore regarded as the most important of all the fast days. In the Talmud one of the sages is quoted as saying: "Any one who eats or drinks on the Ninth of Ab is as if he ate and drank on the Day of Atonement" (Ta'an. 30b). While all other fasts last only from sunrise to sunset, the Ninth of Av, like the Day of Atonement, begins at sunset and continues for twenty-four hours, till the stars are visible to the naked eye. And fasting in the Jewish tradition means abstention from both food and drink. The latter is particularly exhausting on Tishah Be-Av, which falls in midsummer when the days are long and hot. A spirit of mourning prevails throughout the day. No enjoyable activity is permitted—not even the study of Torah—except study of the Books of Job and Lamentations, which evoke sadness and tears, and those prophecies of Jeremiah which speak of the fall of Jerusalem.

The Three Weeks

The observance of Tishah Be-Av actually begins with the fast of the Seventeenth of Tammuz,* which falls three weeks before Tishah Be-Av. These three weeks are a period of official mourning. No enjoyable activities are permitted, and no marriages are scheduled during that period. On the Sabbaths that fall during this period there are special prophetic readings for the Haftarah that speak of the misfortunes awaiting the Jewish people because of their constant backsliding. On the Sabbath preceding the Ninth of Av, both the Torah and the Haftarah readings are related to the approaching fast day. The weekly Torah readings are so arranged that the Book of Deuteronomy is always begun on the Sabbath before Tishah Be-Av. In this portion there is a verse that begins with the same word as the Book of Lamentations, which is read on Tishah Be-Av. Moses reviews the great events of the Exodus and says: "How [*Ekhah*] can I bear unaided the trouble of you, and the burden, and the bickering!" (Deut. 1:12). This verse is chanted in the traditional sad melody of the Book of Lamentations as a reminder that the Black Fast is approaching. The prophetic reading is more directly related to the fast day. Indeed, the Sabbath is known as *Shabbat Hazon*, the Sabbath on which the Haftarah (Isa. 1:1–27) begins with the word *Hazon* (The vision [of Isaiah]). The prophet speaks of the dire consequences that await the people because of their disobedience and backsliding. He describes the desolation that awaits Jerusalem because of its sinfulness, and he concludes with hopeful words: "Zion shall be redeemed with justice, / And they that return of her with righteousness" (Isa. 1:27).

The Evening Service

The most characteristic element of the Maariv service of the fast day is the reading of the Book of Lamentations immedi-

* *See p. 284.*

ately after the *Tefillah*. During the talmudic period it was read only in private. In the geonic period, however, it became part of the synagogue liturgy. The setting for the reading of this book is as impressive as the mournful reading itself. The synagogue is stripped of its adornments. Even the curtain of the ark is removed. All bright lights are extinguished. Only enough light is left to permit the worshipers to follow the service. In some synagogues candles are distributed to the worshipers, and they follow the service by candlelight. The people remove their shoes and sit on the floor or on low stools like mourners, and the prayers are recited in subdued voices. In this setting the mournful melody of the Book of Lamentations is chanted:

How doth the city sit solitary,
That was full of people!
How is she become as a widow!
She that was great among the nations,
And princess among the provinces,
How is she become tributary! [*Lam. 1:1*].

When the reader reaches the last verses, the congregation suddenly comes to life and loudly repeats the verse before the last: "Turn Thou us unto Thee, O Lord, and we shall be turned; / Renew our days as of old" (Lam. 5:21).

The reading of the Book of Lamentations is followed by a number of dirges, or kinot. The reader and the congregation read these somber piyutim with great seriousness. Prof. Eli Ginzberg, in an address delivered on the occasion of his distinguished father's yahrzeit, speaks of "the tears that streamed down his [the father's] face as he read the prayers on Tishah Be-Av." [12] This was characteristic of the solemnity and earnestness with which the Jews of former generations observed the fast day. The reading of the kinot was not just a traditional ritual. Ever since the first century, when the Second Jewish Commonwealth was destroyed, Jews have mourned the destruction of the central shrine of Judaism as an immediate personal loss of tragic dimensions. Just as the Jew rejoiced on Passover "as though he personally went forth out of Egypt," so he wept on the Ninth of Av as though he personally had suffered all the calamities of the Jewish people. This melancholy observance of the Ninth of Av was already the accepted practice during the geonic period. In the Middle Ages the number of dirges increased, the mourning deepened, and the tears flowed even more freely.

The Morning Service

The mournful spirit of Tishah Be-Av is dramatized at the morning service by the absence of the tallit and tefillin.[13] For a congregation to engage in a weekday morning service without these prayer accouterments is like appearing naked at a public function.

The essential elements of the morning service consist of a special prayer, *Anenu* (Answer us), which is interpolated into the *Tefillah;* special scriptural readings; and many dirges which are read at the end of the service.

The *Anenu* prayer is ancient in origin. It is already mentioned in the Talmud (Ta'an. 13b). The prayer is recited in both the morning and the afternoon *Tefillah.* Since this prayer is read on every fast day, it is couched in general terms and does not specify the Ninth of Av. The prayer reads in part: "Answer us, O Lord, answer us on this day of the fast of our humiliation, for we are in great trouble . . . for Thou, O Lord, art He who answereth . . . in all times of trouble and distress." The prayer is inserted into the benediction that implores God to "Hear our voice," and it concludes with the blessing of this benediction: "For Thou hearkenest in mercy to the prayer of Thy people Israel. *Praised art Thou, O Lord, who hearkenest unto prayer.*" [14]

The Torah reading on Tishah Be-Av (Deut. 4:25–40) is part of the sharp warning that Moses gave to the children of Israel in regard to what will befall them when they forsake the teachings of the Torah. The words of Moses vividly describe what in later years actually befell the Jewish people. But they also promise that God will have mercy and will redeem Israel from its exile, once they repent and return to Him:

> Should you, when you have begotten children and children's children and are long established in the land, act wickedly . . . I call heaven and earth this day

> to witness against you that you shall soon perish from the land which you are crossing the Jordan to occupy. . . . The Lord will scatter you among the peoples, and only a scant few of you shall be left among the nations. . . . But if you search there for the Lord your God, you will find Him. . . . For the Lord your God is a compassionate God: He will not fail you nor will He let you perish; He will not forget the covenant which He made on oath with your fathers [Deut. 4:25–29, 31].

These words of warning and hope are obviously suitable for the occasion. The warning has already been realized. The Jewish people is scattered and decimated. It is now for the people to return to God "with all their heart and with all their soul," and redemption will surely follow.

The prophetic reading (Jeremiah 8:13–9:23) is a bitter lament over the misfortunes of the Jewish people:

> *For the hurt of the daughter of my people am I seized*
> *with anguish;*
> *I am black, appalment hath taken hold on me.*
> *Is there no balm in Gilead?*
> *Is there no physician there?*
> *Why then is not the health*
> *Of the daughter of my people recovered?*
> *Oh that my head were waters,*
> *And mine eyes a fountain of tears,*
> *That I might weep day and night*
> *For the slain of the daughter of my people!*
> [*Jer. 8:21–23*].

The Haftarah is a suitable introduction to the kinot that are recited after the Torah is returned to the ark. These dirges sear the heart and depress the spirit. The congregation sits on the floor or on low stools and reads scores of dirges. When the kinot are finished and the congregation has exhausted its ample capacity for mourning and lamentation, the service is ended. The congregation continues its fasting in private until it reassembles in the afternoon for the last service of the day.

THE AFTERNOON SERVICE

The Minhah service on Tishah Be-Av is a somber ritual. The congregation is physically exhausted from the fast, but it rallies by the unusual rite of putting on the tallit and tefillin at a Minhah service.[15] What is normally the simplest and briefest of public services now assumes an air of major importance.

The liturgy, too, lifts the service to a high level of significance. The Torah is taken from the ark, and a special selection is read. It deals with the prayer that Moses uttered in behalf of the children of Israel after they had worshiped the golden calf (Exod. 32:11–14). This portion ends with God's acceptance of Moses' prayer: "And the Lord renounced the punishment He had planned to bring upon His people" (Exod. 32:14). The reading then continues with the narration of God's revelation to Moses of the Thirteen Divine Attributes of mercy (Exod. 34:1–10).* Moses, we are told, prayed once more in behalf of the children of Israel: "If I have gained Your favor, O Lord, pray, let the Lord go in our midst. . . . Pardon our iniquity and our sin, and take us for Your own" (Exod. 34:9). God not only forgave their transgressions, but also renewed His covenant with them: "He said: I hereby make a covenant. Before all your people I will work such wonders as have not been wrought on all the earth or in any nation" (Exod. 34:10).

The choice of this biblical selection for the last service on Tishah Be-Av is understandable. It held out the hope of forgiveness and redemption. Just as God forgave the children of Israel for worshiping the golden calf and renewed His covenant with them, so will He again forgive the Jewish people for their sins and renew His covenant with them, and once more lead them to the Promised Land.

The prophetic reading is a selection from the Book of Isaiah (55:6–56:8) which is replete with words of comfort:

Seek ye the Lord while He may be found,
Call ye upon Him while He is near;
Let the wicked forsake his way,

* *See pp. 229–30.*

And the man of iniquity his thoughts;
And let him return unto the Lord, and He will have compassion upon him,
And to our God, for He will abundantly pardon [*Isa. 55:6–7*].

Thus saith the Lord:
Keep ye justice, and do righteousness;
For My salvation is near to come,
And My favour to be revealed [*Isa. 56:1*].

Saith the Lord God who gathereth the dispersed of Israel [*Isa. 56:8*].

The *Tefillah*, too, is enriched with a special benediction. In addition to the *Anenu* prayer, the reader adds a benediction known by its initial word: *Nahem* (Comfort [the mourners of Zion]). This benediction is mentioned in the Talmud, and it was already a regular part of the Tishah Be-Av service during the geonic period. It is recited after the benediction that implores God to "return in mercy" to Jerusalem. It reads in part:

> Comfort, O Lord our God, the mourners of Zion, and the mourners of Jerusalem, and the city that is in mourning, laid waste, despised and desolate. . . . She sitteth with her head covered like a barren woman who hath not borne. . . . Therefore let Zion weep bitterly, and Jerusalem give forth her voice. O my heart, my heart! How it grieveth for the slain! . . . *Praised art Thou O Lord, who comfortest Zion and rebuildest Jerusalem.*

Words of Comfort

Comforting as is the Haftarah of the Minhah service, it is not enough to offset the scores of dirges read during the fast day and the grim warnings of the prophetic readings on the three Sabbaths before Tishah Be-Av. The fast being over and Israel having repented, the rabbis saw fit to designate selections from the latter part of the Book of Isaiah as prophetic readings for every Sabbath between the Ninth of Av and Rosh Hashanah. These prophecies are replete with words of comfort. The first Sabbath after Tishah Be-Av is known as *Shabbat Nahamu*, the

Sabbath on which the Haftarah (Isa. 40:1–26) begins with the word *Nahamu* (Comfort ye):

> *Comfort ye, comfort ye My people,*
> *Saith your God.*
> *Bid Jerusalem take heart,*
> *And proclaim unto her,*
> *That her time of service is accomplished*
> *That her guilt is paid off* [*Isa. 40:1–2*].

In each of the eight prophetic readings on the Sabbaths after Tishah Be-Av, the restoration of Jerusalem and the vindication of Israel's suffering are depicted in glowing terms. These prophecies revive the dormant hopes of the people and imbue them with renewed fortitude to face the continuing perils of exile and homelessness.

Other Fast Days Commemorating the Fall of the Temple

The fast of Tishah Be-Av has three satellites. The prophet Zechariah lists them in the order of their occurrence during the year and concludes that they "shall be to the house of Judah joy and gladness" (Zech. 8:19). The rabbis of the Talmud comment on the contradiction in the prophecy. How can a day be a day of both fasting and gladness? The answer is illuminating:

> R. Papa replied: What it means is this: When there is peace they shall be for joy and gladness; if there is persecution, they shall be fast days; if there is no persecution but yet not peace, then those who desire may fast and those who desire need not fast. If that is the case, the ninth of Ab also [should be optional]?— R. Papa replied: The ninth of Ab is in a different category, because several misfortunes happened on it, as a Master has said: On the ninth of Ab the Temple was destroyed both the first time and the second time, and Bethar was captured and the city [Jerusalem] was ploughed [R.H. 18b].

Three fasts are optional, according to the rabbis, depending on the state of peace or persecution. The Tenth of Tevet [16] commemorates the day regarded as the beginning of the Babylonians' siege of Jerusalem. The city was besieged for almost two years. On the Seventeenth of Tammuz [17]—the second of the above-mentioned fast days—the city walls were breached. Three weeks later, on the Ninth of Av, the city fell.

But the destruction of Jerusalem and the burning of the Temple were not actually the final blow. There was still a remnant of the people in Jerusalem and in the hinterland. The king of Babylonia appointed a man by the name of Gedaliah to govern the conquered territory. Gedaliah aimed at reconstructing Jerusalem and perhaps rebuilding the Temple. New hope was infused into the hearts of the inhabitants. But there were some who saw in Gedaliah a collaborator with the hated enemies of Judea. On the Third of Tishri, Gedaliah was assassinated. This was regarded as the final and decisive blow. The anniversary of Gedaliah's assassination became a fast day.

These days have been official fast days ever since the fall of the First Jewish Commonwealth more than 2,500 years ago. When the Second Commonwealth was established within a century after these misfortunes, the observance of the fast days was relaxed but not forgotten. They became optional. When the Second Commonwealth was destroyed and the city fell on the very day on which the First Commonwealth collapsed, the fast days ceased to be optional.

The ritual and the liturgy of the three minor fast days are hardly comparable to those of Tishah Be-Av. Their observance is only a faint shadow of the major fast day. The fast itself, as already mentioned, lasts only from sunrise to sunset. Those who observe these fast days usually get up before sunrise and partake of food and drink, which makes the fast considerably easier. The special liturgy consists only of the additional *Anenu* prayer * in the *Tefillah* and the reading of the same Torah portion as at the Tishah Be-Av afternoon service. This Torah reading is repeated at the Minhah service, along with the com-

* *See p. 279.*

forting Haftarah that is read as the Tishah Be-Av service.* A number of special piyutim were composed for the morning services of these fast days. Some of these were written in the early talmudic times, some during the geonic period, and still more during the Middle Ages. By the end of the geonic period, however, the basic liturgy of these fast days had been formulated, and the pattern has remained part of the tradition of the synagogue.

The Fast of Esther

The misfortunes connected with the fall of the First and Second Commonwealths were not the only national calamities that called for fasting. The rabbinic text *Megillat Ta'anit* lists thirty-five fast days observed at that time. In later centuries some of these fast days were discarded, but new calamities called for new fast days. However, only two additional fasts will be mentioned here, because they are still observed in limited circles. Their survival power derives from the fact that they are sanctioned in the Bible. The first of these is the Fast of Esther, which is observed immediately before Purim, and the second one is the Fast of the Firstborn, which is observed on the day before Passover.

The Fast of Esther is popularly associated with the fast that Esther proclaimed before she approached the king to plead for her people. The biblical account reads:

> Then Esther bade them return answer unto Mordecai: "Go gather together all the Jews that are present in Shushan, and fast ye for me, and neither eat nor drink three days, night or day; I also and my maidens will fast in like manner; and so will I go in unto the king, which is not according to the law; and if I perish, I perish" [Esther 4:15–16].

But this is not the reason for the fast—Esther's fast took place long before the fateful days in the month of Adar. According to rabbinic calculations, Esther's fast took place in the month

* *See p. 281.*

of Nisan and, according to the account quoted above, lasted three days.

The Fast of Esther, which is observed on the thirteenth of Adar, is mentioned for the first time in an eighth century geonic work,[18] where it is associated with the verse (Esther 9:18) that speaks of the Jews assembling on the thirteenth day of Adar in preparation for their battle on the following day. To the rabbis, "assembling" means assembling for prayer and fasting. The proper celebration of Purim therefore calls for fasting on the thirteenth of Adar and feasting on the fourteenth, thus reliving the experience of those fateful days. And this is altogether logical in terms of the normal Jewish experiences. Every generation experienced threats to its very survival, but in each case salvation came at the last moment. This was the pattern: a grave danger threatened, the people gathered in the synagogue for prayer and fasting, then came the miraculous, last-minute salvation and celebration.

The liturgy of the Fast of Esther is the same as that of all the minor fast days except for the piyutim, which deal specifically with the threatened extermination of the Persian Jews and their miraculous rescue.

The Fast of the Firstborn

The last of the fast days to be considered in this chapter is the Fast of the Firstborn. Surprisingly, this most ancient and seemingly irrelevant fast day is observed more widely than is suspected. In all Orthodox and in most Conservative synagogues, men who are the firstborn of their mothers gather for the morning service on the day before Passover and participate in the ritual connected with the Fast of the Firstborn. But, as we shall see, the observance turns out to be a feast instead of a fast.

The biblical basis for this fast is the account of the tenth plague that befell the Egyptians at the time of the Exodus. "All the firstborn in the land of Egypt" were slain. But the houses of the Hebrews were passed over, and the firstborn were spared. The firstborn therefore commemorated that event by devoting the day before Passover to a fast which, according to the rabbis, is a form of sacrifice, since fasting "diminishes one's blood and fat."

Completing the Study of a Rabbinic Text

The rationalization of the Fast of the Firstborn is tenuous to the point of unreality. The rabbis were conscious of the vulnerability of this institution and were faced with a difficult dilemma. They could neither defend the fast nor abrogate so ancient a tradition, one with roots in the Bible. So they wisely resorted to a legal fiction. If one could plan his study of a talmudic text so as to complete it on the day before Passover, he would be exempt from the fast, because of the *Se'udat Mitzvah*, the religious feast that is called for on such an occasion. The actual practice has been for the rabbi to invite all the firstborn who attend the morning service on the day before Passover to join him in the study of the last section of the tractate that he has been studying in preparation for this occasion. When the study is completed, everyone celebrates with the rabbi. The fast is thus nullified. It has been superseded by the feast of the Torah.

The celebration of the completion of a talmudic text is known as *Siyum Massekhta*, the completion of a tractate, or just *Siyum* for short. A unique ritual going back to the geonic period is followed meticulously. The first step has already been mentioned: the leader and his guests study the last section of the tractate. The leader then delivers a learned discourse related to the section just studied or to the completed tractate. Then follows a brief service which is introduced by a formula that is in essence a valedictory addressed to the tractate just completed. These words of leave-taking are known as the *Hadran* (Many Returns), which expresses the hope that the students and the text are not parting permanently but will meet again. This singular formula reads:

> Many returns from us to thee and from thee to us, tractate ——.[19] Our thoughts be with thee and thy thoughts be with us, tractate ——. May we not be

> forgotten by thee, nor thou be forgotten by us, tractate ——, neither in this world nor in the world to come.

This ancient Aramaic formula is recited three times and is followed by three talmudic prayers, each of which was originally a prayer that a rabbi of the Talmud used to recite upon the conclusion of his daily study. The first of these, however, is only partly talmudic. The rest of it consists of the names of Rabbi Papa's ten sons, the recitation of which, it was believed, was an antidote to the most dreaded affliction that could befall a scholar, the loss of memory. The prayers are:

> May it be Thy will, O Lord our God, that our Torah may be our occupation [20] [in this world and that it be with us in the world to come]. [The names of Rabbi Papa's ten sons are now listed.]
>
> Make pleasant, therefore, we beseech Thee, O Lord our God, the words of Thy Torah in our mouth and in the mouth of Thy people, the house of Israel, so that we with our offspring and the offspring of Thy people the house of Israel, may all know Thy name and study Thy Torah. Blessed [Praised] art Thou, O Lord, who teachest Torah to Thy people Israel.[21]
>
> I give thanks to Thee, O Lord my God, that Thou hast set my portion with those who sit in the [house of study] and Thou hast not set my portion with those who sit in [street] corners, for I rise early . . . for words of Torah, and they rise early for frivolous talk.[22]

The *Siyum* service is concluded with a personal prayer by the leader:

> May it be Thy will, O Lord my God, that just as Thou hast helped me to complete this tractate, so mayest Thou help me to start and to complete other tractates. . . . And may the merit of the sages of the Talmud stand by me and my offspring, so that the Torah may not depart out of my mouth nor out of the mouth of my seed for ever [Isa. 59:21]. And may it be established in regard to me:

When thou walkest, it [the Torah] shall lead thee,
When thou liest down, it shall watch over thee;
And when thou awakest, it shall talk with thee
[Prov. 6:22].

For by me [the Torah] thy days shall be multiplied,
And the years of thy life shall be increased [Prov. 9:11].

The Lord will give strength unto His people;
The Lord will bless His people with peace [Ps. 29:11].

The scholars' Kaddish * is recited and the feast begins.

The liturgy and the rituals of the fast days were, as already stated, fully formulated during the talmudic and geonic periods. To be sure, a number of piyutim and some other refinements were added during the centuries that followed, but essentially the tradition of the synagogue had assumed its classic form during the period under discussion. The prayers of Israel were ready for their crystallization in the form of an official prayer book.

11 PRIVATE AND HOME WORSHIP

The liturgy which developed during the talmudic and geonic periods met the Jew's private and domestic spiritual needs as adequately as it did those of the congregation and the synagogue. To be sure, the religious Jew worshiped God everywhere and at all times. Every experience was an occasion for a benediction, every place was sanctified by God's presence, and every moment was permeated with divine grace.† The home, however, was the only institution that rivaled the synagogue as an official place of worship; the prayers recited in the home constituted a substantial part of the established liturgy. When

* *See pp. 153–56.*
† *See pp. 91–92.*

the prayer book was published, these private and domestic prayers were included as an integral part of the official Jewish liturgy.

Not even the pious are always free to join the congregation for the daily services. They frequently have to recite their prayers in private. This is not their preferred way of worship, for one cannot respond to the reader's call to worship; * nor can one recite the verses of the Kedushah during the reader's repetition of the *Telfillah;* † and one is deprived of the privilege of participating in the public reading of the Scriptures.‡ But even the Jew who is fortunate enough to participate in public worship every day engages in a rich regimen of domestic devotions. He therefore regards his home as a shrine. This is not a poetic exaggeration, for the Jewish home was, in a sense, a little sanctuary. The family table was regarded as an altar, each meal was a holy ritual, and the parents were the officiating priests. Family worship accompanied many of the daily activities and transformed the biological and social relationships of the family into a spiritual kinship.

Prayers at Rising in the Morning and Retiring at Night

The private devotions of a Jew began when he awakened from his sleep in the morning. Each act of rising, dressing, washing—any act involved in getting ready for the normal activities of the day—had its benediction (Ber. 60b).§ It developed, however, that many Jews did not know these prayers by heart and so did not recite them. These benedictions were therefore transferred to the morning service of the synagogue, where the reader recited them audibly and the congregation responded with the traditional Amen. In later times, when prayer books became available and people no longer had to learn their prayers by heart, the Early Morning Benedictions were not returned to their original role of private devotions. They had

* *See pp. 98–99.*
† *See pp. 134–36.*
‡ *See p. 559.*
§ *See pp. 143–44.*

already become a traditional part of the synagogue service, and to this day the *Birkhot Ha-Shahar* are part of the introductory prayers of the regular morning services.*

Not so with the private devotions at the end of the day. Before retiring at night, the Jew recites an elaborate, well-rounded prayer unit built around the traditional affirmation of faith, the *Shema.*[1] The night prayer is known as *Kriat Shema Al Ha-Mittah*, the Reading of the *Shema* before Retiring for Sleep. This prayer unit was developed in rabbinic times and has remained substantially the same to this day. The Talmud prescribes a rather brief formula for busy scholars:

> Though a man has recited the *Shema* in the [evening service at the] synagogue, it is a religious act to recite it again upon his bed. . . . Abaye says: Even a scholar should recite one verse of supplication, as for instance: *Into Thy hand I commit my spirit. Thou hast redeemed me*, *O Lord*, *Thou God of truth* [Ps. 31:6] [Ber. 4b–5a].

But the recital of the *Shema* followed by one verse of prayer did not satisfy even the busy scholars. A much fuller night prayer is prescribed in the Talmud for normal use, and this prayer with some embellishments has become the accepted prayer ritual. The following is the talmudic statement:

> On going to bed one says from "*Hear, O Israel*" to "*And it shall come to pass if ye listen diligently*" [Deut. 6:4–9]. Then he says: "Blessed [Praised] is He who causes the bands of sleep to fall upon my eyes and slumber on my eyelids. . . . May it be Thy will, O Lord my God [and God of my fathers], to make me lie down in peace. . . . [O] enlighten mine eyes lest I sleep the sleep of death. Blessed [Praised] art Thou, O Lord, who givest light to the whole world in Thy glory [Ber. 60b].

Accordingly, the night prayers as they have come down to modern times begin with the rabbinic benediction, quoted above, followed by the first paragraph of the *Shema.* Then come several appropriate psalms and prayers. Among the

* *For the* Modeh Ani *prayer, see pp. 145–46.*

psalms are the ninety-first psalm, which contains the reassuring words "Thou shalt not be afraid of the terror by night" (Psalms 91:5), and the third psalm, which contains the comforting verse, "I lay me down, and I sleep; I awake, for the Lord sustaineth me" (Psalms 3:6). Among the additional prayers are two which were borrowed from the synagogue evening service—(*Hashkivenu*) "Cause us, O Lord our God, to lie down in peace, and raise us up, O our King, unto life . . ." and (*Barukh Adonai Ba-Yom*) "Blessed be the Lord by day; blessed be the Lord by night; blessed be the Lord when we lie down; blessed the Lord when we rise up." In both prayers the concluding blessings are omitted. These blessings have already been recited in the Maariv service. To repeat them would be to take God's name in vain.

After reciting his night prayers, the core of which is the affirmation of faith, the Jew could sleep peacefully. The Reading of the *Shema* before Retiring for Sleep was a sort of spiritual insurance policy against the frightful possibility of "sleeping the sleep of death." Should he not awaken from his sleep, God forbid, the Jew had the comforting assurance of having finished his mortal existence with the traditional affirmation of God's unity.

Grace before and after Meals

The Early Morning Benedictions and the Reading of the *Shema* before Retiring for Sleep were only the opening and closing acts of daily worship. Between these was a busy day of private worship. The most hallowed of the domestic prayer experiences were those that accompanied every meal, especially the Sabbath and festival meals, when the whole family participated in the recital of the prayers.

The opening benediction before the meal is the brief blessing in which God is praised and thanked for "bringing forth bread from the earth." Bread, in this blessing, is the symbol of all food and includes the whole meal irrespective of the variety of dishes served. The recitation of this blessing, known as the Hamotzi (Who brings forth [bread from the earth]), was already widespread in rabbinic times. Thus an innkeeper is quoted in the Midrash as saying to a fellow Jew: "When I saw that you ate without washing your hands and without a blessing I thought you were an idolator" (Num. Rabbah 20:21).

The devotions after the meal made up for the brevity of the Hamotzi. They constitute a well-constructed and a deeply moving prayer unit of four bulky benedictions. In these benedictions the Jew thanks God in accordance with the biblical injunction: "When you have eaten your fill, give thanks to the Lord your God for the good land which He has given you" (Deut. 8:10). Accordingly, the first benediction thanks God for the blessing of food, and the second benediction thanks God for "the good land" that He gave to Israel as an inheritance. The third benediction thanks God for His merciful restoration of Jerusalem. To be sure, Jerusalem was in ruins. Nonetheless, the benediction is in the present tense—"who rebuildest Jerusalem." The redemption of Israel will materialize at any moment, perhaps at the very moment when the benediction is being recited. The first benediction reads:

> "*Praised art Thou, O Lord our God, King of the universe*, who feedest the whole world with Thy goodness, with grace, with loving-kindness, and tender mercy; Thou givest food to all flesh, for Thy loving-kindness endureth forever. Through Thy great goodness food hath never failed us: O may it not fail us for ever and ever for Thy great name's sake, since Thou nourishest and sustainest all beings and doest good unto all, and providest food for all Thy creatures whom Thou hast created. *Praised art Thou O Lord, who givest food unto all.*

The three initial benedictions of the *Birkat Ha-Mazon* (the Blessing for the Food) are among the most ancient prayers in the Jewish liturgy. The rabbis emphasize their antiquity by ascribing them to Moses, Joshua, and King Solomon respectively. The Talmud says:

> Moses instituted for Israel the [first] benediction [of the grace] "Who feeds" at the time when the

> manna descended for them. Joshua instituted for them the [second] benediction of the land when they entered the land. David and Solomon instituted the [third] benediction which closes "Who buildest Jerusalem" [Ber. 48b].

A fourth benediction, called *Ha-Tov Veha-Metiv* (Who is good and doeth good) is a later addition, attributed by the rabbis to the period immediately after the Bar Kokhba rebellion in the second century. At that time the remnants of the Jewish people were threatened with extinction through a pestilence caused by the many corpses strewn everywhere; when the Romans granted permission to bury the dead this benediction was instituted. It thanks God "who is good and doeth good" and in His mercy does not permit Israel to perish.

With the passage of time the *Birkat Ha-Mazon* expanded considerably beyond the initial core. Thanksgiving prayers for a number of additional blessings were incorporated in the first three benedictions. Among the divine blessings for which thanks are expressed are the gifts of the Torah, the covenant of Abraham, and the dynasty of David, one of whose descendants will be the Messiah. But it was the fourth benediction that really grew to giant size. People took more liberties with it because it was the latest of the benedictions to be officially incorporated into the *Birkat Ha-Mazon.* A number of general supplications were added to this benediction, each of which starts with the word *Ha-Rahaman* ([May] the All-Merciful . . .). For the Sabbath a special prayer was added: "Be pleased, O Lord our God, to strengthen us by Thy commandments, and especially by Thy commandment of the seventh day, this great and holy Sabbath. . . ." For Passover, Shavuot, Sukkot, New Year, and the New Moon days, the *Ya'aleh Ve-Yavo* * prayer was borrowed from the *Tefillah.* And for Hanukah and Purim the *Al Ha-Nissim* † prayer was similarly borrowed.

The *Birkat Ha-Mazon* has thus grown into a prayer unit of substantial proportions, too long for a busy person, especially

* *See pp. 209–10.*
† *See p. 271.*

on weekdays. An abbreviated grace was therefore provided for use by "working people during the workdays." The abbreviated *Birkat Ha-Mazon* summarizes the essence of each benediction and condenses the whole grace after meals into a single paragraph.

When three or more men participate in a meal the *Birkat Ha-Mazon* becomes a formal group service with a leader and an official call to worship. The leader opens with an invocation: *Rabbotai Nevarekh* (Gentlemen, let us say grace). The participants in the meal respond with the traditional "Blessed be the name of the Lord from this time forth and forever." The leader follows up his call for worship and says: "With the sanction of those present we will praise Him of whose bounty we have partaken." Again the participants respond: "Praised be He of whose bounty we have partaken, and through whose goodness we live." Then they all continue with the regular *Birkat Ha-Mazon.*

By the end of the geonic period this service had not only been formulated but also fully accepted. Only minor accretions were added in the subsequent centuries. To this day the *Birkat Ha-Mazon* serves those Jews who choose to express their gratitude to God who feeds "the whole world" with His "goodness, grace, loving-kindness, and tender mercy." Unfortunately, too many Jews today take their blessings for granted. They prefer to emulate Esau, of whom the Bible says: "He ate and drank, and he rose and went away. Thus did Esau spurn the birthright" (Gen. 25:34).

Home Worship on Sabbaths and Festivals

The domestic prayers on the Sabbath and festivals were by far the most impressive. Among these are the rites that inaugurate and conclude the holy and festive occasions.

Kindling the Sabbath and Festival Lights

Sabbaths and festivals are ushered in by the brief but solemn act of kindling the lights. The privilege of kindling the lights belongs to the mother. She recites a benediction before the lights and thanks God "who sanctified us by His commandments and commanded us to kindle the Sabbath [or festival] lights." On the first night of the festival the Sheheheyanu blessing is also recited. It thanks God for having "kept us in life, and preserved us, and enabled us to reach this season."

Strangely enough, the impressive element of this ritual has its origin in a mere legal fiction. The recitation of a benediction precedes the experience for which the benediction is pronounced. But this is not possible with the Sabbath lights—once the woman recites the benediction, the Sabbath has begun for her, and she is no longer permitted to kindle the lights. Hence the woman kindles the lights before the benediction, but shields her eyes from the light till after the benediction is recited. The mother therefore stands before the kindled lights with her hands shielding her eyes while she silently recites the prescribed blessing. She usually prolongs this posture to add a personal supplication in behalf of her home and family. This moment of the mother's prayer usually impresses the children deeply. No Jew ever forgets the moments of his childhood days when he stood silently and watched his mother praying before the Sabbath lights.

The origin of this enchanting ritual is rather prosaic. During the talmudic period an ordinary home consisted of two rooms. On week-nights a single light was lit and carried into the second room if needed there. But on Friday evening two lights were lit, one for each room, because on the Sabbath it was forbidden to carry the light from room to room. This distinction, however, became firmly associated with the ushering in of the Sabbath, and the kindling of two lights on Friday evening came to be regarded as a religious act. There was still no blessing or any other ritual connected with the kindling of the Sabbath lights. However, in the eighth century the Karaite sect * rejected all rabbinic legislation and declared that only biblical law was binding. They quoted the verse "You shall kindle no fire throughout your settlement on the sabbath day" (Exod. 35:3) and insisted that one must sit in darkness on Friday nights. The rabbis, however, interpreted this text to mean that although one may not kindle a fire *on* the Sabbath,

* *See p. 130.*

one may kindle the lights *before* the Sabbath. As is usual in sectarian controversies, the rabbis not only permitted the kindling of lights before the advent of the Sabbath, but proclaimed that it was a religious act to do so in order that the Sabbath be a delightful experience. This, said the rabbis, is in accord with the prophetic designation of the Sabbath as "a delight" (Isa. 58:13). A benediction was prescribed thanking God for His commandment "to kindle the Sabbath lights." This dramatically pointed up the error of the sectarians. It naturally followed that a similar sanctity was bestowed upon the festival lights, and by the end of the geonic period the ritual of kindling the Sabbath and festival lights was firmly established, a ritual that has been followed in all its details ever since.

The Kiddush

There are two important acts of domestic worship on Sabbaths and festivals. The first is the Kiddush, a ritual which proclaims the sanctity of the Sabbath or festival. It is recited over a cup of wine immediately before the family meal.[2] The second is the Havdalah, which declares that God has made a distinction between the holy and the profane, between the Sabbath (or festival) and the weekdays. The Havdalah is pronounced at the end of the Sabbath or festival.

These two domestic acts of worship are ancient in origin. The rabbis ascribe them to the Men of the Great Assembly * who flourished between the sixth and fourth centuries B.C.E. (Ber. 33a). The exact wording of these prayers, however, comes from talmudic times. It was then that the final formulas and their accompanying symbols were determined.

The evening meal on Sabbaths and festivals has always been the high point of Jewish domestic serenity and joy. Unfortunately, this is no longer a characteristic of most Jewish homes. Modern life has not been kind to domestic life in general, but the Jewish home has suffered even more severely because it has lost, among its many distinctive features, that indescribable delight that used to pervade it on Sabbaths and festivals. There

* *See pp. 70–72, 104.*

are still modern Jewish homes that have succeeded in maintaining their traditional pattern. In these homes the Sabbath eve is still an occasion of family serenity and blessedness.

On a Sabbath or festival eve the family gathers around the table for the festive meal. The Kiddush, which precedes the Sabbath meal, is essentially a benediction in which the Jew thanks God for having "in love and favor given us the holy Sabbath as an inheritance."[3] The Sabbath, according to the Kiddush, is both a memorial of the creation of the world and of the Exodus from Egypt.[4] The Kiddush concludes with the traditional formula: "*Praised art Thou, O Lord, who hallowest the Sabbath.*"

On a festival the evening Kiddush makes mention of the festival and the historic event that it commemorates. On Passover the Kiddush refers to "the Feast of Unleavened Bread, the season of our freedom"; on Shavuot the Kiddush speaks of "the Feast of Weeks, the season of the giving of our Torah"; and on Sukkot the Kiddush mentions "the Feast of Tabernacles, the season of our gladness."

After the Kiddush is chanted, everyone partakes of the wine, the symbol of joy which inheres in the observance of the Sabbath and festivals. The blessing over the bread is then recited and the meal is begun.

The noon meals, too, begin with a Kiddush. But this Kiddush is unimpressive, notwithstanding its inflated title—the Great Kiddush. Its name is altogether deceptive, for the noon Kiddush is essentially nothing more than the customary blessing over the wine. This is vividly illustrated in the following incident recorded in the Talmud:

> R. Ashi visited Mahuza [a city in Babylonia]. Said they [the Mahuzaeans] to him: "Let the Master recite the Great *kiddush* for us." They gave him [the cup of wine]. Now [Rabbi Ashi] pondered, What is the Great *kiddush?* Let us see, he reasoned, for all blessings [of *kiddush*] we first say "[*Praised art Thou*] . . . who createst the fruit of the vine" [So] he recited "[*Praised art Thou*] . . . who createst the fruit of the vine," and tarried over it [in order

> to see whether this was deemed sufficient for the Kiddush], [and then] he saw an old man bend [his head] and drink. Thereupon he applied to himself [the verse], *The wise man, his eyes are in his head* [Ecc. 2:14] [Pes. 106a].

While the blessing over the wine is sufficient for the noon Kiddush, some people have felt that this Kiddush should have a little more substance. A suitable scriptural verse was therefore added. For the Sabbath the verse is "Therefore the Lord blessed the Sabbath day and hallowed it" (Exod. 20:11). For festivals the additional verse is: "So Moses declared to the Israelites the set times of the Lord" (Lev. 23:44). Some have felt that the addition of a single verse is still inadequate for a Kiddush with so exaggerated a title as the Great Kiddush. They have therefore enriched the brief Sabbath noon Kiddush with an additional biblical passage (Exod. 31:16–17), the *Ve-Shamru* (And they shall keep [the Sabbath]), a passage in which the Sabbath is labeled as "an everlasting sign" between God and the children of Israel. But these accretions have remained optional. Most people are content with the introductory verse followed by the blessing over the wine. In all probability the name, the Great Kiddush, originally referred to the amount of drink rather than the length of prayer.

The Havdalah

The conclusion of the Sabbath or festival is marked by a ritual rich in symbols and religious significance. The ritual is called Havdalah (literally, separation or distinction). Like the Kiddush it is of ancient origin. But unlike the Kiddush, the Havdalah is recited in a somber mood. The day of joy is gone, and the weekday trials are soon to begin.

Although the Havdalah is of ancient origin and is attributed by the rabbis to the Men of the Great Assembly, its composition was still in a fluid state during the talmudic period. The Talmud discusses at length the contents of the Havdalah. The following two excerpts are illuminating: "R. Huna b. Judah visited Raba's home. Light and spices were brought before them, [whereupon] Raba recited a blessing over the spices first and then one over the light" (Pes. 103a). Then follows a discussion as to whether Raba was right in regard to the order of the blessings. The second talmudic excerpt relates the following incident, again about Raba:

> R. Jacob B. Abba visited Raba's home. . . . When he [Raba] came to perform *habdalah* . . . [he] recited: "He who makes a distinction between holy and non-holy, between light and darkness, between Israel and the nations, between the seventh day and the six working days" [Pes. 103 a–b].

A lengthy discussion follows. But in the end a definitive formula emerges.

The Havdalah consists of three blessings—over wine, over sweet-smelling spices, and over light. The reason for the first blessing is self-evident. The Havdalah, like the Kiddush, is recited over a cup of wine, and a blessing is required before drinking the wine at the conclusion of the ritual. The reason for the second blessing is that sweet-smelling spices symbolize the spiritual farewell "feast" for the departing "additional soul" which the Jew figuratively possesses on the Sabbath. This blessing is omitted from the Havdalah recited at the conclusion of a festival, because the "additional soul" is attributed only to the Sabbath. The reason for the third blessing is that God's first creation, on the first day of the week, was light. Again, this blessing is omitted from the Havdalah at the conclusion of a festival because light was created only on the first day of the week.[5]

The main benediction of the Havdalah, as its name indicates, deals with the separation or distinction that God has made "between the holy and the profane, between light and darkness, between Israel and the other nations, between the seventh day and the six working days—*Praised art Thou, O Lord, who makest a distinction between holy and profane.*"

In the Middle Ages a hymn welcoming the angels of peace was added as an introduction to the Kiddush, and a few introductory verses were added to the Havdalah.[6] But these additions are not essential parts of the Kiddush or the Havdalah.

Both rituals have remained basically as formulated in the Talmud about fifteen hundred years ago.

The Passover Seder

The most elaborate and by far the most impressive of all domestic services is the Seder, the home service on the first and second nights of the Passover. The Seder (literally, the order of the ritual) is a family service in the form of a religiohistorical pageant which dramatizes in word and symbolic act the story of the Exodus from Egypt. This ritual has enabled the Jewish people to relive annually the epic of its birth. It has also planted in the people's heart an attachment to the house of Israel and a commitment to personal and national freedom.

Early Stages in the Development of the Seder

In the Temple days there was already a distinctive home observance of the Passover. Prior to the festival each family searched the house for leaven and removed all traces of it from sight and possession; during the festival everyone refrained from eating leavened bread. The main celebration, however, took place in Jerusalem. The pilgrims and the local residents attended the Temple services, which were conducted by the Kohanim and the Levites. The people also shared in a festive family celebration, the central feature of which was the paschal offering. The lamb was roasted and consumed. The biblical command regarding this Passover ritual is succinctly summed up in a single verse: "They [the family group] shall eat the flesh [of the paschal lamb] that same night; they shall eat it roasted over the fire, with unleavened bread and with bitter herbs" (Exod. 12:8).

The main Passover observance was thus limited to those who could make the pilgrimage to Jerusalem and to those who resided near the Temple. The biblical legislation is strict on this limitation:

> You are not permitted to slaughter the passover sacrifice in any of the settlements . . . ; but at the place where the Lord your God will choose to establish

> His name, there alone shall you slaughter the passover sacrifice [Deut. 16:5–6].

When the Temple was destroyed, the paschal lamb was necessarily eliminated from the Seder. But the other elements of the ritual were transferred to the home. Every Jew could now carry out the main intent of the Seder ritual, which, according to the Bible, is pedagogical:

> When, in time to come, your son asks you, "What mean the exhortations, laws, and rules which the Lord our God has enjoined upon you?" you shall say to your son, "We were slaves to Pharaoh in Egypt and the Lord freed us from Egypt with a mighty hand. The Lord wrought before our eyes marvelous and destructive signs and portents in Egypt, against Pharaoh and all his household; and us He freed from there, that He might take us and give us the land that He had promised on oath to our fathers [Deut. 6:20–23].

The Seder thus became strictly a family ritual. Except for the paschal lamb, all the rites that were formerly performed in the Temple precincts were transferred to the home service. Only a memorial of the paschal lamb was preserved: a roasted bone is placed on the Seder plate as a reminder of the ancient rite in the Temple. During the two centuries after the fall of the Temple, the Seder service assumed its classic form, and since then it has remained essentially unchanged. To be sure, there have been some adjustments and some accretions, but these have been of relatively minor importance. Thus the answer to the child's questions with which the Seder ritual is opened is as prescribed in the Talmud: (Pes. 116a) "We were slaves unto Pharaoh in Egypt, and the Lord our God took us out from there with a mighty hand and an outstretched arm. . . ." So are the homilies and the other basic elements of the service in accord with the rabbinic sources.

The Preliminary Part of the Seder

The book that contains the liturgy of the Seder service is known as the Haggadah. It usually contains an introduction in which there are specific instructions on how to set the table for the Seder. Three cakes of unleavened bread, or matzot, are placed at the head of the table. Each of the matzot is separately covered. Two of them represent the two loaves of bread which are always placed on the table for Sabbath or festival meals. The third is for the afikomen which is broken and put aside for later use. Then there is the Passover platter, on which are placed a number of items that symbolize historic events and religious concepts connected with the Exodus. These items consist of (1) horseradish tops and sliced and ground horseradish to symbolize the bitterness of slavery, (2) a mixture of nuts and apples called haroset, to symbolize the mortar out of which the Hebrews made bricks for Pharaoh, (3) a roasted bone and a roasted egg as memorials of the paschal and the festival sacrifices at the Jerusalem Temple, and (4) some parsley and a bowl of salt water in which to dip it before eating. This symbol has been variously interpreted. The reason most frequently given is that the green vegetable is a reminder of the spring, when vegetation revives and with it the eternal hope for a new world of freedom. Also placed on the table are a decanter filled with wine, a wineglass for each person, and an extra cup of wine for the prophet Elijah, who will bring the good tidings of the Messiah's arrival.

Usually the introduction to the Haggadah also contains a mnemonic device for remembering the order of the service. This formula consists of fifteen words, each of which stands for a specific element of the ritual. This device goes back to the days when there were no handy Haggadot, and people had to rely on memory. Today this device serves mostly as a historic relic of the talmudic days when the prayers and the liturgic rituals were still an oral tradition.[7]

Like all festival meals, the Seder starts with the Kiddush—the first of four cups of wine that everyone drinks at the Seder. This practice had its beginnings in the social customs that prevailed in the talmudic period, when it was customary to start and conclude a festive meal with a cup of wine. The opening cup of wine became the Kiddush.* The concluding cup

* *See pp. 297–99.*

came to be known as the *Kos Shel Berakhah,* the cup over which a special benediction was recited after the completion of the *Birkat Ha-Mazon.** But on Passover there was a long service between the Kiddush and the meal, and a similarly lengthy liturgy after the *Birkat Ha-Mazon.* Hence another cup of wine was served at the end of the initial service (that is, immediately before the meal) and still another cup at the conclusion of the Seder service, before the people left the table. As usual, acts that accompany religious rituals become religious rituals in their own right. The four cups of wine came to be regarded as essential elements of the Seder. Even the poorest man, says the Mishnah, should not drink less than four cups of wine (Pes. 10:1). The four cups were duly rationalized as symbols of our rejoicing over God's fourfold promise of freedom: "I will free you," "[I will] deliver you," "I will redeem you," and "I will take you" (Exod. 6:6–7).

This rationalization of the four cups of wine brought forth a controversial issue. If each divine promise of freedom is celebrated with a cup of wine, then a fifth cup should be drunk in celebration of a fifth promise in the very next verse: "I will bring you [into the land]" (Exod. 6:8). Indeed, what is the value of being taken out of the land of Egypt and not being taken into the Promised Land? A fifth cup is therefore filled but not drunk. When the prophet Elijah comes to herald the coming of the Messiah he will, according to the rabbis, decide all moot questions, among them whether a fifth cup of wine is in order. This extra cup of wine has therefore been named the cup of Elijah. This, of course, is the legal explanation. There is a popular and more poetic explanation, however: the extra cup of wine is to demonstrate our faith in the promise of Elijah's coming to announce the redemption of Israel from its exile.

The Seder service should logically follow the Kiddush. But there are several preliminary rites that must be performed. These rites are not of lesser importance; their symbolism is rich and edifying, and their performance is traditionally regarded as mandatory. First the father washes his hands, in

* *See pp. 292–95.*

Circumcision, Rothschild ms. 24, 1475, The Israel Museum, Jerusalem. PHOTO: ALFRED BERNHEIM

imitation of the Kohanim who used to perform the ritual in the Temple. Then the parsley is dipped in the salt water, the appropriate benediction is recited, and it is eaten by everyone. The leader then breaks off half of the middle matzah and puts it aside to be eaten at the end of the meal as the afikomen.[8] The afikomen is an additional remembrance of the paschal lamb, which was eaten at the end of the Passover feast. The last of the preliminary rites is the recitation of a formula inviting the poor and the homeless to join in the family Seder. This invitation is appropriately phrased in the Aramaic vernacular of the time, otherwise the poor would not understand the invitation extended to them:

> This is the bread of poverty which our ancestors ate in Egypt. All who are hungry, let them come in and eat. All who are needy, let them come in and celebrate the Passover. Now we are here; next year may we be in the land of Israel! Now we are slaves; next year may we be free men![9]

After these preliminaries the main body of the Haggadah is read.

The Organizational Pattern of the Haggadah

At first glance the Haggadah appears to be an unplanned accumulation of material dealing with the Exodus from Egypt and the observance of the Passover. However, a careful reading of the Haggadah reveals an organizational pattern based on a number of principles. To begin with, there are the Hallel psalms, which were an essential part of the Temple service. These psalms, along with their introductory and concluding benedictions, constitute a central part of the Haggadah. The rest of the Haggadah is based on three pedagogic principles. The first is the biblical command that every Jew is duty bound to tell his children about the miraculous redemption from Egyptian slavery:

> And when your children ask you, "What do you mean by this rite?" you shall say, "It is the passover sacrifice to the Lord, because He passed over the

> houses of the Israelites in Egypt when He smote the Egyptians, but saved our houses" [Exod. 12:26–27].

Hence the education of the children is the primary objective of the Seder service.

The second and the third principles delineate the methodology of the educational process. In teaching the children about the redemption from Egypt, the parent is not to be perfunctory or hasty. He is to tell the story in depth. The Haggadah therefore states that "the more one tells about the going out from Egypt, the more praiseworthy is he." It is equally important that the parent not perform his teaching in a listless, uninvolved manner. This would render his teaching fruitless. The story of the Exodus must be told with feeling and conviction:

> In every generation a man is bound to regard himself as though he personally had gone forth from Egypt, because it is said, and thou shalt tell thy son . . . : It is because of that which the Lord did for *me* when *I* came forth out of Egypt" [Pes. 116b].

The first of these principles is implemented quite effectively. The child is placed in the center of the Seder ritual. He opens the service by asking the Four Questions. In ancient times these questions were quite natural, because the Passover meal was eaten first; the child had partaken of the unleavened bread, dipped the parsley in the salt water and the bitter herbs in the haroset, and he had eaten of the roast meat of the paschal lamb. The original questions concerned these three things. And if the child did not ask of his own accord, the Mishnah tells us, the father would coach him to ask these questions. Today the children are taught in advance how to ask the traditional Four Questions.

The Four Questions have had a rather complicated history.[10] By their very nature they remained for a long time in a fluid state. As we have indicated, originally there were only three questions: about the unleavened bread, the roast meat, and the extra dipping of bitter herbs in the haroset. Later a fourth question was added—in all probability to match the four sons mentioned in the Haggadah and the four cups of wine. The additional question was about the bitter herbs. This question, it will be noted, overlaps the question about the dipping of the bitter herbs in the haroset. Another change was made after the Temple was destroyed. Because the question about the roast meat had become obsolete, a new question was substituted—the question about the leaning posture at the Seder service. Leaning at a festive meal was a Roman custom. Free men would lean on couches around the festive table. The Jews had copied this custom, and they regarded this posture as especially suitable for the Seder, since it emphasized that the participants were free men and women. But this last of the Four Questions is now as obsolete as the question about the roast meat which it replaced. Jews no longer recline on couches around a festive board; there is only a clumsy attempt to simulate the ancient custom. What is more perplexing is that the Haggadah provides no direct answer to this question. It is left to the leader of the Seder to explain it orally.

The Four Questions elicit an appropriate response. The father says:

> We were slaves unto Pharaoh in Egypt, and the Lord our God took us out from there with a mighty hand and an outstretched arm. If the Holy One, blessed be He, had not taken our forefathers out of Egypt, then we, and our children, and our children's children would still be slaves unto Pharaoh in Egypt.

Were it not for the second principle, which demanded elaboration and enrichment of the story of the Exodus, this response would logically have been followed by the specific answers to each of the questions. These are given in a later section of the Haggadah: "R. Gamaliel used to say: Whoever does not make mention of these three things on Passover does not discharge his duty, and these are they: the Passover-offering, unleavened bread, and bitter herbs" (Pes. 116a–116b). This statement by Rabban Gamaliel is followed by an explanation of each of these symbols and constitutes an adequate answer to the questions as originally asked when the Temple was in existence. However, the second principle demanded elaboration of the story of the Exodus. This principle is enunciated in the Haggadah immediately after the father's initial answer. A number of rabbinic discourses on the story of the Exodus are now introduced. Parenthetically it is mentioned how each of four types of sons is to be told about the Exodus.

The elaboration begins with a mishnaic homily: "In the beginning, our forefathers were idolators, but the Eternal has brought us near to His service." This introduces a brief summary of the historic events from Abraham to the enslavement in Egypt and Pharaoh's attempt to annihilate the Hebrew people. And this, says the Haggadah, has been the pattern of Jewish history: "For it is not only one man [Pharaoh] who tried to annihilate us, but in every generation there are those who try to destroy us, and the Holy One, blessed be He, rescues us from their hands."

A running commentary on each word of the biblical text (Deut. 26:5–8) follows: "My father was a fugitive Aramean. He went down to Egypt." The commentary leads up to the ten plagues that God inflicted on the Egyptians, followed by some fanciful speculations as to the number and the nature of the plagues. These rabbinic discourses are concluded with a fitting piyut which enumerates the many favors and benefits that God bestowed on Israel at the time of the Exodus. Each boon mentioned is concluded with the refrain "*Dayenu*" (It would have been enough for us).

At this point the Haggadah resumes the direct response to the Four Questions with the statement of Rabban Gamaliel regarding the three essential items of the Seder service. The response to the Four Questions is thus concluded. As noted above, the answer about the paschal lamb relates to a question that is no longer asked, and the question about the leaning posture that replaced it is not answered at all.

The Haggadah now states the third principle, that each man must regard himself as if he personally was redeemed from Egypt. This principle is implemented by means of several symbolic enactments of the national experience, which gives them reality and tends to develop in the child a sense of identification with the historic events. The bitterness of slavery ceases to be an abstraction and becomes a real experience. Freedom is not just a vague ideal but an actuality.

Before the symbolic actions, the reading of the Haggadah has to be completed. The Hallel psalms,* which were recited at the Temple to thank God for His mighty acts of redemption, are now introduced. Only the first two of the six psalms are read at this point. The second of these psalms is especially appropriate, because it is directly related to the Exodus: [11]

When Israel came forth out of Egypt,
The house of Jacob from a people of strange language;
Judah become His sanctuary,
Israel His dominion.

The sea saw it, and fled;
The Jordan turned backward.
The mountains skipped like rams,
The hills like young sheep [*Ps. 114:1–4*].

These psalms are introduced by a prayer which connects them with the story of the Exodus: "We are therefore duty bound to thank, praise, laud, glorify, and exalt . . . Him who performed all these wonders for our fathers and for us. . . . Now let us sing unto Him a new song: Hallelujah!" The reading of the two psalms is followed by a concluding benediction and the drinking of the second cup of wine.

After washing the hands for the meal, two benedictions are recited. The first is the Hamotzi,† the benediction before eating bread, and the second is a benediction thanking God "who sanctified us by His commandments and commanded us concerning the eating of matzah." After the eating of the matzah comes the benediction "concerning the eating of bitter herbs." Slices of horseradish [12] are dipped in the haroset and eaten. Finally there is the eating of the three central Passover symbols in one sandwich, as "a memorial to the days when the Temple was in existence, in accordance with the practice of Hillel":

Thus did Hillel, when the Temple was in existence: He would combine some of the paschal

* *See pp. 210–11.*
† *See p. 292.*

> lamb and some *Matzah* and some bitter herbs, and eat them together to fulfill the biblical command: "They shall eat it with unleavened bread and bitter herbs" [Num. 9:11].

Today's sandwich contains only matzah and bitter herbs.

The festival meal is now served. It is concluded with everyone's eating a piece of the afikomen, after which the grace after meals is recited and the third cup of wine is drunk.

It will be recalled that only two of the Hallel psalms were read before the meal. The balance of the psalms should now be read. But a strange ritual of postgeonic origin precedes the Hallel. The door is opened and some harsh words are uttered:

> *Pour out Thy wrath upon the nations that know*
> *Thee not,*
> *And upon the kingdoms that call not upon Thy name.*
> *For they have devoured Jacob,*
> *And laid waste his habitation* [*Ps.* 7*9:6*–7].

In the popular mind this ritual is associated with the coming of Elijah to bring the good tidings of the impending arrival of the Messiah. The door is opened as a gesture of welcome to the prophet, and little children are usually told that the spirit of Elijah actually enters and takes a sip from the cup reserved for him. In recent times some have eliminated the harsh verses from the Haggadah and have replaced them with a suitable hymn about the coming of Elijah. Appropriate as this innovation is, it does not explain the earlier custom of pronouncing maledictions when the door was opened.

The historic basis for opening the door and reciting the discordant verses quoted above can be traced to the practice of opening the door at the beginning of the Seder, when the invitation to the poor and the homeless was pronounced. Thus the Talmud tells us that "when he [Rabbi Huna] had a meal he would open the door wide and declare, Whosoever is in need let him come and eat" (Ta'an. 20b). But during the Middle Ages this praiseworthy practice became increasingly risky, for unruly Gentiles would take advantage of these situations. Instead of a poor Jew's entering the house, unwelcome and offensive guests would enter, preceded by some missiles. As happens with many practices that become associated with a religious ritual, the opening of the door became a religious ritual in its own right. When it became too hazardous to open the door, this practice was not abolished but was postoned to a later hour, after the meal, when there were no longer any rowdies to disturb the Seder. It was quite natural for the Jews to relieve their frustration by quoting those bitter verses of the psalmist against the heathens "who know Thee not . . . for they have devoured Jacob, and laid waste his habitation."

The Hallel is now completed. Psalm 136, known in rabbinic literature as the Great Hallel, is also read. And finally the concluding benediction, which is the same as the one recited on Sabbaths and festivals after the Verses of Praise,* is read. It starts with the *Nishmat* † prayer, and ends with the blessing "*Praised art Thou, O Lord, God and King, great in praises, God of thanksgivings, Lord of wonders, who delights in song and psalm, O King and God, the life of all worlds.*"

During the geonic period a number of piyutim were added after the conclusion of the Haggadah, and during the Middle Ages a number of hymns, among them several jingles for the children, were attached at the end of the Haggadah. The most popular of the jingles, which deals with an only kid that father bought for two zuzim (coins), is a sixteenth century adaption of an old German poem. But it has been properly reinterpreted and invested with higher significance. It now alludes to several important events in Jewish history, ending with the messianic era.

In Israel this grand religiohistorical pageant, the Seder, is performed only on the first night of the Passover. In the Diaspora, the Orthodox and the Conservative branches of Judaism repeat it on the second night. Unfortunately, the ritual on the second night is an exact repetition of the first night, which renders it something of an anticlimax. The establishment of the state of Israel has led some to question not only the second Seder, but also the propriety of the Second-Day

* *See pp. 141–42.*
† *See pp. 166–67.*

Festival of the Diaspora.* Its solution must be left to the future. Whether the Seder ritual is performed once or twice is not as important as the fact that it has proved itself throughout the centuries to be the most impressive, the most joyous, the most memorable of all domestic rituals in Judaism.

Some Additional Domestic Rites

Of the domestic rituals developed during the rabbinic and geonic times three are of particular interest. The first is the ritual of the removal of leaven before the Passover festival. The second is that of the building of a sukkah for the Feast of Tabernacles. The third is the rite of kindling the Hanukah lights. In all these rituals the children play a central role.

The Search for Leaven

One of the strictest biblical admonitions deals with the removal of hametz, or leaven, before the Passover. This commandment is repeated in two consecutive chapters of the Book of Exodus: "No leaven shall be found in your houses for seven days" (Exod. 12:19); and "No leavened bread shall be found with you . . . in all your territory" (Exod. 13:7). On the basis of these verses the rabbis concluded that leaven is neither to be *seen* nor *found* in anyone's possession during the Passover. From the wording of these commandments they also concluded that the prohibition is absolute. Not even the minutest crumb, not even an infinitesimal amount of hametz is to remain within one's premises. Conscientious women have therefore dreaded the annual task of cleaning the house for Passover. It has been both back-breaking and frustrating. Failure is almost inevitable. How can one be sure that a tiny crumb was not left in some obscure crevice?

Housecleaning for Passover begins long before the festival. But the official ritual of removing the leaven from the house takes place on the evening before the Seder. The talmudic tractate Pesahim, which deals with the observance of the Passover, opens with these words: "On the evening of the four-

* *See pp. 205–208.*

teenth [of Nisan] a search is made for leaven by the light of a lamp" (Pes. 2a).

The ritual of searching for leaven is carefully staged. Crumbs of bread are placed in a number of out-of-the-way places, and during the search they are "found" and whisked away. Children look forward to the search for leaven with much anticipation. The father—holding a lighted candle, a receptacle such as a wooden spoon, and a feather for a brush—recites the benediction: "[Who hast commanded us] concerning the removal of leaven" (Pes. 7a). The search is pursued in earnest. Excitement accompanies the location of each crumb, and the act of brushing it into the spoon is regarded as a special privilege. The search continues till every crumb has been located and safely lodged in the spoon.

At the conclusion of the search the father reads a legal formula, nullifying all hametz that may have been overlooked: "Let all leaven that is in my premises which I have not seen and which I have not removed be as of no avail and be as the dust of the earth." The spoon and the crumbs and the feather are now carefully stored away. Next morning, after ten o'clock, when hametz may no longer be eaten, the bundle that had been stored away on the previous evening is burned along with all other hametz. The house is now ready for the Passover.

Building a Sukkah

The most exciting of the home rituals, as far as the children are concerned, is the annual building of a sukkah for the Feast of Tabernacles. No skillfully planned class project can ever hope to develop as much personal involvement and enthusiastic participation as does the building of a sukkah. There is no artificiality or make-believe about this family project. It is a real adult activity, and the adults are none other than their own parents. The children's enthusiasm usually overflows the bounds of the home and soon involves the children of the whole neighborhood.

The building of a sukkah is clearly ordained in the Bible:

> On the fifteenth day of this seventh month there shall be the Feast of Booths to the Lord, [to last]

> seven days. . . . You shall live in booths seven days; all citizens in Israel shall live in booths, in order that future generations may know that I made the Israelite people live in booths when I brought them out of the land of Egypt, I the Lord your God [Lev. 23:34, 42–43].

The Bible does not specify how the sukkah is to be built. The specifications are provided by the rabbis, who devote to this subject a substantial part of the mishnaic tractate Sukkah. The general principle is that the sukkah is to be "a temporary abode" with a covering that is sufficiently sparse to permit one to see the stars. The sukkot thus resemble the booths in which the Israelites dwelled in the desert. By "dwelling" in such a precarious hut one is expected to experience the insecurity of the Hebrews during their wanderings in the desert for forty years, and to be inspired with a feeling of trust in God who led the Hebrews safely through the desert and brought them to the Promised Land.*

The Mishnah provides the specific rules for the building of a sukkah. The height of the sukkah must not be less than ten and not more than twenty handbreadths. There is no limit to the length or width of the sukkah, but it must not be less than seven by seven handbreaths. The covering must consist of materials that grew from the soil, such as tree branches, straw, or narrow slabs of wood.

Ideally one should really dwell in the sukkah during the seven days of the festival and eat, drink, and sleep in the sukkah. If this is impossible, one should at least eat his meals there. If it rains, however, one should eat in the house, for the Feast of Sukkot is the "season of our rejoicing," and there is absolutely no pleasure in being soaked by the rain during the meal.

The synagogue liturgy of the Feast of Tabernacles is extensive and impressive,† but in the home it is rather scant. The festival lights are kindled by the mother, the Kiddush is recited by the father, and the *Ya'aleh Ve-Yavo* prayer is added to the

* *See pp. 204–205.*
† *See pp. 219 ff.*

grace after meals. These home rituals are not distinctive, for they are part of the home observance of every major festival. Eating in the sukkah and reciting the extra blessing after the Kiddush—"Who sanctified us by His commandments and commanded us to dwell in the sukkah"—are the chief elements of the home observance of the Feast of Tabernacles.

The sukkah is often used during the week of the festival for functions not prescribed in the religious codes, but not contrary to the spirit of the festival. If the sukkah is large enough and properly decorated, guests are entertained in it; children invite their friends, and if a child's birthday falls during the festival, the sukkah is the natural place for the celebration. Studying in the sukkah is especially praiseworthy.

People who live in apartment houses find it difficult if not impossible to erect a sukkah.[13] They discharge their duty by visiting the synagogue sukkah, where the congregation gathers after each service and participates in the Kiddush and partakes of the refreshments. In some synagogues a symbolic meal is served to enable the people to eat a meal in the sukkah.

In recent years many Jews have moved to the suburbs, and the building of family sukkot is beginning to come back into favor. Fortunate are the children whose parents build a family sukkah. Their rewards are very great.

Kindling the Hanukah Lights

The chief characteristic of the Hanukah observance is the kindling of the lights. To be sure, the Hallel is recited at the daily morning services, and special selections from the Scriptures are read in the synagogue.* But it is the home ritual that stands out as the essential ceremony of the festival. The children anticipate the kindling of the Hanukah lights with great pleasure because the home service is followed by the distribution of presents or money known as Hanukah *gelt* (money).

Contrary to expectation, the origin of the ritual of kindling lights on Hanukah is vague and its motivation is weak. A legendary reason for the lights is given in the Talmud:

* *See pp. 271–72.*

> What is [the reason of] *Hanukkah?* For our Rabbis taught: . . . when the [Syrian] Greeks entered the Temple, they defiled all the oils therein, and when the Hasmonean dynasty prevailed against and defeated them, they made search and found only one cruse of oil which lay with the seal of the High Priest, but which contained [oil] sufficient for one day's lighting only; yet a miracle was wrought therein and they lit [the lamp] therewith for eight days. The following year these [days] were appointed a Festival with [the recital of] Hallel and thanksgiving [Shab. 21b].

It is also surprising to learn that the rules regarding the Hanukah lights were in a state of flux for a long time. The schools of Hillel and Shammai, which existed more than a century after the Hasmonean victory, discussed the manner of kindling the lights. The Talmud records their divergent views: "*Beth Shammai* maintain: On the first day eight lights are lit and thereafter they are gradually reduced; but *Beth Hillel* say: On the first day one is lit and thereafter they are progressively increased" (Shab. 21b). The Talmud concludes that the view of *Bet Hillel* is to be followed.

The reason for this state of flux is that the observance of kindling the Hanukah lights was not widespread during the days of the Mishnah.[14] The celebration of Hanukah had lost much of its significance because of the strained relations between the early sages of the Mishnah and the Hasmonean rulers. As a result, the Mishnah hardly mentions the Hanukah festival. This is all the more striking because a whole mishnaic tractate is devoted to the semifestival of Purim. But in the third century Hanukah regained its honorable place in the calendar of Jewish festivals. After the Persian Magians launched their fanatic persecutions against the Jews, the kindling of the Hanukah lights was one of the religious rites that were forbidden. As often happens, persecution of a religious rite awakens special esteem for it. The forbidden rite shares the aura of martyrdom. To kindle the Hanukah lights became an act of kiddush hashem, the sanctification of God's name. The rabbis then provided the ritual with special blessings and found a logical place in the Talmud for a discussion of the Hanukah observance. In a section dealing with the Sabbath lights they digressed to discuss the procedures of kindling the Hanukah lights (Shab. 21a–23b). These lights, the rabbis say, are not to be placed on the family table; their purpose is not to light up the house. They are placed on a windowsill so that they may be seen outside, "to publicize the miracles" that God performed for "our ancestors in those days at this season of the year." These lights are to serve only one purpose, to make known God's saving power.

The liturgy accompanying the kindling of the Hanukah lights was formulated during the talmudic period and has come down to our day with hardly any changes. On each evening of the festival the family gathers for the service. As mentioned above, the procedure of the *Bet Hillel* is followed. On the first night one light is lit, and on each succeeding night an additional light is lit. An extra light, called the shammash, or auxiliary light, is kindled each night. It is used as a glorified match with which to kindle the official lights.

The liturgic element of the service is limited to appropriate blessings and hymns. On the first night three blessings are recited:

> *Praised art Thou . . . who sanctified us by His commandments and commanded us to kindle the light of Hanukah.*
>
> *Praised art Thou . . . who wrought miracles for our fathers in days of old, at this season.*
>
> *Praised art Thou . . . who kept us in life, and preserved us, and enabled us to reach this season.*

On the second night and thereafter the ritual is no longer a novelty. Hence the last benediction is omitted.

During the geonic period a brief prayer known by its initial words—*Ha-Nerot Ha-Lalu* (These lights)—was added. Recited or chanted immediately after the benedictions, it summarizes the purpose and the nature of the ritual.

Another hymn, known from its initial words as *Ma'oz Tzur* (Rock of Ages), was added in the thirteenth century. This postgeonic piyut with its borrowed melody[15] has achieved much popularity and is generally regarded as an integral part of the service.

For the children the climax of the ritual comes immediately after the home service, when Hanukah gifts are distributed. From the children's viewpoint what can possibly be of greater significance in the Hanukah service? And from our viewpoint what can be a pleasanter note on which to close this chapter?

12 RITES OF INITIATION, MARRIAGE, AND BURIAL

The notable junctures of a person's life are usually celebrated by rituals in which the family and the community participate. Liturgic rites have developed for the observance of these significant occasions. Among those that have assumed a special sanctity in Judaism is the initiation of the male infant into the covenant of Abraham. If the male infant happens to be the firstborn of his mother, there is an additional rite, the symbolic redemption of the child from his obligations to serve in the Temple ritual. A similar rite of initiation takes place for adults who renounce the faith into which they were born and apply for admission into the religious fellowship of the Jewish people. Another ritual is marriage, which is accompanied by an ancient liturgy of beauty and significance. Finally, there is the inevitable end of life, which calls for the final rites of burial. During the talmudic and geonic periods a liturgy grew up around each of these crucial moments in the lifetime of the Jew. These rites are both relevant to each of the occasions and meaningful to the community as a whole.[1]

The Covenant of Abraham

When a Jewish male infant is eight days old, he is admitted into the covenant of Abraham by means of the rite of circumcision. This religious ritual is emphatically enjoined in the Bible:

> God further said to Abraham, . . . "Such shall be the covenant between Me and you and your offspring to follow which you shall keep: . . . throughout the generations, every male among you shall be circumcised at the age of eight days [Gen. 17:9–12].

The rite of circumcision, the berith milah, became one of the most deeply rooted institutions in Judaism. When the Romans tried to interfere with this religious rite, the Jews of Palestine rose up in a bitter rebellion which led to one of the bloodiest wars in Jewish history.*

The liturgy of the berith milah had already assumed most of its characteristics in the early centuries of the Common Era. The Talmud (Shab. 137b), quoting an early source of the second century, describes the service in detail, a description which generally corresponds to the service followed today. By the end of the geonic period the liturgy was fully developed. The child is brought to the synagogue and is handed to the mohel, the man who performs the circumcision. The people in attendance greet the infant with the biblical verse "Blessed be he that cometh in the name of the Lord" (Ps. 118:26). The person who holds the child on his lap while the mohel performs the circumcision is known as the sandek.[2] Two chairs are provided—one for the sandek and one for a special "guest," the prophet Elijah, who according to a popular tradition attends every berith milah service and protects the infants from lurking dangers. Some synagogues, especially in oriental communities, have a permanent "chair of Elijah" reserved for these occasions, which no one but the spirit of Elijah ever occupies.

* *See pp. 123–24.*

To make sure that no one sits on this chair, some oriental synagogues suspend it high on a wall.

The mohel recites a number of appropriately chosen verses as an introduction to the service.[3] When the infant is placed on the lap of the sandek, the mohel recites a benediction as prescribed in the Talmud: "*Praised art Thou, O Lord our God, King of the universe, who sanctified us by His commandments and commanded us to perform the rite of circumcision.*" After the circumcision the father recites the benediction prescribed for him in the Talmud: "*Praised art Thou, O Lord our God, King of the universe, who sanctified us by His commandments and commanded us to make him enter into the covenant of Abraham our father.*" The people in attendance respond in accordance with the talmudic prescription: "Even as he has entered the covenant, so may he enter the study of the Torah, the marriage canopy, and the performance of good deeds."

The mohel then takes a cup of wine and recites a special Kiddush. It starts, as usual, with the benediction over the wine, and concludes with a prayer for the infant: "O living God . . . deliver from destruction the dearly beloved of our flesh for the sake of the covenant Thou hast set in our bodies. *Praised art Thou, O Lord, who makest the covenant.*" It should be noted that the blessing is in the present tense. The covenant is conceived of not only as a precious spiritual heritage from Abraham, but also as an immediate personal commitment. God enters into a covenant with each Jew individually.

During the geonic period it became customary to name the child at the berith milah. An appropriate prayer was added to the ritual:

> Our God and God of our fathers! Preserve this
> child to his father and to his mother, and let his name
> be called in Israel——the son of——.[4] Let his
> father rejoice in him that came forth from his loins,
> and the mother be glad with the fruit of her womb;
> as it is written: Let thy father and thy mother
> be glad,/And let her that bore thee rejoice [Prov.
> 23:25].[5] . . . This little child,——, may he become

> great. Even as he has entered the covenant, so may he enter the study of the Torah, the marriage canopy, and the performance of good deeds.

The neophyte is returned to his mother, and the festivities begin.

The ritual of circumcision, which has been practiced for over four millennia, is rooted in both the history and the consciousness of the people. In the nineteenth century some radical Reform leaders advocated the abolition of circumcision on the grounds that it is not consonant with modernity. But most of the membership of the Reform congregations as well as the more moderate Reform leadership vigorously opposed any tampering with this hallowed ritual. Today the rite of circumcision is an accepted religious observance among all the Jewish groups. Although some prefer to have it performed by a medical surgeon, most Jews, especially of Orthodox and the Conservative branches of Judaism, have insisted on the traditional ritual with a mohel performing the rite. The berith milah, they insist, is a religious ritual not a medical operation; only an approved functionary of the Jewish religious community should perform it. Besides, they add, the mohel (who is, as a rule, approved or licensed by the medical staff of the local hospitals) is usually more expert in his specialty.

Redemption of the Firstborn

A ritual as ancient as the berith milah is the pidyon haben, the redemption of the firstborn male child. The origin of this practice has been traced to ancient, pre-Mosaic times, when it was the duty and privilege of the firstborn to perform the priestly duties for his clan. When these duties were transferred in biblical times to the tribe of the Levites, the firstborn continued to be regarded as consecrated to the priesthood from birth. A legal fiction was created whereby the firstborn was freed or redeemed from his priestly obligations. In the Bible the ritual is rationalized as an outcome of that unforgettable event in the nation's history, the sparing of the Hebrew firstborn when the Egyptian firstborn were smitten during the tenth plague. Because of this it is the duty of the Hebrew firstborn to devote their lives to the service of God by performing the priestly duties in the Temple. Since the Levites have taken over these Temple responsibilities, the Bible provided for a formal release of the firstborn from their inherited obligations by means of a symbolic redemption from the priesthood. The Bible stipulates that "their redemption price [shall be] . . . five shekels" (Num. 18:16). A descendant of the ancient priests, a Kohen, performs the service. Upon receiving the symbolic redemption fee, the Kohen assumes the firstborn's responsibilities and frees the child from his Temple duties. As might be expected, a suitable liturgy was developed to accompany the ceremony. The essential elements of this liturgy are specified in the Talmud (Pes. 121b).

The pidyon haben takes place on the thirty-first day of the child's life and applies only to children who are the firstborn of their mothers. No pidyon haben is required if either the father or the mother is a Kohen or a Levite.

The ritual consists of two parts. The first is the prescribed transaction of redeeming the child. This involves the father's payment of five silver coins, corresponding to the five shekels stipulated in the Bible. During the geonic period formulas were developed, prescribing the exact words the father and the Kohen are to say. The second part is a religious service with appropriate benedictions and prayers for the child's well-being.

In the first part, the father presents the child to the Kohen and makes the following declaration: "This, my firstborn son, is the firstborn of his mother, and the Holy One, blessed be He, has commanded to redeem him, as it is said:" (he quotes Numbers 18:16 and Exodus 13:2). The father places before the Kohen the silver coins (five silver dollars).

The Kohen asks in the vernacular Aramaic: "Would you rather give me your firstborn son, the firstborn of his mother, or redeem him for five *sela'im* [coins] which you are obligated to give according to the Torah?"

The father replies in Aramaic: "I desire to redeem my son,

and here is the money for his redemption, which I am obligated to give according to the Torah." The Kohen takes the coins and hands the child back to the father.

With this preliminary transaction completed, the liturgic part of the ritual begins. The father pronounces two blessings:

> *Praised art Thou, O Lord our God, King of the universe, who sanctified us by His commandments and commanded us concerning the redemption of the firstborn son.*
>
> *Praised art Thou, O Lord our God, King of the universe, who kept us in life and preserved us, and enabled us to reach this season.*

The Kohen then holds the coins over the head of the child and pronounces the following formula and blessing:

> This [the coins] is instead of that [the child], this is in exchange for that, this is in remission of that.
>
> May this child enter into life, into the study of the Torah and the fear of heaven. May it be God's will that even as he has been admitted to redemption, so may he enter into the study of the Torah, the marriage canopy, and the performance of good deeds. Amen.

The Kohen then places his hand on the child's head and bestows upon him several biblical blessings, among them the priestly benedictions.[6]

The festivities now begin. Those in attendance extend their good wishes to the happy parents, and bestow their manifold blessings upon the child.

Admission of Proselytes

Contrary to popular belief, Jews were at one time active in winning converts to Judaism. Rabbi Simeon ben Gamaliel is quoted as saying:

> Thus have the Sages [of the Mishnah] taught: When a would-be proselyte comes to accept Judaism, a hand [of welcome] should be stretched out

> towards him to bring him beneath the wings of the *Shekhinah* [God's Presence] [Lev. Rab. 2:9].

The proselyte was regarded as being under God's special protection, as Resh Lakish said: "Whoever wrests the judgment of the proselyte is as if he wrests the judgment of the All-High" (Hag. 5a).

Jews held the proselytes in high esteem—so much so that they traced the ancestry of some of their greatest personalities to proselytes. King David was a descendant of Ruth, the Moabite (Ruth 4:21–22), and the great sages of the Mishnah, Shemaia and Abtalion, as well as Rabbi Akiba and Rabbi Meir, were either proselytes or the descendants of proselytes. In the weekday *Tefillah* one of the benedictions couples the proselytes with the "righteous" and the "pious" upon whom God's mercy and blessing are invoked. However, during the persecutions that followed the disastrous Bar Kokhba rebellion,* Jews began to look upon proselytes with suspicion. Some of the proselytes lapsed and turned against their erstwhile coreligionists. They spied upon the Jews and denounced them to the Romans.

The Talmud defines the status of a proselyte as "a child newly born" (Yeb. 48b). He is therefore initiated into Judaism by means of a well-defined ritual comparable to that for a newborn infant. The first step in the admission of a convert is the establishment of the purity of his or her motives. The would-be convert is admonished regarding the disadvantages and religious burdens which are the lot of a Jew. If the would-be convert remains firm, his candidacy is accepted. However, if it is discovered that his motives are based on personal advantage, his candidacy is rejected. The rabbinic treatise *Gerim* (Proselytes) opens with the following guiding principle:

> One who is about to become a proselyte is not received at once. But he is asked: What has induced you to join us? Do you not know that this nation is downtrodden and afflicted more than all the other nations, that they are subjected to many ills and sufferings? . . . If the candidate replies: "I am

* *See pp. 124–25, 438–39.*

> unworthy to take upon myself the obligations of Him who created the world by mere uttering of of words, blessed be He," he is received at once; if not, he takes leave and departs.[7]

The initiation that follows involves circumcision and ritual immersion, both to be performed in the presence of three witnesses. A woman undergoes only immersion, and proper precautions are taken not to offend her modesty. The Talmud also stipulates that "a proselyte . . . must make [at the time of his ablution] a declaration of acceptance [of the observance of the commandments]" (Yeb. 48a). This necessitates instruction in the basic teachings of Judaism.

At the time of the ritual of immersion the proselyte recites two benedictions in the presence of the witnesses:

> *Praised art Thou, O Lord our God, King of the universe, who sanctified us by His commandments, and commanded us concerning the rite of immersion.*
>
> *Praised art Thou, O Lord our God, King of the universe, who kept us in life, and preserved us, and enabled us to reach this season.*

The neophyte is then given a new name. Since proselytes are regarded as the spiritual children of the patriarch Abraham, who according to the rabbis was actively engaged in the conversion of people to his faith, male proselytes are usually given the name Abraham the son of Abraham, and women are usually given the name Ruth the daughter of Abraham.

In modern times the procedure of admitting proselytes has become more formal. A period of about six months of instruction precedes the ritual, and the proselyte is required to appear before a rabbinic court for an examination. However, the basic principles established in talmudic times are still the guiding rules.

The Marriage Service

The happiest of the rites of passage is that of marriage. This is properly so, for the Talmud says: "Any man who has no wife lives without joy, without blessing, and without goodness"(Yeb. 62b). This ritual, too, had been fully developed during the talmudic period. Only some minor items were added in later centuries.

In the Bible we find no mention of a marriage ritual that can be called religious. The groom, we are told, is to pay the bride's father a *mohar*, or a marriage price. This was not necessarily a purchase transaction. In all probability it was a means of providing the bride with possessions to bring into her new home. This is still the practice among the Moslem Arabs. Be that as it may, we find no marriage liturgy until rabbinic times.

In the talmudic and geonic periods it was customary to perform the marriage ritual in two stages. First there was the betrothal, called *Erusin.* As much as a full year elapsed before the second stage was reached. This permitted the bride to gather her trousseau and to prepare for wedded life. The second stage was the marriage proper, called *Nisuin.*

In postgeonic times, when Jewish life became precarious, leisurely weddings were no longer possible. Nobody could anticipate the nature of the misfortunes ahead. The two ceremonies of betrothal and marriage were therefore combined into one ritual. This has remained the standard practice to this day. However, a separation of the two parts of the liturgy was introduced in the form of a public reading of the marriage writ, known as the ketubah.

In connection with the ketubah it should be noted that marriage was regarded by the rabbis as being at once a religious rite and a social contract. As a religious rite the marriage ceremony was called Kiddushin, an act of sanctification, and was to be implemented by means of a rich and meaningful liturgy. As a social contract the marriage called for a ketubah, a legal writ, in which the bride and groom undertake mutual obligations and the bride is provided with safeguards in case of divorce or widowhood. The language of the religious rite is liturgic, that of the ketubah is legal.

The liturgy of the Jewish marriage ceremony is prescribed in the Talmud as follows:

> [As to] the benediction of betrothal—what does one say? . . . *Blessed* [*Praised*] *art Thou, O Lord our*

> *God, King of the Universe, who has sanctified us by his commandments and has commanded us concerning the forbidden relations and has forbidden unto us the betrothed and has allowed unto us the wedded through* [the marriage] *canopy and sanctification. . . . Blessed [Praised] art Thou, O Lord, who sanctifies Israel through canopy and sanctification* [Ket. 7b].

This formula is preceded by the usual benediction over the cup of wine. The bride and groom taste the wine as a symbol of their commitment to share their life. The betrothal ceremony is concluded with the bridegroom's giving the bride a gold ring and reciting a formula which is also of rabbinic origin: "Behold, thou art consecrated unto me [by this ring, according to the law of Moses and Israel]" (Kid. 5b).

No marriage ceremony takes place without a ketubah's having been executed in the presence of witnesses and officially transmitted to the bride. Originally this was a private transaction in no way connected with the liturgic ritual. But, as mentioned above, the custom of reading the ketubah at the completion of the betrothal service was instituted to provide a separation between the betrothal and the marriage rites.

The marriage rites, known in rabbinic literature as *Birkot Hatanim*, the Blessings of the Bridegrooms, had also been fully developed in the rabbinic period, as we read in the Talmud:

> Our Rabbis taught: The blessing of the bridegrooms is said in the presence of ten [persons]. . . . What does one say? Rab Judah said: "*Blessed [Praised] art Thou, O Lord our God, King of the Universe, who has created all things to his glory,*" *and [Praised art Thou . . .] the Creator of man,*" *and* "*[Praised art Thou . . .] who has created man in his image, in the image of the likeness of his form, and has prepared unto him out of himself a building for ever [i.e., Eve]. Blessed [Praised] art Thou, O Lord, Creator of man.*" "*May the barren [i.e., Zion] greatly rejoice and exult when her children will be gathered in her midst in joy. Blessed [Praised] art Thou, O Lord, who maketh Zion joyful through her children.*" "*Mayest Thou make the loved companions*

> *[bride and bridegroom] greatly to rejoice, even as of old. . . . Blessed [Praised] art Thou, O Lord, who maketh bridegroom and bride to rejoice." "Blessed [Praised] art Thou, O Lord our King, God of the universe, who has created joy and gladness, bridegroom and bride, rejoicing, song, mirth, and delight, love, and brotherhood, and peace, and friendship. Speedily, O Lord our God, may be heard in the cities of Judah, and in the streets of Jerusalem, the voice of joy and the voice of gladness, the voice of the bridegroom and the voice of the bride, the voice of the singing of bridegrooms from their canopies and of youths from their feasts of song. Blessed [Praised] art Thou, O Lord, who maketh the bridegroom to rejoice with the bride."* [Ket. 7b–8a].

These benedictions plus the opening benedictions over a cup of wine constitute the seven benedictions of the marriage rite which have been in use ever since the early centuries of the Common Era.[8]

The marriage rites are performed under a huppah, or canopy. This is an ancient and important rite. So much so that the rabbis saw fit to mention the huppah in the betrothal benediction as a symbol of the sanctification of the couple's life. The origin of the canopy was the bridal chamber where the marriage was consummated. In time the bridal chamber was replaced by a mere symbol, consisting of a cover over the heads of the bride and groom, supported by four rods. Its meaning is that the couple will hereafter live under one roof as husband and wife.

Another symbolic act performed at the conclusion of the ritual is the breaking of a glass. This is to indicate that even at the moment of their greatest joy Jews grieve for Zion which was crushed and destroyed. This symbolic act is in fulfillment of the oath taken by the Hebrews when they were led into captivity in 586 B.C.E.

> *If I forget thee, O Jerusalem,*
> *Let my right hand forget her cunning.*
> *Let my tongue cleave to the roof of my mouth,*
> *If I remember thee not;*

> *If I set not Jerusalem*
> *Above my chiefest joy* [*Ps. 137:5–6*].

Funeral Rites

The acceptance of God's dispensations with absolute faith in His inscrutable justice is one of the ideals of rabbinic Judaism. To be sure, so exemplary a person as Job rebelled against blind faith and questioned the justice of his own suffering. But in the end Job too learned that God's ways are beyond human comprehension and that God's dispensations, however mysterious, must be accepted in utter faith. The prophet Habakkuk summed up this principle: "The righteous shall live by his faith" (Hab. 2:4). The Talmud holds up for emulation the example of the martyrdom of Rabbi Hanina ben Teradion and his family. The sage was one of the ten martyrs tortured to death by the Romans.* Their guilt consisted of defying the Hadrianic laws which forbade the teaching of the Torah and the practice of its commandments. The Talmud relates that

> [the Romans] brought up R. Hanina b. Teradion . . . to be burnt, his wife to be slain, and his daughter to be consigned to a brothel. . . . As the three of them went out [from the tribunal] they declared their submission to [the Divine] righteous judgment. He quoted: *The Rock, His work is perfect, for all his ways are justice* [Deut. 32:4]. His wife continued [the verse]: *A God of faithfulness and without iniquity, just and right is He* [ibid.]. And the daughter quoted: *Great in counsel and mighty in work, whose eyes are open upon all the ways of the sons of men, to give everyone according to his ways, and according to the fruit of his doing* [Jer. 32:19] [Ab. Zarah 17b–18a].

The act of submission to God's dispensations is the essence of the Jewish burial service. It is called *Tzidduk Ha-Din*, the justification of God's judgment, and the verses quoted by Rabbi Hanina and his family are the essential part of the ritual.

* *See pp. 124–25, 461.*

Confession on the Deathbed

There are several subordinate rites which precede the *Tzidduk Ha-Din.* The first of these is the *Vidui,* the confession, which is recited on one's deathbed. This is in accordance with the principle laid down in the Talmud that "if one falls sick and his life is in danger, he is told: Make confession" (Shab. 32a); and in the Mishnah there is the statement that "everyone that makes his confession [before his death] has a share in the world to come" (San. 6:2). The formula of the confession reads: "May my death be an atonement for all the sins, iniquities, and transgressions of which I have been guilty against Thee." A whole prayer unit was eventually built up around this brief formula. It includes the short confession *(Ashamnu)*,* and it concludes with the affirmation of faith, "Hear, O Israel, the Lord is our God, the Lord alone" (Deut. 6:4).

The Funeral Oration

Eulogies were already known in biblical days. The most famous is David's eulogy over Saul and Jonathan:

> *Thy beauty, O Israel, upon thy high places is slain!*
> *How are the mighty fallen! . . .*
>
> *I am distressed for thee, my brother Jonathan;*
> *Very pleasant hast thou been unto me;*
> *Wonderful was thy love to me,*
> *Passing the love of women.*
> *How are the mighty fallen,*
> *And the weapons of war perished!* [*2 Sam. 1:19, 26–27*].

In rabbinic times the delivery of a eulogy was a well-established practice. The eulogy was usually based on scriptural texts and was embellished with parables. Its object was, according to one of the sages, to arouse loud lamentations and weeping (Ber. 6b). But the orators were warned not to exaggerate the merits of the deceased: "Just as the dead are punished [for their sins], so the funeral orators are punished [for exaggerated praise of the dead]" (Ber. 62a).

* *See pp. 230–31.*

The procedure in those days was to cleanse the corpse,[9] clothe it with shrouds, and, in the case of a man, place on his shoulders the tallit which he used to wear at prayer. If the deceased was a person of outstanding piety or scholarship, the corpse was taken into the synagogue for a eulogy; ordinary people were carried directly to the cemetery where the service was held.

Justifying the Divine Dispensations

While carrying the corpse to the place of burial, the bearers recited the ninety-first psalm:

> *I will say of the Lord, who is my refuge and my*
> *fortress,*
> *My God, in whom I trust,*
> *That He will deliver thee from the snare of the*
> *fowler,*
> *And from the noisome pestilence* [*Ps. 91:2–3*].

This reassuring prayer prepared the mourners for their supreme test of faith, the acceptance of God's judgment at the very moment when their dead was being buried.

The *Tzidduk Ha-Din* begins with the verse uttered by Rabbi Hanina ben Teradion and his wife at the time they were condemned to death. A number of rhymed poetic passages proclaiming God's justice follow. The prayer is concluded with several scriptural verses, among which is the one uttered by Rabbi Hanina's daughter (Jer. 32:19) and Job's famous words when he learned of his sons' and daughters' death: "The Lord gave, and the Lord hath taken away; / Blessed be the name of the Lord" (Job 1:21). Finally, when the grave is closed, the mourners recite a special Kaddish which includes an insert confirming the rabbinic doctrine concerning the resurrection of the dead during the messianic era:

> May His great name be magnified and sanctified in the world that is to be created anew, where He will quicken the dead, and raise them up into life eternal; will rebuild the city of Jerusalem, and establish His Temple in the midst thereof; and will uproot all alien worship from the earth, and restore the worship of

> the true God. O may the Holy One, blessed be He, reign in His sovereignty and glory during your life. . . . [The rest is the regular mourners' Kaddish.*]

In postgeonic times opposition developed to taking the dead into the synagogue. To begin with, there was the question of where exactly the line is that separates those who deserve to be honored with a eulogy in the synagogue and those who are not worthy of this honor. Then there was the biblical claim that only the living belong in the house of prayer: "The dead praise not the Lord," says the psalmist (Ps. 115:17). As a result, the custom of delivering the funeral oration in front of the synagogue or at the cemetery arose. In modern times the funeral parlor has become an accepted institution, and the funeral oration is usually delivered there. An appropriate service has been developed around the eulogy. In the popular mind, the service at the funeral parlor is the main ritual, and the recital of the *Tzidduk Ha-Din* at the cemetery is a mere supplement. The reverse is in accord with the historic development of the ritual.[10]

13
RITES, SYMBOLS, AND CEREMONIES OF JEWISH WORSHIP

In addition to the prayers sanctioned by tradition, there are concomitant symbols, ceremonials, gestures, postures, acts of expiation, and special garb which express devotion, adoration, and homage. In a literal sense one worships not with mind and heart alone, but with every part of the body. "All my bones," says the psalmist, "shall say: Lord, who is like unto Thee" (Ps. 35:10).

Symbols and symbolic actions are not mere conventions of worship or religious etiquette. Religious rites and symbols con-

* *See pp. 153 ff.*

vey to the worshiper tangible ideas that would otherwise remain mere abstractions; they awaken emotions that might otherwise remain dormant; and they tend to rouse in the worshiper feelings of holiness. Verbal expressions, though symbols in themselves, are at best intangible; symbolic actions are, as a rule, substantive and dramatic. Thus the Kol Nidre prayer * is lifted by means of its traditional chant from a mere legalistic formula to the very peak of the Yom Kippur devotions. Similarly, the custom of kissing the Torah scroll as it is carried from the ark to the reader's table transforms the act of carrying the scroll to the dais into an expression of reverence and devotion to the Torah.

A considerable number of ceremonials have already been described in earlier chapters. Among these were the recital of the Kiddush over a cup of wine, the blowing of the shofar on Rosh Hashanah, the fasting on the Day of Atonement, the shaking of the palm branch and the citron on the Feast of Tabernacles, the kindling of lights on Hanukah, the eating of unleavened bread at the Seder, and the other symbols of the Seder service. These and other symbols and ceremonies have raised Jewish worship from what might have been anemic verbalizations to meaningful and dynamic acts of worship.

Most of the ceremonials, gestures, and postures of Jewish worship had their beginnings in remote antiquity, when they were natural expressions of religious emotions. But in the course of time they were formalized and made into official rituals of the tradition. Since they had their origin in antiquity, it is not unusual for their original meanings to have been superseded by new ones, their original implications reinterpreted to conform with the rabbinic outlook on life. It should be stressed, however, that the lowly origin of a symbol or ceremonial and its original implications, though of interest to the scholar and intriguing to the layman, is functionally of no significance. Only the higher connotations are significant, because they are the ones that have a functional role in the realm of worship.

When the silent objects and the mute actions that accompany the liturgy became part of the tradition, they were en-

* *See pp. 244–47.*

dowed with firm stability. Just as the prayers maintained their exact formulations for centuries, so did their concomitant gestures and ceremonials. To alter a traditional rite was as shocking as to tamper with a prayer. Change was regarded as the mutilation of a sacred usage; deviation was looked upon as defiance of the religious authorities and rebellion against the saintly personalities of the past. The symbols and ceremonials of Jewish worship have therefore retained their essential features throughout the centuries. When change became necessary because of altered conditions, rituals were usually reinterpreted and endowed with new meaning—but the external forms remained fixed.

In recent times changes have been introduced by the Reform and, to a lesser extent, by the Conservative branches of Judaism. Even the Neo-Orthodox have made some slight changes in the ritual. Some of the changes have been motivated by a desire to be modern. An example of such a change is the widespread practice in American synagogues of the reader's facing the congregation instead of the ark. This change was obviously inspired by the Protestant Church, where the pastor faces the congregation and conducts the service. This seemingly minor change in the reader's posture has changed the tone of the synagogue worship. The reader is no longer a *shaliah tzibbur*, the congregation's emissary in divine worship, but a performer of the prayer ritual.

The Place of Worship

"The world is full of God's glory," says the prophet. Nonetheless, the rabbis taught that a man should have a set place for his prayers (Ber. 6b). They found support for this principle in the biblical account of Abraham's prayer in behalf of the cities of Sodom and Gomorrah. "Abraham," says the Bible, "hurried to the place where he had stood before the Lord" (Gen. 19:27). This indicates that Abraham, though he lived before there was a synagogue, already had a designated "place where he stood . . . before the Lord" in prayer. For Abraham's descendants, the ideal place has been the house of prayer.

Synagogue Architecture

In respect to its architecture the synagogue has at no time reflected any uniquely Jewish style. Being aliens everywhere, the Jews did not build with an eye to permanence. Historians have characterized the medieval Jewish economy as one of liquid cash. The Jew never knew when he would have to pack up and wander forth to a new temporary home. Architectural style was therefore not a primary consideration. In addition, the vast majority of Jews were very poor, this despite their supposed wealth. Unless there was a wealthy patron, the general poverty of the community dictated extreme economy. An added reason for not developing a uniquely Jewish style of architecture was the dispersal of the Jews among many nations, where they were always a small minority of the population. And the prevailing disabilities resulted in a lack of skills in the plastic arts—the Jews produced many scholars but few architects. Hence they usually relied on non-Jewish architects to interpret the Jewish tradition of synagogue practice. Because there were some countries where Jews were not permitted to own land, synagogues were held by non-Jewish trustees or were leased on short terms. Under such conditions elaborate architectural structures were not prudent, and the development of a definitive architectural style was unlikely. Modesty to the point of drabness was the prevailing policy.

Unlike the cruciform of the church, the architectural shape of the synagogue lacked symbolic meaning. The synagogue was usually oblong or square, and its external appearance was usually unobtrusive. Especially in medieval Europe, anonymity and concealment were the better part of wisdom.

In the Eastern lands the situation of the Jews was more stable. The Babylonian Talmud therefore specifies that the synagogue be the tallest building in town—and starkly admonishes that any city in which the roofs are higher than the synagogue will eventually be destroyed (Shab. 11a). This provision, however, was seldom possible of execution, especially in the Christian countries where the Church appropriated this prerogative for itself. Woe to the Jewish community that dared build a synagogue taller than the local church. Still, there were synagogues that dared compete with the dominant faith. They achieved their humble victory by building downward so that the synagogue was "taller" than the church within the structure. Building the synagogue partly below the ground also fulfilled the words of the psalmist: "Out of the depths have I called Thee, O Lord" (Ps. 130:1). This principle also found expression in having the spot where the reader stood somewhat below the synagogue floor, so that he could literally cry out to God "out of the depths."

The Talmud also requires that synagogues always have windows (Ber. 31a). The rabbis based this ruling on the example of Daniel's place of prayer in which, the Bible says, "his windows were open in his upper chamber" (Dan. 6:11). A modern interpretation of this rabbinic requirement was given by the late Rabbi Kook. The windows in the synagogue, said Rabbi Kook, are to teach us that during our prayers we must be aware of the outside world. A Jew must not withdraw from the world and pray only for his own needs. But this architectural pattern, too, was not always followed. Windows at times were a liability because the prayers might be heard without and be considered an affront to the sensibilities of the non-Jews.

The Synagogue Interior

The interior of the synagogue was relatively simple and functional. It was devoid of such bold religious symbols as statues, crosses, crucifixes, icons, censers, fonts, relics, or reliquaries. In comparison with some houses of worship, the synagogue was simplicity itself. But it was not lacking in meaningful symbols.

Functionally the synagogue was well adapted to the usages of the tradition. This became evident the moment one crossed the synagogue threshold. The most striking object, located in the center of the synagogue, was the bimah, the raised platform on which the Torah was read. This boldly emphasized the central role of Torah in the synagogue worship. In the modern American synagogue the bimah has all but vanished. The platform in front of the synagogue has replaced the bimah, and the symbol of the Torah's centrality has been obliterated.

The second prominent fixture of the synagogue interior was the *aron ha-kodesh*, the holy ark, wherein the Torah scrolls were kept. Originally there was only a chest with several shelves on which the scrolls were kept in a lying position. The chest was in a side room, and a curtain set it off from the congregation. During the talmudic period the chest was moved to the center of the east wall and made into a fixed part of the synagogue structure. The scrolls were appropriately adorned and were arranged in a standing position so that they could be seen when the ark was opened. The doors of the ark, too, were ornamented with lions and the tablets of the Ten Commandments. The curtain in front of the ark, known as the paroket, became an essential adjunct of the ark in imitation of the tabernacle built in the desert. The Bible tells us that Moses "put up the curtain . . . and screened off the Ark" (Exod. 40:21). In the Jerusalem Temple, too, the Bible informs us that Solomon "made the veil" for the ark (2 Chron. 3:14).

Another symbol that was transferred from the ancient tabernacle and from the Jerusalem Temple was the eternal light. Here, too, the Bible records that one of the priestly duties was to keep the candelabrum lit "before the Lord [to burn] regularly" (Lev. 24:4). In the synagogue the eternal light (made of gold, silver, or burnished brass, depending on the opulence of the donor) hung in front of the ark and burned constantly. It symbolized the spiritual enlightenment which is forever emanating from the Torah.

Torah Ornaments

The most precious adornments were lavished on the Torah scrolls. Each scroll was dressed in a mantle; the Mishnah mentions "scroll wrappers with figures portrayed on them" (Kelim 28:4). Each scroll had two rods, used for rolling the Torah to the assigned portion; they protruded at either end of the scroll. Ornamentation of the upper rods was a natural development. The ultimate form of this ornamentation was a finial on each of the upper rods or a silver crown over the two rods.[1]

Two additional ornaments of the Torah scroll were added in postgeonic times—the breastplate and the pointer. They were developed for utilitarian reasons. Since certain occasions require reading from more than one scroll, it was necessary to know which scroll had been rolled to which reading of the day. Otherwise the scroll had to be rolled during the service while the congregation waited restlessly. Someone came up with the original idea of suspending on each of the prepared scrolls a plaque with changeable inserts, indicating which of the scrolls are to be taken out for the particular service. In time, the changeable plates were omitted and the purely decorative breastplate came into being.

The pointer, too, can be traced to a utilitarian origin. The reader used to point with his index finger to the words he was reading, but this often made it difficult for the person who was called to the Torah to see the script and to follow the reading. Someone thought of a pointer, the end of which was naturally in the form of a hand with its index finger extended. It was called yad (hand) rather than pointer because it represented the hand of the reader. In all probability the yad originated in Germany in the sixteenth century; like the breastplate, it spread from Central Europe to Jewish communities everywhere.

Women's Gallery

The synagogue pews faced the ark, except those along the east wall, which faced the congregation. The east wall seats were occupied by the notables of the community.[2] The synagogue pews were reserved exclusively for the men. The women were provided with separate quarters. In the Eastern lands a separate room was set aside for the women. It was adjacent to the synagogue with connecting windows to enable the women to hear the prayers. In the Western lands there was usually a more liberal arrangement—a gallery with a porous partition which permitted the women not only to hear the prayers but also to peep into the synagogue below.

Contrary to popular belief the separation of the sexes in the synagogue is not a very ancient tradition. The Jerusalem Temple had a special Women's Court, called *Ezrat Nashim*, which has often been suggested as the precedent for the erection of women's galleries in the synagogues. However, the Women's Court in the Temple was used by both men and women except on Sukkot, when the women were separated from the men. It was feared that the gaiety of the occasion might lead to a spirit of levity. But no strict rule separated the sexes during the other occasions of Temple worship.

In the early synagogue, too, there were no formal rules as to the place of the women at the service.[3] The few references in the Mishnah would imply that women participated in the service and even in the public reading of the Torah. However, there was already a bias against women acting as public readers of the Torah because it might prove embarrassing to the men.[4]

It was quite natural, however, for a policy of separating the sexes to develop. According to rabbinic legislation only men are obligated to participate in worship. It was therefore normal for a woman who came to pray to sit in the rear. In talmudic times attempts were made at formal separation of the sexes, especially during crowded festivities—we read that one of the sages set up rows of pottery to separate the men from the women (Kid. 81a). But the actual setting aside of a section of the synagogue for women developed at a later period. There is no record of the exact process of this development, but we do know that in the thirteenth century separate sections of the synagogue for women were already widespread; they soon became the accepted rule everywhere.

Storeroom for Discarded Sacred Texts

Another adjunct of the synagogue structure was the genizah, a room in which people deposited torn prayer books, Bibles, and other holy texts that had deteriorated and become useless. This was established as an act of reverence for the name of God which these books and documents usually contained; for this reason the discarded materials were called *shemot*, divine names. So that these books would not be exposed to possible profanation, every Jew who had a torn book would bring it to the synagogue and deposit it in the genizah. From time to time the torn books were removed and reverently buried on the cemetery. It was in such a genizah in a Cairo synagogue dating back to the year 882 that the late Solomon Schechter discovered the famous hoard of historic documents.[5] For some unknown reason that genizah was never emptied, and the Egyptian climate preserved these thousands of valuable manuscripts and printed materials for modern scholarship.

Art in the Synagogue

No permanent place of worship is devoid of some form of artistic expression. The synagogue was no exception. In addition to the adornments of the scrolls of the Torah and the ark, there were also decorations on the walls and floors. A number of ancient synagogues going back to the talmudic period have recently been excavated, among them the sixth century synagogue at Bet Alpha, with its beautiful mosaics depicting birds, animals, and human figures.[6] The most important of synagogue excavations was that of the Dura-Europos synagogue, which was erected in 245 C.E. This discovery revealed an ancient synagogue art of surprising beauty and originality. The frescoes and mosaics contain symbols of the zodiac, biblical scenes, and geometric figures. The murals are the earliest representations of biblical scenes on so large a scale, and they are regarded as the prototypes of Christian art. Among the panels are a number of colorful scenes from the Bible, such as the prophet Samuel in the Tabernacle of Shiloh (1 Sam. 3) and the three youths in the fiery furnace (Dan. 3). Apparently the Jews of the talmudic period did not refrain from adorning their synagogues with pictures of human beings, at least not in the third century C.E., when the Dura synagogue was erected.

In later centuries, however, the bias against human forms as synagogue decorations grew and in time prevailed. Such decorations came to be regarded as contrary to the second commandment: "You shall not make for yourself a sculptured image, or any likeness of what is in the heavens above, or on the earth below, or in the waters under the earth" (Exod. 20:4). But the religious authorities were not consistent. Lions and eagles as synagogue decorations were to be found everywhere.

The restriction on synagogue art resulted in an increasing reliance on Hebrew inscriptions for decorative purposes. These inscriptions served a dual purpose: they embellished the synagogue and edified the congregation. As an adornment Hebrew script, like Arabic, is an exquisite art form. As edification, the quotations utilized were mostly biblical verses suitable for creating a proper mood for prayer. The most frequent inscription was "Know before whom you stand" (Ber. 28b). Others were "How lovely are Thy tabernacles, O Lord of hosts" (Ps. 84:2); "O give thanks unto the Lord, call upon His name" (Ps. 105:1); "O Lord, hear my prayer" (Ps. 102:2); and many similar quotations.

Occasionally the glass windows were decorated with symbolic forms, but that was rare. Synagogue windows were usually few and small and their function strictly utilitarian. They were meant to admit some light and in warm weather some fresh air.

The Congregational Quorum

Congregational worship was preferred to private devotions because it enabled one to respond to the reader's call to worship and to recite the Kedushah of the *Tefillah*.* At a public service one could also hear the reading of the scriptural selections, and a mourner could recite the Kaddish.† In addition one experienced the interstimulation that comes from worship with coreligionists.

What constitutes a congregation? The answer is a minyan, a minimum of ten adult Jews (an adult Jew is any Jewish male who has passed his thirteenth birthday). The number ten was derived from the first verse of Psalm 82, which reads: "God standeth in the congregation of God." The word *edah* (congregation) is also applied to the ten spies who, in the days of Moses, rendered a negative report on the land of Canaan. Hence it was established that a "congregation of God" consists of at least ten men.

In the geonic period the definition of the minyan was not rigid. In *Massekhet Soferim* (10:8), a late geonic work, we read that a minyan is required for the recitation of certain

* *See pp. 134–36.*
† *See pp. 155–56.*

prayers—but, it is added, "our Sages in Palestine recite these prayers in the presence of seven . . . and some say even in the presence of only six." The practice of the Palestinians did not prevail, however. The rule of the Babylonian Jews was adopted everywhere, and a full quorum of ten men has been required for public prayer.

It has also been argued whether one may include in the minyan a boy under thirteen when only one person is lacking for the quorum.

> The authorities never agreed in this respect. Whilst the one insisted upon [the boy's] having obtained his majority, the other was satisfied with his showing such signs of intelligence as would enable him to participate in the ceremony in question.[7]

While the authorities have disagreed, congregational practice has usually been uncompromising. A congregation to be hallowed by the divine presence and to deserve the official designation of *kehillah kedoshah* (holy congregation) had to have the required quorum of ten mature worshipers.

The rabbis assumed that a minyan was not a hardship on any community. Larger communities were obviously not affected by this requirement, since they always had at least ten men of leisure known as batlanim. These men constituted the core of the permanent congregation and were highly respected for their piety and learning. In later centuries these men became paid functionaries and were frequently regarded as the ne'er-do-wells, who received a dole from the community in the form of a payment for their availability at all times for a congregational quorum. This tradition has been revived in some modern synagogues which encounter difficulties in maintaining a daily service. These congregations have resorted to hiring a number of idle men to worship daily in their synagogues instead of the synagogues of their own choice.

The requirement of a full minyan for public services has caused hardships to many small communities. A pitiful example is the remnant of the once-thriving Jewish community of Dubrovnik, Yugoslavia, a community that dates back to Roman days. Of the two hundred Jewish residents, only seventeen survived the Nazi slaughter—seven men and ten women. "We hold services on Sabbaths and festivals," said the head of this miserable remnant to the writer, "even though we do not have a minyan. After all these centuries of unbroken Jewish religious life we dare not close the synagogue. In time, Jewish families from elsewhere may settle here. Then a real Jewish congregation will be reconstituted, and we shall again insist on a proper minyan." The sad situation of Dubrovnik is repeated in numerous, though less determined, Jewish communities scattered all over the world. Should such communities be granted official permission to revert to the ancient Palestinian practice? Or should they act independently, as do the Jews of Dubrovnik? This is a question for the rabbinate, not for students of the Jewish liturgy.

Ritual Garb

Among the rituals of Jewish worship there are several that pertain to the suppliant's attire. The sages of the Talmud, we are told, regarded suitable attire at prayer as a mark of reverence for the divine presence (Shab. 10a). Prayer, the rabbis taught, takes the place of the Temple offerings; therefore the worshiper must wear special garments, as did the priests when they performed their sacerdotal functions. Of ritual garb associated with Jewish worship none occupies so important a place in the tradition as the tallit, or prayer shawl, and the tefillin, or phylacteries, that are worn during the weekday morning services. Both the tallit and the tefillin are biblical in origin. The tallit is specifically enjoined in the third paragraph of the *Shema:* *

> The Lord said to Moses as follows: "Speak to the Israelite people and instruct them to make for themselves fringes on the corners of their garments throughout the ages; . . . Thus you shall be reminded to observe all My commandments and to be holy to your God [Num. 15:37–41].

* *See p. 98.*

The biblical injunction regarding the tefillin is contained in both the first and the second paragraphs of the *Shema.*

The Tallit

The tallit was to remind the Jew of the commandments of the Torah. How do the fringes of the tallit remind one of the commandments? The Jews' search for a logical correlation between the tallit and the commandments of God was rewarded with intriguing discoveries. The numerical value of the word tzitzis (fringes) is 600. Each of the fringes contains 8 threads and 5 knots, making a total of 613. This number corresponds to the 613 commandments contained in the Torah. It was also noted that in making the fringes one winds the long thread around the other threads between the 5 knots 7, 8, 11, and 13 times respectively. The first three numbers equal 26, which is the numerical value of the Tetragrammaton. The remaining number equals the numerical value of the word *One*—the last word in the opening verse of the *Shema.* The fringes of the tallit thus not only remind the Jew of the 613 divine commandments, but also underscore the central doctrine of Judaism, that the Lord is one.

Ethical and theological meanings have also been read into the symbolism of the tallit. According to the Midrash [8] wrapping ourselves in the prayer shawl is to aid us in attaining a proper mood of reverence for God and a prayerful spirit during our worship.

> Rabbi Hezekiah also taught: When the children of Israel are wrapped in their prayer-shawls, let them [feel] . . . as though the glory of the [divine] Presence were upon them, for . . . Scripture does not say: "That ye may look upon them" [the fringes], but *That ye may look upon Him* [9] [Num. 15:39], that is, upon the Holy One, blessed be He.[10]

The prayer shawl has remained an inseparable part of Jewish worship. Its importance can be judged from a touching incident that occurred in 1493. In that year the Jews of Sicily were despoiled of all their possessions and expelled from their homes. Before leaving the island they petitioned the authorities for the privilege of taking their prayer shawls with them. Their petition was refused.

In modern times the tallit has remained an essential element of Jewish worship. During the morning prayers the tallit is worn over the garments by every male above the age of thirteen, or in some synagogues only by the married men. A full-size tallit is large enough for the worshiper literally to wrap himself up with it. It reaches from the shoulders to the ankles. Many people, however, prefer the small tallit, which is usually no larger than a scarf. In the American Orthodox and Conservative synagogues, the worshiper is given a tallit as he enters for prayer. In some Reform synagogues the wearing of a tallit is optional; in others only the rabbi and the reader wear it.

The Tefillin

Equally important in Jewish worship are the tefillin, or phylacteries. Actually, the name phylacteries is a misnomer because the tefillin are neither amulets nor charms. They do not serve as prophylactic objects to ward off evil spirits or to protect the wearer from harm. The tefillin are worn during the prayer to remind the Jew of his duty to strive for holiness through the performance of God's commandments. The tefillin contain selections from the Torah which have a direct bearing on Jewish belief and the Jewish way of life.

The rite of wearing tefillin during the weekday morning services is based on a biblical injunction which is repeated several times: "Bind them as a sign on your hand, and let them serve as a symbol on your forehead" (Deut. 6:8, 11:18). The rabbis interpreted these verses literally and ruled that these "signs" should be placed daily on one's arm and forehead during weekday morning prayers. On Sabbaths the tefillin are not worn lest people carry them to the synagogue, which according to rabbinic legislation is forbidden. This reason was later superseded by another explanation: the Sabbath is itself a "sign" and a witness of God's covenant with Israel, as it is written: "[the Sabbath is] a sign for all time between Me and the people of Israel" (Exod. 31:17). Hence there is no need of the tefillin to serve as a sign of the covenant. Since the festivals are equated with the Sabbath in many rabbinic laws, one is exempt from putting on the tefillin on these days, too.

The four biblical selections which are contained in each of the tefillin consist of the first two paragraphs of the *Shema*, which contain references to the tefillin, and two additional selections (Exod. 13:1–10 and Exod. 13:11–16) which deal with the Exodus from Egypt and refer to the tefillin as "a sign" and "a memorial" of God's redemption of the children of Israel from the Egyptian slavery.

These four biblical selections are inscribed on parchment scrolls and placed in small boxes. Leather straps are attached to each of the tefillin to hold them in place on the forehead and on the left arm. The reason for putting the tefillin on the forehead and on the muscle of the arm next to the heart is to teach that one is to serve God with his intellect, his strength, and his emotions. The strap is wound around the forearm seven times to signify that the covenant with God must be a matter of concern, on every day of the week, not only on special occasions. The strap is then wound three times around the middle finger to indicate Israel's triple commitment to God, as stipulated by the prophet:

And I will betroth thee unto Me for ever;
Yea, I will betroth thee unto Me in righteousness, and in justice,
And in lovingkindness, and in compassion.
And I will betroth thee unto Me in faithfulness;
And thou shalt know the Lord [*Hos. 2:21–22*].

On one of the tefillin there is a large Hebrew letter, shin. This was probably meant to indicate that the scrolls inside begin with the *Shema* and not with the Ten Commandments, which at one time were also included in the tefillin.[11] On its opposite side there is a four-pronged shin, to indicate that only four selections are in each of the tefillin and not five, as was the case when the Ten Commandments were also included. But these historic reasons were forgotten and new ones were grafted onto the mysterious letter. One explanation is intriguing. The letter shin is combined with two other "letters" which were discovered in the tefillin, and together they form the word *Shaddai*—Almighty God. The two letters were found in the peculiar knots in the straps; the one on the head resembles the letter daleth and the one on the arm resembles the letter yod. The tefillin are thus to remind the Jew of his obligation to perform the commandments of Almighty God. This explanation is obviously contrived, but it has been accepted these many centuries as the real reason for the shin on the tefillin.

With the passage of the centuries the universal high regard for the rite of the tefillin increased, and new religious meanings and values were discovered in the ritual. Maimonides found that the tefillin serve a singular purpose in the religious life of the Jew. They are a holy institution leading man to humility and the fear of God. The tefillin, says Maimonides, are of

> a high degree of sanctity. As long as the *Tefillin* are on a man's head and arm, he is humble and God-fearing; [he] is not drawn into frivolity and idle talk; and does not dwell on evil thoughts, but occupies his mind with thoughts of truth and righteousness. A man should therefore endeavor to wear *Tefillin* the whole day.[12]

Maimonides did not originate the idea of wearing the tefillin throughout the day. In the early centuries of the Common Era some of the sages wore their tefillin all day, even on hot summer days. The *Shema* within the tefillin signifies "the acceptance of the yoke of the Kingdom of Heaven." By wearing the tefillin, the sages paid homage to the God of Israel and at the same time defied "the wicked kingdom" of Rome. During the talmudic and geonic periods, as well as during the Middle Ages, there were pious Jews who emulated the sages of the Mishnah and wore their tefillin all day. For the average Jew, however, the tefillin have been a sacred symbol to be worn only during the weekday morning service.

Important as the tefillin undoubtedly are, they were not universally used till postgeonic times, when rabbinic learning became the core of Jewish education. The laxity is reported by Rabbi Moses of Coucy. In his travels in Provence and northern

Spain at the end of the thirteenth century, he found it necessary to emphasize in his sermons the importance of the tefillin. He relates that an earthquake frightened the people. They repented and "thousands and tens of thousands pledged to perform the commandment of *Tefillin* . . . which they had not been careful to observe theretofore." [13] The obvious conclusion is that previously tens of thousands did not put on tefillin at prayer.[14] But this laxity disappeared, and the rite of putting on the tefillin at morning prayers became universal in all Jewish communities. Upon reaching his majority at the age of thirteen every boy regarded it a privilege to put on the tefillin at the morning services. It was a public demonstration of his being a full-fledged member of the congregation of Israel, and of his eligibility to be counted into the quorum of ten worshipers and to be called to the Torah. The boy continued to put on the tefillin throughout his life.

In modern times, before reaching their thirteenth birthday Jewish boys are usually taught how to put on the tefillin. But the prevailing laxity in the observance of religious rites soon overtakes these neophytes, and the tefillin are consigned to a safe place where they are gradually forgotten altogether. To be sure, there are notable exceptions. Among the Orthodox Jews, and to a lesser extent among the Conservative Jews, there are some parents who put on the tefillin during their daily devotions. Some of the children of these parents will probably emulate their fathers. These children may yet prove to be the "faithful remnant" who will revive the ritual of the tefillin and restore it to its former dynamic role in Jewish life.

Shoes and Hats

In Western society a gentleman "tips his hat" to a lady, and a Christian removes his hat upon entering a church. Not so in the Moslem world. To be bareheaded is to show disrespect and to be barefooted is a sign of reverence. No one is permitted to enter a mosque without first removing his shoes. In Judaism both the hat and the shoes have retained their symbolic meaning, though not with equal weight or consistency.

The propriety of removing one's shoes before entering a

holy place was already an accepted practice in biblical times. When Moses heard the divine call from the burning bush, he was told: "Do not come closer. Remove your sandals from your feet, for the place on which you stand is holy ground" (Exod. 3:5). When the angel appeared to him near Jericho, Joshua, too, was told: "Put off thy shoe from off thy foot; for the place whereon thou standest is holy" (Josh. 5:15).

This ancient Semitic practice may have been at the outset nothing more than a means of keeping the dust out of the sanctuary. In biblical days, however, it was already an established religious symbol signifying humility before the divine presence. Conversely, to enter a sanctuary with shoes on was an act of arrogance and defiance.

During the talmudic and geonic periods the removal of one's shoes before entering a synagogue was a well-established custom in the Eastern Jewish communities. At prayer the Jews would sit on the floor, cross-legged and barefooted. This practice is still common among the Moslems and in some oriental Jewish communities. In the West, however, seats were provided in the synagogues, and shoes were removed only on special occasions such as on Yom Kippur, as a symbol of humility before the divine seat of judgment. The shoes were also removed by the Kohanim before they ascended the platform to bestow the priestly blessing upon the congregation.* This was a carryover from the Temple ritual, where the priests were barefooted during the performance of their duties.

On two other occasions the European Jews adhered to this ancient custom. During the reading of the lamentations on the Ninth of Av † the people sat without shoes, and mourners did not wear shoes during the seven days of mourning. In both cases, the removal of the shoes expressed grief and acceptance of God's dispensations.

In modern times the removal of the shoes is adhered to by the Kohanim when they bless the congregation and by mourners during their seven-day period of mourning. But on the Day of Atonement and on the Ninth of Av only the Orthodox

* *See pp. 84–85.*
† *See pp. 277–79.*

Jews remove their shoes during the worship. In America even among the Orthodox it is far from a universal practice. The process of acculturation to the dominant Western culture has somewhat eroded these traditions.

If the symbolism of removing the shoes has faded somewhat among the modern Jews, the covering of the head as a symbol of reverence during worship has remained a religious symbol of significance. But the origin and development of this religious symbol is shrouded in uncertainty. We know that among the priestly vestments of Aaron and his sons there was a "headdress" for Aaron (Exod. 28:4) and "turbans" for Aaron's sons (Exod. 28:40). These, the Bible tells us, were "for dignity and adornment." In the Talmud we read a lone but telling reference: "Rabina was sitting before R. Jeremiah of Difti, when a certain man passed by without covering his head [as a sign of respect]. How impudent is that man! he exclaimed" (Kid. 33a).

Moses Maimonides makes reference to this talmudic incident in his famous philosophic work, *The Guide for the Perplexed.* He says: "The great men among our Sages would not uncover their heads because they believed that God's glory was round them and over them." [15]

Though covering one's head was regarded during the talmudic period as a sign of respect, there is scant evidence that Jews in the Temple court or in the early synagogue were required to wear any headgear. In Christian Europe we have evidence of a disregard for this tradition, or at least inconsistency in its observance. "In the thirteenth century," says Israel Abrahams, quoting a contemporary work, "boys in Germany and adults in France were called to the Law in synagogue bareheaded." [16]

With the passage of time, the custom of covering the head during worship increasingly became mandatory. As the persecutions of the Church increased, the Jewish aversion to everything Christian deepened. The uncovering of the head became associated with Church etiquette and therefore became repugnant. To worship or even to go about with an uncovered head was regarded as imitation of the Christians and an act of irreverence to God. Conversely, the covering of one's head became an act of Jewish piety. For convenience the skullcap, or yarmulke,[17] was adopted.

In modern times the headdress is an indispensable part of the Jew's attire at worship. It is quite unthinkable for anyone to enter an Orthodox or Conservative synagogue, let alone participate in the worship, with an uncovered head.

When the Reform movement was launched in the last century, the head covering at prayer was abolished. Hatless worship in the Reform synagogues became a mark of distinction and a barrier between the Reform and the other branches of Judaism no less than the theological differences and the liturgic changes.

Deportment at Worship

Worship always encompasses a number of rituals which involve specific postures and a variety of gestures. Silence, loudness, and bodily movements such as bowing, kneeling, and "falling on the face" are familiar rituals of worship. In the Jerusalem Temple there were many impressive rituals, some of which were transferred to the synagogue; others have been all but forgotten. Among the latter are those rites which were inseparable parts of the sacrificial cult and those which were adopted and used excessively by the Gentiles. The early Christians, for example, kneeled repeatedly at their services. Jews came to regard kneeling as a characteristically Christian rite and therefore all but eliminated kneeling from the synagogue services, except on the High Holy Days. Similarly, the spreading of the hands at prayer, a symbol of heartfelt entreaty, was eliminated from the synagogue worship, because the early Christians frequently spread their hands during their services and claimed that the gesture symbolized the cross. Also, the rite of "falling on the face," still a prominent feature of Moslem worship, was all but eliminated from the synagogue service, despite its having been an integral part of the Temple ritual. Nonetheless, a considerable number of rituals have remained in the synagogue worship, and their symbolism has contributed much to the meaning and inspiration of the services. By the end of the geonic period most of these rites and symbols had been fully crystallized, and they have become an essential part of the established pattern of synagogue worship.

Silence and Loudness

Is prayer to be silent or audible? Is it to be a mere whisper or a loud shouting? In the Bible one can find support for each of these modes of prayer. In Deuteronomy (11:13) we read that one is to serve God "with all your heart." This, the rabbis say, means that prayer is "the service of the heart." One is therefore to refrain from reciting the *Tefillah* loudly or even audibly. The rabbis also make a distinction between prayer and study. They say that a person "who says the *Tefillah* so that it can be heard is of the small of faith" (Ber. 24b). By praying loudly he implies that God does not hear silent prayer. To the rabbis this type of prayer suggested the Greek manner of worship, which was as a rule done in a loud voice. Hence the rabbis say:

> The Heathen has his god in his own house and yet he cries aloud to him . . . but his god does not hear him and does not save him. . . . A Jew enters the synagogue . . . prays in a whisper, and the Holy One, blessed be He, hearkens to his prayer (Jer. Ber. 203a).

The rabbis found conclusive support for their view in Hannah's prayer. "Hannah," says the Bible, "spoke *in her heart. . . . Only her lips moved. . . . But her voice could not be heard* [1 Sam. 1:13]" (Ber. 31a). It thus became a custom for Jews to recite the *Tefillah* in silence. Even in oriental synagogues, where the prayers are generally recited in unison, the *Tefillah* is recited in total silence. But, like Hannah's, their lips are in constant movement. This "reading with the lips" should not be taken as a sign of low mentality or of faulty teaching. Jewish children are deliberately taught to read their silent prayers with the lips, as ordained by the ancient tradition.

The precentor who leads the congregation in prayer was an obvious exception: he was expected to recite the prayers audibly. And the congregation, when responding to the reader's chanting of the prayers, was likewise not restrained, as we read in the Talmud: "Resh Lakish said: He who responds 'Amen' with all his might has the gates of paradise opened for him" (Shab. 119b).

If silence was considered a virtue at prayer, it was regarded as a hindrance to concentration at study. Since the *Shema* was classified by the rabbis as being partially study, the Talmud does not require silence during the recitation of the *Shema* during prayer. "When one recites the *Shema*, he must let himself hear what he says, as it says: '*Hear, O Israel, the Lord our God, the Lord is One*' " (Ber. 15a). As a result of these varied principles, the synagogue service is totally quiet during the *Tefillah*, only partially so during the recitation of the *Shema* and its benedictions, and quite noisy at certain other parts of the service. A stranger entering a synagogue during the *Tefillah* is impressed with the decorum and the earnestness of the worshipers. But this initial impression is soon dispelled when the congregation rises for the Kedushah * and everyone vociferates the responses without reference to the lusty responses of the other worshipers. At this point the service sounds to the visitor more like pandemonium. One can readily understand why it was necessary to include in the charter granted to the Jews in 1320 by the Infante Alfonso of Aragon the provision that "within the synagogue walls the Jews might sing their prayers in a loud or a low voice by day or by night." [18] Without such a provision there was the danger of the prayers being heard outside and becoming a pretext for mob action against the Jews.

Postures at Prayer

Standing is a universal symbol of reverence. In the Bible there are many references to rising before honored people and standing up during worship. "You shall rise before the aged" (Lev. 19:32) is a well-known biblical commandment. And Hannah, whose prayer has already been quoted, says to Eli, the high priest: "I am the woman that stood by thee here, praying unto the Lord" (1 Sam. 1:26). Standing has therefore come to be regarded as the normal posture at prayer. The rabbis added a

* *See pp. 571–73.*

detail: "When one prays, he should place his feet in proper position [i.e., close together], as it says, *And their feet were straight together* [Ezek. 1:7]" (Ber. 10b).

The Jewish posture at the more important prayers has therefore been one of standing, and the *Tefillah* is also known as the Amidah, that is, the prayer that is recited in a standing position. Among the other prayers similarly recited are the call to worship,* the recitation of the Kedushah,† and the Hallel.‡ The congregation also stands up when the Torah is taken out and returned to the ark.

If standing is the proper posture for prayer, sitting is the normal posture at study. Hence the congregation is seated during the reading of the Torah. The *Shema* and its benedictions are also recited in a sitting position, because the three paragraphs of the *Shema* are selections from the Torah, and their reading is regarded as study. In many modern congregations the worshipers rise for the recitation of the first verse of the *Shema.* This is a recent innovation derived from the feeling that this verse is so central in Judaism that it should be given special emphasis.

When rising for the *Tefillah* the congregation faces toward Jerusalem. This is based on Solomon's prayer at the dedication of the Jerusalem Temple: "Hearken Thou to the supplication . . . of Thy people Israel, when they shall pray toward this place" (1 Kings 8:30). Similarly we read that Daniel prayed before his windows which were open "toward Jerusalem" (Dan. 6:11). In the Talmud this practice was formulated in detail:

> If he is in the east [of Palestine] he should turn his face to the west; if in the west [of Palestine] he should turn his face to the east; if in the south he should turn his face to the north; if in the north he should turn his face to the south. In this way all Israel will be turning their hearts towards one place [Ber. 30a].

* *See pp. 98–99.*
† *See p. 135.*
‡ *See pp. 210–11.*

Ever since the talmudic period Jews have turned in prayer toward Jerusalem. In the Western countries the custom has been to construct synagogues with the ark of the Torah in the east wall, so that the congregation will face the Holy Land. In the Eastern countries the architecture of the synagogue is reversed. In Israel, worshipers in Galilee face south, while those in the Negev face north. In Jerusalem, synagogues are built so that the worshipers face the Temple Mount. In this way, all Jews turn their eyes "toward one place" when they pray, toward the spot whereupon the holy Temple stood.

Symbolic Gestures

Bodily gestures are normal expressions of worship. At the Jerusalem Temple kneeling, the spreading of the hands, and prostration of the body face downward [19] were frequent accompaniments of the services. The prophets never reproached the people for these forms of adoration. The Bible speaks of these gestures as normal acts which needed no explanation or rationalization whatever. King Solomon, the Bible tells us, "arose . . . from kneeling on his knees with his hands spread forth toward heaven" (1 Kings 8:54).

During the Second Temple kneeling and prostration were the favored forms of adoration. The Bible records the memorable scene of Ezra's reading the Torah to the great assemblage in Jerusalem:

> And Ezra opened the book in the sight of all the people. . . . And Ezra blessed the Lord, the great God. And the people answered: "Amen, Amen," with the lifting up of their hands; and they bowed their heads, and fell down before the Lord with their faces to the ground [Neh. 8:5–6].

And the Mishnah informs us that one who visited the Temple had to make no less than thirteen prostrations with the face touching the ground (Shek. 6:1).

Christians and Moslems borrowed many of their symbolic gestures of worship from the Jews and with some modifications still practice them. As the Christians became increasingly hostile to the Jews, the forms taken over by them came to be regarded as characteristic of Christianity and were avoided in the synagogue services. In Palestine, where Christianity was especially in disfavor because of the severe persecutions, the rite of prostration was altogether forbidden. In Babylonia it was partially retained, and the Babylonian practice has prevailed during the Yom Kippur service. When the congregation recites the account of the ancient Temple service,* and the reader describes how the high priest pronounced the ineffable name of God and the people in the Temple court knelt and prostrated themselves and fell on their faces, the synagogue worshipers likewise perform these rites.[20]

The elimination of these impressive gestures of worship from the synagogue services has been regretted by some. In the thirteenth century, Rabbi Abraham ben Maimon, son of Moses Maimonides, made a vigorous attempt to reintroduce the ceremonials that had been eliminated after the fall of the Temple. He was impressed by the decorum at Moslem services and the expressive gestures of Moslem worship. These, he felt, were important aids to piety. Besides, he argued, they were originally Jewish and should be recaptured for the enhancement of the synagogue prayers. But he was successfully opposed by his contemporaries, who defended the simplified and less decorous procedures of the synagogue. They quoted the biblical prohibition "nor shall you follow their laws" (Lev. 18:3). They also pointed with horror to the practice of the Jewish sectarians, the Karaites, who fall on their faces like the Moslems and recite the formula:

> O God, behold, I am attaching the most honored part of my body—the head—to the place that I tread with my feet, that is, the dust to which I am destined to return, as Thou hast made known unto us in the words of Scripture, "For dust you are / And to dust you shall return" [Gen. 3:19].

Rabbi Abraham ben Maimon lost the battle and Judaism lost a number of powerful aids to fervent prayer.

Although kneeling, prostration, and the spreading of the hands are no longer normal parts of Jewish worship, bowing,

* *See p. 253.*

kissing, and stepping forward and backward have remained acceptable symbols of synagogue prayer. In the recitation of the *Tefillah* it is customary for the worshiper to bow his head or bend the upper part of the body at the beginning and end of the first benediction, and again at the opening and the closing of the thanksgiving benediction. It is also customary for the reader to bow his head during his call to service,* and for the congregation to do so during the response. In the *Alenu* prayer when the congregation recites or chants the words "We bend the knee, bow down, and give thanks unto the King of kings, the Holy One, blessed be He," everyone bows reverently.

Too much bowing, however, was discouraged. "If one," says the Talmud, "wants to bow down at the end of each benediction and at the beginning of each benediction, he is instructed not to do so" (Ber. 34a). Too much bowing is ostentatiously pious and savors of hypocrisy.

Is bowing at prayer just a formal rite or is it a symbol of worship? The Talmud records divergent opinions, but the following is the most noteworthy:

> Rabbi Tanhum said in the name of R. Joshua b. Levi: in saying the *Tefillah* one should bow down [at the appropriate places] until all the vertebrae in the spinal column are loosened. . . . R. Hanina said: If he simply bows his head, he need do no more [Ber. 28b].

The prevailing practice follows the opinion of Rabbi Hanina. The act of bowing is a symbol of reverence and homage; one need not overdo it.

A similar gesture of reverence is the act of taking three paces forward at the start of the *Tefillah* and three paces backward at the conclusion. At the start of the *Tefillah* one symbolically draws near to God, as we read in the Bible: "Abraham came forward" (Gen. 18:23) and prayed in behalf of the inhabitants of Sodom and Gomorrah. At the conclusion of the *Tefillah* the worshiper takes leave, as it were, from the divine presence with which he has been in communion. The accepted

* *See pp. 98–99.*

procedure is not to turn one's back on an important personage the moment one finishes his petition. On taking leave of royalty one steps backward a few paces.[21]

Then there is the symbolic act of kissing the fringes of the tallit during the recitation of the last paragraph of the *Shema*. One also kisses the Torah as it is carried from and to the ark. Everyone within reach touches the Torah mantle and then kisses the object that touched the scroll. In the same spirit one kisses the tefillin when they are taken out to be put on the head and the arm, and again when they are being returned to their receptacle. And when a Jew leaves or enters a house he kisses the mezuzah on the doorpost. And if a person accidentally drops a prayer book or any religious book, he lifts it to his lips and kisses it as a pious apology for his carelessness. In each case the kiss is a symbol of love and devotion to the Torah and to the divine commandments symbolized by the fringes of the tallit, the mezuzah on the doorpost, or the religious book.

The most curious of bodily movements associated with Jewish prayer is that of swaying to and fro. These bodily movements did not, as many erroneously believe, originate with the Hasidic movement in the seventeenth century. The Hasidim merely intensified an old practice as a means of inducing greater concentration and deeper devotion at prayer. Actually, rocking and swaying were common in the geonic period and even during the talmudic period. Thus the Talmud tells us that when Rabbi Akiba prayed privately he would start his devotions in one part of the room and end up in another (Ber. 31a). This was due to his vigorous bodily movements.

Many have been puzzled by this strange custom. Judah Halevi, who lived in Spain during the twelfth century, explained this widespread Jewish practice in his philosophic work, *The Kuzari*:

> *Al Khazari*: "I should like to ask whether you know the reason why Jews move to and fro when reading Scripture."
>
> *The Rabbi*: ". . . As it often happened many people read [a given book] at the same time. . . . Each of

> them was obliged to bend down in turn in order to read a passage, and to turn back again. This resulted in a continual bending and sitting up, the book lying on the ground. . . .Then it became a habit through constant seeing, observing, and imitating which is human nature."[22]

Most scholars share Judah Halevi's view that the swaying at prayer originated in the academies and in the study rooms attached to the synagogues. Students would sway at study, not so much because of the scarcity of books, but because each student read his text aloud. As mentioned above, "one must let himself hear what he is saying." In order to concentrate on his text in the midst of the many others reading texts aloud, each one resorted to swaying as a means of shutting out the competing texts. This habit was transferred from the study room to the synagogue.

The symbolic gestures developed in the talmudic and geonic periods spread to communities everywhere; most of them promise to remain part of the synagogue liturgy.

Acts of Expiation, Atonement, and Mourning

Deep-seated emotions, such as regret and sorrow, atonement for sins, or mourning over tragic events, demand expressions that are more substantive than words, however poetic and fitting. In all societies there are specific actions that help to express these emotions and afford release to one's inner tensions.

The most effective gesture of regret for wrongdoing is fasting. The suppliant wants to humble himself before God as a sign of his repentance, and he hopes to awaken God's mercy through his act of expiation. In Judaism fasting is not regarded as meritorious in itself. Asceticism is not an essential element of Judaism. But the religious person craves atonement, and fasting is the most efficacious means of satisfying this religious need. It provides the suppliant with a sense of relief. He feels that God will surely see his distress and grant him forgiveness.

The act of "afflicting one's soul," as fasting is called in the Bible, is regarded by the rabbis as a personal sacrifice, an offering of one's "blood and fat" upon the altar (Ber. 17a).

Judaism provided for a number of fixed fasts. The most important of these is the great White Fast of Yom Kippur.* Fasts commemorating national calamities, especially those connected with the fall of Jeursalem, were instituted from time to time, and some of these have remained in the Jewish calendar to this day.† In addition, fasts were proclaimed when calamities threatened the community—most frequently in Palestine during periods of drought.‡

The rabbis emphasized repeatedly that the act of fasting is only a means to an end. It is not for the purpose of arousing God's pity, but rather to induce repentence and righteous living. Judaism thus filled the old ritual of "practicing self-denial" with new spiritual content. This is why the rabbis chose chapter 58 of Isaiah for the Yom Kippur Haftarah. This selection contains a moral definition of fasting which the rabbis wanted to impress on the people.[23]

There were also a number of self-imposed fasts: the very pious would fast on Mondays and Thursdays as auxiliary acts of worship, and the overpious also fasted on additional days. As Israel Abrahams so aptly put it: "The medieval Jew's calendar was thickly studded with fasts, indeed some must have abstained from food for quite half the year." [24]

Though fasting was the most important act of repentance and atonement for sins, it was not the only one. Weeping is another obvious symbol of regret and sorrow. Weeping is not necessarily a spontaneous phenomenon—it can be induced. With practice tears can be turned on as easily as some turn on a smile. Such tears, notwithstanding their artificiality, can deeply affect the weeper. In ancient days there were professional weeping women who were hired to participate in funerals and honor the dead with their ample flow of tears. The weepers not only worked themselves up to real mourning

* *See p. 244.*
† *See pp. 276 ff.*
‡ *See pp. 137–38.*

but roused others to shed real tears. Many contemporary American Jews remember how, a generation or so ago, the loud weeping in the women's gallery could be heard throughout the synagogue, especially during the prayers that accompanied Blessing the New Month.

Weeping was characteristic of the women's gallery, but breast-beating was indulged in by every worshiper in the synagogue. When one recited the sixth benediction of the weekday *Tefillah* and said: "Forgive us, O our Father, for we have sinned; pardon us, O our King, for we have transgressed," he would beat his breast on uttering the words *sinned* and *transgressed*. On the Day of Atonement breast-beating accompanied each of the many confessions.* Breast-beating, though not spontaneous nor painful, helped induce a sense of penitence.

Modern Jewish worship has been impoverished by the omission of some of these symbolic acts. Reliance on the utterance of the lips is hardly adequate.

The Music of the Synagogue

We do not have detailed documentary accounts concerning the ancient Jewish liturgic music, but there is enough historic evidence to indicate that both vocal and instrumental music played an important role in the Temple worship and that much of the synagogue music has its roots in great antiquity. Music was a focal element in the worship tradition of the ancient Hebrews, and it has maintained its key position in Jewish worship to this day. By the end of the geonic period the musical tradition had already assumed its classic form.

The tenacity of the synagogue musical tradition is remarkable, its enrichment of Jewish worship inestimable. While the words of a prayer may lift the worshiper to modest devotional heights, the addition of a suitable chant—especially if it is rooted in tradition—often lifts one to lofty heights of inspiration.

Musical instruments were accepted elements of the Temple

* *See p. 249.*

service. The Bible repeatedly speaks of singers and musicians in the Temple. Thus we read of King Hezekiah who reigned in the days of the first Temple:

> And he set the Levites in the house of the Lord with cymbals, with psalteries, and with harps. . . . And when the burnt-offering began, the song of the Lord began also, and the trumpets, together with the instruments of David king of Israel (2 Chron. 29:25,27).

When the Temple was rebuilt after the Babylonian captivity, the elaborate sacrificial cult, with its stately vocal and instrumental music, was reinstituted. In those days there was already, in addition to the Temple ritual, the simple synagogue service, guided by a reader who chanted some of the prayers.* The Mishnah records the testimony of Rabbi Joshua ben Hananya, who had been a chorister at the Temple and survived the fall of Jerusalem. He testified that on certain occasions the choristers of the Temple went in a body from the altar ritual to a synagogue service that was conducted within the Temple precincts, and they sang at both services (Suk. 53a). But the nature of the synagogue music is unfortunately not indicated.

After the tragedy of the year 70 C.E., the Jews expressed their feelings of sorrow by banning music from all public functions. This was quite normal, for Jewish mourners traditionally refrain from musical entertainment as a sign of grief. This abstention from listening to music was also applied in part to the synagogue services. How long this state of mourning lasted is conjectural at best, but it is certain that by the third century of the Common Era this abstention from music was widely disregarded, especially in Babylonia. In the synagogue it was probably never fully observed. A state of mourning cannot be maintained for centuries. Vocal music remained part of the synagogue service and has never been dislodged from it.

Outside the synagogue the geonim tried hard to prohibit, or at least restrict, nonreligious music. But they found it neces-

* *See pp. 76–79.*

sary to make an exception of weddings. The rabbinic view was crystallized in a responsum of Rabbi Hai Gaon, who insisted that the memory of the destruction of the Temple had to be kept alive. Musical instruments at banquets and even weddings should therefore be banned, especially since frivolity induced by wine and song might lead to lewdness. This view found its way into the codes. But the late Boaz Cohen concludes his scholarly essay "The Responsum of Maimonides Concerning Music" by saying: "In spite of the rigor of the law, music could not be suppressed. . . . The law prohibiting music was never fully observed, because it ran counter to human nature." [25]

The ban on music after the destruction of the Temple succeeded in excluding all musical instruments from the synagogue liturgy except the ram's horn, if that can be called a musical instrument. Only in recent years have the Reform and some of the Conservative synagogues begun to introduce musical instruments, especially the organ, into the synagogue service. This innovation, however, has been vigorously rejected by the majority of synagogues. Only when the Temple is restored, say they, will musical instruments be introduced into the Jewish service. Till then, vocal music will suffice.

Cantillations of the Bible

Vocal music in the synagogue was never really suspended. When the Temple fell the voice of song at worship was subdued but not eliminated. The psalmist's admonition to "serve the Lord with gladness" and to "come before His presence with singing" (Ps. 100:2) was not forgotten. In later years the sages of the Talmud were constrained to list among the qualifications of a reader that he be "skilled in chanting [and] has a pleasant voice" (Ta'an. 16a). The traditional chants of the synagogue were therefore not forgotten. They were transmitted from generation to generation, from century to century. Indeed, the tenacity of synagogue music has surprised many a musicologist. This tenacity is especially characteristic of the rendition of the Torah and other scriptural portions which are read at the services. They have stubbornly resisted change or adaptation to new musical influences and have remained authentic to this day. These renditions, usually called cantillations, are the oldest elements of synagogue music.

The cantillations of scriptural texts are expressed through a system of musical notations known as tropes.[26] The identical notations serve the chanting of the Torah, the Prophets, and the five small books of the Bible known as the scrolls.[27] But the rendition of the tropes differs with each book. Thus the Book of Lamentations, which is read on the fast of the Ninth of Av,* is appropriately chanted in a mournful melody. But the Book of Esther, which is read on Purim,† is chanted in a melody that suggests a narrative. Despite these different renditions there is a marked similarity between them, which makes it relatively easy to learn all the renditions once a person has mastered any one of them.

The cantillations are the product of the normal situations of life in ancient times. To begin with, there were no punctuation marks in any text. They are still nonexistent in the Torah scroll which is read in the synagogue. The ancients resorted to a kind of prosody, a combination of reading with singing, which was an effective aid to comprehension. To this day the Talmud, which has hardly any punctuation marks, is studied in the yeshivot in a singsong intonation. The cantillations group the words into phrases and provide vocally the punctuation marks which are printed in a modern text. While the cantillation of a narrative or didactic text developed from the rhythmic rendition of the readers, the cantillation of a sorrowful text, such as the Book of Lamentations, derived its melody from the sad, rhythmic singsong of the professional wailing women. These sorrowful cantillations were used by the prophets when they lamented the fate of Israel at the time of their deportation to Babylonia. In time these mournful cantillations, as well as the didactic and happy cantillations, assumed definitive forms and were recorded by a set system of musical notations (tropes) which have served as accents, punctuation marks, and musical interpretations of the texts. These cantillations were fully developed long before the end of the geonic period and have survived with little alteration to this day.

* *See pp. 277–78.*
† *See pp. 273–74.*

TRADITIONAL CHANTS OF THE LITURGY

In addition to the scriptural cantillations there are a number of traditional prayer chants that go back to Temple days. These ancient melodies, associated with particular prayers or whole prayer units, are designated as the official *Nusah*, or musical tradition, of the synagogue.

In the Temple the psalms were usually rendered in a rhythmic, responsive antiphony. The parallelism characteristic of biblical poetry lends itself to a rhythmic, monotone recitation, out of which the more formal renditions at the Temple service developed. (The plainsong of the Catholic, Byzantine, and Armenian Churches traces its origin to the same source.) These simple responsive and unison readings in the Temple gave rise to the ancient synagogue melodies which became the core of the synagogue *Nusah*, as we read in the Talmud:

> At the time the Israelites ascended from the Red Sea . . . how did they render the song [of Moses]? . . . R. Nehemiah declares: Like a school-teacher who recites the *Shema* in the Synagogue, viz., he begins first and they respond after him [Sotah 30b].

By the geonic period there was already a definite *Nusah* for a number of prayers, such as the one for the benediction that introduces the *Shema (Ahavah Rabbah)*, the benedictions of the *Tefillah*, the special prayers for rain *(Geshem)*,* the closing service of Yom Kippur, and others. To this day these melodies and motifs are essential elements of the synagogue service. When a congregation is about to elect a cantor, his audition takes into account not only the quality of his voice and his musical training, but also his knowledge of the *Nusah*. The candidate may be a fine musician, but if he lacks a knowledge of the synagogue *Nusah* he is considered inadequate for the post.

The End of the Matter

The rites, symbols, and ceremonial traditions of the synagogue have added substance and meaning to the liturgy. They have

* *See pp. 221–22.*

helped lift the experience of Jewish worship to a level bordering on real communion with the divine presence. The symbolism of the synagogue structure and its furnishings, the special garb worn at prayer, and the unique postures and gestures of the service have contributed greatly to the total religious sentiment and to the spiritual exaltation of the Jewish worshiper. Similarly, the traditional cantillations and chants have added immeasurably to the worship experience. They help awaken both the emotional sentiments and the intellectual insights of the worshiper.

Unfortunately, some modern Jews have tried to strip the synagogue worship of what they call the "external elements." To do so is to reduce the Jewish liturgy to a state of spiritual nakedness. To be sure, there are some who can do without the symbolic accompaniments of traditional prayer. These people are the rare exceptions, however; most people need the additional bulwarks to bolster their spiritual security and to enhance their religious experience.

There are also some who seek to enrich the worship by adding new rituals and new musical renditions. These efforts deserve the support of everyone, provided the new elements do not clash with tradition. But those who seek to replace ancient expressions of worship with new symbolism and new music are sowing seeds of destruction. Such "modernization" of the worship robs it of its authenticity and reduces it to a performance. Radical surgery of this type can be justified only in time of emergency; the spiritual surgeons should be cautious.

14
THE FIRST *SIDDUR*

In the year 856 Rabbi Amram became the gaon of the Sura Academy in Babylonia. As the head of this famous seat of learning he received letters from the scattered Jewish communities asking for guidance in matters of Jewish law and learning. Among the questions that reached Rabbi Amram Gaon was one from far-off Spain asking for guidance in the matter of prayers. Unfortunately, we do not have the original letter, but we know the essence of the question, for Rabbi Amram summarized it in the introduction to his responsum. The letter asked for "the prayers and benedictions for the entire year." Rabbi Amram Gaon's responsum is a historic document: the first Jewish prayer book ever produced authoritatively. To comprehend the significance of this responsum we must digress to examine the state of the prayers and benedictions in the ninth century and the historic factors that necessitated this radical departure from tradition.

The Oral Tradition of the Synagogue

It is difficult for the modern reader to conceive of a prayer book as being anything but a book that contains the order of worship. But this was not always the case with the Jewish book of prayer. For many centuries the liturgy of the synagogue was solely an oral tradition, and the prayers were recited from memory. There was a strict rabbinic ban against committing the prayers to writing. The reader who led the congregation in prayer had to know the prayers by heart, and the worshipers either knew the prayers by heart or repeated them after the reader as best they could. The less knowledgeable worshipers only responded with the traditional Amen after each benediction. That is why the *Tefillah* is recited twice during the morning and afternoon services: those who knew the prayers by heart recited them silently, and then the reader repeated the *Tefillah* for those who could only respond with the time-honored Amen.*

As mentioned in an earlier chapter,† the ban on committing the prayers to writing had applied to all nonbiblical lore, including the Mishnah, the Palestinian and Babylonian Talmuds, and the homiletic teachings known as the Midrash. Only the

* *See p. 427.*
† *See pp. 125–28.*

Scriptures were definitive and authoritative. Only the Scriptures were sacred in every word and title. All other traditional lore, however authentic, was to remain oral. This principle was clearly recorded in the Talmud:

> R. Judah b. Nahmani . . . discoursed as follows: . . . The words which are written [i.e., the Scriptures] thou art not at liberty to say by heart, and the words transmitted orally [i.e., the Oral Torah] thou art not at liberty to recite from writing [Gittin 60b].

Prayers were included in this ban, and the rabbinic stricture against writing down the prayers was quite incisive. The *Tosefta*, a rabbinic work of the early centuries of the Common Era, sharply censures those who write down prayers: "They who write down benedictions commit as grave a sin as those who burn the Torah" (Tos. Shab. 13:4). Thus two complementary Torahs came into being, the Written Torah (that is, the Bible) and the Oral Torah, which encompassed every other element of traditional lore, including the prayers of the synagogue.

But the oral tradition could not endure forever. At the end of the second century Rabbi Judah Ha-Nasi took the bold step of causing the Mishnah to be edited and prepared for publication.* He felt that the situation was critical and that emergency action was called for. Prevailing persecutions and the crushing poverty of the Jewish people in Palestine were so demoralizing and degrading that all learning was in danger of being forgotten and lost forever. In order to save the accumulated rabbinic lore and scholarship, Judah Ha-Nasi took the unprecedented step of gathering the oral learning developed over the centuries and preparing it for transcription.

The rabbis justified this courageous deed by a principle based on a biblical verse (Ps. 119:126): "*Aggada* is not meant to be written down? We say, however, that since [the writing down of the Haggadah] cannot be dispensed with [lest it be forgotten], we say 'when it is time to work for the Lord, they [may] break the law' " (Gittin 60a). Two centuries later Rav Ashi, head of the Sura Academy in Babylonia, took similar action

* *See pp. 125–26.*

in regard to the Babylonian Talmud. Again there was the danger of losing the vast accumulation of rabbinic learning. To quote the late Solomon Schechter: "The continuous and ever-growing stream of oral doctrine, flowing and swelling in volume through the centuries, had at last begun to exceed the powers of human memory, and recourse to transcription became inevitable."[1] Rav Ashi took the decisive step of gathering the vast amount of rabbinic teachings that were built upon and around the Mishnah. He organized the material and prepared it for eventual commitment to writing.

The liturgy, however, continued to be an oral tradition for a long time to come. Its dimensions were relatively limited, and its regular use precluded the danger of its being forgotten. Ultimately, however, the prayers, too, had to be reduced to writing. In the ninth and tenth centuries the geonim reluctantly lifted the ban, and the prayers of the synagogue were published.

The Development of Local Rites

The reasons for committing the prayers to writing are to be found in the nature of oral traditions. People take liberties with an oral tradition which they would not take with written material. They "improve" on the diction and eliminate what they regard as superfluous or repetitious. Some are just careless with the exact wording of an oral text. Thus Rabbi Saadia Gaon, who published a prayer book in the tenth century, says in his introduction * that he found it necessary to commit the prayers to writing because they had suffered from "neglect, additions, and omissions."

But the most perilous challenge to the oral tradition of the synagogue was the ever-widening dispersion of the Jewish people. As long as the Jews were concentrated in Palestine and Babylonia their respective traditions were fixed and well known. The heads of the academies diligently watched over them and protected them from corruption and even from slight mutilation. However, when the Diaspora widened, contacts with the sources of authority became infrequent and

* *See pp. 385–88.*

tenuous. By the ninth century there were Jewish communities in Europe from the Iberian Peninsula to the Russian Empire and from Italy to England. In Asia and Africa there were substantial Jewish communities from the Straits of Gibraltar to Persia and beyond, reaching as far east as China and as far south as India. Under these circumstances the oral tradition, however tenaciously and lovingly guarded, could not escape the impact of local influences. Even musical renditions of the prayers were affected by the indigenous music in the many lands of the dispersion—the chanting of the Torah began to differ from area to area. It was inevitable, therefore, that a variety of local usages should develop in the scattered communities.

Differences in the wording of the prayers also became a common feature of local usage. As long as these differences were not at variance with the rabbinic guidelines established at Yavneh and with the exact formulations found in the Talmud, they were accepted and approved as valid local minhagim, or rites.

Another source of local minhagim was the rise of the new synagogue poetry.* For understandable reasons the people preferred piyutim by authors whose fame had reached them; but the fame of many a poet was localized and limited. It was therefore inevitable that variations in local rites would increase with the multiplication of the piyutim.

Some local variations were not just matters of diction; they were total innovations caused by purely local circumstances, often of a temporary nature. But these new prayers tended to survive the circumstances that gave rise to them and continued to be used as local minhagim. In a responsum by Rabbi Yair Hayim Bacharach, a sixteenth century talmudist, we read about an interesting though unusual example of the birth and survival of a local minhag in the city of Worms:

> I once had a discussion with a learned old man in Worms about a curious custom. One of the piyutim recited on the Sabbath of Hanukah starts in the middle of the piyut instead of the beginning. The old man

* *See pp. 168–74.*

> told me that he had heard from the elders of the congregation that during the persecutions all the prayer books were burned. . . . After a long period had elapsed and the storm had passed, the remnants of the congregation returned and they made use of whatever they rescued from the destruction. As to the above-mentioned piyut, they found only the second half of it. So they recited it as is, as a temporary device. But in time this practice became a set custom. And to this day they recite this piyut from the middle instead of from the beginning.[2]

This intriguing minhag may not be typical of the origin of local customs, but it clearly describes how local rites often come into being by fortuitous circumstances, especially during critical periods, and then survive the circumstances that gave rise to them.

Another striking example of the development of local rites is in the *Alenu* prayer with which all services are concluded.* This ancient and beloved prayer was altered to suit Christian sensitivities,† because the Church objected to one sentence which implied that Christianity is a form of idolatry. Today the Church no longer censors the prayers of the synagogue, but the objectionable sentence has remained expunged from the *Alenu* prayer in all communities of the Christian lands. Even the most Orthodox have not seen fit to restore that sentence officially to its rightful place. The censored reading has become a minhag, and a minhag clings to the ritual with a tenacity that transcends reason or historic developments. Among the Jews of the Moslem countries the original text remained intact, and to this day the objectionable sentence is part of the prayer.

The Crystallization of Local Rites

The rabbis of the Talmud tried to safeguard the unity of the tradition. It will be recalled that the guiding motivation behind Rabbi Gamaliel's enactments at Yavneh ‡ was the preservation

* *See pp. 241–42.*
† *See pp. 455–57.*
‡ *See pp. 86–88.*

of the unity of the Jewish people. Rabbi Gamaliel and his colleagues successfully met the challenge of their day. They evolved a system of religious practice that brought the Jewish people an enduring unity without imposing a rigid, stifling uniformity. This rabbinic wisdom is also reflected in the liturgy, which they carefully nurtured and guarded. On the one hand, they resisted a multiplicity of variant practices, and on the other hand they recognized the validity of local minhagim.

In some localities the people regarded their minhagim as sacred traditions handed down by their fathers. There was also a general assumption that variant practices did not arise by chance; they were surely introduced by eminent authorities. How else, they reasoned, could changes in the liturgy have been made in the first place? This reverence for local custom was recognized in the Mishnah, where it is legislated that local custom is generally binding. In the mishnaic tractate *Pesahim* there is a chapter called, from its initial words, *Makom She-Nahagu* (Where it is customary), which deals with the theme of local custom. The Talmud states this principle in sweeping terms: "The minhag of fathers is to be regarded as Torah" and "A minhag of Israel is in the category of Torah."

The geonim, too, accepted local customs and advocated their retention. In postgeonic times Moses Maimonides began his work on the *Order of the Prayers* * with the words "It is the custom of the people. . . ." In his great code the *Mishneh Torah*, Maimonides frequently enunciates the principle that in some situations "everything depends on local minhag."

In the fourteenth century the validity of local minhag was given final and definitive force by the talmudic scholar Rabbi Jacob Mölln (Maharil). He even extended this principle to the melodies of the prayers. His overwhelming authority bestowed on local custom the power of law. As a result, the custom of each locality assumed a permanence never dreamed of before.

If Rabbi Jacob Mölln gave local custom its effective legal authority, it was Rabbi Isaac Luria,† the father of what is

* *See p. 388.*
† *See pp. 489–92.*

called "the practical kabbala," who provided local custom with a rationale. To be sure, its rationality can be questioned since his reasoning is purely mystical in character. Nonetheless, it carried weight because in the Middle Ages mysticism was an overriding intellectual preoccupation in many influential circles. According to Rabbi Isaac Luria, there are twelve heavenly gates through which the prayers of Israel ascend to heaven. Each minhag has its own gate. Hence it is the duty of each Israelite to adhere to his own rite, lest he bring confusion into the higher realms. Minhagim are therefore valid and binding.

The Mainstreams of the Tradition

There is a persistent belief that the Jewish prayer book is monolithic in its structure and content. It is assumed that the prayer book was composed by divinely inspired men and that its text is therefore sacred and immutable. The assumption that the traditional prayer book has a definitive form which has remained fixed and unaltered to this day led Rabbi Judah He-Hasid and his medieval school of mystics to search the text of the prayers for divine mysteries in the same way that the kabbalists searched the biblical text for divine secrets. These mystics counted the words and even the letters of the prayers, hoping to decipher their esoteric implications. But these assumptions of the mystics were unfounded. The prayer book has never been uniform in content. Even before it was committed to writing there were already a number of well-defined versions with variant readings. To be sure, the essential framework remained the common element of all the versions. But a framework can be finished in a variety of ways, reflecting local color and temporal characteristics. What dialect is to a mother tongue, local custom, or minhag, has been to the prayer tradition of the synagogue. And like a dialect, each local minhag has clung tenaciously to its locality and has distinguished it from all others.

Out of the welter of many local customs two fundamental rites crystallized: the Ashkenazic, or German, minhag and the Sephardic, or Spanish, minhag. Consolidation was due in large measure to the invention of the printing press.* The term *Ashkenazic* embraced the Jewries scattered over the dominions of the Christian potentates, while the term *Sephardic* embraced the Jewries under Mohammedan rule. These major rites, notwithstanding their geographic names, are neither German nor Spanish in origin. Their origins go back to the two ancient centers of Judaism: the Ashkenazic tradition traces its roots to Palestine, the Sephardic tradition had its beginnings in Babylonia. These major streams of the tradition have had tributaries, large and small. The Yemenite Jews now living in Israel, for example, justly protest their inclusion in the Sephardic community; their rites and customs, they say, are quite different from those of the Sephardim. Because they lived in isolation from the rest of the Jewish people for many centuries, their rite developed independently and is different in many respects from those of the two dominant groups. Hence they want to be under the religious jurisdiction of a chief rabbi of their own.

The Jews of Italy, too, have a minhag that fits neither the Ashkenazic nor the Sephardic rite. The Roman Jewish community was founded when the Temple was still standing. Its rite goes back to early rabbinic times, before the completion of Mishnah. Hence their minhag contains many independent elements.[3]

And within the two main rites there are a number of local practices,[4] some of which are of great interest to the specialist but are too technical for our purpose. However, the two major minhagim deserve more than passing mention.

Ashkenazic and Sephardic Minhagim

The differences between the Ashkenazic and Sephardic rites are not limited to the wording of the prayers; they are to be found in almost every area of the liturgy. A person of occidental background entering a Sephardic synagogue immediately becomes aware of several striking characteristics that reflect not merely superficial customs but characteristics of an anthropological nature. A different civilization is evident. The

* *See pp. 541 ff.*

first noticeable difference is that the Hebrew pronunciation is strikingly different from the one current among the Ashkenazim. It is hard to say which pronunciation is closer to the original Hebrew—in all probability the prophet Isaiah would find both pronunciations unlike the one he used when he uttered his prophecies. However, since the scientific world and the state of Israel have accepted the Sephardic pronunciation, it has gained ascendancy;[5] it can be assumed that in time most Ashkenazic congregations will abandon their traditional pronunciation in favor of the Sephardic. For the present the Western Jew visiting an oriental synagogue hears what is to him a strange pronunciation of the Hebrew, and he immediately becomes aware of the wide gulf between the two minhagim.

Our hypothetical visitor is equally surprised when he opens the Sephardic prayer book. He is struck by the strange design of the printing. The Tetragrammaton, he notes, is ingeniously interwoven with the word *Adonai* (Lord) or with the names of certain angels. These kabbalistic combinations are usually contrived by printing the word *Adonai* in smaller letters under the enlarged last letter of the Tetragrammaton or by alternating the letters of these two words and forming a single unpronounceable mystic word. Since these strange mystic symbols are to be found in almost every line, the Sephardic prayer book is exotic and confusing to the Western visitor. He soon realizes that mysticism has exerted a more profound influence on the Sephardim than on the Ashkenazim.*

But our visitor's greatest surprise comes when the service starts. To begin with, the reader stands on the bimah, which is in the center of the synagogue (in contradistinction to the practice in the Ashkenazic synagogue, where the reader stands at the *amud* (stand), located in the front of the synagogue at the foot of the ark). However, the most striking discovery is that the worshipers read most of the prayers in unison, in a rhythmic, monotonous singsong. Our visitor inevitably contrasts this strange mode of praying with the familiar procedure in his own synagogue, where the worshipers recite the prayers silently and the reader repeats the concluding verses tunefully.

* *See pp. 493–94.*

ואנחה (לידית). ומלוך עלינו מהרה אתה
יהוה יאהדונהי לבדך. בחסד וברחמים בצדק
ובמשפט: ברוך אתה יהוה יאהדונהי מלך
אוהב צדקה ומשפט:

בעשרת ימי תשובה אומרים המלך המשפט:

אם טעה ואמר מלך אוהב וכו' כיון שוכר מלך אינו חוזר.

למינים ולמלשינים אל תהי תקוה וכל הזדים
כרגע יאבדו. וכל אויביך (סמאל) וכל
שונאיך (לידית) מהרה יכרתו. ומלכות הרשעה
מהרה תעקר ותשבר ותכלם ותכניעם
במהרה בימינו: ברוך אתה יהוה יאהדונהי
שובר אויבים ומכניע מינים:

על הצדיקים ועל החסידים ועל שארית
עמך בית ישראל. ועל פליטת בית
סופריהם. ועל גרי הצדק ועלינו. יהמו נא
רחמיך יהוה יאהדונהי אלהינו ותן שכר טוב
לכל הבוטחים בשמך באמת. ושים חלקנו
עמהם. ולעולם לא נבוש כי בך בטחנו.

Facsimile of a page from a Sephardic *Siddur*. Note how the Tetragrammaton is interwoven with *Adonai*. Names of angels are interspersed throughout the text. This version of the prayer *Velamalshinim* contains phrases that are no longer found in the Ashkenazic *Siddur*. TAKEN FROM SIDDUR TEFILLAT YESHARIM, PUBLISHED BY S. J. MANSOUR, JERUSALEM.

He wonders why the Sephardim persist in this monotonous droning.[6] In all probability this Sephardic custom goes back to the days when the prayers were recited from memory, and only a few knew the prayers by heart. It was therefore necessary for the reader to recite the prayers in unison with the congregation to enable the less knowledgeable worshipers to follow the service.

Finally, our visitor notes that the content of the prayer book differs considerably from the one used in his own Ashkenazic congregation. Although these differences do not violate the basic rabbinic tradition, nonetheless they are numerous and prove a stumbling block to the visitor. The many differences and likenesses of the two minhagim can be illustrated in parallel columns, but this would prove too technical and of little interest to the average reader. Anyone who wishes to pursue this subject is advised to open an Ashkenazic and a Sephardic prayer book and compare the parallel readings of the *Tefillah.* He will find that except for the statutory portions that were established in the talmudic period, the wording of practically every benediction differs in the two minhagim.[7]

Some Liturgic Differences

While an examination of the exact wording of each prayer in the two major rites is hardly an exciting prospect, there are some differences that one can easily note without recourse to detailed research. For example, the Ashkenazim recite two benedictions when they put on the tefillin, one for each tefillin. Not so the Sephardim. They recite only the first of these benedictions. The Sephardim do not put on the tefillin during the intermediate days of Passover and Sukkot, the Ashkenazim do put them on during these semiholidays. Another example chosen at random from among many is the call to prayer, or *Barkhu,** in the morning and evening services. The Sephardim recite it twice in each service, one at the beginning of the service (as is also the practice among the Ashkenazim)

* *See pp. 98–99.*

and a second time before the conclusion of the service. The second *Barkhu* is to enable latecomers to join the congregation in reciting the doxology: "Praised is the Lord who is to be blessed for ever and ever." The Sephardic minhag is to recite the Hallel * at both the evening and morning festival services; the Ashkenazim, however, recite the Hallel only during the morning services.

One more interesting distinction between the two rites is to be found at the Passover Seder. The Ashkenazim recite a benediction before each of the four cups of wine prescribed for the ceremony, but the Sephardim recite the benediction only before the first and the third cups of wine; the second and the fourth cups of wine are drunk without a benediction.

Enough differences have been mentioned to indicate the gulf that separates the two major minhagim. But one more striking difference should be mentioned, that of their respective hymnologies. The hymns and songs of praise of the German minhag were composed by poets from Palestine or from Europe. The piyutim of Eleazar Kalir, for example, dominate the Yom Kippur service of the Ashkenazim. In the Spanish minhag this prolific poet is almost unknown. Instead, one finds piyutim by such gifted poets as Solomon Ibn Gabirol, Judah Halevi, Moses Ibn Ezra, and Abraham Ibn Ezra,[8] all of whom lived in Spain.

Coexistence of the Minhagim

The Ashkenazim and the Sephardim have clung to their respective rites, and when they wandered from one exile to another, they carried their spiritual baggage with them. The coexistence of these rites thus became a feature of many Jewish communities. In Italy, for example, before the Nazi holocaust, there were many rites existing peacefully side by side. In central Italy the "Roman," or Italian, rite was generally in use; in northern Italy the German rite was dominant; in the seaports the Spanish rite generally prevailed; in larger com-

* *See pp. 210–11.*

munities, such as Venice, all three existed; and in Rome, where for a long time only one synagogue building was permitted, five conventicles existed within the synagogue, each following its own minhag.

Today one finds both Ashkenazic and Sephardic synagogues almost everywhere. In America the Ashkenazim are the dominant group. They came in overwhelming numbers from Central and Eastern Europe during the nineteenth and early twentieth centuries. Actually, the Sephardim had come to America earlier. The first group of Jewish immigrants, who landed in New Amsterdam (New York) in the year 1654, were Sephardim, and they still have several synagogues which are of historic importance. In more recent times a number of Sephardic immigrants have settled in America. These, too, founded synagogues of their own. Both the descendants of the early settlers and the recent arrivals proudly adhere to their Sephardic minhag. But they constitute a small minority of the American Jewish community, and their minhag is unknown in most American cities.

In Israel the Jewish population is almost equally divided between the Ashkenazim and the Sephardim. Each of the two branches of Judaism has its own chief rabbi and its own rabbinic courts. This community organization was inherited from the British Mandatory government and has been continued by the Israeli government as a convenient framework for administrative purposes.

Reciprocal Influence

The strict adherence to local custom did not preclude a measure of reciprocal influence, especially during the geonic period, when the Babylonian academies and their scholars wielded a powerful influence on the whole Diaspora. Many a Babylonian minhag was adopted by the Palestinian Jewish community and its followers in the Diaspora. The most striking of these is the procedure followed at the Sabbath morning reading of the Torah. The minhag in Palestine was to read the Torah in a three-year cycle. This practice was abandoned in favor of the Babylonian minhag of reading the Torah in a one-year cycle, which became the rule everywhere.

Similar examples of this type are the acceptance by the Palestinian Jews of the Kedushah * and the Half Hallel,† both of which had originated in Babylonia.

In the postgeonic period the stream of influence was reversed and the Sephardim took over a number of minhagim from the Ashkenazim. For example, the Ashkenazim associated the ark of the Torah with the Holy of Holies in the Jerusalem Temple. A curtain was therefore hung on the ark of the Torah in imitation of the Holy of Holies, where a curtain or paroket, hung on the ark which contained the tablets of the Ten Commandments.‡ The Sephardim did not have this association, and their ark of the Torah had only doors to permit the taking out and the returning of the Torah scrolls. The Ashkenazic practice of hanging a paroket on the ark appealed to the Sephardim and they adopted it. The paroket on the ark has thus become a universal practice in the synagogue.

Several prayers also crossed over from the Ashkenazic to the Sephardic minhag. One of these is the High Holy Days prayer known as the *Unetaneh Tokef* (Let us declare the mighty [holiness of the day]).§ This prayer is traditionally ascribed to the martyr Rabbi Amnon, who, in his dying moments, uttered this hymn. Rabbi Amnon lived and died in Mayence, and the story of his martyrdom reflected the historic experiences of German Jewry. The touching background of this prayer appealed to the Sephardim, however, and they adopted it; it occupies an honored place in the Sephardic rite.

Should There Be a Uniform Minhag in All Synagogues?

The possibility of uniting the two major minhagim and their subsidiaries into a single rite has been discussed at various times.

* *See pp. 134–37.*
† *See pp. 210–11.*
‡ *See pp. 253–54.*
§ *See p. 461.*

At the World Conference of Ashkenazic and Sephardic Synagogues held in Jerusalem in January 1968, a resolution was submitted by the Association of Youth Synagogues in Israel, asking for a uniform liturgy for all traditional synagogues. The chief rabbi of the Ashkenazim, Rabbi I. Y. Unterman, opposed the resolution. He said that such a liturgy would develop "naturally" in the course of time. His statement would have been far more penetrating had he said that the appeal of uniformity should not blind people to the enriching qualities of harmonious diversity. Rabbi Jacob Emden, in his famous commentary on the *Siddur*, wisely remarked: "The custom of the Sephardim is to recite the prayer *Hodu* before the prayer *Barukh She-Amar*.* The minhag of the Ashkenazim is to recite it after the *Barukh She-Amar*. There is support for each custom. . . . Therefore let everyone follow the minhag of his congregation." The approach of Rabbi Jacob Emden is altogether sound. The goal of the Jewish communities should be mutual respect and harmonious coexistence, not uniformity. The chief rabbi might have underscored the talmudic principle that "both are the words of the living God" (Erub. 13b). It has been claimed that cultural pluralism bestows color, beauty, and vitality on a people's way of life. It follows that the liturgy of the synagogue, containing as it does a variety of minhagim, should prove a source of spiritual vigor. Israel Abrahams has summarized this phase of Jewish reality in his inimitable way:

> Custom is a tyrant. Custom survives the circumstances which give it birth, and because the retention of it is based on sentiment, it is not amenable to the assaults of reason. But despite the evils resulting from this multiplicity of custom, despite the disorder accruing, for instance, from the constant presence in a town of immigrant Jews who were held free to follow their own imported *Minhagim*, Jewish life gained more than it lost by the freedom of the individual, the freshening of the atmosphere, and the avoidance of clerical arrogance, by the co-existence of many smaller varieties within the body of Judaism.[9]

* *See p. 142.*

Relaxation of the Ban on Transcribing the Prayers

Rabbi Amram Gaon made history with his responsum to the Jews of Spain. But he was not quite the revolutionary that some have imagined him to be. It should be noted that prior to the ninth century the ban on writing down the prayers had already been considerably relaxed. Thus in the eighth century we find a responsum by Rabbi Yehudai Gaon in which he permits the reader to use a written compilation of the prayers on the Day of Atonement. He yielded to this innovation because the service on Yom Kippur is long and elaborate. But on other occasions he expected the reader to recite the prayers from memory.

By the ninth century it must have been quite common for readers to use privately compiled prayer books. This can be established from a responsum by Rabbi Natronai Gaon, Rabbi Amram Gaon's immediate predecessor as head of the Sura Academy. He was asked whether a blind man may act as reader. Had the general practice still been for the reader to recite the prayers from memory, the question about a blind man's eligibility could not possibly have arisen. The blind man can recite the prayers by heart like everyone else. It seems that by the middle of the ninth century, however, readers generally used written prayers not only on the Day of Atonement but on every occasion. These written prayers had no stamp of approval by a recognized authority; they were privately written down for use by the reader as aids to his memory. Officially there was still no prayer book that a Jew could use as a guide to his devotions in the synagogue or at home.[10]

The private compilations of the prayers not only were without authority, they were often infested with errors due to faulty copying or erroneous local practices. Each person copied the service in his own way, adding or omitting what seemed helpful to him. This tended to compound the confusion and rendered the situation more critical than it had been when the oral tradition was in full force. It is not surprising, therefore, to find a community turning to an authority for guidance. The community, as already indicated, was located in Spain and the authority was Rabbi Amram Gaon, head of the Sura Academy from 869 to 881, a man endowed with sufficient vision and courage to act on so pressing a question.

Rabbi Amram Gaon's *Siddur*

The declared purpose of *The Book of Common Prayer* published by the Anglican Church in 1549, as stated in its preface, was that it be "to God's glory, the edifying of the people, and for the advancement of true religion." [11] No such grandiloquent declaration introduced the first official Jewish prayer book. Because its prayers had been in use for many centuries, no ringing statement of purpose was necessary. When a preface was written to a prayer book, about half a century later, by Rabbi Saadia Gaon, it only pointed to the practical needs of the day and not to any pretentious aims. According to the rabbis, the glory of God is reflected in the lives of the pious; the edification of the people is achieved by the teaching of Torah; and the true faith is advanced by Israel's loyalty to the divine covenant. Rabbi Amram Gaon introduced his compilation of the prayers in a rather perfunctory manner: "Regarding the prayers and benedictions for the whole year, about which you asked me, I found it proper to arrange them in order and to send them to you as they have been transmitted to us by the *tanna'im* and *amora'im*." [12]

The original *Order of the Prayers* that Rabbi Amram Gaon prepared for the Spanish Jews, or even an early copy of it, is not extant. What we have are "badly worked-over versions," which differ widely from each other. This is not due to a lack of reverence for the gaon or his authoritative work. It is because the responsum recorded the prayers used in Babylonia; in Spain and elsewhere there were well-established local customs which even an authority of Rabbi Amram Gaon's stature could not dislodge. It naturally followed that copyists in Spain and elsewhere substituted their own local prayers, so that the *Seder Rav Amram Gaon* as copied in the various communities in no way represented the original. To quote the late Prof. Louis Ginzberg: "The [original responsum] was so modified, abridged, and extended, that we now have very little of what it was . . . when it left the hands of Rav Amram." [13]

The importance of the *Seder Rav Amram Gaon* was not diminished by the corruption of the original text, however, because it also contained extensive notes and comments which corrected the prayer texts and clearly presented the basic principles of the liturgy as developed by the rabbis of the Talmud. These comments set the limits of deviation. Rabbi Amram Gaon thus provided the Jews of Spain with an authoritative guide to which their leaders could resort in cases of doubt or dispute. The leaders of the communities were now enabled to control the local minhagim and prevent their straying from the basic liturgy. In the course of time the *Seder Rav Amram Gaon* spread beyond the boundaries of Spain. The copyists of the far-off communities, too, had little compunctions about replacing the prayers of the gaon's *Siddur* with their local versions. The commentary, however, they left intact. To be sure, some copyists "improved" on the commentary by adding relevant material from Rabbi Amram's responsa, but in general the commentary has remained fairly true to the original.

The *Seder Rav Amram Gaon* is regarded as the "father" of the Jewish prayer book, especially of the Sephardic version. It was widely disseminated and has been extensively referred to as an authority. The historic significance of Rabbi Amram Gaon's responsum lies in the fact that the ban on writing down, or in later centuries printing, the prayers for use by the synagogue worshiper had been permanently lifted. Never again did anyone question the propriety of publishing a *Siddur*. Worship ceased to be the monopoly of those who knew the prayers by heart and became "the heritage of the congregation of Jacob."

RABBI SAADIA GAON'S *Siddur*

The first authoritative *Siddur* for use by the ordinary worshiper was produced by a brilliant successor of Rabbi Amram Gaon. Its author was Rabbi Saadia Gaon (882–942), a man of surprising scholarly stature and originality. To quote the late Prof. Louis Ginzberg "Anything that he touched in the wide range of his studies bears the stamp of his personality and originality."[14] And the range of his studies was extensive. He was an outstanding philosopher and talmudist, a poet and grammarian, a translator of the Bible into Arabic, and a successful polemicist in the continuing battle of words between the Karaites and the Rabbinites.

The story of Saadia's *Siddur* is intriguing. It was produced in the early tenth century but was presumed lost for about five hundred years. In view of the author's fame, modern scholars tried to reconstruct it from scattered quotations in medieval writings. All the while a copy of this valuable book was lying undisturbed in the Bodleian Library of Oxford University, where the eminent scholar Moritz Steinschneider rediscovered it in 1851. This discovery was followed at the end of the century by a still greater find: the Cairo genizah,* in which there were many fragments of Saadia's *Siddur*. These fragments made it possible to fill in gaps in the Bodleian manuscript where pages were missing. Scholars could also compare, analyze, and evaluate the authenticity of Saadia's *Siddur*. Critical studies of the parallel texts and careful analyses of the manuscripts and the quotations from Saadia's *Siddur* found in medieval texts have established that the *Siddur* discovered in the Bodleian Library is essentially as it was composed by Saadia Gaon. It is the oldest authentic *Siddur*, the actual parent of all *Siddurim*. To be sure, the *Seder Rav Amram Gaon* was written before Saadia was born. But as already stated the available copies had been worked over so thoroughly that they are far from the original. And what is more significant, Rabbi Amram Gaon's aim was not a *Siddur* for the worshiper but a guide for the community leaders. In contrast, Saadia's *Siddur* is essentially like the original (notwithstanding the fact that the available copy is dated centuries after its composition and surely contains some errors) and was compiled for actual use by the average synagogue worshiper. Saadia's objective in compiling the *Siddur* is clearly stated in his introduction. In the course of his travels, he says, he noted that there were three evils that corrupted the order of prayer—omissions, additions, and abridgments. He therefore resolved

* *See pp. 340–41, 426.*

> to collect and arrange the established prayers, praises and benedictions so that the original form should be restored. But as to the omissions and additions, I shall point out which are contrary to the fundamentals of prayers and which are not; the former I prohibit; the latter I permit though they have no foundation in tradition.[15]

Rabbi Saadia Gaon was familiar with his predecessor's *Siddur* and followed in his footsteps to the extent of compiling the text of the prayers and composing a running commentary. However, he produced a more logical and more economical arrangement of the prayers, which made it possible for the average layman to follow the service. Rabbi Amram's chronological arrangement of the prayers, which made it necessary to repeat many prayers (such as the *Tefillah* of the festivals, which is the same for each of the three major holidays), was abandoned by Saadia. Rabbi Amram Gaon's *Siddur* had also contained a miscellaneous section, a sort of catchall. The layman would find it extremely difficult to locate the prayers grouped in this section, so Saadia devised a simple and original organization. He arranged the prayers in logical groups: festival prayers constituted one coherent group, fast day prayers constituted another, and all benedictions were grouped together and logically classified. This simple device not only precluded repetition, but made the *Siddur* a handy manual for all Jews, laymen and scholars alike. Anyone with average intelligence could locate the prayers for every occasion. Although some of Saadia's prayer groupings have been improved upon in later compilations, his overall approach has remained as the basic arrangement of the traditional *Siddur*, and the rules Saadia recorded in his commentary are essentially those of the traditional synagogue today.

Since Saadia's *Siddur* was meant for the people, his commentary was written in the vernacular, that is, in Arabic.[16] It contains no references to the sources. The law is stated and that is sufficient for the average man, who has neither the time nor the training to check the sources. The commentary deals with the rules of prayer—the time, the mode, the posture at worship. Saadia was a master of the art of brevity. Complicated legal matters are summarized in a few lines or a few words. The prayers for the New Moon contain the rules of the calendar. The prayers for Yom Kippur contain the laws of fasting, repentance, and the importance of asking forgiveness from one's neighbor.

Saadia's *Siddur* enjoyed great popularity and exerted great influence on the synagogue rites. Its popularity continued till the appearance of Moses Maimonides' monumental code, the *Mishneh Torah*, which included a section on the liturgy entitled "The Order of the Prayers of the Whole Year." But Saadia's *Siddur* was not altogether forgotten. When Rabbi David Abudarham published his scholarly commentary on the *Siddur* in the fourteenth century, he quoted extensively from Saadia's *Siddur*. After that Saadia's *Siddur* fell into oblivion till it was rediscovered in the mid-nineteenth century. In the year 1941, which was the thousandth anniversary of Saadia's death, his *Siddur* was published in Jerusalem under expert editorial guidance.[17] The publication contains a Hebrew translation of the Arabic commentary as well as scholarly notes for the specialist.

While the *Seder Rav Amram Gaon* is historically the "father" of the *Siddur*, the *Seder Rav Saadia Gaon* is its actual parent. But Saadia's *Siddur* followed mainly, though not exclusively, the Sephardic rite. An authoritative *Siddur* for the Ashkenazic synagogue was not compiled till the eleventh century. Surprisingly, this *Siddur* does not bear the name of an outstanding scholar but that of a French town: Vitry.

The First Ashkenazic *Siddur*

After the tenth century leadership in Jewish life passed from the Babylonian geonim to the European scholars. After Rabbi Saadia Gaon there were two more geonim of scholarly stature whose prestige gave them unchallenged leadership—Rabbi Sherira Gaon and his son Rabbi Hai Gaon. When the latter died in 1038 the leadership of Babylonian Jewry faded rapidly. To be sure, scholars continued to rise among the Sephardim, and their scholarship was acknowledged throughout the Diaspora. A shining example is Moses Maimonides (1135–1204).

But Maimonides did not head either of the two famous Babylonian academies.

The fame and prestige of Sephardic scholars was usually limited to their own communities. And the fame of Spanish Jewry rested not so much on talmudic scholarship as on other areas of creativity, especially philosophy, poetry, and linguistics. One need only mention the names of Solomon Ibn Gabirol, Judah Halevi, and the Ibn Ezras to establish the grandeur of Spanish Jewry's achievements. But the great talmudists who wielded religious authority and were the spiritual successors of the geonim were to be found mainly in the Central European lands. This historic development is highlighted by such luminaries in the field of talmudic scholarship as Rabbenu Gershom (960–1040), who was lovingly called by the Ashkenazic Jews "the Light of the Exile"; Rabbi Solomon Yitz'haki (1040–1105), generally known as Rashi; Rashi's famous grandsons, Rabbi Samuel ben Meir (d. about 1158), known as the Rashbam,[18] and Rabbi Jacob ben Meir (d. 1171), known as Rabbenu Tam; and, to mention just one more luminary, the martyred Rabbi Meir of Rothenberg (d. 1293), upon whom the title "the Light of the Exile" was also bestowed. It is significant that the greatest talmudic scholars of Spain, the family of Rabbi Asher, were imported from Central Europe. Rabbi Asher ben Yehiel (d. 1328), known as the Rosh,* and his famous sons, Judah ben Asher and Jacob ben Asher, were all born in Germany. In later centuries, when persecutions dimmed the light of talmudic scholarship in Central Europe, it did not return to the Near Eastern lands. It moved to Eastern Europe, where it maintained its eminent position till it was tragically extinguished by the Nazi holocaust in the 1940s.

By the eleventh century the synagogues of the Ashkenazim were ripe for an official compilation of their own *Siddur*. The person who met this need was Rabbi Simhah ben Samuel, a pupil of Rashi. The compiler of this pioneer work lived in Vitry, France, and his *Siddur* is known as *Mahzor Vitry*, the Cycle of Prayers from Vitry. This compilation is regarded by

* *See p. 537.*

some as the most important of the early *Siddurim.* It was the basis of the Ashkenazic minhag, and in the thirteenth century it was introduced by the French rabbis as the official liturgy of their communities.

The *Mahzor Vitry* is an ambitious work, ten times as voluminous as the *Siddur* of Rabbi Amram Gaon. It contained both the text of the prayers and a running commentary, which included not only notes on the prayers for every occasion, but also the laws pertaining to the occasions themselves. It was in fact a comprehensive religious manual built around the liturgy. It contained almost everything a Jew needed to know to live a full religious life. In dealing with the prayers of a festival, for example, the *Mahzor Vitry* also includes the laws of the festival. The author frequently quotes his predecessors, especially Rabbi Amram Gaon, but he goes beyond the bounds established by them. He included material which had previously not been regarded as an inherent part of the liturgy, such as the mishnaic tractate Avot (Fathers), which is studied by observant Jews during the summer Sabbath afternoons,* and the Passover Haggadah.† Commentaries were provided for each. Most important, the author included material that was indigenous to the minhag of French Jewry, especially the piyutim which were locally in use. For the first time, the *Alenu* prayer is found as the concluding prayer of all services.

The *Mahzor Vitry* remained in manuscript form for almost eight centuries. When the printing press was invented, less voluminous prayer manuals were printed for the Ashkenazic Jews. They followed the *Mahzor Vitry* but did not contain the copious commentary, nor were the prayers copied exactly as they appeared in the *Mahzor Vitry.*

The *Mahzor Vitry* was finally printed for scholarly use in Berlin in 1893. The printed volume contains over nine hundred pages. Its significance, however, is not its amplitude, but its historic distinction of being the first *Siddur* of the Ashkenazic synagogue. It can be said that with certain adjustments it is still the prayer book of the Ashkenazic Orthodox synagogue.

* *See pp. 194–96.*
† *See pp. 301 ff.*

With the compilation of the *Mahzor Vitry*, an era in the development of the *Siddur* was completed.[19] The oral tradition of the synagogue officially ended in the ninth century when Rabbi Amram Gaon wrote his famous responsum for the Jews of Spain. In the tenth century Rabbi Saadia Gaon compiled his *Siddur* and provided an official prayer book for the ordinary worshiper in the Sephardic synagogue. In the eleventh century Rabbi Simhah ben Samuel compiled his *Mahzor Vitry* for the Ashkenazic synagogue. The oral tradition of the synagogue thus became fully a matter of history.

But the *Siddur* was never a finished work. It has always been a living organism, sensitive to the religious needs of each generation. It constantly grew and adjusted. The adjustments, however, were not permitted to mutilate in the least the liturgic foundations laid by the rabbis of the Talmud. Notwithstanding this limitation, significant additions were made, reflecting the changing historic and intellectual climates of the passing centuries. The *Siddur* thus continued to be a living instrument of the spiritual life of the Jewish people. The story of the *Siddur*'s growth and its adjustments to the new situations of the postgeonic centuries will constitute the contents of the balance of this book. But before we start that story, we must digress and examine the theology of the *Siddur*, for the rabbinic doctrines of Judaism were both the foundations and the building bricks of the synagogue's liturgy.

15
THE THEOLOGY OF THE *SIDDUR*

The *Siddur* is the Jewish book of piety. In it are reflected most clearly the Jew's intellectual and emotional attitudes to God. It not only contains the Jew's fervent petitions for God's mercy, his thanksgivings for God's blessings, and his praises for God's glorious manifestations in the world of nature and man, but it also records the Jew's dependence on God's fatherly love and his certainty of God's merciful response to the reasonable yearnings of his heart. This piety—or inwardness, as some call it—is based on a number of theological premises: the nature of God, the essence of sin, the efficacy of repentance, and similar articles of faith. These beliefs constitute the backdrop of Jewish piety, and they are fully and clearly expressed in the traditional prayers of the synagogue.

All prayer is based on a number of assumptions which represent the essential truths and the highest good to which a person or a people is committed. In the prayers of the synagogue one can find the Jew's traditional ideals, beliefs, values, attitudes, and feelings toward God, Israel, and mankind. These essentials of the faith are the authentic doctrines of rabbinic Judaism.

The *Siddur*, however, is not to be regarded as a text on Jewish theology. The prayers do not elucidate any theological dogmas, nor do they defend any tenets of belief. What we find scattered in the various prayers are only the accepted assumptions of rabbinic Judaism, the sifted and recognized articles of faith. While the Talmud contains the views of numerous scholars, the *Siddur* contains the distilled convictions of Judaism as a whole. These convictions were reiterated by the geonim and thereafter were diligently taught by the authorities of the post-geonic times. They constitute the essential theology of Orthodox Judaism to this day. It was only in the nineteenth century, when modernity began to penetrate Jewish life, that some Jews began to question a number of these doctrines.[1]

Prior to the onset of modernity the ordinary Jew was wont to recite his prayers thrice daily. In doing so he gained more than a superficial acquaintance with the essential teachings of rabbinic theology. He learned from the *Siddur* about God, His nature, His will for man, and His special relationship with Israel. Thus Sholom Aleichem's well-known character Tevyeh the Dairyman[2] constantly quoted from the *Siddur*, and his quotations—though twisted to suit his needs—reflected a general understanding of the essentials of rabbinic theology. Tevyeh's grasp of the religious doctrines was fragmentary and lacked logical system, not only because Tevyeh was not a theologian, but also because the *Siddur* from which he learned most of his religious doctrines does not contain a systematic presentation of rabbinic thought. Indeed, nowhere in the writings of the rabbis is there a logically organized presentation of Jewish religious belief. To quote the late Louis Ginzberg:

> The most characteristic features of the rabbinical system of theology is its lack of system. With God as a reality, revelation as a fact, the Torah as a rule of life, and the hope of redemption as a most vivid expectation, one was free to draw his own conclusions from these axioms and postulates in regard to what he believed.[3]

It should be indicated, however, that the concepts of rabbinic theology, notwithstanding their lack of logical system, constitute "a unitary pattern . . . wherein the . . . concepts are interrelated with each other." Inherent in the complex of rabbinic concepts is a unique "organic relationship" which endows it with a distinct inner coherence.[4]

It was only among the Hellenistic Jews of ancient Alexandria and among the medieval Jews, especially those of the Iberian Peninsula, that Jewish philosophers tried to combine rabbinic concepts with Greek philosophy. But their attempts to prove the validity of rabbinic teachings by means of philosophic reasoning was at best only partially successful, because the basic concepts underlying prayer, forgiveness, holiness, and similar doctrines are ultimately rooted in faith as much as in reason. To be sure, these beliefs are reasonable and follow logically from basic assumptions. But the rabbis were not philosophers. They were religious teachers who taught their disciples and the people at large how to live in accordance with God's will, as revealed in the Torah. They did not teach religious doctrines as an independent intellectual discipline. Theological concepts were propounded as the occasion arose, within the framework of discussions on religious conduct, biblical exposition, and other related subjects. The principles of the faith were thus taught incidentally and were scattered within the rabbinic teachings of the law and lore of Judaism without any logical sequence or orderly arrangement. If the scattered rabbinic statements on religious doctrine were collated and arranged in logical and historical sequence, however, they would constitute the authentic raw material for a notable work on rabbinic theology.[5]

The prayers of the synagogue, as already indicated, reflect the rabbinic doctrines of Judaism. These doctrines are not only implied in the substance of divine praise and thanksgiving and in the private and public petitions of the *Siddur*, but they are also stated with meticulous clarity. No wonder that some persons have actually used the *Siddur* as a basic source book in the teaching of rabbinic theology.

A thorough treatment of all the explicit and implicit theological ideas to be found in the *Siddur* would surely prove illuminating. But the scope of this book is too limited for so ambitious an exposition. Only several doctrines of rabbinic Judaism as they are crystallized in the *Siddur* will be presented. These cardinal beliefs will be drawn from the essential prayer units of the *Shema* and the *Tefillah*, as well as other prayers which will help to clarify the doctrines under discussion.

"Our Father, Our King"

The relevancy of prayer depends on one's conviction that there is a God who hears prayer and who, in His great love and mercy, chooses to be influenced by the prayers of the devout. Anyone who questions that there is a living and loving God questions the validity of prayer, and his prayers are reduced to mere wishful utterances. In a sense, such a worshiper actually prays to himself. This type of prayer may have psychological value and in that sense be efficacious, but it is at best only a shadow of real prayer as traditionally conceived in rabbinic Judaism. As we shall see, this cardinal principle is repeatedly stressed in the prayers of the synagogue and is clearly implied in the classic formula of the Jewish liturgic benediction.*

The opening words of the benediction formula read: "*Praised art Thou, O Lord our God, King of the universe.*" In this formulation are to be found the dual aspect of the Jew's relationship with God. On the one hand, there is the direct, personal, intimate approach in which he addresses God as "Thou." The suppliant requires no intermediary; he engages in a personal dialogue with God. In this relationship God is very near; He hears the worshiper's prayer; and in loving-kindness He answers his prayers. The rabbis base this principle on the text "For what great nation is there that has a god so close at hand as is the Lord our God whenever we call upon Him?" (Deut. 4:7).

It is in this context that God is often addressed as Father.[6] In one of the best-known litanies recited during the High Holy Days, the *Avinu Malkenu*, God is repeatedly addressed as "Our Father, our King." And after appealing for God's compassion on the basis of the martyrs who died for the sanctification of God's name, the congregation rests its appeal on God's mercy:

> Our Father, our King! do it for the sake of them that
> went through fire and water for the sanctification
> of Thy name.
>
> Our Father, our King! be gracious unto us and
> answer us, for we have no good works of our own;
> deal with us in charity and kindness, and save us.

This theme is emphasized in the Yom Kippur services, in which God's compassion and love and His nearness to those who repent of their transgressions and return to Him "with a perfect heart" are the central assumptions of the service. In the *Tefillah* of the closing service the divine attribute of mercy is forcefully stressed:

> O do Thou, in Thy abounding compassion, have
> mercy upon us, for Thou delightest not in the

* *See pp. 91 ff.*

> destruction of the world, as it is said, "Seek ye the Lord while He may be found, call ye upon Him while He is near" [Isa. 55:6]. And it is said: "Let the wicked forsake his way, and the man of iniquity his thoughts; and let him return unto the Lord, and He will have compassion upon him; and to our God, for He will abundantly pardon" [Isa. 55:7]. For Thou art a God ready to forgive, gracious and merciful, slow to anger, plenteous in lovingkindness, and abounding in goodness . . . [Exod. 34:6].

On the other hand, the benediction formula speaks of God as the "King of the universe." Here God is the awesome, transcendent, distant Ruler of all that exists; God is no longer the near and intimate Father, but the ineffable, the mysterious, the holy God, whose majesty transcends all human comprehension. He is the Almighty God who sits in judgment over nations and empires. Before Him the worshiper can only prostrate himself in humble adoration. Before His awesome presence the angels in Isaiah's vision cover their faces and exclaim: "Holy, holy, holy, is the Lord of hosts; / The whole earth is full of His glory" (Isa. 6:3). And Job learns of God's incomparable and incomprehensible power when God answers him "out of the whirlwind." Job can only respond: "I abhor my words, and repent, / Seeing I am dust and ashes" (Job. 42:6).

The concept of God as the transcendent King of the universe occupies a central place in the liturgy of Rosh Hashanah. God sits in judgment over all His creatures. In the third benediction of the Rosh Hashanah *Tefillah* we read: "Holy art Thou and awesome is Thy name, and there is no God beside Thee, as it is written: And the Lord of Hosts is exalted in judgment, and the Holy God is sanctified in righteousness [Isa. 5:16]. *Praised art Thou, O Lord, the Holy King.*" The kingship of God is also the theme of an entire prayer unit known as *Malkhuyot.** The prayer unit concludes with the exalted supplication for the establishment of God's kingdom:

> Our God and God of our fathers, reign Thou in Thy glory over the whole universe, and be exalted

* *See pp. 240–42.*

> above all the earth . . . and shine forth in the splendor and excellence of Thy might upon all the inhabitants of Thy world that . . . whatsoever hath breath in its nostrils may say, The Lord God of Israel is King and His dominion ruleth over all. . . .

On the Day of Atonement God forsakes His seat of judgment, as it were, for the seat of mercy in order to receive those who confess their sins and return to Him wholeheartedly. The stern Judge becomes the compassionate Father; the "King of the universe" becomes the ever-so-near "Thou" of the benediction formula.

The devout Jew finds no contradiction in this polarity of sentiment. In his approach to God he readily combines love and fear, love of God the merciful Father and fear of God the just and awesome King of the universe. He prays to God, who, he knows, is near to those who turn to Him in truth; and he trembles before God who, in His infinite greatness, is utterly incomprehensible. The two concepts are often united in the prayers, as they are in the benediction formula. But most frequently the devout worshiper stresses God's nearness and His compassionate love. He invokes the God of mercy who hears and answers the prayers of those "that call upon Him in truth," as we read in one of the benedictions of the daily *Tefillah:* "Hear our voice, O Lord our God . . . and accept our prayers in mercy and favor; for Thou art a God who hearkenest unto prayers and supplications. . . . *Praised art Thou, O Lord, who hearkenest unto prayer.*" This benediction is expanded on fast days with an additional paragraph: "Answer us, O Lord, answer us on this day of our fast . . . for Thou, O Lord, art He who answerest in time of trouble. . . ."

"The Lord Is One"

Twice daily the devout Jew recites the prayer unit known as the *Shema.** This prayer unit, it will be remembered, consists of three biblical paragraphs and several benedictions that precede and follow the scriptural selections. In this prayer unit are

* *See pp. 96 ff.*

to be found a number of fundamental doctrines which are at the heart of Judaism. One of these is the declaration "Hear, O Israel, the Lord our God, the Lord is One" (Deut. 6:4).

Commentators have discovered in this verse many profound meanings. For the ordinary Jew, however, this verse represents primarily the doctrine of the unity and the uniqueness of God. This Jewish belief has been placed above all other doctrines of the faith. The declaration that "the Lord is One" is recited not only in the morning and evening services, but also when the Torah is taken out of the ark and at the conclusion of the day-long prayers on the Day of Atonement. It is recited before retiring for the night and before retiring for one's "eternal sleep" in the dust.

In rabbinic times the affirmation of God's unity was a revolutionary challenge to the accepted doctrines of the Gentiles. It boldly denied the pagan deities who constituted whole dynasties of male and female gods. In Babylonia the doctrine of God's unity challenged the concept of divine duality which was basic in Zoroastrianism. It denied that there were two deities, one of whom created light and the other darkness. It denied the idea of opposing forces that are in eternal conflict. In order to negate this doctrine firmly and decisively the rabbis composed the first benediction before the *Shema:* "*Praised art Thou, O Lord, our God, King of the universe, who formest light and createst darkness, who makest peace and createst all things.*" [7]

In the proclamation that "the Lord is One," the rabbis also denied and challenged the Christian concept of the Trinity. In Judaism God is conceived as an absolute and indivisible oneness, and this faith in the one God was so deep and firm that Jews were ready to be "slaughtered for Thy unity."

The absolute oneness of God was only the obverse of this tenet of the faith; its reverse was the doctrine of God's uniqueness. Unlike the pagan deities, God is not subject to any of the human desires and weaknesses, nor is He subject to the powers of magic and incantations by means of which the pagans influenced and even controlled their gods. "There is none like unto Thee among the gods, O Lord" (Ps. 86:8) was therefore included by the rabbis in the liturgy.

More significant is God's uniqueness in His concern for the nature of human conduct. Among all the attributes of God this is probably the most relevant, because it alone explains why God gave the Torah to Israel and why God sent prophets to teach the ways of justice and righteousness. Not only is God just, righteous, and compassionate, but He wants man to emulate His divine character and be righteous and compassionate in his dealings with his family, his neighbor, and his fellow man. It is God's will that man live the good life, as is indicated in one of the benedictions of the daily *Tefillah: "Praised art Thou, O Lord, the King who lovest righteousness and judgment."*

The affirmation of God's unity and uniqueness became the touchstone of the Jewish faith. This doctrine is repeated in the prayers over and over again, and Israel is expected to emulate God and be a unique people. In the Saturday afternoon *Tefillah* we read: "Thou art One and Thy name is One and who is like Thy people Israel an only nation on the earth?" The same theme is touchingly repeated in the hymn "O Guardian of Israel," which is part of the penitential prayers * recited on Monday and Thursday mornings:

> *O Guardian of Israel, guard the remnant of Israel,*
> *and suffer not Israel to perish, who say, "Hear,*
> *O Israel."*
> *O Guardian of a unique people, guard the remnant*
> *of this people and suffer not this unique people*
> *to perish, who proclaim the unity of Thy name,*
> *saying, "The Lord our God, the Lord is One."*

And in the *Alenu* prayer, which concludes every synagogue service, we find the theme of God's unity firmly reasserted: "He is our God; there is none else. In truth, He is our King; there is none besides Him."

God's "Treasured Possession"

Every man yearns for a world outlook which will raise his life to a plane of significance. The Jewish people succeeded in finding such a world outlook in its belief that God is not only

* *See p. 463.*

the Source of all that is good and noble, but is also concerned with man's goodness and nobility. That is why He revealed His will to Israel and taught Israel to walk in His ways.

According to the rabbis, the concept of God's revelation at Sinai encompassed not only the Ten Commandments, but the whole Written Torah as well as the Oral Torah—that is, the future teachings of the rabbis. This expansion of the concept of revelation was not accepted without challenge. As mentioned in an earlier chapter,* a central portion of the morning service was excised because of the vigorous controversy around this concept of divine revelation. Thus we read in the Talmud:

> By right the Ten Commandments should be recited daily [in the morning service]. Why are they not recited? So that the sectarians should not be able to claim that only the Ten Commandments were revealed at Mount Sinai. [The sectarians would find proof for their views and would say that only what God said and the people heard at Sinai is recited in the prayers] [Jer. Ber. 27a].

The controversy between the rabbis and the sectarians was ominous and sharp. The rabbis therefore resorted to the radical measure of removing the Ten Commandments from the liturgy.

With the acceptance of the all-embracing concept that both the Written Torah and the Oral Torah are of divine origin, the Jews had a complete way of life that reflected God's will. Their daily activities were thus filled with transcendent meaning.

The peoplehood of Israel, too, assumed preeminent significance. Of all the nations Israel alone was chosen to receive the Torah. Of all the nations, Israel alone was selected to become "a kingdom of priests and a holy nation" (Exod. 19:6). God's revelation at Mount Sinai and the election of Israel became basic doctrines of rabbinic theology and frequent themes of the synagogue worship.

Some moderns have found these twin doctrines unpalatable,† and they have reinterpreted these concepts so as to coincide

* *See p. 73.*

† *See pp. 594–96.*

with their contemporary ideas. To the rabbis of the Talmud, however, the revelation represented the literal, verbal transmission of the Torah to Moses at Mount Sinai. Similarly, in regard to the election of Israel, God chose Israel "from all the peoples" and gave them the Torah.

The doctrine of the election of Israel requires some elucidation, because it has been grossly misunderstood. The concept of the chosen people has never implied any inherent superiority of the people of Israel, nor has it meant that the people of Israel was elevated to a position of privilege. Nowhere is it stated that God's choice was due to the superior qualities, intellectual or spiritual, of the Jewish people. What is frequently stressed is that the merit of the fathers, of Abraham, Isaac, and Jacob, was a decisive factor in the election of Israel to be the recipient of the Torah. Thus we read in the Pentateuch: "It is not because you are the most numerous of peoples that the Lord set His heart on you and chose you—indeed, you are the smallest of peoples; but it was because the Lord loved you and kept the oath He made to your fathers" (Deut. 7:7–8). And the choice of Israel bestowed upon it no privileges. On the contrary, it only conferred upon the Jews added obligations. It became their duty to obey the commandments of the Torah. As a corollary of this commitment they became subject to greater punishment if they failed to live up to the high divine expectations. To quote the prophet: "You only have I known of all the families of the earth; Therefore I will visit upon you all your iniquities" (Amos 3:2).

To be sure, there is a clear assumption of the superiority of Judaism over all the existing faiths. Judaism alone had its origin in divine revelation. It obviously is the only true faith. This posture of superiority is characteristic of all revealed religions. Thus Christianity and Islam are constantly proclaiming their preeminence over all faiths and insisting that they exclusively possess the truth. In Judaism this doctrine is saved from being arrogant and intolerant by the limiting creed that righteous Gentiles, though they are theologically in error, have a share in the world to come, provided they observe the seven moral laws revealed to Noah.[8]

That Judaism is the only authentic faith is frequently indicated in the prayers. In one of the morning benedictions the Jew thanks God "*who has not made me a heathen.*" He thanks God for the privilege of having been born a Jew and thus obliged to perform the commandments of the Torah. This idea is expressed even more boldly in the *Alenu* prayer:

> It is our duty to praise the Lord of all things, to ascribe greatness to Him who formed the world in the beginning, since He hath not made us like the nations of other lands, and . . . hath not assigned unto us a portion as unto them [for they bow down to vanity and emptiness, and worship a god who cannot save]. But we bend the knee and bow down before the supreme King of kings, the Holy One, blessed be He.

This posture of possessing a superior faith was a luxury that a small, scattered, and helpless people could hardly afford. The excision of the words in the brackets therefore became necessary * in the Christian countries where Church censorship was persistent and watchful.

These cardinal doctrines of the revelation at Sinai and the election of Israel are clearly and repeatedly stated in the prayers. In the benedictions which accompany the *Shema* we read: "Thou hast chosen us from all peoples and tongues, and hast brought us near to Thy great name for ever in faithfulness, that we might in love give thanks unto Thee and proclaim Thy unity. *Praised art Thou, O Lord, who hast chosen Thy people Israel in love.*" In the central benediction of the festival *Tefillah*, too, we read: "Thou hast chosen us from all peoples; Thou hast loved us and taken pleasure in us, and hast exalted us above all tongues; Thou hast sanctified us by Thy commandments, and brought us near unto Thy service, O our King, and hast called us by Thy great and holy name." And when one is called to the reading of the Torah, he declares publicly: "*Praised art Thou, O Lord our God, King of the universe who chose us from all peoples, and gave us His Torah. Praised art Thou, O Lord, who givest the Torah.*" These tenets of God's revelation and of Israel's election as God's "treasured possession" (Exod. 19:5) were thus kept fresh in the

* *See pp. 455–57.*

mind of the Jew, and his obligations were constantly reiterated so that he was always aware of them.

God's Covenant with Israel

The revelation at Sinai was not in the nature of an imposition by an all-powerful King on a small, helpless people. The democratic impulse in Israel would hardly have permitted such an authoritarian concept to take root. The giving of the Torah is represented in Scripture as a mutually agreed-upon covenant between God and Israel, with specific mutual obligations and sanctions. If God chose Israel to be His people, so did Israel choose God to be its Deity. If Israel agreed to live in accordance with the commandments of the Torah, so did God agree to give Israel the land of Canaan and to make Israel "high above all nations . . . in fame and renown and glory." Thus Moses, addressing the children of Israel in his last testament, emphasizes this concept of mutuality:

> You have affirmed this day that the Lord is your God, that you will walk in His ways, that you will observe His laws and commandments and rules, and that you will obey Him. And the Lord has affirmed this day that you are, as He promised you, His treasured people which shall observe all His commandments, and that He will set you, in fame and renown and glory, high above all the nations that He has made; and that you shall be, as He promised, a holy people to the Lord your God [Deut. 26:17–19].

The covenant idea did not originate at Mount Sinai. It goes back to the days of the patriarchs. God promised Abraham that He would make his descendants into a great nation and would give them the land of Canaan for an inheritance. This covenant between God and Abraham was sealed with the rite of circumcision as an everlasting sign between God and Israel. This is emphatically recorded in the Scriptures: "Such shall be the covenant between Me and you and your offspring to follow which you shall keep: every male among you shall be circumcised . . . and that shall be the sign of the covenant between

Me and you" (Gen. 17:10–11). The Jewish commitment to this rite has been deep and constant. Jews have made untold sacrifices in order to practice the rite of circumcision. They even fought bloody wars, when tyrants tried to interfere with this sacred "sign of the covenant." [9]

The covenant between God and Israel not only imposed clearly defined obligations on both parties, but also provided for sanctions in case of failure to abide by its terms. If Israel betrayed the covenant, exile from the Promised Land was one of the inexorable consequences. Instead of being "high above all the nations," Israel would become an object of scorn and contempt. But if Israel felt that God did not abide by the terms of the covenant, as it were, it could remonstrate with the Almighty. The covenant idea has thus endowed Jewish prayer with a tone of intimacy with God which is a unique characteristic of the Jewish liturgy. On a number of occasions Israel admits in the prayers that it has failed to abide by the terms of the covenant. Nonetheless, God is reminded of the covenant either in the name of the patriarchs or "because of Thy name." If God permits Israel to suffer in exile His name will be desecrated. "Wherefore should they say among the peoples: Where is their God?" (Joel 2:17). This taunt of the Gentiles is a clear hillul hashem which God should not permit.

In resorting to this argument the Jews are emulating Moses, who prayed in behalf of the Israelites when they threatened to return to Egypt and God communicated His plan to destroy them and make of Moses "a nation far more numerous than they": "If then You slay this people to a man, the nations who have heard Your fame will say, 'It must be because the Lord was powerless to bring that people into the land which He had promised them on oath that He slaughtered them in the wilderness' " (Num. 14:15–16). Hence we find many prayers, such as the one in the Musaf *Tefillah* of the festivals, in which the Jewish people admits that it has betrayed the covenant: "On account of our sins we were exiled from our land, and removed far from our country." But this admission of failure is balanced by the prayer that calls upon God to remember the covenant and restore the Jewish people to its homeland and to its former glory. Also in the penitential prayers * recited on Monday and Thursday mornings there are several such appeals to the covenant: "Remember unto us the covenant of our fathers, and save us for Thy name's sake." "Remember unto us the covenant of our fathers, and the testimony we bear every day that the Lord is One."

In the Early Morning Benedictions † there is a tender prayer in which the worshipers' all too human limitations are compared with God's omnipotence: "What are we? What is our life? What is our piety? What is our righteousness?" Then the prayer recovers from this self-abnegation and boldly asserts: "Nevertheless we are Thy people, the children of Thy covenant." Later in the morning service, in the Verses of Praise,‡ there is another reminder of the covenant: "[And Thou] madest a covenant with [Abraham] to give the land of the Canaanite . . . unto his seed" (Neh. 9:8).

In the Rosh Hashanah service God is boldly reminded of His covenant. The Scriptures are quoted in support of Israel's claim, clearly indicating that God had assumed a firm obligation in His covenant with Israel:

> Remember unto us, O Lord our God, the covenant and the loving-kindness and the oath which Thou swearest unto Abraham our father. . . . As it is said: "I will remember . . . the covenant with the ancients, whom I freed from the land of Egypt in the sight of the nations to be their God" [Lev. 26:45].

References to the covenant in the liturgy are many. But more telling is the rabbinic choice of the second paragraph of the *Shema* as part of the core of the daily service. In this biblical selection the Jew is not only reminded of the covenant between God and Israel, but is also made aware of his accountability in terms of the obligations assumed in that covenant—to "walk in His ways, and observe His laws and commandments and norms." This section of the *Shema* also indicates the dire consequences of a betrayal of these commitments: the land which

* *See pp. 461–63.*
† *See pp. 143 ff.*
‡ *See pp. 141 ff.*

God gave to Israel in accordance with His promise will become a curse, and the children of Israel will be spewed out of the Promised Land.

The Messianic Ideal in Judaism

God's wisdom and power are the vital factors in the history and destiny of mankind. This truth, say the rabbis, was demonstrated most vividly in the annals of Israel, especially in the redemption of the children of Israel from the Egyptian bondage. This event has impressed itself on the consciousness of the Jewish people as the most decisive in their history. The Exodus from Egypt above all other events demonstrated God's role as the Redeemer of Israel. This never-to-be-forgotten national experience is constantly stressed in the prayers of the synagogue and in the rituals of the home, especially those connected with the Passover festival. Every service in the *Siddur* refers to the divine role as the Redeemer of Israel. Thus the *Shema* concludes with the definitive words: "I the Lord am your God, who brought you out of the land of Egypt to be your God: I, the Lord your God" (Num. 15:41). God's role as the Redeemer of Israel is also the central theme of the concluding benediction after the *Shema*. The benediction summarizes the story of the Exodus and concludes with a supplication for the deliverance of Israel: "O Rock of Israel, arise to the help of Israel, and deliver, according to Thy promise, Judah and Israel. Our Redeemer, the Lord of hosts is His name, the Holy One of Israel. *Praised art Thou, O Lord, who hast redeemed Israel.*"

The redemption of Israel from bondage and oppression is regarded in Judaism not merely as a historic event, but as one of the divine attributes. God not only redeemed Israel from the Egyptian bondage, but He will also redeem Israel from its current exile and humiliation and vindicate Israel in the sight of the nations.

The belief that God is the Redeemer of Israel has been one of the seminal doctrines out of which grew the powerful conviction concerning the messianic era and the world to come. The doctrine concerning the world to come has played a pivotal role in Jewish theology and has contributed decisively to the survival of the Jewish people.

The essentials of the messianic doctrine are not as simple as they seem. They are not presented systematically in the Bible or in the rabbinic literature; one must construct them from scattered biblical and rabbinic sources. The vagueness of some statements and the real or seeming contradictions of others increase the difficulties. Nevertheless, a fairly clear system emerges.

The Kingship of God

Among the loftiest ideals in Judaism is the concept of the "world to come." In the Bible there are a number of prophetic pronouncements regarding the "end of days." The prophets speak in glowing terms of a time when God will redeem Israel and establish His kingship in all the earth. All peoples will then recognize and serve the God of Israel. Unlike the ancients, who looked back to a golden age in the remote past, the Jews looked forward to an era when justice and righteousness, prosperity and happiness, national independence and eternal peace would be instituted. In that idealized future the scattered children of Israel will be gathered from the four corners of the earth and restored to their homeland. The prophet Isaiah says of that era:

> *And it shall come to pass in that day,*
> *That a great horn shall be blown;*
> *And they shall come that were lost in the land of*
> *Assyria,*
> *And they that were dispersed in the land of Egypt;*
> *And they shall worship the Lord in the holy mountain*
> *at Jerusalem* [*Isa. 27:13*].

And the prophet Jeremiah, who had the misfortune to witness the fall of Judea, speaks of the days to come with similar optimism: "For, lo, the days come, saith the Lord, that I will turn the captivity of My people Israel and Judah, saith the Lord; and I will cause them to return to the land that I gave to their fathers, and they shall possess it" (Jer. 30:3).

During the rabbinic period the concept of the kingship of God[10] grew, till it encompassed the loftiest universal ideals.

Eternal peace and prosperity, justice and truth, personal piety and brotherly love will then prevail. And this state of bliss will not be limited to the righteous of Israel. It will be shared by the righteous among the Gentiles, who will join the faithful. All others, both Jews and Gentiles who are sinners, will perish. Sin itself will disappear from the earth. The faith of Judaism will become the universal faith. That glorious era the rabbis called the world to come, or the kingship of God.

These anticipations were supported by a number of prophetic utterances, such as the famous prophecy of Isaiah:

> *And it shall come to pass in the end of days,*
> *That the mountain of the Lord's house shall be*
> *established as the top of the mountains,*
> *And shall be exalted above the hills;*
> *And all nations shall flow unto it.*
> *And many peoples shall go and say:*
> *'Come ye, and let us go up to the mountain of the Lord,*
> *To the house of the God of Jacob;*
> *And He will teach us of His ways,*
> *And we will walk in His paths.'*
> *For out of Zion shall go forth the law,*
> *And the word of Lord from Jerusalem. . . .*
> *And they shall beat their swords into plowshares*
> *And their spears into pruning-hooks;*
> *Nation shall not lift up sword against nation,*
> *Neither shall they learn war any more* [*Isa. 2:2–4*].

Not only will Jerusalem be the religious capital of mankind, but Gentiles who accept the true faith will become part of God's people and will minister in the Holy Temple as Kohanim and Levites:

> *Also the aliens, that join themselves to the Lord, to*
> *minister unto Him,*
> *And to love the name of the Lord,*
> *To be His servants, . . .*
> *Even them will I bring to My holy mountain,*
> *And make them joyful in My house of prayer;*
> *Their burnt-offerings and their sacrifices*
> *Shall be acceptable upon Mine altar;*
> *For My house shall be called*
> *A house of prayer for all peoples* [*Isa. 56:6–7*].

The kingship of God, the rabbis taught, will be ushered in by the Messiah, the anointed of God, who will be of Davidic lineage. It was quite natural that the future glory of the Jewish people be associated with the Davidic dynasty, since David's reign was considered to have been the most glorious era of Jewish history. The Messiah is therefore referred to both in rabbinic literature and in the prayers as *Tzemah David*, the offshoot of David. Among the biblical proof texts are the words of Jeremiah:

Behold, the days come, saith the Lord,
That I will raise unto David a righteous shoot
[Tzemah],
And he shall reign as king and prosper,
And shall execute justice and righteousness in the land.
In his days Judah shall be saved,
And Israel shall dwell safely [Jer. 23:5–6].

The Messiah, the offshoot of David, was conceived of by the rabbis as a human being of superior spiritual and intellectual gifts. This is in accord with the prophet Isaiah's well-known prophecy:

The spirit of the Lord shall rest upon him,
The spirit of wisdom and understanding,
The spirit of counsel and might,
The spirit of knowledge and of the fear of the Lord
[Isa. 11:2].

His reign will therefore be wiser and more righteous than that of any ruler before him.

The rabbis elaborated and expanded the messianic hope into a complex pattern of theological doctrines,[11] some of which were incorporated into the prayers. During the long exile, as the estate of the Jews sank ever lower, the messianic hope shone ever brighter; and as the oppression grew harsher, the prayers for Israel's redemption became more fervent.

Prayers for the Coming of the Messiah

The restoration of Israel through the agency of the Messiah occupies a major part of the Jewish liturgy. There is no service that does not contain an affirmation of the messianic hope and a prayer for the coming of the Messiah. Every benediction speaks of God as the King of the universe. By this the rabbis indicated not only that God rules the destiny of the world, but also that the ultimate goal of history is the establishment of the kingship of God. "To perfect the world through the establishment of the kingship of the Almighty" was, for the rabbis, more than a theological principle; it was a program of action.

In the daily *Tefillah* there are no less than five benedictions that deal with the messianic hope. They reflect the depth of the rabbinic conviction and the extent of the Jewish yearning for the coming of the Messiah. These benedictions are precise and explicit:

> Return to Jerusalem, Thy city, in mercy, and dwell therein as Thou hast spoken . . . and speedily set up therein the throne of David. *Praised art Thou, O Lord, who rebuildest Jerusalem.*
>
> Speedily cause the offspring of David, Thy servant, to flourish, and let his horn of glory be exalted by Thy salvation, because we wait for Thy salvation all the day. *Praised art Thou, O Lord, who causest the horn of salvation to flourish.*

The messianic prayers are to be found in the grace after meals and in the prayers on retiring at night, in the benedictions after reading the Haftarah and in the benedictions of the wedding ceremony, in the festival prayers and in the fast day prayers. But most significant are the messianic prayers of the Rosh Hashanah service. In the prayers, known as *Malkhuyot*,* or kingship prayers, the national and universal hopes of Israel are merged into a single divine plan.

The pious Jew regarded it his duty to expect the Messiah's arrival every day of his life. But he knew from experience that the Messiah's arrival was a long way off. During the long period of waiting the Jew needed a clear, consistent policy to guide him in his relationships with the dominant gentile world. This policy was provided by a prophetic verse: "Let all the peoples walk each one in the name of its god, / But we will walk in the name of the Lord our God for ever and ever" (Micah 4:5). This policy statement enabled the Jew to live

* *See pp. 241–42.*

with dignity while waiting for the coming of the Messiah. The Jew engaged in a holding action, as it were. To be sure, the Gentiles constituted the overwhelming majority of the world's population, and they possessed the massive power of the contemporary world. But these are not of ultimate significance. Let the Gentiles go on worshiping their gods, and let them glory in their power. As for the Jew, it is his duty to persevere in his loyalty to the true and living God. This policy is both an admission of helplessness and a declaration of stubborn resistance to the blandishments of power by the Gentiles. These prophetic words therefore became the standard Jewish response to persistent missionary pressures. They were also the peroration of the welcoming address by Israel's president, Shneour Zalman Shazar, to Pope Paul VI, during the pope's pilgrimage to the Holy Land. They are recited immediately before the *Alenu* prayer which concludes every synagogue service. The *Alenu* prayer closes with these comforting words: "The Lord shall be King over all the earth; / In that day shall the Lord be One, and His name one" (Zech. 14:9).

The messianic ideal played a powerful role in the spiritual and national life of the Jewish people. It released powers of undreamed-of magnitude. Although the idea originated with the prophets, it was the rabbis of the Talmud who nurtured it, developed it, and elevated it to the rank of a religious dogma. The idea took root in the hearts of the Jewish people and kindled in them a hope and a faith that no persecutions could dim, let alone extinguish.

The Rabbinic Theodicy

If God is just, as Judaism insists, retribution in kind and measure should prevail. In the Bible there is a catalog of unforgettable blessings in store for those who fulfill the terms of the covenant, and an extensive inventory of appalling maledictions awaiting those who fail to hearken unto God and fulfill the commandments of the Torah (Lev. 26; Deut. 28). But these blessings and curses were of a collective nature. In the life of the individual these chastisements did not always find fulfillment. This disturbing discrepancy between the justice of God and the injustices that often prevail in the affairs of man was boldly posed by Job. He could not find any justifiable reason for his personal suffering. But Job does not resolve this dilemma. He concludes his lucid argument without a logical theodicy. His own finitude is matched against God's infinite greatness, and the outcome is a humble surrender to faith.

The rabbis of the Talmud were neither satisfied with Job's indecisive conclusion nor with the prophetic assertion that "the righteous shall live by his faith" (Hab. 2:4). They were troubled by the continuing challenge to the doctrine that God rules the destinies of men with absolute justice. A partial answer to their disturbing problem was provided by the claim that God chastises the righteous man out of love. He wants to induce him to repent of his sins, rare though they be. In the Bible there is ample support for this thesis: "Whom the Lord loveth He correcteth, / Even as a father the son in whom he delighteth" (Prov. 3:12).

But this thesis, too, did not fully satisfy the rabbis. Everyone knew of wicked men who prospered and of righteous men who suffered far beyond the chastisement of divine love. The nagging question continued to plague the sensitivity of the rabbis. Why do the righteous suffer? And why do the wicked prosper?

This perplexing question received a definitive and irrefutable answer in a rabbinic doctrine that became a touchstone of Judaism. One cannot, said the rabbis, explain God's justice in terms of man's short earthly existence. Just retribution cannot possibly be administered in this world, because God's justice is tempered by His tender mercy, which demands that the sinner be given ample opportunity to repent and return to God. Every day offers man an opportunity to repent. Man can repent even on the last day of his life. Retribution must therefore wait for the hereafter, when divine justice is dispensed to each man according to his deserts. But if full justice is to be dispensed in the hereafter, each man must be revived and brought before the divine seat of judgment. This dispensation of justice, said the rabbis, will take place at "the end of days," after the coming of the Messiah.

The doctrine of the Messiah was thus amplified to include the resurrection of the dead and the final judgment. Rabbinic opinions on these tenets are not always consistent, let alone ordered. In general there is a refreshing silence in regard to conditions after death; there is hardly any attempt to catalog in detail the joys or sorrows in the heavenly spheres of the world to come. There is only a confirmation of the broad basic doctrines of the immortality of each person and the reward or punishment that awaits him in accordance with his deserts. The righteous and those who have been purified through their just punishment will live in eternal bliss, while the thoroughly wicked will perish. The nature of this bliss is not clearly defined in rabbinic literature. An inkling of rabbinic views on this subject is to be found in a statement attributed to Rav, one of the outstanding talmudic authorities. Rav used to say: "In the future world there is no eating nor drinking nor propagation nor business nor jealousy nor hatred nor competition, but the righteous sit with their crowns on their heads feasting on the brightness of the divine presence" (Ber. 17a).

In the popular mind the prospect of passing one's existence in eternity basking in the radiance of God's presence was hardly enticing. Hence one finds varied and not always consistent speculations on the world to come in which other forms of eternal bliss are specified, such as plenty and prosperity, good health and painless childbirth, peace and general well-being. But one principle the rabbis regarded as basic. The whole human being must appear before the divine seat of judgment. Unlike the Greek thinkers, the rabbis did not regard the body as a mere abode of the soul, an abode which the soul vacates and abandons at the time of death. The rabbis distinguish between body and soul, but they do not regard either as the totality. Nor do they support the thesis that there is a state of conflict between body and soul. The rabbis conceived of the body as an intrinsic part of the human totality. God's Torah encompassed all conduct—mental, emotional, and physical. The whole human being will therefore stand for judgment as he was during his lifetime: body and soul reunited. The bodies of the dead will be resurrected from their tombs; their souls will join them; and together they will appear for judgment.[12] As proof texts for the doctrine of the resurrection, the rabbis quoted a number of biblical verses, such as the one from Daniel: "And many of them that sleep in the dust of the earth shall awake, some to everlasting life, and some to reproaches and everlasting abhorrence" (Dan. 12:2).[13] The final judgment, the rabbis taught, was not limited to the Jewish people. Righteous Gentiles will also appear before God, because "the pious of the nations have a share in the world to come" (Ṭosef. San. 13:2).

The theological dilemma arising from the prosperity of the wicked as contrasted with the suffering of the righteous was thus fully resolved. The rabbis succeeded in establishing a tight theodicy which is beyond challenge. In the world to come God's justice will become evident to all, and even those who scoffed and mocked at the faithful will acknowledge God's justice and will accept His sovereignty.

The doctrine of the resurrection of the dead became a cardinal dogma of rabbinic Judaism and Christian theology.[14] Belief or disbelief in this doctrine was a basic issue in the controversy between the Pharisees and their opponents, the Sadducees. But the Pharisees won over the mass of the people and thus won a total victory over their opponents. Judaism has continued to uphold this dogma with unswerving fidelity, so that twentieth century Orthodox Judaism is as committed to belief in the resurrection of the dead as were the Pharisees of two thousand years ago.

The victory of the Pharisees, however, did not come without a bitter struggle. In order to meet the formidable challenge by their opponents the Pharisees resorted to strict measures. They permitted no dissent on this doctrine. No one could question, let alone deny, this theological dogma and remain among the faithful. Anyone who denied the doctrine of the resurrection, said the rabbis, had no share in the world to come (San. 10:1). In the bitter struggle between the Pharisees and their opponents, the liturgy was utilized as a means of separating the faithful from the heretics. The Pharisees were able to do this because they were in full control of the synagogue. They simply turned this theological dogma into a sort of "admission card" to public worship by inserting into the *Tefillah* a special benediction in which the worshiper committed himself to this doctrine. This benediction reads in part: "Yea, faithful art Thou to quicken the dead. *Praised art Thou, O Lord, who quickenest the dead.*"

The worshiper thus had to make his choice: either accept this key pharisaic dogma at the very beginning of the *Tefillah* or be excluded from the congregation. If anyone failed to recite this benediction or failed to respond to it with the conventional Amen, he was immediately spotted as a heretic. But there were not many such dissenters. The doctrine of the resurrection was not only theologically sound in that it provided a logical theodicy, but it was also emotionally comforting, because it robbed the grave of its victory. So deep was the conviction regarding the resurrection that in many Jewish communities it was customary to bury the dead with their feet toward the east, so that when they rise from their graves, they will stand up facing the Holy Land, to which they will immediately make their way.[15]

The People and the Land of Israel

The salvation of the individual Jew, as we have seen, was tied to the restoration of the nation. The resurrection of the dead and the final judgment were part of a total divine program, which also envisaged the redemption of Israel and its restoration to the land of Israel. An organic relationship has thus existed between the individual Jew, the people of Israel, and the land of Israel. The individual Jew can achieve his complete salvation only as a member of the community of Israel and in the land of Israel. The Christian's confession of belief in the doctrines of the Church constitutes his membership in the Christian community and renders him eligible for salvation. In Judaism, however, one is born into the Jewish people and is initiated into the teachings of the Torah during his lifetime.[16] A denial of the doctrines of Judaism is regarded as sinful but does not exclude one from the community of Israel. And being a faithful member of the community of Israel in the Diaspora affords one only partial salvation, because some divine commandments can be fulfilled only in the land of Israel. Indeed, the concept of a creed as the essence of a religious community is, as far as Judaism is concerned, as unreal as a disembodied spirit. To achieve his salvation a Jew had to be part of the people of Israel. And to achieve it fully he had to live in the land of Israel.

It should be stressed, however, that the peoplehood of Israel is not limited to those who were born into the Jewish people. Any Gentile can enter into the covenant of Abraham, can join the community of Israel by the process of conversion. But he must accept both the faith and fate of the people of Israel. Converts who meet these prerequisites are welcomed, and a special benediction in the *Tefillah* couples these converts with the righteous of Israel: "Toward the righteous and the pious . . . toward the true proselytes and toward us also may Thy tender mercies be stirred, O Lord our God!"

The concept of the community of Israel is therefore more than the sum total of all Jews. It even transcends the concept of the Jewish nation. The community of Israel is conceived as possessing a collective personality not only in a legal sense as the concept of the corporation but in a mystical and psychological sense. Thus the benediction before the *Shema* of the evening service concludes: "*Praised art Thou, O Lord, who lovest Thy people Israel.*" The Jew experiences even God's love as a member of the community of Israel.

The significant aspect of this elusive concept is that the Jew felt and responded to his being a part of the community of Israel not as a matter of biological accident or of enlightened self-interest, but as something tinged with emotion. To this day the Jew taxes himself for the benefit of the community of Israel in the same spirit as one incurs expenditures in behalf of one's children. The Jew is not just a member or a citizen of the community of Israel. He is part of it as one is part of his family. The community of Israel is therefore called *Bet Yisrael*, the house or family of Israel.

This seemingly abstract idea became quite tangible to the Jew during his long exile when he experienced persecution not as a person but as part of the Jewish people. In modern times, too, during the Nazi holocaust, Jews died in the millions not as individuals but as part of the community of Israel. The individual Jew and the peoplehood of Israel were thus welded into an inseparable unity.

The peoplehood of Israel is an integral part of the liturgy. The overwhelming majority of the prayers are corporate in their formulation.* Typical of the synagogue prayers are the benedictions of the *Tefillah:* "Forgive us, O our Father, for we have sinned," "Look upon our affliction, and plead our cause," and so on. This corporate formulation of the prayers is especially to be wondered at since the synagogue prayers are rooted in the psalms, which are personal and therefore in the singular. Even prayers that were originally uttered in the singular were deliberately changed to the plural. Thus Jeremiah's prayer "Heal me, O Lord, and I shall be healed; / Save me, and I shall be saved; / For Thou art my praise" (Jer. 17:14) was changed in the *Tefillah* to read: "Heal us, O Lord, and we shall be healed; save us, and we shall be saved, for Thou art our praise." The deliberate shift from the singular of the psalm to the plural of the *Siddur* indicates that in Judaism the worshiper is expected to merge himself with the community, for the individual Jew can best find his way to God as part of the community of Israel.

Equally significant are the many prayers for the redemption of Israel. As mentioned,† the core of the weekday *Tefillah* is made up of messianic prayers, imploring God to redeem the people of Israel from exile and restore it to the land of Israel. Most touching is the prayer recited on Monday and Thursday mornings, in which the Jew prays in behalf of his fellow Jews of the house of Israel, as one would pray in behalf of members of his immediate family:

> As for our brethren, the whole house of Israel, such
> of them as are given over to trouble or captivity . . .
> may the All-present have mercy upon them and
> bring them forth from trouble to enlargement, from

* *See pp. 31–32.*
† *See p. 73.*

darkness to light, and from subjugation to redemption, now speedily and at a near time; and let us say, Amen.

The peoplehood of Israel was more than a concept; it was a personal identification, real and deep. And the prayers fully reflected this identification of the individual Jew with the people of Israel.

Similarly close was the Jew's identification with the land of Israel. Zion and Jerusalem were idealized and transformed into the holiest and most glorious spot on earth. And during the gloomy years of persecution the Jew found solace in the shining beauty of Zion which, in its desolation, was waiting for Israel's return. This attachment to the land of Israel resulted in a strange liturgic development. In the fall, when people in the northern countries are anticipating the winter with its frost and snow, the Jew prayed for ample rain (*Geshem*) * during the coming winter months. And in midwinter, on the fifteenth day of the Hebrew month of Shevat, the Jew observed the coming of spring and recited appropriate benedictions for the occasion. This sounds incongruous. But for the Jew it was altogether logical—no matter where he was physically, in his prayers he was transplanted to the land of Israel. His spiritual life was centered in Zion and Jerusalem. It was quite logical to pray for plentiful rain during the winter months and to observe the coming of spring in February, because in his spiritual homeland winter is the season of rain and mid-February is early spring, when green vegetation and wild flowers are in evidence everywhere.

In the daily prayers of the synagogue the supplication for the rebuilding of Zion and Jerusalem is repeated over and over again. Typical of these is the benediction of the Haftarah: "Have mercy upon Zion, for it is the home of our life, and save her . . . speedily, even in our days. *Praised art Thou, O Lord, who maketh Zion joyful through her children.*" And in the introductory benediction to the *Shema* we read: "O bring us in peace from the four corners of the earth, and make us go upright to our land; for Thou art a God who worketh salvation."

* *See pp. 221–22.*

These prayers fostered a love of Zion which accounts in large measure for the powerful identification of the Jew with the land of Israel. The love of Zion was so deeply rooted in the heart of the Jew that on the Ninth of Av he would sit on the floor of the synagogue and read innumerable dirges * and mourn the destruction of Jerusalem as one who was bereaved of a beloved child; he longed for its restoration as a young man for his beloved bride.

"I Am the Lord Your God"

One of the anomalies of biblical legislation is that there is no commandment to believe in God. This is especially remarkable when contrasted with the Christian emphasis on salvation by faith. The rabbis were aware of this theological gap. They filled it by declaring that the opening words of the Ten Commandments, "I am the Lord your God," constitute the first of the Ten Commandments and that their intent is to teach belief in the existence of God and faith in His justice and mercy. Actually, there was no need for a commandment on faith in God. The pious Jew expressed his faith in God by means of his daily act of prayer. He demonstrated his faith in God when he recited the benedictions dealing with the resurrection of the dead, the redemption of Israel, and the restoration of Jerusalem in the present tense, as if they were taking place at the very moment when he was praying for their fulfillment. This expression of absolute faith in the divine providence, says the Midrash, has rewarded Israel with eternal life, as it is written in Scripture: "The Lord preserveth the faithful" (Ps. 31:24).[17]

Circumstances, however, forced the rabbis to formulate a number of definitive articles of faith and to insist that every Jew subscribe to them. The rabbinic era was marked by several polemics, which demanded a firm declaration by every Jew as to where he stood on certain theological doctrines. Mere inferences in the wording of some prayers was hardly enough at a time when heretics and sectarians were openly challenging the basic doctrines of the faith. These considerations led the rabbis

* *See p. 280.*

to make a number of changes in the liturgy. The first of these had to do with the Ten Commandments, which along with the three paragraphs of the *Shema* used to be the core of the morning service. The Ten Commandments were excised from the service because some heretics claimed that the Ten Commandments alone were revealed at Sinai and that they alone constituted the divine revelation. This view challenged the very foundation of rabbinic Judaism, which rested on the belief that both the Written Torah and the Oral Torah were of divine origin. The rabbis therefore removed the Ten Commandments from the daily service to indicate that they are only part of God's revelation and not all of it.*

Another powerful challenge came from those Jews who denied the doctrine of the resurrection of the dead. As already mentioned, the rabbis met this challenge not only by arguments from the Torah but also by inserting in the *Tefillah* a special benediction which indicated one's acceptance of this doctrine. The benediction on the quickening of the dead was placed at the beginning of the *Tefillah*, so that no one who denied this dogma could possibly lead the congregation in prayer.

Still another challenge derived from the presence in the synagogue of sectarians who subscribed to Christianity. The controversy between the Jews and the early Christians was especially bitter because some of the Christians had acted as informers for the Romans during the tragic Judeo-Roman war. In order to cleanse the synagogue of these sectarians, the rabbis added a special benediction to the *Tefillah* pronouncing a malediction on the informers.† This benediction has undergone many changes, mainly because of Christian censorship. But it still reflects its original purpose:

> And for informers let there be no hope, and let all wickedness perish as in a moment; let all Thine enemies be speedily cut off, and the dominion of arrogance [18] do Thou uproot and crush, cast down and humble speedily in our days. *Praised art Thou, O*

* *See p. 400.*
† *See pp. 105–106.*

> *Lord, who breakest the enemies and humblest the arrogant.*

Originally the prayer began with the phrase "And for the sectarians" (*minim*), but this was later changed to the less offensive word *informers.*

More significant than the polemical prayers was the insertion of an emphatic declaration of faith into the prayer unit of the *Shema.* To be sure, the recital of the *Shema* is in itself a declaration of faith. But the addition is in the nature of a credal statement. In its original form it probably read as follows:

> True and firm . . . is this word unto us for ever and ever. . . . It is true that Thou art indeed the Lord our God and the God of our fathers; our King, the King of our fathers; our Redeemer and the Redeemer of our fathers; our Maker, the Rock of our salvation; our Deliverer and Rescuer, from everlasting, such is Thy name; there is no God beside Thee.[19]

This creed lacks the precise, logical presentation of a philosophical thesis. It has, however, the merit of being a clear statement of rabbinic beliefs. It reflects deep conviction and is couched in a powerful idiom.

By incorporating this affirmation of faith into the daily prayers, the rabbis provided every Jew with the opportunity of daily renewing his acknowledgment of God as his King and Savior, and with renewed faith to carry out his obligations under the covenant. The worshiper, as it were, received the Torah every day and by implication restated the national pledge at Sinai: "All that the Lord has spoken we will faithfully do" (Exod. 24:7).

For many centuries this confession of faith adequately served the requirements of the synagogue. However, there came a time when a more philosophical statement became necessary. The confrontation with other faiths, especially with that of the Moslems, and the challenge of Greek philosophy, which had become popular among the Jewish intelligentsia of the Middle Ages, led to the composition of a number of philosophical formulations of the basic doctrines of Judaism. Of all the creeds formulated, the one composed in the twelfth century by Moses Maimonides is by far the best known and the most widely accepted. It consists of Thirteen Articles of Faith, each of which begins with the formula "I believe with perfect faith that. . . ." The first of these articles is the belief in the existence of a Creator. Then comes the belief in God's unity, His incorporeality, and His eternity and the belief that all worship and adoration are due to Him alone. Then comes a group of articles which specify the belief in prophecy, that Moses was the greatest of all prophets, that the Torah was revealed to Moses at Sinai, and that the Torah is immutable. Finally comes the belief that God knows the actions of men, and rewards and punishes in justice, that the Messiah will come, and that the dead will be resurrected. It will be noted that some of the articles were of a polemical nature, especially the article that states categorically that "this Torah [of Moses] will not be changed, and there will never be any other Torah from the Creator, blessed be His name." Obviously this was aimed at the Christians' claim that the New Testament superseded the Torah and the Moslems' claim that the Koran superseded both the Jewish and Christian Bibles.

These Thirteen Articles of Faith were incorporated in the *Siddur* at the conclusion of the morning service as one of the optional selections available to the pious for daily review. These articles of faith also became a popular theme for Jewish poets. The hymn *Yigdal* (Magnified [be the living God]), written at the end of the thirteenth cenury by Daniel ben Judah Dayan, is based on Maimonides' creed and was included in the *Siddur* as an opening or closing hymn. The *Yigdal* became the model for many such hymns.[20]

As we have seen, the *Siddur* was not only a handbook of prayers which enabled the Jew to participate in the synagogue and home services; it was also the repository of Jewish belief. In it the Jew found the authentic doctrines of Judaism, such as the nature and character of God, His revelation to Israel, His relationship to the people of Israel and to the individual man, the nature of man and his obligations to God and to his fellow man, the consequences of transgression and sin, the remedies for failure, the means of expiation, the hope of the resurrection, and the bliss in the world to come. These and other articles of faith were incorporated into the *Siddur* in the form of implicit and explicit statements. No wonder the Jew treasured the *Siddur* and treated it as a trustworthy life companion.

16
ETHICAL TEACHINGS IN THE *SIDDUR*

When the Hebrews received the Torah at Mount Sinai, they pledged: "All that the Lord has spoken we will faithfully do" (Exod. 24:7). They thus assumed the obligation to live in accordance with the divine statutes, commandments, and ordinances, be they ritual observances, civil and criminal laws, or moral and ethical rules of conduct. These divine teachings were later explained and amplified by the rabbis, and many of them are affirmed in the prayers of the *Siddur*.

Ritual observances are represented in the *Siddur* by several biblical and rabbinic selections dealing with the sacrificial service of the Temple.* But of greater significance are the moral and ethical duties emphasized in the prayers.[1] These duties, however, are not derived from any overriding philosophical premises. The rabbis do not distinguish between ritual and ethical laws; [2] they make no sharp distinctions between man's duties to God and his duties to his fellow man.[3] According to the rabbis all human conduct derives its validity from the revealed will of God. To be sure, some of these teachings are more important than others. Some originate in the Bible, while others originate in rabbinic sources. There are even some

* *See p. 149.*

commandments for which one should suffer martyrdom rather than transgress. But these distinctions apply to individual commandments rather than to broad categories derived from philosophical principles. According to the rabbis, all human actions and sentiments derive their authority from the one authentic Source, the word of God. Virtuous conduct is sanctioned because it is God's will; sinful conduct is condemned because it is contrary to God's will. Since God is by definition the embodiment of goodness, justice, compassion, and love, His laws embody these qualities and are by definition good.

Moral Behavior in the Liturgy

Generally the ethical teachings of Judaism are not taught in the prayers directly and explicitly. But they are implied clearly and at times forcefully. Thus we read in the introductory prayers of the daily morning service that God gives man a soul that is pure and unsullied. But man contaminates the soul with his sins—forty-four such sins are enumerated in the Yom Kippur confession.* It is remarkable that not a single one of these sins is of a ritualistic nature. Such sins as desecrating the Sabbath or eating forbidden food are not mentioned. The catalog of sins listed in the confession are all of an ethical nature: "For the sin which we have commited before Thee with the utterance of the lips; and for the sin which we have committed before Thee by wronging a neighbor; . . . by violence; . . . by taking bribes; . . . by slander; . . . in business; . . . by effrontery; . . . by contentiousness; . . . by envy; . . . by levity; . . . by tale-bearing; . . . by causeless hatred; . . . by breach of trust."

The liturgy also singles out many good deeds that are incumbent upon a Jew to perform. Moral behavior, says one of the daily prayers, has no measure or norm. No one can measure filial piety or hospitality. These and several similar moral duties are listed in the Talmud and quoted in the morning prayers. They are to be left to the conscience of the individual, say the rabbis:

* *See pp. 249–50.*

> These are the things which man performs and enjoys their fruits in this world, while the principal remains for him for the world to come, viz.: honouring one's parents, the practice of loving deeds, [timely attendance at the house of study morning and evening, hospitality to wayfarers, visiting the sick, dowering the bride, attending the dead to the grave, devotion in prayer], and making peace between man and his fellow; while the study of the Torah surpasses them all [Pe'ah 1:1] [Shab. 127a].

After the reading of the Torah at the Sabbath services, the reader chants a prayer invoking God's blessing on the congregation. The prayer then enumerates those who are especially deserving of God's blessing, among them persons who support the synagogue, provide food for wayfarers and charity for the poor, and "occupy themselves faithfully with the wants of the congregation." *

But the most edifying section of the prayer book is the short mishnaic treatise Avot (Fathers), which the Jew is expected to study during the long Sabbath afternoons throughout the summer.† In this treatise the favorite sayings of many teachers of the Mishnah are preserved. These sayings were gathered and lovingly treasured by their disciples. The inclusion of this mishnaic tractate in the prayer book is not an anomaly, because according to the rabbis the study of the Torah is an act of worship. Unfortunately, the many lofty teachings of this tractate cannot be summarized here, because they range over the whole gamut of ethics and piety; even a sampling will not illustrate the contents of this precious compendium of rabbinic ethics. One can only urge the reader to examine this notable digest of rabbinic teachings.

Restraint in the Face of Abuse

The confession of sins does not exhaust the moral and ethical ideals explicitly mentioned in the prayers. Indeed, there are

* *See pp. 188–89.*
† *See pp. 194–96.*

too many to be listed, let alone discussed, in this brief presentation. But one moral teaching deserves special note, that of restraint in the face of abuse. The Midrash says: "Any man who remains silent when he hears himself reviled, even though he has at hand the means to strike back, becomes a partner of the Holy One, blessed be He, who likewise remains silent as He hears the nations of the earth revile Him to His face." [4]

A private prayer by one of the rabbis bespeaks this high ideal. It was incorporated into the *Tefillah* and is recited thrice daily: "My God! keep my tongue from evil and my lips from speaking guile. May my soul be silent to them that curse me and may my soul be as the dust to all" (Ber. 17a).

Reverence for God's Name

It has often been said that the Jew's relationship with God is intimate and informal. Yet reverence for the name of God is strictly maintained. God's name is never pronounced, not even during divine worship. Though the Tetragrammaton is spelled out in every prayer, the Jew reads it as if it were the word *Adonai*, the Lord. And when a prayer book or any other volume which contains the name of God is no longer useful because of long usage, it is deposited in the genizah * and in due time given a respectful burial.

Reverence for parents was also dramatized in the synagogue during worship. When a man was called to the reading of the Torah, his sons rose from their seats and remained standing until their father returned to his place.

Concern for the Unlettered

Concern for the underprivileged implied more than the dispensation of charity to the poor; it applied equally to those who are poor in knowledge. The Early Morning Benedictions, as was indicated in an earlier chapter,† were introduced into the public service expressly for the benefit of those who did not know how to recite these blessings privately. These bene-

* *See p. 340.*
† *See pp. 144–45.*

dictions are read aloud in the synagogue in order to afford the unlettered the opportunity of answering Amen and thus not be deprived of the privilege of thanking God for His wonders and blessings.

For similar reasons the rabbis instituted the repetition of the *Tefillah.** After the congregation has recited these benedictions silently, the reader repeats them audibly so that the ignorant may hear them and respond with the conventional Amen.

Concern for the unlettered is demonstrated in still another part of the morning service. The rabbis taught that a Jew is obliged to study Torah daily and specified that everyone should study daily a selection from the Bible, the Mishnah, and the Gemara.† But what is an unlettered Jew to do? Is he to be deprived of this important religious duty? The rabbis introduced into the service selections from the Bible, Mishnah, and Gemara to be read as part of the prayers, thus affording the unlettered Jew the opportunity to perform the commandment of studying the Torah, symbolically if not actually.

The Jewish sensitivity to the feelings of the ignorant is demonstrated most strikingly when the service was deliberately changed to prevent embarrassing the unlettered. The rabbis taught that "one who causes his fellow-man's face to blanch in public has not a share in the life of the world to come" (Avot 3:11). This principle is demonstrated each time the Torah is read at the services. It used to be the practice that everyone called to the Torah read his portion. But there were some who could not read for themselves and had to have someone read for them. This, however, proclaimed publicly that the person called up could not read for himself. In order not to embarrass anyone, it was established that no one should read his portion. A functionary was appointed to read the Torah for everyone. Even the rabbi only recites the requisite blessings when called to the Torah, and the reading is done for him by the congregational reader. ‡

* *See p. 368.*
† *See p. 147.*
‡ *See pp. 183–84.*

The Sanctification of God's Name

The summit of moral action is the performance of deeds that hallow God's name, and conversely the most reprehensive of immoral action is the desecration of God's name. This principle is stated forcefully in the Bible: "You shall not profane My holy name, that I may be sanctified in the midst of the Israelite people" (Lev. 22:32). To be sure, Israel sanctifies God's name when the congregation recites the Kaddish * and exclaims: "Magnified and sanctified be His great name," and when the congregation recites the Kedushah: † "We will sanctify Thy name in the world even as they sanctify it in the highest heaven." But it is more important to hallow God's name by moral action, so that men shall see and say that the God of Israel is the true God. Extraordinary acts of justice and compassion, when performed in the sight of the Gentiles, are kiddush hashem, the sanctification of God's name. Acts that reflect dishonor on the Jewish faith, such as defrauding a Gentile, are hillul hashem, the desecration of God's name, for people judge Judaism by the conduct of Jews.

The spiritual hero in Judaism is the martyr who hallows God's name with his very soul. The precedent for kiddush hashem through martyrdom was set by Rabbi Akiba, a second century teacher. The Talmud relates that Rabbi Akiba defied the Roman decree forbidding the Jews to study and practice the teachings of the Torah. He was apprehended, tortured, and executed for his defiance of the Roman edict. The time of his execution happened to be "the hour for the recital of the *Shema.*" While the Romans were torturing him and "combing his flesh with iron combs," Akiba recited the *Shema.* His disciples seeing this marveled and asked: "Our teacher, even to this point?" [5] Akiba answered:

> All my days I have been troubled by this verse, "[*Thou shalt love the Lord thy God with all thy heart,*] *with all thy soul,* [*and with all thy might*]," [which I interpret] "even if He takes thy soul." . . .

* *See pp. 153 ff.*
† *See pp. 134–37.*

> When shall I have the opportunity of fulfilling this? Now that I have the opportunity shall I not fulfil it? He prolonged the word *ehad* [one] [6] until he expired while saying it [Ber. 61b].

Rabbi Akiba's example has been emulated by numerous Jews, and martyrdom has come to be regarded in Judaism as the highest religious triumph. Since the martyr's act of self-sacrifice is performed before the very eyes of his persecutors, his deed bears weighty witness to Israel's loyalty to God. By his defiance of evil and suffering, the martyr confirms the Jew's spiritual potential. The martyr, as it were, crowns God as the Holy One of Israel.

One of the great scholars, Rabbi Asher (1250–1327), composed an ethical work entitled *Rules*. In it he offers advice on how to pray, and especially how to recite the *Shema*:

> Pray not as a matter of rote, for prayer is the service of the heart. . . . And when thou recitest the verse which bids thee love the Lord thy God, speak as one ready to deliver up life and substance for the sanctification of God, thus fulfilling the words of the Singer: "For Thy sake are we killed all the day" [Ps. 44:23].[7]

In the Middle Ages the Church performed many an auto-da-fé to burn heretics *ad majorem dei gloriam*, and many a Jew offered his soul, not for God's glory but for God's holiness. The opportunities to sanctify God's name were frequent. Many a Jew, faced with the choice between apostasy and a martyr's death, chose to die for kiddush hashem.

Kiddush Hashem in the Liturgy

The liturgy of the synagogue took note of the martyrs of Israel. It even provided the martyr with a special blessing which he was to recite before breathing his last breath. The martyr was to bless God "who sanctified us by His commandments and commanded us to love the glorious and awe-inspiring name, that was, is, and shall be eternally, with all our soul, and to sanctify Thy name before the many. *Praised art*

Thou, O Lord, who hallowest Thy name among the many."[8] This blessing will not be found in the *Siddur* because dying for the sanctification of God's name is not a daily occurrence. Considerations of economy have dictated its omission. However, the daily morning service provides a declaration on the duty of every Jew to sanctify God's name. This declaration is followed by the verse "Hear O Israel, the Lord our God, the Lord is One," and concludes with the blessing "*Praised art Thou, O Lord, who sanctifiest Thy name among the many.*" *

During the High Holy Days, the martyrdom of Jews is featured prominently. In the Yom Kippur service, there is a martyrology † in which there is a heartrending account of how the Romans tortured and put to death ten leading Jewish scholars—among them the exemplar of Jewish martyrdom, Rabbi Akiba. The recital of the martyrology on the Day of Atonement was calculated to awaken the congregation to greater piety and to more ardent repentance. Similarly, the prayer *Unetaneh Tokef* (Let us declare the mighty [holiness of the day]),‡ which is ascribed to the martyr Rabbi Amnon, is calculated to arouse sentiments of piety during the High Holy Days worship. And in the litany *Avìnu Malkenu* § there is a moving appeal to God on the ground that so many Jews have died for kiddush hashem:

> *Our Father, our King! do this for the sake of them that were slain for Thy holy name.*
> *Our Father, our King! do it for the sake of them that were slaughtered for Thy unity.*
> *Our Father, our King! do it for the sake of them that went through fire and water for the sanctification of Thy name.*

The persecutions of the Middle Ages made their gory contributions to the annals of Jewish martyrdom, and these in turn left their imprint on the liturgy of the synagogue. But this sad story is reserved for the next section of the book.

* *See pp. 92, 148–49.*
† *See pp. 458–60.*
‡ *See p. 461.*
§ *See pp. 234–35.*

Woman of Valor, Rothschild ms. 24, 1475, The Israel Museum, Jerusalem.
PHOTO: ALFRED BERNHEIM

"You Shall Be Holy to Your God"

The greatest reward promised to the children of Israel for living up to the terms of the covenant was the opportunity to develop their spiritual potentialities and become a holy people: "You shall be to Me a kingdom of priests and a holy nation" (Exod. 19:6). This principle is concisely expressed by Solomon Schechter in his felicitous definition of the concept of revelation:

> The Holy One of Israel revealed His holy will through His holy Torah to teach Israel ways of holiness so that they become a holy people, tamed in their appetites, separated from their neighbors, and standing aloof from the vanities and abominations of the world around them, and responsible for every action of theirs, be it ever so unimportant or trifling in their eyes.[9]

The concept of holiness has been defined as the highest moral perfection. In Judaism one of the major attributes of God is holiness. In Isaiah's vision the angels cover their faces and exclaim: "Holy, holy, holy is the Lord of Hosts." And in reciting the Kedushah * Israel joins the angels on high in declaring God's holiness. But God's holiness is beyond human comprehension, let alone emulation. Nonetheless, it is the duty of the Jew to strive for holiness. Some saintly people have succeeded in approximating it by achieving a state as close to moral perfection as a human being can achieve. The children of Israel, the Bible says, can achieve a state of holiness by living in accordance with the teachings of the Torah. Israel was therefore directed to emulate the Holy One, blessed be He: "You shall be holy, for I, the Lord your God, am holy" (Lev. 19:2). *Imitatio dei* is the road to holiness.

In the prayers of the synagogue this goal of the religious life is stressed in every benediction recited before the performance of a religious act. God is praised and thanked for having "sanctified us by His commandments." † And in the

* *See pp. 134–37.*
† *See p. 93.*

Kiddush recited on festivals this principle is reiterated: "For Thou hast chosen us and sanctified us above all peoples." The sanctification of Israel consisted of God's giving them the Torah in which are the commandments that lead to the goal of becoming "a holy nation."

To become a holy nation, all of life had to be sanctified: the spiritual and the sensual, the intellectual and the physical. By prescribing blessings for every act of life—including such physical acts of eating, drinking, sleeping, and dressing—the rabbis implied that Judaism aimed at the sanctification of the whole of life. The Havdalah prayer * notwithstanding, Judaism does not separate life into two distinct dominions, that of the holy and that of the profane. The rabbis recognized the obvious fact that in life there are different levels of holiness and that the lowest level is absolutely profane. But Judaism tries to extend the sphere of the holy by sanctifying even what is generally regarded as profane. Obviously, the total elimination of the profane is impossible. Only "at the end of days" † will holiness prevail on all levels of life. For the present, the Jew's task is to strive for the achievement of holiness in his own life and to raise the state of holiness in society as a whole.

Modern Hasidic lore is replete with anecdotes about the exemplary life of the tzaddik, about how he hallows life by infusing every act with divine significance. The holy, according to Hasidism, will penetrate every act of life if we only create the proper conditions for it. "Where is God?" asked the rebbe of Kotzk. "Where we open the door to let Him in," was his answer. This profound teaching is in conformity with rabbinic Judaism. The profane can be made holy, and it is the duty of the Jew to help and support this process.

The emphasis on holiness is characteristic of the synagogue liturgy. The third benediction of the *Tefillah*, which is recited three times daily, reads: "Thou art holy, and Thy name is holy, and holy beings praise Thee daily. *Praised art Thou, O Lord, the holy God.*" Israel's duty is to emulate the Holy One and to strive for holiness, as is indicated in the last paragraph

* *See pp. 297–99.*
† *See pp. 406 ff.*

of the *Shema*, in which the Jew is instructed about the fringed garment, the tallit: * "Thus you shall be reminded to observe all My commandments and to be holy to your God" (Num. 15:40). This basic goal of Judaism is repeated in numerous public and private prayers, indeed on every occasion when prayer is uttered. At no time was the Jew permitted to forget this central objective of the faith. No wonder so many Jews were ready for kiddush hashem when the occasion demanded a choice between apostasy and death.

* *See p. 98.*

PART III

EXPANSION OF THE *SIDDUR* DURING THE MIDDLE AGES

17 THE SYNAGOGUE'S CONFRONTATION WITH THE CHURCH

The Christian liturgy as it had developed by the fourth century included many Jewish elements. This is not surprising since Jesus and the early Christians, including Paul, participated in the synagogue and Temple services. Thus the Eucharist had its origin in the Passover Seder, in which the eating of matzah and the drinking of wine are essential rituals. The use of Amen as a public declaration of faith is almost exactly as it is in the synagogue. Psalms and hymns, reading from the Bible, and preaching of sermons based on biblical texts are all derived from the practices of the synagogue. Also, the literary style and the terminology of the Lord's Prayer are identical with those of ancient Jewish prayers as preserved in the *Siddur*. Such phrases as "Our Father who art in heaven," "Thy kingdom come," "hallowed be Thy name," "give us this day our daily bread," and others are derived from the pharisaic teachings of the rabbis.[1] To be sure, non-Jewish influences also played decisive roles in determining the nature of the Christian liturgy. But Jewish worship of the mishnaic period was the original foundation on which the Christian liturgy was built.

The Parting of the Ways

When the separation of Judaism and Christianity was effected, the Christian liturgy followed its own path completely outside Jewish influence. In time the Church was converted into a shrine, and it became largely a place of sacred rites performed by priests as intermediaries between the worshipers and the Deity. The Jewish liturgy, however, continued on the original path paved by the sages of the Mishnah. The synagogue continued to be a house of prayer, study, and public assembly. In discussing the separation of Christianity from Judaism, R.

Travers Herford describes the parting of the ways in these graphic words:

> In actual fact, Judaism was hardly at all affected by the rise and separation of Christianity except while the process was going on. The stream of Pharisaic Judaism which had been flowing for four centuries before the Christian era, flowed on in its own channel with no interruption at that time and ever since. . . . Judaism took but little notice of Jesus and none whatever of Paul, so far as the talmudic literature is evidence.[2]

Hostility between the Jews and the Early Christians

Although Christianity did not divert the stream of Judaism, it did have more than a peripheral impact on Jewish religious life. Unfortunately, the contacts between the two religious communities were hostile from the beginning. When Christianity achieved power, it assumed a superior attitude and initiated its ceaseless efforts to convert the Jews to the dominant faith. These efforts were always obnoxious to the Jews, and when the means employed turned into severe persecutions, the Jews responded with bitterness born of helplessness.

The Jewish liturgy reflects the painful rupture between the synagogue and the Church. The separation of the daughter religion from the parent faith began after the war with Rome in the years 66–70 C.E. and lasted till after the Bar Kokhba rebellion in 135–137 C.E. In both wars the Christians were suspected of pro-Roman sentiments and accused of spying for the enemy. More irritating were the Christian taunts that the defeat at the hands of the Romans and the destruction of the Temple were conclusive evidence that God had rejected the Jews in favor of the Christians. What had been a sectarian group within Judaism now became a treacherous enemy. What had been merely a religious disagreement within Judaism now became a violent struggle between incompatible theologies, each laying claim to absolute divine truth. The controversy was therefore sharp and bitter. The New Testament, which was produced at that time, presents the controversy from the

Christian point of view. It reflects the bitterness and ill will on the Christian side. Some of the prayers of the synagogue reflect the controversy and the bitterness from the Jewish side.

Resentment on the part of the Jews can easily be grasped. They had fought a heroic war against "the power of wickedness," as they called Rome. The defeat on the battlefield was devastating. But the destruction of the Temple, which was their center of worship, threatened the very survival of Judaism. To be sure, the synagogue was already a fully developed institution, and it readily filled the void left by the burning of the Temple. Nonetheless, the threat to the survival of Judaism was real and distressing.* The challenging provocations by the early Christians naturally produced bitter animosity against the erstwhile Jews turned first sectarians, then open enemies.

Anti-Christian Polemics in the Jewish Liturgy

After the first war with Rome the rabbis added a benediction to those that are recited after the reading of the Haftarah.† Its aim was to refute the Christian claim that the Messiah had come. The benedicion supplicates God to restore the kingdom of David under the Messiah and concludes with a blessing in which God is called the Shield of David. The benediction reads:

> Gladden us, O Lord our God, with Elijah the prophet, Thy servant, and with the kingdom of the House of David, thine anointed. Soon may he come and rejoice our hearts. Suffer not a stranger to sit upon his throne, nor let others any longer inherit his glory; for by Thy holy name Thou didst swear unto him, that his light should not be quenched forever. *Praised art Thou, O Lord, the Shield of David.*

This newly added benediction was mild. It merely reasserted the Jewish faith in the coming of the Messiah who would redeem Israel from the Roman yoke. Obviously, its aim was to negate the central dogma of Christianity. But it was not offensive. However, there is another prayer that was then added

* *See pp. 79–80.*
† *See pp. 184–86.*

to the liturgy which is not so mild and whose purpose was not merely to negate a Christian dogma. Its objective was to weed out the Judeo-Christians from the Jewish congregations.* This was not easy: the Christians were indistinguishable from the Jews because they observed all the Jewish religious practices. This new prayer actually contained a malediction upon the early Christians or, as they were called, the Nazarenes. The benediction began: "And for the Nazarenes and the sectarians let there be no hope, and let all wickedness perish." [3] The inclusion of this prayer in the *Tefillah* made it unpleasant for the early Christians to participate in the synagogue services. If one of them was chosen to be the reader and omitted the word *Nazarenes*, he was immediately detected as a Christian. Anyone who did not respond to the benediction with a loud Amen was recognized as one of the sectarians. The word *Nazarenes* was later eliminated from the prayer; the Christian censors saw to that. In its day, however, it was eloquent evidence of the prevailing animosity between the Jews and the early Christians.

Another liturgic remnant of those days was inspired by Paul's antinomianism, which led to the Christian abrogation of the rite of circumcision. The rabbis chose to give this rite special emphasis and thereby negate the new Christian teaching. The rabbis added the rite of circumcision to the list of the divine blessings for which the Jew thanked the Almighty in the grace after meals. To emphasize its centrality they placed it ahead of the gift of the Torah. The prayer of thanksgiving as it now appears in the grace after meals reads in part:

> We thank Thee, O Lord our God, . . . for Thy covenant which Thou hast sealed in our flesh, Thy Torah which Thou hast taught us, Thy statutes which Thou hast made known unto us, the life, grace, and loving-kindness which Thou hast vouchsafed unto us, and for the food wherewith Thou dost constantly feed and sustain us every day, in every season, at every hour.[4]

* *See pp. 105–106.*

Adjustment under Adversity

The period of controversy between the mother and daughter religions came to an abrupt end when Christianity became the official religion of the Roman Empire. The triumphant Church not only marked Judaism with the sign of inferiority, but began to interfere with Jewish religious expression in the synagogue. In the Theodosian Code, promulgated in the year 438 C.E., Judaism was already referred to as "the abominable superstition." Similar degrading terms were used in Church literature throughout the Middle Ages and well into the modern era. From the Theodosian period on, synagogue building was strictly limited. No new synagogue might be erected without special permission, and old synagogues, if rebuilt, were not to exceed the existing ones in size and height.

More odious were the Church's indefatigable efforts to convert the Jews to Christianity. The proud posture of the Church not only offended the Jews but inflicted endless suffering through persecutions inspired by missionary zeal. The Jew's steadfastness was seen by the Church as nothing but blind, obstinate defiance. Jewish resistance to baptism aroused in the Church feelings of anger and frustration. Persecutions were therefore launched to force the Jew to abandon his stubborn resistance to the dominant religion. Yet the Jew continued to persist in his constancy. This constancy in the face of almost insufferable persecutions prompted many a historian to marvel at the miracle of the Jewish survival. Henry Charles Lea, in his monumental *History of the Inquisition of Spain*, characterizes the Jewish resistance to the conversionary efforts of the Church in these trenchant words:

> The annals of mankind afford no more brilliant instance of steadfastness under adversity, of unconquerable strength through centuries of hopeless oppression, of inexhaustible elasticity in recuperating from apparent destruction, and of conscientious adherence to a faith whose only portion in this life was contempt and suffering.[5]

Obviously it was not mere obstinacy that endowed the Jews with the strength to withstand unending and often bloody persecutions. It was their unswerving faith in the tenets of Judaism and in the comforting conviction that their spiritual tenacity would in time be vindicated in the sight of all the nations. Indeed, their humiliation and suffering at the hands of the Church was part of the divine scheme, as the rabbis so aptly pictured it:

> The Holy One, blessed be He, spoke to our father Jacob: *And thy seed* [*descendants*] *shall be as the dust of the earth* (Gen. 28:14). As the dust of the earth is trodden down by all, so shall thy children be trodden down by all; but as the dust of the earth wears down vessels of metal and itself lasts for ever, so shall thy children wear down the nations of the earth and themselves shall last forever.[6]

The persecutions were not limited to the social and economic spheres. They were often religious in nature and frequently found their expression in the proscription or censorship of certain prayers. In the prayers of the synagogue the Church not infrequently discovered doctrines which negated its own doctrines. These prayers were regarded as too offensive to remain unchallenged. And the simplest way to meet a theological challenge by a weak and helpless antagonist is to suppress the offensive prayers. The Jews had no choice but to bow to the vastly superior power of the Church, at least ostensibly. But they resisted nonetheless. Jewish resistance was typical of a weak but determined foe who cannot meet the enemy in open battle—the Jews resorted to clever stratagems and subterfuges. One of the simplest evasions of the Church's proscription of a prayer was to change the scheduled time of prayer and to recite it when the appointed censor was not present in the synagogue. More intriguing was the substitution of new prayers into which veiled allusions to the proscribed prayers were incorporated. These allusions were usually clear enough to the Jews but sufficiently vague to escape the censor's vigilance. What intrigues the student of Jewish liturgy is that the end of the persecutions and the restoration of the traditional services did not lead to the elimination of the emergency prayers. They were usually retained in the service because their usage over a long period of time endowed them with a sanctity of their own. A number of these prayers are still statutory parts of the liturgy.

The Justinian Edict

As mentioned earlier,* the persecution of Judaism began immediately after the triumph of Christianity. From the time of Constantine the Great to the time of the conquest of Palestine by the Arabs (312–636 C.E.) the Jews suffered religious persecutions of varying severity. These persecutions left permanent marks on the Jewish liturgy. But the really massive persecution did not start till the middle of the sixth century, when the Justinian Edict, which aimed at suppressing Judaism altogether, was issued. The Justinian Edict clearly spelled out this policy. To begin with, the Church objected to the *Shema*, which forcefully declares the unity of God. The Jews' vociferous recitation of the *Shema* at each morning and evening service was, the Church felt, a deliberate challenge to the Christian dogma of the Trinity. Hence the recitation of the *Shema* was proscribed.[7]

The Church also found one of the benedictions of the *Tefillah* most objectionable: the one added during the early controversies with the Judeo-Christians invoking God's wrath on informers, apostates, and Nazarenes.† The Church therefore proscribed not only this benediction but all the benedictions of the *Tefillah*.

The final blow to Jewish worship was the prohibition of the rabbinic teaching which took place during the services. The edict expressed concern over the fact that the Jews "have given themselves over to irrational explanations and have to this day gone astray from the true [Christian] interpretation [of Scripture]." Justinian felt that the rabbinic interpretations of the Torah were responsible for the stubborn Jewish rejection of

* *See pp. 169–70.*
† *See pp. 105–106.*

Jesus. He could not very well prohibit the reading of the Scriptures because the Church too regarded them as holy, but he was determined to silence the rabbinic explanations of the text. He therefore decreed that:

> the Holy Scripture may be read in the synagogues in Greek . . . so that the text may be understood by those present. . . . The interpreters [the rabbis] shall not be allowed to corrupt the Hebrew text. . . . We strictly forbid what they call Deuterosis [rabbinic interpretations]. . . . This our will is to be observed [by officials who] shall subject those who dare resist it or hinder it in any way to corporal punishment first, then force them to live in exile and confiscate their property, so that they may not act disrespectfully against God and the Emperor.[8]

Justinian thus struck at the heart of Jewish worship. By excising the *Shema* and the *Tefillah* and the teaching of the Torah, he suppressed the essence of Jewish worship. What was now left of Jewish worship was merely the right to gather in the synagogue and to hear the reading from the Torah without any rabbinic comment. They could also recite religious poems devoted to the praise of God and the Kedushah.* The latter was condoned because Christians saw in the threefold sanctification of God—"Holy, holy, holy is the Lord of hosts"—a hint of the Trinity.

Strategy of Resistance

The Jews exploited these seemingly minor concessions and by means of ingenious subterfuges restored some of the traditional worship. They regularly gathered in their synagogues and recited the Kedushah. Surreptitiously they inserted into the Kedushah the opening verse of the *Shema*—"Hear, O Israel, the Lord our God, the Lord is One"—and also the concluding words of the last paragraph of the *Shema*—"I am the Lord your God."[9] These insertions are still part of the Kedushah of every Musaf service. But the Kedushah, too, was in time prohibited. The Christians became aware that when recit-

* *See pp. 134–37.*

ing the verse "Holy, holy, holy, is the Lord of hosts," the Jews not only failed to perceive in it a trinitarian implication, but actually saw in it a confirmation of the absolute unity of God. This verse is specifically translated into Aramaic to mean that "God is holy in the heavens above; God is holy on the earth below; and God is holy to all eternity." Indeed, the recitation of the Kedushah became a sort of demonstrative proclamation of God's unity—and by implication a repudiation of the Christian trinitarian dogma. Hence the recitation of the Kedushah also became offensive to the Church. This prohibition, however, was also circumvented. The Kedushah was inserted into another prayer, *Uva Le-Zion Go'el*, which was recited at a time when the government censors were not in attendance (at the conclusion of the homily on Sabbath afternoons when the congregation reassembled for the afternoon service). Not only was the Kedushah inserted but also its polemical Aramaic translation. The practice of reciting *Uva Le-Zion Go'el* and its inserted Kedushah at the Sabbath afternoon service has continued to this day. At a later date this prayer was taken over by the Babylonian Jews, and they included it in the daily service, where it has remained to this day.

But it was the prohibition of rabbinic homilies that called for the most ingenious strategy. This prohibition had left the people without guidance in both religious belief and ritual practice, for the rabbis would not only interpret the text and extract from it the theological doctrines of Judaism, but also would instruct the congregation in the practices and observances of the Jewish faith. As we showed earlier, the rabbis resorted to a most skillful subterfuge: they utilized religious poems in which were incorporated allusions to the rabbinic interpretations of the Torah readings, as well as timely religious laws for the people's guidance. The composition of religious poems containing allusions to biblical and rabbinic teachings was an accepted form of literary expression. Now this literary activity was greatly intensified and became a means of circumventing the edict. The veiled language and the vague allusions of these piyutim were clear enough to many Jews, but quite incomprehensible to the government censors. To be sure, many of the Jews did not quite catch the implications of these piyutim either. But they recited them in the knowledge that they were appropriate substitutes for the traditional prayers and teachings proscribed by the authorities.

In the year 636, about a century after the issuance of the Justinian Edict, the Arabs conquered Palestine and restored to the Jews their freedom of worship. The traditional synagogue services were fully reinstated, but the innovations of the emergency period did not disappear from the liturgy. Thus the first and last verses of the *Shema* were retained in the Kedushah of the Musaf * service on Sabbaths and festivals; and the Kedushah which was inserted into the prayer *Uva Le-Zion Go'el* has remained to this day. But the most important legacy of that period was the intensified practice of composing liturgical poems, or piyutim, for all special occasions. This practice, which gained momentum during the persecutions, developed into a powerful religioliterary movement in Judaism. (The story of this development has already been discussed in an earlier chapter.†)

The Legacy of the Crusaders

In the year 1096 the First Crusade was launched with the avowed purpose of rescuing the holy sepulcher from the hands of the Saracens. But some of the Crusaders could not wait until they reached Jerusalem, and they vented their unholy zeal on the infidels who dwelled in their midst. The victims of the Crusaders touched the heart of the Jewish people most deeply, so that the liturgy of the synagogue still mourns the martyrs of those massacres who died "for the sanctification of God's name."

The Slaughter of the Jews in the Rhineland

In the Rhineland there were a number of ancient Jewish communities, some of which were founded in the days of the Roman Empire. When the Crusaders reached these Rhenish

* *See p. 192.*
† *See pp. 168 ff.*

towns they began their ungodly work in earnest. They murdered and plundered the Jews mercilessly. Entire Jewish communities perished for the "glory" of the cross, and the trail of Jewish blood left by the Crusaders has never been forgotten by the Jewish people. These events are memorialized in the synagogue liturgy and in some of the Jewish mourning customs.

It should be noted that the Crusaders, unlike the Nazis, offered the Jews a choice—baptism or death. To the astonishment and frustration of the Crusaders the Jews chose death.

The Crusaders performed the wholesale slaughter with holy zeal. They did their bloody work with such thoroughness that few survivors remained. As the Crusaders passed the Rhenish towns of Treves, Speyer, Worms, Mayence, and Cologne, the Jewish corpses multiplied by the thousands, and the plunder increased proportionately. In some communities, however, the Crusaders were cheated of their dubious acts of piety. The Jews anticipated their fate and committed suicide rather than fall into the hands of the Crusaders. In the tradition of the defenders of Masada against the Roman legions almost a thousand years earlier, many Jews killed their wives and children and then themselves. Among these were some who were widely known for their piety and scholarship. Thus the liturgic poet Kalonymus ben Meshullam, head of the community of Mayence, was among those who committed suicide.[10] Rabbi Yom Tov ben Isaac, author of piyutim which are still part of the *Siddur* [11] was among the martyrs who met their collective death at York, England, in 1190 during the Third Crusade. Rabbi Eleazer ben Judah of Worms suffered an even worse fate. "On the fatal day in November 1196, the Soldiers of the Cross burst into his house, as he was engaged in writing his commentary on Genesis, plundered it of its contents, cruelly maltreated his wife and then murdered her and their children. The Rabbi alone escaped with bare life." [12] But the crowning deed of the Crusaders' zeal was their slaughter of the entire Jewry of Jerusalem. When the Crusaders finally took possession of the Holy City, they herded all the Jews—men, women, and children—into a synagogue, set it on fire, and thus cleansed the city of its Jewish infidels. The new kingdom of Jerusalem was thus founded on the ashes of Jewish martyrs.[13]

Yahrzeit and Yizkor Observances

As the years passed, the Rhenish Jewish communities slowly rose from their ashes. There were some Jews who survived the slaughter because they happened to be away on a journey; there were others who managed to hide; and there were those who were forcibly baptized and then returned to the fold. These survivors along with new arrivals slowly rebuilt the devastated towns. But they never forgot the thousands of martyrs who died for the sanctification of God's name. The steadfastness of the martyrs stirred the hearts of the survivors as few tragedies ever did. They mourned the victims and memorialized them on the anniversaries of their deaths. These annual commemorations gave rise to the institution of the yahrzeit, the annual memorials observed by Jews for the deceased members of their immediate families. The transition from the annual memorials for the victims of the Crusaders to the annual memorials by private people for their near relatives was quite natural, for the passing of a close relative is as great a blow and as painful a tragedy to those directly concerned as is the death of thousands of anonymous martyrs to a community.

The observance of the yahrzeit on the anniversary of the death of parents spread from Germany to Jewish communities far and near. Among the Sephardim this memorial ritual was unknown until the sixteenth century, when the kabbalist Isaac Luria * of Safed gave it a kabbalistic explanation. Ever since, the yahrzeit has also been one of the mourning customs of the oriental Jews. As time passed the yahrzeit observance became an increasingly sacred family rite. A memorial light is kindled at home in accordance with the biblical words "The spirit [soul] of man is the lamp of the Lord" (Prov. 20:27), and the children of the deceased recite the mourner's Kaddish † at each of the three services on that day.

* *See pp. 489–92.*
† *See pp. 153 ff.*

The custom of memorializing the dead members of the family during the Yom Kippur services goes back to the geonic period, but it was only after the massacres of the Crusaders that the yizkor service became a statutory part of the ritual. These services are mentioned in the Midrash Tanhuma, which dates back to the fifth century. In its comments on Deuteronomy 32:1 we read: "It is the duty of the living to redeem the dead. Therefore it is our custom to memorialize the dead on the Day of Atonement." Some scholars, however, suspect that this reference to the Day of Atonement is a later addition, for it is only after the period of the Crusaders that the memorial service of Yom Kippur is clearly mentioned in various sources. Thus the *Mahzor Vitry* (1208)* speaks definitely of this practice. Later the yizkor service was also introduced into the liturgy of the festivals.[14]

The essential prayers of the yizkor service are simplicity itself. The service begins with a brief formula which each worshiper recites silently:

> May God remember [*yizkor*] the soul of my revered
> father, ——, son of ——, who has gone to his repose.
> May his soul be bound up in the bundle of life [15]
> with the souls of all the righteous men and women.
> May his rest be glorious with fullness of joy in Thy
> presence, and pleasure for evermore at Thy right hand.
> Amen.[16]

A solemn feeling of filial piety pervades the congregation as the worshipers rise and silently recite this simple formula. Many a reverential tear is shed by children who recall the loving devotion of their parents and by bereaved parents who recall the loss of beloved children.

The yizkor formula is followed by the reader's haunting chant of the prayer *El Malei Rahamim* (God, full of mercy). In content this prayer adds nothing new, for it generally repeats what was already said in the yizkor prayer. But the traditional chant stirs the heart and evokes tender memories of the dead. Unfortunately, the yizkor service has lost much of its

* *See pp. 389–91.*

spiritual power. Not only has it shared the fate of all prayer in our days, but also it has been vulgarized by many well-meaning people who have embellished it with exaggerated eulogies of "the dearly beloved who have been called to their eternal rest." These flowery but artificial additions have vitiated the simplicity and the dignity of the yizkor service.

The Unending Medieval Persecutions

The Crusades were not the only landmarks in the history of Jewish repression during the Middle Ages. Among the outstanding milestones of medieval Jewish history there are several that deserve at least passing note because they exerted an influence on the liturgy. One is the establishment of the permanent Inquisition in 1233 by Pope Gregory IX. This powerful institution was entrusted to Dominican friars, who performed their work with severity and cruelty. Heretics and those suspected of heresy were frequently condemned to the stake. Among those suspected of heresy were the Marranos, the Jews of Spain and Portugal who had been forcibly baptized. These suspects provided thousands of martyrs for the glory of the Church and the entertainment of the aristocracy and the mob.[17] The Inquisition functioned with cunning efficiency—first against Christian heretics, including the Marranos, and eventually against the Jews, whose very existence, it was argued, encouraged the new Christians to relapse. The story of these heresy hunts, the torture chambers, and the spectacular autos-da-fé is too gruesome to be detailed here. It must be pointed out, however, that these activities of the Inquisition had a most depressing effect on Jewish life and that they left their marks on the liturgy of the synagogue.

There were other depressing persecutions during the Middle Ages, among them those triggered by the Black Death in the mid-fourteenth century. This plague, which was blamed on the Jews, naturally caused untold suffering to the innocent victims. Periodic accusations that Jews had desecrated the host invariably kindled the mob's passion for murder and plunder. And there were the recurring Eastertime accusations of ritual murders supposedly committed by Jews who, it was claimed, needed Christian blood for the Passover observance. These blood accusations, which originally had been leveled against the Christians, were now directed against the Jews and were usually followed by bloody massacres.

But transcending these periodic outbursts were the persecutions unleashed by the bull issued by Pope Paul IV in the mid-sixteenth century. Among its provisions was the order that the Jews be herded within walled ghettos with only one gate, which was to be locked from sundown to sunrise.[18] The crucial effect of the ghetto on Jewish history is that it prolonged the Jewish Middle Ages to the end of the eighteenth century, when the ghetto walls were officially pulled down by the French Revolution. Because of the segregation of the Jews within ghetto walls, the Renaissance had little effect on the Jewish people. They were effectively excluded from the cultural awakening that was initiated at that time. To be sure, the social insulation imposed on the Jews was not airtight. Some Jews were in contact with Gentiles, but largely in the field of commerce. Socially and culturally the Jews were almost totally excluded from non-Jewish society. The Jews remained within the framework of medieval life when Western Europe was slowly breaking out of the confines of medievalism.

The Jews of Eastern Europe too were quite effectively segregated. The Russian government confined them to limited areas of residence and even more limited areas of economic activity. Crowding and poverty were their lot. What was equally decisive was the backwardness of the people among whom the Jews lived. The Russians and other East European nationalities were hardly capable of stimulating new cultural movements. The Jewish Middle Ages therefore did not begin to expire until the end of the eighteenth century.

The most pernicious curse of the medieval Jews was the Jewish apostate, who often turned against his erstwhile coreligionists with venomous hate and brought upon the Jews untold suffering. These informers were feared and hated.[19] When the medieval Jew recited in the *Tefillah* "And for informers let there be no hope,"* he did so with a deep sense of immediacy. The informer was the canker of the medieval Jewish community. He was the guide and mentor of those who censored and expurgated Jewish books, among them the *Siddur*.

Solomon Schechter summed up the medieval persecutions of the Jews by saying:

> The persecutions from the times of the First Crusade in 1096 till perhaps the end of the fifteenth century are so continuous that we can hardly speak of frequency, which at least suggests moments of breath and recuperation. Confiscation followed confiscation, massacre followed massacre, and expulsion followed expulsion so closely during these terrible centuries that it is the greatest miracle how the Ashkenazi Jews survived.[20]

However, the Jew did manage to survive. He yielded neither to the harsh fate of degradation and suffering nor to the blandishments of ample rewards for submission to baptism. He sought and found strength and hope in the prayers of the synagogue and in the study of God's word as revealed in the Torah and amplified by the teachings of the rabbis.

Christian Sermons in the Synagogue

The Church was indefatigable in its proselytizing zeal. Failing to bring the Jews to the Church, it decided to bring the Church to the Jews. This crudest of religious persecutions is clearly spelled out in a bull issued in 1415 by Pope Benedict XIII. Three times annually Christian preachers were to deliver sermons in the synagogues. "All Jews above twelve years of age," specified the edict, "shall be compelled to attend and hear these sermons."[21] The ludicrous aspects of these missionary efforts are satirized by Robert Browning in his poem "Holy Cross Day." The poem is subtitled "On which the Jews were forced to attend an annual Christian sermon in Rome." Forcing the Jews to hear Christian sermons led to such ab-

* *See pp. 104–105.*

surdities as examining each Jew's ears as he entered, for the Jews were suspected of stopping their ears with cotton. Overseers were stationed in the aisles to compel the unwilling auditors to listen to the lengthy sermons. As late as the eighteenth century the Jews of Rome were still required to listen to conversionary sermons.

Censorship of the *Siddur*

The Inquisition enjoyed a remarkable longevity. A Judaizer was burned at an auto-da-fé as late as 1826.[22] But there was also a gentler arm of the Inquisition whose energies were directed to expurgation of heresies from literature. This department of the Inquisition has continued well into the twentieth century and is still active under a different name—the index expurgatorius.

Jewish books also fell prey to the scrutiny of the Inquisition, and their fate was not infrequently that of the auto-da-fé. Jewish apostates played leading roles in this sad performance. Some of these apostates were at home in Jewish literature, and they provided the Dominican friars with the necessary guidance for their censorship. As a result, Jewish books were often burned at autos-da-fé, and others were mutilated by the expurgation of passages which the censors regarded as offensive to Christian doctrine. What was worse, they often substituted more acceptable readings for the expurgated material. The story of these literary mutilations is both shocking and intriguing.

The *Siddur*, though not a primary object of the censors' wrath, has nonetheless had its modest share. It cannot compare with the Talmud, carloads of which were repeatedly burned;[23] but it was periodically subjected to the critical eye of the Inquisition, and certain prayers or expressions were found repugnant to the Church.[24]

Although Church censorship of books became a concern of the clergy in the thirteenth century, Hebrew books were not subjected to a systematic censorship until the period of the Reformation, when the Church was challenged by many deadly heresies and its very survival was threatened.

Attacks against the Kol Nidre Prayer

No sooner was the *Siddur* subjected to the scrutiny of the censors than the Jews were called upon to defend the Kol Nidre prayer, which is recited on the eve of the Day of Atonement. This prayer, as indicated earlier,* is an expression of Jewish piety at its best. Before a Jew dares to appear before God with his supplications on the holiest day of the year, he is overcome by a sense of unworthiness, because he may have inadvertantly violated a vow during the past year. The Kol Nidre does not deal with vows between man and man; these can be absolved only by the person to whom the vow was made. The Kol Nidre is concerned only with vows between man and God. It is for these private vows that the Jew seeks absolution before he starts the Yom Kippur services. But the inquisitors, guided by Jewish apostates, saw in this prayer evidence that the Jew cunningly absolves himself of all vows and thus enables himself to renege on promises and oaths. According to these accusations, the Kol Nidre prayer enables the Jew to defraud his unsuspecting neighbors. It should therefore be expurgated from the synagogue liturgy.

The Jews vigorously denied these accusations. But denials, however well documented, did not stop the accusations from being revived from time to time. As early as the thirteenth century, during a public disputation forced upon the Jews, Rabbi Jehiel of Paris and several other rabbis had to face a Jewish apostate, Nicholas Donin, and refute his charge that the Kol Nidre prayer enables the Jews to defraud the Gentiles. Commentaries have been included in the prayer books reminding the worshipers that the Kol Nidre applies only to private oaths. Nonetheless, these attacks were repeated with such monotony that in modern times the Reform Jews decided to eliminate this prayer altogether. But this attempt has not succeeded. In the vast majority of synagogues the Kol Nidre has not only remained an integral part of the Yom Kippur service, but also has retained its powerful appeal to the heart of the Jewish worshiper.

* *See pp. 244–47.*

Censorship of the *Alenu* Prayer

Another prayer that has repeatedly come up for judgment before the Inquisition is the *Alenu* prayer. This exalted prayer deals with Israel's uniqueness as God's chosen people, and it supplicates God for the speedy initiation of the "kingship of the Almighty," when idolatry will vanish and all mankind will worship the one God.* The author of this prayer was Rav, one of the greatest of the talmudic sages; he lived in Babylonia during the early third century. The popularity of this prayer also derives from its association with the martyrdom of thirty-four men and seventeen women who were burned at the stake in the town of Blois in the year 1171. These martyrs, who had been accused of a ritual murder, were offered their lives in exchange for baptism: but they refused the offer and died in the auto-da-fé, chanting the *Alenu* prayer. This prayer has thus endeared itself to the Jews, and they chose to include it in every service.

The first paragraph of the *Alenu* prayer drew the censure of the Inquisition because it contained an objectionable sentence. The prayer used to read as follows:

> It is our duty to praise the Lord of all, to ascribe greatness to the Creator of the universe, for He hath not made us like the nations of the world, nor fashioned us like the families of the earth. He has not made our portion like them and our lot like that of their multitude. For they worship and bow before idols and vanity and pray to that which availeth not; but as for us, we bend the knee and bow down and give thanks before the supreme King of kings, the Holy One, blessed be He.

The censors claimed the words "idols and vanity" (Isa. 30:7) referred to the Christian divinity. The Jews defended the objectionable sentence by saying that it could not possibly refer to Christianity. The author of this prayer lived in Persia, a non-Christian land, and he obviously referred to the people in whose midst he lived. This defense might have succeeded had not a Jewish apostate "proved" by a curious kabbalistic

* *See pp. 241–42.*

method that the Jews did mean the Christians. Since the Hebrew alphabet also serves as numerals, one can add up the arithmetical value of the letters of any word and thus derive for it a numerical value. The letters of the Hebrew word for vanity equal 316. By coincidence the letters of the Hebrew word for Jesus also add up to 316. The apostate therefore claimed that the Jews equated Jesus with vanity.[25]

This argument was readily accepted by the inquisitors as convincing proof. Nevertheless, the Jews, represented by the illustrious scholar Rabbi Lippmann of Muhlhausen, successfully fought off the spurious argument and averted the condemnation of the *Alenu* prayer. This victory, which took place in 1399, was short-lived, however. In the year 1440 the printing press was invented, and the Church sensed a new danger. A manuscript book was available to a small circle of readers, but a printed book was available to an incalculable number of readers; a printed heresy could infect a whole community. So the Church bestirred itself and introduced a strict censorship of the printed word. All books were subjected to thorough examination before printing, and approval had to be obtained from the local archbishop. The Inquisition was given the task of enforcing the censorship.

As the violence against Hebrew books increased, the Jews of Europe instituted a system of self-censorship. In 1554, at a meeting of congregational representatives at Ferrara, Italy, it was decided to establish what was generally called the *haskamah*, or the system of book approval. According to the *haskamah* no Hebrew book was to be published without the prior approval of the local authorities, consisting usually of three rabbis. The self-censorship led to the omission of dangerous words, phrases, and even longer passages from all printed Hebrew books. But the censors of the Inquisition were not always satisfied with this self-censorship. They made additional "corrections" and substituted acceptable words or phrases for those that they considered objectionable. Since the censors were frequently ignorant, they corrupted the text of many a Hebrew book, especially the Talmud, and rendered many sections of these books almost meaningless.[26]

The system of self-censorship was also applied to the *Siddur*. By the end of the sixteenth century, the objectionable sentence—"for they worship and bow down before idols and vanity and pray to that which availeth not"—began to disappear from the *Siddur*. But children were taught in the Jewish schools to recite this sentence by heart.

Early in the eighteenth century two Jewish apostates brought charges against the *Alenu* prayer before Frederick, king of Prussia. The king acted with moderation: he called the leading rabbis together and had them swear that the Hebrew word for vanity did not refer to Jesus. But the accusations persisted. Finally, the king ordered that the *Alenu* prayer always be recited loudly at public services and that Christian observers be present to make sure that the offensive words are really omitted.

Since censorship was exercised with greater rigor in Christian than in Moslem lands, some of the texts eliminated or mutilated by the Christian censors have remained unaltered among the Sephardic Jews. Thus the objectionable sentence which was expurgated from the *Alenu* prayer in the Ashkenazic prayer books is to be found in the Sephardic *Siddur*. It is interesting to note that in those modern states where censorship of Jewish prayers no longer exists the expurgated sentence of the *Alenu* prayer has not been restored. Many Jews are still afraid lest that troublesome sentence be utilized by modern anti-Semitic elements in their eternal war against the Jews.

The Somber Nature of Medieval Prayers

The medieval persecutions introduced a mournful spirit into the liturgy. The piyutim written during these centuries reflected the anguished feelings of the Jews. The synagogue poets incessantly reminded the Almighty of the sufferings endured by the Jews and of the constancy exhibited by the martyrs who died for the sanctification of God's name. They mourned over the destruction of the holy Temple and the interminable exile. But the rabbinic theodicy never changed.

The poets continued to proclaim Israel's guilt as the cause of the exile and Israel's transgressions as the reason for the Messiah's not coming to redeem the Jewish people from its homelessness. Many of these mournful piyutim are still part of the liturgy. An example of these prayers is the piyut which is recited during the Neilah service on the Day of Atonement. The prayer is known by its initial words—*Ezkerah Elohim* (I remember, O God)—and its opening verses read:

I remember, O God, and I am deeply vexed
When I see every city built on its own site,
While Jerusalem, the city of God, is razed to the ground.
Yet for all this, our faith in Thee does not falter.[27]

Dirges and Martyrologies

The martyrs who died at the hands of the Crusaders were mourned in all European Jewish communities. The liturgic poets composed numerous tearful prayers in which they described the victims' readiness for martyrdom and held up their piety and steadfastness for the emulation of the worshipers. Notwithstanding their occasional appeal that God avenge the blood of the innocent victims, these prayers had an uplifting effect on the congregations. To quote Israel Abrahams, these prayers "generated heroic endurance in the worshipper's mind rather than vindictiveness. . . . These laments . . . inspired [the Jews] with courage to endure all things for that which they held more precious than all things." [28]

These dirges were produced in great abundance, and some are still part of the kinot of the Ninth of Av.* Typical of these elegies is the dirge by Kalonymus ben Judah (the Younger) who lived in Speyer in the twelfth century. This dirge is still read in the Ashkenazic synagogues. The poet introduces his lamentation with the mournful words "O that my head were water, and my eyes a fountain of tears, / That I might weep all the days and nights [of my life]." He then describes the massacres of the Jews of Speyer, Worms, and Mayence, as well as the wanton destruction of the holy books, and he continues:

* *See pp. 277–79.*

Reader: *So for these do I weep, and my heart groans exceedingly,*
And I call to the hired mourning women and to the skilled keeners.
All moan, mourn, and wail; is there any anguish that can be compared to my anguish?
Without does the sword bereave, and within terror [reigns];
My wounded, and those who are riddled with sword thrusts, lie naked;
Sucklings, young men, and maidens [together] with hoary old men,
Their corpses are like carrion for the wild beasts of the land.

Cong.: Alas for the house of Israel, and for the people of the Lord, for they are fallen by the sword!

Reader: *My oppressors mock and increase their reproach:*
"Where is their God," they say, "the Rock in whom they trusted till death?
Let Him come and save [them] and restore their souls [to life]";
O Thou, who art mighty! Who is like Thee, O Lord, who bearest [all] burdens?
Wilt Thou be quiet and restrain Thyself and not gird Thyself in wrath
When those that scoff at me say: "If He be a God, let Him contend [for thee]"?

Cong.: Alas, for the house of Israel, and for the people of the Lord, for they are fallen by the sword! [29]

Another example of the dirges written during that period is the one by Rabbi Meir of Rothenberg, who was lovingly called the Light of the Exile. The author lived in the thirteenth century, and his elegy, which is part of the kinot of the Ninth of

Av, is a lamentation on the burning of the Talmud in Paris in 1242. One of the stanzas reads:

O [Torah] that hast been consumed by fire seek the welfare of those who mourn for you,
Of those who yearn to dwell in the court of your habitation,
Of those who gasp [as they lie] in the dust of the earth,
Who grieve and are bewildered over the conflagration of your parchments.
They grope in the dark, bereft of light,
Indeed, they wait [in longing] for the daylight that will shine upon them and upon you.

The author describes the public burning of the holy books. He appeals to Mount Sinai and to Moses and Aaron not to be silent and concludes his elegy on a note of hope. He addresses "the daughter of Zion":

You will again adorn yourself with ornaments of scarlet;
You will take up timbrel, lead the circling dance, and rejoice in your revels.
Then shall my heart be uplifted . . . when your Creator will afford you light,
And will brighten your darkness and illuminate your [sorrowing] gloom.[30]

The memory of the martyrs was also drawn upon to arouse pious sentiments and repentance of sins at services other than those of the Ninth of Av. One such prayer is recited on Sabbath mornings in all Ashkenazic synagogues. It is known by its initial words: *Av Ha-Rahamim* (Father of mercy). It was composed during the First Crusade by an anonymous author who left it on the reader's desk in the synagogue of Worms. Its mysterious origin no doubt added to its prestige and helped it become part of the official liturgy. The prayer is a mixture of tender recollection of the martyred victims and bitter denunciation of those who perpetrated the massacres. The prayer reads in part:

May the Father of mercy, . . . in His mighty compassion, remember those loving, upright and blameless ones, the holy congregations, who laid down

> their lives for the sanctification of the divine name, who were lovely and pleasant in their lives and in their death were not divided [2 Sam. 1:23]. . . . May our God remember them for good with the other righteous of the world, and avenge the blood of His servants which hath been shed.

In the Yom Kippur service, too, there is a well-known martyrology known as *Eleh Ezkerah* (These things I do remember).* It is a touching account of the torture and agony suffered by the martyred scholars at the hands of the Romans after the ill-fated Bar Kokhba revolt. The piyut describes the piety, saintliness, and courage of these scholars. The worshipers associated the suffering of the martyrs with their contemporary experience and shed copious tears when they read this martyrology.

Another medieval piyut connected with the theme of martyrdom is the well-known High Holy Days prayer, *Unetaneh Tokef* (Let us declare the mighty [holiness of the day]). This prayer, though published by the well-known eleventh century author of piyutim Rabbi Kalonymus ben Meshullam, has been generally attributed to Rabbi Amnon of Mayence. Its powerful appeal derives from the alleged martyrdom of the presumed author. Rabbi Amnon, according to this story, was faced with the familiar choice of apostasy or death; he chose the latter. Before he died from the inflicted tortures, he had himself carried to the synagogue, where the congregation was assembled for the holy day services. He asked for the privilege of reciting a personal prayer, the *Unetaneh Tokef*. As he finished his hymn he expired. This hymn is recited during the High Holy Days services both as a memorial to the martyr and as an example for emulation by the worshipers.

Penitential Prayers (*Tahanun*)

Also typical of medieval Hebrew poetry are the numerous penitential prayers which were composed during that period. A substantial prayer unit known as the *Tahanun* (Penitential Prayers) [31] came into being during the Middle Ages and has

* *See p. 125.*

since become part of the weekday services. The *Tahanun* prayers are recited immediately after the *Tefillah* of the morning and afternoon services. A longer *Tahanun* is recited on Monday and Thursday mornings.[32]

The *Tahanun* consists of a number of devotional supplications pleading for God's mercy and grace. On Monday and Thursday mornings the *Tahanun* is introduced by seven heart-rending elegies. They speak repeatedly of Israel's unending suffering, which, they say, are a just retribution for Israel's unfaithfulness to the covenant. Nonetheless, they plead for God's forgiveness. Underlying all these pleas is the abiding faith that the "living and everlasting God" will not forsake His people. He will surely save them from the hands of their enemies, for He is "a gracious and merciful God."

The shorter *Tahanun*, which is recited on the other weekdays, omits these seven elegies and starts with an introductory biblical verse. The Bible relates that the prophet Gad offered King David a choice of punishment for a grave sin that the king had committed. His punishment was to be either at the hands of man or God. The introductory words to the *Tahanun* are King David's reply to the prophet: "And David said unto Gad: 'I am in a great strait; let us fall now into the hand of the Lord; for His mercies are great; and let me not fall into the hand of man" (2 Sam. 24:14). The relevance of these words to the situation of the medieval Jews is obvious. If the Jews deserve punishment, let it not be at the hands of Crusaders or other human beings.

This opening verse is followed by a brief confession: "O Thou who art merciful and gracious, I have sinned before Thee. O Lord, full of mercy, have mercy upon me, and receive my supplications." This brief confession is followed by Psalms 6:2—"O Lord, rebuke me not in Thine anger."

The introductory verse, the confession, and the psalm are recited silently, in a sitting posture with the head resting on the arm, face downward, suggesting private weeping. This posture is derived from the ancient custom of prostration at prayer and "falling on the face." *

* *See p. 253.*

The *Tahanun* is completed with a touching piyut: *Shomer Yisroel* (O Guardian of Israel). The first verse of this prayer reads: "O Guardian of Israel, guard the remnant of Israel, and suffer not Israel to perish, who say, 'Hear, O Israel.' " On Mondays and Thursdays this concluding hymn is preceded by an additional piyut which contrasts Israel's suffering with its steadfastness: "Look from heaven and see how we have become a scorn and a derision among the nations; we are accounted as sheep brought to the slaughter, to be slain and destroyed, or to be smitten and reproached. Yet, despite all this, we have not forgotten Thy name; we beseech Thee, forget us not."

The recitation of the *Tahanun* prayers was originally optional. The congregational service used to be concluded with the recitation of the *Tefillah*. Only the more pious would stay on and recite additional prayers of a devotional nature. For a long time these prayers were in a fluid form, varying from locality to locality. It was only in the sixteenth century that the *Tahanun* assumed the fixed form in which we now find it in the *Siddur*. As more and more people emulated the pious, these prayers became a statutory part of the service and are now recited by everyone. The *Tahanun* is omitted only on semifestivals and on other days when it is not proper to recite such tearful supplications.

Effects of Persecution on the Religious Poetry

The religious poems produced in Central Europe during the Middle Ages were affected adversely by the prevailing climate of persecution. The Jewish poets of the Christian lands suffered from the stagnation that comes from cultural segregation and continued repression. Their poems were usually involved, their Hebrew was tortured by artificialities, and the contents of the piyutim were obscured by many biblical and rabbinic allusions.* Many profound religious sentiments and inspired poetic sparks were lost in the stylistic tangle.

To be sure, there were occasional contacts between the Jew-

* *See pp. 168 ff.*

ish and Christian cultures. There were even some Jewish troubadours and minnesingers. The finest of these was Susskind of Trimberg who, lute in hand, recited and sang his lyrical poems before the nobility. But he, too, bewailed the intolerance and prejudice of the time, which eventually drove him back into the seclusion of the ghetto. In one of his poems he laments his fate:

Full well they know the singer
Belongs to race accursed;
Sweet Minne *doth no longer*
Reward me as at first.
Be silent, then my lyre,
We sing 'fore lords in vain,
I'll leave the minstrels' choir,
And roam a Jew again.[33]

The medieval poets of the synagogue were numerous. In his classic work on the history of the Jewish liturgy Leopold Zunz counts over nine hundred authors who lived after the tenth century. Obviously it will serve no purpose to list even the best known of these poets, let alone discuss the various types of piyutim they wrote. This is too involved and intricate a subject for so brief and untechnical a presentation.

Church and Synagogue—Two Views

The medieval Church was confident of its victory over the synagogue, and it proudly expressed its hegemony and power in the decorative art of the period. The most boastful of these artistic presentations was a set of allegorical figures, such as those of the Strasbourg Cathedral, which present the Church and the synagogue in two contrasting statues. The Church is presented as a woman who stands erect with a crown on her head. In her right hand she holds the banner of the cross and in the left hand a chalice. In contrast, the synagogue is represented as a woman with head bent and eyes veiled. Its banner hangs on a broken staff, and in its left hand is a fragment of the Ten Commandments.

The allegory needs no commentary. Even the medieval Jews

would admit that there was a measure of truth in the allegorical figures. The Christian gospel, aided by the Crusader's lance, the inquisitor's auto-da-fé, and the mob's brutalities, made deep inroads into the ranks of the scattered and bedeviled Jewries of Christendom. It was obvious that the Church could afford to be proud and that the synagogue could only bow its head under the burden of persecution. But that the synagogue's eyes were veiled and its banner broken, that it held on to nothing more than a fragment of the Decalogue, the medieval Jews would firmly deny. On the contrary, they would insist that their eyes clearly saw the truth of Judaism and the falsehood of all other faiths. Their banner was far from broken. To be sure, it was not held up prominently because of the persecutions, but it was held in readiness to be unfurled when the Messiah would come and vindicate their sufferings in the sight of all the nations.

And above all the Jews held on to the complete revelation as contained in both the Written and the Oral Torahs. In the end, the Jews asserted, God will humble the proud and will raise up the lowly. Within the humble synagogue, it should be added, there was a wealth of piety and learning, which added to the Jew's conviction that the Church's power was only physical. In the realm of the spirit the synagogue was the Jew's citadel and his assurance of eternal life. In his spiritual fortress, the Jew ardently prayed for the advent of that glorious day when "the Lord [will] be One and His name one" (Zech. 14:9).

18 NEW INSTITUTIONS AND NEW PRAYERS

When God created man, said the rabbis, He blessed him with the gift of forgetfulness. Man was thus able to leave off mourning his dead and resume normal living. Thus it was that medieval Jews were able, during periods of relative calm, to return to normality and to thank God for the joys of life. There were births and marriages, festivals and anniversaries. These were celebrated with joy and occasionally with abandon. New customs and institutions of a happy character even came into being during those peaceful intervals.

The Bar Mitzvah Observance

One of the new institutions that had its origin in the Middle Ages is the celebration of a boy's thirteenth birthday, when he officially attains his legal and religious majority. The boy becomes a bar mitzvah, a person obliged to observe the religious duties of an Israelite.

The bar mitzvah observance as it is known today did not exist during biblical or rabbinic times. The concept of the thirteenth birthday as the date of attaining one's legal majority did exist during the rabbinic period, but it was purely a legal concept. As Solomon Schechter pointed out: "It was only in the times of the Rabbis, when Roman influence became prevalent in juristic matters at least, that the date of thirteen, or rather the *pubertas*, was fixed as giving the boy his majority." [1]

However, as a religious concept worthy of special observance in the synagogue, the bar mitzvah was unknown prior to the fourteenth century. The term *bar mitzvah* did not even exist. From the fourteenth century on, however, the bar mitzvah celebration became a permanent and festive part of the synagogue service. On the first Sabbath after his thirteenth birthday, the boy is called to the Torah. He is usually given the last aliyah so that he may also read the Haftarah.[2] After the service the parents usually celebrate this event as a joyous family occasion. In former times it was customary for the bar mitzvah to deliver a learned address before the invited guests. Then he received his presents. Thenceforth, the boy was required to wear tefillin during his weekday morning prayers, and he was counted into the minyan of ten men required for a congregational service. In modern times the learned discourse has generally been discontinued, but the festivities and the presents have more than compensated for the abandoned discourse.

The Torah Processions on Simhat Torah (Hakafot)

Another joyous institution that had its beginnings in the Middle Ages is the ceremony of hakafot, the processions with the scrolls of the Torah around the reader's desk on Simhat Torah.* This ritual was introduced in the sixteenth century and has gained momentum insofar as exuberance and gaiety are concerned.

The ceremony is altogether appropriate. On that day the annual cycle of Torah reading is completed and the new cycle is immediately begun. The last section of Deuteronomy is read and is followed by the reading of the first chapter of Genesis. A truly happy achievement for a "holy congregation" in Israel!

The ceremony of hakafot takes place during the evening service of Simhat Torah. The congregation is in a jubilant mood. Men, women, and children crowd around the reader's desk, where the processions with the scrolls take place. Everyone strains himself to kiss the Torah scrolls, or at least to touch each scroll as it is carried in the hakafot and then kiss the fingertips that touched the sacred scrolls. Every adult male is given an opportunity to march with a Torah in his arms. The children, too, participate in the hakafot. They carry flags with suitable illustrations and inscriptions. At least seven hakafot take place, each one accompanied by the chanting of a verse from the hymn *Elohei Ha-Ruhot Hoshiah Na* (God of all souls, save us). Singing and dancing follow each circuit.

In Israel the festival of Sukkot is concluded on the eighth day. Simhat Torah is therefore observed on Shemini Atzeret.† It is celebrated with gaiety and abandon. The observance usually bursts out of the confines of the synagogues, and gay processions with the Torah scrolls take place in the streets. The

* *See pp. 222–24.*
† *See pp. 205–206.*

scrolls are carried under improvised canopies and, like King David of old, the people sing and dance "with all [their] might" (2 Sam. 6:14). Tourists in Israel are usually amazed by the exuberance of these dancing processions. For the pious Jew, however, these acts of rejoicing with the Torah are acts of devotion and reverence, notwithstanding the exhilaration and high spirits that characterize the celebration.

Casting Away the Sins (Tashlik)

Another custom that had its origin in the Middle Ages and is still observed by many Jews is the symbolic self-purification from the contamination of sin. On the afternoon of the first day of Rosh Hashanah people gather near a river or some other body of water. They recite a number of prayers and then shake their garments and empty their pockets of crumbs of bread, which are thrown into the water. Thus they symbolically cast off their sins into the water, which is the symbol of purity.

In all probability the ceremony had its origin in ancient heathen acts of worship.[3] Among the Jews, however, it has assumed spiritual meaning. Through this ceremony the Jews express their yearning for forgiveness. The official rationalization of this practice is a verse in Micah: "And Thou wilt cast all their sins into the depths of the sea" (Micah 7:19). The name of the ceremony, tashlik, is derived from the initial word of this verse: *Ve-Tashlikh* (And Thou wilt cast).

The famous sixteenth century rabbi Moses Isserles gives this ceremony a highly rationalistic explanation. When the Jew goes for tashlik, he sees the waters and contemplates God, who created the mighty seas. These thoughts tend to awaken feelings of penitence, which lead to God's forgiveness of his sins. According to this interpretation it is the repentance that rids the people of their sins; the casting of the sins into the depths of the sea is a mere dramatization of the central theme of the Rosh Hashanah service.

In some cities it is difficult to observe the ceremony, because there are no rivers or lakes within walking distance. In the city of Jerusalem, for example, prior to the Six-Day War one would see groups gathered for the tashlik service near old houses where rainwater is still allowed to gather in underground pools during the rainy season. They would stand near the rusty, unused pumps and recite the tashlik service.[4]

The service consists of a number of penitential prayers and the three verses in Micah which contain God's promise to "cast all their sins into the depths of the sea" (Micah 7:18–20). The medieval mystics also introduced the recitation of the Thirteen Divine Attributes of mercy. (Exod. 34:6–7).*

The origin of the service took place no earlier than the fourteenth century. Since then the tashlik service has been widely observed, especially among the Jews of Eastern Europe. In modern times the ceremony has been on the decline. Some people have suspected the ceremony of superstitious roots. Others have denounced the custom on the grounds that it creates the impression among the common people that they have thrown their sins into the river and therefore need no further repentance or making of amends. Still others have abandoned the custom because in large cities it is often difficult to reach a body of water without violating the holy day. But the most prevalent reason is the modern drift from religious observance. The lengthy service in the synagogue on the morning of Rosh Hashanah amply satisfies the religious needs of most modern Jews.

The Sabbath Evening Parental Blessings

One of the most beautiful Jewish customs which had its beginnings in the Middle Ages is the blessing that parents bestow on their children on Friday evenings. Precedents for this custom are to be found in the biblical stories of the patriarchs. The classic example is Isaac's blessing, which he bestowed on the mother's favorite son, Jacob. Esau's heartrending cry: "Have you but one blessing, Father? Bless me too, Father!" (Gen. 27:38) has awakened sympathy throughout the centuries. In

* *See pp. 228–30.*

ancient days the paternal blessing was the most valuable part of one's heritage. A father or mother's blessing or curse was regarded as possessing divine power.

Directly related to the custom of blessing the children on Friday evenings is Jacob's blessing of Joseph's sons. "By you [said Jacob] shall Israel invoke blessings, saying: God make you like Ephraim and Manasseh" (Gen. 48:20). These words became the formula for the blessing of boys. Its equivalent for girls is "God make you like Sarah, Rebecca, Rachel, and Leah." These formulas are followed by the priestly blessing.*

Though the precedents of this custom go back to the biblical period, the custom itself is mentioned for the first time in a treatise on morals published in 1602 in which the author, Moses Henochs, discusses the education of children and says: "Before the children can walk they should be carried on Sabbaths and holidays to the father and mother to be blessed. After they are able to walk they shall go on their own accord . . . and shall incline their heads and receive the blessing."[5] In the seventeenth century this custom was widely observed throughout Europe. In the Jacob Emden prayer book originally published in the middle of the eighteenth century we also read that "it is the custom in Israel to bless the children on Sabbath eve after the services or upon entering the house."[6]

In our days this beautiful custom has suffered along with most traditional practices. The general laxity in religious observance has resulted in the transfer of many home observances to the synagogue, where the rabbi observes them for the congregation. But the rabbi's blessing at the conclusion of the Friday evening service is not even a pale substitute for the parent's blessing of his children. Unfortunately, this exquisitely sublime Jewish custom is for all practical purposes nonexistent in the American Jewish community.

Occasional Prayers

Prayers were in great demand in the Middle Ages. This accounts for the numerous collections of prayers published as

* *See p. 216.*

supplements to the *Siddur*. Some of these prayers found their way into the prayer book. A typical example is the *Tefillah Zakkah* (A Prayer of Purity), which used to be printed as an introduction to the Yom Kippur services and was read by the pious before the Kol Nidre service. Most of these special prayers, however, remained outside the official liturgy and were published separately for private use.

In these special prayer collections one could find prayers for almost any situation. Some of the prayers were of medieval origin, others go back to talmudic sources. The most important among the latter was the *Tefillat Ha-Derekh*, The Prayer for a Journey. The medieval Jew was not only frequently forced to wander forth in search of a new home, owing to expulsions and other intolerable conditions, but he also wandered about in search of bread for his family. And many a medieval Jew wandered from his home because he was engaged in international trade; some of his trips lasted several months and were fraught with grave dangers. Robbers lurked on the lonely roads and pirates roamed the seas. Many a traveler ended up in an unmarked grave or in a slave market, where his captors offered him for sale to the highest bidder. A prayer for the traveler was obviously called for, and the Talmud provided for this contingency:

> R. Jacob said in the name of R. Hisda: . . . Whoever sets forth on a journey should say the prayer for a journey. What is it?—'May it be Thy will, O Lord my God, to lead me forth in peace, and direct my steps in peace and uphold me in peace, and deliver me from the hand of every enemy and ambush by the way, and send a blessing on the works of my hands, and cause me to find grace, kindness, and mercy in Thy eyes and in the eyes of all who see me. Blessed [Praised] art Thou, O Lord, who hearkenest unto prayer.' [Ber. 29b].

To this talmudic prayer were added several suitable verses from the Bible and a number of psalms; together they formed the *Tefillat Ha-Derekh,* which is still widely used in modern travel, especially by plane.

In one collection [7] there was, among other useful prayers, one written by the famous scholar Nahmanides when he sailed for the Holy Land in 1267, a prayer that is recommended for all travelers by sea. Another prayer in this handy book is to be recited in time of epidemics. But the editor does not rely on the prayer alone, for he also included a medical prescription "from a great man" on the kinds of food to eat and prescribes rules of cleanliness and other practices which will ward off the plague. There is a prayer for one who is in prison, composed by Leon da Modena and worthy of that author's gifts.

Another special prayer that had its roots in the Talmud and was included in many of the medieval prayer collections was the prayer recited on the occasion of a self-imposed fast. Such fasts were not rare. Many a Jew indulged in frequent fasts—as frequent as twice weekly, on Mondays and Thursdays *—because of excessive piety or in expiation of sins. Such private fasts surely required some suitable prayers. For this contingency, too, the Talmud provided the core supplication, as we read:

> When R. Shesheth kept a fast, on concluding his prayer he added the following: Sovereign of the Universe, Thou knowest full well that in the time when the Temple was standing, if a man sinned he used to bring a sacrifice, and though all that was offered of it was its fat and blood, atonement was made for him therewith. Now I have kept a fast and my fat and my blood have diminished. May it be Thy will to account my fat and blood which have been diminished as if I had offered them before Thee on the altar, and do Thou favour me [Ber. 17a].

This prayer was augmented with additional supplications to meet the needs of those engaged in private fasts. These prayers were among the most frequently used during the Middle Ages.

In a mid-nineteenth century publication [8] we find personal prayers to be recited by members of a burial society, by a

* *See p. 70.*

learned man in behalf of those who support him, by physicians before treating their patients, by soldiers and sailors before battle, by matrimonial suitors, and by preachers, to enable them to deliver their sermons fluently and in a manner pleasing to their auditors.

There were also prayers for occasions that were not apt to occur frequently. Among these were prayers on the occasion of the coronation of a king, for the recovery of an ailing monarch, for peace or victory during a war. Not to be overlooked are the prayers composed for the benefit of pilgrims, to be recited upon reaching the Western Wall in Jerusalem or Mother Rachel's tomb in Bethelehem. Thus Rabbi Meshullam of Volterra reports on his itinerary: "On Wednesday, the 29th July, we reached the Holy City of Jerusalem, and when I saw its ruins, I rent my garments a hand breadth, and in the bitterness of my heart recited the appropriate prayer which I had in a small book." [9]

These "small books" were handy and useful. They were published in large quantities and in many editions. They supplemented the *Siddur* and were treasured by the medieval Jews almost as must as the *Siddur* itself.

Devotional Prayers in the Vernacular (Tehinnot)

In the later Middle Ages collections of devotional prayers in the Judeo-German vernacular began to appear. These were known as tehinnot (supplications) and were meant for the womenfolk. The authors of these prayers were often women who understood the religious needs of their sex. Thus one finds in these tehinnot prayers to be recited when baking the Sabbath bread, when putting on the Sabbath garments, before lighting the Sabbath candles, before taking the ritual bath, during pregnancy, before childbirth, when giving charity, and on similar occasions in the life of a Jewish woman. These tehinnot were written in a tearful and heartrending style, and the medieval Jewish women shed copious tears as they read them. Some of the menfolk ridiculed the women and their tehinnot, but the women paid no attention to the mocking of the men and lavished their affections and their tears on these prayers. The tehinnot evidently served a real religious need. The Jewish women lacked the education to comprehend the Hebrew prayers of the *Siddur;* they needed these devotional prayers in the vernacular. So they read their favorite tehinnot, they wept profusely, and they relieved their aching hearts of the fears and pains that were their lot in life.

In the long Jewish Middle Ages, which lasted until the end of the eighteenth century, prayers played a central role in the life of the Jew. The liturgies of the various religious observances and the occasional prayers composed for special contingencies were more than mere adjuncts of the Jew's normal life. They were intrinsic elements of life itself.

19
THE MYSTIC STREAM IN JEWISH LITURGY

Judaism teaches that a pious Jew experiences God's nearness whenever he performs a divine commandment. This mystic experience is especially discerned during worship. Since this experience is within reach of every person, it has been called "normal mysticism." [1] But there is another type of mysticism which only few can hope to experience. This type of mysticism is based on the assumption that there is a vast abyss between the infinite, eternal God and finite, mortal man, between the transcendent Creator of the universe and His earthbound human creature. But God has endowed man with a measure of intelligence, which enables him to penetrate to some extent the baffling mystery that surrounds him and to gain a glimpse of the divine reality. To achieve this mystic illumination requires self-discipline, concentration, and an unceasing search for the divine realities that are normally hidden from man.

Most men accept the mysteries that surround them and find a measure of peace and contentment, notwithstanding the darkness that envelops them. Not so the mystics. They find it impossible to live peacefully while the divine mystery is challenging them intellectually and emotionally. The mystics are therefore in constant search of a way to bridge the terrible abyss that separates them from the divine. They not only seek understanding of the divine mystery, but also they strive for direct and intimate communion with the Source of all reality. They are thus engaged in an unending search for the road that will enable them to traverse the frightening chasm which alienates them from the Essence of their very being. The means employed by the mystics have varied with different faiths and times. But prayer has invariably played a role in these mystic pursuits.

This type of Jewish mysticism has been called kabbala, a word that means tradition and implies that these mystic speculations are of ancient origin. The kabbala has engaged the minds of many great Jewish thinkers and philosophers. Among the students of Jewish mysticism there have also been a number of outstanding non-Jews, such as the famous scholar and humanist Pico della Mirandola, who became a serious student of the kabbala. He was thoroughly convinced that in it were profound truths, including the secrets of life itself. Similarly, the famous German humanist Johann Reuchlin was caught up with the kabbala and became a serious student of the Jewish mystic lore. It was through Reuchlin's kabbalistic studies that Jewish mysticism exerted an influence on the Protestant Reformation.

Some Aspects of Jewish Mysticism

Jewish mystics, as a rule, began their speculations with a firm assertion that God's revelation at Sinai is the starting point of divine knowledge. But, said the mystics, the Torah has more than one level of meaning. When studied superficially, the

Torah discloses only a small part of the divine truth; the deeper truths are revealed only to the initiated. The ordinary student sees the divine reality, as it were, through a thick veil. His vision is so limited that he is spiritually almost blind. But man can discipline himself through intensive study and prolonged meditation. He can thus reach an intellectual and emotional state which will enable him to catch a glimpse of what is behind the veil. In this state of mystic illumination, he may come to comprehend the essence of God's revelation. He may be able, as it were, to peel away the husk that envelops the kernel of reality. He may actually be able to peer directly at the inner mystery. The specific ways of achieving this mystic illumination, the descriptions of that mystic state, and the mysteries revealed to some of the initiates constitute the Jewish mystic lore, or the kabbala. These writings are all in veiled language which only the initiated can follow. They deal with such mysteries as the nature of the divine creative act, the composition of the heavenly hosts, and some of the guideposts on the road to the messianic era.

It should be noted that the kabbalists, despite their search for the esoteric or deeper meaning of God's revelation, did not deny the validity of both the Written and the Oral Torahs. While the mystics chose to concentrate on the search for the divine mysteries, they also accepted the Jewish way of life and remained integral parts of the Jewish community. True, there were some mystics who arrived at heretical conclusions in the course of their search for the deeper meaning of the Torah. These kabbalists, however, were the exceptions. On the whole, says Solomon Schechter, "the tendency of Jewish mysticism was in the direction of self-denial, which developed into an austere life and renunciation of all appetites as far as it was compatible with the spirit of the Torah which held always the right balance between the flesh and the spirit." [2]

Among those who did stray from the path of normative Judaism were those who tried not merely to comprehend the divine mysteries, but also to master the divine powers and to engage them for the achievement of certain momentous goals. The chief goal of these mystics was to hasten the coming of the Messiah and the redemption of the Jewish people from the unbearable sufferings of the exile. These preoccupations often proved pernicious. Not infrequently they led to disastrous messianic movements, which induced inflated anticipations followed by tragic disillusionments.

Another characteristic of Jewish mysticism has been its emphasis on the divine nature of the Hebrew tongue. For the kabbalists Hebrew is not merely a system of symbols by means of which ideas are communicated; it is the sacred bond between God and man. Hebrew was the means of God's revelation at Sinai. Through the utterance of Hebrew words the world was created. "Blessed be He who spoke and the world came into being," says the benediction that introduces the Verses of Praise.* And the words that were the medium of the divine creative act were, of course, in the holy tongue. There are, therefore, Hebrew words that contain within them special creative powers. Among these are words whose letters constitute the various names of God in their various combinations and permutations. The utterance of the right Hebrew words at the right time and under the proper conditions can release incalculable powers.

The Early Mystics and Their Impact on the Liturgy

Popular opinion notwithstanding, the kabbala is not a product of the Middle Ages. It is the outgrowth of a long historic process, the roots of which are to be found in the continuing and earnest Jewish search for the divine. The kabbala is the product of an ever-widening current of religious experience within Judaism going back to earliest times. Gershom G. Scholem sums up this essential fact:

> Kabbalah is not the name of a certain dogma or system, but rather the general term applied to a whole religious movement. This movement . . . has been going on from talmudic times to the present day. . . . It leads from Akiba [who lived in the second century]

* *See pp. 141–42.*

> to the late Rabbi Abraham Isaac Kook [of our own generation].[3]

Actually one finds a number of seminal mystic statements in the Bible. Thus the prophet Isaiah relates a mystic vision in which he

> saw the Lord sitting upon a throne high and lifted up, and His train filled the temple. Above Him stood the seraphim; each one had six wings: with twain he covered his face, and with twain he covered his feet, and with twain he did fly. And one called unto another, and said: Holy, holy, holy, is the Lord of hosts; / the whole earth is full of His glory [Isa. 6:1–3].

Similarly, the prophet Ezekiel saw "visions of God." In his mystic illuminations he saw "the appearance of the likeness of the glory of the Lord" (Ezek. 1:28), and he heard the voice of the heavenly host, calling: "Blessed be the glory of the Lord from His place" (Ezek. 3:12).

During the first century there were already a number of Jewish esoteric circles, some of them among the disciples of Rabbi Yohanan ben Zakkai.* There is a telling statement in the Mishnah which says: "Whosoever speculates upon four things it were better for him if he had not come into the world—what is above, what is beneath, what before, what after" (Hagiga 2:1). This admonition against mystic speculations proves that these speculations were occupying the minds of some people. But they were kept secret among the initiates, because mysticism was considered dangerous for people of unripe age and limited intelligence. According to a significant talmudic account, it can be inferred that these speculations were dangerous even for men who had attained maturity of age and intelligence. Thus we read in the Talmud:

> Our Rabbis taught: Four men entered the 'Garden' [of mystic speculation], namely, Ben Azzai and Ben Zoma, Aher [i.e., Elisha ben Abuyah], and Rabbi Akiba. . . . Ben Azzai cast a look and died. . . . Ben Zoma looked and became demented. . . . Aher

* *See pp. 80–83.*

> mutilated the shoots [i.e., he abandoned Judaism]. R. Akiba departed unhurt [Hag. 14b].

This talmudic testimony and a number of similar statements point to the presence of secret mystic circles that existed centuries before the Middle Ages.

The mystic experiences of the prophets Isaiah and Ezekiel baffled the early mystics no end. These mystics, who lived in Babylonia during the talmudic and geonic periods, searched for an understanding of the prophetic visions. In time they succeeded in seeing visions of their own. After lengthy ascetic preparations some of them achieved a state of ecstasy and saw heavenly visions which dealt with the "celestial mansions" (*hekhalot*), the divine "throne of glory" (*ma'aseh merkavah*) with its mysterious "wheels" (*ofanim*), and the hosts of heaven, such as the "fiery creatures" (*seraphim*) and the "holy creatures" (*hayot ha-kodesh*). All this is undoubtedly incomprehensible to the modern reader who was raised on rational and scientific thought. But it should be realized that these visions dealing with the celestial realms were real experiences and that they exerted a profound influence on Judaism. Especially important for us is the fact that these mystics influenced the liturgy of the synagogue and that their influence has survived to our day.

According to the early mystics the angels on high sing hymns of praise to the divine glory, as indicated in the visions of Isaiah and Ezekiel. It is altogether proper, said they, that similar hymns be sung by the congregation of Israel. The mystics, therefore, composed hymns to be sung in the synagogue, and some of these hymns have become part of the liturgy. These early mystic hymns tend to arouse a feeling of ecstasy rather than to stimulate thinking. They are devoid of the rational theology which is characteristic of the later kabbala. One of these early hymns which is still part of the Yom Kippur service is called "The Song of the Angels," or in Hebrew, *Ha-Aderet Veha-Emunah* (Excellence and Faithfulness). It is an acrostic piyut, listing alphabetically the praises that are due "to Him who lives forever." This refrain is repeated after every two words of praise. The repetition builds up to an emotional state, though it adds nothing to the hymn's central idea. Unlike the psalm, its structure does not develop. Its rhythm, however, produces a cadence, an emotion, and an ecstasy. It captures the feeling of God's majesty through the crescendo of repetitious praises. This hymn and others of its kind, says Gershom G. Scholem "reflect marvelously the religious mood of those who conceived them. They are, indeed, outstanding paradigms of what Rudolf Otto called 'numinous hymns.'"[4]

The early mystics' most important contribution to the liturgy is the prayer known as the Kedushah, or the Sanctification of God. (This significant addition to the service was discussed in an earlier chapter.*) Three times the Kedushah is recited in the daily morning service, and once again in the afternoon service. On Sabbaths and festivals the Kedushah is also recited in the Musaf *Tefillah*. And the congregation recites each Kedushah, especially the ones of the *Tefillah*, with much concentration.

The Central European Mystics and the Cult of the Prayer Book

As indicated above, the early mystics of Babylonia were obsessed with the celestial mysteries and introduced into the liturgy prayers attuned to the angelic choirs. The Central European mystics of the postgeonic times, however, concentrated on God's imminence and focused their energies on prayer, which assumes God's nearness to the suppliant. Through deep concentration at prayer, they believed, one can achieve great spiritual power and thereby affect the natural order of creation. One can, for example, exorcise evil spirits from the afflicted and restore these pitiful men and women to normal, healthful life. These Central European mystics, often called *Hasidei Ashkenaz*, the Hasidim of Germany, are not to be confused with the East European Hasidim of the seventeenth century, who have persisted to this

* *See pp. 134–37.*

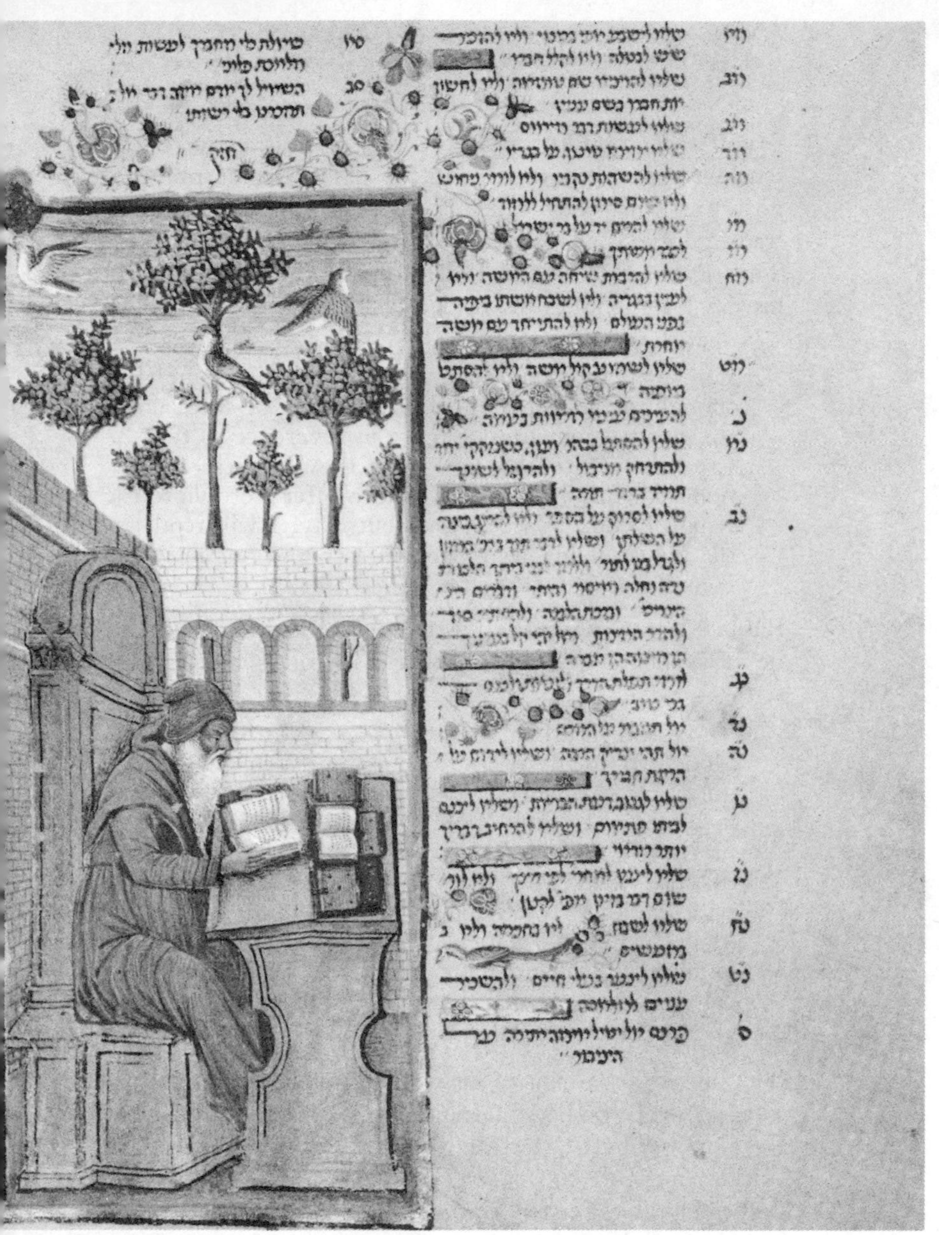

The Scholar, Rothschild ms. 24, 1475, The Israel Museum, Jerusalem. PHOTO: ALFRED BERNHEIM

day. The Central European or German mystics were not content with deep concentration, or kavvanah, at prayer; their goal was what they called *devekut*, a kind of spiritual self-transfiguration which induced a feeling of God's closeness. Thus Rabbi Eleazer ben Judah, one of the leading mystics of his day,[5] admonishes his readers:

> Fix thy mind upon the Almighty when thou standest before Him in prayer, and should some alien thought come to thee in thy devotions, be silent until thy heart is joined once more in reverence to thy Creator. Say to thyself whilst thou prayest, "How honored am I in being suffered to offer a crown to the King of Glory!—I, who am but clay; I will rend the bonds of my heart, and in awe and humility will I enter the Divine Gates."

Rabbi Eleazer speaks eloquently of God's imminence, which, he says, should lead one to pray with one's whole heart and soul:

> My son, hearken to my voice; love the Lord thy God. Let thy heart know Him, and declare His unity. Do thy work until eventide; but remember to love Him at *all* times. See, He stands before thee! He is thy Father, thy Master, thy Maker; submit thyself to Him. Ah, happy is he whose heart trembleth with the joy of God and is forever singing to its Maker! He bears patiently the divine yoke, he is humble and self-denying, he scorns the world's vain pleasures, he lives by his faith.[6]

The author of these words, it will be remembered, witnessed the cruel maltreatment of his wife and then her murder, as well as the murder of his children, at the hands of the Crusaders. He alone survived after the massacre.

In their effort to achieve total concentration during their devotions these Central European mystics came to regard the prayers as holy writ almost on a par with the Scriptures. To quote Marvin Lowenthal: "There grew up a cult of the prayer book, which fondled its every phrase, counted every word, played kabalistic games with the letters, and left a library of some seventy-three volumes of commentaries [on the prayer book]." [7] These mystics put great emphasis on the numerical value (gematria) of the words of a prayer and the relationship of these words to other words or phrases of similar value. An example of this type of kabbalistic activity is the discovery that Psalm 136, which is recited on Sabbath and festival mornings, contains the refrain "for His mercy endureth forever" twenty-six times, which corresponds to the numerical value of the Tetragrammaton. To the medieval mystics this was a most important discovery. Since it bestowed on this psalm transcendent significance in the prayer ritual, the congregation always rises for the recitation of Psalm 136.

A similarly important mystic revelation was the fact that Psalm 67 consisted of seven verses and a total of forty-nine words. This corresponded to the counting of the omer between Passover and the Feast of Weeks, that is, seven weeks or a total of forty-nine days.* There was evidently a correlation between this psalm and the omer period. The kabbalists therefore introduced the reading of this psalm during the counting of the omer.

Similarly, the mystics found that the congregational response during the recital of the Kaddish,† "Let His great name be blessed forever and to all eternity," contains in its Aramaic formulation seven words composed of twenty-eight letters. This corresponds to the number of words and letters in the first verse of the Bible. This, the mystics said, is the reason why the Talmud attaches great importance to the utterance of this response (Ber. 57a). One who responds to the Kaddish with these words becomes, as it were, God's partner in the creation of the world, which is the theme of the first verse in the Scriptures.[8]

The mystics of Central European Jewry weighed and counted the words of the prayers. The more difficult or complicated a prayer, the more attention it received. All this seems strange to the modern reader. Yet these mystic activi-

* *See pp. 218–19.*
† *See pp. 153 ff.*

ties engaged the greatest minds of medieval Jewry. One of the beneficent results of these word games was the standardization of the prayer book. By counting the words and letters of a prayer to discover its hidden meanings, the mystics established the prayer's exact formulation and precluded any tampering with it. Any change, accidental or deliberate, would disturb the established count and would immediately reveal that an error had crept into the text.

The central figure of the *Hasidei Ashkenaz* was Rabbi Judah He-Hasid.[9] His *Sefer Hassidim* (Book of the Pious), which we have quoted on several occasions, is one of the classics of that period. Its lofty ethical ideals have been a source of inspiration to the Jewish people,[10] and its kabbalistic teachings have been a source of frustration to the uninitiated. The book lacks orderly arrangement and is replete with superstitious beliefs, which are characteristic of both the author's time and his place of residence.

Another outstanding personality of this school of mystics was a disciple of Judah He-Hasid, Rabbi Eleazer ben Judah, quoted above.* Both master and disciple were noteworthy liturgic poets and contributed a number of piyutim to the prayer book. It was Judah He-Hasid who wrote the lovely hymn *Shir Ha-Kavod*, The Hymn of Glory, which is chanted in many congregations as a fitting conclusion to the Sabbath morning service. This hymn, popularly known by its initial words, *An'im Zemirot* (I will chant sweet hymns), clearly reflects the author's mystic bent, as can be seen from the initial couplets of the hymn:

I will chant sweet hymns and compose songs;
For my soul panteth after Thee.

My soul hath longed to be beneath the shadow of
Thy hand,
To know all Thy secret mysteries.

Even whilst I speak of Thy glory,
My heart yearneth for Thy love.

* *See p. 482.*

Therefore will I speak glorious things of Thee,
And will honor Thy name with songs of love.

I will declare Thy glory, though I have not seen Thee;
Under images will I describe Thee, though I have not known Thee.

By the hand of Thy prophets, in the mystic utterance of Thy servants,
Thou hast imaged forth the grandeur and the glory of Thy majesty.[11]

The *Hasidei Ashkenaz* did not build any sophisticated kabbalistic systems on the mystic hints they discovered in the prayer book. It was sufficient for them to discover that certain prayers contained mysteries. The building of a quasi-philosophical structure was the preoccupation of the kabbalists in Spain, whose intellectual tradition equipped them for greater mystic feats.

The Zohar (The Book of Splendor)

The Spanish Jewish community produced what has been called the golden era of Jewish history. Its scholars, poets, and philosophers left a rich literary heritage for the Jewish people. The personalities of Solomon Ibn Gabirol, Judah Halevi, Abraham and Moses Ibn Ezra, and Moses Maimonides still stand out as the shining stars of the Jewish Middle Ages. But as the Christians gradually reconquered the Iberian Peninsula the atmosphere became increasingly unfavorable to enlightened cultural activity, and mysticism became a dominant preoccupation of Spanish Jewry. The growth of mysticism was also helped by the realization on the part of many Jewish religious leaders that the rationalism of the previous centuries had brought with it defections from the faith. The rationalism of the golden era therefore declined, and mysticism engaged some of the best minds of Spanish Jewry.

The mysticism of the Spanish Jews was intellectual and quasi-philosophical. It concerned itself with a number of classic philosophical problems: How is it possible for the transcendent, infinite God to become imminent and to communicate with finite creatures? How can the spiritual God create a material world? How can the unknowable God become the Creator of the knowable world? How can God, the perfect, create an imperfect world?

Toward the end of the thirteenth century a mystic work known as *The Zohar* (The Book of Splendor) appeared in Spain. Its fame spread rapidly, and it soon overshadowed all the kabbalistic writings in circulation among the mystics. In time it rose to such eminence that it ranked as a central authority in Judaism, virtually on a par with the Bible and the Talmud.

The Zohar was written in a pseudoepigraphic style. It is presumably the work of Rabbi Simeon ben Yohai, a second century mishnaic teacher. The mystic writers often assigned their writings to personalities of biblical or talmudic fame, so that they might be readily accepted as authoritative. This was not regarded as fraud—it was a means of getting a hearing.

The style of *The Zohar* is midrashic and homiletic in its organization. Rabbi Simeon wanders about with his disciples and discourses with them each portion of the Torah. *The Zohar* may be described, therefore, as a mystical Midrash on the Pentateuch and a couple of other biblical books. It is not a running Midrash on the Bible. It wanders from text to text utilizing any verse that is suitable for the mystic thoughts propounded in the discussion. The homiletic method is in line with Jewish scholarly tradition. The language of *The Zohar* —Aramaic—is in line with the scholarly tradition of the rabbis too. All this added to the work's wide acceptance as a genuine classic of the mishnaic time.[12]

The author's purpose seems to have been at least in part to stem the dangerous rationalism of his day, which was leading some Jews to abandon the traditions of Judaism. His mystical Midrash, he hoped, would lead to a deeper understanding of the Torah and thus preserve the Jewish faith in God and His revelation.

The book was launched in the 1380s by a kabbalist, Moses de Leon, who is generally assumed to have been its author.

The book was an immediate success. It soon reached many Jewish communities beyond the borders of Spain and exerted a profound influence on Jewish thought and life far beyond the author's anticipations.

The kabbalists saw in every word of the Torah an overt and a covert meaning. For the kabbalists the hidden meaning is the essence. Among these are the divine names which are embedded in the biblical texts. Those divine names are not only the keys to deep mysteries but they also contain great forces, both creative and destructive.

Creation, revelation, and the messianic era are among the great mysteries that engaged the minds of the kabbalists. The messianic era is conceived of in *The Zohar* as the time when the gulf between God and His creation will be bridged, when the divine unity will be perfected and restored to its original state before the sin of Adam. Originally, the kabbalists claimed, man was God-like, but sin polluted man's purity and created a gulf between God and man. In the messianic era the spiritual unity of heaven and earth will be restored.

One of the mysteries that plays an important role in *The Zohar* is that of sex. Sexual union is seen as the joining of the active and passive forces in life, a principle which the kabbalists applied universally, even to the divine Essence. The Shekinah, the divine imminence, is often spoken of as the Princess, the Matron, or the Bride, The sexual imagery which is frequently used in *The Zohar* brought forth the fiercest opposition of many talmudists and philosophers. Yet this strange concept spread and took root even among the masses.

The kabbalists were also troubled by the eternal question: *Unde malum*? (Whence comes evil?). Since the kabbalists accepted the reality of evil, they were disturbed by the problem of its source. Pain, suffering, moral wrong, and sin itself must have their source in God. But how can evil emanate from the Source of all goodness and purity? One of the answers given in *The Zohar* is the principle of *kelipah*, literally "bark" (of a tree). Adam's sin generated the *kelipah*, which became part of the divine essence, and man's continued sinning activates the *kelipah*, the source of evil. The mystery of the *kelipah* occupied much of the mystics' attention. But in the messianic era, they said, the *kelipah* will disappear. Man will not sin anymore, and God's kingdom will be established—a kingdom without sin and suffering, without evil and corruption.

The intense concentration of the kabbala on the problems we have mentioned and on many other problems replaced the intellectual discipline of the Talmud. The frenzied acclaim of *The Zohar* drowned out the distress of those who clung to the rabbinic texts and to a rational view of Judaism. Superstitions and profound insights, dull probings for mystic secrets and poetic gems are all commingled in *The Zohar*. It is not surprising that these mystic activities also affected the liturgy. What is surprising is that some of these kabbalistic influences are still part of the *Siddur*.

Before examining the mystic stream in the synagogue liturgy, one more school of kabbalists will be mentioned. This school is known as the Lurianic school of kabbalists, so named after its founder, Rabbi Isaac Luria, who lived in Safed during the sixteenth century.

The Golden Age of Kabbalism

The year 1391 was the turning point of Spanish Jewish history. In that year a wave of massacres engulfed the Jews of Spain. Like a plague it spread from city to city and from town to town. Tens of thousands of Jews were slaughtered, and even larger numbers accepted baptism in exchange for their lives. Thus started the tragic history of the Marranos, the secret Jews of Spain. A century later, in the year 1492, the remnants of Spanish Jewry were expelled from Spain. A large number of them perished during their wanderings in search of new homes, and those who survived settled in several countries which opened their doors to them. These countries were amply rewarded because the Spanish Jews brought with them skills and experiences which stimulated trade and learning.

The medieval persecutions and expulsions had a profound

effect on the Jews. The catastrophes in Spain and in Central Europe turned the Jews increasingly to mysticism. While the kabbalists of the preexpulsion period were an elect group, preoccupied with the mysteries of the divine, the postexpulsion kabbalists concentrated on the process of hastening the arrival of the Messiah. They were concerned not so much with the mystery of the creation as with the process of bringing about redemption to Israel. The new trend which was initiated under the shock of intolerable persecutions grew and reached its peak among the kabbalists of the city of Safed, which had become the center of Jewish mysticism. The kabbalistic circles of Safed gave birth to the new kabbala.

The new kabbala ceased to be the concern of small esoteric circles. *The Zohar*, the people were informed, promised that the Messiah would come if a single Jewish community would repent wholeheartedly. Hence there were attempts to whip up passionate remorse in whole communities. Organized group action, rather than secluded individual meditation, became the accepted kabbalistic process. This kabbalistic propaganda spread the mystic doctrines among the masses, and the new kabbala captured the heart of almost every Jew. The basic doctrines of the kabbala, in rudimentary form, thus became the religious outlook of the average Jew.

Rabbi Isaac Luria and His Disciples

The central figure of the new mystic movement was Rabbi Isaac Luria, who exerted a powerful influence on his disciples. After Luria's death his disciples circulated many legendary accounts of his life, and his fame became worldwide.

Isaac Luria was born in Egypt in 1534 and spent his youth mastering the kabbalistic teachings of his day. In 1569 he arrived in Safed, where he developed his kabbalistic thinking. When Luria died in 1572 at the age of thirty-eight, he left practically no literary legacy. His stay in Safed lasted only three years. But his disciples idolized him and referred to him as *Ha-Ari,* the Lion. He left some commentaries to parts of *The Zohar* and a number of mystical hymns for the Sabbath meals which are still part of the liturgy. His literary legacy is too meager to be a reliable guide to his kabbalistic system. But his disciples recorded and published his conversations with them. One of these disciples, Rabbi Hayim Vital, (1543–1620), published the Lurianic doctrines in a large work entitled *Etz Hayim* (A Tree of Life). Luria's personal traits were also recorded by his disciples in great detail. His personality is thus known despite the many legends that have grown up about him. We know that he was an extreme visionary. He saw souls everywhere, even in inanimate objects, and he insisted that one could communicate with these souls.

His teachings, though kept secret among his immediate disciples, spread and dominated the kabbalistic thinking of the seventeenth century and thereafter. The speculative thinking of the Lurianic school is too complex for a brief summary. However, a few of its doctrines will be mentioned because of their direct bearing on the liturgy.

One of the central doctrines is known as tikkun (literally, "mending") the damaged process of creation. This concept is highly anthropomorphic. But so are many other kabbalistic speculations about God. The doctrine of tikkun claims that Adam was not merely the first human being; he was the soul of all mankind, and his soul is diffused in humanity. When Adam sinned, his soul—and therefore the whole world of purity—collapsed and mingled with the world of *kelipot* (outer shells), or the material essences of life. However, man's actions can not only restore his own soul, but can help in the tikkun of the whole world. Every time one sins, the cosmic process of tikkun is retarded or even reversed. Good deeds accompanied with proper intention help to unravel this admixture of the spiritual and material and advance the process of tikkun. When tikkun has been achieved, the Messiah will come.

Prayer occupies a central position among the good deeds that can advance this cosmic process. But prayer without kavvanah (intention) is worthless. Kavvanah, however, is not mere concentration on one's supplications; it now assumed a new meaning. When the kabbalists spoke of kavvanah they had in mind mystical intention. Therefore they recited a formula before each prayer, declaring that the prayer was being recited "for the sake of uniting the Holy One, blessed be He, and His Shekinah . . . and to unite the mystic letters of the Tetragrammaton in complete unity."

Prayer was thus transformed. It became not just an outpouring of one's heart or an expression of praise and thanksgiving to God for His many mercies. Each prayer became a mystical weapon with infinite power. New prayers were composed containing divine names (*shemot*) with powers against the evil forces that impede the Messiah's arrival. The prayers were widely accepted and devoutly used. But the power latent in these divine names were not released merely by uttering them. One had to know how, when, and where to pray. And the worshiper had to be the proper instrument for the release of these mystic powers.

The gulf between mysticism and magic narrowed, since mystical prayer with the proper kavvanah had become a potential means of influencing God. The wearing of amulets and charms with mystic inscriptions for prophylactic purposes became a widespread practice. Their popularity grew with each tale of their marvelous efficacy. Kabbalistic charms, it was related, had saved whole communities from imminent destruction, halted deadly plagues, and restored life to corpses. Generally speaking, the kabbalists did not concentrate on this aspect of mysticism, but neither did they deny the efficacy of these charms.

By the seventeenth century the Lurianic kabbala dominated Jewish life. "The lurianic Kabbalah," says Gershom G. Scholem, "was the last religious movement in Judaism, the influence of which became preponderant among all sections of the Jewish people in every country of the disapora, without exception." [13] Its doctrines, such as that of gilgul, or the transmigration of souls, and the omnipresence of ghosts, disembodied souls, and other spirits, became the religious baggage of most Jews. And it was generally believed that anyone who knew the secret of the *Shem Ha-Meforash*, the ineffable name of God, could perform miracles. Such a person could cure the sick, fend off evil spirits, and even bring the Messiah.

With the intensification of persecution the search for the

Shem Ha-Meforash assumed paramount importance. The kabbalists became increasingly preoccupied with the complicated combinations, permutations, and letter substitutions that make up the various divine names. Some mystics reputedly succeeded and achieved great power; they actually performed miracles. So went the reports. But the ultimate goal was to force God's hand, so to speak, and bring the Messiah to redeem Israel.

As we have said, the Lurianic school stressed the principle of tikkun, the consummation of which was the coming of the Messiah. When the divine holy name, which was torn apart through Adam's sin, is restored to unity, the exile will come to an end. The redemption of the Jews, personal and national, will be ushered in. However, the Messiah's arrival will be accompanied by a catastrophic eruption. The expected eruption actually came. It came in the mid-seventeenth century in the form of the tragic Sabbatian movement. The defection to Islam of Sabbatai Zevi, the proclaimed Messiah, brought with it such painful disillusionment that it halted the wild speculations of the mystics.

The impact of the Lurianic kabbala on the liturgy was impressive and enduring. Many new prayers came into use, and a number of new institutions with kabbalistic liturgies sprang up and have remained part of the synagogue tradition. However, before we focus attention on these contributions to the liturgy a brief digression on the nature of mystic prayer as developed among the kabbalists of the Lurianic school will prove profitable.

Kabbalistic Prayer Books

In addition to enriching the *Siddur* with prayers and hymns of superb quality, the kabbalists took the ultimate step of transforming all prayer into an esoteric exercise and the whole *Siddur* into a kabbalistic tract. The central objective of prayer was to effect the union of the Shekinah and the Holy One, blessed be He, or to restore the divine perfection that was damaged by sin. The process of prayer consisted of concentration, or kavvanah, on the esoteric significance of each prayer and especially on the divine names in it. This kind of kavvanah, said the kabbalists, can bring unity into the divine essence and thus achieve the redemption of Israel. In order that the mystic may be ever aware of this central aim and properly apply mystic kavvanah to his prayers, each prayer was preceded by preparatory introductions. From the point of view of religious inwardness and piety, this kabbalistic use of kavvanah represents a considerable decline in the concept as used in the Talmud and in the Jewish philosophical and ethical literature of the Middle Ages.* Instead of being a pious concentration on prayer, a pouring out of one's heart before God, kavvanah was turned into a concentration on mystic intentions that aimed at affecting the cosmic order and thus insuring divine aid.

Kabbalists became increasingly absorbed in diverse kavvanot. They arranged each prayer according to involved mystic formulas and added to each prayer elaborate commentaries of a most abstruse nature. Only the initiated could begin to understand the involved thoughts that were to accompany each phrase and each word of every prayer. The traditional prayers were not altered in the least. But they were infused with occult significance of a most obscure nature. This process naturally led to the publication of special prayer books for the exclusive use of the mystics.

The most important of these kabbalistic prayer books was published by Rabbi Hayim Vital, the leading disciple of Rabbi Isaac Luria. The *Siddur* was widely accepted because it was reportedly the work of the master kabbalist himself, who wrote it under the direct instruction of his mentor, the prophet Elijah. In addition, its title page assured everyone who prayed according to this rite that "his prayer will not return empty-handed; it will ascend to the 'Ancient of Days,' and may bring salvation to the whole exiled community, and may speed the coming of the Messiah and the gathering of our scattered people to His holy place." [14]

The *Siddur Ha-Ari*, as this kabbalistic prayer book is called, generally follows the Sephardic rite and is accompanied by an

* *See pp. 24–25.*

extensive running commentary, which guides the worshiper in the concentration of his thoughts as he utters each prayer. The commentary is a thoroughly esoteric text, strictly for the initiates. It presupposes a knowledge of the Lurianic kabbala. The principles of the *Siddur Ha-Ari* were further developed in subsequent prayer books, and the mystic concentrations were carried to such extremes that the kavvanot, the concentrations, indicated in the commentaries totally eclipsed the prayers themselves. The commentary on the *Shema*, for example, directs the worshiper to prolong the articulation of the word *Ehad* (One) in order to concentrate on the union of the Tetragrammaton and the word *Adonai* (the Lord); so that they become a single divine name.[15] In one kabbalistic prayer book the simple hymn *Ein Kelohenu* is made into a vehicle for major kabbalistic doctrines, requiring deep concentration on the esoteric meanings hidden in the simple text. In the four synonyms for God used in the jinglelike verses the kabbalists saw weighty hints regarding the mystery of creation. The hymn reads:

> *There is none like our God. There is none like our Lord. There is none like our King. There is none like our Savior.*
>
> *Who is like our God? Who is like our Lord? Who is like our King? Who is like our Savior?*

The four synonyms, said the kabbalists, refer to the four divine powers involved in the process of creation. The worshiper is to concentrate on these forces during the recitation or the chanting of this hymn. By properly concentrating on these four divine creative forces, the worshiper contributes to the ultimate goal of mystic prayer, as defined above.[16]

Kabbalistic Influences on the *Siddur*

The kabbalists not only transformed their own prayer into a mystic ritual requiring deep concentration on various aspects of their esoteric system, but also influenced the official liturgy of the synagogue. Although they did not alter the traditional prayers, they read into them many esoteric doctrines. These new mystic meanings gained wide acceptance even among the uninitiated. They penetrated the liturgy with hardly any resistance.

Mystic Meditations

In order to direct the worshiper's thoughts to the "real" meaning of the prayers, the kabbalists provided introductory meditations, especially before the various rituals of the liturgy. Thus we find an introductory prayer which is still recited before putting on the prayer shawl for the morning service: "Even as I cover myself with the tallit in this world, so may my soul deserve to be clothed with a beauteous tallit in the world to come in the Garden of Eden. Amen." The kabbalistic content of this prayer is unmistakable. Its mystical symbolism of the soul wrapped in a tallit in the world to come survived even after the modernists had applied their fine comb to the prayer book and eliminated almost all the kabbalistic elements.

While wrapping oneself in the tallit one recites four biblical verses:

How precious is Thy lovingkindness, O God!
And the children of men take refuge in the shadow of Thy wings.
They are abundantly satisfied with the fatness of Thy house;
And Thou makest them drink of the river of Thy pleasures.
For with Thee is the fountain of life;
In Thy light do we see light.
O continue Thy lovingkindness unto them that know Thee;
And Thy righteousness to the upright in heart [*Ps. 36:8–11*].

And while putting on the tefillin two biblical verses are recited:

And I will betroth thee unto Me forever;
Yea, I will betroth thee unto Me in righteousness and in justice,

And in lovingkindness, and in compassion.
And I will betroth thee unto Me in faithfulness;
And thou shalt know the Lord [*Hos. 2:21–22*].

The selections are obviously not kabbalistic compositions. But the mystics saw in the biblical figures of speech kabbalistic hints, such as taking "refuge in the shadow of God's wings," "the fountain of life," "them that know Thee," and of course the obvious kabbalistic doctrine of the "betrothal" of God to His "bride," Israel. These verses were introduced into the rituals of putting on the tallit and tefillin by a seventeenth century kabbalist, Rabbi Nathan Shapira, and they are still part of the ritual.

Most of the introductory meditations initiated by the kabbalists do not rely on mystic hints. They speak clearly of the central goal of the prayer—"to effect the union of the Holy One, blessed be He, and the Shekinah." Thus the meditation read before putting on the tallit starts off with this typical declaration:

> I am hereby ready to put on the fringed tallit in accordance with the halakah (Law) as the Lord our God commanded us in His holy Torah . . . in order to effect the union of the Holy One, blessed be He, and the Shekinah in reverence and love . . . and to unite the first two letters and the last two letters of the Tetragrammaton in a complete union.

Most modern prayer books have eliminated this meditation, along with most other mystic prayers. The Sephardim, however, still use them. Indeed, no modern censorship has been applied to the Sephardic prayer book.[17] It is therefore replete with mystic symbolism and kabbalistic prayers.

Kabbalistic meditations penetrated into the services of the entire prayer cycle. Thus we find a mystic meditation before the sounding of the shofar * during the Rosh Hashanah services. In addition to the usual formula indicating that the intention of the ritual is to "effect the union of the Holy One,

* *See pp. 237–40.*

blessed be He, and the Shekinah," there is an allusion to the concept of a divine court with a celestial "district attorney" in the person of Satan. When the shofar is sounded, its shrill sounds ascend to heaven and confuse Satan, thus permitting God's attibute of mercy to prevail.[18] This mystic concept is spelled out in the acrostic of the biblical verses recited on that occasion.[19] The acrostic reads *Kra Satan* (Destroy Satan).

Still another example of the kabbalistic penetration into the yearly cycle of the synagogue prayers is the practice of reciting the Thirteen Divine Attributes before taking the Torah from the ark during the major festivals. This is followed by a silent prayer: "O Lord of the universe, fulfill for good the desires of our heart." Both the recital of the Thirteen Divine Attributes and the prayer after it are of kabbalistic origin. Their source is a seventeenth century kabbalistic work, entitled *Sha'arey Tzion* (The Gates of Zion) by Nathan Hannover. Because the prayer aroused opposition on the part of the modernists, some modern prayer books omit the prayer, though they retain the Thirteen Divine Attributes. The Sephardic prayer books, of course, contain the full prayer with all its kabbalistic formulas.

Kabbalistic Prayers

"The mystics," says Israel Abrahams, "were the best prayer writers of the Middle Ages, and one would seek in vain for a Jewish Thomas a Kempis outside the ranks of the mystics."[20] The prayers composed by the kabbalists are often not recognized as mystic prayers, because the mystical ideas contained in them are usually stated in simple liturgic style, without recourse to the esoteric terminology of the kabbala. To be sure, this rendered their doctrines somewhat inexact. But the prayers benefited from the avoidance of controversy. They easily lent themselves to reinterpretation and thus became acceptable to all elements of the community. A good example is the kabbalistic prayer recited before the Torah is removed from the ark. This prayer is known by its initial words as *Brikh Shemei* (Blessed be the name). The prayer is taken verbatim from *The Zohar*[21] and was introduced into the liturgy by Rabbi

Isaac Luria. Its wide acceptance in modern synagogues, despite its kabbalistic origin, is due to its genuine liturgic quality, which is evident even in translation:

> Blessed be the name of the Sovereign of the universe. Blessed by Thy crown and Thy abiding-place. Let Thy favor rest with Thy people Israel forever: show them the redemption of Thy right hand in Thy holy temple. . . . Thou art He that feedeth and sustaineth all; Thou art He that ruleth over kings, for dominion is Thine.
>
> I am the servant of the Holy One, blessed be He, before whom and before whose glorious Torah I prostrate myself at all times: not in man do I put my trust, nor upon any angel do I rely, but upon the God of heaven, who is the God of truth, and whose Torah is truth, and whose prophets are prophets of truth, and who aboundeth in deeds of goodness and truth. In Him I put my trust, and unto His holy and glorious name I utter praises.
>
> May it be Thy will to open my heart unto Thy Torah, and to fulfill the wishes of my heart and of the hearts of all Thy people Israel for good, for life, and for peace. Amen.

Another kabbalistic prayer will be quoted in full because of its unique history: the transformation from an ordinary supplication for God's acceptance of the congregation's prayers to a mystic prayer with deep kabbalistic allusions. This prayer, usually called by its initial words, *Ana Be-Kho'ah*,[22] is altogether innocent of mystic concepts. It does not even deal with God or His attributes. In all probability it was written by a medieval reader in a Palestinian synagogue. But the kabbalists discovered that the prayer consists of forty-two words, which corresponds to a mystic divine name of forty-two letters.[23] Equally important is the attribution of the prayer to one of the early teachers of the Mishnah.[24] This attribution is as apocryphal as that of *The Zohar*. Be that as it may, the mystics discovered in this prayer deep kabbalistic allusions. The prayer reads:

> We beseech Thee, release Thy captive nation by the mighty strength of Thy right hand. Accept the joyful shout of Thy people; lift us and purify us, O revered God. O Thou mighty One, guard as the apple of Thine eye them that meditate upon Thy unity. Bless them; purify them; have mercy upon them; ever vouchsafe Thy righteousness unto them. O powerful and holy Being, in Thine abounding goodness lead Thy congregation. Thou who art the only and exalted God, turn unto Thy people, who are mindful of Thy holiness. Accept our prayer and hearken unto our cry, Thou who knowest all secrets.

The prayer became an integral part of every *Siddur*. Among the Sephardim it is still part of the daily services. In the modern Ashkenazic synagogues it has been restricted to the Yom Kippur service and to the ritual of counting the omer.* The reason for the prayer's association with the omer is again its forty-two words, which correspond to the number of days between the last day of Passover and Shavuot when the omer is counted at each evening service.

Table Hymns (Zemirot)

The medieval mystics produced a number of outstanding liturgic poets. Among the disciples of Isaac Luria were several poets whose compositions have survived the centuries and have remained part of the liturgy. Among their piyutim are a number of table hymns, generally known as zemirot.

As already mentioned, the kabbalists believed in the ubiquity of celestial and terrestrial spirits, many of which were friendly and helpful to man. On the Sabbath heavenly guests visited Jewish homes and participated in the holy joy that prevailed in the Jewish households. Thus the Talmud relates in the name of Rabbi Jose son of Rabbi Judah:

> Two ministering angels accompany man on the eve of the Sabbath from the synagogue to his home, one a good [angel] and one an evil [one]. And when he arrives home and finds the lamp burning,

* *See pp. 218–19.*

> the table laid and the couch [bed] covered with a spread, the good angel exclaims, "May it be even thus on another Sabbath [too]," and the evil angel unwillingly responds "amen." But if not [if everything is disorderly and gloomy], the evil angel exclaims, "May it be even thus on another Sabbath [too], and the good angel unwillingly responds, "amen" [Shab. 119b].

If angels come into one's home, they should be welcomed appropriately. The hymn *Shalom Aleichem* (Welcome unto You) is therefore sung upon entering the home on Friday evening to welcome the "angels of peace." During the meal it was considered proper to chant zemirot in honor of the spiritual guests. This practice was not invented by the medieval kabbalists, but they gave it a powerful impetus. The presence of spiritual guests was to them not just a figure of speech; the kabbalists literally sensed the presence of these guests. No wonder that most of the zemirot were composed by them.

Among the kabbalists whose zemirot are still sung in Jewish homes is the master kabbalist himself, Rabbi Isaac Luria, who composed three table hymns, one for each of the three Sabbath meals. These hymns reflect some of the author's doctrines. Thus God is spoken of as *Attika Kadisha*, the Holy Ancient One, a standard kabbalistic term. Notwithstanding their mystic content, these hymns are to be found in almost every prayer book of Eastern Jewry. But the most popular of Isaac Luria's table hymns is the one entitled *Yom Zeh Le-Yisroel* (This Day Is for Israel). The first stanza sets the mood of the table song—a mixture of spiritual and physical pleasure, a divine commandment coupled with bodily enjoyment:

This day is for Israel light and rejoicing,
A Sabbath of rest.

Thou badest us, standing assembled at Sinai,
That all the years through we should keep Thy behest
To set out a table full-laden, to honor
The Sabbath of rest.

This day is for Israel light and rejoicing,
A Sabbath of rest.

And the last stanza naturally deals with the messianic days when life will become one great Sabbath:

Restore us our shrine—O remember our ruin
And save now and comfort the sorely opprest
Now sitting at Sabbath, all singing and praising
The Sabbath of rest.

This day is for Israel light and rejoicing
A Sabbath of rest.[25]

Another liturgic poet belonging to the Safed circle of mystics was Israel Najara. He was a prolific writer. It is claimed that he composed 650 hymns. His best known is the table song *Yah Ribbon Olam* (Lord, Master of the Universe), which has remained a favorite among Jews everywhere.

Israel Abrahams speaks of these table hymns in ecstatic terms. He describes them as "the bridge between the human and the divine; they were at once serious and jocular; they were at once prayers and merry glees." [26]

In the sixteenth century, when the kabbala was generally accepted among the Jews, the practice of singing zemirot at each of the Sabbath meals became universal. And when the Sabbath was coming to an end special zemirot were sung in honor of the departing Queen Sabbath. The melodies for the zemirot were usually borrowed from folk songs, Jewish and non-Jewish alike.

"These table-songs," says Israel Abrahams, "belong entirely to the Middle Ages, and are all later than the tenth century. On Friday evenings in the winter, the family would remain for hours round the table, singing these curious but beautiful hymns." [27]

Welcoming the Sabbath

The best-known liturgic poet of the Safed circle of kabbalists is Solomon Alkabez, author of the hymn *Lekhah Dodi* (Come, My Friend). This hymn is the climax of the *Kabbalat Shabbat*, the prayer unit in which the congregation welcomes the Sabbath before the official Friday evening service.

In the sixteenth century Rabbi Isaac Luria and his disciples used to form a procession every Friday afternoon and go to the outskirts of Safed to receive the Sabbath Bride with song and praise. They recited psalms and sang hymns composed for the occasion. This mystic ceremony spread to other communities, where the Sabbath Bride was welcomed not in the fields, but in the synagogue immediately before the Friday evening service. In time the *Kabbalat Shabbat* was standardized to consist of six psalms, corresponding to the six days of the week,[28] and the hymn *Lekhah Dodi.* These are followed by the Sabbath psalm (92).

Alkabez composed the hymn *Lekhah Dodi* in 1529. In it the Sabbath is compared to a bride who is joyously welcomed by the community of Israel. The refrain which follows each verse exclaims: "Come, my friend, to meet the bride; / Let us welcome the presence of the Sabbath." The idea of welcoming the Sabbath as a bride is not original with the author. The Talmud relates that Rabbi Hanina used to exclaim on Fridays at sunset. " 'Come and let us go forth to welcome the queen Sabbath,' and Rabbi Jannai . . . exclaimed, 'Come, O bride, Come, O bride' "! (Shab. 119a). Nonetheless, the hymn "stands out as a strikingly original composition, fresh, fragrant, full of new charm," says Israel Abrahams.[29]

Moments of Divine Grace

With the spread of the Lurianic kabbala, a number of mystic practices became part of Jewish life. Among these none was as touching as that of the pious Jew rising at midnight to pray and weep over the destruction of the Temple and the exile of Israel from the Holy Land.

Midnight Vigils

The widespread practice of rising at midnight for special devotional prayers can be approached from a purely pious or a strictly mystic point of view. Thus the philosopher Bahya

Ibn Pakuda recommends midnight prayers because at night man is alone, removed from the worldly preoccupations and worries of the day, and is more apt to concentrate on his prayers. This rational approach was not adequate for the mystics. In the kabbala, the midnight hour is a time when the Almighty is especially attentive to prayers and is prone to be influenced if the worshiper knows how to pray and on what kabbalistic doctrines to concentrate. The mystics of Safed would therefore rise in the middle of the night and repair to the synagogue dressed in black. There they would seat themselves on the floor and read a special liturgy, the burden of which was mourning over the destruction of the Holy Temple and the dispersion of the Jewish people, and a confession of the sins of Israel which have been delaying the coming of the Messiah.

These midnight vigils proved contagious. They spread throughout the Diaspora, so that every Jewish community had a number of pious men who regularly rose for the midnight prayers. There are still some pious men who partake of midnight vigils and pray for the restoration of Israel and the rebuilding of the Holy Temple.

The institution of midnight prayer did not originate in sixteenth century Safed. Indeed it is mentioned in the Bible. The psalmist declares: "At midnight I will rise to give thanks unto Thee / Because of Thy righteous ordinances" (Ps. 119:62).[30] In the Talmud, too, there are a number of references to the midnight hour as a time suitable for prayer. In allusion to the verse just quoted, the rabbis say: "A harp was hanging above David's bed. As soon as midnight arrived, a North wind came and blew upon it and it played of itself. [David] arose immediately and studied the Torah till the break of dawn" (Ber. 3b). And a more telling talmudic statement says: "The night has three watches, and at each watch the Holy One, blessed be He, sits and [laments]: . . . Woe to the children, on account of whose sins I destroyed My house and burnt My temple and exiled them among the nations of the world!" (Ber. 3a). In the kabbalistic literature these and other poetic statements of the rabbis are literalized, and mystic doctrines are singled out for concentration during the midnight prayers.[31]

In the Middle Ages a whole liturgy known as *Tikkun Hatzot* (The Order of Midnight Prayers) was developed. It consists of a number of psalms and biblical verses which express Israel's grief over the destruction of the Holy Temple and the sufferings of the dispersed children of Israel. These readings are followed by several soul-stirring dirges and are concluded by a confession of sins and a study session. The piyutim of this service, says Solomon Schechter, "are mostly of a deep spiritual nature [and] of matchless beauty."[32] These prayers were always recited while sitting on the floor as a sign of mourning, and weeping invariably accompanied them.[33]

The Early Risers

It was also an ancient tradition for the pious to rise early and watch for the first rays of the sun, in order to synchronize their morning prayers with the sunrise. This ancient tradition probably antedates the talmudic period—the Bible hints at this practice several times. Thus the psalmist declares:

> *I rose early at dawn and cried;*
> *I hoped in Thy word.*
> *Mine eyes forestalled the night-watches,*
> *That I might meditate in Thy word* [*Ps. 119:147–8*].

In the Talmud there is a reference to the *vatikin* (the pious men of old) who used to start the *Tefillah* exactly at the break of day (Ber. 9b). One of the sages specifically enjoined that "it is a religious duty to pray with the first . . . appearance of the sun." In support of this injunction the psalmist is quoted: "They shall fear Thee while the sun [rises]; / And before the moon [rise] throughout all generations" (Ps. 72:5).[34]

The practice of synchronizing the morning prayers with the sunrise received a strong impetus from the kabbalists during the seventeenth and eighteenth centuries, and the number of early risers increased. Several collections of special prayers for the early risers were published. To this day there are societies of *vatikin* in Jerusalem who worship at sunrise. In order that the first benediction of the *Shema*—"who formest light and createst darkness"—should coincide with the first rays of the sun, these *vatikin* used to prepare annual tables of the sunrise based on observations taken from the Mount of Olives in Jerusalem. The number of early risers, however, never equaled that of the lonely individuals who rose regularly at midnight to mourn the destruction of the Holy Temple and the dispersion of the Jewish people.

Whole-Night Vigils

Yet another institution, consisting of whole-night vigils, was instituted by the medieval kabbalists and has survived to this day. The kabbalists felt that on the festival of Shavuot one should not merely observe the anniversary of the giving of the Torah at Mount Sinai; one should experience the receiving of the Torah. For such an experience one needed special preparation. Hence they instituted the practice of spending the whole night of Shavuot in the study of Torah. This is specifically recommended in *The Zohar*.[35]

A special regimen for this vigil was developed in the sixteenth century under the influence of Rabbi Isaac Luria. It is called *Tikkun Lel Shavuot* (The Ritual for the Night of Shavuot). It consists of excerpts from every portion of the Torah which are read in the synagogue during the annual cycle, plus excerpts from the Prophets and from each of the talmudic tractates. The scriptural selections consist of several verses from the beginning and from the end of each Torah portion, and from each of the other biblical books, and from each rabbinic tractate. This type of abbreviation is based on the theory that reading the beginning and the end of a Torah portion or a tractate is tantamount to reading the whole. Important biblical sections, such as the account of the creation, the Ten Commandments, and the *Shema*, are included in full. Added to this "anthology" of the Written and Oral Torahs are a number of selections from *The Zohar* and several prayers and piyutim built around the theme of the revelation at Sinai and the 613 commandments of the Torah.

Tikkun Lel Shavuot is still in practice in many Jewish communities. In Jerusalem hundreds of synagogues, both Ashkenazic and Sephardic, are lit up all night on Shavuot. In each synagogue there are circles of men who are preparing themselves, through the night-long study of Torah, for the privilege of receiving the Torah anew during the morning service.

Another whole-night vigil takes place on the seventh day of Sukkot, or Hoshana Rabba, on which the divine judgment initiated on Rosh Hashanah is concluded.* During the Middle Ages it was commonly believed that on the night of Hoshana Rabba the souls of the dead emerge from their graves and engage in prayer. It was also the common belief that anyone who did not see his shadow on that night would not live out the year. It is not surprising that it became customary to spend that night in prayer and study. In time the kabbalists developed a regular regimen known as *Tikkun Lel Hoshana Rabba* (The Ritual for the Night of Hoshana Rabba). It consisted of the reading of the Books of Deuteronomy and Psalms, as well as the biblical account of the creation, and selections from *The Zohar* and the Midrash. Special piyutim and penitential prayers *(selihot)* are read after each of the seven sections of the psalms. This vigil is not as widely observed as that of Shavuot but is practiced far more than is commonly suspected.

The Impact of the Kabbala on the *Siddur*

The mystics, especially those of the Lurianic school, left a lasting impression on the *Siddur*. Some of their prayers, especially those whose contents were not too obviously mystic, found a permanent place in the synagogue ritual, among them some of genuine poetic quality. To be sure, the modernists opposed the mystic intrusions into the liturgy, and they succeeded in eliminating most of the kabbalistic prayers. But even the fierce opposition of the modernists could not altogether free the liturgy from the mystic influences. The mystic prayers that have remained in the *Siddur* have been adequately reinterpreted, so that they do not clash with the rationalism of the modern age. The *Siddur* has thus emerged from the Middle Ages much the richer because of the kabbalists.

* *See pp. 219–20.*

20
THE LITURGY OF THE HASIDIM

In thc mid-eighteenth century a Jewish dissenting religious movement arose which has influenced Jewish life profoundly and is still flourishing in some Jewish communities. This movement, known as Hasidism, was in part a revolt against the rabbinic leadership of that day which overemphasized scholarship and, by implication, excluded the uneducated Jew from the religious experiences leading to communion with the divine.

Some Hasidic Doctrines

The Hasidim shifted the emphasis from the intellect to the emotions. "God craves for the heart of man" became a kind of Hasidic slogan. This emphasis had its roots in traditional Jewish teachings no less than the opponents' emphasis on the study of Torah. Indeed, these two emphases have always represented polar tensions in Judaism. Ideally the two should be in balance, but the overemphasis on scholarship brought about an imbalance which led to the creation of the dissenting movement. Needless to say, Hasidism led to a counter imbalance that was equally dangerous.

The new emphasis on the emotions appealed to the mass of poor Jews in Poland and southern Russia, whose learning was limited but whose piety was deep and genuine. The Hasidic movement took root and spread rapidly in the Polish provinces and in the Ukraine. From there it spread to other Russian provinces as well as Hungary and Romania.

The roots of Hasidism were planted deeply in the soil of mysticism, especially in the Lurianic kabbala. The latter had suffered a stunning blow during the preceding century. Its emphasis on bringing the Messiah by kabbalistic means had awakened in the hearts of the Jewish people powerful cravings for redemption and fervent anticipations of the imminent termination of the exile. But these overwhelming hopes ended tragically in the Sabbatian catastrophe when Sabbatai Zevi, the proclaimed "Messiah," apostatized to Islam. To be sure, he defended his apostasy on kabbalistic grounds—it was only a phase, he said, which the Messiah had to go through in order to fulfill his mission. But this did not convince the vast majority of the Jews. Their high anticipations were shattered and their disillusionment was heartbreaking. This severe blow to messianism did not extinguish the mystic flame which burned in the hearts of many pious Jews, however. These mystic yearnings for communion with the divine formed the fertile soil in which the Hasidic movement took root and flourished. Hasidic leaders leaned heavily on *The Zohar* and often quoted it in support of their teachings.

Hasidism was founded by the saintly Israel Baal Shem (Master of the Holy Name). His teachings stressed the mystic forces of true piety and the central importance of ecstasy *(hitlahavut)* in divine worship. God is to be found everywhere and can be reached by everyone. Indeed, God rejoices in receiving the penitent just as a father rejoices in the return of a wayward child. God's revelation is a continuing process. Through faith one can sense God's unending revelation. Faith is also the key to the recognition of God's imminence. While learning can lead only to a comprehension of the divine, faith can lead to a personal knowledge of God. And faith is open to all, to the learned and to the simple. What is equally important, man's piety is not judged in absolute terms but in accordance with his capabilities. The simple man or woman who serves God in a childish manner but with a whole heart is more precious to God than the learned man who serves God in a sophisticated manner but only with his lips.

These doctrines were expanded and elaborated by the disciples of Israel Baal Shem, and they proved to be as powerful a reaction to the rabbinic scholasticism of the eighteenth century as the kabbala had been to the rationalism of the Jewish Aristotelians of the thirteenth century.

In its early period the movement was virile. It produced a vast literature, much of it truly magnificent. Unlike the kabbala, Hasidic writings expressed themselves in epigrams and parables rather than the veiled, esoteric style of the earlier mystics. The new movement was revivalist in nature, seeking a mass following. The Hasidim therefore spoke to the people rather than to small circles of initiates. They popularized their mysticism by preserving those elements of the kabbala which appealed to the masses and passing over those elements that were abstruse and complicated. The focal effort of the movement was on achieving personal redemption or salvation. "Its early purposes," says Solomon Schechter, "were high, its doctrines fairly pure, its aspirations ideal and sublime." [1] It attracted numerous followers in whom it kindled great devotion to its leadership and its doctrines.

How to Pray

Prayer occupies a central position in the life of a Hasid. The motivation of prayer, said the Hasidim, is the love of God, and its aim is to bring the worshiper closer to the object of his love. To achieve this mystic goal of prayer one had to have faith in God's nearness and love. Prayer ignites one's religious fervor and keeps the flame of faith burning. Prayer provides the worshiper with the experience of God's nearness and goodness.

But prayer is not just a ritual; it must come from the heart and must be expressed with ardor and concentration, with enthusiasm *(hitlahavut)*. Each word of prayer requires concentration to the point of losing one's consciousness of the world about him and even of one's own corporeal existence. Mystic intoxication is a concomitant of true prayer. Israel Baal Shem is quoted as having said: "Let your worship and your service be a fresh miracle every day to you. Only such worship, performed from the heart, with enthusiasm, is acceptable." [2]

True prayer, said the Hasidim, does not depend on one's knowledge or wisdom. Depth of feeling is within the grasp of the simple and the ignorant no less than the learned and the wise. Even ignorance of the meaning of the words of prayer is no obstacle, because God looks to the heart. Many Hasidic stories deal with the prayers of the ignorant, the simple, and even the foolish, which were accepted by God because of their sincerity. One such story tells how an ignorant farmer boy was once overcome with an irresistible desire to pray during the Neilah * service of the Day of Atonement. But the boy did not know how to read the prayers. Suddenly he put his whistle to his lips and blew it with all his might. The congregation was shocked. The people were about to expel the offender from the synagogue when the Baal Shem joyfully congratulated the congregation and exclaimed: "God has opened the gates of prayer."

Also basic to the doctrine of Hasidism is the element of joy. One must serve God with gladness (Ps. 100:2). Mortification does not hallow life. Life is hallowed through the service of God, which must be joyful. Sadness is a negative, spiritually sterile quality which blocks the channels of fervor. Indeed, sorrow is a manifestation of one's disbelief in God's goodness and love. Joy, on the other hand, enables one to serve God with the whole heart, with ardor and ecstasy. The Bratzlaver Tzaddik therefore advised his followers: "If you feel no joy when you are beginning your prayers, compel yourself to be joyful, and real joy will follow. A joyful melody is a genuine aid." [3]

The Hasidic commitment to joy as a religious duty is not a hedonistic approach to life. The joy of the Hasid is derived from spiritual conviction and experience. His joy springs from doing God's will, which for the Hasid is a thrilling experience. Prayer must be uttered with joy as well as with fervor; song, therefore, played a crucial role in the Hasidic movement. This, of course, is not an innovation. Both Scriptures and the Talmud speak of song and joy as suitable media of worship. "O sing unto the Lord a new song," says the psalmist. "Sing unto the Lord, all the earth. Sing unto the Lord, bless His name" (Ps. 96:1–2). And the Talmud teaches: "One should not stand up to say *Tefillah* while immersed in sorrow"

* *See pp. 258–61.*

(Ber. 31a). The Hasidim, however, gave these teachings a new emphasis and made them into central doctrines of their movement.

Because the purpose of song was not to entertain but rather to rouse the spirit of joy and ecstasy, the Hasidim rebelled against the formal, concertlike performances of the hazanim, or cantors. The Hasidim refused to be a passive audience. So they did away with cantors altogether. To be sure, when they chose their readers they took into consideration the quality of their voices, but this was secondary to the qualifications of piety and ardor in their prayers.

Besides song, the Hasidim also regarded dancing as a potent stimulant to joyful prayer. Dancing, too, engenders enthusiasm and ecstasy in the service of God, so it was brought into the Hasidic service and became, along with the distinctive Hasidic chants, an intrinsic element of worship. In some Hasidic congregations no service is complete without the worshipers forming a circle around the reader's desk for a period of song and dance. A recent visitor in a Hasidic synagogue in Jerusalem reports what he witnessed:

> One of the elders began singing a quick little tune, "Sing to Him; rejoice in Him." A few voices joined the song. Soon everybody in the room, including the children, had formed a circle, a kind of chain with hands held in front and in back. This was the Bratzlaver dance I had heard about—a simple kind of quick step in the rhythm of the sprightly tune which all were now singing. . . . Both the singing and the dance were rather quiet. A few of the Hassidim had smiles on their faces, and others were simply relaxed, peaceful . . . [unlike] the hypnotically stimulated emotion worked up in the dance of other hassidic groups.[4]

Aids to Prayer

It will be recalled that the rabbis of the Talmud taught that prayer should be preceded by a period of preparation.* One

* *See pp. 28–29.*

must develop a proper frame of mind in order to pray with kavvanah. The Hasidim made this rabbinic teaching into an important doctrine of their movement. They insisted that one must spend considerable time and effort in order to be able to pray with one's heart. Contemplation, study of mystic texts, and ablutions are aids to divine service, as we read in a letter by a Hasidic leader to one of his followers:

> Arise before daylight and commune with thy God in solitude. . . . Confess your sins with a broken heart. Tear your heart into twelve pieces by considering how much anguish your sins have brought to the *Shekhinah,* and how you have lengthened its Exile. Devote, also, an hour during the day for communion with God in solitude. . . . Pray to the Lord that he may lead you on the pathway to truth, that you may no longer waste your days in unworthiness. . . . Beware of uttering a single word before your prayers, as your mind must be wholly engrossed in contemplation of God to whom you are about to offer prayer.[5]

The Hasidim therefore delayed the hour of worship in order to achieve a proper frame of mind, and it became their practice to pray at a late hour. This shocked their opponents. It constituted a flagrant breach of the ancient practice of praying at an early hour. But the Hasidim persisted in praying at a late hour, because they regarded the preparation as an indispensable precondition of true prayer.

More characteristic of Hasidic prayer is its ardor and enthusiasm, which the Hasidim regard as means of arousing the heart to the service of God. They insist that bodily movement and gesticulation during prayer arouse one's emotions and maintain one's state of concentration throughout the period of worship. One of the Hasidic leaders is quoted as having said: "If you see one praying, standing upright without emotion, know that he does not pray with thoughts inviolate and with a whole heart; his mind is not with God." [6] And Israel Baal Shem said:

> When a man is drowning in a river, and splashes about trying to pull himself out of the waters that are

> overwhelming him, those who see him will certainly not make fun of his splashing. So, when a man prays with gestures, there is no reason to make fun of him, for he is saving himself from the raging waters that come upon him to distract him from his praying.[7]

Hence the Hasidim have dispensed with formality and decorum during their services. Loud chanting and shouting have been the rule. Frantic movements of the body and constant agitation are the normal accompaniments of prayer. Clapping of hands, gesticulating, and crying out periodically are not simply acceptable expressions of one's rapture; they are necessary adjuncts of true prayer. Each Hasid concentrates on his own prayer and expresses his ardor in his own way. Each one sings with ecstasy his own chant. As he chants or shouts, he sways and see-saws, lurches and leaps, shakes his body and claps his hands. Some, in the fervor of their prayer, jump, while others "are rapt in a motionless ecstasy." To the outsider it all adds up to pandemonium. Not so to the Hasid. He is so immersed in his own prayers that he is completely unaware of the commotion about him. He has disciplined himself to concentrate on his own prayers so completely that he is oblivious to any chant or noise except his own. And he is convinced that God hears him individually, even as He hears everyone else individually, provided he prays with his whole heart.

Changes in the Liturgy

As the adherents of the new movement increased, they became bold enough to introduce not only external changes, such as the time and the manner of prayer, but also innovations in the liturgy itself. The boldest breach in the tradition was the daring changeover from the Ashkenazic to the Sephardic ritual.* Although the Hasidim retained many Ashkenazic elements in their prayers, they took over enough Sephardic characteristics to create a wide gulf in the ranks of East European Jewry. To this day prayer books published for use by East European Jews and for their offspring all over the

* *See pp. 375–78.*

world are distinguished on their title pages as being either in accordance with the Minhag Ashkenaz (German rite) or the Minhag Sepharad (Spanish rite). The latter is the ritual introduced by the Hasidim.

This definitive break with their opponents was not motivated by partisan interests. It was the logical result of the movement's mystic orientation. Many of the Hasidic leaders were dedicated students of the mystic literature, and they frequently turned to the kabbala for guidance. It will be recalled that the greatest of the kabbalists, Rabbi Isaac Luria, had published a *Siddur* * based on the Sephardic rite. This *Siddur* found wide acceptance among the mystics of the sixteenth and seventeenth centuries. So it is not surprising that the Hasidim needed no urging to accept the *Nusah Ha-Ari*, the liturgic rite of "The Lion" among the mystics. But Luria's *Siddur* was not entirely Sephardic. It contained some Ashkenazic elements. which the Hasidim also incorporated into their rite. The most important of these is the retention of many Ashkenazic piyutim, which were generally inferior to those of the Sephardic rite.† The Hasidim cannot be accused of poor literary taste—they were merely consistent. It was Rabbi Isaac Luria who detected mystic implications in the tortured verses of Kalir, and the Hasidim followed the master kabbalist all the way.

In most other respects the Minhag Sepharad of the Hasidim was similar to the Sephardic ritual. For example, the Hasidim do not put on tefillin ‡ during the intermediate days of Passover and Sukkot, in accordance with the custom of the Sephardim. And the Kedushah of the Musaf service starts with the Sephardic formula, *Keter Yitnu L'kha*: "*A crown is given unto Thee*, O Lord our God, by the angels who dwell on high and Thy people Israel who are gathered below. Thrice they jointly ascribe unto Thee holiness, . . . saying: Holy, holy, holy is the Lord of hosts." In the Ashkenazic *Siddur*, this Kedushah starts with the formula *Na'aritzkha Ve-Nakdishkha:* "*We will reverence and sanctify Thee* according

* *See pp. 493–94.*
† *See pp. 171–72.*
‡ *See pp. 346–49.*

to the mystic utterance of the holy Seraphim who hallow Thy name, . . . saying: Holy, holy, holy is the Lord of hosts." In the Kaddish * the Hasidim insert the words *Ve-Yatzmah Purkanei* (And may He cause His salvation [the coming of the Messiah] to be fulfilled). There are many other digressions from the Ashkenazic ritual (including the order of several prayers), all of them in accord with the Sephardic rite.

The *Shtiebel*

As time passed the gulf between the Hasidim and their opponents, the mitnagdim, widened, and their antagonism sharpened. Having adopted a ritual of their own, the Hasidim necessarily had to establish synagogues of their own where they could pray as they chose and where they would be free to exercise their enthusiasm at prayer. These independent Hasidic synagogues were called *shtiebels*, little houses. Actually, they were not even little houses. A *shtiebel* was usually just a room and the congregation only a conventicle. Despite its smallness the *shtiebel* served a multitude of purposes. Officially it was dedicated as a bet hamidrash, a house of study, rather than a synagogue. This permitted a number of activities that are forbidden in a synagogue. The Hasidim could not only hold services on all occasions and study their religious and mystic texts, but they could also hold congregational repasts and partake of refreshments, which usually included strong drink—in moderation, of course. The latter served to stimulate the spirit of joy and comradeship. The *shtiebel*, therefore, resounded with loud prayers, resonant songs, and lusty dancing, all of which shocked their opponents no end.

Conflict with the Mitnagdim

It is the usual fate of dissenting religious movements to become embroiled in sharp disputes with the entrenched institutions. The Hasidim and their opponents were no exception. The mutual recriminations were bitter and often exaggerated.

* *See pp. 153 ff.*

The mitnagdim were justly suspicious of the new movement. They feared a new sectarianism, akin to the Sabbatian messianic movement—or worse, the antinomianism of an offshoot of the Sabbatians known as the Frankists, who ended up in the Catholic Church. The emotional enthusiasm of the Hasidim, the liberties they took with the schedule of services, their adoption of an independent liturgic rite, and their challenge to the traditional authority of the rabbis inevitably led to furious opposition. Even the famous scholar, the Gaon of Wilna, emerged from his scholarly seclusion to take up battle with what he was convinced was a new sectarian movement. The Hasidim were persecuted; they were excommunicated; and they even suffered persecutions by the Russian government, which was called into the feud.

But the Hasidim weathered the storm. The persecutions did not drive them out of the fold—it only intensified their solidarity. They remained an integral part of the community of Israel because they were in fact not sectarians and were free from antinomian tendencies. To be sure, they had exchanged the liturgic tradition of the Ashkenazim for that of the Sephardim, and a change of ritual is contrary to the tradition, but the rite they adopted is fully in line with the teachings of the rabbis. They also prayed at unorthodox hours and adored their tzaddikim almost to the point of idolatry. But they never elevated their religious leaders to any divine status. Most important, their religious behavior was impeccable.

When the smoke of battle cleared, the mitnagdim realized that Hasidism was not a sectarian movement. It was just another minhag within Judaism. And the Hasidim, too, lost much of their original ardor. The fire of revolt burned itself out, and the Hasidim gradually abandoned their dissenting posture. They even began to hold in high esteem those among them who were scholarly. Study of the Torah was recognized as a desirable occupation for a Hasid. However, the Hasidim have not compromised on their positive principles. They have remained loyal to their respective tzaddikim and to their Minhag Sepharad. Their manner of praying has also remained a characteristic of their movement.

An Enlightened View of Hasidism

The nineteenth century modernists never tired of attacking the Hasidim. They saw in their unyielding orthodoxy nothing but obscurantism and medievalism. They ridiculed their manner of prayer and their veneration of the tzaddikim. But much of this antagonism was born of prejudice and blind enmity rather than enlightened understanding. During the past few decades, however, the Hasidim have been presented by a number of outstanding scholars in a totally new light. The new evaluation of Hasidism is based on sound study and sympathetic understanding. Among these scholars are such men of fame as S. M. Dubnow, Solomon Schechter, Martin Buber, and Gershom G. Scholem. Hasidism has thus emerged as a religious movement worthy of respect and even admiration. Those who have written off Hasidism as a mere vestige of the Middle Ages must reevaluate the movement. Hasidism may have inner strength and staying power far beyond the expectation of the nineteenth century modernists. There are even some signs of renewed growth and reawakened vigor among the Hasidim. Their religious enthusiasm and their dedication to heartful and joyful worship have been admired by rationalists no less than mystics, and their influence has been felt in many a synagogue that regards itself as sharply opposed to Hasidism.

21
THE RISE OF HAZANUT

Every liturgy has its musical modes and melodies which serve to heighten the worshiper's identification with the tradition and to deepen his ardor at prayer. And the Jewish liturgy is no exception. In the days of the First Temple, when the sacrificial cult occupied the center of worship, both vocal and instrumental music were constant elements of the service.* Thus the prophet Amos chastises the worshipers of his day in the name of God: "Take thou away from Me the noise of thy songs; / And let Me not hear the melody of thy psalteries" (Am. 5:23). When the Temple service was reinstated in Jerusalem after the Babylonian captivity, Nehemiah reports that the Levites and the Kohanim participated in the thanksgiving prayers with choirs and instrumental music. And when Ezra instituted the reading of the Torah in the synagogue, he set the precedent of reading it "distinctly" (Neh. 8:8), which is traditionally understood to mean that the scriptural selections were chanted, as they have been to this day. In the first century of the Common Era, when the synagogue and the Temple were fully accepted as complementary institutions, the Kohanim and Levites (who participated in both the Temple and synagogue services) † chanted some of the Temple melodies in the synagogue; thus was some Temple music transmitted to the synagogue.

When the Second Temple was destroyed in the year 70 C.E., music was banned as a sign of mourning. But inspired worship could not be maintained without melodic expression, so the prohibition of music applied to instruments only. In all probability vocal music did not cease to be part of the synagogue liturgy even immediately after the destruction of the Temple.

The Role of the Hazan

The officiant at the synagogue services during rabbinic times was known as *korei* (reader) or more frequently as *shaliah tzibbur* (the emissary of the congregation). In the Talmud the term hazan was applied to another synagogue functionary, a sort of professional superintendent of the house of prayer (Sotah 7:7–8). The word hazan is probably borrowed from the Assyrian language, in which *hazani* means a director or overseer. In the El Amarna tablets *hazanuti* refers to the governors stationed by the Egyptian rulers in the subjugated cities of Palestine.

* *See pp. 49–51.*
† *See pp. 72–73, 78–79.*

The hazan's duties in the synagogue were varied, similar to those of the shamash in the contemporary synagogue. He was in charge of the synagogue building and its furnishings. On Friday afternoons he announced the time of the stoppage of work at the approach of the Sabbath by three blasts of the trumpet (Shab. 35b). He kept order in the synagogue. He took the scroll out of the ark for the reading and returned it to the ark after the reading. At times he also taught the children to read and occasionally led in the services and read the Torah, as does the shamash today. But these functions were incidental. In time, however, these occasional duties became central, and the hazan became principally the precentor of the congregation. When the musical rendition of the service began to play a central role in the worship in the Middle Ages, the title hazan became associated exclusively with the person who distinguished himself in the musical rendition of the prayers. The hazan thus became the cantor of the congregation. Since instrumental music was strictly banned, the hazan performed as a soloist, often assisted by a male choir. The quality of his voice and the nature of his renditions became his primary qualifications. If someone not qualified musically to be a hazan conducted the services, even if he possessed a pleasant voice and performed his task competently, he was called by the secondary title of *ba'al Tefillah*, one who leads the congregation in prayer.

The hazan, though frequently called *shaliah tzibbur*, the emissary of the congregation, was never regarded as a minister who prays in behalf of the congregation. His religious function was to lead the congregation in prayer. The worshipers read the prayers silently, and the hazan chanted the concluding verse or verses of each prayer. One exception was the *Tefillah*, which the hazan repeated in full for the benefit of those who could not read the prayers. The unlettered worshipers listened to the precentor and responded with the traditional Amen.

To lead the congregation in prayer was regarded as an act of piety and a great privilege. Hence many a famous rabbi acted as reader, especially during the High Holy Days. Rabbenu Gershom and Rabbi Meir of Rothenberg, both of whom were accorded the distinguished title of *Me'or Ha-Golah* (the

Light of the Exile) used to lead the services on the High Holy Days. So did Rashi and Rabbi Jacob Mölln (Maharil).* But these outstanding scholars were not hazanim. In all probability they possessed pleasant voices and therefore availed themselves of the opportunity to perform a pious deed. To be a hazan one had to possess superior vocal talent. Musical distinction rather than scholarly attainment was the hallmark of the hazan. To be sure, some hazanim were scholars of note, but this was not a prerequisite for the cantorate in most congregations.

Since the hazan was the emissary of the congregation, he was expected to possess certain religious qualifications in addition to his musical talent. Above all, his character and his piety were to be irreproachable. The *Shulhan Arukh*, which is recognized by Orthodox Jews as the official religious code, specifies the qualifications of a hazan:

> He should be a man free of transgressions and with a good reputation that has not been soiled even in his youth. He should be of humble and pleasing personality. He should possess a sweet voice, and should be fluent in the reading of the Torah, the Prophets, and the Writings. If such a person is not available, the best man in terms of scholarship and piety is to be chosen. [If there is a choice between an old man with a sweet voice but an ignoramus, and a young boy who is only thirteen years old, possessing no sweet voice, but understands what he reads, the boy is to be preferred.] [*Shulhan Arukh, Orah Hayim* 53:4–5].

Since he was a representative of the congregation, it was also felt that a perfect harmony should exist between the hazan and the worshipers. Some communities therefore required a unanimous vote for the election of the hazan, especially for the High Holy Days services. In the Rhine district this rule was adhered to with special strictness. Elsewhere some glaring faults in the candidate for hazan were readily overlooked for the sake of his pleasant voice and his expressive delivery.

Despite their popularity the hazanim were hardly professionals in the modern sense. Generally the hazan had neither a

* *See pp. 523–24.*

formal musical education nor did he devote all or a major part of his time to the cultivation of his musical talent. He was born with a fine voice, and he learned the traditional renditions of the service by ear, usually from the local hazan. His livelihood he earned only partly from his musical talent and usually supplemented his earnings from such additional occupations as that of ritual slaughterer, teacher, or scribe. There were also some who were full-time functionaries of the synagogue. But they carried many communal responsibilities, and their preoccupation with the music of the synagogue was generally limited to the actual rendition of the services.

In the later Middle Ages and especially in the nineteenth century [1] many hazanim became fully professional and devoted their time mainly to their musical art. The post was elective, salaried, and frequently handed down from father to son for several generations. The hazan's duties were mainly the chanting of the prayers and the scriptural readings of the services. In some cases his duties were limited solely to the rendition of the prayers. He was usually a highly esteemed functionary of the community, second in importance only to the rabbi.

The Musical Tradition of the Synagogue

Musicologists have shown that in the early centuries of the Common Era the music of the synagogue exerted a profound influence on the Church and later also on the mosque; conversely, the synagogue has absorbed musical elements from non-Jewish sources. They point to the common ingredients of synagogue music and the Gregorian chants of the Catholic tradition. There are also points of contact with the chants of the muezzin and the Koran reader in the Moslem tradition. The intonation of the services in the Sephardic synagogue often recalls the plainsong of the Mozarabian Christians, in whose proximity the Spanish Jews lived until the thirteenth century.

As the dispersion of the Jews widened, the musical renditions of the services were increasingly influenced by the local musical traditions in the many lands of the exile. Wide differences began to develop, especially between the oriental and occidental synagogues: "While most of the western musicians prefer open, so-called 'natural' vocal productions, the Middle Eastern singer masks his voice, making it nasal, guttural, throaty." [2] These and other characteristics affected the synagogue music of the far-flung Jewish communities, and even the chanting of the Torah began to differ from area to area. Despite these differences the various traditional renditions have much in common, especially in those parts of the services that are of ancient origin. The differences in the rendition of the ancient passages, such as the *Tefillah* and the benedictions which precede and follow the *Shema*, are not to be found in the basic melody but in their tonality. The musicologist realizes that these differences are superficial, but the untrained layman finds them to be an insuperable barrier between the oriental and occidental Jewish communities, necessitating separate services for each community, sometimes in the same building.

The liturgy of the synagogue, it will be remembered, took definite shape during the geonic period. But the music of the synagogue did not assume distinctively recognizable expression until after the geonic period. The shaping of the distinctive music of the liturgy and its acceptance into the synagogue corpus of sacred song took place between the eighth and thirteenth centuries. This is obviously a long time, but not quite as long as it took the liturgy to develop. In those days social change and growth were not as rapid as today. During these postgeonic centuries the musical renditions of the prayers were given the official name of *Nusah*. Although the modes of the *Nusah* vary somewhat from synagogue to synagogue because they are not chanted absolutely in the same way, note for note, nevertheless they are recognizable and are guarded as part of the sacred tradition. This has been especially true of the East European Jews, who conscientiously protect the *Nusah* against corruption. A reader who substitutes a tune of his own for the accepted *Nusah* is usually reprimanded.

As a rule the *Nusah* applies only to the rendition of the last passages of the ancient prayers. The hazan may improvise in his rendition of the earlier parts of these prayers, but when he reaches the concluding passages he is expected to lead smoothly back to the *Nusah*. This insistence on the *Nusah* has preserved the unity of the musical tradition of the synagogue services, despite the innumerable improvisations and compositions by hazanim throughout the centuries.

The famous scholar Rabbi Jacob Mölln (Maharil) played a crucial role in the preservation of the *Nusah.* He lived in Mayence between 1365 and 1427, a period of disorganization and demoralization in the Jewish communities of Central Europe. The Black Death of the mid-fourteenth century had decimated the Jewish communities. In addition, they suffered from severe persecutions and massacres resulting from accusations that the Black Death was caused by Jews who plotted the extermination of the Christians. These accusations found willing ears among the harassed and frightened Christians, many of whom turned against the Jews with violence born of desperation. Disorganization and a lowering of morale devastated the Jewish communities. Rabbi Jacob Mölln, who directed all his authority and prestige toward reconstruction of the communities, approached his difficult task with energy and persistence. Among his achievements was the reinforcement of the principle that established customs, or minhagim, are valid even if they have no basis in rabbinic literature and even if their scope is only local. He thus restored order and stability.

In his emphasis on the validity of local custom Rabbi Mölln specified that traditional melodies of the synagogue are binding and must not be changed by the hazan. To be sure, this emphasis on the validity of custom did not originate with Rabbi Mölln; it was already stressed in the Talmud.* Still, many people took liberties with established practices that were based only on custom. This was especially true of the musical renditions of the services. Rabbi Mölln ruled that "One must not change the *Minhag* of a place in any matter even in regard to the introduction of melodies to which the people are not accustomed."[3] The authority of Rabbi Mölln was recognized in Jewish communities throughout Northern Europe, from France to Poland. His ruling therefore became a unifying force among the Ashkenazic Jews, and the *Nusah* was firmly established as the official music of the synagogue.

Rabbi Mölln's ruling restricted the hazan only where estab-

* *See p. 373.*

lished custom was involved; it left him free to introduce his own tunes in all other prayers, especially in the piyutim.

Foreign Music in the Synagogue

On Sabbaths and festivals the hazan exercised his talent to the delight of the worshipers. In some cases the hazan was also the local poet. He would then introduce both his piyut and its musical setting, the latter not infrequently borrowed from the non-Jewish community. At times even a church melody found its way into the synagogue. It should be noted that borrowing music from outside sources is not necessarily an undesirable practice, depending on what one borrows and whether the borrowed material is properly digested and absorbed into the spirit of the tradition. If the borrowed tune remains an obviously foreign element, unadapted to the traditional setting of the synagogue, it is jarring. But if the borrowed melodies are blended into the tradition, so that their origin is recognizable only to the specialists, they may enrich the service. Many a borrowed tune has thus been introduced into the synagogue liturgy and has remained in the synagogue unchallenged and undisturbed.

Among the hazanim who introduced borrowed tunes into the Jewish tradition was Israel Najara, author of the popular Friday evening hymn, *Yah Ribbon Olam.** We are told that he composed many piyutim to Arabic and Turkish melodies, some of them love songs. He was criticized for not being more selective in the choice of his melodies. But he was not the only hazan who, knowingly or not, introduced foreign tunes into the service.

The Florid Style of Hazanut

During the Middle Ages, when the cultural contact between Jew and Gentile became increasingly rare, the Jew fell back on his own cultural resources. The synagogue became the place where the genius of the Jew found its motivation and its form of expression. At the synagogue service the hazan gave expression to his musical talent. On the festivals his music ex-

* *See p. 501.*

pressed jubilant praise of God's saving power; on penitential days, pleading supplication for God's mercy; and on fast days, agonized lament over Israel's exile and suffering. These renditions of the services were the bright moments in the Jew's otherwise bleak existence. As he listened to the hazan, the Jew forgot the harsh realities of his life and rejoiced in his Sabbaths and festivals. No wonder the Jew showed such enthusiastic appreciation of the hazan's musical virtuosity. This appreciation encouraged the hazan to enlarge his repertoire and expand on his musical renditions. Occasionally, in a moment of inspiration or deep emotion, the hazan gave utterance to a musical phrase of beauty and power which was especially expressive of the spirit of the service. The congregation would catch the tune and repeat it until it became a permanent element of the liturgic tradition. The synagogue was thus not only the Jew's house of prayer, study, and assembly, but also his house of creativity.

To please their appreciative audiences, the hazanim exerted themselves to show their vocal agility. This gave rise to the florid intonations which became the characteristic style of the Ashkenazic synagogue, especially of East European Jewry. A stranger who visited an Ashkenazic synagogue at the turn of this century described the music of the service in these penetrating words:

> What most strikes a stranger present for the first time at a synagogue service . . . is the strange weirdness of the liturgy, chanted with a curious swaying, pendulum-like motion, peculiarly suggestive of those alternations of joy and sorrow, exultation and self-abasement, passionate pleading and ineffable repose, which are specially characteristic of the Hebrew Prayer Books. Now it is an arid monotony of long and minute legal enactments; anon, the recital is broken by piercing lyric cries of yearning. This, again, swiftly modulates into a major key in which is trumpeted forth, with triumphant assertiveness, some dominating certitude of faith. Thereafter follows, in broken accents of entreaty, confession of sin, merging at length in an exalted song of praise that would rend the very heavens! [4]

It should be noted that the Sephardic synagogue did not develop this type of hazanut. One reason is that the oriental Jews emphasize unison reading of the prayers, which has limited the reader's opportunities for solo singing. Another restriction is the relative absence of piyutim in the Sephardic service. As mentioned above, the piyutim provided the hazan with many of his opportunities for musical self-expression. The Sephardic Jews were thus saved from the cantorial excesses to which the Ashkenazic congregations were eventually exposed. On the other hand, the absence of the Ashkenazic hazanut has resulted in a monotonous rendition of the services which the occidental Jew finds almost intolerable.

Excesses and Decline

The role of the hazan is to lead the congregation in prayer; his music is to awaken in the worshiper a prayerful mood and move his heart to greater devotion. But the adulation of admiring listeners prompted many a hazan to forget his primary function and to see himself as a virtuoso. Instead of striving to arouse in the congregation feelings of piety, the hazan has often striven to entertain his appreciative audience. "The Hazan became less a reader than a singer, less a singer than a spirited declaimer. He gave to his emotions an expression which can only be described as dramatic; he wept or was glad as the prayers called for it." [5] The more the service was turned into a professional concert, the less the congregation identified itself with the hazan as its *shaliah tzibbur*. No matter how plaintive the rendition, the congregation remained an audience. As a virtuoso the hazan gained the plaudits of the people, but he failed to elicit from them devout worship.

Some cantors began to violate good musical taste. They indulged in excessive vocal gymnastics and even corrupted the sense of the prayers for the sake of demonstrating their vocal agility. At times they employed incongruous tunes.[6] A kind of musical pilpul of technical intricacy became the goal of hazanut, and emotionalism of a ludicrous nature often climaxed the hazan's performance. It fascinated many of the listeners. This in

Book of Esther, 1730, The Israel Museum, Jerusalem. PHOTO: ALFRED BERNHEIM

turn encouraged many a hazan to increase the musical embellishments ad nauseum. Abraham J. Heschel bewails the decline of hazanut and sees in it no less than a tragedy:

> Hazanut has become a skill, a technical performance, an impersonal affair. As a result the sounds that come out of the Hazan evoke no participation. They enter the ears; they do not touch the hearts. The right Hebrew word for Cantor is *ba'al tefillah*, master of prayer. The mission of a Cantor is to lead in prayer. He does not stand before the Ark as an artist in isolation, trying to demonstrate his skill or to display vocal feats. He stands before the Ark not as an individual but with a Congregation. He must identify himself with the Congregation. His task is to represent as well as to inspire a community. Within the synagogue, music is not an end in itself, but a means of religious experience. Its function is to help us to live through a moment of confrontation with the presence of God; to expose ourselves to Him in praise, in self-scrutiny, and in hope.[7]

The music of the hazan not only ceased to stir the heart to piety, but prolonged the service to the point of weariness. This naturally led to sharp protests, and some of these protests are worthy of note.

Reactions to the Excesses of the Hazanim

Within the general acclaim of hazanut during the Middle Ages there were many echoes of protest. Indeed, no other communal official of the ghetto occasioned so many complaints as the hazan. These complaints were directed against the foreign melodies often derived from folk songs and love songs, the vanity of some hazanim, the undue length of the service, and occasionally against the conduct of some hazanim. There were hazanim who possessed masterful voices but little scholarship; they mispronounced the Hebrew of the prayers and at times rendered the prayers incomprehensible by disregard of the text's punctuation.

As early as the twelfth century the saintly Rabbi Judah He-Hasid complained against some of the hazanim: "They repeat large parts of the prayers, merely to show how competent they are musically. It is a sin to do so. Besides it is an imposition upon the people's patience. . . . Those who fear God will not do so."[8] The *Shulhan Arukh*, the official code of Jewish religious law, also rebukes the hazanim sharply: "An Emissary of the Congregation who prolongs the service in order that people may hear his sweet voice . . . is a vulgar person. Whatever the motivation, he who prolongs the service is not acting properly because he is inconsiderate of the congregation's inconvenience."[9] A word of advice is offered by Abraham ben Shabbati Horowitz in his ethical will. He recommends the study of the Mishnah at those places in the service where the hazan prolongs his singing.[10] But the most devastating attack on hazanim is contained in a seventeenth century publication *Reshit Bikurim* (First of the New Fruits) by Rabbi Enoch ben Abraham. The author was a talmudist and a preacher of note. According to the author the hazanim were destroying true prayer in the synagogue by their vain and irrational conduct:

> The hazanim in these areas are generally not learned men and do not understand the prayers. They pay no attention to the sense of the text and thus render the prayers meaningless. . . . When it comes to the piyutim they recite them with such rapidity that even a horseman could not overtake them. . . . The hazan's intentions are primarily to show off his voice. . . . He chants one word at length . . . and then he recites many benedictions in one breath. And in the middle of one benediction he suddenly lets out a loud and bitter cry that frightens everyone who hears it. . . . All this is only to entertain the people. Actually it is only a mockery and a travesty, so that anyone who hears it laughs.[11]

Renewal of Hazanut in the Modern Synagogue

The above strictures and many more were leveled against many of the medieval cantors. However, one can say with satisfaction that in modern times the situation has been changing rapidly. The hazanim in many synagogues are trained and disciplined musicians who aim to inspire their congregations and to arouse in them a spirit of devotion. Rather than performing, they lead their congregations in the chanting of the prayers. Some of the modern hazanim are also enriching the music of the synagogue with their creative talent. A brighter future for hazanut is definitely on the horizon.

22
THE DECLINE OF PREACHING

In an earlier chapter it was shown that the homily was a central feature of Jewish worship.* Ezra the Scribe set the example of expounding the Scriptures to the people, and the Pharisees followed in his footsteps. They developed the intricate rules that governed the pattern of the homily.† By the beginning of the Common Era homilies, or religious discourses, were regularly delivered in the synagogues on Sabbaths and festivals. Aramaic was used in Palestine and Greek in Alexandria. There is ample evidence to support the view that the homilies were a successful educational means of popular enlightenment and edification.

The Master Preachers of Old

Some of the Pharisees were master preachers. Their scholarly proficiency earned them the respect of their contemporaries, and their masterful preaching won them the loyalty and trust of the people. It was largely because of their effective preaching that in periods of national emergency the Pharisees were able to give the people effective leadership. Thus in the first century of the Common Era neither the irritating challenge of the early Christians nor the devastating catastrophe of the Roman war could undermine the rabbinic influence among the Jews. Indeed, the very survival of the Jewish people was due

* *See p. 116.*
† *See pp. 117–19.*

in large measure to the people's loyalty and love for their religious leaders.

The homily continued to be an established part of the synagogue service throughout the talmudic and geonic times. It provided the people with an awareness of the basic beliefs of Judaism and guided them in the observance of both the ethical and ritual laws of their faith. The Bible and the Talmud are replete with moral preachments and the vast literature of the Midrashim is devoted almost exclusively to the homilies preached by the rabbis of the talmudic and posttalmudic periods. These Midrashim contain many poetic gems selected from the preachers' utterances, and many captivating parables and anecdotes illustrating the moral lessons of the homilies. This literary legacy, especially the folios of the *Midrash Rabbah*, is still used by synagogue preachers as source material for the enrichment of their sermons.

As late as the turn of the tenth century, the bishop of Lyons complained bitterly "that many Christians openly declare that the sermons of the Jewish preachers please them better than those of the Christian clergy." [1] But in the succeeding centuries such compliments became increasingly rare, especially in the Ashkenazic communities of Northern and East European countries.

Prolongation of the Services by Piyutim

In postgeonic times the homily began to cede its place in the service to two attractive and fashionable liturgic innovations which were introduced by the poets and singers of the synagogue. The beginning of this process can be traced to the Church persecutions in the sixth and seventh centuries of the Common Era when, in accordance with the Justinian Edict,* it was forbidden to expound the Scriptures during the synagogue services. It was then that the reader began to take over the function of the preacher. He would recite religious poems which contained in veiled language some of the rabbinic teachings which were normally presented in the homily.† This

* *See pp. 443–44.*
† *See pp. 169 ff.*

makeshift strategy was useful and even effective in the synagogue's resistance to the persecutions of the dominant faith. But it ultimately caused the decline of the homily and, in time, its total exclusion from the official worship periods. When the Arabs conquered Palestine in 636 and the Jews were allowed to worship freely, the recitation of liturgic poems, or piyutim, during the services was retained. In the postgeonic period, the writing of piyutim became a mark of creative distinction, and local poets were honored for their religious poems. The stream of religious poems became a veritable flood, and the synagogue services—especially those of the special Sabbaths, festivals, fasts, and holy days—became cluttered with piyutim. The worship periods were thus prolonged, and the piyutim began to impinge on the time required for the delivery of the sermon.

Prolongation of the Services by Hazanut

In the postgeonic period the synagogue service was further prolonged by the hazanim, whose popularity had risen and who increasingly occupied the center of the pulpit. This was especially true of the Ashkenazic synagogues, where the people were excessively fond of the cantorial renditions of the service. But the hazan's virtuosity often prolonged the service to the point of weariness. Something had to give. The hazan's singing was too popular to yield to the pressure of time, and the piyutim had already become fixed elements of the service because of their uninterrupted usage over long periods of time. So it was that the homily yielded, notwithstanding its ancient and honorable history. It yielded because it never became a constant ingredient of the service. Whenever there was no preacher in the synagogue, the homily was omitted. Hence the sermon came to be regarded as an optional element and was squeezed out of the service.

The Medieval Rabbi

In blaming the decline of preaching on the synagogue poets and singers we have put the proverbial cart before the horse.

For the primary cause of the decline of the sermon was the deterioration of the rabbis' competence as preachers. Had the rabbis maintained the pharisaic tradition of public education and continued to be, like their predecessors, effective preachers, it is doubtful whether the homily would have yielded to the pressure of the piyutim and the musical embellishments of the hazanim.

The story of the decline of preaching actually begins as early as the first century of the Common Era, at the very time when preaching was a most effective instrument in the public education of the people. When the Temple was destroyed in the year 70 C.E., the disciples of Yohanan ben Zakkai revived the formal procedure of ordaining spiritual leaders. The ceremony consisted of semikhah, the laying on of the hands.[2] This ceremony affirmed the candidate's scholarly erudition and conferred on him the title of rabbi, along with certain spiritual and communal powers. Among these was his eligibility to be a member of the Sanhedrin. In later years the ceremony of laying on of the hands was abolished—probably because the Christians had adopted this ceremony and it had become associated with Church practice. In the Middle Ages the word *semikhah* continued to be used to designate the act of ordination. The word merely implied that a document had been awarded to the candidate, affirming that he had mastered sufficient learning to be worthy of the title rabbi and that he possessed the qualifications of character and piety befitting the rabbinate. This document was awarded by any rabbi whose scholarship was widely recognized or by the head of the talmudical academy where the recipient of the "semikhah" had been a student.[3]

It will be noted that in both the actual semikhah of ancient times and in the nominal "semikhah" of the Middle Ages the emphasis was on scholarship and piety. And the rabbis lived up to these requirements. They devoted much of their time and energy to the pursuit of study, and they strove to be examples of conscientious dedication to the rabbinic guidelines of ethical and ritual conduct.

The rabbi's scholarship was not altogether an academic quest for knowledge. His learning enabled him to perform a number of rabbinic functions, such as the supervision of ritual slaughter and of the community's educational institutions. Sometimes the rabbi conducted or headed a yeshivah. But the most practical of the rabbi's use of his learning was in connection with his function as the official judge in both religious and civil litigation among Jews. Judging the disputes in his community was both exacting and time-consuming. A vast literature consisting of the more important decisions rendered in the rabbinic courts has accumulated during the centuries. More than a thousand collections of published responsa are extant, and still more have remained in manuscript form. So exacting was the rabbi's function as judge that larger communities usually appointed special functionaries, known as dayanim (judges), to relieve the rabbis of the more ordinary judicial duties. To be the judge of the community, the rabbi had to be master of the Law.

The rabbis therefore cultivated the Law. But as their proficiency in the Law increased, their mastery of the art of preaching decreased. A homily had to deal with matters that were relevant to the people's daily life, and to hold the listeners' attention it had to be embellished with appropriate anecdotes and parables. The homily had to be morally uplifting and emotionally stirring. The medieval rabbis were not prepared for such discourses. They were so fully involved in their scholarly activities that they had no time for such mundane matters as popular sermons. To cultivate the art of preaching was for them to forsake the Torah, "the fountain of living waters." Hence it developed that when an opportunity to address the congregation presented itself, the rabbis used it to demonstrate their scholarly attainments and their legal erudition. They aimed at impressing the few scholars rather than enlightening and edifying the people at large.

The Rabbinate as an Honorary Occupation

The medieval rabbi could afford to choose his field of specialization because he was not a professional. The rabbi did not deign to accept any recompense for his labors; his reward would come from the Almighty in the "real world." To say that a man was a rabbi by profession was, to use Solomon Schechter's simile, as accurate as to say that a man is a philanthropist by profession.[4] The rabbi's office was purely honorary. He earned his livelihood from various private occupations. He followed in the footsteps of his illustrious predecessors, the rabbis of the Talmud, who considered it improper and even sinful for rabbis to receive remuneration for the performance of their duties. The Talmud tells of some talmudic sages who earned their livelihood as shoemakers, blacksmiths, and similar humble occupations. To be sure, the medieval communities tried to compensate the rabbis indirectly. Rabbis who were merchants were usually given priority in the sale of their merchandise so as to free them for their studies. Rabbis also had a number of tax privileges. But these fringe benefits can hardly be regarded as professional compensation. The rabbis earned their livelihood in a variety of occupations: some were merchants, others were physicians, still others were brokers. Thus the famous Rashi (Rabbi Solomon Yitz'haki) was rabbi of the community of Troyes, but he received no emoluments from his office. He earned his livelihood as a vine-grower.

The rabbi's preoccupation with earning a living often restricted his rabbinic activities. His mundane labors often exhausted much of his time and energy and interfered with his spiritual duties. Preaching, which can be a full-time occupation in itself, was thus effectively squeezed out of the rabbi's functions, except for two annual addresses which he delivered on the Sabbath before Passover and the Sabbath before Yom Kippur. The former dealt with the legal aspects of Passover observance, and the latter dealt with repentance and piety necessary for the proper observance of Yom Kippur. But these discourses were usually lengthy, learned, and involved—they served to demonstrate the rabbi's scholarly aptitude. The discourse before Passover was usually unrelated to the practical needs of the people in regard to the Passover observance, and the discourse before Yom Kippur hardly ever moved the people to repentance or to greater piety. While the Pharisees of old taught rabbinic law in the academy and preached rabbinic lore in the synagogue, the medieval rabbi concentrated solely on the halakah (law) and almost totally abandoned the Haggadah (lore). The services could not possibly accommodate lengthy dissertations, hence the semiannual discourses were transferred to the Sabbath afternoon after the weekly postprandial siesta. Attendance was then optional, but most people honored the rabbi by their attendance. The rabbi's delivery was usually unhurried. Eloquence was replaced by dialectics. Thus didactic and hortatory homilies almost ceased to be part of the synagogue tradition among the Ashkenazim.

Preaching in the Sephardic Synagogue

Though emphasis on scholarship was also strong among the Sephardim, preaching continued to be one of the Sephardic rabbi's duties. As mentioned above, the Sephardic services were not overloaded with piyutim, and their hazanim did not consume an inordinate amount of time during the services.* The homily therefore continued to flourish in the Sephardic synagogue throughout the Middle Ages. In Spain and later in Italy, Holland, England, the Orient, and North Africa there was preaching in the Sephardic synagogue during the services. Some of the preachers achieved fame, among them Nahmanides, Leon of Modena, and Menasseh ben Israel.

The Sephardic sermon was skillfully elaborated and was delivered in the vernacular. It usually contained a double text—a verse from the Scriptures and a passage from rabbinic sources. These led into the sermon proper, which contained numerous biblical and rabbinic quotations, each one shedding light on the preceding one. The last quotation led back to the original text. The sermon closed with the standard formula: "May the Redeemer come to Zion; may this be the will of God. Amen."

The Professionalization of the Rabbinate

The medieval rabbis found it increasingly difficult to serve their communities and at the same time support their families. As the persecutions continued to restrict the economic activities of the Jews, competition for the bare necessities of life

* *See p. 526.*

increased. One had to invest all his time and ingenuity just to earn a meager livelihood. It therefore became almost impossible for rabbis to support their families and perform their rabbinic functions. Professionalization of the rabbinate became inevitable. By the fourteenth century the transition from the honorary status of the rabbinate to that of a salaried profession had already been made, not infrequently accompanied by pangs of conscience. Thus Rabbi Judah ben Asher, who was rabbi of Toledo, Spain, in the early fourteenth century,

> still retained his antiquated German prejudices, and could never reconcile himself to the idea of accepting a remuneration for his services to the community as rabbi and teacher. As the community insisted on his accepting the salary, he saved up all the money which he received from his congregants and converted it in his will into a bequest for various educational and charitable purposes.[5]

To be sure, the rabbi's salary was usually inadequate. But he was no longer a volunteer in the service of the community. One historian bewailed this change: "When the rabbis . . . lost their amateur standing, the soul of Jewry suffered a loss from which it has never recovered."[6] However, this development was not only inevitable but actually beneficial. Without it the rabbinate would have disappeared altogether, and the consequences would have been far more grievous.

Since the rabbi's salary was usually meager, it was customary to supplement it with fees for personal services, such as marrying a couple. The rabbi also received emoluments for judging court cases. Despite their salaries and professional fees, the medieval rabbis only provided their families with the bare necessities of life. Under strained economic conditions bordering on poverty they performed their duties with utter dedication. And the Jewish communities saw in their rabbis shining examples of piety and devotion. Intellectually and spiritually they were indeed pillars of light in the medieval ghettos. They cultivated the light of knowledge and kindled the people's faith in God and in Israel's redemption.

The Itinerant Preacher (Maggid)

The semiannual lectures delivered by the rabbis did not quench the popular thirst for moral instruction. On holy days the people craved for soul-stirring sermons, and on fast days they yearned for words of comfort. But the rabbis could not provide this. With rare exceptions, preaching was not within their competence.

The spiritual vacuum was eventually filled by a new type of religious functionary, known as the maggid, the preacher. The maggid was not an ordained rabbi, nor was he a trained preacher. He was a man whose natural gifts inclined him to the poetic and dramatic, and he craved self-expression among men rather than scholarly activity in the proverbial ivory tower. When a personal talent for preaching is coupled with a fervent desire to teach God's will and to raise the moral tone of life, a forceful preacher is an almost inevitable result. Preaching becomes for such a person a calling. It is thus that a new religious functionary was added to the medieval Jewish communities of Northern, Central, and Eastern Europe.

The life of the maggid was hardly to be envied. While the hazan's audience was assured because everyone in those days came to pray, the maggid had to attract his audience by the appeal of his sermon and by the eloquence of his delivery. The maggid would usually deliver his sermon on a Saturday afternoon or on a weekday evening. His moral exhortations had to be moving and appealing or he would have no audience. The maggid therefore embellished his homily with homely parables, folk tales, epigrams, and of course suitable quotations from biblical and rabbinic sources. The maggid was also at a disadvantage vis-à-vis the rabbi. While the community honored its rabbi and provided him with a post, it rarely recognized the maggid as part of the community's religious staff. The maggid was received everywhere with eagerness and at times with enthusiasm, but he was seldom provided with a stable source of sustenance. Multitudes of people came to hear the maggid's sermon, but they did not accord him the social status commensurate with his popularity. Only the few who achieved wide fame were rewarded with official posts in the large and relatively affluent congregations. But even in these communities the maggid was regarded as a luxury and was usually expected to perform additional functions, such as teaching.

Most often the maggid was not attached to any post. He was an itinerant free lance, wandering from town to town. His rewards depended on the popular appraisal of his sermons. His recompense consisted of the meager collection made after the sermon. If the sermon was delivered on a Sabbath afternoon, someone would collect the offerings after the Sabbath and transmit them to the maggid. Obviously the greater the maggid's fame, the larger the audience; the better the sermon, the more generous the offerings.

The Framework of the Maggid's Sermon

The traditional framework of the maggid's sermon was the exposition of a biblical text from the scriptural selections read at the service. The overt and covert meanings of the text were established with the help of corresponding texts from the Bible and from rabbinic teachings. In the course of the exposition the emphasis would shift to a religious message which was illuminated by apt and at times original illustrations. Religious conduct and theological belief were duly stressed.

The basic ingredients of the maggid's art consisted of novel and ingenious interpretations of a difficult text, fortified by numerous quotations from the classic sources. The listeners were familiar with many of the quotations and enjoyed recognizing them. The numerous quotations also served to establish the maggid as a man of learning. His utterances thus gained an aura of authenticity.[7] But the effectiveness and popularity of the maggid's homily depended mainly on the relevant and captivating illustrations, especially his apt anecdotes and parables, which he wove into his sermon. It was this ingredient that held the listeners' attention and impressed them with the validity of the message. Finally, there was the ingredient of stirring oratory. The maggid's eloquence would reach a climax by shifting into a rhythmic singsong, especially during the peroration—a technique which often moved the listeners to heights of emotion and even to tears. Needless to say, a religious message ran through the quotations and the illustrations as a string runs through a pearl necklace. It was the religious burden that raised the homily to a level of significance.

The maggid was frequently a creative person. He usually spun his own parables out of the daily experiences and the humble ambitions and dreams of the common folk. To be sure, some of the maggidim were hardly men of stature, and their mediocrity revealed itself in their attempt to demonstrate their ingenuity. They would seek out real or imaginary incongruities or contradictions in the biblical or rabbinic texts and then, by an intricate combining and weaving of unrelated texts, folk sayings, and parables, they would finally emerge with the startling discovery that the original verses were really not contradictory at all. In fact these verses contained an obvious truism, which no one had hitherto perceived. The listeners were often intrigued by the clever solution, diverted by the parables and the homely illustrations. They were entertained, not edified. But the talented maggidim who achieved fame were different. They, too, resorted to intriguing textual problems, but lurking behind the intricacies of the homily there was always a refreshing message of spiritual content, such as a call to greater faith in God's benevolence, a deeper belief in a theological dogma, or a stronger determination to remove some social evil. This type of maggid usually left his listeners morally uplifted and spiritually refreshed.

The Dubno Maggid

Among the talented maggidim whose fame has survived to this day was Jacob Kranz (1741–1804), popularly known as the Dubno Maggid. This name derives from the Polish city of Dubno, where he served as official maggid for eighteen years. He was an extraordinary preacher. His eloquence moved people to tears or raised their spirits to great religious exaltation. But his fame rests on the numerous parables with which he embellished his sermons. These parables have become legendary, and Jewish preachers to this day use some of these parables with telling effect. The parables of the Dubno Maggid have been collected by anthologists, and his life story has been a subject of considerable interest. Many a striking parable is now ascribed to the Dubno Maggid only because of its charm or brilliance. Who else could have thought of such an apt parable but the Dubno Maggid? Unfortunately, many other maggidim deserving of admiration beyond their own time have been forgotten. Their fame died with them and their creative work was not preserved for posterity.

Renewal of Rabbinic Preaching in Modern Times

In modern times, especially in America, the homily has returned to its original place in the synagogue service, and it is generally regarded as an integral part of Jewish worship. The rabbi has resumed his original function in the field of religious public education. To be sure, preaching is only one of the many functions of the modern rabbi. But preaching is no longer regarded as an optional element which can be squeezed out of the service. In many synagogues a Sabbath or festival service without a sermon is as inconceivable as a service without a Torah reading. And the content of the sermon has shifted from clever solutions of textual incongruities to that of teaching, inspiring, and uplifting the congregation. This revival of preaching has proved itself a wholesome and promising development in the liturgy of the modern synagogue.

23 THE INVENTION OF THE PRINTING PRESS

In the year 1440 the printing press with movable type was invented by Johann Gutenberg. The invention seems rather simple to modern people. Nonetheless it was an event of historic proportions. It initiated an intellectual and spiritual revolution of vast proportions. The eradication of illiteracy and the dissemination of knowledge, the scientific revolution, and the development of democracy as a political system can all be traced to this invention.

Prior to the invention of the printing press, education was a luxury available only to the elect. Books were scarce and expensive. Only a rich Jew could afford to own a manuscript *Siddur*. This is why only one *Siddur* has come down to us from English Jewry of the preexpulsion period.[1] Before the advent of printing it was not unusual for a synagogue to possess only one *Siddur*, for the reader. The precentor would recite most of the prayers aloud, and the worshipers either followed the reading in an undertone or just listened and responded at the appropriate places with the traditional Amen. To this day oriental Jews recite most of the prayers in unison, and Yemenites chant their prayers jointly in a rhythmic singsong, which helps them memorize the prayers. Should memory fail, one just falls in with the recitation of the others.[2]

The printing press revolutionized the synagogue service as it did all cultural and spiritual activities. It was appropriately referred to by medieval Jewish writers as "a scribe with many quills." A single printing could produce thousands of volumes. The price of books was thus reduced sharply, and copies of the *Siddur* were placed in the hands of many and in time all worshipers. The prayers and piyutim which had accumulated during the centuries could now be read by the congregation. No longer was it necessary for the reader to recite each piyut loudly. Thus the congregation began to read the prayers and piyutim in an undertone and, of course, more rapidly. But the services were not appreciably shortened. The time saved was usually utilized by the hazan for more elaborate renditions of the concluding verses.

The Printed *Siddur*

Soon after the invention of printing from movable type, a veritable stream of printed Hebrew books appeared on the market. The demand for Hebrew books was enormous, and printers vied with each other for the profitable trade.

The most famous of the early Hebrew printers was Nathan

Soncino, a physician by profession, who founded a publishing house in Italy in the year 1483. The Soncino family continued the founder's historic enterprise, and the firm is still functioning in England. The story of this historic press and its contributions to the advancement of general and Jewish culture is noteworthy. In 1486 the Soncino Press published the first Hebrew prayer book for use by the Italian Jews. This prayer book follows the *Nusah Romi* (the Roman rite) * and was known by the name of *Sidurello*.

Actually a *Siddur* had been published earlier for use among the crypto-Jews of the Iberian Peninsula. A Marrano, Juan de Lucena, operated a secret printing press in the town of Montalban as early as 1475. At the peril of his life he published a *Siddur* for use by his fellow Marranos. This *Siddur* is repeatedly mentioned in Inquisition trials. In one such trial, in the year 1485, a Marrano woman testified that eight years previously the daughters of Juan de Lucena had inadvertently left in her house a small book which was later identified as a Hebrew prayer book. One of these Marrano prayer books is now in the library of The Jewish Theological Seminary of America. Its format is small and oblong, of proper size to be slipped into the sleeve of one's garment in case of a surprise visit by a stranger who might denounce the worshiper to the Inquisition. This rare volume is not dated, but it is assumed to have been printed in 1475 or earlier.[3]

The first Ashkenazic *Siddur* was printed in Prague in 1512. Thereafter the number of printed editions of the *Siddur* increased from decade to decade. In the catalog of the Jewish National and University Library in Jerusalem more than eight thousand *Siddurim*, *Mahzorim*, and handy prayer collections are listed. And these do not begin to exhaust the vast number of printed prayer books.

Competition among Publishers

The demand for Hebrew prayer books was enormous, and publishers competed aggressively for this lucrative trade. Each one tried to enhance the usefulness of his publication in order

* *See p. 375.*

to attract customers. If one included in his *Siddur* the mishnaic tractate Avot (Fathers), which Jews studied during the summer Sabbaths,* his competitor included the Book of Psalms, which many Jews read systematically every day. If one added the Haggadah, which is read during the Passover Seder, the other added the Book of Esther, which is read at the Purim services. In time some *Siddurim* included commentaries on the prayers, while others contained kabbalistic annotations, and still others boasted of legal guides with special emphasis on the laws of prayer. Finally, some enterprising publishers included Judeo-German translations.

The title pages paraded the special advantages of each edition. Most frequently these advantages consisted of new commentaries by famous scholars or mystics. Some boasted of less visible but more persuasive advantages. Thus one *Siddur* published in Jerusalem solicits customers on the ground that the publisher will help those who pray from his *Siddur* to be heard on high. He states on the title page: "I hereby make it known that I pray at the holy places that God hearken to the prayers of everyone who prays in my *Siddur*, and I am certain that everyone who prays in my *Siddur* will attain a state of repentance, and God will hearken to his prayers, because I always pray for that."[4] Publishers also improved the *Siddur*'s design and format. The more important prayers were usually printed in bold type, and the prayers of the monthly service of the Consecration of the Moon,† which are read by moonlight, were generally printed in giant letters. It became the practice of teachers to use the *Siddur* as a primer for teaching children the elements of Hebrew reading. The alphabet and the vowels were printed in the introductory section, and the prayers in bold type were used for reading exercises by the young scholars.

The format of the *Siddur* also received due attention. Various sizes, from folio volumes to pocket-sized miniatures, were published. The former were meant for the reader's desk, while the miniatures were designed for those who traveled to fairs

* *See pp. 194–96.*
† *See pp. 266–68.*

and other trading centers. One late sixteenth century publisher, Jacob Polak by name, states the reason for publishing a small-sized *Siddur:* "Seeing that Jews constantly travel from country to country, from city to city, and from place to place with merchandise and for other purposes, it occurred to me to publish a small prayer book to lighten their burden and to enable everyone to have it handy." The miniature *Siddurim* usually contained, in addition to the traditional prayers, an invocation for God's protection on the perilous medieval highways. As a rule a calendar was appended, so that the lonely traveler might know when the holy days and festivals fell.[5]

The Genesis of the Ashkenazic *Mahzor*

The Bible informs us that Moses' intercession in behalf of his sister, Miriam, consisted of only five Hebrew words, truly a world record for liturgic brevity.[6] And what is equally remarkable is that his prayer was granted. Later Moses once more uttered a most urgent prayer: "Oh, let me behold Your Presence" (Exod. 33:18). And again his prayer was granted. Unfortunately, these efficacious prototypes of prayer were not taken to heart by Jews of succeeding generations. "Liturgies," says Israel Abrahams, "are inclined to prolixity," and the liturgy of the synagogue has been no exception. Each generation swelled the Jewish store of intercessions, invocations, laments, and thanksgivings. Numerous additions to the prayers were composed by poets, mystics, and ordinary men of piety. These compositions were at first optional. But the optional prayers of one generation tend to become the obligatory prayers of succeeding generations. Thus the *Siddur* grew until it became quite bulky. Then came the printing press, and many additional liturgic elements were included in the *Siddur*. Several biblical books were now permanent parts of the prayer book, and one or more commentaries were included. The *Siddur* thus became unwieldy, and it became necessary to subdivide it into several volumes. This was obviously a matter of simple logic. But logic is not as decisive in human affairs as one might expect. To divide the *Siddur* into two volumes must have appeared to some as a break with tradition and making this simple change required a measure of courage. The man who took this step was a publisher of the early sixteenth century who apologizes for his initiative in the introduction to his *Siddur:*

> Observing that the material in this work is constantly increasing, that it is attaining the size of the *Shulkan Arukh* . . . and has become too cumbersome to be carried into the synagogue, the present publisher, with a pure heart, decided to print the *Siddur* in two volumes, the first to contain the daily prayers and the second, the prayers for the holy days. This arrangement will enable one to purchase either part, as he may desire.[7]

It is thus that the *Mahzor* was born. The part of the prayer book which contains the daily and Sabbath services has retained the original name, and to this day is called the *Siddur*. The part that was detached, containing the prayers of the holidays, was called the *Mahzor* (Cycle [of holiday prayers]). In time the *Mahzor*, too, was subdivided into the High Holy Days *Mahzor* and the festival *Mahzor*.[8]

Consolidation of Minhagim

The printing press also influenced the minhagim, the local customs, of synagogue worship. It helped to standardize and consolidate the local customs that had developed over the centuries. These local customs never deviated from the tradition as set by the rabbis of the Talmud, but they did diverge in regard to the later accretions, especially the piyutim. Many localities had their own firmly established customs, so that a Jew visiting a neighborhood town often found it difficult to follow the service.

When the printing press was invented, the printers followed the prevailing customs. But it soon developed that the prevailing customs began to follow the printed *Siddurim*. The minhagim that existed only in limited areas tended to disappear. There were a few notable exceptions, the most famous of which was the community of Frankfort am Main, which has tenaciously held on to its local customs. But practically all other minhagim which prevailed only in limited areas merged with those of their regions. A consolidation of synagogue practice thus developed. This proved a blessing to the Jewish people. The minhagim that survived were only those that characterized relatively large sections of Jewry, such as Ashkenazim, the Sephardim, the Hasidim, the Yemenites, and a few others.

Handy Collections

Enterprising publishers soon discovered that the Jewish hunger for liturgic material was not limited to the traditional prayers of the synagogue. Prayer was an adjunct of every phase of Jewish life. To paraphrase a well-known biblical verse, the Jew engaged in prayer at all times: when he sat in his house, and when he walked by the way, and when he lay down, and when he rose up (Deut. 6:7). Why not publish handy prayer collections for these religious needs? The answer was a profusion of handy prayer collections. Among them were prayer booklets for young children and for travelers, for mealtime and for nighttime. There were handy collections of blessings for all occasions and hymns for the Sabbath table, daily midnight prayers (*Hatzot*) * and the special predawn prayers for the High Holy Days season (*selihot*),† Haggadot for the Passover Seder and special prayers for the Shavuot vigils,‡ lamentations for the Ninth of Av, and prayers for miscellaneous occasions. As the competition sharpened, publishers added commentaries and translations. Thus a handy booklet for use on Saturday afternoons, called *Oneg Shabbat* (Sabbath Delight), proudly announces on its title page that it contains "*The Ethics of the Fathers*, the *Barkhi Nafshi* [Ps. 104], precious pearls, and the Sabbath afternoon service, together with one hundred and ten commentaries, all with Judeo-German translations." [9]

There was still another potential market for liturgic materials, and the printers were quick to discover it—women. The Jewish woman had practically been left out of participa-

* *See pp. 502–505.*
† *See pp. 226 ff.*
‡ *See pp. 505–506.*

tion in Jewish worship. To be sure, women could attend the synagogue services within the special quarters designated for their use, but this privilege did not fully satisfy the religious cravings of the women. Because they had been excluded from the intensive education provided for the male children, the meaning of the Hebrew prayers was a total mystery to them. As was already pointed out,* the women's need for suitable prayer material was met by the devotional prayers in the vernacular known as tehinnot. The invention of the printing press made this development possible. Venturesome publishers and printers exploited this unsuspected demand, and thus enriched themselves as well as the Jewish legacy of liturgic materials.

The Beloved *Siddur*

Before the printing press was invented it was customary to adorn the manuscript *Siddur* with beautiful illuminations. Some *Siddurim* contained elaborate initial letters, decorative margins, and colorful illustrations of the text.[10] These pictorial illustrations have been studied and admired. And the writing, too, was often masterful. The specimens that have survived are few, especially when compared with the favorites of Jewish illuminators—the Haggadah, the *Megillah*, and the marriage contracts—but the few illuminated *Siddurim* that have endured are exquisite and are deservedly treasured with pride in the British Museum, the Jewish National and University Library in Jerusalem, the library of The Jewish Theological Seminary of America, and several other important collections.

When the printing press was invented, the woodcut replaced the hand-painted embellishments of the manuscripts. Unfortunately, the woodcuts were often crude. Their favorite subjects were the signs of the zodiac which accompanied the prayers for rain (*Geshem*).† In this service there is a piyut which sketches the agricultural work performed during the twelve months of the year. Each month was usually accompanied by an illustration of the corresponding sign of the zodiac. Other pictorial symbols frequently found in the

* *See pp. 473–74.*
† *See pp. 221–22.*

printed *Siddur* were the seven-branched candlestick, the six-pointed star (popularly called the "Shield of David"), and the palm branch and citron used during the Sukkot services. The title pages often contained a stylized picture of the Temple in Jerusalem—a wall with several trees upon it, flanked by imposing towers. It can be said generally that the introduction of printing led to the discontinuance of the artistic illumination of the prayer book.

But the Jew did not cease to express his love of the *Siddur* by artistic means. During the Middle Ages bookbinding was often an art rather than a craft. When the prayer book was handwritten, it was usually bound in parchment which was hand painted in vivid colors. The printed book was often adorned with silver covers, frequently of delicately wrought filigree. During the Renaissance it was quite fashionable for a young man to present his bride with a prayer book bound in an exquisite silver binding, and many a bride would proudly carry her gift to the synagogue.

Beginning with the sixteenth century an increasing number of Jews began to possess their own *Siddurim*. These prayer books were generally not bound in silver covers, but they were just as precious to their owners. The *Siddur*, adorned or unadorned, was the Jew's daily companion from the time he was enrolled in the heder, usually at the age of five, to the day of his death. And each time the Jew closed his *Siddur* after his devotions, he bestowed upon it a reverent and affectionate kiss.

24
THE SYNAGOGUE IN PREMODERN TIMES

At the end of the eighteenth century Europe was shaken by the eruption of the French Revolution. Among the historic changes initiated by that epoch-making event was the official demolition of the ghetto walls and the termination of the Jewish Middle Ages. At the opening of the eighteenth century, however, the Jewish Middle Ages was still at its height. This is dramatically demonstrated by an event which took place on Yom Kippur of the year 1705. On that day an auto-da-fé was celebrated in the public square of Lisbon in the presence of the king and queen. Sixty-six hapless victims of the Inquisition were on hand. They were addressed by an archbishop, who opened his address with an intemperate harangue: "O degraded remnants of Judaism . . . the last spoil of Judea! . . . You are the wretched fragments of the Synagogue, for all of its former greatness is come to an end."[1] The eloquent archbishop's theme was not original. For centuries the Church had repeatedly proclaimed that the synagogue was utterly degraded and defeated.*

But the institution of the synagogue, no less than Judaism itself, continued to represent a defiant challenge. Despite its lowly state, the synagogue succeeded in stirring up heretical doubts in the mind of many a Christian. The Church could have crushed its helpless opponent, but its doctrines had assigned to the Jews a special role, to be "the living witnesses of the true religion." The Jews were to be preserved, but in a state of humiliation, so as to demonstrate what happens to those who reject the true faith. The remnant of the Jewish people was therefore allowed to survive despite its obstinate persistence in its "error."

The Synagogue Triumphant

The medieval Jew, however, saw the situation in a totally different light. To begin with, he was utterly convinced of the truth of his faith. What is more, he did not see the synagogue as lowly and defeated. For the Jew, the synagogue was triumphant. It was for him "a fountain of living waters." It unfailingly provided him with spiritual light and strength. Indeed, it was the center of his life. As to the Church's splendor

* *See pp. 464–65.*

and might, they were inconsequential when viewed in the context of the divine scheme of universal history. When the Messiah comes, justice and truth will triumph, and the synagogue will emerge triumphant in the sight of all the nations.

For the present the Jews were content to build their synagogues in a relatively inconspicuous manner. Unlike the Christian cathedrals, which reflected in their magnificence both glory and power, the medieval synagogue was often indistinguishable from the houses on either side of it. The obvious purpose of this outward modesty was to remain unnoticed by outsiders as much as possible. In its outward obscurity the synagogue sought and frequently found a measure of security.

Where anonymity was not an adequate protection, the medieval Jews fortified their synagogues to resist attacks. After the cossack slaughter of the Polish Jews in the mid-seventeenth century, the Jews built many of their synagogues as defensive strongholds. These synagogues had thick walls, heavy buttresses, and crenellations for sharpshooters along the roof. The synagogue thus helped the Jew to achieve both salvation of soul and safety of life and limb.

Inside the synagogue the Jew was relaxed. He was shielded from the watchful eye of the Church and from the insolence of the mob. There he was part of the Holy Congregation of Israel. The institution itself he proudly identified with the divine prophecy of Ezekiel: "Thus saith the Lord God: Although I have removed them far off among the nations, and although I have scattered them among the countries, yet have I been to them as a little sanctuary in the countries where they are come" (Ezek. 11:16). The "little sanctuary," the rabbis taught, is an obvious reference to the Jewish houses of worship (Meg. 29a).

For the medieval Jew the synagogue was also the successor and heir of the Jerusalem Temple. The synagogue is to maintain this holy status until "the end of days," when the Messiah comes and restores the Holy Temple to its former glory. Occasionally a synagogue was sufficiently resplendent in its physical appearance actually to reflect the grandeur of the ancient Temple, as can be judged from the charm and magnificence of the Church of Santa Maria la Blanca in Toledo, which was originally the local synagogue. In the eighteenth century, however, the synagogues were generally humble in their physical appearance. Their structures reflected the insecurity and poverty of the ghettos and the unsettled nature of Jewish life. Why invest the meager resources of the people in magnificent structures if the community may be expelled at any time? Notwithstanding the synagogue's humble exterior, it served the Jew as a "portable homeland." Through its spiritual, cultural, and social impacts on his life, the synagogue provided the Jew with extraordinary resilience in his recurring crises, with inexhaustible hope in his darkest moments, and with moral strength in the face of interminable humiliations.

The Synagogue as a House of Prayer

The synagogue, being the "little sanctuary" of prophecy, was treated with due respect. Acts of commerce or frivolity were forbidden. But the Jew did not regard God as a superior Being whom one was to approach with "formal etiquette." Generally, a reverential attitude was maintained in the synagogue but without any pietistic affectations. Nor did he regard fund-raising activities for the maintenance of the synagogue or for other philanthropic institutions as commerce. The Jew did not find it irreverent to announce during the service financial pledges for worthy causes or even to sell the "honors" by auction at certain set occasions in order to obtain the wherewithal to maintain the synagogue's needs.

As a house of prayer the synagogue was almost in constant use. It was open all day and much of the night for private and public worship. In time of adversity the Jew went to the synagogue to seek God's help, and in time of rescue he went to the synagogue to rejoice in his deliverance and to chant psalms of praise and thanksgiving to God, his deliverer. One might say that the voice of prayer was always heard in the synagogue. Even during the midnight and predawn hours there were in the synagogue some saintly men who wept over the fate of Israel and implored God to make an end of the exile. And during the hours of regular daily services, the synagogue was well attended. However, it was on Sabbaths and festivals that the synagogue was resplendent with its multitude of worshipers. Each worshiper occupied his own seat, which he held by the principle of tenant right, often inherited from his father or purchased from an heirless widow. It was on these occasions that the Jew experienced the exaltation of being a descendant of Abraham, Isaac, and Jacob, and a member of the Holy Congregation of Israel.

Informality at Worship

Sanctimonious piety has not been a characteristic of Jewish worship. But in the Ashkenazic synagogue of Central and Eastern Europe the lack of decorum often exceeded even the norms of informality. And in the conventicles of the Hasidim it bordered on outright disorder. To be sure, if one entered a synagogue during the recitation of the *Tefillah* he could hear the proverbial pin drop. But during the other parts of the service, especially during the reading of the Torah, the Jew felt sufficiently at home in his "little sanctuary" to walk about whenever he felt restless or to exchange gossip with his neighbors. He also felt free to chant his prayers out loud, totally unconcerned as to whether his favorite melodies were in harmony with those of the hazan or his neighbors. If the result was a cacophony, he was hardly aware of it. He was so engrossed with his personal dialogue with God that he hardly heard the noises around him. But should the reader inadvertently introduce a slight departure from the local minhag, almost everyone would immediately note it, and corrections would rain down on the hapless reader from the remotest corners of the synagogue. The climax of noise and confusion was reached on Purim, when the Jew celebrated the rescue of the Persian Jews from the plot of wicked Haman, and on Simhat Torah, when he celebrated the annual completion of the reading of the Pentateuch. Samuel Pepys reports in his famous diary that he visited a London synagogue [2] on October 13, 1663. He arrived during the noisy procession with the scrolls * on Simhat Torah. His opinion was, to say the least, uncomplimentary. How could he grasp the unique nature of this joyous celebration? His reaction was understandably one of revulsion. In his diary he exclaims: "But Lord! to see the disorder, laughing, sporting, and no attention, but confusion in all their service, more like brutes than people knowing the true God." [3]

It should be noted, however, that the indecorous behavior in the medieval synagogue reflected in large measure the general European culture in which the Jew lived. If the Jews talked to their neighbors during the services, so did the Gentiles in their churches, especially in the pre-Reformation period.[4]

Despite the lack of decorum, the synagogue was not devoid of piety and inwardness. Israel Abrahams warns against such a conclusion:

> It must be remembered that a free and easy attitude in worship was associated with a very sincere piety. . . . On the whole, the abuses of the great principle that the Jew was at home in his place of worship did not appreciably lessen devotion. It was only at the close of the eighteenth century, when the Jews hovered between the old and the new, that this familiar attitude towards God [came to be regarded as] undecorous.[5]

The Synagogue as a House of Study

The medieval synagogue was more than a house of prayer. It was the "mother of all the ghetto institutions." Within its precincts there were study halls, schools, and the social and philanthropic institutions of the community.

The most important adjunct of the synagogue was the bet hamidrash, the study hall. Within the bet hamidrash there was a library in which one would find Bibles with various commentaries, several sets of talmudic folios, a number of useful codes, especially the authoritative *Shulhan Arukh*, a few kab-

* *See pp. 467–68.*

balistic tracts with *The Zohar* occupying the place of honor, and a variety of other miscellaneous religious texts. While the scholarly Jew would spend his leisure time in the bet hamidrash studying his favorite rabbinic or mystic texts, the ordinary Jew would go to the bet hamidrash to participate in one or more study groups which met there regularly. There was quite a choice of study groups. There was usually a Talmud study group for the more learned members of the community and several study groups for the simple folk. Some met for the study of the weekly portion of the Torah and its commentary of Rashi,* the Midrash,† or some other uncomplicated religious texts. The teachers were, as a rule, volunteers who taught Torah for the reward in the hereafter. On a Sabbath afternoon the bet hamidrash was alive with many groups engaged in the study of Torah.[6]

In addition to the informal adult study groups, the synagogue also housed the community school where the children were taught to read the prayers and to comprehend the contents of the Bible and its commentary of Rashi. Older children were taught the rabbinic texts with their commentaries. In some cities the synagogue also housed an academy for advanced students, a yeshivah, in which the studies led to rabbinic ordination.

In the Jewish tradition study is superior to prayer. The rabbinic emphasis on the importance of study was formulated in the Mishnah:

> The following are things for which a man enjoys the fruits in this world while the principal remains for him in the world to come: the honoring of father and mother, the practice of charity, and the making of peace between man and his friend; but the study of the Torah is equal to them all [Peah 1:1].

Added to its high rank in the hierarchy of divine commandments, the study of Torah was also regarded as a kind of divine worship.‡ It was therefore considered improper to in-

* *See pp. 389, 535.*
† *See p. 531.*
‡ *See pp. 108 ff.*

terrupt one's study for the purpose of prayer. If such an interruption was unavoidable, it was considered expedient to reduce it to a minimum. It therefore became customary to hold regular services in the bet hamidrash for the convenience of the scholars and students. However, a considerable number of nonscholars preferred to pray in the bet hamidrash because there the rules of conduct were somewhat relaxed: one was permitted to eat, sleep, and smoke, which were prohibited in the synagogue. These liberties were especially sought after by the Hasidim, who usually partook of refreshments after each service. Their *shtiebel*s were therefore dedicated as study halls rather than synagogues.

By the eighteenth century the synagogue and its adjunct the bet hamidrash were the religious and cultural centers of Jewish life. When the Jew was not engaged in the pursuit of his livelihood, he knew of only two places where he could raise his head with a measure of dignity—his humble home and his equally humble synagogue. And he usually spent as much time in his synagogue as in his home.

The Synagogue as a Center of Community Life

The synagogue was the nerve center of the Jewish community; around it all communal activities revolved. The Jew therefore made sure to live as close to the synagogue as he could. A man who was forced to live in the countryside was a man to be pitied, for he was cut off from much of Jewish life. Even before the ghetto walls were erected, the Jewish quarter was a compact settlement, a de facto ghetto.

The synagogue was usually the center of a constellation of institutions, some with physical quarters of their own. In addition to the bet hamidrash, the synagogue usually housed the community offices, the courtroom, the ritual bath, the matzah bakery, the hospice for needy travelers, and the *Tanzhaus*, the hall where weddings and other festivities were held. A large courtyard was an important adjunct of the synagogue. There the canopy would be set up for marriages, which were performed in the open as a symbol of abundant blessings for the couple. The monthly service of the Consecration of the Moon, too, was held in the synagogue courtyard. In those cities where the Jews were allowed to police their own community, a number of prison cells were installed in the synagogue quarters.

The Seat of Self-government

The synagogue was used for town meetings to transact communal business. In larger cities there were special synagogues not only for the different rites, such as those of the Ashkenazim, Sephardim, and the *shtiebel*s of each Hasidic group, but there were also special synagogues for the different crafts. For example, as late as the early twentieth century the city of Lublin, Poland, held "the Kotlerschul, belonging to the coppersmiths guild, the M'schorsimschul for the business clerks, . . . the Lauferschul, dedicated to the carters and porters, and the Schneiderschul to the tailors." [7] The members of these guilds would meet in their synagogues for prayer and study as well as the transaction of business.

Ordinances endorsed by the community leadership were submitted to the people for approval at special meetings in the synagogue. Transgressors were brought before the court of justice which met in the synagogue precincts. When an oath was to be administered, the person was brought near the ark of the Torah, from which a scroll was taken and held as a witness.

There were, however, cases where strong measures were necessary, and the ban of excommunication was invoked. The ban was solemnly pronounced by the rabbi or the reader in the synagogue. The externals of this penalty were weird and humiliating. The proclamation of the ban was made with lighted black candles and a blast of the shofar. Awesome maledictions were also invoked upon the head of the excommunicated culprit. This frightful ceremony was performed in front of the ark, and the Torah scrolls were held as witnesses.

But the most striking practice, one which insured justice for all, was directly tied with the synagogue services. When an individual, man or woman, found himself helpless before the mighty power of what is nowadays called "the establishment" or before anyone who was mighty because of wealth or government connections, the aggrieved could resort to a unique tactic sanctioned by Jewish tradition. He could rise during the congregational services and call for a halt in the prayers. The service would immediately come to a stop and would remain silenced until the aggrieved was satisfied that justice would be done and without delay. How this remarkable tradition developed is hard to say. But it was a recognized procedure, and it was resorted to by the orphan, the widow, the stranger, the injured.[8] That this tactic did not become a communal nuisance is only because of the integrity of the Jewish courts, which seldom gave anyone the feeling that he was deprived of justice.

Since the synagogue occupied so central a position in the life of the Jewish community, it is not surprising that it was frequently exploited for political purposes. Thus the elector of the Palatinate decreed in 1733 that a Jew's oath was invalid unless it was taken in the synagogue before a scroll of the Torah. The king's demands were read in the synagogue. And when someone of the royal blood or the king himself passed through the town, the Jews would gather in the synagogue, don their prayer shawls, take the scrolls in their arms, and march to receive the dignitary.

But political partisanship was rare in the synagogue. The prayer for the government was dutifully recited at the Sabbath service, irrespective of who was in power. Politics was too dangerous a game for so helpless a community. In all political battles between the princes, both lay and ecclesiastical, the Jews were, as a rule, strictly neutral.

Democracy in the Synagogue

In the synagogue everyone was a person: everyone was counted into the quorum of ten adult men needed for a congregational service,[9] and everyone had a say in all communal matters. More remarkable, everyone was eligible to lead the congregation in prayer. The only requirement was a person's ability to be the reader. (A more important limitation was due to the professionalization of the leadership of the Sabbath and festival services,* which limited this egalitarian principle mainly to the weekday services.) On the anniversary of a parent's death, the humblest worshiper could claim his right to lead the congregation in prayer.

Every Jew was also eligible to be called to the Torah. Ever since the reading of the Torah was professionalized † and it was no longer required that the person called should read his portion, even the illiterate could be honored with an aliyah. Here, too, the poorest man had his rights. On certain important occasions, such as the Sabbath after he reached his majority, the Sabbath before his marriage, and the anniversary of a parent's death, every Jew was called to the Torah. And on Simhat Torah ‡ no Jew was deprived of an aliyah. The congregation would subdivide itself into several parallel congregations, and the Torah portion would be read repeatedly in each of the subcongregations until everyone who desired an aliyah was called to the Torah. Generally, everyone wanted an aliyah on Simhat Torah. So the services would last well past the midday hour.

There was only one exception to the egalitarian principles of the synagogue. The descendants of the Kohanim and the Levites who had ministered in the ancient Temple in Jerusalem had a number of prerogatives. The first two men called to the Torah were always a Kohen and a Levite respectively. These theoretical Kohanim also bestowed on the congregation the ancient priestly benediction, and the Levites dutifully poured water on the hands of the Kohanim prior to their blessing the congregation. But these hereditary Kohanim and Levites included both rich and poor, learned and ignorant. Indeed, the ritual of blessing the congregation was a demonstration of democracy in action, for the proudest and humblest

* *See pp. 518–21.*
† *See pp. 183–84.*
‡ *See pp. 222–24.*

men stood next to each other and performed their hereditary duty as equals before the congregation.

The Functionaries of the Synagogue

The rabbi, the dayan (judge), and the hazan have already been discussed in earlier chapters. There was another important functionary, however: the shammash, or beadle.[10] Although his official duties were lowly, he often became the de facto ruler of the synagogue. It was his duty to see to it that the synagogue was clean and warm, that the lamps were lit for evening services, and that the Torah scrolls were rolled to the exact portion of the day. He ran official errands for the rabbi and for the lay officers of the congregation. One of his humble duties was to wake the people early in the morning to come to the synagogue for the "service of the Creator." [11] Notwithstanding these unimpressive duties, the shammash was often a power to reckon with because of his ubiquity. He attended all public and private affairs. This gave him access to a good deal of intimate knowledge of people's private affairs, which raised him from the status of a servant to that of a confidant. His relationship with people was often on the level of familiarity rather than servility.

The lay officials of the synagogue were democratically elected, as were the religious functionaries.[12] To be sure, the poor man seldom if ever stood for election. He usually had neither the ambition nor the following. But this is a universal situation, prevailing even in the most advanced democracies of the Western world. In theory, however, the poorest man had the same rights in the synagogue as the richest. His limitations arose from the proverbial truth that "the ruin of the poor is their poverty" (Prov. 10:15).

The chief lay official of the synagogue was the parnas, who corresponded to what is now called the synagogue president. The parnas was seldom a man of outstanding scholarship. He was usually a person endowed with leadership ability and an abundance of ambition to wield power. The parnas presided over a council of elders, which was the policy-making body.

These offices were not hereditary, and the officers could be deposed by popular vote.

The parnas was assisted by two gabbaim, originally in charge of the collection and administration of the congregational charity fund. In the course of time their function changed, so that in the eighteenth century the gabbaim were the ones who regulated the synagogue services. They assigned the honors during the reading of the Torah and decided who was to lead the congregation in prayer.

The Synagogue Aristocracy

Notwithstanding the prevailing democracy in the synagogue there was an unofficial aristocracy which commanded respect and even a measure of power. It consisted of the men of learning. But this aristocracy was open to talent. "Be heedful [not to neglect] the children of the poor," says the Talmud, "for from them Torah goeth forth" (Ned. 81a). From its earliest beginnings the synagogue honored the scholar rather than the wellborn. There were poor artisans among the sages of the Talmud. Since the door to scholarship was always open, promising young men rose up in each generation and achieved the rank of scholar. The man of learning was assured of lifelong honor and also several unchallenged privileges. This tradition was in accord with the remarkable statement of the Mishnah: "If a bastard was a scholar and a *Kohen Gadol* an ignoramus, the learned bastard takes precedence over the ignorant *Kohen Gadol*" (Hor. 3:8). The above is the concluding decision on the priorities in the calling of people to the reading of the Torah. "A priest," says the Mishnah, "takes precedence over a Levite, a Levite over an Israelite," and the scholar precedes everyone in his category, even the *Kohen Gadol.*

Women in the Synagogue

There was a fly in the democratic ointment. Women had almost no status in Jewish worship. In the ancient Temple in

Jerusalem they had no share in the performance of any important ritual. They were required to offer certain sacrifices, and they could always bring free-will and thanksgiving offerings, but they could not enter the inner court where the ceremony of the imposition of hands was performed. This exclusion of women from the center of worship became a firm precedent for later generations. Hence women were neither preachers nor readers. They were not counted into the quorum needed for public worship, nor could they participate in the synagogue worship except as backbenchers or in their own special quarters.

A woman might be called to the reading of the Torah but this was disapproved on grounds of propriety. It might embarrass the menfolk who were not able to read from the scroll. This principle is laid down by the rabbis of the Talmud: "All are qualified to be among the seven [who read], even a minor and a woman, only the Sages said that a woman should not read in the Torah out of respect for the congregation" (Meg. 23a). But the most decisive restriction on the Jewish woman was her segregation in special quarters during worship.

Though women were not obliged to recite the prescribed prayers, they could not be denied the right to pray. Precedents for this are plentiful. In the Bible we read about Miriam leading the women in a song of thanksgiving after crossing the Red Sea (Exod. 15:20–21) and Deborah singing her famous song of triumph and thanksgiving (Jud. 4, 5). Hannah prays for a child, and when her prayer is granted she utters a song of thanksgiving (1 Sam. 1:10–13; 2:1–10). Women went to prayer meetings on Sabbaths and festivals (2 Kings 4:23). In the synagogue, however, the Jewish woman was, from the start, practically silent. The rabbis exempted the woman from the daily recitation of the *Shema* and the putting on of the tefillin. However, women were required to recite the *Tefillah* (Ber. 3:3). Hence they were permitted to enter the synagogue for prayer (Sotah 22a).

Welcome though the women were in the synagogue, they were nonetheless segregated from the men. This is not surprising since women in those days had their own quarters in the household as well.[13] By the eighteenth century the women's gallery was a standard feature of the synagogue.* The women in the gallery were permitted to pray in the vernacular, a practice on which the rabbis would have looked with horror in the male section of the synagogue.

The majority of Jewish women were not literate enough to read the Hebrew prayers. Nonetheless they flocked to the synagogue on Sabbaths and festivals, and their gallery was usually crowded. If the women could not read, they could feel the general nature of the prayers. So they prayed with their hearts. And during the monthly Blessing the New Month,† they wept loudly when the hazan mournfully chanted the prayer for a month of blessings.

Women's weeping at prayer had its biblical precedent. In the well-known prophetic portion read on Rosh Hashanah the touching words of Jeremiah describe Mother Rachel weeping for her children in exile (Jer. 31:15). Jewish women emulated Mother Rachel, and their loud weeping could be heard in the male section of the synagogue, often drowning out the hazan's soulful chanting.

In response to a need felt by many women in the gallery there arose a unique institution among the Jews of Eastern Europe. Female precentors, known as *forzuggerins*, read the prayers out loud, enabling the clusters of women around them to repeat the prayers after them. The *forzuggerins* would also read the translations of the prayers. This created a market for *Siddurim* with Judeo-German translations. Numerous editions of such prayer books were published in Eastern Europe.

In her subordinate position in the synagogue the medieval Jewish woman was not unhappy. She fully accepted her segregation at the services and her secondary role in the synagogue no less than her sex. She found her satisfaction in the performance of the religious duties assigned to her, and she found her fulfillment in the scholarship of her husband and her sons.

* *See pp. 547–48.*
† *See pp. 264–66.*

Children in the Synagogue

If the woman was underprivileged in the synagogue, children were definitely overprivileged. In the children the congregation saw its potential scholars and saints. The congregation therefore lavished upon the children its collective affection and patiently tolerated their noisy presence at the services.

Actually the congregation had no alternative. Prayer had to be taught, and the habit of prayer had to be cultivated from earliest childhood. Learning to pray is not just a matter of learning how to read the prayers. Nor is it a matter of learning the order of the services. The mastery of these skills could well be left to the school, where instruction in the classroom and prayer practice in a children's congregation could adequately impart these skills. But a child can learn to pray only by the example of his parents and by continued participation in the official services of the synagogue. A children's service is make-believe; an adult service in which his parents participate is authentic worship. The medieval synagogue accepted both the nurture and training of the children as a congregational responsibility no less than the parents. The home and the synagogue were the instruments for the implementation of the child's religious education. At home the child not only emulated his parents in the recitation of his prayers every morning when he rose from sleep and every night before he retired to sleep,* but he also learned to recite the many benedictions prescribed for every meaningful experience. At home he actively participated in all the daily and the festive family rituals. He joined in the recitation of the grace after meals; he recited the Kiddush with his father before the Sabbath and festival meals; he held the candle at the Havdalah service at the conclusion of the Sabbath; he assisted in the kindling of the Hanukah lights; and on Passover he was the hero at the Seder, which he initiated with the traditional Four Questions. The child was a partner in the planning and the execution of the family rituals.

In the synagogue, too, the child played a clearly defined

* *See pp. 291–92.*

role. As soon as he was old enough to respond to the benedictions with Amen, he was brought to the synagogue and taught by his father to join the congregation in this response. He was taught to handle the *Siddur* with reverence. If it accidentally fell to the ground, he learned to kiss it penitently, and when he closed it at the conclusion of the service, he learned to kiss it reverently. Gradually the father introduced him to new sections of the service until the boy was able to join fully in the congregational worship.

But until the child was old enough to joint the congregation in prayer, he was a nuisance and a source of disorder. He would run from the men's section of the synagogue to the women's section and then back again. Occasionally he would fall on the path between his parents and emit a loud cry that would startle the congregation, frighten his mother, and cause his father to run to the scene of the "catastrophe." But the congregation did not protest. From the time the boy was brought to the synagogue at the age of eight days to be initiated into the covenant of Abraham to the time he was initiated as a full-fledged member of the house of Israel at the age of thirteen, the congregation willingly and patiently accepted him and even granted him a number of privileges.

At the Friday evening service a child would be given the privilege of sipping the wine from the cup over which the reader had recited the Kiddush. And after the service he would kiss the rabbi's hand and receive the rabbi's blessing. On Sabbath mornings he kissed the Torah scrolls as they were carried to the reading desk or back to the ark. And when he was old enough, he was honored with the chanting of the prophetic portion. On Sukkot the child would join his father in the procession with the lulav and etrog. Usually the father would allow him to carry these religious symbols during at least part of the procession. The climax of his participation in the services was on Simhat Torah, when he partook in the procession with the scrolls, bearing a flag and chanting with the congregation the appropriate verses. Finally, when he reached his majority at the age of thirteen,* he was ceremo-

* *See pp. 466–67.*

niously called to the Torah as a bar mitzvah, and he officially became a part of the congregation. Thereafter his participation in the congregational worship was as regular as his father's. The congregation's hopeful anticipations were then fully realized, and the educational pattern in which the synagogue had shared achieved its objectives. The child had grown up to be a Jew who prayed both in the privacy of his home and in the public services of the synagogue.

The End of an Era

During their long Middle Ages the Jews had established the fact that the synagogue was truly triumphant. There was no Jewish community without a synagogue. Thus a synod of Castilian Jews held in 1432 adopted an ordinance that was typical of Jewish life throughout the Middle Ages. The ordinance prescribed that "any community having ten families or more shall establish a place for prayers. They shall either buy or rent a house for that purpose so that they may not interrupt the prayers even for a single day." [14] And in the larger communities there were many synagogues, all of them alive with prayer and study, with communal and philanthropic activities. From dawn to dusk and far into the night the synagogue building and its adjoining institutional structures were in constant use. Hardly anyone suspected that a world-shattering event was about to topple the ghetto walls and initiate a new era in Jewish life, an era that was seriously to affect the institution of the synagogue and challenge the essence of Jewish worship. Hardly anyone anticipated the critical challenge to prayer, a challenge that would shake the firm foundations of Jewish worship developed during the millennia of uninterrupted growth and development.

CONCLUSION

JEWISH WORSHIP IN MODERN TIMES

Modernity has been defined as the postmedieval period, extending from about the sixteenth century to the present day.[1] During these centuries, Western Europe slowly and painfully broke with the scholastic modes of thought which were based on traditional texts, such as the religious classics and Aristotelian philosophy, and turned to creative originality based on experimentation and objective research. Modernity, thus defined, did not begin to make its appearance in the ghettos of Central and Western Europe until the turn of the nineteenth century. It did not reach the East European Jewish communities until the latter half of the nineteenth century. And in the oriental countries the impact of modernity was not felt by the Jews until the beginning of the twentieth century.

When modernity reached the Jews it provoked many perplexing problems, among them the adjustment of the liturgy to the new world. Adjustment to new situations was not unknown to the Jewish people. The institution of the synagogue and its liturgy were the outcomes of such adjustments.* At times foreign rituals even found their way into the Jewish tradition. These foreign elements were slowly and imperceptibly assimilated. Judaism stamped its own character on them, thus converting them into authentic parts of the tradition. In the later Middle Ages, however, this process practically ceased. Everything new was stubbornly resisted and rejected. In modern times, changes or innovations along the pattern of the olden times are rejected not only by the Orthodox but also by the non-Orthodox who find the historical process too slow for the tempo of modern life. Besides, say they, Judaism received such a powerful jolt when it was suddenly catapulted from medievalism into modernity that an emergency

* *See pp. 63–67.*

situation has been created and emergency measures are called for. Some Jews have therefore set out to inaugurate the necessary adjustments and changes in order to meet the challenge of modernity.

Correcting the Text of the *Siddur*

No sooner were the gates of the Central European ghettos opened than young Jews began to flock to the universities. Many applied themselves to the mastery of professional skills. Others concentrated on scholarly pursuits. From among the latter emerged a number of ranking scholars who applied their scholarly techniques and their critical minds to the study of the Jewish classics. They initiated what came to be called the "science of Judaism." They examined the biblical, rabbinic, and medieval texts and discovered that many corruptions had crept into them. Some of these scholars set out to correct the classic texts by careful comparative study of old manuscripts. One of the classic texts thus studied was the *Siddur*, and it was found that many errors had crept into the prayers and that some of the prayers had been seriously corrupted. This is not surprising, since the *Siddur* has been the most popular book among the Jews, and, to quote the late Louis Ginzberg, "the more popular a book is, the more it is copied, and the more it is copied, the more its text is apt to become corrupt." [2] It will be recalled that Saadia Gaon's reason for publishing his *Siddur* was that during his travels he had found "many errors in the prayers" which he resolved to correct.* When the printing press was invented and numerous editions of the prayer book were published, the errors multiplied, especially in the seventeenth century when the publishers, in their haste to feed the market, became careless.

In the eighteenth century a number of scholars began to concern themselves with the rectification of the text of the *Siddur*, but it was not until the nineteenth century that the task was fully accomplished through the dedicated and scholarly efforts of Seligman Baer. In 1868 Baer's *Siddur*, *Avodat*

* *See pp. 385–88.*

Yisrael (The Worship of Israel), was published, and it was immediately recognized as a definitive work. Baer had access to old manuscripts and old editions of various *Siddurim.* He corrected, revised, emended, and finally published what has justly been called the "*Siddur* par excellence."

The text of the Baer *Siddur* is accompanied by a commentary in which changes in the text are explained and supported by references to variant readings. He also gives a digest of the customs and the order of the prayers. Baer's *Siddur* became the basic text for subsequent publications of the *Siddur.*

Decorum at Prayer

In the early nineteenth century the Jews of Central Europe became sensitive to Christian opinion of the Jews and of Judaism. As contacts with non-Jews increased, this sensitivity grew and became an obsession. The problem of decorum at worship thus became a live issue.

The vast majority of Gentiles were neither aware of nor concerned with the nature or content of Jewish worship. The few Gentiles who had visited a synagogue service did so purely out of curiosity. Their recorded impressions vary, depending on the section of the service they witnessed. Thus Aimé Palliere, a French Roman Catholic priest, begins the story of his conversion to Judaism with a description of how he strayed into a synagogue on Yom Kippur when the congregation was reciting the silent *Tefillah* of the Neilah service.

> The spectacle of that large number of men assembled, their shoulders covered by *Talliths*, suddenly disclosed to my eyes a far-off past. The Hebrews of the Doré Bible were there on their feet before me. . . . At first, on seeing the prayer shawls uniformly worn by all the participants in the service, I thought that in a way they were all officiating. . . . In the second place, it seemed to me that this silent assembly was in expectancy of something about to happen.[3]

This impression of Jewish worship, which ultimately led to the priest's conversion to Judaism, is not universal. More often the impression has not been complimentary.* Thus an American visitor to England in 1815, Joseph Ballard, describes his reactions:

> It being the Jewish Sabbath, I was induced to visit the synagogue, near Duke Street, the residence exclusively of these Shylocks. . . . The service was chanted in Hebrew, the congregation joining at times, in a din most horrible. I came away disgusted with the little reverence they seemed to pay to the Being who pronounced them His chosen people.[4]

The lack of decorum at the synagogue services was due, in large measure, to each worshiper's practicing the cantor's role at the conclusion of each prayer. Thus several hundred Jews would more or less simultaneously—but not in unison—erupt into cantorial chanting. The result was both vociferous and cacophonous. This time-honored medieval practice was carried over into the modern era.

Another discordant element was that of conversation during the reading of the Torah and during the reader's repetition of the *Tefillah*. It was the practice of almost every Jew to review the weekly portion before the Sabbath services. Since the worshiper had read each verse of the portion thrice—twice in the original and once in the Aramaic translation—the reading in the synagogue could not possibly hold his attention. The reader's recitation of the *Tefillah*, too, was only a repetition of what each worshiper had just recited silently with proper devotion. Hence conversation was quite common during these parts of the service. These breaches of decorum were vigorously protested.[5] Maimonides, sensitive to the taunts of Moslems who said that the Jews were not reverential at worship, went so far as to abolish the silent *Tefillah* so that the people would of necessity listen to the reader and refrain from conversation.[6] This radical reform was in force in Egypt, Palestine, and Syria from the twelfth to the sixteenth century, when it was abolished by Rabbi David Ibn Zimra (the Radbaz).[7]

* *See pp. 554–55.*

With the coming of modernity some synagogues began to take drastic action to enforce decorum. In the eighteenth century Rabbi Menachem Navarra pronounced an excommunication on a worshiper who was in the habit of talking at the services. He based his severe penalty on an old regulation of the community of Verona.[8] In the Great Synagogue of London, we are informed, it was forbidden to chew tobacco; a fine of two shillings and sixpence was imposed on transgressors. Since the transgressors were usually from among the poor, the fine was sufficient to be a deterrent. And when the building of the Great Synagogue of London was dedicated in 1790, the chief rabbi composed a prayer which contained an admonition against indecorous behavior at worship: "May we restrain our mouths from idle discourse during the prayer and reading of the Law. Of this let the presidents and elders be careful strictly to admonish the community."

These sporadic efforts were of little avail until the Reform movement was launched in Western Europe and in America. The Reform Jews were strongly motivated by a desire to be accepted in the non-Jewish community as moderns. Strict decorum therefore became a characteristic of the Reform ritual. When the Conservative synagogues broke away from the Reform, they retained this asset. And in time the Neo-Orthodox synagogues in Europe and America fell in line, so that decorum generally prevails at Jewish worship except in the synagogues of the extreme Orthodox, where the spirit of modernity has not yet penetrated. However, a word of caution is necessary: "A minus of decorum does not always mean a plus of devotion; just as little as a maximum of respectability and stiffness are not to be taken as signs of true piety." [9]

Translation of the Prayers

As long as the vernacular of the Jews was Hebrew there was linguistic harmony in Jewish worship. The psalmists composed their psalms in the language of the people. In the rabbinic period, however, a gulf developed between the language of prayer and the vernacular of the people. The Jews of

Palestine and Babylonia spoke Aramaic, and the Jews of the Hellenistic Diaspora spoke Greek. But the rabbis composed their prayers in pure Hebrew, because they regarded Hebrew as the holy tongue.

The rabbis were cognizant of the linguistic disharmony, and therefore permitted the use of the vernacular in prayer. But Hebrew was their preference. Among the rituals which one may recite "in any language," the rabbis included the *Shema* and the *Tefillah* (Sotah 7:1–2; Ber. 40b).[10] Indeed, several prayers were formulated in the Aramaic language, and these prayers became permanent parts of the liturgy.*

In Caesarea, Alexandria, and other cities of the Hellenistic Diaspora, Greek was generally used as the language of prayer. In Rome, too, the service was conducted in Greek,[11] and the translation of the Pentateuch into Greek, known as the Septuagint, was not just a literary exercise. It met a need among the Jews of Alexandria who did not know Hebrew. The Greek translation was used in the services in place of the Hebrew original. The fact that these Jewish communities did not survive has often been cited as evidence of the danger of abandoning the Hebrew tongue as the medium of prayer. Maimonides underscored the importance of praying in Hebrew on purely pragmatic grounds. He says that the use of foreign languages by the exiles in Persia, Greece, and other countries caused Ezra and his synod to formulate the prayers in pure Hebrew, so that all Israelites might pray in unison.[12]

The Pitfalls of Translation

The translation of the Bible into Greek in the second century before the Common Era was welcomed by the Alexandrian Jews with jubilation. The rabbis, however, regarded this historic event as a catastrophe and instituted an annual fast on the eighth day of Tevet to mourn that fateful event.[13] In this act the rabbis showed deep insight. For, in truth, how can one punctiliously translate the Hebrew text into a foreign tongue? A translation is at best an approximation. Overtones and nuances are inevitably lost or replaced by those of the culture of the new language. Thus Franz Rosenzweig, himself a trans-

* *See pp. 33–34.*

lator of the Bible into German, says: "Anyone who translated into the German language must, to some extent, translate into Christian language."[14] The language of Hebrew prayer is especially difficult to translate because its spirit, mood, and fervor are often lost in translation. The replacement of archaic metaphors with modern figures of speech often alters not only the text's flavor but also its character. The Kedushah, for example, has always transmitted to the synagogue worshiper an ineffable feeling of holiness. This mystic ingredient is lost in the translation. The nuances and the delicate shadings of the Hebrew idiom are lost.

These difficulties become insuperable when it comes to the translation of the piyutim * because of their obscure style. "The tyranny of the acrostic, the wealth of cryptic allusions [to the classic texts], and the enormous divergence between the ways and habits of thought peculiar to the liturgists of the Rabbinical and Poetanic Schools and those of a modern European, especially of an Englishman,"[15] make the translation of the piyutim a rugged and stubborn task.

Some translators have taken the liberty of departing from the classic text in order to make their translations more lucid and relevant. Others have resorted to vague renditions in order to make the rabbinic prayers acceptable to the varying shades of religious belief. These procedures can be forgiven because they are motivated by the desire to meet the contingencies of modernity. However, the deliberate falsification of the content of the prayers by incorporating into them modern concepts is to be condemned. The original composers would shudder to read as their compositions what they would regard as outright heresies. This kind of "translation" misleads the trusting but uninformed worshiper. What he utters is not a classic Hebrew prayer in translation, but a modern prayer composed by the "translator."

English Translations of the *Siddur*

In the year 1641 John Evelyn recorded in his diary an incident involving "a Burgundian Jew, who had married an apostate Kentish woman. . . . He showed me," writes Evelyn, "several

* *See pp. 168 ff.*

books of their devotion, which he had translated into English for the instruction of his wife." [16] Unfortunately, that first English translation of the *Siddur* has not come down to us.

Even more intriguing is the story of a translation of the *Siddur* dated 1738, which has the distinction of being the first published work of its kind. The translation was done by an apostate. He concealed his identity and used the pseudonym of Gamaliel Ben Pedahzur, because he was afraid that the leaders of the London Jewish community would not sanction a translation by an apostate. The title of the translation was strange and long even for the eighteenth century, when long titles were not unusual.[17] The translation was really, as the author claimed, "remarkable." It was full of distortions aimed at besmirching his former coreligionists. Added to the willful distortions are gross ignorance and barbaric English style. The work has aroused interest solely because it was the first full translation of the *Siddur* and because it carried so tantalizing a pseudonym, the name of a prince of the tribe of Manasseh (Num. 7:54). The publication of this translation must have amused the Gentiles and aroused the indignation of the contemporary Jews. Otherwise it is no more than a literary curiosity of interest only to antiquarians.

Shortly after this curious translation a number of accurate translations appeared which revealed the stately diction of many of the Hebrew prayers.[18] The first authentic translation, which originated in London but was published in New York City, appeared in 1766. The translator, Isaac Pinto, stated in his introduction that since Hebrew was "imperfectly understood by many, and by some not at all, it has been necessary to translate our prayers in the language of the country wherein it hath pleased the Divine Providence to appoint our lot." He hoped that his translation would lead to "the improvement of my brethren in the devotion."

Notwithstanding the author's good intentions and the fairly accurate and dignified devotional style of the translation, the wardens of the Spanish and Portuguese congregation in London refused to approve the publication. This is strange since the congregation had approved a Spanish translation twenty-

Marriage Contract, 1871, The Israel Museum, Jerusalem. PHOTO: ALFRED BERNHEIM

eight years earlier. Perhaps they feared that the English translation would transplant their beloved Castilian, as it eventually did. Whatever the reason, Isaac Pinto betook himself to the colonies, where a thriving congregation of Spanish and Portuguese Jews existed, the Shearith Israel Congregation in New York City, and had his translation published there. Thus the first authentic translation of the Jewish liturgy into the English vernacular is a joint venture of London and New York and is proudly claimed by both British and American Jews.

One more eighteenth century translation is of interest because its author, David Levi, was a fascinating personality. He was a self-made scholar, endowed with inexhaustible energy and industry. He produced prodigious works, all in the midst of crushing poverty. In addition to his prolific literary achievements, he seems to have loved a good controversy. When Joseph Priestley in his "Letters Addressed to the Jews" invited the Jews to a friendly discussion of the evidences of Christianity, David Levi could not resist the invitation and entered the polemic with his usual vigor. This polemic grew and expanded. Then he took on no less a personality than Thomas Paine. In a series of letters addressed to the author of the *Age of Reason* he ably defended the Bible.

David Levi's greatest achievement is his translation into English of practically the whole of the Sephardic and Ashkenazic liturgies. He applied himself to this gigantic and pioneering task with diligence and competence. His translation has been a model for future translations and has made the task much easier for his successors.

In the nineteenth century numerous translations of the *Siddur* were published. There were translations into German, French, Italian, Polish, Russian, Dutch, Spanish, Hungarian, Danish, Bohemian, Romanian, Croatian, and others. England and America had their full share of new translations.

One of these is worthy of special note. It was published in 1891 under the title of *The Authorized Daily Prayer Book of the United Hebrew Congregations of the British Empire*. The translation by S. Singer was printed opposite the corresponding Hebrew pages. Its purpose was not to replace the Hebrew by the vernacular but to help the worshiper to understand the traditional prayers. This *Siddur* was authorized by Chief Rabbi N. M. Adler, and the cost of its production was defrayed by Mrs. Nathaniel Montefiore. It sold at the nominal price of one shilling, which resulted in a large export trade with America. In 1904 a *Mahzor* with an English version, edited by H. N. Adler, became a sort of companion to the Singer prayer book. Some of the piyutim in this *Mahzor* were translated by Israel Zangwill, Nina Salaman, Elsie Davis, and other distinguished British Jews. The *Adler Mahzor*, as this publication is generally called, was also widely used in America.[19]

In recent years a plethora of new translations have appeared in America. Each one tried to improve on the Singer translation, but they hardly succeeded. To be sure, the style of most of the new translations is smoother and more modern. But in their attempt to make the text more lucid, they took liberties which in some cases border on falsification of the Hebrew text. This writer, as noted in the preface, has chosen to quote the Singer translation because it is by far the most authentic.

Providing the prayer book with a translation into the vernacular was not an innovation. Translations had appeared as early as the sixteenth century. The old translations into Spanish, Italian, and Judeo-German vernaculars were usually published in Hebrew script and were intended primarily for women. In modern translations Latin script is used. This accords with the education of modern Jews, which is, as a rule, derived from the secular school systems of the countries of their residence.

Enrichment of the Traditional Prayer Book

The traditional synagogue has tried to meet the challenge of modernity in several ways. In addition to improving the decorum at the services and incorporating translations of the prayers into the vernacular, it has tried to explain the prayers and to make them intelligible to the layman. Historical and homiletical notes were added to the prayers. The most successful effort of this type is the commentary to the *Authorized*

Daily Prayer Book by the late Chief Rabbi Joseph H. Hertz.[20] Rabbi Hertz also provided an English commentary to the Torah readings, entitled *The Pentateuch and Haftorahs.* This commentary has tended to lift the reading of the Torah from a boring ritual to a potentially meaningful learning experience.

More significant have been the liturgic enrichments of the traditional services by the addition of responsive readings and meditations. These optional prayers are usually printed as supplements to the statutory prayers. Their intent is to give the traditional services a measure of relevancy. Thus one of the traditional prayer books saw fit to include a "Meditation before Kol Nidre" composed by the late chief rabbi of the Holy Land, Rabbi Abraham Isaac Kook.[21] But most significant is the inclusion of a number of new Hebrew prayers in the spirit of the traditional practice of adding piyutim and other prayers to meet specific situations. Some of these new prayers meet the criteria of good liturgic literature.

Among the new prayers included in some modern *Siddurim* is the prayer for the state of Israel composed by the chief rabbinate in Israel. Another is the prayer *Al Ha-Nissim* (For the miracles), which was included in the *Tefillah* of one prayer book[22] for recitation on Israel Independence Day. This new prayer parallels the *Al Ha-Nissim* prayers recited on Hanukah and Purim,* and like them thanks God "for the heroism, the triumphs, and for the miraculous deliverance of our fathers in other days at this season." Another prayer was incorporated into the Passover Haggadah as a memorial for the victims of the holocaust.[23] Recently the New York Board of Rabbis published a prayer in behalf of the Jews in Russia and suggested that it "be read each Sabbath."

Israel Independence Day has inspired the creation of a considerable amount of liturgic material. A meaningful service for that occasion was published by the Kibbutz Ha-Dati in Israel. A comprehensive service for that day was also published in England "with the approval of the Very Reverend Israel Brodie, Chief Rabbi."[24] The holocaust, however, has not yet found adequate expression in the liturgy.

* *See pp. 272–73.*

The Six-Day War stimulated the writing of new prayers. The chief rabbis of Israel declared the day of the liberation of Jerusalem as a semireligious holiday, and they authorized the inclusion of the Hallel with its benedictions into the service of the day. Several new prayers for the full redemption of Israel were composed and are recited on that day in many Orthodox synagogues.

The Neo-Orthodox have seen in these liturgic developments an adequate response to the demands of modernity. They claim that the introduction of decorum at the services and the addition of a translation in the vernacular, explanatory notes to the prayers, and the composition of new prayers for important historic events have given the traditional liturgy vitality and relevancy.

Radical Reform of the Liturgy

When the modern Jew became a citizen of his state and was permitted to participate freely in the cultural, political, and economic life of modern society, he was faced with some novel choices never encountered by his forefathers. Some Jews opted out of modernity and chose to continue their medieval way of life. These Jews have no need of any adjustments. They live in their secluded communities in the Williamsburg section of Brooklyn, in the Me'ah She'arim section of Jerusalem, and in other segregated places, and have thus kept the spirit of modernity out of their lives. This extreme wing of Orthodox Jewry has remained firm in its devotion to the medieval pattern of worship. They reject the validity of modern experience. The traditional *Siddur*, say they, represents "the tradition of our fathers." It has served well the saints and scholars of many generations and is equally valid for this generation. This argument carries deep emotional appeal, and as far as these Jews are concerned the problem has been settled for all time. Not even the slightest change in any custom is tolerated. The pattern of Jewish life is, as far as they are concerned, frozen for all time.

Discounting for the moment the considerable segment of Jewry which has no need of adjustments in the liturgy because prayer has lost its validity in their lives, all other Jews—whether they label themselves Orthodox, Conservative, Reform, or Reconstructionist—have felt the challenge of modernity and have responded in varying degrees, ranging from that of the Neo-Orthodox to the radical Reform. While the Neo-Orthodox made a valiant attempt to adjust the liturgy without infringing on tradition, other groups within Judaism have felt that changes even in the essentials of Judaism were called for. The most revolutionary of these groups was the Reform movement, which had its beginning in Germany in the early nineteenth century.

It should be noted and stressed that these Reformers were not, as some have claimed, simply wreckers of the tradition. Among them were men of dedication who earnestly sought a way to meet the critical situation of their day. This does not mean that everything they did was either justified or constructive. But their motives were sincere. To understand their innovations in the liturgy one must realize that in early nineteenth century Germany there was a veritable stampede of young Jews to the baptismal fonts. These Jewish apostates saw in Judaism nothing but a hindrance on the glorious road opened to them by the emancipation. They saw a new world of universal brotherhood just around the corner, and they threw themselves into the race for its immediate achievement. The early Reformers were likewise obsessed by the rosy optimism of their day. But they were attached to their Jewish heritage and therefore tried to meet both the general demands of modernity and the painful challenge posed by the mass exodus from Judaism. To stem the flood of desertions, the early Reformers declared emphatically that the euphoric ideals which beckoned the Jewish youth to apostasy were all derived from the biblical teachings of justice and righteousness and from the prophetic visions of "the end of days" when a new humanity of brotherhood and love would be inaugurated. It can be safely assumed that some young Jews on their way to a church stopped at the Reform temple and reintegrated themselves into the Jewish community.

The early Reformers tried to modernize Judaism and to restore to Jewish worship deeper devotion and piety. To achieve this they tried not only to make the synagogue worship decorous and outwardly attractive, but they also tried to harmonize the liturgy and its underlying theology with the prevailing ideas and beliefs of their day. These changes, they thought, would remove from Judaism the stigma of medievalism and foreignism, and make Jews worthy of full citizenship in the countries of their residence.

The Prayer Book of the German Reform Synagogue

The first Reform prayer book for public worship was published in Hamburg in 1818 and has been popularly called the *Hamburg Temple Prayer Book.*[25] It contained a number of practical and theological changes which were to characterize, in greater or lesser degree, the liturgy of Reform congregations everywhere. Its principal innovations consisted of the abridgment of the text, the substitution of the vernacular for some of the Hebrew prayers, and the excision of references to the coming of the Messiah, the reestablishment of a Jewish state in the land of Israel, and the restoration of the sacrificial worship in the Jersualem Temple. But there was little consistency in the prayer book, because it retained a number of references to the traditional doctrines that had been consigned to excision. This inconsistency was too obvious to have been an oversight. In all probability these early Reformers did not want to stir up too much controversy. Nevertheless, Orthodox leadership, as might have been expected, was shocked by these radical reforms. They denounced the *Hamburg Temple Prayer Book* in all the synagogues of the city and strictly banned its used. This outcry of the rabbinate succeeded in confining the use of the new prayer book to a narrow circle and also led to a number of modifications in the second edition of the prayer book, which appeared in 1841. But the modifications did not satisfy the rabbinate, and again the prayer book was excommunicated.

Among the Reform leaders of the early nineteenth century the *Hamburg Temple Prayer Book* met with considerable approval. Some even asked for more radical changes. However, there were other Reform leaders who argued for a more traditional approach. Among the latter was the scholarly and respected Abraham Geiger, who argued that

> a celebration, especially a religious one, does not affect the soul merely by its content, but also by all the memories connected with it from early times. When we change its form, we thereby snap the band of continuity, and the celebration is no more the loved one of old, but something new and cold, and contains little of the glow which warms the soul.

Geiger was instrumental in having one of the rabbinical conferences of the Reform movement in Germany, held in 1845, pass a resolution that "Hebrew be retained for the present." In 1854 Geiger published a Reform prayer book,[26] which was regarded as highly authoritative. It was far more traditional than the *Hamburg Temple Prayer Book.* It contained almost the whole text of the Hebrew service. The changes were so few that it could almost have passed for a traditional prayer book. References to the Messiah and the restoration of Zion were untouched, and the reading of the prayers was from the right. By the middle of the nineteenth century the German Reform movement had lost its revolutionary character and aroused little further controversy. However, the German Reform movement was carried over to America, where it was reinvigorated and its initial radical tendencies were reawakened.

The Reform Movement in America

The seeds of reform were brought over to America by some of the German Jewish immigrants in the mid-nineteenth century. In America the ideas of the German Reform movement took root and grew into a vigorous movement.

In 1824 the first "Reformed Society of Israelites" was founded in Charlestown, South Carolina. It started with a group of forty-seven men who seceded from the parent Orthodox congregation after its demands for change in the liturgy had been refused. By today's standards their demands were relatively mild. But in those days they were regarded as daring. They asked that the service be shortened, that some of the prayers be read in English translation, that discourses in the vernacular be instituted, and that decorum be maintained. They pointed to the reforms introduced in Germany as worthy of emulation. Among these reforms they noted the elimination of the sale of honors at the reading of the Torah, the suppression of the custom of see-sawing during the prayers and of repeating the prayers in too loud a voice, and the prohibition "of striking the impious Haman at the festival of Purim." [27]

When the Reformed Society of Israelites began its independent services, they eliminated not only references to the Messiah and the Temple, but also the prayers for the resurrection of the dead. By the mid-nineteenth century several Reform congregations had been founded and several leaders endowed with convictions and zeal had arrived in America. These men gave the Reform movement courageous leadership and developed its organizational structure. Among these new leaders were two men—Isaac Mayer Wise and David Einhorn—whose leadership gave the American Reform movement its definitive character and led to the movement's rapid growth and to its massive prestige.

Rabbi Isaac Mayer Wise, generally regarded as the father of the American Reform movement, arrived in New York in 1846 and assumed the post of rabbi in an Orthodox congregation in Albany. He introduced a number of reforms, such as sermons in English and a choir with mixed voices. Meeting with firm opposition, he resigned and organized a new congregation where he might inaugurate the reforms he sought. However, his real opportunity came in 1853 when he was called to the pulpit of Congregation B'nai Jeshurun in Cincinnati. In 1857 Rabbi Isaac Mayer Wise published his prayer book, *Minhag America* (American Rite). A year later Rabbi David Einhorn, who was rabbi at Sinai Congregation in Baltimore, published his prayer book *Olat Tamid* (The Daily Offering). Einhorn's prayer book was reissued in 1896 with some emendations and an English translation by Rabbi E. G. Hirsch.[28] This prayer book was generally accepted as an authentic source for the liturgy of the American Reform movement.

To understand the motivation and the reasoning that led to the radical surgery performed on the *Siddur* one must grasp some of the guiding principles which were formulated at a number of rabbinical conferences and especially at the Pittsburgh Conference in 1885.[29] Israel's destiny, it was decided, is not tied to the Holy Land or the national restoration under the Messiah or the restoration of the Temple in Jerusalem. Indeed, Israel is not in exile. The dispersion of the Jews is in fact the divine plan for the realization of Israel's mission to spread the truth of ethical monotheism among the nations of the world. Israel's mission is to bring about the messianic era of universal justice, righteousness, and brotherhood by the example of the rectitude and nobility which characterize the life of the Jews. Reform Judaism must therefore abandon the hope of a Messiah and must annul all laws pertaining to the priesthood and the Temple sacrifices. The liturgy must be purged of all references to the exile, to the land of Israel as a Jewish national state, and to the Temple service. Jews are citizens of the countries of their residence and may not pray for another citizenship. The doctrine of the resurrection during the time of the Messiah is also to be eliminated from the prayers. Rabbinic law, said they, was valid in its day but does not apply to modern life. Biblical law, too, was largely nullified. Only the ethical, moral, and universal teachings of the Bible had validity for modern man.

In 1895 the Central Conference of American Rabbis published an official prayer book for the American Reform synagogues, entitled *The Union Prayerbook*.[30] It implemented the new theology and was more radical than anything produced in Germany. This publication shocked the traditional elements in American Jewry and a wide rift was thus created in the American Jewish community.

Abbreviation of the Liturgy

The traditional *Siddur* matched the faith of the medieval Jew. It reflected his desire to worship God at all times. The *Siddur* therefore grew constantly, and its growth was regarded as a boon. In the nineteenth century, however, the traditional liturgy exceeded the Jew's spiritual needs. The lengthy services were burdensome. The adherents of the Reform movement wanted shorter services.

Abbreviation of the prayers was not an unprecedented procedure in the Jewish tradition. The rabbis of the Talmud provided for the abridgment of a number of prayers for people who were pressed for time.* An abbreviated *Tefillah*, known as *Havinenu*, was composed by the rabbis and is to be found in many a *Siddur*.[31] However, the abridgments introduced by the Reform leaders were not emergency provisions. Their excisions were meant to be the normal ritual of the Reform synagogue.

One of the principles adopted, though not followed consistently, was to discard those prayers which were last to enter the *Siddur*, the assumption presumably being that the older a prayer is, the more sacred it is. A second guiding principle was to eliminate those prayers which originally entered the *Siddur* as optional elements. Accordingly, the first prayers to be jettisoned as surplus baggage were almost all the piyutim.† Then came the almost total elimination of three large prayer units—the Early Morning Benedictions,‡ the Verses of Praise,§ and the Penitential Prayers *(Tahanun)*.¶ This reduced the morning service to less than half its original length. But this surgery was relatively painless. The most controversial excisions were those motivated by the new theological doctrines. These changes were regarded by the Orthodox as outright heresy.

Changes Motivated by the New Theology

In order to implement the doctrines of Reform Judaism, it became necessary to rewrite many of the essential prayers. The most striking changes were those motivated by the rejection

* *See p. 140.*
† *See pp. 168 ff.*
‡ *See pp. 143 ff.*
§ *See pp. 141–42.*
¶ *See pp. 461–63.*

of the age-old Jewish yearning for a return to Zion and the revival of the Jewish nation in the Holy Land. The Messiah was replaced by the concept of a messianic era when all peoples will live in brotherly love. Zion and the land of Israel practically disappeared from the liturgy. The doctrine of the chosen people was replaced by the doctrine of Israel's mission to spread ethical monotheism among the nations of the world. The doctrine of the resurrection of the dead was replaced by the immortality of the soul. References to the restoration of the Temple offerings were eliminated. The Musaf *Tefillah*, with its emphasis on the restoration of the Temple and its worship, was severely amputated.

The Torah reading, too, was radically altered. The traditional portions were disregarded; aliyot were abolished; and the cantillations were dispensed with. Each rabbi selected a few verses from the Torah which he regarded as suitable for public edification and recited them in accordance with the best rules of elocution.

Transformation of the Rituals

Only rituals that symbolize ethical principles or universal ideals were considered valid. All others, the Reformers felt, were irrelevant survivals from ancient times. These rituals were eliminated with little regard to their historic or emotional roots. The very word *synagogue* was abandoned in favor of the term *temple*, a misnomer because it implies a ritual built around a priestly cult. The religious calendar, too, was altered. The Second-Day Festival of the Diaspora * was abolished—even Rosh Hashanah was observed for only one day. The minor feast days, with the exception of Hanukah and Purim, were abolished, as were all fast days except Yom Kippur.

Inside the temple the manner of worship was greatly changed. The officiating clergy was dressed in clerical robes and conducted the service from a platform situated in front of the congregation. Organ music and mixed choirs intoned

* *See pp. 205–208.*

the prayers. Strict formality characterized the worship. The men, bareheaded and without prayer shawls, sat beside their women and followed the service in accordance with the rabbi's directions.

The final touch was the reduction of Hebrew almost to the vanishing point. This was a reversion to the practice of the extinct Hellenistic Jewish communities. This radical departure from the synagogue tradition was defended on the ground that from the strictly legal point of view there is no obligation to pray in Hebrew.* Besides, the Hebrew language is only a national aspect of Jewish life, and the Reform movement has divested Judaism of its national garb. Furthermore, the vernacular is understood by the worshipers and will stir them to greater devotion and piety. It was only logical that the Reform prayer book be read from the left, like an English book.

The end result of these earnest labors was a small, predominantly non-Hebrew prayer book which enunciated admirable universal ideals with which no one could argue. Nonetheless, the Reform liturgy called forth sharp criticism, some of which the next generation of Reform leaders accepted as valid.

Criticism of the Reform Prayer Book

The authors of the Reform prayer book were proud of their handiwork. It was thoroughly purged of medievalism, superstition, and nationalism; it was consistent with the Reform theology; it was replete with universal ideals; and in no way did it jeopardize the loyalty of the Jew to his country. Yet the prayer book aroused sharp antagonism. Orthodox Jews naturally saw it as an abomination, and they excommunicated it. But it was also criticized by others on both objective and subjective grounds; Franz Rosenzweig wrote to his mother in 1918 that he had visited the "German synagogue" and that he found it "very gorgeous, very assimilated, coiffured, and *so* cold!"[32] These criticisms were also applied to the liturgy of the American Reform synagogue. It lost its Jewish character and its religious warmth, said the critics. The new liturgy, they

* *See p. 33.*

said, was motivated by a powerful craving for acceptance by the non-Jews. This led the Reformers into a double pitfall. They tended to imitate the ritual of the Church, and they tended to look over their shoulder to glimpse the impression their services were making on the Gentiles. The former tendency gave the Reform liturgy a distinctly foreign character and helped to widen the gulf between themselves and the more traditional Jews. The latter tendency gave the liturgy an apologetic tone. Judaism was presented as the pinnacle of universal idealism, as a faith worthy of admiration and praise. The service thus became, in large measure, a recitation of glorious platitudes addressed mainly to the world at large instead of prayers to the God of Israel.

Some of the critics denounced the wholesale excisions which reduced the Reform prayer book to a mere shadow of the traditional *Siddur*. In the passion of revolt the Reformers dispensed with some of the basic doctrines of Judaism, including the peoplehood of Israel, the centrality of the land and the tongue of Israel, many age-old traditions and practices, and many prayers with deep historic roots. Many a prayer with profound religious associations disappeared, and others with rich evocative powers, such as the Kol Nidre, were excised. New prayers were composed but they lacked "the faith of the mystic, and the pen of the poet." Unfortunately, the Reform movement did not produce poets of the stature of Judah Halevi. Nor did the liturgic genius of the talmudic sages find an echo in the new prayers of the Reform temple.

There were also those who criticized the Reformers' excessive faith in the god of reason. The early Reformers seemed to feel that the rationality of modern man would soon bring about the messianic era. Jews would be emancipated from their disabilities, and all mankind would soon achieve the hoped-for state of universal brotherhood. This buoyant optimism led the Reformers to believe that they were standing on a universal escalator, moving irresistibly to the peak of human redemption. Reason was the motive power behind that onward and upward movement of humanity. Anything mystical was suspect. Anything not clearly rational was superstition.

The Reform prayer book thus lost that element of mystery which is at the center of religion. In its place was injected a rational theology which easily obtained the assent of the worshipers but did not win their hearts.

In the mid-twentieth century, with the crematoriums of Auschwitz, Treblinka, and their like still fresh in the memory of many Jews, faith in man's pure reason and man's steady, uninterrupted progress has been shaken. The sense of mystery is no longer dismissed as mere obscurantism. Reason will always play a vital role in human affairs, but in the hands of evil men reason can become a tool for evil. Man needs, in addition to a keen mind, a feeling heart and a sensitive spirit. The rationalistic foundation of the nineteenth century Reform prayer book, therefore, appears to some modern critics as old-fashioned.

There were also those who sharply criticized some of the new doctrines of the Reform prayer book. The doctrine of the mission of Israel came under special censure. In Judaism, said the critics, the Jewish people was always regarded as a nation and the land of Israel as its national homeland. All authentic Jewish sources clearly reflect this central assumption. The Jewish yearning for Zion has therefore been a central theme of synagogue prayer. Its deletion from the Reform liturgy has destroyed the Jewish character of *The Union Prayerbook*. Besides, added some of the critics sarcastically, a religion "whose great virtue is adaptability" cannot possibly convert the world.

Counterreform

The daring reforms of the Pittsburgh Conference called forth not only criticism but also counteraction. There were a number of rabbis and scholars who had been cooperating with the Reformers in the hope of winning them over to moderation. They accepted the principle of the need of adjustment to American life, but they were against submerging the tradition within the dominant culture to the point of spiritual suicide. Judaism has succeeded in maintaining its uniqueness in times of persecution. It should surely be able to maintain its integrity in time of emancipation. The adoption of the Pittsburgh Platform created too wide a gulf to permit further cooperation.

The Founding of the Conservative Movement

Rabbi Sabato Morais took the initiative and founded a new seminary for the training of American rabbis committed to traditional Judaism. The Jewish Theological Seminary of America was officially opened in 1887, and it became the fountainhead of what came to be known as Conservative Judaism. The new movement emphasized the observance of the Sabbath and the dietary laws, Hebrew as the language of prayer, and the land of Israel as one of the central themes of synagogue prayer. In 1902 Solomon Schechter was brought from England to head the seminary. He gathered a distinguished faculty and reinvigorated the institution. By the beginning of the twentieth century the number of East European Jews had grown considerably, and they became the principal source of strength of the Conservative movement.

The liturgy of the Conservative synagogues was at first quite diverse. In some synagogues the Szold-Jastrow prayer book, which was only a little less reformed than *The Union Prayerbook*, was in use. Others used the Orthodox *Siddur*. In its early stages, the Conservative movement was a coalition of opponents to the Pittsburgh Platform. As the movement coalesced, the leftist synagogues either moved over to the Reform movement or were overwhelmed by the mass of traditional elements who flocked to the Conservative synagogues.

The Conservative synagogue was definitely American in character. Sermons were delivered in English, and several prayers were usually read in English translation. But the language of prayer was essentially Hebrew. The men worshiped with covered heads and wore the tallit at morning services. The main departures from the tradition were the introduction of mixed pews and the elimination of prayers for the restoration of the sacrificial worship.

In the traditional *Siddur* there were many prayers for the restoration of the Temple and its service. In these prayers the word *Avodah* is generally used, a word which in rabbinic literature refers to the sacrificial service of the Temple. But this word can also mean prayer worship.* The Conservative rabbis and informed laymen were thus able to live with these prayers, notwithstanding their personal rejection of the sacrificial cult as a means of worship. In the Musaf *Tefillah*, however, there is a prayer which not only spells out the sacrifices to be offered, but also pledges the worshipers to perform these sacrifices in the restored Temple. The Conservatives could not live with this prayer. When the organization of Conservative rabbis published its prayer book in 1946,[33] this prayer was revised. In the *Siddur* it reads:

> May it be Thy will, O Lord our God and God of our fathers, to lead us up in joy unto our land, and to plant us within our borders, *where we will prepare unto Thee the offerings that are obligatory for us*, the continual offerings according to their order, and the additional offerings according to their enactment; and the additional offering of this Sabbath day *we will prepare and offer up unto Thee* in love, according to the precept of Thy will, as Thou hast prescribed for us in Thy Torah.

In the new prayer book the italicized sections were changed to read: "where our fathers prepared unto Thee the offerings that were obligatory for them" and "they [our fathers] prepared and offered up unto Thee." This change was vigorously attacked by the Orthodox rabbis as conclusive proof that the Conservative synagogues are not traditional, but are a milder type of Reform.

The Conservative movement has often been criticized for its state of indecision. It has never produced a clear platform of principles. It has never defined the limits of digression permitted within the movement. This indecision, say the apologists, is a source of strength. It permits a wide range of opinion and practice within the Conservative ranks; it enables the movement to grow unhindered by restrictive definitions

* *See pp. 81–82.*

and allows each congregation and each rabbi to experiment. Actually, say the apologists, there are limits—the left wing never strays as far as the Reform temple, and the right wing never clings to the tradition as fully as the Orthodox.

The Reconstructionist Prayer Book

The almost complete swing of the Conservative synagogue back to the traditional *Siddur* left many religious problems and theological questions unanswered. Some of the Conservatives questioned the validity of such rabbinic doctrines as the belief in a personal Messiah, the resurrection of the dead, the restoration of the Jerusalem Temple with its sacrificial offerings, the election of Israel, and the revelation at Sinai as a historic fact in the literal sense. These doctrines are never officially approved or rejected by the Conservative movement, but they are clearly spelled out in the liturgy used in the Conservative synagogues. Those who raised these questions were just as troubled by the Reform theology, which denied the peoplehood of Israel, rejected the land of Israel and the Hebrew tongue as part of the pattern of Jewish values, and denied the validity of most of the Jewish traditions. Those who raised these questions were not satisfied with vague reinterpretations which are valid for individual worshipers in the privacy of their own thinking. They wanted these doctrines clearly defined.

These dissidents, who were mostly within the ranks of the Conservative synagogues, found in Mordecai M. Kaplan a brilliant spokesman. In his *Judaism as a Civilization*[34] Kaplan clearly and convincingly stated his case, outlined a rational approach to the problems of the modern Jew, and proposed a practical program for Jewish community life in America. He asked for a reconstruction of Judaism in the light of "the profound changes in life and thought during the last century and a half." He defined Judaism as the evolving religious civilization of the Jewish people. The emphasis was placed on the peoplehood of Israel and the religious civilization which it has developed during its existence. The nature of Judaism, restated in terms of modern thought, rendered the traditional

Siddur inadequate. The Reconstructionists, as Mordecai M. Kaplan's followers called themselves, set out to revise systematically the traditional prayers to conform with their outlook. They hoped that their prayer book would help the Jew "to experience the presence of God in his personal and communal life" and would "so unite the worshiper with Israel as to put him in possession of the living truth which Israel has learned concerning man's task on earth." [35]

In revising the prayers the Reconstructionists retained the Hebraic character of the services. They replaced the rabbinic theology with their own doctrines by small emendations of the traditional prayers. By changing a phrase here and omitting a sentence there they succeeded in purging a prayer of its objectionable doctrine or grafting onto it their own principles. The ritual of the synagogue was generally like that of the Conservatives except for the excision of the Musaf from the Sabbath and festival services. The Musaf *Tefillah* is so preoccupied with the sacrificial cult that it was deemed altogether superfluous. The Reconstructionists also granted women the privilege of being called to the Torah.

The strength and weakness of the Reconstructionist movement was its rationalism. It refused to accept ambiguities. It clearly defined its principles and doctrines. Thus it defined God as "the Power that makes" for justice, righteousness, human cooperation, and similar ideals. It rejected supernaturalism and miracles. In the Reconstructionist prayer book the prayers are not only translated into the vernacular, but are also accompanied by "interpretive versions" which reflect the religious views of the movement. This double rendering of the Hebrew prayers permitted both integrity in the translation of the old prayers and a reinterpretation of the prayers to make them relevant to modern life. New prayers were also added. Some were selected from Hebrew literature, both modern and premodern, and some prayers were especially composed for the new prayer book.

The publication of the Reconstructionist prayer book aroused sharp criticism. As might have been expected, the Orthodox rabbinate was shocked, and the prayer book was banned and burned. The Conservatives reacted with restraint in the hope of retaining the Reconstructionists within their ranks despite their dissident views. Others argued—at times sharply—against the Reconstructionist reforms. Why, asked these critics, was it necessary to expurgate all references to the chosen people? Is it not a historic fact that the Torah was entrusted to or evolved in Israel? Many of the other expurgated doctrines, said the critics, can be reinterpreted in line with modern thought. Only the few prayers which do not lend themselves to reinterpretation should have been censored. But the strongest criticism was leveled against the depersonalization of God. Somehow people find it difficult to pray to "the sum total of man's highest ideals" or to "the Power that makes" for justice, freedom, and all the other worthy human ideals. Judaism, say the critics, has been made into a philosophy instead of the national faith. The Reconstructionists, however, defend their prayer book on the grounds of its integrity and rationality. It reckons with tradition yet is thoroughly modern and relevant. Their doctrines can be accepted by a modern Jew without reservation. Their program, say the Reconstructionists, has the potentiality of reintegrating the modern Jew within the Jewish people.

Revisions of *The Union Prayerbook*

More than a century has passed since the Reform movement was launched in America. New generations were born and new leaders took their places at the head of the movement. It was natural for these leaders to take a new look at the reforms enacted by their predecessors. The new leaders were not hampered by the blinding light of sudden emancipation. They were not in need of any proof that they were worthy of citizenship. Nor were they imbued with a spirit of revolt against the tradition. The new leaders of the Reform movement had witnessed the forces of bestiality unleashed in the center of Western Europe—forces which the early Reformers thought impossible anywhere in the modern world, least of all in enlightened Europe. The certainties of the early Reformers surely had to be reexamined. Then came the birth of the state of Israel, which awakened in the hearts of most Jews a sense of pride and a feeling of identity, the depth of which the early Reformers never knew. The peoplehood of Israel and the centrality of the Hebrew tongue in the ritual of the synagogue suddenly ceased to be subjects for discussion. The new situation called for a rethinking of the doctrines and institutions of Reform Judaism.

The Union Prayerbook was reexamined and found to be in need of revisions. A revised edition was issued in 1927, a newly revised edition was issued in 1961, and still another revision is now in the making. It is not possible to give a detailed analysis of the revisions, except to note that they have generally been in the direction of a return to the tradition. For example, in the 1885 edition the Sabbath morning *Tefillah* had only three benedictions in Hebrew—the first, second, and fourth. In the 1927 revised edition the Hebrew version of all the seven benedictions was included. In the newly revised edition of 1961 the Hebrew version of the concluding prayer *(Elohai Netzor)* was also included. Needless to say, the Hebrew benedictions were accompanied by free translations which were used in many temples. But those congregations that wished to recite the *Tefillah* in Hebrew now had an option.

As to the revisions now in the making, there are wide differences of opinion among the leaders of the Reform movement. While one leading rabbi asks for free and uninhibited experimentation,[36] another rabbi asks that *The Union Prayerbook* be primarily in the Hebrew language and that the silent *Tefillah*, the Early Morning Benedictions, the Half Kaddish, the *Kaddish De-Rabbanan*, and even the *Tahanun* ("recast in appropriate form and content") be restored.[37] Obviously the revisions will follow neither of these extremes. But in all probability they will take another step in the direction of the tradition. The gap between the Reform and the other non-Orthodox groups is narrowing. Will it ultimately lead to a unification of the Reform, Conservative, and Reconstructionist groups into a single, strong, religious movement in Judaism? There are some who see clear evidence of such a development in the not too distant future.

The Dilemma of the Modern Jew

The several groupings in American Judaism are, on the whole, satisfied with their respective liturgies. Where revisions are contemplated, only details are involved. One might therefore assume that the American synagogue is flourishing. Actually, this is far from the truth, for the synagogues are more often than not empty of worshipers, even on Sabbaths and festivals. Opulent but poorly attended synagogues have become a characteristic of most American Jewish communities.

The religious fervor of the Jew which once expressed itself in daily prayer has all but vanished. Although many Jews are synagogue members, they hardly ever engage in prayer. Occasionally they go to a synagogue service, they behave decorously, and they follow the rabbi's instructions politely. But it is not the "service of the heart" that the rabbis spoke of. A spiritual void has thus been created in the hearts of many a sensitive Jew. They have lost the spiritual vitality which in past generations enabled the Jews to face the future with confidence. Their "fountain of living waters" has dried up, and "empty cisterns" have become their lot.

The dilemma of the American Jewish youth is especially agonizing. If on a rare occasion he enters a synagogue, he is bewildered and usually does not return. Uprooted from his heritage, he is spiritually confused. He therefore turns to every fashionable new god of the day. By the time he realizes that his new god has clay feet, he is no longer young and his best energies have already been sacrificed to the false gods.

Why Many Have Ceased to Pray

Before the advent of modernity the Jew wanted to know *how* to pray; now he wants to know *why* he should pray. While waiting for an answer he has lost the habit of praying; then he forgot how to pray; and by now he does not know to whom to pray. To be sure, there are Jews who adhere to the tradition of daily prayer, but these Jews are only a small minority within the American Jewish community.

Among those who have ceased to pray there are some who

are sensitive by nature and religious in sentiment. They want to pray but they cannot. Modernity has filled their minds with a searching skepticism. They ask the classic question: "Does God hear and answer prayer?" The claim that God answers prayer in His own inscrutable way does not satisfy them. They do not necessarily dismiss this answer lightly, because any concept of God assumes an element of mystery. The old saying "If I could comprehend God, I would be God" has much to recommend it. The human intellect is obviously limited. But many a modern man feels that within his intellectual limits he should continue to search for answers to his questions, and he expects his faith to be reasonable and credible. Once his faith moves beyond these bounds blind faith becomes his alternative. Some sophisticated Jews have chosen this alternative. They have succeeded in departmentalizing their minds, so that their mastery of the natural or social sciences is not permitted to impinge upon their religious faith. Most modern Jews, however, cannot live peacefully with a divided personality.

Some modern theologians have identified God with the cosmos and the moral forces in it. But this hardly solves the problem. Aware of his own uniqueness as a personality and conscious of his ability to make choices and initiate actions, how can he pray to a God who is devoid even of the qualities of a human being? Theologians can surely defend a naturalistic religion, but one can hardly pray to a philosophic concept.

"The Righteous Shall Live by His Faith"

The alienation of so many Jews from prayer suggests painful questions: Is the age-old Jewish dialogue with God coming to an end? Or is it only passing through a critical period which will be followed by a revival of prayer? Or is prayer perhaps forever doomed to the limited circle of the faithful remnant? "The righteous shall live by his faith," said the prophet. The righteous in Israel will persist in their faith that "God will give His people strength; God will bless His people with peace." Israel's strength will come from a revival of the Jew's historic dialogue with God, and Israel's peace will come through God's answer to the prayer of His people.

NOTES

Introduction

1. The Vatican Council met in Saint Peter's Basilica in Rome from June 1962 to December 1965.
2. Israel Abrahams, "The Mission of Judaism," *The Jewish Quarterly Review*, o. s. 9 (1897):197.
3. The word *prayer* is derived from the Latin word *precaria*, which means "a begging." The word *prayer* therefore implies petition.
4. *Sefer Hassidim*, Parma edition, no. 1570.
5. Quoted in Israel Abrahams, *Hebrew Ethical Wills* (Philadelphia, 1926) 2: 334–35.
6. William G. Braude, trans., *The Midrash on Psalms* (New Haven, 1959), 1:498.
7. Ibid., 2:202.
8. Ibid., 1:272; Ber. 33b.
9. Solomon Ibn Gabirol, *Selected Religious Poems*, trans. Israel Zangwill (Philadelphia, 1923), p. 2.
10. Solomon Schechter, *Studies in Judaism*, 1st ser. (Philadelphia, 1911), pp. 85–86.
11. Braude, *Midrash on Psalms*, 1:23.
12. George Foot Moore, "The Idea of Torah in Judaism," *The Menorah Journal* 8 (1922):6.
13. The Hebrew word *demiah* is generally translated as "waiteth," but it can also be rendered as "silence."
14. Braude, *Midrash on Psalms*, 1:273.
15. Quoted in William J. Wolf, *The Almost Chosen People* (New York, 1959), p. 125. I am indebted to Dr. Simon Greenberg for this quotation.
16. Braude, *Midrash on Psalms*, 1:374. The talmudic stories about Honi Ha-Me'aggel (Ta'an. 23a), whose prayer could bring rain in time of drought, are widely known, as is the story of Hanina ben Dosa's efficacious prayer for the son of Rabbi Gamaliel II (Ber. 34b).
17. Quoted in *Hebrew Ethical Wills*, 2:288.
18. A distinction is often made between efficacy and effectiveness of prayer. If the results correspond with the worshiper's own wishes, the prayer is efficacious. If, however, it merely results in desirable outcomes which are not congruent with the supplicant's wishes, the prayer is effective but not efficacious. What follows in this chapter belongs largely in the latter category. No distinction is made in the text, however, in order not to complicate the discussion.
19. Abraham J. Heschel, *The Insecurity of Freedom* (Philadelphia, 1966), p. 256.

20. Braude, *The Midrash on Psalms,* 2:199.
21. Rabbi Eliezer enunciated three guiding principles: (1) how scholars are to relate to their colleagues, (2) how to educate one's children, and (3) how to pray.
22. Quoted in Abrahams, *Hebrew Ethical Wills,* 1:39.
23. Quoted in ibid., p. 98.
24. Bahya Ibn Pakuda, *Duties of the Heart,* trans. Moses Hyamson (Jerusalem, 1962), 2:207–11.
25. Israel Abrahams, "Some Rabbinic Ideas on Prayer," *Pharisaism and the Gospels,* 2nd ser. (Cambridge, 1924), p. 84.
26. Milton Steinberg, *Basic Judaism* (New York, 1947), p. 137.
27. Abraham J. Heschel, *Man's Quest for God* (New York, 1954), p. 32.
28. Louis I. Newman, *The Hasidic Anthology* (New York, 1934), p. 332.
29. *Sefer Hassidim,* Parma edition, no. 11.
30. Among these are the response to the reader's call to worship, the traditional response of "Amen!" to each of the benedictions pronounced by the reader, the recitation of the Kedushah during the reader's repetition of the *Tefillah,* and, if the worshiper is a mourner, the recitation of the Kaddish in memory of the deceased.
31. Braude, *The Midrash on Psalms,* 1:398.
32. The biblical books of Daniel, Ezra, and Nehemiah are largely in Aramaic.
33. Moses Maimonides, *Mishneh Torah,* "The Book of Adoration," trans. Moses Hyamson (Jerusalem, 1962).
34. Theodore N. Lewis, *Temple Topics,* 7 May 1965.
35. George Foot Moore, *Judaism in the First Centuries of the Christian Era* (Cambridge, Mass., 1927), 2:227.

Chapter 1

1. See Amos 5:22–24, Hosea 6:6, and Isaiah 1:11–17.
2. A detailed account of this service is included in the Day of Atonement service. See pp. 252–54.
3. The ceremony of the priestly blessing is still part of the synagogue liturgy. It is called to *dukhan,* i.e., "to ascend the (Temple) steps" (to bless the assemblage of worshipers). See p. 74.
4. The psalm of the day, too, is still part of the synagogue service.
5. For denunciations of human sacrifice, see Lev. 20:2–7 and Deut. 18:9–13.
6. The biblical condemnation of these practices is uncompromising. See Deut. 18:9–13. In the Temple the priests and Levites practiced no magic or "mysteries." What there remained of ancient mysteries and oracles had fallen into disuse to such an extent that contemporaries of the Temple could no longer define the nature of the Urim and Thummim (Exod. 28:30).
7. Yehezkel Kaufmann, *The Religion of Israel,* trans. and abr. Moshe Greenberg (Chicago, 1960), p. 303.
8. For the biblical condemnation of such rites, see Deut. 23:18–19.
9. There was also a tithe levied on the agricultural produce of the field

for the maintenance of the priests and Levites. Also, a share of the first crops and fruits, a portion of the dough (hallah), and a specified share of the sacrifice were revenues that helped maintain the priests (Lev. 10:14–15; Deut. 18:3–4).

10. J. Israelstam and Judah J. Slotki, trans., *Midrash Rabbah on Leviticus* (London, 1939), p. 44.
11. Ibid., pp. 38–39.

Chapter 2

1. Other conditional prayers in the Bible are Jacob's prayer for sustenance (Gen. 28:20–22), the prayer of the Israelites for victory over the Canaanites (Num. 21:2), and Hannah's prayer for a child (1 Sam. 1:11).
2. Other biblical prayers of this type are Jacob's prayer before meeting with Esau (Gen. 32:11–13), Moses' prayer in behalf of the Israelites after they had worshiped the golden calf (Exod. 32:31–32), and Jeremiah's prayer after purchasing Hanamel's field (Jer. 32:16–25).
3. This blessing is bestowed on the congregation by the reader every time he repeats the *Tefillah*. On certain occasions the blessing is bestowed on the congregation by the Kohanim, who are the descendants of the Temple priests. See p. 216.
4. The round number of 150 has not remained unchallenged. The Greek translation of the Bible, known as the Septuagint, contains an additional psalm, usually referred to by scholars as Psalm 151, and the Dead Sea Scrolls contain an additional five psalms. But these additional psalms belong to a class of religious literature which the rabbis deliberately excluded from the Bible, because they regarded it as not authentic. These extra psalms, like all the books of the Apocrypha, were not used in the synagogue, and therefore have no relationship to the synagogue liturgy.
5. F. Max Müller, "On Ancient Prayers," *Semitic Studies in Memory of Rev. Dr. Alexander Kohut* (Berlin, 1897), p. 40.
6. According to Yehezkel Kaufmann, all the psalms were composed before the Babylonian exile. "There is no psalm," says he, "whose plain sense . . . requires a dating later than the exilic psalm 137." See Yehezkel Kaufmann, *The Religion of Israel*, trans. and abr. Moshe Greenberg (Chicago, 1960), p. 311.
7. Psalm 90 is ascribed to Moses and Psalms 72 and 127 are ascribed to King Solomon. The rest are ascribed to Levites. Psalms 50 and 73 to 83 are credited to Asaph, and Psalms 42, 44–49, 84, 85, and 87 to the sons of Korah. Psalm 88 is assigned to one—Heman—and Psalm 89 to one—Ethan.
8. The Hallel consists of Psalms 113–118. Hallel means "praise."
9. See 2 Kings 4:23.
10. Quoted in J. H. Hertz, *The Pentateuch and Haftorahs* (London, 1938), p. 562.
11. There were several other occasions when the Torah was publicly read to the people. On the festival of Sukkot during sabbatical years the Torah was read to the people (Deut. 31:4–12; Sotah 7:8). Also,

King Josiah read the Torah to the people (2 Kings 23:2). And on Yom Kippur the high priest read to the people a couple of relevant selections from the Torah (Yoma 7:1). But these public Torah readings were either one-time occurrences or took place in connection with isolated ceremonies that had little impact on the nation.

12. George Foot Moore, *Judaism in the First Centuries of the Christian Era* (Cambridge, Mass., 1927), 1:281.
13. This practice is no longer in vogue. See pp. 113–14, 182.
14. Soferim 10:1.
15. Louis Ginzberg, *Students, Scholars and Saints* (Philadelphia, 1928), p. 106.
16. Tamid 5:1; Ber. 11b.
17. In his *Prayer in the Period of the Tanna'im and the Amora'im* (Jerusalem, 1964), Joseph Heinemann discusses this challenging subject perceptively. See chapter 5 ("Prayers in the Temple"), pp. 78–87, or the English abstract of this chapter on pp. vi–vii.
18. This rite was described above, p. 59, as part of the early Temple ritual in the days of the First Commonwealth.
19. Each day of the week had its own psalm. The seven psalms in the cycle are still recited in the daily morning services. These psalms are 24, 48, 82, 94, 81, 93, 92.
20. Two of these biblical selections are still read in the synagogue service on the Day of Atonement. They consist of Lev. 16 and Num. 29:7–11.
21. For a listing of the themes of these benedictions, see Yoma 7:1.
22. The Ten Commandments were deliberately eliminated from the liturgy. See chapter 4, note 9.
23. Ket. 105a.
24. The word *synagogue* was originally applied to any association or guild. Eventually it became associated exclusively with the Jewish association, and it has remained the specific term for the Jewish place of worship, study, and general assembly.
25. These men were known as *Anshei Ma'amad*, Men of the Station. For a rabbinic discussion of the *Ma'amadot* see Ta'an. 4:2–4.
26. Josephus, *The Jewish Wars*, trans. H. S. J. Thackery (London, 1927), 4:9, 3, par. 424, claims that on the Passover of the year 66 C.E., 255,600 paschal lambs were counted by the priests. He therefore estimates the attendance to have been about three million persons. Granted that this figure is a gross exaggeration, we can still safely conclude that the number of pilgrims was enormous.

Chapter 3

1. *Avot de Rabbi Nathan* 4; see Judah Goldin, trans., *The Fathers According to Rabbi Nathan* (New Haven, 1955), p. 34.
2. William G. Braude, trans., *The Midrash on Psalms* (New Haven, 1959), 2:300.
3. Ibid., 1:26.
4. Ibid., 2:93.
5. Thus the superscription for Sunday reads: "This is the first day of the week on which the Levites in the Temple used to say:" (Ps. 24 follows).

6. As late as the sixth century, the priestly families knew the precise two weeks of the year when their families' turn (*Ma'amad*) would have been at the Temple service, and they took note of that fact by reciting a special prayer. Among the many piyutim by Yannai, discovered in the genizah, there are a number of *Mishmarot*, corresponding to the twenty-four priestly divisions who took turns at the Temple twice annually. The memory of the specific weeks when each priestly family used to be on duty at the Temple is no longer perpetuated.
7. See Num. 6:22–27 and Deut. 21:5.
8. In Jerusalem the priestly blessing is bestowed by the Kohanim at every morning *Tefillah*.
9. The "black Jews" of Cochin, India, who have no Kohanim and *Levi'im* in their midst, have resorted to hiring impoverished "white Jews" who are of priestly and Levitical descent to perform the functions assigned to them by the rabbis.

   The rabbis also perpetuated the ancient principle of priestly holiness. This has proved, in some cases, rather troublesome to Orthodox Jews. Among the applications of this principle has been the marital restriction imposed on the descendants of the priestly families. A Kohen, the Bible prescribes, may not marry a divorcee. It happens occasionally that the dictates of a Kohen's heart clash with his technical holiness, and he wants to marry a divorcee. Difficulties have also arisen from the law forbidding a Kohen to be near a corpse, lest his "holiness" be contaminated. Hence a Kohen may not be in the same house with a dead body, except that of a near relative. Nor may he enter a cemetery. This imposes difficulties on Orthodox rabbis who happen to be of priestly descent. They are prevented from officiating at funerals. Some legal fictions have been resorted to in order to enable such rabbis to perform their duties, but it is still a burdensome obstacle.
10. Among the biblical selections in the prayer book that describe the sacrifices are Num. 28:1–14.
11. See "The Messianic Doctrine in Contemporary Jewish Thought," *Great Jewish Ideas*, ed. Abraham E. Millgram (Washington, D.C., 1964), pp. 237–59.
12. Ber. 26b. See also Braude, *The Midrash on Psalms*, 1:492–93.

Chapter 4

1. G. E. Biddle, "A Theist's Impression of Judaism," *The Jewish Quarterly Review* 19 (1907):219.
2. The benediction is recited when a person is called to the Torah during his first participation in a public service after his deliverance. The congregation responds: "May He who bestowed all good upon thee, further bestow good unto thee. Amen."
3. A similar biblical use of these words is to be found in Ps. 119:12.
4. William G. Braude, trans., *The Midrash on Psalms* (New Haven, 1959), 1:200.
5. For similar biblical responses of "Amen," see Pss. 72:18–19; 106:48; Neh. 8:6.

6. Only scholars were permitted to act as reader, because only a scholar could formulate the prayers at a public service.
7. "Who formest light and createst darkness" is clearly aimed at negating the Persian dualism which assigns the creation of light and darkness to different divinities. This benediction emphasizes that both light and darkness are the creation of the one God. Compare Isa. 45:7 with the concluding words, "who makest peace and createst all things."
8. For the full text of these benedictions, as formulated in the *Siddur* now in use, see *The Standard Prayer Book,* Authorized English Translation, by Rev. S. Singer, American Edition (New York, 1951), pp. 44 ff.
9. It will be recalled that in discussing the liturgy of the Temple (pp. 72–74), it was stated that the affirmation of faith recited by the priests consisted of the three biblical selections of the *Shema* and the Ten Commandments. The inclusion of the Decalogue was altogether logical, since it contains several basic doctrines of the faith. But the recitation of the Decalogue in the daily service proved embarrassing to the rabbis because certain sectarians claimed that the Ten Commandments alone were revealed at Mount Sinai. The Ten Commandments were therefore removed from the affirmation of faith (Ber. 12a). Despite the rabbinic opposition, the Ten Commandments continued to be part of the daily service in some isolated places for many centuries. In the Palestinian synagogue of Old Cairo this practice continued down to the thirteenth century.
10. When the liturgy was canonized at Yavneh, the body of each benediction was still in a fluid state and continued so for many centuries. Hence there were several forms of the prayers in use in various localities. When the rabbis of a later time made the final and definitive selection of the benediction formulas, they occasionally accepted more than one form. Thus in the benedictions of the *Shema*, they assigned one form for the morning service and another for the evening service.
11. The discrepancy between the name, Eighteen Benedictions, and the actual number of nineteen is discussed below, pp. 105–106.
12. In rabbinic literature these benedictions are called (1) *Avot* (Fathers), in which the God of Abraham, Isaac, and Jacob is exalted, (2) *Gevurot* (Powers), in which God's might is acknowledged, and (3) *Kedushat Hashem* (Hallowing God's Name), in which God's holiness is invoked.
13. The petitions of the thirteen benedictions are:
    - (4) to grant us understanding
    - (5) to cause us to return to His Torah and His worship
    - (6) to pardon our sins
    - (7) to deliver us from our afflictions and oppressions
    - (8) to heal our sick
    - (9) to bless the crops of our fields
    - (10) to gather the scattered exiles of Israel
    - (11) to restore our judges as of old
    - (12) to destroy the apostates and heretics
    - (13) to have mercy on the righteous proselytes

(14) to rebuild Jerusalem
(15) to restore the Davidic dynasty
(16) to hear our prayers and fulfill our petitions

14. Prayer units are usually concluded with the recital of the Half Kaddish (see p. 157). But there is no Half Kaddish between the last benediction of the *Shema* and the beginning of the *Tefillah*. This is to indicate that the two prayer units are one service.
15. Kedushot are prayers that emphasize the holiness of God or the holiness of the sacred days, such as Sabbaths and festivals. Havdalot are prayers recited at the conclusion of the sacred days. They declare that God separated the holy from the profane, the Sabbath (or festival) from the weekdays, etc.
16. This benediction has undergone many changes because of pressure on the part of the Church. In the Ashkenazic rite it now reads: "For slanderers let there be no hope, and let all wickedness perish as in a moment; let all Thine enemies be speedily cut off, and the dominion of arrogance do Thou uproot and crush, cast down and humble speedily in our days. *Praised art Thou, O Lord, who breakest the enemies and humblest the arrogant.*"
17. Braude, *The Midrash on Psalms*, 1:38.
18. The intermediate benediction for Rosh Hashanah concludes with the blessing *Praised art Thou, O Lord, King over all the earth, who sanctifies Israel and the Day of Remembrance.*

    The intermediate benediction on Yom Kippur is more elaborate. It concludes *Praised art Thou, O Lord, Thou King, who pardons and forgives our iniquities and the iniquities of His people, the house of Israel, and causes our trespasses to pass away year by year, King of the whole earth, who sanctifies Israel and the Day of Atonement.*
19. The Hebrew word *Avodah* (Service) originally meant the performance of the Temple ritual. Later it also came to mean worship through the utterance of prayers.
20. At first the meturgeman used to expand on the text with illustrations drawn from past and current events as well as other haggadic material. But in later mishnaic times he was limited to translation. But even then the translation reflected rabbinic interpretations of the text.
21. From the commentary in Saadia's *Siddur*, published by the *Mekitzei Nirdamim* (Jerusalem, 1941), pp. 359–60.
22. Judah Goldin, trans., *The Fathers According to Rabbi Nathan* (New Haven, 1955), p. 91.
23. The description of the structure of the rabbinic homily is based on *The Bible as Read and Preached in the Old Synagogue* by Jacob Mann (Cincinnati, 1940), vol. 1.
24. Homiletics is generally defined as a branch of rhetoric that deals with "the composition and delivery of sermons."

Chapter 5

1. Solomon Schechter, *Studies in Judaism*, 1st ser. (Philadelphia, 1911), p. 177.
2. Louis Ginzberg, *Geonica* (New York, 1909), 1:viii.

Chapter 6

1. Some scholars claim that the nineteenth benediction is the anti-Christian benediction which was added during the days of Rabbi Gamaliel II. See pp. 105–106.
2. The three Kedushot of the daily morning service are known as (1) *Kedushah De-Yotzer,* (2) *Kedushah De-Amidah,* and (3) *Kedushah De-Sidra.* In the afternoon service only the *Kedushah De-Amidah* is included.
3. The weekday *Tefillah* had been fixed, while the Sabbath and festival *Tefillah*s were still fluid. Hence they felt free to introduce the Kedushah into the Sabbath and festival *Tefillah*s but refrained from incorporating it into the weekday *Tefillah.*
4. When the Palestinian Jews finally admitted the Kedushah into their liturgy, they omitted the introductory phrase used in Babylonia—*Keter Yitnu Lekha* (A crown is bestowed upon Thee [by the angels above and Thy people Israel, the dwellers below]). This introduction expresses the mystic concept that Israel is "crowning God" when it recites the Kedushah. The opening words in Palestine were *Nekadesh et Shimkha* (We sanctify Thy name). The oriental Jews generally follow the Babylonian ritual and open their Kedushah with the words *Keter Yitnu Lekha.* The Jews of Northern and Eastern Europe and most American Jews follow the Palestinian custom and start the Kedushah with the words *Nekadesh et Shimkha.*
5. Additions to the *Tefillah* that are recited only on special occasions will be discussed in later chapters in connection with those occasions.
6. The oriental Jews use the first version in all services. The second version (*Shalom Rav*) is unknown to them.
7. Some of these prayers are recorded in Ber. 16b–17a. According to Louis Ginzberg there are about two dozen such private prayers in the Talmud. See Abraham A. Neuman and Solomon Zeitlin, eds., *Saadia Studies* (Philadelphia, 1943), p. 315.
8. The first of these prayers, known by its initial words as *Hodu Ladonai* (O give thanks unto the Lord) (1 Chron. 16:8–36), precedes the psalms. It contains the prayer which David recited when he brought to Jerusalem the ark with the Ten Commandments. It also contains a number of other assorted but fitting biblical verses.

   Another prayer before the central group of psalms is known by its initial words as *Yehi Khevod* (Let the glory [of the Lord endure forever]). It, too, consists of selected biblical verses.

   The seven psalms are followed by three biblical prayers. The first is the prayer which David uttered before his death (1 Chron. 29:10–13). The second is a prayer from the Book of Nehemiah (9:6–11). The third is the Song of Moses (Exod. 14:30–15:18) in which he praised and thanked God for the miraculous rescue of the children of Israel from the pursuing Egyptians at the Sea of Reeds. This last prayer was introduced in Germany by Rabbi Moses ben Kolonymus in the eleventh century. See Louis Ginzberg, *Geonica* (New York, 1909), 1:127.
9. The private prayer that Rabbi Judah Ha-Nasi used to recite after

the conclusion of the *Tefillah* is somewhat similar to the above prayer. It reads: "May it be Thy will, O Lord our God, and God of our fathers, to deliver us from the impudent and from impudence, from an evil man, from evil hap, from the evil impulse . . ." (Ber. 16b). It was natural for informed worshipers to associate Rabbi Judah Ha-Nasi's prayer with the one in the text. In time it was added to the morning blessings, next to its related prayer.

10. Rabbi Meir derives this rule by a simple emendation of a biblical word. He reads the word *mah* (what) in the verse "And now, O Israel, *what* does the Lord your God demand of you?" (Deut. 10:12) as *me'ah* (a hundred).
11. Moses Maimonides, *Mishneh Torah, Hilkhot Tefillah*, 7:9, trans. Moses Hyamson (Jerusalem, 1962), p. 160a.
12. See Abraham Berliner, *Ketavim Nivharim* (Jerusalem, 1945), 1:55–56.
13. Some mss. have a variant reading for the first blessing, and formulate it in the positive: "who hast made me an Israelite."
14. This blessing savors of conceit.
15. The reading in our prayer books is "a brutish man."
16. The talmudic list also contains the blessings that accompany the putting on of the tallit and the tefillin. These benedictions, however, were deferred to the actual time when the worshiper puts on these prayer appurtenances.
17. When the persecutions ended and these prayers were no longer private and secret, the phrase "as well as in public" was added.
18. Rabbi Solomon B. Freehof describes the *Birkhot Ha-Shahar* as a "preview of the morning service" and as a miniature "duplicate of the complete morning service." See *Hebrew Union College Annual* 23, (1950–1951): 339–54.
19. The prayer *Uva Le-Zion Go'el* is also recited at the Sabbath afternoon service and on Saturday nights at the end of the Maariv service. This practice, too, goes back to the ancient custom of reading selections from the Prophets on Saturday afternoons and selections from the Writings after the Saturday evening service. These readings were discontinued long ago, but the prayer *Uva Le-Zion Go'el* has remained in the ritual. For other occasions on which this prayer is recited, see Louis Ginzberg, *Geonica*, 2:298 ff.
20. That the Christian Paternoster has many parallels to the Kaddish is not surprising, since Jesus was a Jew and derived his theology as well as his religious practices from the teachings of the rabbis.
21. When the high priest uttered the Tetragrammaton, the people would exclaim: "Blessed be His name whose glorious kingdom is for ever and ever." Similarly, in the opening verses of the Hallel (see pp. 210–11) there is a call to worship and a response that is similar to that of the Kaddish. The response is: "Blessed be the name of the Lord from this time forth and for ever" (Ps. 113:2).
22. A concluding sentence, this time in Hebrew, was added at a much later time. It reads: "He who maketh peace in His high places, may He, in His mercy, make peace for us and for all Israel, and say ye, Amen!"
23. When the mourners began to recite the Kaddish after a discourse or a study period, it became obvious that a prayer for the scholars who

teach the Torah should be included in the Kaddish. Thus the *Kaddish De-Rabbanan*, as we have it now, came into existence.

24. Actually, the mourners recite the Kaddish for only eleven months. The reason is to be found in a talmudic statement which implies that the wicked are judged in purgatory for twelve months (Shab. 152b). Obviously, no son would designate his parents as wicked. Hence the period of reciting the mourners' Kaddish was shortened to eleven months.
25. There is also a special version of the Kaddish used at the time of the burial service. The first paragraph of this Kaddish contains an interpolation aimed at consoling the mourners with a reminder that in the messianic time God will "quicken the dead and raise them up unto life eternal."
26. Additional reasons for the importance of the Ashre are given in Louis Ginzberg, *Ginzei Schechter* (New York, 1928), 1:300–1.
27. This is not an altogether new discovery. Scholars had reconstructed the missing verse from ancient translations of the Bible.
28. *Barukh Adonai Le-Olam* (Blessed [Praised] be the Lord for evermore [Ps. 89:53]).
29. Several communities, among them the city of Jerusalem, omit these eighteen verses and their concluding benediction.
30. Some commentators have claimed that the reason for these introductory verses is that the Maariv service had no *Tefillah*. Since the *Tefillah* was a substitute for the Temple offerings, it atoned for the people's sins. Because the Maariv service lacked this atonement these verses were added to implore God's mercy to "forgive iniquity."

Chapter 7

1. See Exod. 31:13, 16, 17; Ezek. 20:12 ff.
2. George Foot Moore, *Judaism in the First Centuries of the Christian Era* (Cambridge, Mass., 1927), 2:22.
3. The Sabbath *Tefillah* is popularly called *Shemoneh Esreh*. But this is a misnomer because there are only seven benedictions in a Sabbath *Tefillah*.
4. Joseph Heinemann in his scholarly and original work *Prayer in the Period of the Tanna'im and Amora'im* makes a convincing case for the hypothesis that the Sabbath *Tefillah* is not an adaptation of the weekday *Tefillah*, but is an independent and parallel development. See *Prayer in the Period of the Tanna'im and Amora'im* (Jerusalem, 1964), pp. 143–44 (Hebrew).
5. See Shab. 24b and Rashi ad loc.
6. Traditions assume importance apart from their original purposes. They live on, assume new meaning, and perform new functions which are often more important than those responsible for their inception. An example of this process of reinterpretation of religious practices is to be found in Rabbi Asher ben Yehiel's commentary on the Talmud. In regard to the Kiddush recited at the Friday evening services we read in this thirteenth century commentary: "Since there are people who do not know how to make Kiddush, it was established that the Kiddush be recited in the synagogue, so that these

people may fulfill their duty of making Kiddush which is prescribed in the Torah" (Commentary to Pes. 101a).

In thirteenth century Spain, the home of Rabbi Asher ben Yehiel, the social situation had changed and necessitated a new justification of the tradition. Rabbi Asher ben Yehiel's reinterpretation applies with equal logic to modern times. It applies to both the recitation of the Kiddush and the reader's repetition of the Friday evening *Tefillah* in the form of the *Magen Avot*. There are many Jews who attend Friday evening services who do not know how to read the silent *Tefillah* or how to make the Kiddush at home. The repetition of the *Tefillah* in the *Magen Avot* and the chanting of the Kiddush affords these worshipers the opportunity to hear these essential parts of the Friday evening liturgy and to respond with the traditional Amen.

7. The blessing of the concluding benediction after the *Shema* was adapted to the Sabbath situation. On weekday it reads: *Praised art Thou, O Lord, who guardest Thy people Israel for ever.* On Friday evening this blessing reads: *Praised art Thou, O Lord, who spreadest the tabernacle of peace over us and over all Thy people Israel, and over Jerusalem.*
8. Psalms 19, 34, 90, 91, 135, 136, 33, 92, and 93.
9. The authorship of the *Nishmat* prayer, especially its last section, has been the subject of speculation. Among the suggested authors is the patriarch Isaac. This is based on the discovery that the initial letters of the four nouns in the four consecutive verses spell out the Hebrew name Isaac. But there have been many Isaacs. Fortunately, the field was narrowed by the additional discovery that the name Rebecca is to be found in the verbs of these verses. The third letter in each of these verbs constitute the four letters of the Hebrew name Rebecca. This discovery necessitated a reshuffling of the verbs to be valid. The Sephardic Jews have rearranged these verbs and print the letters that spell out the names of Isaac and Rebecca in bold type for everyone to see the presumed author's name. According to this line of reasoning, the author is obviously a man by the name of Isaac whose wife was named Rebecca, hence the patriarch Isaac.

   Others have discovered acrostics of the name Simon in the verses which precede the above verses. Hence they concluded that the author was named Simon. And what Simon was more famous than Rabbi Simon ben Shetah, who lived in Palestine about one hundred years before the Common Era? There have even been some who ascribed this noble prayer to the apostle Peter whose Hebrew name was Simon.

   Actually, the authors of this composite prayer are unknown. Nor is it known when the separate parts of the *Nishmat* prayer were composed. We can only say with certainty that the prayer is of talmudic origin and that the authors must have been men of piety and inspiration.
10. See Heinemann, *Prayer in the Period of the Tanna'im and the Amora'im*, pp. vii–viii.
11. Quoted in Israel Davidson, *Mahzor Yannai* (New York, 1919), p. xvii.
12. Other such psalms are Pss. 34 and 119. Prov. 31 also contains an alphabetic acrostic.

13. H. Brody, *Diwan des Jehudah ha-Levi* (Berlin, 1901), 2:93–99.
14. This addiction was even allowed to overshadow the sense of the piyut. Thus the favorite hymn *Ein Kelohenu* as it now appears in all prayer books hardly makes sense. It begins with the affirmative declaration "There is no one like unto our God" and immediately proceeds to ask "Who is like unto our God?" Obviously these two verses should be reversed. And originally their sequence was reversed. But someone spotted an acrostic. If the lines are reversed, as they now are, the initial letters of the first three lines read "Amen." This was irresistible.
15. Morris S. Goodblatt, *Jewish Life in Turkey in the Sixteenth Century* (New York, 1952), p. 141.
16. *Siddur Bet Jacob* (Lemberg, 1904), p. 172a.
17. Solomon Schechter, *Studies in Judaism*, 3rd ser. (Philadelphia, 1924), p. 11.
18. Quoted in ibid., "Leopold Zunz," p. 110.
19. Israel Davidson, *Thesaurus of Mediaeval Hebrew Poetry* (New York, 1924–1933), 4:viii–xiv.
20. Leopold Zunz, *Die synagogale Poesie des Mittelalters* (Berlin, 1855), pp. 70–71.
21. This line is composed of the first part of each of three biblical verses: Pss. 10:16 and 93:1; Exod. 15:18.
22. The rabbis interpreted this verse as referring to the Torah, which is the source of Israel's strength and peace. See Zev. 116a.
23. The reading of the Torah was discussed in an earlier chapter; see pp. 108 ff.
24. The second verse is abbreviated. The initial part of the verse was omitted either for the sake of brevity or because it was considered superfluous for the purpose at hand.
25. In 1845 the triennial cycle was revived at the Conference of Reform Rabbis in Frankfort am Main. Today it is also gaining favor in many Conservative congregations in America.
26. Elkan N. Adler, *Jewish Travellers* (London, 1930), pp. 69–70.
27. The prophetic portions read between the fast of the Ninth of Av and Rosh Hashanah were chosen from Isaiah 40–66, because they contain words of comfort.
28. In the Palestinian ritual it was customary for the congregation to respond at this point: "Faithful art Thou, O Lord our God, and faithful are Thy words. Faithful, ever living, and existing God, Thy name and Thy memorial will reign over us for ever and ever." The reader then continued with "Faithful art Thou," and so on.
29. See Heinemann, *Prayer in the Period of the Tanna'im and the Amora'im*, pp. 143–44.
30. Other examples of parallel versions preserved in the prayer book are (1) the benediction after the *Shema—Emet Ve-Yatziv* and its parallel in the evening service, *Emet Ve-Emunah*—and (2) the last benediction of the *Tefillah—Sim Shalom* and its parallel in the afternoon and evening *Tefillah, Shalom Rav*.
31. Josephus, *The Jewish Wars*, trans. H. S. J. Thackery (London, 1927), 2:10, 4.
32. This commentary by David Abudarham was written in 1340. It enjoyed great popularity and was republished many times.

33. A. Alexander's edition contains an English translation and the Hebrew text according to the ritual of the Spanish and Portuguese Jews, 5531–5534 (1770–1773).
34. This translation of the Hebrew text does not appear in the translation that accompanies the prayer in the official Conservative prayer book. Instead there is a brief paraphrase.
35. See Louis Ginzberg, *Geonica* (New York, 1909), 2:49.
36. Pss. 119:142; 71:19; 36:7.
37. See Ginzberg, *Geonica*, 2:299–300.
38. The biblical selections include Gen. 27:28–29; 28:3–4; 49:25–26; Deut. 7:13–15; Gen. 48:16; Deut. 1:10–11; 28:3,6,5,4,8,12; 15:6; 32:29.

Chapter 8

1. See Pes. 68b.
2. See Franz Delitzsch, *Jewish Artisan Life* (London, 1902), chapter 4.
3. The land was divided into twenty-four districts, each called a *Ma'amad*. See pp. 77–78.
4. See Sukkah 55b, *Pesikta*, ed. Buber, 193b–194a, and others.
5. For the two-day observance of Rosh Hashanah, see pp. 231–32.
6. The Samaritans would light beacons on other days to confuse the Jews.
7. The phrase "Thou hast chosen us from all peoples" was never understood by the Jews to mean that they were in any way superior to other nations and were therefore entitled to a privileged status among the peoples of the world. It meant that God had bestowed on the Jewish people special duties involving obedience to the teachings of the Torah. It also implied severer punishment for failure to live up to these high expectations. See pp. 401–402.
8. The *Ya'aleh Ve-Yavo* prayer is also included in the *Tefillah* of Rosh Hashanah and Yom Kippur and the New Moon days. It is also to be found in the grace after meals on each of those days.
9. Rosh Hashanah and the New Moon days are known as Days of Remembrance. Hence the *Ya'aleh Ve-Yavo* prayer is included in their liturgy.
10. When the Hallel psalms were recited on the festival of Sukkot, each worshiper who had a lulav and etrog waved them during the recitation of Psalm 118:25: "We beseech Thee O Lord, save now!/We beseech Thee, O Lord, make us now to prosper!" The lulav was waved in six directions—the four points of the compass, upward, and downward.
11. It has been conjectured that the reason for omitting these verses is that they were originally not part of the Hallel and were later additions; hence they were detached when a distinction was to be made.

    The above discussion of the Hallel is based on an article by Solomon Zeitlin in *The Jewish Quarterly Review* 53 (1962–1963): 22–29.
12. There is also a homiletic explanation for reciting only the Half Hallel during the last six days of the Passover. This explanation is based on the biblical verse "Rejoice not when thine enemy falleth" (Prov. 24:17). The seventh day of Passover is traditionally the anniversary of the Egyptians' drowning in the Sea of Reeds. To demonstrate that the Jewish people is not rejoicing because of the calamity

that befell the Egyptians but only because of their own liberation from bondage, the psalms of rejoicing were shortened on that day. But obviously if you recite the Half Hallel on the seventh day, which is a full festival day, you will not recite the Full Hallel on the intermediate semifestival days. Hence the Half Hallel is recited during the last six days of the Passover.

13. See Ps. 22:4 and Exod. 15:11.
14. The chanting of the Thirteen Divine Attributes (Exod. 34:6–7) before the scroll of the Torah is taken out of the ark is of late medieval origin.
15. The other two *megillot* are Esther and Lamentations. Esther is read on Purim, and Lamentations is read on the fast of the Ninth of Av. See pp. 273–74, 278.
16. The functions of the Kohanim and the *Levi'im* were usually recorded on their tombstones. Two hands outstretched in blessing are the token of a Kohen, and the ewer used by the Levites to wash the hands of the Kohanim is the token of a Levite.
17. There is a tradition going back to the geonic period that during the messianic days the resurrection will take place on the Passover, and the cataclysmic wars of Gog and Magog will take place on Sukkot. Hence the Haftarah for the Sabbath of Hol Hamoed of Passover is Ezek. 37, which deals with the vision of the dry bones coming to life, and the Haftarah for the corresponding Sabbath on Sukkot is Ezek. 39, which deals with the wars of Gog and Magog.
18. In the Diaspora the counting of the omer on the second evening of Passover is usually done at the second Seder.
19. The practice of staying up all night on Shavuot and reading the *Tikkun Lel Shavuot* is not dealt with here because it is a late medieval development. See pp. 505–506.
20. The ceremony of hakafot, the procession with the Torahs, is of postgeonic origin. See pp. 467–68.

Chapter 9

1. William G. Braude, trans., *The Midrash on Psalms* (New Haven, 1959), 1:370.
2. The word *selihot* is the plural of the Hebrew word *selihah,* a penitential prayer.
3. When Rosh Hashanah falls on Monday or Tuesday, the first *Selihot* service is held on the Saturday night of the preceding week. The number of penitential services before Rosh Hashanah is therefore never less than four and can be as high as eight.
4. In the weekday *Tefillah* of the intermediate days between Rosh Hashanah and Yom Kippur there is a similar change in the eleventh benediction: the concluding words of the blessing, "King who lovest righteousness and justice," are changed to "King of justice." During this season God not only loves justice but dispenses justice in His role as the universal Judge.
5. For illuminating comments on the contents of these as well as all

other High Holy Day prayers, see Max Arzt, *Justice and Mercy* (New York, 1963).

6. The shofar has retained some of its nonliturgical uses. During the Middle Ages, the shofar was sounded when excommunication was imposed on someone who was derelict in the performance of certain important duties. The sound of the shofar added a note of solemnity and finality to the decree. During plagues and other communal calamities the shofar was blown to arouse the community to repentance.
7. A discussion in the Talmud (R. H. 27b) of the legal aspects of sounding the shofar into a pit or a vat reflects periods of persecution when the sounding of the shofar was prohibited and clandestine methods had to be resorted to.
8. In the later Middle Ages another emphasis, which had its origin in the esoteric teachings of the kabbalah, became popular. The purpose of the shofar was to confuse Satan, Israel's adversary. See pp. 496–97.
9. Moses Maimonides, *Mishneh Torah, Teshuvah* 3:4, trans. Moses Hyamson (Jerusalem, 1962), p. 84a.
10. The day on which God, the Sovereign of the universe, judges all his creatures.
11. Rosh Hashanah 4:6.
12. The Yom Kippur services are exceeded in length only by the Samaritan Day of Atonement services, which last twenty-four consecutive hours.
13. The tallit is not put on at an evening service. However, it is worn on Yom Kippur evening because it is put on before Kol Nidre, while it is still daytime. Since the Maariv service continues without a break, the congregation continues to wear the tallit through the evening service.
14. For geonic opposition to the Kol Nidre, see Jacob Mann, *Texts and Studies* (Philadelphia, 1935), 2:52.
15. Nahum N. Glatzer, *Franz Rosenzweig: His Life and Thought* (New York, 1953), chapter 2.
16. This does not imply that the ritual and ceremonial observances of Judaism are deprecated in the liturgy. The importance of ritual can be judged by the inclusion in the Yom Kippur service of a detailed description of the sacrificial rites that were performed at the Jerusalem Temple.
17. Translated by Elsie Davis in Herbert M. Adler and Arthur Davis, ed. and trans., *Mahzor for Yom Kippur* (London, n.d.), p. 39.
18. In many traditional prayer books, the *Selihot* are included only in the Maariv and the Neilah services.
19. Poems of this type, describing in detail the Temple service on Yom Kippur, had been written by earlier poets, and these poems were used as *Avodot* in various communities.
20. The Talmud provides a different formula for the beautiful maidens whom the above formula placed at a disadvantage. "Our Rabbis have taught: The beautiful amongst them called out, Set your eyes on beauty for the quality most to be prized in woman is beauty" (Ta'an. 31a).
21. The memorial service which follows the Haftarah in the modern liturgy is postgeonic. See pp. 448–50.

Chapter 10

1. If Rosh Hodesh falls on a Sunday, there is a special Haftarah on the preceding Sabbath. The prophetic selection is 1 Sam. 20:18–42, which begins with the words: "And Jonathan said unto [David]: 'To-morrow is the new moon; and thou wilt be missed, because thy seat will be empty.' "
2. This prayer is quoted in full in Ber. 16b.
3. The Books of the Maccabees will be found in R. H. Charles, ed., *The Apocrypha and Pseudepigrapha of the Old Testament* (Oxford, 1913), 1:59–173. The Scroll of the Hasmoneans is included in Philip Birnbaum, ed. and trans., *Daily Prayer Book* (New York, 1949), pp. 714–26.
4. The addition of the Second-Day Festival of the Diaspora has extended the observance of the festival of Passover to eight days. See pp. 205–208.
5. The school of Shammai held that eight lights should be kindled on the first night of Hanukah and thereafter the number of lights should be progressively reduced until the eighth night, when only one light is kindled. One of the reasons given for this procedure is that the lights should "correspond to the bullocks of the Festival [of Sukkot]" (Shab. 21b). On Sukkot the number of offerings was progressively reduced each day. On the first day thirteen bullocks were sacrificed, on the second day twelve, and so on (Num. 29:12–34).
6. The twenty-fifth of Kislev was chosen as the date because on that day, exactly three years after the desecration of the Temple, the rededication took place. The choice of the date for the desecration of the Temple by Antiochus Epiphanes may have been connected with the winter solstice.
7. In the *She'iltot (Vayishlah)* by the Gaon Aha we read: "One is obliged to recite the *Al Ha-Nissim* in the thanksgiving benediction."
8. The others are Song of Songs, Ruth, Lamentations, and Ecclesiastes. These scrolls are read at synagogue service on Passover, Shavuot, Tishah Be-Av, and Sukkot respectively.
9. Obviously, the Day of Atonement is in a different category.
10. The four fasts listed in Zech. 8:19 are, in the order of their occurrence, the Fast of Gedaliah, the Tenth of Tevet, the Seventeenth of Tammuz, and the Ninth of Av.
11. See also Ta'an. 26b and R. H. 18b.
12. *Proceedings of the Rabbinical Assembly*, vol. 28 (1964), p. 119.
13. The prayer vestments are regarded as (religious) ornaments and are therefore forbidden.
14. During the reader's repetition of the *Tefillah*, the prayer *Anenu* is recited after the seventh benediction, that is, after "*Praised art Thou, O Lord, the Redeemer of Israel.*"
15. The tallit and tefillin are put on to compensate for the omission of these rites in the morning service.
16. The months of Tevet, Tammuz, and Av correspond approximately to the months of January, July, and August respectively.

17. These tragic events are related briefly but poignantly by the prophet Jeremiah (52:4–13).
18. *She'iltot* by the Gaon Aha (*She'ilta* 79).
19. The name of the tractate is inserted.
20. Rabbi Hiyya's prayer on concluding his study (Ber. 16b).
21. Rabbi Johanan's prayer on concluding his study (Ber. 11b).
22. This prayer is introduced in the Talmud as follows: "Our Rabbis taught . . . On his leaving [the house of study] what does he say?" (Ber. 28b).

Chapter 11

1. The requirement to repeat the *Shema* before retiring originated when it became customary to recite the Maariv service immediately after the Minhah service, even if it was before sunset. This made it necessary to repeat the *Shema* after nightfall in accordance with the biblical injunction to recite the *Shema* "when thou liest down [at night] and when thou risest up [in the morning]." See Louis Ginzberg, *Geonica* (New York, 1909), 1:136.
2. The paternal blessing of the children is of late medieval origin. See pp. 469–70.
3. The Sabbath is not sanctified over a cup of wine. The Sabbath is holy by virtue of its having been sanctified by God, as we read in the Scriptures: "Therefore the Lord blessed the sabbath day and hallowed it" (Exod. 20:11).
4. The double memorial is in accordance with the variant texts of the Sabbath commandment in Exodus (20:11) and Deuteronomy (5:15).
5. For the origin of these and other Sabbath rituals, see Abraham E. Millgram, *Sabbath: The Day of Delight* (Philadelphia, 1944), pp. 14–22.
6. These verses are Isa. 12:2–3; Pss. 3:9; 46:12; 84:13; 20:10; Esther 8:16; Ps. 116:13.
7. Ever since the Haggadah was made available, at first in manuscript and then in print, Jewish artists have lavished their talents on it. In an article on illustrated Haggadot published in *The Jewish Quarterly Review* 16 (1925–26):471, the late Alexander Marx welcomes the publication of an old illuminated Haggadah to be sold at a reasonable price "to replace its ugly modern successors." He was reacting to the modern Haggadah produced as an advertising medium. These are surely unworthy successors to the charming Haggadot illuminated by artists of skill and taste. The revulsion against the modern cheap Haggadot has had its beneficial effects. A number of beautiful old Haggadot have been republished, and several new ones of exquisite taste and charm have recently been published.
8. The word *afikomen* is derived from the Greek and means "after meal dessert," or the last item of the meal.
9. Nowadays it is customary to donate to a fund called *Ma'ot Hittin* (Money for the Purchase of Wheat) to enable every poor Jew to conduct his own Seder.
10. This account is based on Israel Davidson, *Thesaurus of Mediaeval Hebrew Poetry* (New York, 1930), 3:95.

11. The Hallel (Pss. 113–118) is often called the Egyptian Hallel to distinguish it from the Great Hallel (Ps. 136).
12. Although horseradish is most commonly used, other varieties of bitter herbs may be substituted.
13. In Israel many apartment houses are planned so as to enable each tenant to erect a sukkah on his balcony.
14. The Mishnah was compiled at the end of the second century C.E.
15. The melody is an adaptation of an old German folk song.

Chapter 12

1. The rite of bar mitzvah is omitted from this section because it is postgeonic in origin. See pp. 466–67.
2. The word *sandek* is a corruption of the Greek word *sunteknos*, which in the Greek Church meant godfather.
3. The verses are Gen. 49:18; Ps. 119:156, 162–166; Ps. 65:5.
4. The child's name and the father's name are inserted.
5. The following verses are also recited at this point: Ezek. 16:6; Ps. 105:8–10; Gen. 21:4; Ps. 118:1.
6. The biblical blessings consist of the following verses: Gen. 48:20; Num. 6:24–26; Ps. 121:5; Prov. 3:2; Ps. 121:7.
7. Michael Higger, ed. and trans., *Seven Minor Treatises* (New York, 1930), p. 47.
8. The last benediction is based in part on the prophecy of Jeremiah: "Thus saith the Lord: Yet again there shall be heard in this place, whereof ye say: It is waste, without man and without beast, even in the cities of Judah, and in the streets of Jerusalem . . . the voice of joy and the voice of gladness, the voice of the bridegroom and the voice of the bride. . . . For I will cause the captivity of the land to return as at the first, saith the Lord" (Jer. 33:10–11).
9. This part of the rite of burial is known as taharah, or laving of the body.
10. The yahrzeit is a postgeonic institution. See pp. 448–50.

Chapter 13

1. A Torah crown is mentioned in a responsum by Hai Gaon, who lived in the tenth century. The oriental Jews developed solid containers for the scrolls, with finials on the protruding rods at the top. These ornaments were usually made of silver and often embellished with bells.
2. In the Sephardic synagogues the pews ran lengthwise, along the north and south walls, facing the centrally located bimah.
3. The early Christians strictly segregated the women at worship, and in some churches there were women's galleries. This bias is not surprising since a woman was the cause of "original sin," which is a fundamental doctrine in Christian theology. See Solomon Zeitlin, "The Segregation of Women during Prayers," *The Jewish Quarterly Review* 38 (1947–48):305–8.
4. See Meg. 23a.
5. Actually this treasure was discovered in 1864 by the Jewish traveler

Jacob Saphir, but it was the rediscovery by Solomon Schechter that led to its availability to scholars. For an illuminating description of the Cairo genizah, see Paul E. Kahle, *The Cairo Geniza* (Oxford, 1959), pp. 3–13.

6. See Eleazar L. Sukenik, *The Ancient Synagogue of Beth Alpha* (Jerusalem, 1932).
7. Solomon Schechter, *Studies in Judaism*, 1st ser. (Philadelphia, 1911), p. 311.
8. William G. Braude, trans., *The Midrash on Psalms* (New Haven, 1959), 2:99.
9. The actual translation is "That ye may look upon *it*." But in Hebrew there is no word for *it*, because there are only two genders, the masculine and the feminine.
10. During the geonic period the wording of the tallit commandment added fuel to the burning issues of the great schism that gave birth to the Karaite sect. The rabbis interpreted the phrase "that ye may look upon it" (Num. 15:39) to mean that the obligation to put on the tallit at prayer applies only to the daytime. A blind man is therefore obligated to put on the tallit at prayer even though he cannot "look upon it." The Karaites, however, took this biblical phrase to mean that one is to "look" at the tzitzis. In their literalness they removed the phrase from its context which clearly indicates that it is a garment and is therefore to be worn. They ruled that the tzitzis are to be hung up on a wall, so that everyone may "look upon it."
11. On the elimination of the Ten Commandments from the prayers and, for the same reason, from the tefillin, see p. 400.
12. Moses Maimonides, *Mishneh Torah: The Book of Adoration*, trans. Moses Hyamson (Jerusalem, 1962), p. 126b.
13. Moses of Coucy, *Sefer Mitzvot Gadol* (SeMaG), book 2, *The Positive Commandments*, end of no. 3 (Munkacs, 1905).
14. See also B. Lewin, ed., *Otzar Ha-Geonim*, vol. 1, *Berakhot* (Haifa, 1928), p. 41, no. 90.
15. Moses Maimonides, *Guide for the Perplexed*, trans. M. Friedlander (London, 1925), pp. 391–92.
16. Israel Abrahams, *Jewish Life in the Middle Ages* (London, 1932), pp. 301–2.
17. According to W. Gunther Plaut, the word *yarmulke* is derived from the head covering of the medieval clergy, called *armucella*. See W. Gunther Plaut, "The Origin of the Word '*Yarmulke*,'" *Hebrew Union College Annual* 26 (1955):567–70.
18. James Parkes, *The Jews in the Medieval Community* (London, 1938), p. 189.
19. For rabbinic definitions and descriptions of these rites, see Ber. 34b and Meg. 22b.
20. Another remnant of the ritual of prostration is to be found in the *Tahanun* prayers. The worshipers place their heads on their left arms and silently confess their sins. This rite is considered as a symbolic "falling on the face." See pp. 461–63.
21. See Yoma 53b.
22. Judah Halevi, *Book of Kuzari*, trans. Hartwig Hirschfield (New York, 1946), pp. 112–13.

23. See Ta'an. 2:1.
24. Israel Abrahams, *Jewish Life in the Middle Ages*, p. 157.
25. Boaz Cohen, *Law and Tradition in Judaism* (New York, 1959), p. 181.
26. In Hebrew they are known as *ta'amei ha-mikra*, or scriptural notations.
27. The Song of Songs, Ruth, Lamentations, Ecclesiastes, and Esther.

Chapter 14

1. Solomon Schechter, *Studies in Judaism*, 3rd ser. (Philadelphia, 1924), p. 148.
2. Yair Hayim Bacharach, *Hovat Yair*, Responsum 238 (Frankfort am Main, 1699), p. 222b.
3. Another widespread minhag that differs considerably from the two main rites is that of the Hasidim, known as *Nusah Sepharad*. See pp. 513–15.
4. An example of variant local rites within each of the major minhagim are the rules governing the priestly benediction pronounced by the Kohanim during the reader's repetition of the *Tefillah*. In most Ashkenazic synagogues it is pronounced only during the three major festivals. The Hasidim perform this ritual even if the festival falls on a Sabbath. In Jerusalem it is performed at every morning service and on a Sabbath or festival, at both the Shaharit and the Musaf services.
5. The Sephardic pronunciation was adopted by the Christian scholar Johann Reuchlin and thus became the official pronunciation in Christian circles, and subsequently in all universities. In modern times the Zionists, in their rebellion against the ghetto, rejected the pronunciation used in the European ghettos in favor of the Sephardic pronunciation. They thought that the Ashkenazic pronunciation was a corruption resulting from the miserable ghetto life in the Christian lands.
6. The fourteenth century talmudic scholar Rabbi Isaac ben Sheshet (Rivash) gave a rational explanation of this custom. He was asked "whether it is proper for the reader to recite the prayers in unison with the congregation, instead of the reader and congregation reciting the prayers silently, and then the reader just repeating loudly the conclusion." In his responsum Rabbi Isaac ben Sheshet says: "It appears that this custom came into being in those countries because the majority were ignorant and could not pray even from a book. . . . Therefore they pray together with the reader" (*The Responsa of the Rivash*, no. 37).
7. For a fuller appreciation of the wide differences that developed in the minhagim, compare the Ashkenazic *Tefillah* with the Palestinian version discovered in the Cairo genizah, published by Ismar Elbogen in his *Der jüdische Gottesdienst* (Frankfort am Main, 1931), pp. 517–18.
8. The Sephardim have often pointed with pride to the superiority of their piyutim. See pp. 171–72.
9. Israel Abrahams, *Jewish Life in the Middle Ages* (London, 1932), pp. 50–51.
10. The above is based mainly on Louis Ginzberg, *Geonica* (New York, 1909), 1:119–23. See also idem, "Saadia's Siddur," *Saadia Studies*, ed.

Abraham A. Newman and Solomon Zeitlin (Philadelphia, 1943), pp. 316 ff.

11. *The Two Books of Common Prayer* (1549–1551) (Oxford, 1838), p. vii.
12. The *tanna'im* were the teachers of the Mishnah who lived in Palestine prior to the third century. The *amora'im* were the teachers of the Talmud who lived after the compilation of the Mishnah, between the third and fifth centuries.
13. Ginzberg, *Geonica*, 1:144.
14. Louis Ginzberg, "Saadia's Siddur," *The Jewish Quarterly Review* 33 (1942–43):324.
15. Quoted in ibid., p. 327.
16. In later centuries the Arabic of Saadia's *Siddur* limited its usefulness to the Arabic-speaking countries. But in his day these countries contained the leading Jewish communities—the Babylonian community with its famous academies and its influential geonim, the important Jewries of North Africa, especially that of Kairowan (now Tunisia), and Spanish Jewry, which was then in the early stages of its "golden era."
17. Israel Davidson, S. Asaf, and B. I. Joel, eds., *Siddur R. Saadja Gaon* (Jerusalem, 1941).
18. The names of famous scholars were usually abbreviated. Thus Rashi consists of the initials of *R*abbi *Sh*lomoh *I*tzhaki, and Rashbam is made up of the initials of *R*abbi *Sh*muel *B*en *M*eir.
19. The *Mahzor Vitry* did not end the process of transcribing the liturgy for the synagogue. Thus the first definitive *Siddur* of the Italian rite was not formulated till the twelfth century, by Menahem ben Solomon of Rome.

Chapter 15

1. Theologians usually distinguish between dogmas, doctrines, and precepts. In this chapter these terms are used interchangeably. The fine distinctions of the specialists will only confuse the uninitiated. It should also be noted that the word *dogma*, like the word *taboo*, has become a loaded word. To use it is to arouse irrational prejudice against the idea under discussion. The words *doctrine, precept, tenet,* and *belief* are frequently used in its place.
2. See Maurice Samuel, *The World of Sholom Aleichem* (New York, 1943), pp. 8–20.
3. Louis Ginzberg, *Students, Scholars and Saints* (Philadelphia, 1928), p. 92.
4. Max Kadushin, *Organic Thinking: A Study in Rabbinic Thought* (New York, 1938), pp. 6 ff.
5. A number of pioneering attempts of this type have been made. Among these are Solomon Schechter's *Aspects of Rabbinic Theology* (Schocken Books, Schocken Paperbacks, 1961) and George Foot Moore's *Judaism in the First Centuries of the Christian Era*, 3 vols. (Cambridge, Mass., 1927–1930).
6. God is referred to in the Bible as the Father of Israel in Hos. 11:1 and in Jer. 31:9. In Ps. 103:13 we read: "Like as a father hath com-

passion on his children, So hath the Lord compassion upon them that fear Him." Rabbinic literature is replete with references to God as "Father," "Father in heaven," "our Father who art in heaven." (See *Mishnah Yoma* 8, end.) Similarly, the synagogue prayers repeatedly refer to God as "Father."

7. Compare the wording of this benediction with Isa. 45:7, on which it is based.
8. The seven laws of Noah prohibited (1) blasphemy, (2) theft, (3) idolatry, (4) murder, (5) incest, and (6) eating flesh from a living animal; also, (7) courts of justice were to be established.
9. The interdiction of the rite of circumcision was a primary cause of both the rebellion against Antiochus in the second century B.C.E. and the rebellion against Rome in the second century C.E.
10. The rabbinic term *Malkhut Shamayim* is frequently translated as the kingdom of heaven. But in rabbinic literature the word *Shamayim* is a synonym for God. *Malkhut Shamayim* means the kingship of God.
11. This brief statement does not deal with several basic messianic concepts. Nor does it include the role of Elijah or the catastrophic wars of Gog and Magog. The concept of the resurrection is discussed below, pp. 411–15. The presentation of the messianic doctrine is abbreviated to fit the scope of this book.
12. For an illuminating talmudic parable demonstrating the logic of the resurrection of both body and soul, see San. 91a–b.
13. Ezekiel's vision of the dry bones is another obvious support of the doctrine. See Ezek. 37:1–14 and Isa. 26–19.
14. In Christianity the speculations are concentrated on the salvation of the individual. In Judaism the restoration of the people of Israel is of equal importance to that of the individual Jew. The Jew is an inseparable part of the community of Israel.
15. Another view holds that the dead will roll underground till they reach the Holy Land, and there they will rise. To avoid this unpleasant prospect some Jews arranged to be buried in the Holy Land.
16. A convert not only accepts Judaism but also becomes a "son of Abraham." He is technically "reborn" into the Jewish people.
17. William G. Braude, trans., *The Midrash on Psalms* (New Haven, 1959), 1:399.
18. "The dominion of arrogance" referred to the Roman Empire.
19. The parts of this prayer that were omitted are in all probability later accretions which were added to emphasize and amplify the essential articles of the creed.
20. Alexander Marx, "A List of Poems on the Articles of the Creed," *The Jewish Quarterly Review* 9 (1918–19):305 ff., lists eighty-eight such poems.

Chapter 16

1. The words *ethical* and *moral* are used interchangeably, although there is a clear distinction between them. In *Crabb's English Synonyms* this distinction is made: "When we speak of something as being ethically right, we suggest that we are going back to first

principles and judging it as a matter of abstract right and wrong. When we speak of something as being morally wrong, we are thinking especially of the act in relation to society and social judgments." In Judaism, both ethics and morals are part of God's revealed will.

2. Some modern writers have tried to read into the ethical teachings of the rabbis a system of rabbinic ethics involving first principles. One such attempt was made by M. Lazarus in his *Ethics of Judaism*, 2 vols. (Philadelphia, 1900–01). All such attempts are doomed to failure because rabbinic literature is not governed by philosophic systems of thought. See pp. 391–94.
3. To be sure, there is the rabbinic statement that repentance is effective only in matters between man and God. In matters between man and man restitution must precede repentance. While the rabbis prescribe the procedures of repentance, they do not distinguish between these types of transgressions in terms of their essential validity.
4. William G. Braude, trans., *The Midrash on Psalms* (New Haven, 1959), 2:69.
5. That is, does the obligation to recite the *Shema* demand that one do so even in the midst of agonizing torture?
6. The last word in the opening verse of the *Shema*.
7. Israel Abrahams, *Hebrew Ethical Wills* (Philadelphia, 1948), 1:124–25.
8. Quoted in Yosef Yuzpa Han Norlingen, *Yosef Ometz* (Frankfort am Main), 1723, p. 59.
9. Solomon Schechter, *Studies in Judaism*, 3rd ser. (Philadelphia, 1924), p. 56.

Chapter 17

1. Compare the Lord's Prayer (Luke 11:2–4; Matt. 6:9–13) with the parallels given in C. Taylor, *Sayings of the Jewish Fathers* (London, 1897), pp. 128–29.
2. R. Travers Herford, "The Separation of Christianity from Judaism," *Jewish Studies in Memory of Israel Abrahams* (New York, 1927), p. 210.
3. There are many versions of the benediction, owing to Christian censorship, which necessitated not only the elimination of the word *Nazarenes*, but other changes as well. Sephardic and Yemenite prayer books contain versions which are closer to the original. For the original form of the prayer, see Paul E. Kahle, *The Cairo Geniza* (Oxford, 1959), p. 41.
4. A later rabbinic justification for this seemingly illogical order of the divine blessings is that the word *brit* (divine covenant) occurs thirteen times in the biblical section dealing with the circumcision of Abraham (Gen. 17), while it occurs only three times in the section dealing with the giving of the Torah (Exod. 19–24) (Ber. 48b–49a).
5. Henry Charles Lea, *A History of the Inquisition of Spain* (New York, 1906), 1:35.
6. William G. Braude, trans., *The Midrash on Psalms* (New Haven, 1959), 2:259.
7. A parallel to the Christian proscription of the *Shema* was that of the Magians in Persia. They, too, found the proclamation of God's unity

offensive, because it contradicted the doctrine of dualism which is central in Zoroastrianism. There, too, the Jews circumvented the edict. See pp. 148–49.

8. For the full text of the edict see Kahle, *The Cairo Geniza*, pp. 315–17.
9. Louis Ginzberg, *Geonica* (New York, 1909), 2:49 ff.
10. Rabbi Meir of Rothenberg in his responsa refers to Kalonymus ben Meshullam. See Irving A. Agus, *Rabbi Meir of Rothenberg* (Philadelphia, 1947), 2:679 (resp. no. 784).
11. The prayer *Omnam Ken* (True Indeed), which is read on Kol Nidre night, is one of the piyutim by Rabbi Yom Tov ben Isaac.
12. Solomon Schechter, *Studies in Judaism*, 3rd ser. (Philadelphia, 1924), p. 22.
13. For a vivid description of the massacres during the First Crusade, see Marvin Lowenthal, *The Jews of Germany* (Philadelphia, 1936), pp. 39–49.
14. The yizkor prayers are recited four times annually—on the Day of Atonement, on the last days of Passover and Shavuot, and on Shemini Atzeret (the eighth day of Sukkot).
15. This figure of speech for immortality is based on 1 Sam. 25:29.
16. The same formula is recited for a mother and for other members of the family with appropriate changes in the designation of relationship and gender. A special yizkor is also recited for those who died as martyrs for the faith.
17. The martyrs were burned to the applause of the best people. In some cities it was an annual event, and in others it was a more frequent entertainment. The nobility and Church dignitaries came from great distances. They occupied balconies overlooking the auto-da-fé. The performances were often accompanied by great festive banquets and were often staged on the occasion of a royal visit or in honor of the marriage of a prince.
18. The redeeming feature of the ghetto was that it often protected its inhabitants against mob violence.
19. See D. Kaufmann, "Jewish Informers in the Middle Ages," *The Jewish Quarterly Review* 8 (1896):217–38.
20. Schechter, *Studies in Judaism*, 3rd ser., p. 16.
21. Forcing Jews to hear conversionary preaching was not initiated by Pope Benedict XIII; early in the thirteenth century this was already practiced in several localities. But now it became widespread. See Israel Abrahams, *Jewish Life in the Middle Ages* (London, 1932), p. 442.
22. For a moving account of the Inquisition at work in the Western Hemisphere, see Seymour B. Liebman, *The Enlightened: The Writings of Luis de Carvajal, el Mozo* (Coral Gables, Fla., 1967).
23. The first book burning took place at Montpelier in 1233, when Maimonides' works were burned in public. This was followed in 1242 by the famous auto-da-fé in Paris where twelve thousand manuscript volumes of the Talmud were burned.
24. The policy of book censorship actually began as early as the year 325 C.E., when Constantine decreed that the works of Arius, who challenged some of the Church doctrines, be condemned to the flames.

25. A similar "proof" was found to establish that the prayer had the Moslems in mind. See J. D. Eisenstein, *Otzar Masa'ot* (New York, 1926), p. 94b (Hebrew).
26. A curious example of the censors' mutilation of Hebrew texts is based on their abhorrence of the word *goy*, which in classic Hebrew means nation and later came to be used colloquially for Gentile. In their ignorance the censors concluded that *goy* was an obnoxious word. So they often substituted for the word *goy* the word *akum*, which means idolator. This resulted in many an absurdity. During the Russian-Turkish war in 1830, the Russian censor saw fit to substitute for *goy* the word *Turk*. The results were even more absurd.
27. The author of this piyut was Amittai ben Shephatiah, who lived in the eleventh century. The translation is by Morris Silverman.
28. Abrahams, *Jewish Life in the Middle Ages*, p. 27.
29. *Kinot for the Ninth of Av*, trans. Abraham Rosenfeld (London, 1965), pp. 132–34.
30. Ibid., pp. 161–62.
31. The name *Tahanun* is derived from the word *Hanun* (gracious God) in the opening words—*Rahum Ve-Hanun* (O merciful and gracious God).
32. On Monday and Thursday mornings the Torah is read. The services are therefore regarded as of greater importance.
33. Gustav Karpeles, *Jewish Literature and Other Essays* (Philadelphia, 1895), p. 188.

Chapter 18

1. Solomon Schechter, *Studies in Judaism*, 1st ser. (Philadelphia, 1911), p. 307. See also Avot 5:21.
2. On some occasions the bar mitzvah is called to the Torah on a Monday or Thursday morning. This practice is unusual, though traditionally acceptable.
3. See Jacob Z. Lauterbach, "Tashlik," *Hebrew Union College Annual* 11 (1936):207–340.
4. Since the Six-Day War, the Jerusalemites go for tashlik to the "waters of the Shiloah" in the eastern part of the city.
5. This excerpt from *Brantspiegel* by Moses Henochs is quoted in M. Güdemann, *Quellenschriften zur Geschichte des Unterrichts und der Erziehung bei den Deutschen Juden* (Berlin, 1891), p. 165.
6. Jacob Emden, *Siddur Bet Jacob* (Lemberg, 1904), p. 150a, par. 7.
7. David Savivi, *Matzil Nefashot* (Venice, 1743).
8. Eliezer Papu, *Bet Tefillah* (Belgrade, 1860).
9. Elkan N. Adler, *Jewish Travellers* (London, 1930), p. 189.

Chapter 19

1. Max Kadushin, *Organic Thinking: A Study in Rabbinic Thought* (New York, 1938), pp. 237–240.
2. Solomon Schechter, *Studies in Judaism*, 3rd ser. (Philadelphia, 1924), pp. 18–19.

3. Gershom G. Scholem, *Major Trends in Jewish Mysticism* (New York, 1946), p. 18.
4. Gershom G. Scholem, *Jewish Gnosticism, Merkabah Mysticism, and Talmudic Tradition* (New York, 1965), p. 21.
5. Rabbi Eleazer ben Judah lived in Worms in the late twelfth century.
6. Quoted in Schechter, *Studies in Judaism*, 3rd ser., pp. 22–23.
7. Marvin Lowenthal, *The Jews of Germany* (Philadelphia, 1936), p. 109.
8. For an illuminating example of mystic scrutiny and discovery in the prayer book see Shalom Spiegel, "On Medieval Hebrew Poetry," *The Jews: Their History, Culture, and Religion*, ed. Louis Finkelstein (Philadelphia, 1949), 2:537–38.
9. Rabbi Judah He-Hasid lived in Regensburg in the twelfth century.
10. Several excerpts from the *Book of the Pious* will be found in Abraham E. Millgram, *An Anthology of Medieval Hebrew Literature* (New York, 1961), pp. 136–41.
11. The Hymn of Glory contains thirty-one couplets. See *The Standard Prayer Book*, trans. S. Singer (New York, 1951), pp. 246–47.
12. For a fine analysis of *The Zohar* and its authorship, see Scholem, *Major Trends in Jewish Mysticism*, pp. 156 ff.
13. Ibid., pp. 285–86.
14. *Siddur Ha-Tefillah Meha-Ari* (Zalkwa, 1781).
15. In Sephardic prayer books this combination of the divine names is regularly in use. See facsimile of a page from a Sephardic *Siddur*, p. 377.
16. In Jerusalem there are a number of kabbalists who engage in mystic prayer in accordance with the Lurianic doctrines. Their prayer book, published in Jerusalem in 1911–16, is called the *Siddur of Rabbi Shalom Sharabi*. For an appreciation of the lengths to which the kabbalists went in their emphasis on mystic kavvanah, the reader is advised to examine this *Siddur*.
17. An exception is the prayer book—*Seder Ha-Tefillot*—translated by David de Sola Pool, Union of Sephardic Congregations (New York, 1960).
18. An allusion to the concept of confusing Satan is found in the Talmud (R. H. 16b).
19. The verses are Ps. 118:5; Lam. 3:56; Ps. 119:160, 122, 162, 66, 108.
20. Israel Abrahams, *Jewish Life in the Middle Ages* (London, 1932), p. 169.
21. According to *The Zohar* the prayer was composed by Rabbi Simeon ben Yohai himself: "Rabbi Simeon said: When the scroll of the Torah is taken out, in the presence of the congregation to be read therein, the heavenly gates of mercy open, and divine love awakens; therefore one should recite the following: Praised be the name. . . ." See *The Zohar*, trans. Harry Sperling and Maurice Simon (London, 1949), 2:199 (206a).
22. These initial words correspond to the italicized words in the translation of the first sentence: *We beseech* Thee, release Thy captive nation *by the* mighty *strength* of Thy right hand.
23. The kabbalistic concept of a special forty-two-letter name of God is based on a talmudic statement. See Kid. 71a.

24. The prayer was attributed to Nehumyah ben Ha-Kanah, who lived in the first century C.E.
25. Translated from the Hebrew by Nina Salaman.
26. Abrahams, *Jewish Life in the Middle Ages*, p. 149.
27. Ibid.
28. Pss. 95–99, 29. The Sephardim do not recite the six psalms. They start with the *Lekhah Dodi* prayer.
29. Spiritual guests also visited the Jew in his sukkah. The mystics therefore composed official welcomes for each of the honored guests. These compositions were called *ushpizin,* from the Latin word *hospes,* guests. Isaac Luria composed the *ushpizin* for Abraham, Isaac, Jacob, Joseph, Moses, Aaron, and David, who consecutively visit on each day of the festival.
30. See also Isa. 26:9; Ps. 119:55.
31. See *The Zohar, Lekh Lekha,* trans. Harry Sperling and Maurice Simon (London, 1949), 1:303 (92a).
32. Solomon Schechter, *Studies in Judaism,* 2nd ser. (Philadelphia, 1908), p. 156.
33. A number of special collections of prayers for *Tikkun Hatzot* were published, and some of the collections were included in the regular prayer books as adjuncts for voluntary devotions.
34. The translation is midrashic.
35. *The Zohar, Emor,* trans. Harry Sperling and Maurice Simon (London, 1949), 5:123 (97b–98a).

Chapter 20

1. Solomon Schechter, "The Chassidim," *Studies in Judaism,* 1st ser. (Philadelphia, 1911), p. 3.
2. Louis I. Newman, *The Hasidic Anthology* (New York, 1934), p. 337.
3. Ibid., p. 340.
4. Herbert Weiner, *The Wild Goats of Ein Gedi* (Garden City, N.Y., 1961), p. 143.
5. Newman, *The Hasidic Anthology,* pp. 280–81.
6. Ibid., p. 334.
7. Quoted in S. Y. Agnon, *Days of Awe* (New York, 1948), p. 52.

Chapter 21

1. In Eastern Europe the nineteenth century was still in many respects part of the Middle Ages.
2. Johanna Spector, "On Jewish Music," *Conservative Judaism* 21, no. 1 (1966):71.
3. *Sefer Maharil* (Sklow, 1796), p. 46b. Maharil's view was accepted by Moses Isserles, who incorporated it into the *Shulhan Arukh* (*Orah Hayim,* 619:1).
4. G. E. Biddle, "A Theist's Impressions of Judaism," *The Jewish Quarterly Review* 19 (1907):218–19.
5. Israel Abrahams, *Jewish Life in the Middle Ages* (London, 1932), p. 277.

6. An example of an incongruous tune was the employment of the melody of the "Marseillaise" for the rendition of the Kaddish, as happened in Lorraine in the early nineteenth century.
7. Abraham J. Heschel, "The Vocation of the Cantor," *The Insecurity of Freedom* (Philadelphia, 1966), p. 244.
8. *Sefer Hassidim* (Frankfort am Main, 1924), p. 124, no. 418.
9. *Shulhan Arukh, Orah Hayim,* 53:11.
10. Abraham ben Shabbatai Horowitz, *Yesh Nohalin* (Jerusalem, 1965), pp. 58–59.
11. Enoch ben Abraham, *Reshit Bikurim* (Frankfort am Main, 1708), pp. 29a–b.

Chapter 22

1. Quoted in H. Graetz, *History of the Jews* (Philadelphia, 1894), 3:172–73.
2. The precedent for semikhah is the biblical account of the ordination of Joshua as Moses' successor. Moses laid his hands upon Joshua, and a portion of Moses' spirit was transferred to Joshua (Num. 27:22–23). According to tradition Moses also ordained the elders by the laying on of hands. This procedure was followed thereafter, so that the elders of each generation passed their spiritual propensities to their successors. During the Second Temple semikhah was a firm institution, and the members of the Sanhedrin were thus ordained.
3. This type of "semikhah," or document, is still given by some rabbis (or more frequently by the heads of talmudical academies) as confirmation of the holder's fitness to act as rabbi. Without such a "semikhah" no Orthodox congregation would consider an applicant's candidacy for its pulpit.
4. Solomon Schechter, *Studies in Judaism,* 1st ser. (Philadelphia, 1911), p. 102.
5. Ibid., 3rd ser. (Philadelphia, 1924), p. 15.
6. Marvin Lowenthal, *The Jews of Germany* (Philadelphia, 1936), p. 137.
7. Secular literature was hardly ever tapped by the maggidim. Even Leon da Modena's (1577–1648) published sermons are totally lacking in references to secular literature, though he was at home in the Renaissance literature of his day.

Chapter 23

1. This *Siddur* is a manuscript by Jacob ben Judah, hazan of London. It is now in the Municipal Library of Leipzig. It is a small parchment volume which the hazan wrote three years before the expulsion in 1290.
2. In Israel the Yemenite synagogues are well stocked with prayer books, but most of the people still recite the prayers by heart in their traditional singsong.
3. Joshua Bloch, "An Early Spanish Mahzor," *The Jewish Quarterly Review* 30 (1939–40):51–57.

4. *Siddur Bet Abraham,* published in "The Holy City of Jerusalem (May it be restored and rebuilt speedily in our days, Amen!) by Abraham the son of Rabbi Aharon Yoseph, 1932."
5. In modern times pocket-sized *Siddurim* have been published in large quantities. In the mid-nineteenth century they were produced for use by Jewish emigrants to America, and in larger quantities for Jewish soldiers and sailors serving in various armies. During the two world wars large numbers of such prayer books were issued in America, Great Britain, and other countries. See Isaac Rivkin, "A Pocket Edition Prayer Book for German-Jewish Emigrants to America, 1842," *Publications of the American Jewish Historical Society,* no. 35 (1939):207–17.
6. Moses' prayer was: "O God, pray heal her" (Num. 12:13).
7. M. Roest, *Catalog der Hebraica und Judaica aus der L. Rosenthal'schen Bibliothek* (Amsterdam, 1875), 1:734.
8. This definition of the word *Mahzor* applies only to the Ashkenazic usage. Among the Sephardim the term *Mahzor* applies to a prayer book that includes the cycle of prayers for the whole year, including the weekday and Sabbath prayers.
9. Printed in Pietrikov, 1926.
10. Rabbi Meir of Rothenberg mildly disapproved of figures of birds and beasts in the prayer book, because they tend to distract the worshiper and thus interfere with his kavvanah. "But," he added, "there is no infringement on the prohibition, 'Thou shalt not make unto thee a graven image' (Exod. 20:4), . . . because these pictures have no substance, being made only of paints" (Isaac Ze'ev Cahana, *Responsa of Maharam* [Jerusalem, 1960], vol. 2, no. 56, p. 50).

Chapter 24

1. This sermon and a reply by Rabbi David Nietto were published in an English translation entitled *The Inquisition and Judaism* by Moses Mocatta (London, 1845), pp. 1–2.
2. The synagogue was probably the one on Creechurch Lane.
3. John Warrington, ed., *The Diary of Samuel Pepys* (London, 1953), 1:441.
4. In the oriental countries the synagogue services were quite decorous during the Middle Ages, as they are today. So were the Moslem services. See Elkan N. Adler, "The Travels of Petachia of Ratisbon," *Jewish Travellers* (London, 1930), p. 82.
5. Israel Abrahams, *Jewish Life in the Middle Ages* (London, 1932), pp. 37–38.
6. In Central and Eastern Europe the synagogue was called *shul,* which is generally associated with the German word *Schule* (school). This association is fully justified, because teaching has always been a major function of the synagogue. However, the actual origin of the word *shul* goes back to the days of the Romans, who called the Jewish community *schola,* a term which the Romans applied to a corporation or the place where a professional corporation met. See Cecil Roth, *The History of the Jews of Italy* (Philadelphia, 1946), p. 24.

7. Marvin Lowenthal, *A World Passed By* (New York, 1933), p. 373.
8. This procedure could easily have become a source of annoyance if resorted to in trifling matters. It was therefore restricted somewhat for purely regulative purposes. A person had to try this tactic three times at weekday services before he could stop a Sabbath service.
9. For some theories regarding the origin of the number ten of the minyan, see George Foot Moore, *Judaism in the First Centuries of the Christian Era* (Cambridge, Mass., 1930), 3:99–100, n. 77.
10. Another public official was the shohet, the ritual slaughterer, but his functions were in no way connected with the synagogue or the services.
11. See "The Testament of Alexander Suesskind," *Hebrew Ethical Wills,* ed. Israel Abrahams (Philadelphia, 1926), 2:337.
12. For methods of electing the synagogue officials and their qualifications see Salo W. Baron, *The Jewish Community* (Philadelphia, 1942), 2:52–122.
13. Louis M. Epstein, *Sex Laws and Customs in Judaism* (New York, 1948), pp. 75–83.
14. Louis Finkelstein, *Jewish Self-government in the Middle Ages* (New York, 1924), p. 355.

Conclusion

1. Webster's Third New International Dictionary, 1966.
2. Louis Ginzberg, "Saadia's Siddur," *Saadia Studies,* ed. Abraham Newman and Solomon Zeitlin (Philadelphia, 1943), p. 335.
3. Aimé Palliere, *The Unknown Sanctuary* (New York, 1929), pp. 20–21.
4. Quoted in J. Rumney, "Anglo-Jewry as Seen through Foreign Eyes," *Transactions of the Jewish Historical Society of England* 13 (1932–35):327.
5. See Judah He-Hasid, *Sefer Hassidim,* Parma edition no. 1589.
6. Naphtali Wieder, *Islamic Influences on Jewish Worship* (Oxford, 1948), pp. 27–28.
7. The Radbaz argued that the Gentiles hold us in contempt anyway, and it makes no difference whether we talk or do not talk at the services. Hence why not return to the talmudic tradition of recitin_ the *Tefillah* first silently and then loudly by the reader?
8. Cecil Roth, "Rabbi Menachem Navarra," *The Jewish Quarterly Review* 15 (1924–25):451.
9. Solomon Schechter, *Studies in Judaism,* 1st ser. (Philadelphia, 1911), p. 334.
10. For rabbinic opposition to Aramaic prayers see Sotah 33a.
11. See Harry J. Leon, *The Jews of Ancient Rome* (Philadelphia, 1960), pp. 246, 258. See also Joshua Starr, *The Jews in the Byzantine Empire, 641–1204* (Athens, 1939), pp. 65–66.
12. *Mishneh Torah, Tefillah,* 1:4.
13. *Soferim* 1:7.
14. Nahum N. Glatzer, *Franz Rosenzweig: His Life and Thought* (Philadelphia, 1953), p. 101.
15. S. Singer, "Early Translations and Translators of the Jewish Liturgy,"

Transactions of the Jewish Historical Society of England 3 (1896–98):67.
16. John Evelyn, *The Diary of John Evelyn*, ed. William Bray (London, 1818), p. 31.
17. The title consisted of seventy-six words. Its opening words were *The Book of Religion, Ceremonies, and Prayers of the Jews, as Practised in Their Synagogues and Families on All Occasions*, etc., etc.
18. In 1740 Isaac Nieto, hakham of the Spanish and Portuguese congregation in London, published an elegant translation of the *Siddur* in Spanish. Many members of the congregation were recent Marrano arrivals or descendants of Marranos who knew no Hebrew. In his introduction the author says: "There is the problem of people not understanding what they uttered. How can people's devotion be aroused by words without meaning?"
19. The translation by David Aaron de Sola (revised by M. Gaster), which was published in London in 1901, became the official translation of the Sephardic communities.
20. It should be noted that these modern commentaries differ from those of their medieval predecessors in that the older commentaries were concerned mainly with providing the layman with the rules of worship, while the modern commentaries are mainly inspirational. The former were concerned with instructing the people how to pray; the modern commentaries tell the people why they should pray.
21. *Ha-Mahzor*, ed. and trans. Ben Zion Bokser (New York, 1959), p. 255.
22. *Weekday Prayer Book*, Rabbinical Assembly of America (New York, 1961), pp. 64–65.
23. This prayer has been included in the Haggadah largely as a result of the initiative of the late Rufus Learsi.
24. *Order of Service and Customs for the Synagogue and the Home for Israel Independence Day, as Instituted by Our Sages in Israel, Adapted for Diaspora Jewry*, ed. and trans. Moses Friedlander (London, 1964).
25. Actually, it was entitled *Seder Ha-Avodah* (Order of the Services) and it was subtitled *Minhag Kehal Bayit Hadash* (The Rite of the New Temple).
26. It was entitled *Seder Tefilla Devar Yom Be-Yomo* (Order of the Daily Prayers).
27. See "Petition to the Charleston Congregation, 1824," *The Jews of the United States, 1790–1840*, eds. Joseph L. Blau and Salo W. Baron (New York, 1963), 2:554–60.
28. The original had a German translation.
29. For the text of the Pittsburgh Platform see Moshe Davis, *The Emergence of Conservative Judaism* (Philadelphia, 1963), pp. 226–27.
30. The full title was *The Union Prayerbook for Jewish Worship*. Its Hebrew name was *Seder Tefillot Yisrael* (Order of the Prayers of Israel).
31. There is also an abbreviated grace after meals and an abbreviated *Tefillah* in the Sabbath evening service. See p. 163.
32. Nahum N. Glatzer, *Franz Rosenzweig: His Life and Thought* (Philadelphia, 1953), p. 76.

33. The prayer book is entitled *Sabbath and Festival Prayer Book.* In Hebrew it is called *Seder Tefillot Yisrael Le-Shabbat Ule-Shalosh Regalim* (Order of the Prayers of Israel for Sabbath and the Three Festivals).
34. Mordecai M. Kaplan, *Judaism as a Civilization* (New York, 1934).
35. *Sabbath Prayer Book* (Seder Tefillot Le-Shabbat) (New York, 1945), p. xxviii.
36. Maurice N. Eisendrath, *Can Faith Survive?* (New York, 1964), pp. 245 ff.
37. Dudley Weinberg, in *C.C.A.R. Journal* 14 (Oct. 1967):41–44.

BIBLIOGRAPHY

General

Abrahams, Israel. *A Companion to the Authorized Prayer Book*. London, 1922.

Arian, Philip, and Eisenberg, Azriel. *The Story of the Prayer Book*. Hartford, 1968.

Cohen, Boaz. "Liturgic Literature." *The Jewish People: Past and Present*, vol. 3. New York, 1952.

Dembitz, Lewis N. *Jewish Services in Synagogue and Home*. Philadelphia, 1898.

Freehof, Solomon B. *The Small Sanctuary: Judaism in the Prayerbook*. Cincinnati, 1942.

Friedlander, M. "Divine Worship." *The Jewish Religion*. London, 1913.

Garfiel, Evelyn. *The Service of the Heart*. New York, 1958.

Glatzer, Nahum N. *Language of Faith*. New York, 1967.

Idelsohn, Abraham Z. *Jewish Liturgy and Its Development*. New York, 1932.

Jacobson, B. S. *Meditations on the Siddur*. Tel Aviv, 1966.

The Jewish Encyclopedia, s.v. "liturgy," "prayer." New York, 1907.

Munk, Elie. *The World of Prayer*. New York, 1961.

Perles, Felix. "Prayer (Jewish)." *Encyclopaedia of Religion and Ethics*. 1918. Edited by James Hastings.

Some Pioneering Works in Jewish Liturgy

Berliner, Abraham, *Randbemerkungen zum täglichen Gebetbuche (Siddur)*. Berlin, vol. 1, 1909, vol. 2, 1912.

———. *Ketavim Nivharim*. Jerusalem, vol. 1, 1945, vol. 2, 1949. A Hebrew translation of the German edition.

Davidson, Israel. *Thesaurus of Mediaeval Hebrew Poetry*. New York, 1924–1933. 4 vols. (Hebrew).

Elbogen, Ismar. *Der jüdische Gottesdienst in seiner geschichtlichen Entwicklung*. Leipzig, 1913.

Heinemann, Joseph. *Prayer in the Period of the Tanna'im and the Amora'im: Its Nature and Its Patterns*. Jerusalem, 1964. (Hebrew.)

Zunz, Leopold. *Die gottesdienstliche Vortrage der Juden*. Berlin, 1832.

———. *Die synagogale Poesie des Mittelalters*. Berlin, 1855.

———. *Der Ritus des synagogale Gottesdienstes*. Berlin, 1859.

———. *Literaturgeschichte der synagogalen Poesie*. Berlin, 1865.

The *Siddur*: A Precious Spiritual Possession

Abrahams, Israel. "Some Rabbinic Ideas on Prayer." *Studies in Pharisaism and the Gospels*. 2d ser. Cambridge, 1924.

Agus, Jacob B. "The Meaning of Prayer." *Great Jewish Ideas*. Edited by Abraham E. Millgram. Washington, D.C., 1964.
Baumgard, Herbert M. *Judaism and Prayer: Growing Towards God*. New York, 1964.
Berkowitz, Eliezer. "Prayer." *Studies in Torah Judaism*. Edited by Leon D. Stitskin. New York, 1969.
Cronbach, Abraham. "The Social Implications of Prayer." *Hebrew Union College Jubilee Volume*. Cincinnati, 1925.
Dresner, Samuel H. *Prayer, Humility, and Compassion*. Philadelphia, 1957.
Enelow, H. G. "*Kawwana:* The Struggle for Inwardness in Judaism." *Studies in Jewish Literature* (Issued in Honor of Professor Kaufmann Kohler). Berlin, 1913.
Freehof, Solomon B. *In the House of the Lord*. Cincinnati, 1942.
Gordis, Robert. *The Ladder of Prayer*. New York, 1956.
Greenberg, Hayim. "Prayer." *The Inner Eye*, vol. 2. New York, 1964.
Heschel, Abraham J. *Man Is Not Alone*. Philadelphia, 1951.
———. *Man's Quest for God*. New York, 1954.
———. "Prayer as Discipline." *The Insecurity of Freedom*. Philadelphia, 1966.
Jacobs, Louis. *Jewish Prayer*. London, 1956.
Maimonides, Moses. *Mishneh Torah: The Book of Adoration*. Translated by Moses Hyamson. Jerusalem, 1962.
Steinberg, Milton. *Basic Judaism*. New York, 1947.
Werner, Eric. *The Sacred Bridge: The Interdependence of Liturgy and Music in Synagogue and Church*. New York, 1959.

1 Hebrew Worship in Ancient Days: The Temple Cult

Albright, W. F. *Archaeology and the Religion of Israel*. Baltimore, 1942.
Benzinger, I. "The Temple." *Encyclopaedia Biblica*. Edited by T. K. Cheyne and J. Sutherland Black. London, 1903.
Box, G. H. "Worship, Hebrew." *Encyclopaedia of Religion and Ethics*, 1918. Edited by James Hastings.
———. "The Temple-Service." *Encyclopaedia Biblica*.
Büchler, A. "Atonement of Sin by Sacrifice." *Studies in Sin and Atonement in Rabbinic Literature of the First Century*. New York, 1967.
Gaster, M. "Sacrifice, Jewish." *Encyclopaedia of Religion and Ethics*.
Gray, George Buchanan. *Sacrifice in the Old Testament: Its Theory and Practice*. Oxford, 1925.
Hertz, Joseph H. "The Sacrificial Cult." *The Pentateuch and Haftorahs*. London, 1938.
Hirsch, Emil G. "Sacrifice." *The Jewish Encyclopedia*. New York, 1907.
Hirschfeld, H. "Priest, Priesthood." *Encyclopaedia of Religion and Ethics*.
Moore, George Foot. "Sacrifice: Description of the Developed Jewish System." *Encyclopaedia Biblica*.
Oesterley, W. O. E. *Sacrifices in Ancient Israel: Their Origin, Purposes and Development*. London, 1937.
———. "Worship in the Old Testament." *Liturgy and Worship*. Edited by W. K. L. Clarke. London, 1932.

Parrot, André. *The Temple of Jerusalem.* London, 1957.
Wright, G. Ernest, et al. "The Significance of the Temple in the Ancient Near East." *The Biblical Archeologist* 8, nos. 3, 4 (1944).

2 Prayer in Bible and Temple Days

Bacher, W. "Synagogue." *The Jewish Encyclopedia.* New York, 1907.
Braude, William G., trans. *Midrash on Psalms.* 2 vols. New Haven, 1959.
Buttenweiser, Moses. *The Psalms: Chronologically Treated with a New Translation.* Chicago, 1937.
Finkelstein, Louis. "The Origin of the Synagogue." *Proceedings of the American Academy for Jewish Research* 1 (1928–30):49–59.
Hirsch, Samson Raphael. *The Psalms: With a Translation and Commentary.* Translated by Gertrude Hirschler. 2 vols. New York, 1960, 1966.
Kohler, Kaufmann. *The Psalms and Their Place in the Liturgy.* Philadelphia, 1897.
Levertoff, Paul Philip. "Synagogue Worship in the First Century." *Liturgy and Worship.* Edited by W. K. L. Clarke. London, 1932.
Levy, Isaac. *The Synagogue: Its History and Function.* London, 1963.
Moore, George Foot. *Judaism in the First Centuries of the Christian Era,* vol. 1. Cambridge, Mass., 1927.
Prothero, Rowland E. *The Psalms in Human Life.* London, 1917.
Zeitlin, Solomon. "The Origin of the Synagogue." *Proceedings of the American Academy for Jewish Research* 2 (1931):69–81.
———. "The Morning Benediction and the Readings in the Temple." *The Jewish Quarterly Review* 44 (1953–54): 330–36.

3 National Tragedy and Spiritual Consolidation

Baron, Salo W. "Closing the Ranks." *A Social and Religious History of the Jews,* vol. 2. New York, 1958.
Moore, George Foot. *Judaism in the First Centuries of the Christian Era,* vol. 1. Cambridge, Mass., 1927.
Zeitlin, Solomon. "An Historical Study of the First Canonization of the Hebrew Liturgy." *The Jewish Quarterly Review* 36 (1945–46):211–229; 38 (1947–48):289–316; 54 (1963–64):208–49.

4 The Framework of Jewish Worship

Bettan, Israel. "Early Preaching in the Synagogue." *Studies in Jewish Preaching.* Cincinnati, 1939.
Büchler, A. "The Reading of the Law and Prophets in a Triennial Cycle." *The Jewish Quarterly Review,* o.s. 5 (1892–93):420–68; 6 (1893–94):1–73.
Cohen, F. L. "Cantillation." *The Jewish Encyclopedia.* New York, 1907.
Elbogen, Ismar. "Studies in Jewish Liturgy" in *The Jewish Quarterly Review,* o.s. 18 (1906):587–99; 19 (1907):229–49, 704–20.
Finkelstein, Louis. "The Development of the *Amidah.*" *The Jewish Quarterly Review* 16 (1925–26):1–4, 127–70.
Hertz, Joseph H. "The Shema." *The Pentateuch and Haftorahs.* London, 1938.

Hertz, Joseph H. "On the Shema." *The Authorized Daily Prayer Book,* New York, 1948.

The Jewish Encyclopedia, s.v. "benedictions," "*Shemoneh Esreh.*" New York, 1907.

Liber, M. "The Structure and History of the *Tefilah.*" *The Jewish Quarterly Review* 40 (1949–50):331–57.

Mann, Jacob. *The Bible as Read and Preached in the Old Synagogue,* vol. 1. Cincinnati, 1940; vol. 2. New York, 1966.

Moore, George Foot. *Judaism in the First Centuries of the Christian Era,* vol. 2. Cambridge, Mass., 1927.

Oesterley, W. O. E. "The Jewish Liturgy." *The Jewish Background of the Christian Liturgy*. Oxford, 1925.

Waxman, Meyer. "The Agadic Collections (Midrashim)." *A History of Jewish Literature,* vol. 1. New York, 1930.

5 A Glance at Eight Centuries of Jewish History

Baron, Salo W. "Worship: Unity Amidst Diversity." *A Social and Religious History of the Jews,* vol. 7. New York, 1958.

Cohen, Gerson D. "The Talmudic Age." *Great Ages and Ideas of the Jewish People*. Edited by Leo W. Schwarz. New York, 1956.

Goldin, Judah. "The Period of the Talmud." *The Jews: Their History, Culture, and Religion,* vol. 1. Edited by Louis Finkelstein. Philadelphia, 1949.

6 Expansion of the Weekday Services

Hertz, Joseph H. "The Mourner's *Kaddish.*" *The Authorized Daily Prayer Book*. New York, 1948.

The Jewish Encyclopedia, s.v. "*kedushshah,*" "*Shemoneh Esreh.*" New York, 1907.

Liebreich, Leon J. "The Compilation of the *Pesuke de-Zimra.*" *Proceedings of the American Academy for Jewish Research* 18 (1948–49): 255–67.

Luban, Marvin. *The Kaddish: Man's Reply to the Problem of Evil.* New York, 1962.

Mann, Jacob. "Changes in the Divine Service of the Synagogue Due to Religious Persecutions." *Hebrew Union College Annual* 4 (1927): 241–310.

Pool, David de Sola. *The Kaddish*. New York, 1964.

7 The Crystallization of the Sabbath Services

Abrahams, Israel. "Sabbath (Jewish)." *Encyclopaedia of Religion and Ethics*. 1918. Edited by James Hastings.

Barak, Nathan A. *The History of the Sabbath*. New York, 1965.

Heschel, Abraham J. *The Sabbath: Its Meaning for Modern Man.* New York, 1951.

Kaplan, Mordecai M. *The Meaning of God in Modern Jewish Religion.* New York, 1937.

Millgram, Abraham E. *Sabbath: The Day of Delight*. Philadelphia, 1944.
Schauss, Hayyim. *The Jewish Festivals*. New York, 1938.

THE NEW SYNAGOGUE POETRY (PIYUT)

Davidson, Israel. Introduction to *Mahzor Yannai*. New York, 1919.
Spiegel, Shalom. "On Medieval Hebrew Poetry." *The Jews: Their History, Culture, and Religion*, vol. 2. Edited by Louis Finkelstein. Philadelphia, 1949.
Waxman, Meyer. *A History of Jewish Literature*, vol. 1. New York, 1930.

MISCELLANEOUS

Büchler, A. "The Reading of the Law and Prophets in a Triennial Cycle." *The Jewish Quarterly Review*, o.s. 5 (1892–93):420–68.
The Jewish Encyclopedia, s.v. "Abot or Pirke Abot," "Law, reading from the," "Musaf." New York, 1907.
Mann, Jacob. *The Bible as Read and Preached in the Old Synagogue*, vol. 1. Cincinnati, 1940; vol. 2. New York, 1966.

8 The Liturgy of the Major Festivals

Gaster, T. H. *Passover: Its History and Tradition*. New York, 1949.
Goodman, Philip. *The Passover Anthology*. Philadelphia, 1961.
The Jewish Encyclopedia, s.v. "Passover," "Pentecost," "Tabernacles." New York, 1907.
Kaplan, Mordecai M. *The Meaning of God in Modern Jewish Religion*. New York, 1937.
Levy, Isaac. *A Guide to Passover*. London, 1958.

THE SECOND-DAY FESTIVAL OF THE DIASPORA

Kreitman, Benjamin Z. et al. "Yom Tov Sheni." *Conservative Judaism* 24 (Winter 1970):21–59.
Plaut, W. Gunther. "Second Day of the Festival." *The Rise of Reform Judaism*. New York, 1963.
Zeitlin, Solomon. "The Second Day of the Holidays." *Central Conference of American Rabbis Journal*, April 1969, pp. 48–57.
———. "The Second Day of the Holidays in the Diaspora." *The Jewish Quarterly Review* 44 (1953–54): 183–93.

THE HALLEL

Finkelstein, Louis. "The Origin of the *Hallel*." *Hebrew Union College Annual* 23 (1950–51):319–37.
Zeitlin, Solomon. "The *Hallel*." *The Jewish Quarterly Review* 53 (1962–63):22–29.

9 The Liturgy of the High Holy Days

Agnon, S. Y. *Days of Awe*. New York, 1948.
Arzt, Max. *Justice and Mercy: Commentary on the Liturgy of the New Year and the Day of Atonement*. New York, 1963.
Barish, Louis. *High Holy Day Liturgy*. New York, 1959.
Hirsch, Samson Raphael. *Selected Essays on Rosh Hashanah*. Edited and translated by Ismar Lipschutz. New York, 1954.

Jacobs, Louis. *A Guide to Yom Kippur*. London, 1957.
———. *A Guide to Rosh Ha-Shanah*. London, 1959.
Kaplan, Mordecai M. *The Meaning of God in Modern Jewish Religion*. New York, 1937.
Kieval, Herman. *The High Holy Days: A Commentary on the Prayer Book of Rosh Hashanah*. New York, 1959.
Schauss, Hayyim. *The Jewish Festivals*. New York, 1938.

KOL NIDRE

Davidson, Israel. "Kol Nidre." *American Jewish Year Book*. New York, 1924.
———. "Kol Nidre." *Thesaurus of Mediaeval Hebrew Poetry*, vol. 2. New York, 1929.
Kieval, Herman. "The Curious Case of Kol Nidre." *Commentary* 46, no. 4 (Oct. 1968):53–58.
Petuchowski, Jacob J. "New Versions of Kol Nidre." *Prayerbook Reform in Europe*. New York, 1968.
Schloessinger, Max. "Kol Nidre." *The Jewish Encyclopedia*. New York, 1907.

MISCELLANEOUS

Seligsohn, Max. "Selihah." *The Jewish Encyclopedia*. New York, 1907.
Zeitlin, Solomon. "The Second Day of Rosh Hashanah in Israel." *The Jewish Quarterly Review* 44 (1953–54):326–29.

10 The Liturgy of the Minor Festivals and Fast Days

Book of Esther. *The Holy Scriptures*. Philadelphia, 1917.
Charles, R. H., ed. "Books of the Maccabees." *The Apocrypha and Pseudepigrapha*, vols. 1 and 2. Oxford, 1913.
Finkelstein, Louis. "Hanukkah and Its Origin." *The Jewish Quarterly Review* 22 (1931–32):169–73.
Gandz, Solomon. "Studies in the Hebrew Calendar." *The Jewish Quarterly Review* 39 (1948–49):259–80; 40 (1949–50):157–72, 251–77.
Gaster, T. H. *Purim and Hanukkah in Custom and Tradition*. New York, 1950.
Goodman, Philip. *The Purim Anthology*. Philadelphia, 1949.
Kaplan, Mordecai M. *The Meaning of God in Modern Jewish Religion*. New York, 1937.
Morgenstern, Julian. "The Chanukkah Festival and the Calendar of Ancient Israel." *Hebrew Union College Annual* 20 (1947):1–136.
Solis-Cohen, Emily. *Hanukkah, the Feast of Lights*. Philadelphia, 1937.
Schauss, Hayyim. *The Jewish Festivals*. New York, 1938.
Zeitlin, Solomon. "Hanukkah: Its Origin and Its Significance." *The Jewish Quarterly Review* 29 (1938–39):1–36.

11 Private and Home Worship

Abrahams, Israel. *A Companion to the Authorized Prayer Book*. London, 1922.

Finkelstein, Louis. "The *Birkat Ha-Mazon.*" *The Jewish Quarterly Review* 19 (1928–29):211–62.
———. "Pre-Maccabean Documents in the Passover Haggadah." *Harvard Theological Review* 31 (1938):291–317 and 36 (1943):1–38.
Friedmann, M. "The Sabbath Light." *The Jewish Quarterly Review*, o.s. 3 (1891):707–21.
Gaster, T. H. *Passover: Its History and Tradition.* New York, 1949.
The Jewish Encyclopedia, s.v. "Habdallah," "Kiddush," "lamp, Sabbath." New York, 1907.
Kaufmann, David. ""The Ritual of the Seder and the Agada." *The Jewish Quarterly Review*, o.s. 4 (1891–92):550–61.
Landsberger, Franz. "The Cincinnati Haggadah and Its Decorator." *Hebrew Union College Annual* 15 (1940):529–58.
———. "The Washington Haggadah and Its Illuminator." *Hebrew Union College Annual* 21 (1948):73–103.
Marx, Alexander. "Illustrated Haggadahs." *The Jewish Quarterly Review* 13 (1922–23):513–19.
Rivkin, Isaac. *The Passover Haggadah through the Generations.* New York, 1961.
Schechter, Solomon. "The Child in Jewish Literature." *Studies in Judaism.* 1st ser. Philadelphia, 1911.
Wischnitzer, Rachel. "Illuminated Haggadahs." *The Jewish Quarterly Review* 13 (1922–23):193–218.
Ya'ari, Abraham. *Bibliography of Passover Haggadahs from the Beginning of the Printing Press to Our Day.* Jerusalem, 1961 (Hebrew).
Zeitlin, Solomon. "The Liturgy of the First Night of Passover." *The Jewish Quarterly Review* 38 (1947–48):431–60.

12 Rites of Initiation, Marriage, and Burial

Bender, A. P. "Beliefs, Rites, and Customs of the Jews, Connected with Death, Burial, and Mourning." *The Jewish Quarterly Review*, o.s. 6 (1893–94):317–47; 7 (1895):101–18.
Cohen, Boaz. "On the Theme of Betrothal in Jewish and Roman Law." *Proceedings of the American Academy for Jewish Research* 18 (1949):67–135.
Epstein, Louis M. *Marriage Laws in Bible and Talmud.* Cambridge, Mass., 1942.
Finkelstein, Louis. "The Institution of Baptism for Proselytes." *The Journal of Biblical Literature* 52 (1933):203–11.
Goodman, Philip, and Goodman, Hanna. *The Jewish Marriage Anthology.* Philadelphia, 1965.
Jakobovitz, Immanuel. *Order of the Jewish Marriage Service.* New York, 1959.
Lauterbach, Jacob Z. "The Ceremony of Breaking a Glass at Weddings." *Studies in Jewish Law, Custom, and Folklore.* New York, 1970.
———. "Burial Practices." *Studies in Jewish Law, Custom, and Folklore.* New York, 1970.
Morgenstern, Julian. *Rites of Birth, Marriage, Death, and Kindred Occasions among the Semites.* Chicago, 1966.

13 Rites, Symbols, and Ceremonies of Jewish Worship

Ginzberg, Louis. "Adoration." *The Jewish Encyclopedia.* New York, 1907.

Goodenough, Erwin R. *Jewish Symbols in the Greco-Roman Period.* Princeton, 1968.

Greenberg, Simon. "Symbols and Symbolism." *Foundations of a Faith.* New York, 1967.

Gutmann, Joseph. *Beauty in Holiness: Studies in Jewish Ceremonial Art and Customs.* New York, 1969.

Heschel, Abraham J. *Man's Quest for God.* New York, 1954.

———. "Symbolism and Jewish Faith." *Religious Symbolism.* Edited by F. Ernest Johnson. New York, 1955.

Hirsch, Samson Raphael. "A Basic Outline of Jewish Symbolism." *Timeless Torah: An Anthology of the Writings of Rabbi Samson Raphael Hirsch.* Edited by Jacob Breuer. New York, 1957.

Jacobson, B. S. *Meditations on the Siddur.* Tel Aviv, 1966.

Kaplan, Mordecai M. "The Future of Religious Symbolism—A Jewish View." *Religious Symbolism.* Edited by F. Ernest Johnson. New York, 1955.

Levy, Isaac. *The Synagogue: Its History and Function.* London, 1963.

Lowenthal, Marvin. *A World Passed By.* New York, 1933.

Tillich, Paul J. "Theology and Symbolism." *Religious Symbolism.* Edited by F. Ernest Johnson. New York, 1955.

Decorative Art in Ancient Synagogues

Goldman, Bernard. *The Sacred Portal* (Art in the Bet Alpha Synagogue). Detroit, 1966.

Rostovtzeff, M. *Dura-Europos and Its Art.* Oxford, 1938.

———, ed. *The Excavations at Dura-Europos.* 6 vols. New Haven, 1943–59.

Sonne, Isaiah. "The Paintings of the Dura Synagogue." *Hebrew Union College Annual* 20 (1947):255–362.

Sukenik, Eleazar L. *The Ancient Synagogue of Beth Alpha.* Jerusalem, 1932.

Wischnitzer-Bernstein, Rachel. "The Samuel Cycle in the Wall Decoration of the Synagogue at Dura-Europos." *Proceedings of the American Academy for Jewish Research* 11 (1941):85–103.

Miscellaneous

Greenup, Albert William. "Fasts and Fasting." *Essays Presented to J. H. Hertz.* London, 1938.

Gutmann, Joseph. *Jewish Ceremonial Art.* New York, 1964.

Idelsohn, Abraham Z. *Jewish Music in Its Historical Development.* New York, 1948.

Kayser, Stephen S. *Jewish Ceremonial Art.* Philadelphia, 1959.

Kraus, Samuel. "The Jewish Rite of Covering the Head." *Hebrew Union College Annual* 19 (1945):121–68.

Landsberger, Franz. *A History of Jewish Art.* Cincinnati, 1946.

———. "The Origin of European Torah Decorations." *Hebrew Union College Annual* 24 (1952–53):133–50.

Lauterbach, Jacob Z. "Should One Cover the Head When Participating in Divine Worship?" *Year Book of the Central Conference of American Rabbis* 38 (1928):589–603.

Rosowsky, Solomon. *The Cantillations of the Bible.* New York, 1957.

Rothmüller, Aaron Marko. "The Biblical Accents." *The Music of the Jews.* New York, 1954.

Werner, Eric. *The Sacred Bridge* (The interdependence of liturgy and music in synagogue and church during the first millennium). London, 1960.

Wischnitzer, Rachel. *The Architecture of the European Synagogue.* Philadelphia, 1964.

14 The First *Siddur*

The Development of Minhagim

Hyamson, Albert M. *The Sephardim of England: A History of the Spanish and Portuguese Jewish Community, 1492–1951.* London, 1951.

Jacobson, B. S. *Meditations on the Siddur.* Tel Aviv, 1966.

Mann, Jacob. "Genizah Fragments of the Palestinian Order of Service." *Hebrew Union College Annual* 2 (1925):269–338.

Roth, Cecil. *The World of the Sephardim.* Tel Aviv, 1954.

Zimmels, H. J. *Ashkenazim and Sephardim.* London, 1958.

The First *Siddur*

Davidson, Israel; Asaf S.; and Joel, B. I., eds. *Siddur R. Saadja Gaon.* Jerusalem, 1941.

Elbogen, Ismar. "Saadia's Siddur," *Saadia Anniversary Volume.* New York, 1943.

Ginzberg, Louis. *Geonica,* vol. 1. New York, 1909.

———. "Saadia's Siddur." *Saadia Studies.* Edited by Abraham A. Neuman and Solomon Zeitlin. Philadelphia, 1943.

Hurwitz, S., ed. *Mahzor Vitry.* Nuremberg, 1923.

Malter, Henry. *Saadia Gaon: His Life and Works.* Philadelphia, 1942.

15 The Theology of the *Siddur*

Finkelstein, Louis. "The Jewish Religion: Its Beliefs and Practices."*The Jews: Their History, Culture, and Religion,* vol. 4. Edited by Louis Finkelstein. New York, 1949.

———. *The Pharisees: The Sociological Background of Their Faith.* 2 vols. Philadelphia, 1962.

Ginzberg, Louis. "The Religion of the Pharisee." *Students, Scholars and Saints.* Philadelphia, 1928.

Glatzer, Nahum N., ed. *Faith and Knowledge: The Jew in the Medieval World.* Boston, 1963.

Herford, R. Travers. *The Pharisees.* New York, 1924.

Heschel, Abraham J. *Between God and Man: An Interpretation of Judaism.* Edited by Fritz A. Rothschild. New York, 1965.

Jacobson, B. S. *Meditations on the Siddur.* Tel Aviv, 1966.

Kadushin, Max. *Organic Thinking: A Study in Rabbinic Thought.* New York, 1938.

Kohler, Kaufmann. *Jewish Theology.* New York, 1918.

Lauterbach, Jacob Z. "The Pharisees and Their Teachings." *Hebrew Union College Annual* 6 (1929):69–139.

Montefiore, C. G., and Loewe, H. *A Rabbinic Anthology.* New York, 1963.

Schechter, Solomon. "The Dogmas of Judaism." *Studies in Judaism.* 1st ser. Philadelphia, 1911.

———. *Some Aspects of Rabbinic Theology.* New York, 1961.

Silberman, Lou H. "God and Man." *Great Jewish Ideas.* Edited by Abraham E. Millgram. Washington, D.C., 1964.

Steinberg, Milton. *Anatomy of Faith.* New York, 1960.

MISCELLANEOUS

Greenberg, Hayim. "The Universalism of the Chosen People." *The Inner Eye.* New York, 1953.

Heschel, Abraham J. "A Preface to an Understanding of Revelation." *Essays Presented to Leo Baeck.* London, 1954.

Plaut, W. Gunther. *The Case for the Chosen People.* New York, 1965.

Schwarzschild, Steven S. "The Messianic Doctrine in Contemporary Jewish Thought." *Great Jewish Ideas.* Edited by Abraham E. Millgram. Washington, D.C., 1964.

16 Ethical Teachings in the *Siddur*

Baron, Salo W. "Equality of Ritual and Moral Law." *A Social and Religious History of the Jews,* vol. 2. New York, 1952.

Bernfeld, Simon. *The Foundations of Jewish Ethics.* New York, 1968.

Cohen, Boaz. "Law and Ethics in the Light of the Jewish Tradition." *Law and Tradition in Judaism.* New York, 1959.

Glatzer, Nahum N. ed. *Faith and Knowledge: The Jew in the Medieval World.* Boston, 1963.

Greenberg, Simon. *The Jewish Prayer Book: Its Ideals and Values.* New York, 1957.

Kadushin, Max. *Worship and Ethics.* Evanston, Ill., 1964.

Lauterbach, Jacob Z. "The Ethics of the Halakah." *Year Book of the Central Conference of American Rabbis* 23 (1914):249–87.

Lazarus, M. *The Ethics of Judaism.* 2 vols. Philadelphia, 1900–1901.

17 The Synagogue's Confrontation with the Church

Abrahams, Israel. "Sorrows of Tatnu." *By-Paths in Hebraic Bookland.* Philadelphia, 1920.

Adler, Elkan N. *Auto da Fé and Jew.* London, 1908.

———. "Lea on the Inquisition of Spain." *The Jewish Quarterly Review,* o.s. 20 (1908):509–71.

Baron, Salo W. "The Age of the Crusaders." *A Social and Religious History of the Jews,* vol. 4. New York, 1957.

Freehof, Solomon B. "The Origin of the Tahanun." *Hebrew Union College Annual* 2 (1925):339–50.
Friedlander, Gerald. *The Jewish Sources of the Sermon on the Mount.* London, 1911.
Gavin, F. *The Jewish Antecedents of the Christian Sacraments.* London, 1928.
Grayzel, Solomon. *The Church and the Jews in the XIIIth Century.* Philadelphia, 1933.
———. "The Talmud and the Medieval Papacy." *Essays in Honor of Solomon B. Freehof.* Pittsburgh, 1964.
Jacobs, Joseph. "The Church and the Jews." *Jewish Contributions to Civilization: An Estimate.* Philadelphia, 1919.
Kraus, Samuel. "The Christian Legislation on the Synagogue." *Ignace Goldziher Memorial Volume.* Jerusalem, 1958.
Lea, Henry Charles. *A History of the Inquisition of Spain.* 4 vols. New York, 1906–7.
Lowenthal, Marvin. *The Jews of Germany.* Philadelphia, 1936.
Mann, Jacob. "Changes in Divine Service of the Synagogue Due to Religious Persecution." *Hebrew Union College Annual* 4 (1927):241–310.
Marcus, Jacob R. *The Jew in the Medieval World: A Source Book, 315–1791.* Cincinnati, 1938.
Oesterley, W. O. E. *The Jewish Background of the Christian Liturgy.* Oxford, 1925.
Parkes, James. *The Conflict of the Church and the Synagogue.* Philadelphia, 1961.
Popper, William. *The Censorship of Hebrew Books.* New York, 1969.
Porges, N. "Censorship of Hebrew Books." *The Jewish Encyclopedia.* New York, 1907.
Rosenthal, Erwin I. J. "Mediaeval Judaism and the Law." *Judaism and Christianity,* vol. 3. London, 1938.
Roth, Cecil. *A History of the Marranos.* Philadelphia, 1932.
———. *The Ritual Murder Libel and the Jew: The Report of Cardinal Lorenzo Ganganelli* (Pope Clement XIV). London, 1935.
———. *The Spanish Inquisition.* New York, 1964.
Steinberg, Milton. *The Making of the Modern Jew.* New York, 1949.
Strack, Hermann L. *The Jew and Human Sacrifice: Human Blood and Jewish Ritual.* London, 1909.
Trachtenberg, Leopold. *The Devil and the Jews.* New Haven, 1943.
Zunz, Leopold. *The Sufferings of the Jews in the Middle Ages.* New York, 1907.

18 New Institutions and New Prayers

Abrahams, Israel. "The Parents' Blessing." *A Companion to the Authorized Prayer Book.* London, 1922.
Freehof, Solomon. "Devotional Literature in the Vernacular." *Year Book of the Central Conference of American Rabbis* 33 (1923):375–424.
The Jewish Encyclopedia, s. v. "bar mizwah," blessing of children," "hakkafot." New York, 1907.
Lauterbach, Jacob Z. "Tashlik: A Study in Jewish Ceremonies." *Hebrew Union College Annual* 11 (1936):207–340.

19 The Mystic Stream in Jewish Liturgy

Abelson, J. *Jewish Mysticism: An Introduction to the Kabbalah*. London, 1913.

Franck, Adolph. *The Kabbala or the Religious Philosophy of the Hebrews*. New York, 1926.

Ginzberg, Louis. "The Cabala." "*On Jewish Law and Lore*." Philadelphia, 1955.

Heschel, Abraham J. "The Mystical Element in Judaism." *The Jews: Their History, Culture, and Religion*. Edited by Louis Finkelstein, vol. 2. New York, 1949.

Schechter, Solomon. "Safed in the Sixteenth Century—A City of Legists and Mystics." *Studies in Judaism*. 3d ser. Philadelphia, 1924.

———. "Jewish Saints in Medieval Germany." *Studies in Judaism*. 3d ser. Philadelphia, 1924.

Scholem, Gershom G. *Major Trends in Jewish Mysticism*. New York, 1946.

———. *Zohar: The Book of Splendor*. New York, 1949.

———. *Merkabah Mysticism and Talmudic Tradition*. New York, 1965.

———. *On the Kabbalah and Its Symbolism*. Translated by Ralph Manheim. New York, 1965.

Sperling, Harry, and Simon, Maurice, trans. *The Zohar*. 5 vols. London, 1949.

Waxman, Meyer. "The Kabbala." *A History of Jewish Literature*, vol. 2. New York, 1933.

20 The Liturgy of the Hasidim

Buber, Martin. *Tales of Hasidism: The Early Masters*. New York, 1947.

———. *Tales of Hasidism: The Later Masters*. New York, 1948.

———. *The Legend of the Baal-Shem*. London, 1956.

———. *Hasidism and Modern Man*. New York, 1958.

———. *The Origin and Meaning of Hasidism*. New York, 1966.

Dresner, Samuel H. *The Zaddik: The Doctrine of the Zaddik According to the Writings of Rabbi Yaakov Yosef of Polnoy*. New York, 1960.

Dubnow, S. M. "Hasidim, Hasidism." *The Jewish Encyclopedia*. New York, 1907.

Heschel, Abraham J. *The Earth Is the Lord's*. New York, 1950.

Horodezky, S. A. *Leaders of Hassidism*. London, 1928.

Levin, Meyer. *Classic Hassidic Tales*. New York, 1966.

Lipschitz, Max A. *The Faith of a Hassid*. New York, 1967.

Minkin, Jacob. *The Romance of Hassidism*. New York, 1935.

Newman, Louis I. *The Hasidic Anthology: Tales and Teachings of the Hasidim*. New York, 1934.

Schatz, R. "Contemplative Prayer in Hasidism." *Studies in Mysticism and Religion*. Jerusalem, 1967.

Schechter, Solomon. "The Chassidim." *Studies in Judaism*. 1st ser. Philadelphia, 1911.

Scholem, Gershom G. *Major Trends in Jewish Mysticism*. New York, 1946.

Waxman, Meyer. "Hassidism." *A History of Jewish Literature,* vol. 3. New York, 1936.

21 The Rise of Hazanut

Cohen, Francis L. "Music, Synagogal." *The Jewish Encyclopedia.* New York, 1907.

Heschel, Abraham J. "The Vocation of the Cantor." *The Insecurity of Freedom.* Philadelphia, 1966.

Idelsohn, A. Z. "Song and Singers of the Synagogue in the Eighteenth Century." *Hebrew Union College Jubilee Volume.* Cincinnati, 1925.

———. *Jewish Music in Its Historical Development.* New York, 1948.

Rothmüller, Aron Marko. *The Music of the Jews: An Historical Appreciation.* London, 1953.

Spector, Johanna. "On Jewish Music." *Conservative Judaism* 21, no. 1 (1966):57–72.

Werner, Eric. *From Generation to Generation: Studies in Jewish Musical Tradition.* New York, 1968.

Wohlberg, Max, "Music, Synagogal." *The Universal Jewish Encyclopedia.* New York, 1942.

22 The Decline of Preaching

Bettan, Israel. *Studies in Jewish Preaching: Middle Ages.* Cincinnati, 1939.

———. "The Dubno Maggid." *Hebrew Union College Annual* 23 (1950–51):267–93.

Cohen, A. *Jewish Homiletics.* London, 1937.

Freehof, Solomon B. *Modern Jewish Preaching.* New York, 1941.

Glatt, Herman A. *He Spoke in Parables: The Life and Works of the Dubno Maggid.* New York, 1957.

Heinemann, Benno. *The Maggid of Dubno and His Parables.* New York, 1967.

Joseph, Morris. "About Preaching." *The Jewish Quarterly Review,* o.s. 3 (1891):120–45.

Newman, Louis I. *Maggidim and Hasidim: Their Wisdom.* New York, 1962.

Rabinowitz, H. R. *Portraits of Jewish Preachers.* Jerusalem, 1967 (Hebrew).

Waxman, Meyer. "Homiletic Literature." *A History of Jewish Literature,* vol. 3. New York, 1936.

Zunz, Leopold. *Homiletics of the Jews in Divine Worship.* Berlin, 1919 (German).

23 The Invention of the Printing Press

Amram, David Werner. *The Makers of Hebrew Books in Italy.* Philadelphia, 1909.

Bloch, Joshua. "Venetian Printers of Hebrew Books." Reprinted from the *Bulletin of the New York Public Library,* Feb. 1932.

———. "Hebrew Printing in Naples." Ibid., June 1942.

The Jewish Encyclopedia, s. v. "Bomberg, Daniel," "Soncino." New York, 1907.
Marcus, Jacob R. *The Jew in the Medieval World: A Source Book, 315–1791*. Cincinnati, 1938.
Marx, Moses. "Gershom (Hieronymus) Soncino's Wander-Years in Italy, 1498–1527: Exemplar Judaicae Vitae." *Hebrew Union College Annual* 11 (1936):427–501.
Rivkin, Isaac. "A Pocket Edition Prayer Book for German-Jewish Emigrants to America, 1842." *Publications of the American Jewish Historical Society*, no. 35 (1939): 207–17.
Roth, Cecil. "Hebrew Printing in Venice." *Venice*. Philadelphia, 1930.
———. "The Printed Book." *The Jews in the Renaissance*. Philadelphia, 1959.

24 The Synagogue in Premodern Times

Abrahams, Israel. *Jewish Life in the Middle Ages*. London, 1932.
Neuman, Abraham A. "The Synagogue and Its Auxiliary Institutions." *The Jews in Spain*, vol. 2. Philadelphia, 1942.
Philipson, David. *Old European Jewries*. Philadelphia, 1943.
Zborowski, Mark, and Herzog, Elizabeth. *Life Is with People: The Culture of the Shtetl*. New York, 1962.

The Status of Women in the Synagogue

Epstein, Louis M. "Sex Segregation in Public Places." *Sex Laws and Customs in Judaism*. New York, 1948.
Schechter, Solomon. "Women in Temple and Synagogue." *Studies in Judaism*. 1st ser. Philadelphia, 1911.
Zeitlin, Solomon. "The Segregation of Women during Prayers." *The Jewish Quarterly Review* 38 (1947–48):305–8.

Jewish Worship in Modern Times

English Translation of the *Siddur*

Roth, Cecil. "Gamaliel Ben Pedahzur and His Prayer Book." *Miscellany of the Jewish Historical Society of England*. Part 2. London, 1935.
Singer, S. "Early Translations and Translators of the Jewish Liturgy in England." *Transactions of the Jewish Historical Society of England* 3 (1896–98):36–71.

Adjustments to Modernity: The Orthodox Approach

Belkin, Samuel. "The Jewish Community in a Non-Jewish World: Problems of Integration and Separation." *Essays in Traditional Jewish Thought*. New York, 1956.
Hertz, Joseph H. "The Jewish Prayer Book." *The Authorized Daily Prayer Book*. New York, 1952.
Hirsch, Samson Raphael. "Our Mission." *Timeless Torah: An Anthology of the Writings of Rabbi Samson Raphael Hirsch*. Edited by Jacob Breuer. New York, 1957.
Jakobovits, Immanuel. "Jewish Law Faces Modern Problems." *Studies in Torah Judaism*. Edited by Leon D. Stitskin. New York, 1969.

Jung, Leo. "What Is Orthodox Judaism?" *The Jewish Library*. 2d ser. Edited by Leo Jung. New York, 1930.
Lookstein, Joseph H. "Traditional Judaism in America: Problems and Achievements." *The Jewish Quarterly Review* 45 (1954–55):318–33.

Adjustments to Modernity: The Reform Approach

Bemporad, Jack, ed. *The Theological Foundations of Prayer: A Reform Jewish Perspective*. New York, 1967.
Cohon, Samuel S. "The Theology of the Union Prayer Book." *Year Book of the Central Conference of American Rabbis* 38 (1928):246–70.
Freehof, Solomon B. *Reform Jewish Practice and Its Rabbinic Background*, 2 vols. Cincinnati, 1944.
Petuchowski, Jakob J. *Prayerbook Reform in Europe*. New York, 1968.
Philipson, David. *The Reform Movement in Judaism*. New York, 1931.
Plaut, W. Gunther. *The Rise of Reform Judaism: A Sourcebook of Its European Origins*. New York, 1963.
———. *The Growth of Reform Judaism: American and European Sources*. New York, 1965.
Rauch, Joseph. "The Hamburg Prayer-book." *Year Book of the Central Conference of American Rabbis* 28 (1918):253–72.
Weiner, Max, ed. *Abraham Geiger and Liberal Judaism: The Challenge of the Nineteenth Century*. Philadelphia, 1962.

Adjustments to Modernity: The Conservative Approach

Bokser, Ben Zion. "Conservative Judaism in America."*The Jewish Quarterly Review* 45 (1954–55):334–49.
Davis, Moshe. *The Emergence of Conservative Judaism*. Philadelphia, 1963.
Gordis, Robert. *Conservative Judaism*. New York, 1945.
———. *Conservative Judaism: A Modern Approach to Jewish Tradition*. New York, 1956.
Parzen, Herbert. *Architects of Conservative Judaism*. New York, 1964.
Sklare, Marshall. *Conservative Judaism: An American Religious Movement*. New York, 1955.
Waxman, Mordecai, ed. *Tradition and Change: The Development of Conservative Judaism*. New York, 1958.

Adjustments to Modernity: The Reconstructionist Approach

Kaplan, Mordecai M. *Judaism as a Civilization*. New York, 1934.
———. *The Future of the American Jew*. New York, 1948.
———. *The Greater Judaism in the Making*. New York, 1960.
———. *The Purpose and Meaning of Jewish Existence*. Philadelphia, 1964.

Revisions of the *Union Prayerbook*

Commentary to Union Prayer Book, vol. 1. Newly revised, experimental edition. New York, 1962.
Freehof, Solomon B. "Reform Judaism in America." *The Jewish Quarterly Review* 45 (1954–55):350–62.

Silberman, Lou H. "Union Prayer Book: A Study in Liturgical Development." *Year Book of the Central Conference of American Rabbis* 75 (1965):72–73.

"The Union Prayer Book: A Symposium." *Year Book of the Central Conference of American Rabbis* 40 (1930):251–303.

Hertzberg, Arthur. "The American Jew and His Religion." *The American Jew: A Reappraisal.* Edited by Oscar Janowsky. Philadelphia, 1964.

"The State of Jewish Belief." *Commentary*, August 1966 (38 contributors).

INDEX

INDEX *

Definitions will be found on those pages appearing in boldface type

* *Compiled by Jerome H. Kanner, Ph.D., L.H.D.*